PERGAMON GENERAL PSYCHOLOGY SERIES

EDITORS
Arnold P. Goldstein, Syracuse University
Leonard Krasner, Stanford University & SUNY at Stony Brook

Behavioral Assessment

A Practical Handbook, Third Edition

edited by

ALAN S. BELLACK
The Medical College of Pennsylvania at
Eastern Pennsylvania Psychiatric Institute

MICHEL HERSEN
University of Pittsburgh School of Medicine

PERGAMON PRESS

New York · Oxford · Beijing · Frankfurt
São Paulo · Sydney · Tokyo · Toronto

U.S.A.	Pergamon Press, Maxwell House, Fairview Park, Elmsford, New York 10523, U.S.A.
U.K.	Pergamon Press, Headington Hill Hall, Oxford OX3 0BW, England
PEOPLE'S REPUBLIC OF CHINA	Pergamon Press, Room 4037, Qianmen Hotel, Beijing, People's Republic of China
FEDERAL REPUBLIC OF GERMANY	Pergamon Press, Hammerweg 6, D-6242 Kronberg, Federal Republic of Germany
BRAZIL	Pergamon Editora, Rua Eca de Queiros, 346, CEP 04011, Paraiso, São Paulo, Brazil
AUSTRALIA	Pergamon Press Australia, P.O. Box 544, Potts Point, N.S.W. 2011, Australia
JAPAN	Pergamon Press, 8th Floor, Matsuoka Central Building, 1-7-1 Nishishinjuku, Shinjuku-ku, Tokyo 160, Japan
CANADA	Pergamon Press Canada, Suite No. 271, 253 College Street, Toronto, Ontario, Canada M5T 1R5

Copyright © 1988 Pergamon Books Inc.

First edition 1988

Library of Congress Cataloging-in-Publication Data

Behavioral assessment.
(Pergamon general psychology series; 65)
Includes bibliographies and indexes.
1. Behavioral assessment.   2. Mental illness–
Diagnosis.   I. Bellack, Alan S.   II. Hersen, Michel.
III. Series.   [DNLM: 1. Behavior.   2. Mental Disorders–
diagnosis.   WM 141 B4179]
RC473.B43B44   1987   616.89'075   87-2740

British Library Cataloguing in Publication Data

Behavioral assessment.—3rd ed.
1. Man. Behaviour. Assessment
I. Bellack, Alan S. II. Hersen, Michel
152.8

ISBN 0-08-032796-6 Hardcover
ISBN 0-08-032795-8 Flexicover

Printed in Great Britain by A. Wheaton & Co. Ltd., Exeter

Behavioral Assessment (PGPS-65)

Pergamon Titles of Related Interest

Related Journals *

To Barbara, Jonathan, and Adam
Victoria, Jonathan, and Nathaniel

Contents

Contents

Preface to the Third Edition

We are pleased to be able to present the Third Edition of this book. The need for this edition reflects two factors. First, the scholarship of the contributors to the first two Editions attracted a large and enduring audience. We are gratified by the fact that this book has become a standard textbook in the field. Second, the previous Edition is already outdated, due to the continued growth and development of the field. This Edition is much more than a cosmetic overhaul of its predecessor. There have been substantive changes in both the range of material covered and the content of chapters retained.

This Edition contains 17 chapters in four sections, compared to the 15 chapters in three sections in the Second Edition. Behavior therapy has become much more of a mainstream discipline than it was 10 years ago. In the process, we have become much more cognizant and tolerant of the seminal contributions made by our psychiatric and non-behavioral colleagues. Most notably, diagnosis and psychiatric nosology have become important parts of behavioral research and practice. In consequence, structured diagnostic interviewing plays an increasingly central role in our research. In response to this change, we have added chapters on Behavioral Assessment and DSM-III (Chapter 3), and Structured Interviews and Rating Scales (Chapter 8).

Perhaps the fastest growing area within behavior therapy is behavioral medicine. It would be impossible to cover the entire gamut of assessment techniques in this area in a volume such as this. However, we have added one overview chapter on Health Related Disorders (Chapter 12) to complement updated chapters on Psychophysiological Assessment, Assessment of Sexual Dysfunction, and Assessment of Appetitive Disorders.

We do not claim to be omniscient, but we have also added a chapter on Future Directions in an effort both to predict and help guide the further development of the field. Regretfully, we were forced to omit some material from the previous Edition in order to accommodate to the expanded focus. We elected not to include an update of Charles Wallace's excellent chapter on the Assessment of Psychotic Behavior. Unfortunately, this decision reflects the diminishing involvement of behavior therapists with psychotic patients. We also combined the separate chapters on assessing children in inpatient and outpatient settings into one chapter on the Assessment of Childhood Behavior Problems (Chapter 16).

Once again, we wish to thank the many people whose efforts made the revision possible. First and foremost, we wish to thank our contributors for their excellent work. Second, we could not have produced this volume (or much of our other work) without the dedication and tolerance of Florence Levito and Mary Newell. Last but not least, we are grateful to our friends at Pergamon, most notably our long-time editor Jerome B. Frank.

Alan S. Bellack, Ph.D.
Michel Hersen, Ph.D.

PART 1

FUNDAMENTAL ISSUES

1
On the Changing Nature of Behavioral Assessment

Billy A. Barrios

Through the years behavior therapy has escaped formal definition (e.g., Kazdin, 1979; Wilson, 1978, 1982); it has not, however, escaped change. What was once an identifying feature of behavior therapy is no longer one; what was once antithetical to the practice of behavior therapy is no longer antithetical. Amid all of the change there has been one constant: behavior therapy's outlook toward the future. Behavior therapists have always looked to the future with great hope and optimism (e.g., Barlow, 1980; Hersen, 1981; Kazdin, 1979; Ross, 1985; Wilson, 1982). They have always seen the future as a time when behavior therapy's potential will be fully realized. This vision of the future has been sustained by the continuing successes of the behavioral approach to clinical treatment (e.g., Kazdin & Wilson, 1978; Rachman & Wilson, 1980).

What of the behavioral approach to clinical assessment? Has it, too, changed over the years? Has its outlook toward the future also remained constant over the years? We are certain that the nature of behavioral assessment has changed markedly. There is, however, uncertainty as to whether the promise of behavioral assessment will be realized in the near future. This chapter describes the substantive ways behavioral assessment has changed over time by contrasting previous and current conceptualizations/practices of behavioral assessment. This chapter also examines the questions raised about the future of behavioral assessment by revealing the widespread confusion and controversy that exist over the nature and goals of assessment and the methods of achieving those goals.

Behavioral assessment is not and never has been a discipline separate from the discipline of behavior therapy. The fabric of behavior therapy is very much the fabric of behavioral assessment; the theories and assumptions that guide the practice of behavior therapy are the same ones that guide the

3

practice of behavioral assessment. Thus, as the nature of behavior therapy has changed, so has the nature of behavioral assessment. The close ties between the two disciplines are due to behavioral assessment having arisen out of the behavioral approach to clinical treatment in order to meet the special needs of clinical treatment (e.g., Hersen & Barlow, 1976; Nelson, 1983). Simply put, it is because we have a behavioral approach to clinical treatment that we have a behavioral approach to clinical assessment — and not vice versa. Behavioral assessment's *raison d'être* is behavior therapy, and its motto, if it had one, would be *Ad Serviam.*

ON THE PAST NATURE OF BEHAVIORAL ASSESSMENT

Most early attempts to define behavioral assessment did so by contrasting the aims, assumptions, and applications of the behavioral approach to clinical assessment with those of the traditional approach to clinical assessment (e.g., Bornstein, Bornstein, & Dawson, 1984; Ciminero, 1977; Goldfried & Kent, 1972; Hartmann, Roper, & Bradford, 1979; Mash & Terdal, 1976). A summary of these comparisons is presented in Table 1.1.

All measurement is constructed and carried out with specific aims in mind. In the behavioral approach, the major aims of assessment are to assist in the identification of problem behaviors; the identification of the factors maintaining the problem behaviors; the selection of the optimum treatment for the problem behaviors; the evaluation of the effectiveness of treatment; and, if needed, the revision of treatment. The major aims of traditional assessment are to assist in the diagnosis of the problem condition, the classification of the problem condition, the identification of the etiology of the problem condition, and the prognostication of the problem condition.

The focus and scope of all measurement is a direct function of one's assumptions about the nature of human performance. In the behavioral approach, performance is thought to be a function of current environmental conditions — antecedent and consequent stimuli. Performance is expected to be stable as long as the specific environmental conditions remain stable. Given this view of performance as situationally specific, the behavior therapist constructs tests with specific situations in mind and judges (in part) the adequacy of tests in terms of how well these specific situations are represented. The traditional approach, on the other hand, assumes performance to be a function of enduring, underlying intrapsychic states or person variables; performance is expected to be consistent across time and settings. Given this view of performance as cross-situationally consistent, the traditional therapist constructs tests only with specific performances (and not specific situations) in mind.

The two approaches differ not only in their assumptions about the causes

TABLE 1.1. A Summary of the Aims, Assumptions, and Applications of the Behavioral and Traditional Approaches to Assessment

	BEHAVIORAL APPROACHES	TRADITIONAL APPROACHES
I. Aims	To assist in the identification of problem behaviors and their maintaining conditions To assist in the selection of an appropriate treatment To assist in the evaluation of treatment effectiveness To assist in the revision of treatment	To assist in the diagnostication or classification of problem conditions To assist in the identification of etiological factors To assist in prognostication
II. Assumptions 1. Causes of performance	Performance is thought to be a function of situational variables or the interaction of situational and person variables	Performance is thought to be a function of intrapsychic or person variables
2. Meaning of performance	Test performance is viewed as a sample of a person's repertoire in a specific situation	Test performance is viewed as a sign of an enduring, underlying state or trait or person variable
III. Applications 1. Instrument construction	Adequate representation of the contextual features of the setting of interest is emphasized (in that performance is seen as situationally determined) Adequate representation of the repertoire of interest is emphasized (in that test performance is seen as a sample of the repertoire)	Little emphasis on the representation of contextual features (in that performance is seen as consistent across time and settings) Adequate representation of the underlying state or trait or person variable of interest is emphasized (in that test performance is seen as a sign of the underlying variable)
2. Scope of assessment	Broad focus encompassing the problem behaviors and their maintaining conditions, treatment prerequisites, treatment administration, treatment outcome, etc.	Narrow focus encompassing the problem condition
3. Schedule of assessment	Repeated assessment: at key junctures in the course of treatment or throughout the course of treatment	Infrequent assessment: typically prior to and after treatment
4. Method of assessment	Preference for direct methods of measurement	Methods of measurement are by definition indirect (in that test performance is seen as a sign of an underlying state or trait)

Note: Table adapted from Barrios & Hartmann (1986) and Barrios, Hartmann, Roper, & Bradford (1979).

of performance and the construction of tests of performance, but also in their assumptions about the meaning of test performance. The behavioral approach considers performance on a specific test to be a sample of the person's behavioral repertoire in a specific situation. The emphasis, then, in the behavioral approach is on gathering a representative sample of the person's behavior in that situation. The representativeness of the sample determines, in part, the adequacy of the assessment. In the traditional approach, performance on a specific test is considered to be a sign of some underlying state or trait. Emphasis is on gathering a representative picture of this underlying trait. The adequacy with which the trait is addressed determines, in part, the adequacy of the assessment.

The very different aims and assumptions of the two approaches have very different implications for the exact form assessment will take. Oriented toward treatment, behavioral assessment is much broader in scope than traditional assessment. Behavioral assessment seeks out information on contextual variables, controlling variables, treatment requisites, treatment side effects, etc. — all information which will facilitate the orderly course of treatment. Traditional assessment, on the other hand, seeks out only information that will facilitate the accurate classification of the person's problem condition. Given that treatment is a fairly dynamic process, assessment in the behavioral approach will be carried out repeatedly, at key junctures in the course of treatment or throughout the course of treatment. Given that classification is a fairly static process, assessment in the traditional approach will be carried out sporadically, perhaps only before and after treatment. The two approaches differ in both their scope and schedule of measurement and in their methods of measurement. In the behavioral approach, there is interest in the test performance per se because it is seen as a sample of the performance pattern of interest. The emphasis, therefore, is on the use of direct methods of measurement (e.g., observation of performance in the naturalistic setting). In the traditional approach, there is interest in the test performance only insomuch as it serves as a sensitive sign of the underlying state or trait of interest. Measurement of performance qua performance is secondary to measurement of performance as correlate of underlying condition. There is, therefore, less emphasis on the use of direct methods of measurement.

ON THE PRESENT NATURE OF BEHAVIORAL ASSESSMENT

Many of the aforementioned differences between behavioral assessment and traditional assessment are no longer as sharp and pronounced as they once were. Changes in the practice of behavior therapy have prompted changes in the practice of behavioral assessment, which in turn have blurred many of the original distinctions between behavioral and traditional assessment. To wit, the practice of behavioral assessment has become more heterogeneous in the level of measurement, in the method of measurement, and in the evaluation of measurement (e.g., Mash, 1979; Mash & Terdal, in press; Nelson & Barlow, 1981; Nelson & Hayes, 1986; Ollendick & Hersen, 1984). Amid all of this heterogeneity, we do find a common core; it is this common core which distinguishes behavioral assessment as it is practiced today from other approaches to clinical assessment.

Distinguishing Features

The common core of behavioral assessment is a broad philosophy concerning the purposes, precision, and premium of clinical assessment. Clinical assessment is carried out solely to help clinical treatment. The purposes of clinical assessment are, therefore, inextricably tied to the purposes of clinical treatment. Stated briefly, the primary purposes of clinical treatment are to identify the problem area and to develop an intervention for the problem area. Execution of each one of these purposes of clinical treatment is predicated on a decision, which in turn is predicated on an inference. Clinical assessment facilitates the conduct of clinical treatment by facilitating the generation and selection of tenable inferences. The precision with which a particular assessment aids in the generation and selection of tenable inferences is a function of its network of empirically established relationships. That is, the precision of a particular assessment is a function of the extent to which we can legitimately generalize other occasions, settings, responses, and persons. The ultimate worth of an assessment does not, however, lie in its precision; the ultimate worth of an assessment lies in its usefulness vis-à-vis the practice of behavior therapy. The measurement concept of utility subsumes and supersedes the measurement concept of precision. It is, therefore, the measurement concept of utility which has the final say as to the value of an assessment (e.g., Barrios & Hartmann, 1986; Nelson & Hayes, 1986).

The paragraphs that follow discuss at greater length these shared and varied aspects of the behavioral approach to clinical assessment. Specifically described are the discrete goals of behavioral assessment, the diverse methodologies for achieving these goals, and the diverse methodologies for evaluating the exactness with which these goals are achieved. In so doing, special attention is paid to the most recent developments and dissensions in the practice of behavioral assessment and to the apparent link between these recent developments and dissensions and recent developments in the practice of behavior therapy.

PURPOSES OF ASSESSMENT

One hallmark of the behavioral approach to clinical practice is the dynamic interplay between treatment and assessment (e.g., Bornstein, Bornstein, & Dawson, 1984; Hersen & Barlow, 1976; Rimm & Masters, 1979). Assessment provides us with the basis for various types of inferences; the various types of inferences provide us with the bases for the design and conduct of our therapeutic operations. Each different step in the design and conduct of therapy is founded upon a different inference, and each different inference is founded upon different assessment data. Assessment data, then, do not and cannot perform many of the functions that many have mistakenly ascribed to them. Assessment data do not and cannot identify problem areas or determine controlling variables or select an intervention or evaluate an intervention (e.g., Nelson & Hayes, 1981). Assessment data can give rise to inferences, which in turn can give rise to decisions vis-à-vis identification of problem areas, determination of controlling variables, selection of an intervention, and evaluation of an intervention. The different phases and purposes of assessment are, therefore, simply different attempts to fulfill requests for different types of information — the exact nature of the request being a function of the exact point in the course of therapy.

The various phases and purposes of behavioral assessment are summarized in Table 1.2. The phases of behavioral assessment resemble a funnel in that they begin with a broad scope and progressively narrow to a circumscribed focus (Cone & Hawkins, 1977b; Hawkins, 1979). Within each phase are couched several questions that need to be addressed; the purposes of assessment at each phase are to supply information relevant to the questions of the phase. From this information, answers to the questions are formulated, actions are taken, and the questions of the next phase are addressed.

Screening

In the initial phase of screening and general disposition, the need is to determine whether or not the person is suitable for the type of services offered, and to do so quickly. If the person is deemed suitable, the need is to determine what additional information may be pertinent. If the person is deemed unsuitable, the need is to determine to whom the person should be referred. Assessment data are used to assist in making each one of the determinations. From assessment data, a rough sketch of the prospective client is fashioned. This rough sketch is compared to selection or screening criteria, and the degree of match is ascertained.

Problem Identification and Analysis

Assessment in the initial phase of screening and general disposition yields only a broad, surface view of the client's functioning because the clinician is

TABLE 1.2. The Purposes of Behavioral Assessment

PHASE OF TREATMENT	QUESTIONS ADDRESSED BY ASSESSMENT
Screening	Is the prospective client suitable for services?
	If the prospective client is not suitable for services, to whom should the person be referred?
Problem identification and analysis	What is the nature of the client's difficulties?
	Does the client's difficulties constitute a problem warranting treatment?
	What are the factors maintaining the client's problem condition?
Treatment selection	Which prerequisites of the available treatment alternatives does the client satisfy?
	Which prerequisites of the available treatment alternatives does the client's environment satisfy?
	Which prerequisites of the available treatment alternatives does the therapist satisfy?
	What is the optimum treatment for the client's problem condition?
Treatment evaluation	Has the treatment been administered faithfully?
	What changes have occurred in the problem condition and collateral behaviors?
	Can these changes be attributed to the treatment?
	What costs have been incurred in treatment?
	Are the benefits of treatment adequate?
	Should treatment be terminated or altered?

Note: Table based upon Barrios & Hartmann (1986), Cone & Hawkins (1977), Hawkins (1979), Haynes (1978), and Mash & Terdal (1976).

interested in making only a general determination of acceptable or unacceptable for services. In the second phase, problem definition and analysis, the clinician is interested in making much finer discriminations. Specifically, the therapist is interested in identifying (a) the aspects of the client's functioning that are problematic, (b) the order in which these problematic aspects should be addressed, and (c) the variables that underlie the maintenance of each.

The initial phase's broad, surface view of the client's functioning provides clues as to which aspects might be problematic and which might be unproblematic. Exactly how we follow-up on these clues depends on how we conceptualize a problem space — the universe of acceptable targets for treatment (Mash, 1985). Historically, the universe of acceptable targets for behavioral treatments has been limited to the isolated behavior. Thus, assessment during this phase has historically been limited to gathering information on isolated behaviors. From this information, the custom has been to select one behavior as the target of treatment. Which behavior one selected as the target of treatment depended on which set of guidelines one adhered to. Among the guidelines proposed for designating an isolated behavior a problem are (a) the behavior is harmful to the client or others, (b) the behavior deviates significantly from optimal level of performance, (c) the behavior deviates significantly from the norm, (d) the behavior disturbs important persons in the client's environment, and (e) the behavior differs from the behavior of others identified as competent (e.g., Foster & Ritchey, 1979; Goldfried & D'Zurilla, 1969; Hartmann et al., 1979; Nelson & Hayes, 1979, 1981). Among the guidelines proposed for selecting one isolated problem behavior over another as the target of treatment are (a) select the most noxious behavior, (b) select the easiest behavior to change, (c) select the behavior most likely to generalize to other behaviors, and (d) select the earliest behavior in a chain of behaviors (e.g., Angle, Hay, Hay, & Ellinwood, 1977; Nelson & Hayes, 1981; O'Leary, 1972; Tharp & Wetzel, 1969).

In recent years, a deep dissatisfaction with such a traditional view of treatment targets has surfaced, which in turn has prompted a number of reconceptualizations of the problem space. This deep dissatisfaction stems from therapists' reasons for selecting a particular behavior as a treatment target and the representativeness of that behavior as a treatment target (Mash, 1985). All too often the sole reason for our selecting a particular behavior as the focus of treatment has been convenience. The target behavior has been one that could be easily operationalized, easily measured, and easily interpreted via visual inspection. Such a behavior has all too often been an inadequate representation of the client's concerns (Evans, 1985), and in those cases where it has not been a trivialization of the client's concerns, it has all too often been an incomplete representation of those concerns (Hersen, 1981;

Kazdin, 1985). That is, even in those cases where the isolated target behavior has been a relevant feature of the client's difficulties, it has not been the embodiment of the client's difficulties.

Reconceptualizations of the problem space have sought to expand the problem space — to make it more commensurate with what goes on in clinical practice. Implicit in the traditional definition of the problem space is the limiting of treatment targets to overt, observable behaviors. Recent formulations of the problem space have placed no such limits on the nature of our treatment targets. In fact, recent formulations explicitly cite both overt and covert (i.e., cognitions) phenomena as acceptable targets for treatment (Kratochwill, 1985; Nelson & Hayes, 1981). In addition to expanding the nature of acceptable treatment targets, recent reformulations of the problem space have expanded the number of phenomena that collectively may serve as an acceptable treatment target. Traditionally, the number of phenomena that could serve as a legitimate treatment target has been limited to one. Tradition is not, however, as strong a force as it once was. Clusters of responses such as those denoting the diagnostic categories of the American Psychiatric Association (1980) are now seen by most as acceptable targets for behavioral treatments (Nelson & Barlow, 1981; Kazdin, 1983; Kratochwill, 1985; Nathan, 1981; Nelson & Hayes, 1981; Taylor, 1983) and by many as the most acceptable targets for behavioral treatments.

From this discussion it is clear that one's assessment of the client during this second phase is guided by one's conceptualization of the problem space and one's definition of the problem. It is also clear that an in-depth analysis of an identified problem is guided by the conceptualization of problematic functioning. Among the conceptual models traditionally drawn upon in the assessment of an identified problem are the Stimulus-Response-Contingency-Consequence model (Lindsley, 1964), the Stimulus-Organism-Response-Consequence model (Goldfried & Sprafkin, 1976), and the Stimulus-Organism-Response-Contingency-Consequence model (Kanfer & Saslow, 1969). In each of these models, the stimulus variable refers to the environmental events that elicit or evoke the problem behavior, the response variable to the elements that constitute the problem behavior, and the consequence variable to the internal and external events that succeed the problem behavior. In the first and third models, the contingency variable refers to the schedule by which these internal and external events succeed the problem behavior; in the second and third models, the organism variable refers to the physical and hypothetical states of the client that mediate the problem behavior. All three of the frameworks view the maintenance of the problem behavior as a function of the internal and external events that succeed it (i.e., consequence variable). The three frameworks differ, however, in their views of the instigation of the problem behavior. The oldest of the models — the Stimulus-Response-Contingency-Consequence model

— regards the expression of the problem behavior as a function of only situational events. On the other hand, the two most recent models regard the expression of the problem behavior as a function of both situational and internal events. The two most recent models are clearly the most compatible with contemporary experimental psychology's interactionist view of human performance (e.g., Endler & Magnusson, 1976; Magnusson & Endler, 1977). It is not surprising, then, that the two most recent models are the most widely employed of the three problem analysis frameworks (e.g., Bornstein et al., 1984; Gelfand & Hartmann, 1984; Nelson & Hayes, 1981).

Carrying out an in-depth assessment of an identified problem also draws upon one of three other conceptual models: the linear-linkage model, the hierarchical model, and the systems model (Kanfer, 1985). The three frameworks described in the previous paragraph provide a broad conceptualization of the problem behavior's controlling variables; the three frameworks just described provide a broad conceptualization of the problem behavior's response structure. Both types of frameworks are needed to perform a detailed analysis of the client's problem. In the linear-linkage model, the problem behavior is seen as an organized collection, or chain, of individual responses; the individual responses are seen as connected to one another in a sequential or horizontal fashion, not causing or controlling one another but simply preceding or succeeding one another. In the hierarchical model, the problem behavior is seen as one of several intricately organized response classes that bear a definite causal relationship to each another; certain response classes are seen as the precursors and producers of other response classes. In the systems model, the problem behavior is seen as an element of the dynamic network of relationships among the client's cognitive, affective, physiological, and behavioral components.

For those problem behaviors that occur with some regularity across clients, there are more refined versions of these two sets of conceptual schemes. These problem-specific or disorder-specific conceptual frameworks offer a finer blueprint for assessing a client's problem behavior; they pinpoint with greater precision the possible causal and structural features of a client's problem behavior. Among the problem behaviors that frequently require in-depth assessment are anxiety, depression, marital discord, schizophrenia, sexual disorders, and appetitive disorders. Each of these problem behaviors occurs with such regularity that this handbook has devoted a separate chapter to the assessment of each one of them. Each one of these chapters gives examples of these problem-specific conceptual frameworks.

Treatment Selection

The purpose of carrying out an intensive assessment of problem behavior is to help identify the variables that are maintaining said behavior, which in turn helps in selecting the most appropriate treatment for said behavior. Assessment data from phase two (problem identification and analysis) are, therefore, quite relevant to this phase-three task. The data for these two tasks alone, however, are not sufficient for an efficient and judicious selection of the optimum treatment. In order to select the most appropriate treatment for a particular problem, we need information on both the variables maintaining the problem behavior and the variables mediating the efficacious treatment of the problem behavior. In the third phase of treatment selection, the purpose of assessment is to provide this latter information — information on the requisites and mediators of the treatment alternatives available.

For many of the problem conditions we encounter there are few proven behavioral interventions from which we can choose. For these problem conditions, the task assigned to assessment is a relatively simple one. Having few proven behavioral interventions, we have relatively few treatment requisites and mediators on which to gather information. There are, however, a great many problem conditions for which we have several behavioral interventions. In these situations, the challenge is to select from this pool of proven behavioral interventions the treatment that will be most effective for the client. Though the techniques in this pool of proven techniques may have comparable records of success across groups of clients, they may not have comparable probabilities for success with one individual client. Techniques may not be equally successful because the conditions necessary for optimal administration may not be equally present for all clients. Assessment tells us how well the present situation meets each of the necessary conditions for optimal employment of the various treatment alternatives. On the basis of such information, the treatment option that best fits our client's situation is selected.

Earlier we saw that it is the conceptualization of an identified problem that guides us in the assessment of the problem. The same is true of the assessment of a prospective treatment for the problem: It is the conceptualization of a prospective treatment which guides us in the assessment of its potential for success. The conceptualization of a prospective treatment specifies the conditions under which the treatment will be operative and the factors that will influence the precision of its operation. At present, we have few such broad conceptual frameworks to direct us in the assessment of a prospective treatment. One that we do have is the elaborate framework developed by Haynes (1986). In this general working model for treatment selection, the fidelity and integrity of a prospective treatment (and thus the likelihood of success with that prospective treatment) are seen as a function of a host of client, social-environmental, and therapist variables. Among the client variables seen as influencing a given intervention's likelihood for success are motivation, resistance, resources, and competing problems; among the social-environmental variables are social mediators, social supports, organization resources, and environmental constraints; and among the therapist variables are experience, expertise, and values.

More numerous than general models for treatment selection are problem-specific models for treatment selection. Table 1.3 presents such a model for the specific problem of children's fears and anxieties. For each of the treatment alternatives listed, there is a listing of the requisite setting, child, and parent characteristics. From an assessment of each one of these treatment requisites, we can gauge the feasibility and intensity of a given treatment alternative. This information and the information from an in-depth assessment of the problem condition are both drawn upon in deciding which is the most appropriate intervention to employ with a particular child client. Examples of other problem-specific frameworks for treatment selection can be found in this volume's chapters on the assessment of specific problem conditions.

Treatment Evaluation

Having selected and implemented a treatment that we believe to be the most appropriate for a client's life circumstances, our concern is now with the fidelity with which our treatment has been implemented and the effects that it has produced. At this juncture in therapy, we wish to determine whether or not our treatment is having the desired impact on the client's problem condition. If it is, then we wish to determine whether or not treatment should be discontinued and maintenance strategies initiated. And if it is not, then we wish to determine whether treatment should be renewed, revamped, or replaced. Underlying each of these determinations is the supposition that treatment has been carried out as was intended. In this phase of treatment evaluation, the function of assessment is to assist us in determining the validity of that supposition.

Our assessment of the faithfulness and exactness with which our treatment has been administered is, of course, directed by our conceptualization of the treatment — the conditions deemed necessary and sufficient for its operation. Take, for example, the widely employed behavioral technique of systematic desensitization. The technique is commonly seen as having three components: training in deep muscle relaxation, construction of a hierarchy of anxiety-eliciting situations, and pairing of hierarchy items with a relaxed state (Wolpe, 1982). According to this breakdown of the technique, the client must imagine the hierarchy scenes while in a relaxed state in order for the treatment to be active. Failure on the part of the client to do so renders the treatment inert. Assessing the fidelity with which systematic desensitization has been carried out would thus involve assessing whether or not the client imagined the anxiety-eliciting scenes while in a relaxed state. Other breakdowns of the technique specify different foci for an assessment of the

TABLE 1.3. Assessment Considerations in the Selection of a Behavioral Treatment for Children's Anxiety Disorders

Treatment Prerequisite	BEHAVIORAL TECHNIQUE							
	Systematic Desensitization	In Vivo Desensitization	Emotive Imagery	Imaginal Flooding	In Vivo Flooding	Implosion	Reinfor Practice	Contingency Management
Setting characteristics								
Identification of discriminative stimuli								+
Identification of eliciting stimuli	+	+	+	+	+	+	+	
Identification of cognitive mediators		+						
Identification of response consequences		+						+
Child characteristics								
Repertoire with the feared stimulus	+ +	+ +	+	+	+	+	+	
Concept of ordinality	+ +	+	+					
Imagery ability	+		+ +	+ +		+ +		
Autonomic perception	+ +	+	+	+	+	+	+	
Self-management skills	+	+						
Attention deficit	+ −	−						
Defensiveness	−	−						
Parental characteristics								
Monitoring skills	+ +							+
Dispenses consequences contingently	+ +						+	+
Mood disturbance	−							−
Misattributions towards child's behavior								−

Note: A plus (+) indicates that the characteristic is a prerequisite of the technique. A minus (−) indicates that the presence of the characteristic contraindicates the technique. An open cell indicates that the characteristic is not thought to be pertinent to the technique. Portions of this table adapted from Barrios & Hartmann (in press-a) and Barrios, Hartmann, & Shigetomi (1981).

technique's integrity. These models and models for other behavioral interventions can be found in any of the recent tomes on behavioral treatment (e.g., Barlow, 1985; Bellack, Hersen, & Kazdin, 1982; Hersen, 1983, 1985).

Relatively certain that the treatment has been carried out as planned, clinicians then wish to know whether the treatment has been successful in correcting the client's problem condition. Measuring the success the treatment has had is, of course, dependent upon how we define success. Behavior therapists do not yet agree with one another on what are acceptable outcome criteria for the common problems (e.g., Mash, 1985). Behavior therapists do, however, agree with one another that change in an isolated target response of an isolated individual in an isolated setting at an isolated time is not an acceptable treatment outcome. For a treatment to be successful, there must be some spread of therapeutic effects to nontreated responses, nontreated persons, nontreated settings, or nontreated points in time (Barrios & Hartmann, in press-b; Krantz, 1984; Stokes & Baer, 1977; Yates, 1981). Various grids have been developed for charting the spread of desired effects from treatments. One such grid is the Generalization Map developed by Drabman, Hammer, and Rosenbaum (1979). The map consists of 16 different types of generalized effects: maintenance (the complete absence of generalization); generalization across persons; generalization across responses; generalization across persons and responses; generalization across settings; generalization across persons and settings; generalization across responses and settings; generalization across persons, responses, and settings; generalization across time; generalization across persons and time; generalization across responses and time; generalization across persons, responses, and time; generalization across settings and time; generalization across persons, settings, and time; generalization across responses, settings, and time; and generalization across persons, responses, settings, and time. Other such grids for use with specific problem conditions have been developed. Examples of these grids can be found in any of the recent handbooks on behavioral treatments (e.g., Barlow, 1985; Bellack et al., 1982; Hersen, 1983, 1985). Be they problem-specific or problem-nonspecific, these generalization grids are important in that they define the scope of our assessment of treatment outcome.

There is always some cost involved in treating a client's problem condition. There is the expenditure of time, energy, and money; there is endurance of discomfort and the possibility of future discomfort. These costs must be taken into account when evaluating the success of a treatment. We thus need information on the costs incurred in treating a client's problem condition. Collecting such information is the job of assessment.

To collect such information we must first specify the variables that make up the costs associated with treatment; it is these variables that will be the focus of our assessment of the costs incurred in treating our particular client's problem condition. Having specified the variables that make up the cost associated with treatment, we must then define each one of these variables. Among the cost variables behavior therapists commonly cite are personnel, facilities, equipment, materials, and personal loss (Haynes, 1986; Yates, 1985). Each cost variable may be defined from a number of different perspectives (e.g., client, institution, community, society), with each different perspective defining each cost variable in a somewhat different way (Yates, 1985). Having defined and collected data on this set of cost variables, we must then compare the benefits of the treatment to the expenses of the treatment, having compared the two, we must then decide on the overall success we have had in ameliorating our client's problem condition. There are several different approaches to comparing the benefits of treatment to the costs of treatment. Among these approaches are statistical significance tests, cost-outcome matrices, cost/benefit ratios, and mathematical modeling of cost-outcome relationships (Yates, 1985). A detailed discussion of the steps and advantages and disadvantages of each of these approaches can be found elsewhere (Yates, 1985). Suffice it say that at this time, behavior therapists have no widely agreed-upon definitions of cost variables or widely agreed-upon strategies for handling cost variables.

Whatever we determine to be the overall success of the treatment, we would like to be able to attribute that success to the treatment with considerable confidence. The soundness of assessment data is one factor that determines the confidence with which we can make that attribution (e.g., Campbell & Stanley, 1966; Cook & Campbell, 1979; Kazdin, 1980; Kratochwill, 1978). Precisely how we go about determining the soundness of assessment data is, however, a matter of some contention (e.g., Barrios & Hartmann, 1986; Nelson & Hayes, 1986). A later section describes the various methods that have been recommended for evaluating the soundness of assessment practices.

In discussing the role assessment plays in estimating the costs born by treatment, in estimating the overall success of treatment, and in attributing that overall success to treatment, we have assumed that the treatment has in fact been successful. If in fact treatment has not been successful in correcting our client's problem condition, we look to assessment for insights into this lack of success and into possible improvements. Such insights may come from an assessment of the integrity of the treatment and an assessment of the variables thought to undermine the integrity of the treatment. If our assessment of the integrity of the treatment reveals that it has not been carried out as intended, then our assessment of the variables thought to undermine our treatment may help to pinpoint the source of the breakdown. Pinpointing the source of the breakdown of the treatment may in turn help to devise and enact steps to rectify the situation (i.e., enhance the integrity and potency of treatment). In sum, the steps clinicians take to correct the situation are predicated on their conceptualization of the situation — the situation in this case being the operations of treatment and the forces that may sabotage those operations. Though at this time there are no general frameworks to guide us in assessing the integrity of treatments and the threats to that integrity, we do have a number of technique-specific frameworks. Examples of these frameworks can be found in any of the several recent sourcebooks on behavioral interventions (e.g., Barlow, 1985; Bellack et al., 1982; Hersen, 1983, 1985).

LEVELS OF ASSESSMENT

From the previous discussion it is clear that the purposes of behavioral assessment are many; it is also clear that the procedures used to carry out these many purposes are largely a function of the conceptual framework we adhere to (Mash, 1985). The level at which we assess our client's problem condition is thus largely a function of our definition and conceptualization of the problem space (Mash, 1985). Assessment of our client's problem condition generally takes place at one of three levels: the symptom, the syndrome, or the system. Each level of measurement has its advantages and disadvantages, its supporters and detractors, and each is discussed in this section.

Symptom

Assessment at the level of the symptom is assessment at the level of the individual behavior (Kazdin, 1983). A client's problem condition is framed as a disturbance in an isolated behavior; assessment of a client's problem condition is focused on the measurement of that isolated behavior; and treatment of a client's problem condition is directed to alteration of that isolated behavior. Such a tack is consonant with the roots of the behavioral approach to clinical practice: the emphasis on behavior as the primary datum of therapy, the emphasis on a discrete focus to our assessment and treatment operations, the emphasis on an isomorphism between the target of assessment and the target of treatment (e.g., Barrett, Johnston, & Pennypacker, 1986; Nelson, 1983). Though consonant with the historical underpinnings to the behavioral approach to clinical practice, many behavior therapists find assessment at the level of the symptom discordant and detrimental to the current practice of behavior therapy (cf Kratochwill, 1985). Those who object to defining the problem space as an isolated behavior object to assessing the client's problem condition at the level of the symptom. They do so for the same reasons cited earlier. Too often the isolated behavior selected for assessment and treatment is selected for its convenience and not for its representativeness. Too often those isolated behaviors selected for their representativeness are neither adequate nor accurate representations of the problem condition. Those who object to assessment at the level of the symptom, believe that the syndrome, or system are better able to capture the complexity of the client's problem condition.

Syndrome

Assessment at the level of the syndrome reflects a conceptualization of the problem space as a cluster of symptoms that systematically covary with one another (Kazdin, 1983); assessment at the level of the syndrome, therefore, entails measurement of each one of the symptoms thought to cluster with one another. Both the syndrome and the symptom are constructions. The syndrome, though, is a construction of a higher order than the symptom; the syndrome is more of an abstraction than the symptom. There are advantages to conceptualizing and assessing a client's problem condition at the more abstract level of the syndrome than to conceptualizing and assessing a client's problem condition at the less abstract level of the symptom. Foremost among these advantages is the better fit with the clients' descriptions of their problem conditions and our clinical observations of those problem conditions. In other words, assessment at the level of the syndrome appears to be more face valid and content valid than assessment at the level of the symptom: more in accord with the client's experence and more in accord with the clinician's experience. Another advantage of assessment at the level of the syndrome is the potential increase in the predictive powers of individual measures. If the individual symptoms covary with one another as they are thought to covary, then knowledge of the activity of one symptom allows the therapist to predict the activity of another symptom. Such knowledge may be of great service to clinicians in screening potential clients for treatment, designing a potential treatment for clients, selecting a proven treatment for clients, and evaluating the success of treatment. In general, the more phenomena a measure can predict with precision, the more useful the measure. Assessment at the level of the syndrome holds greater promise of producing such useful measures than does assessment at the level of the symptom. A final advantage of assessment at the level of the syndrome is the harmonious relationship it bears to the operations of science. The ultimate aim of science is to account for the greater number of phenomena with the fewest number of variables. Construction and condensation are two of the ways science goes about accomplishing this aim. Construction is the process of carving nature into discrete units; condensation is the process of combining discrete units into larger units. Both processes are involved in assessment at the level of the syndrome; thus, assessment at the syndrome is in keeping with the overall aim of science.

Assessment at the level of the syndrome is not without its shortcomings (e.g., Kanfer & Saslow, 1969). Implicit is the assumption that the individual symptoms have common causal, maintenance, and modification factors. The less tenable this assumption is, the less tenable the concept of the syndrome is and the less useful an assessment at the level of the syndrome is. For many a proposed syndrome, this assumption of shared factors has proven to be false. A second shortcoming of an assessment at the level of the syndrome is the seemingly trivial nature of many of the individual symptoms and the inordinate attention given to these individual symptoms. For many a proposed syndrome, many of the isolated symptoms appear neither disruptive nor debilitating. In cases such as these, questions arise as to the appropriateness of spending so much time assessing symptoms of so little consequence. To many of us, assessing symptoms that are neither disruptive nor debilitating is not an appropriate way to spend valuable therapy time. We should note that neither one of these two shortcomings is an indictment against an assessment at the level of the syndrome per se. Each is an indictment against a particular application of assessment at the level of the syndrome: the first against an ill-conceived syndrome and its assessment, the second against a well-conceived but insignificant syndrome and its assessment.

System

Assessment at the level of the system springs from the increasingly popular view of the client as a living system — a living system comprised of cognitive, affective, behavioral, and biological component (e.g., Kanfer, 1985). Each component is inextricably tied to all other components such that a change in one component begets a change in all other components. Inextricably tied to one another, a disturbance in one component is seen as indicative of a disturbance in the entire system of components. Correcting a disturbance in one component, therefore, entails correcting the fabric of the entire system of components. And the key to correcting this disturbance in the fabric of the system lies in pinpointing the smallest parts of the system with the largest spheres of influence.

From this view of the client as a living system, it follows that an assessment of the client's problem condition will take place at the level of the system. Broader in focus, an assessment at the level of the system better captures the complexity of the client's problem condition than does an assessment at the level of the symptom or an assessment at the level of the syndrome (Evans, 1985; Mash, 1985). A broader focus and a better picture may not, however, make for a more useful assessment of the client's problem condition. With a broader focus comes a bulkier framework for assessing our client's problem condition. The bulkier the framework, the more unwieldy the assessment and the assessment data (Mash, 1985). For those of us who favor assessment at the level of the system, the challenge facing us is the development of a workable model with adequate scope and adequate guidelines for collecting and managing data (Kazdin, 1985; Mash, 1985).

In selecting the level at which to assess a client's problem condition, we are in essence selecting the degree of molecularity with which to analyze and manipulate a client's problem condition. We, of course, wish to select the degree of molecularity (and, in turn, the level of assessment) that leads to the most sweeping and enduring changes in the client's problem condition (Evans, 1985). Unfortunately, we have yet to discover the optimum degree of molecularity. Until we do so, behavioral therapists will continue to disagree with one another on the level at which to assess our client's problem condition.

METHODS OF ASSESSMENT

Whatever level therapists choose to assess a client's problem condition — level of the symptom, level of the syndrome, or level of the system — they will be measuring the responses of the client. The client's responses will fall into one of three different content areas (Cone, 1977, 1978) or systems (Evans, 1986; Lang, 1968, 1971) or channels (Borkovec, 1976; Paul & Bernstein, 1973): cognitive, motor, or physiological. Cognitive responses refer to private events that are not publicly verifiable, motor responses to molar muscular activities that are observable to the naked eye, and physiological responses to activities of the striated and smooth muscles (Cone, 1978).

Numerous instruments have been developed for the measurement of each type of response. For example, in a recent review of the assessment of children's fears and anxieties, Barrios and Hartmann (in press-a) discovered over 100 instruments for measuring the specific cognitive, motor, and physiological responses that are referred to collectively as fear or anxiety. Other reviews of the assessment of other collections of cognitive, motor, and physiological responses offer similar lengthy lists of instruments. Such reviews and their lists of instruments can be found among the chapters in this volume and volumes like it (e.g., Barlow, 1981; Ciminero, Calhoun, & Adams, 1977; Cone & Hawkins, 1977a; Mash & Terdal, in press; Ollendick & Hersen, 1984).

All assessment instruments are employed with a particular purpose in mind (e.g., Green, 1981; Guion, 1980; Nunnally, 1978). Behavioral assessment instruments are no exception. Given that behavioral assessment has many different purposes, the aim is to select the instrument or instruments that best meet the particular purpose. For help in selecting the most appropriate instrument for the particular purpose, there is the Behavioral Assessment Grid developed by Cone (1978). The grid classifies assessment instruments along three dimensions: content, directness, and generalizability. *Content* refers to the nature of the response or responses being assessed; as stated earlier, the responses are seen as being of one of three content types: cognitive, motor, or physiological. *Directness* refers to the immediacy and authenticity with which the responses are assessed. Instruments that measure the problem responses at the time and place they occur are considered direct methods of assessment; instruments that do not measure the problem responses at the time and place they occur are indirect methods of assessment. Instruments of each type are further classified into one of several subtypes, descriptions and examples of which will be presented shortly. *Generalizability* refers to the consistency or repeatability of response scores across a domain or universe of scores. The grid lists six major universes across which we typically wish to generalize: scorer, item, time, setting, method, and dimension. The particulars and purport of each type of generalizability will also be discussed shortly.

Indirect Methods

The further removed an assessment of a problem response is from the time and place of its natural occurrence, the more indirect is the method of measurement. Interviews, questionnaires, and retrospective ratings by others are all indirect methods of assessment. Both interviews and questionnaires make use of word representations of time and place in their assessment of the client's problem response: interviews use the spoken word, questionnaires use the written word. Both interviews and questionnaires ask for word representations of the client's responses in their assessment of the client's problem response: interviews ask for the client's verbal report, questionnaires ask for the client's written report. Interviews and questionnaires, thus, measure word representations of responses to word representations of stimuli. Little wonder, then, why they are considered the most indirect of the methods for assessing a client's problem response.

Less indirect than interviews and questionnaires are the retrospective ratings of others. In this method of assessment, persons other than the client observe the client at times and places at which the problem response is thought to occur; the persons observe the actual responses of the client to the actual stimuli (as opposed to measuring the word representations of responses to word representations of stimuli). There is, however, considerable lag in their observing of the client and their reporting of said observations. The greater the lag, the greater the retrospective nature of the assessment. And as we all know, the greater the retrospective nature of the assessment, the more indirect is the measurement of a client's problem response.

Direct Methods

Assessment procedures that call for little passage of time between the monitoring of a client's performance and the recording of said observations are considered direct methods of measurement. The grid lists five such methods of assessment: self-observation, analog role play, analog free behavior, naturalistic role play, and naturalistic free behavior. The five methods differ from one another in terms of the "cleanliness" of their observations and the verisimilitude of the situations under which their observations are collected. In self-observation, the client monitors the problem response as it occurs in the natural environment and records the information obtained from those observations. In self-observation, the real life setting is the assessment context; therefore, we have no questions about the verisimilitude of the assessment context. We do, however, have questions about the purity of the measures that such an assessment of clients' problem responses yield. In self-observation, the act of observing is inherently confounded with the act of responding. There is no way around this confound; thus, there is no way around questions concerning the authenticity of the procedure's measures.

The other four methods of assessment avoid this confound by having persons other than the client observe the client's response. The four methods differ from one another in terms of the context that they carry out their observations and the constraints that they place on the client's response. Analog role play and analog free behavior are carried out in settings similar to but not identical to the actual settings in which the problem response occurs; naturalistic role play and naturalistic free behavior are carried out in the actual settings in which the problem response occurs. Analog and naturalistic role play impose limits on a client's ability to respond; they restrict the nature and range of possible responses. Analog and naturalistic free behavior impose no such limits on the client's responding; they grant responding complete freedom to vary.

Table 1.4 presents the two-dimensional content area by method of measurement portion of the third-dimensional grid. Examples for all but 10 of the 24 instrument categories are provided vis-à-vis the cognitive, motor, and physiological response cluster known as children's anxiety disorders (Barrios & Hartmann, in press). The 10 instrument categories for which we could provide no examples are at this time only a theoretical possibility.

Until recently there has been little confusion and controversy as to which instrument to employ in the assessment of a client's problem condition. Of the three content areas, behavior therapists have tended to favor the motor responses. Of the two major methods of assessment, behavior therapists have tended to favor the direct methods (e.g., Ciminero, 1977; Hartmann et al., 1979). In favoring the measurement of motor responses over the measurement of cognitive and physiological responses, behavior therapists have been assuming that an assessment of our client's motor responses constitutes an adequate assessment of our client's problem condition; in favoring the use of direct methods of measurement over the use of indirect

TABLE 1.4. A Framework for Classifying Instruments for Assessing Children's Fears and Anxieties

	CONTENT AREA		
Method of Measurement	Cognitive	Physiological	Motor
Indirect			
Interview	Children's Fear Survey Schedule (Ryall & Dietiker, 1979)	Children's Fear Survey Schedule-Revised (Barrios, Replogle, & Anderson-Tisdelle, 1983)	Children's Fear Survey Schedule-Revised (Barrios, Replogle, & Anderson-Tisdelle, 1983)
Self-report	Children's Cognitive Assessment Questionnaire (Zatz & Chassin, 1983)	Fear Thermometer (Giebenhain, 1985)	Nighttime Coping Response Inventory (Mooney, 1985)
Rating by other			Fear Strength, Questionnaire (Graziano & Mooney, 1980)
Direct			
Self-observation	Cognitive State Anxiety Inventory (Fox & Houston, 1983)	Somatic State Anxiety Inventory (Fox & Houston, 1983)	Fear & Avoidance Hierarchy Ratings (Barlow & Seidner, 1983)
Analog role-play			Modified Timed Behavior Checklist (Giebenhain, 1985)
Analog free behavior			Role Play Test (Esveldt-Dawson, Wisner, Unis, Matson, & Kazdin, 1982)
Naturalistic role-play			Behavioral Approach Test (Matson, 1981)
Naturalistic free behavior			Direct Home Observation (Graziano & Mooney, 1980)

Note: The classification scheme is based upon Cone's (1978) Behavioral Assessment Grid: the examples for the instrument categories are drawn from Barrios & Hartmann (in press-b).

methods of measurement, behavior therapists have been assuming that direct methods of assessment yield more veridical, higher fidelity information regarding a client's problem condition. Recently, the wisdom of continuing to be guided by these time-honored assumptions has been challenged. For some problem conditions, motor responses are not the most suitable referents (e.g., delusions, hallucinations, mood, pain); for many other cases, motor responses are not adequate representatives of the domain of content thought to cause the problem conditions (e.g., Barrios & Hartmann, in press; Barrios & Shigetomi, 1985; Jacobson, 1985a; Lang, 1984; Nelson & Hayes, 1981). Direct methods of measurement are not inherently superior to indirect methods of measurement nor are they thoroughly immune to bias and distortion (e.g., Harris & Lahey, 1982a, 1982b; Haynes & Horn, 1982; Jacobson, 1985a). Direct methods of measurement must prove their worth: through empirical demonstrations of their usefulness. Being neither inherently superior nor inherently exact, direct methods of measurement are therefore no more likely to prove to be useful to us in our assessment and treatment of our client's problem condition than are indirect methods of measurement (e.g., Jacobson, 1985a, 1985b).

Generalization

Rather than selecting assessment instruments on the basis of how well they meet preferences for motor responses and direct methods of measurement, it is better to select such assessment instruments on the basis of how well they meet the particular purposes in mind. Each of the many different purposes of assessment is simply a request for information — information that will facilitate accurate inferring which will facilitate effective treatment. Inferring is simply the process of generalizing from one phenomenon to another. Accurate inference is simply a function of the generalizability of the measures of one phenomenon to the measures of another.

At different junctures in treating a client's problem condition, we wish to infer different phenomena. That being the case, we seek different types of information from assessment. Specifically, we seek different estimates of the generalizability of our measures. For example, in the initial therapy phase of screening and general disposition we wish to infer quickly and accurately whether or not a prospective client is suitable for services. To do so we ask for information on the extent to which we can safely generalize from our response scores to the response scores of other scorers, to the response scores of other settings, to the response scores of other instruments, and to the response scores of other responses. In inferring other phenomena at other points in therapy, we ask for information on the extent to which we can safely generalize our response scores across some combination of six domains of response scores: item, scorer, time, setting, method; and dimension (Cone,

1977, 1978). Only instruments with established estimates of the appropriate types of generalization can provide us with such information. They are, of course, the instruments we wish to employ in our assessment of our client's problem condition and our treatment of said condition. To assist us in selecting instruments of appropriate generality, the grid classifies assessment devices along a third dimension — generalizability. It does so in terms of the generality of each instrument's measures across each of the aforementioned domains of scores. This breakdown of instruments by content area, method of measurement, *and* domains of generalization greatly simplifies the task of selecting suitable instruments for each of the different purposes of assessment.

Selecting instruments on the basis of the generality of their measures is not without its problems. *First*, there is the problem of few available instruments with proven estimates of generalizability. This being the case, there are few occasions when we are able to select instruments on the basis of the generality of their measures. On most occasions, then, we will be forced to invoke some other rule in our selection of assessment instruments. The question is: What other rule do we invoke? *Second*, there is the problem of how best to estimate generalization. Various analytical techniques exist for quantifying the generality of our measures (e.g., Cronbach, Gleser, Nanda, & Rajaratnam, 1972), but the techniques vary in their assumptions and their complexity and their ease of interpretation. No one technique or set of techniques has yet to emerge as the preferred method of estimating the generality of measures. *Finally*, there is the problem of how best to utilize these estimates of the generality of measures. The degree to which we can confidently generalize from one set of scores to another set of scores and thus confidently infer one phenomenon from another is certainly an important consideration in deciding whether or not to employ an instrument. It is, however, not the sole consideration. Other factors such as the cost of implementing the instrument, the feasibility of implementing the instrument, and the expertise in implementing the instrument also have a say in whether or not to employ the device. How great a say such factors should have in relation to the generalizability of the instrument's measures has yet to be formalized. Generating such a formula for instrument selection is but another one of the difficult assignments facing therapists.

INTERPRETATION OF ASSESSMENT

For assessment data to be helpful in formulating and evaluating the inferences on which the actions of therapy hinge, they must be interpreted. Contrary to popular belief, assessment data do not speak. Assessment data in and of themselves have no voice meaning. Assessment data take on meaning only when viewed against a backdrop of other data (e.g., Messick, 1980).

Among behavior therapists, the custom has been to have one of three sets of data serve as the backdrop against which we interpret our assessment data: client performance, criterion performance, or norms. With each backdrop comes a particular approach to the interpretation of assessment data. For the backdrop of client performance, it is the client-referenced approach; for the backdrop of criterion performance, the criterion-referenced approach; and for the backdrop of norms, the norm-referenced approach.

Client-Referenced Approach

In the client-referenced approach to interpretation, one assessment of a client's performance is placed beside another performance and meaning is ascribed to the scores on the basis of how well they match up. For example, we may compare the assessment of a client's posttreatment performance to that of a client's pretreatment performance. Or we may compare the assessment of a client's follow-up performance to that of a client's posttreatment performance. Whatever two assessments are compared, one assessment always serves as the referent for judging the significance and importance of the other. It is always the client, then, who serves as his or her own yardstick. For the client, there is perhaps no more sensible or relevant a yardstick for evaluating his or her assessment data. For many therapists and many of the clients' significant others, however, it is a most insensitive and insular yardstick (e.g., Kazdin, 1977).

Criterion-Referenced Approach

In the criterion-referenced approach to interpretation, assessment of the client's performance is not placed beside some other assessment of the client's performance but is placed beside some predetermined standard of performance. Meaning is ascribed to assessment data directly on the basis of how well the client's performance approximates this standard. For example, the therapist may have some set of criteria for adaptive responding. If the client matches this set of criteria, then the client is said to be responding adaptively; if the client does not match this set of criteria, then the client is said to be responding maladaptively. In the case of the therapist having some set of criteria for maladaptive responding, he or she would be making similar types of judgments about the client's responding. Having such performance criteria is certainly preferable to not having such performance criteria. Much of the ambiguity and subjectivity associated with data interpretation disappears when there are objective indices of adaptive and maladaptive functioning. Data interpretation becomes a surprisingly quick and easy and reliable affair when there are objective indices of adaptive and maladaptive functioning. The problem is that few performance patterns exist for which we have established, objective indices of adaptive and maladaptive responding (Barrios & Hartmann, 1986). Hence, there are few occasions on which a criterion-referenced approach to data interpretation can be employed. To increase the number of occasions on which a criterion-referenced approach to data interpretation can be used, clinicians must propose objective standards of problematic and nonproblematic responding for more performance patterns, and as a group we must agree to abide by these objective standards and the interpretive rules that accompany them. As unlikely as it might seem of this ever happening, steps are already being taken toward this end (e.g., Himadi, Barlow, & Boice, 1985).

Norm-Referenced Approach

In the norm-referenced approach to data interpretation, assessment of the client's performance is placed beside the performance of a suitable reference group. Meaning is assigned to the assessment data on the basis of where the client's performance falls in relationship to the performance of the members of that reference group (Ebel, 1972; Green, 1981; Nunnally, 1978). The comparison is an interindividual one: The individual client side-by-side with the reference group. Traditionally, therapists have shied away from making such interindividual comparisons, for they believe that group data were not particularly pertinent to the individual case (e.g., Barlow & Hersen, 1984; Hartmann et al., 1979; Nelson & Hayes, 1979). As a consequence, there are few assessment devices for which we have norms for various reference groups (Barrios & Shigetomi, 1985; Evans & Nelson, 1977). Thus, we have a few occasions on which to use a norm-referenced approach to data interpretation. Lately, we have come to look more kindly toward group data and have come to temper the belief that group data are irrelevant to the individual case. This turnaround in therapists' attitudes toward group data is due largely to an increased awareness and appreciation of the role that norms can play in the practice and progress of behavior therapy (Barrios & Hartmann, 1986; Hartmann et al., 1979). Norms can be of great help in screening prospective clients, identifying performance deficits, defining problematic behaviors, determining treatment targets, designing powerful treatments, selecting optimum treatments, establishing treatment goals, forming homogeneous groups, describing client samples, comparing alternative measures, and gauging treatment outcomes (e.g., Cone & Hawkins, 1977b; Evans & Nelson, 1977; Hartmann et al., 1979; Kazdin, 1977; Wolf, 1978). Of course, norms are of no help in carrying out any of these therapeutic functions if there are no normative estimates for the instruments employed and for the clients with whom they are employed. This is, in fact, the situation for most of the instruments used with the majority of clients. It may, however, be a situation that is changing. For with the changing view toward group data, we are seeing more collection of normative data (e.g., McGlynn & McNeil, in press; Ollendick, 1983). We are thus seeing the creation of more opportunities for the use of a norm-referenced approach to data interpretation.

It has been the custom of behavior therapists to use the three approaches to data interpretation in isolation rather than in tandem, for intraindividual comparisons have been viewed customarily as incompatible with interindividual comparisons. There is, however, no compelling reason to continue adhering to either one of these two customs. The two types of comparisons are not antithetical to one another nor are the three types of approaches antagonistic to one another. The different comparisons and different approaches facilitate the formation and evaluation of different inferences. Different types of inferences, though, are exactly what we need to render a single therapeutic decision. For example, the single therapeutic decision of whether or not a client's performance is a problem is ostensibly based upon the multiple inferences of whether or not that client's performance is distressing to the client, whether or not the client's performance differs from the criterion for persons like him or her, and whether or not the client's performance differs from the performance of persons like him or her. If it is indeed the case that single therapeutic decisions are arrived at by way of multiple isolated inferences, then it is indeed the case that we should employ multiple approaches to the interpretation of assessment data. How it is that the different approaches should be used in conjunction with one another has yet to be determined. How it is that differences of the various approaches should be combined such that they give rise to a single therapeutic decision has also yet to be determined. Naturally, the objective is to integrate the different approaches and their various inferences in ways that best serve the purposes of assessment. How to go about determining what best serves the purposes of behavioral assessment is discussed in the following section.

EVALUATION OF ASSESSMENT

Defining the problem space, identifying the level of analysis, selecting the method of measurement, and choosing the approach to data interpretation are all matters of contention. So, too, is the evaluation of each one of these assessment practices. At present, there are four major approaches to evaluating the soundness of assessment data and assessment practices: (a) the classic psychometric model (e.g., Barrios & Hartmann, 1986), (b) the generalizability model (e.g., Cone, 1977), (c) the accuracy model (e.g., Cone, 1981), and (d) the treatment validity model (e.g., Nelson & Hayes, 1979, 1981, 1986). Each model has its own set of premises about the nature of measurement and its own set of guidelines for the soundness of measurement. Each model also has its own set of advantages and disadvantages. All of these are now discussed.

Psychometric Model

At the heart of the classic psychometric model is the notion that all measurement is fallible. The assessment of a client's problem condition, the assessment of the treatment of a client's problem condition, etc., all contain some error. All assessment data reflect phenomena that are of interest to us (e.g, our client's performance) and that are of no interest to us (i.e., error). For an assessment instrument to be a sound instrument, it must yield data that reflect very much of the former and very little of the latter. The more it does so, the more reliable the instrument. The reliability of an instrument is ascertained by correlating scores on one-half of the items with the other half of the items, correlating scores on one form of the instrument with scores on alternate forms of the instrument, or correlating scores on one assessment occasion with scores on other assessment occasions. In ascertaining the reliability of an instrument, we are in essence estimating how well the instrument correlates with itself or with replicas of itself. If an instrument does not correlate well with itself, it cannot possibly correlate well with any other instrument (e.g., Green, 1981). It is for this reason that we place a premium on the reliability of an instrument when evaluating the worth of that instrument.

Reliability is the cornerstone of the classic psychometric model, but *validity* is the touchstone of the classic psychometric model (e.g., Guion, 1980). Validity is the degree to which we can safely generalize from the scores of one instrument to the scores of another instrument and the degree to which we can confidently infer scores on one instrument from scores on another instrument (e.g., Guion, 1980). With each different type of inferred score comes a different type of validity (e.g., Messick, 1980). If scores on one instrument correlate highly with scores on another instrument of presumably the same content, then both instruments are said to be of high *content validity*. If scores on one instrument correlate highly with scores on a criterion measure, then the former is said to be of high *criterion-related validity*. If scores on one instrument correlate highly with scores on another instrument of different but presumably related content, then both instruments are said to be of high *construct validity*. If scores on one instrument in one setting correlate highly with scores on the same instrument but in a different setting, then the instrument is said to be of high *ecological validity*. Other types of validity are known by other descriptors, each descriptor denoting the type of score we can generalize to or infer from a given instrument (e.g., concurrent validity, discriminant validity, nomological validity, population validity, temporal validity).

In the classic psychometric model, a reliable instrument is not necessarily a valid instrument. Reliability is fundamental to validity, but it does not insure validity. What reliability does insure is the possibility of validity. When scores on an instrument correlate well with themselves or replicas of themselves, we can freely generalize across scores, we can freely infer one score from another. For scores on an instrument to correlate well with scores on another instrument, they must first correlate well with themselves. In other words, in order for an instrument to be valid, it must be reliable (Nunnally, 1978).

Both reliability and validity allow for certain types of inferences: reliability intrainstrument inferences and validity interinstrument inferences. The treatment of a client's problem condition is predicated on a series of intra- and inter-instrument inferences — inferences formulated through the help of reliable and valid assessment data. The helpfulness of a particular instrument is judged always with reference to a particular inference. If the instrument has the specific properties of reliability or validity — or both — that are needed for accurate inferring, then the instrument is judged to be helpful. If the instrument does not have the specific properties that are needed, then the instrument is judged to be not helpful. In the classic psychometric model, the usefulness of our assessment practices lies exclusively in the reliability and validity of the assessment instruments (e.g., Guion, 1980).

The psychometric method of evaluating the quality of assessment data has come under much criticism, much of it having to do with the model's handling of three topics: response consistency, response variability, and response causality (e.g., Cone, 1981; Hayes, Nelson, & Jarrett, 1986; Nelson, 1983). Critics see the model as equating consistency in responding with adequacy of measurement. The more consistent the response scores are across different portions of the same instrument, and across different versions of the same instrument or different administrations of the same instrument, the more reliable the measures are. The more consistent the response scores are across different administrations of the same instrument in different settings and across different instruments of different but presumably related content, etc., the more valid the measures are. According to the psychometric model, the more reliable and valid the measures, the more trustworthy and useful the assessment data. If, however, we adhere to an interactionist view of performance — which behavior therapists now tend to do — there will be many occasions on which such consistency in responding is not expected. On such occasions, measures judged to be useful by the psychometric model will not prove to be very useful to us in treating of a client's problem condition. This being the case, critics question the wisdom of evaluating the quality of the measures by their psychometric properties of reliability and validity.

Critics also see the psychometric model as equating variability in responding at the level of the group with variability in responding at the level of the individual. Estimates of reliability and validity are based upon the response scores of all group members; the estimates of reliability and validity represent intra- and inter-instrument relationships that are applicable for the group as a whole. Although pertinent for the group, the relationships may not be pertinent for the individual. It is, however, at the level of the individual client that these relationships are inferred in the treatment of an individual client's problem condition. If the relationships that are inferred in the treatment of a client's problem condition are suspect, then is not the psychometric model for evaluating the quality of the assessment data also suspect? The critics say yes.

The critics also say that the model equates correlation with causation and that the model ascribes causal properties to person variables but not to situation variables. For example, criterion-related validity coefficients are often construed as causal relationships between predictor variables and criterion variables. The predictor variables are often person variables, and it is these person variables that are construed as the cause of the criterion variables. Coefficients of ecological validity are often interpreted in a similar manner. Consistency in responding across different settings is seen as being caused by a common variable — the common variable being a person variable not a situation variable.

As devastating as these criticisms of the psychometric model may appear to be, they are, upon careful consideration, not very devastating at all. Each of the criticisms stem from a misunderstanding of the nature and application of the model, which upon clarification lessens or eliminates the criticism (Barrios & Hartmann, 1986). For a measure to be useful, the psychometric model does not require identical response scores across different versions of the same instrument, across different instruments of the same content, etc. For a measure to be useful, the model requires that there be a consistent relationship among the response scores. Through a consistent relationship, we are able to infer one response score from another. The precision with which we are able to do so for the scores of an individual client depends upon the strength of this group-based relationship. The stronger the relationship, the more precise the inferences at the level of the individual; the stronger the relationship, the greater the relevance of group data for the individual client. Finally, the blame for misinterpretation of correlational relationships as causal relationships lies not with the psychometric model, but with the careless use of the psychometric model. The same applies to the ascription of causal properties to person variables as opposed to situation variables or the interaction of the two.

Generalizability Model

The concept of *measurement error* is also at the heart of the generalizability model for evaluating the quality of our assessment data (e.g., Cronbach et al., 1972). The model's handling of measurement error is, however, quite different from that of the classic psychometric model. According to generalizability theory, a response score is defined by the specific conditions under which it is determined. Variability in response scores across different forms of the same instrument, across different instruments of presumably the same content, etc., is not attributed to measurement error but to the different conditions under which the scores are determined. Of chief interest are the specific conditions of test item, scorer, method, setting, time, and response dimension (Cone, 1978). These are the specific conditions that we wish to generalize from one response score to another, to infer one response score from another in our treatment of our client's problem condition (Barrios & Hartmann, 1986). When variations in any of these conditions produces substantial variability in response scores, then generalizations or inferences from one level of a condition to another will be faulty. Insomuch as the goal of assessment is to facilitate accurate inferring, instruments yielding scores of established generalizability across the desired levels of one or more conditions are judged to be good measurement devices; instruments yielding scores of unknown or poor generalizability are judged to be poor measurement devices.

Many of the criticisms that have been leveled against the classic psychometric model have been leveled against the generalizability model (e.g., Hayes et al., 1986). And they, too, upon close inspection are not as damaging as they might first appear (Barrios & Hartmann, 1986). The model provides formula for the computation of generalizability coefficients — estimates of the degree to which we can generalize across response scores of different levels of the same condition. The coefficients are in essence a type of correlation coefficient (i.e., intraclass correlation coefficient). Like the judicious interpretation and use of reliability and validity coefficients, the judicious interpretation and use of generalizability coefficients can obviate many of the objections to this approach toward evaluation of assessment practices.

Accuracy Model

The concept of *accuracy* serves as the cornerstone and touchstone for the accuracy model of data evaluation (Cone, 1981). The more accurate the measure, the more useful it is. To determine the accuracy (and thus the usefulness) of an instrument, we simply compare its scores to an incontrovertible index of the performance pattern of interest. Herein lies the major problem with the accuracy model; there are few performance patterns for which we have incontrovertible standards.

Treatment Validity Model

The treatment validity model evaluates the quality of our assessment data in terms of their function, not in terms of their fabric (e.g., Hayes et al., 1986; Nelson & Hayes, 1981). Assessment data are said to be *treatment valid* if they expedite the orderly course of treatment or enhance the outcome of treatment. The more treatment valid the measures, the more useful they are. Treatment validity is established through experimental demonstrations. For example, if treatment carried out with the help of certain assessment data is shown to be more successful than treatment carried out without the help of such data, then those assessment data are said to be treatment valid. If treatment carried out with the help of certain assessment data is shown to be less time consuming or less costly but nevertheless as effective as treatment carried out without the help of such data, then those assessment data are said to be treatment valid. Other demonstrations of treatment validity may take other forms. All offer proof of incremental gains in treatment efficiency or effectiveness as a function of the collection and utilization of assessment data.

In the treatment validity model, we are evaluating the quality of our assessment data on the basis of experimental data. The obvious question is: How do we evaluate the quality of the experimental data on which we base our evaluation of our assessment data? According to the model, we do so by inspecting the integrity or validity of the design of the experiment (e.g., Campbell & Stanley, 1966; Cook & Campbell, 1979). A thorough inspection of the integrity of the experiment's design does, however, call for an inspection of the integrity of the experiment's measures. The treatment validity model offers no guidelines for carrying out such an inspection. It appears, then, that the treatment validity model begs the question of how to evaluate the quality of assessment data.

Conspicuously absent from each of the four data evaluation models is an explicit formulation of the concept of utility. Each of the four models is, therefore, an incomplete approach to evaluating the quality of assessment data. In the psychometric and generalizability models, there is the implicit equating of generalizability with utility; in the accuracy model, there is the implicit equating of accuracy with utility; and in the treatment validity model, there is the implicit equating of incremental gains in treatment efficiency and effectiveness with utility. The usefulness of our assessment procedures would appear to be a function of all three of these properties (e.g., Wiggins, 1973). Exactly how the three properties are to be combined so as to yield a single quantitative index of usefulness has yet to be determined. Development of such a formula is another one of the pressing tasks the future holds.

ON THE FUTURE NATURE OF BEHAVIORAL ASSESSMENT

The great diversity with which we define, analyze, and measure the problem conditions of clients; interpret the data from our assessments; and evaluate the quality of assessment data is a source of great distress to some. It should not, however, be a source of distress provided we do not lose sight of the common enemy — inefficient clinical practice. Clinicians can hope that from this diversity will emerge a unified and useful discipline of behavioral assessment. For such a discipline to emerge, advances must be made in the areas of instrument development, instrument utilization, and instrument evaluation.

In the area of instrument development, we need to begin constructing assessment batteries for the common, complex problem conditions of our clients and to begin administering these batteries in a standardized fashion. Only through standardized assessment can a sizable data base be accrued, and it is a sizable data base that we need in order to carefully determine the value of our assessment practices.

Throughout this chapter, note has been made of the fact that the aim of assessment is to provide information for the purposes of making treatment decisions. In determining the value of assessment data, we are also determining the value of the rules by which the data are utilized and the decisions are reached. In other words, we are also determining the value of our decision-making strategies. Heretofore there has been a conspiracy of silence among us with regard to our decision-making strategies. To sensitively and systematically study the worth of assessment data, we must delineate the models we are using to arrive at treatment decisions (Evans & Wilson, 1983).

Critical appraisal and refinement of data-collection and data-interpretation practices will depend upon our meeting two other conditions: agreement on the criteria against which we judge how well an assessment satisfies its stated purpose and establishment of rules for combining and interpreting the different outcomes (Mash, 1985). Given that we draw upon assessment data for many different purposes (e.g., for assistance in problem identification, treatment selection, and treatment evaluation), we will need to set suitable outcome criteria for each of the different purposes. The task embodied in each of these functions — assistance — is a complex, multifaceted one; the criteria we set forth for data evaluation will, therefore, also need to be complex and multifaceted (e.g., the accuracy of the therapeutic action, the cost of data collection and interpretation, the cost of the therapeutic action, the benefits of the therapeutic action, client satisfaction with the therapeutic action, etc.). For evaluations of our assessment practices to be of service to us, we must also devise rules for combining the various outcomes into a meaningful index of usefulness.

Though the behavioral approach to clinical assessment owes its existence to the behavioral approach to clinical treatment, the futures of the two approaches are inextricably bound. Advances in our assessment procedures will lead to advances in our theories and techniques; advances in our theories and techniques will lead to advances in our assessment procedures. The interplay between the two approaches will lead to iterative refinements in each. We, therefore, cannot afford to neglect either the area of assessment or the area of treatment. Our hope is that constant nurturance of each will bring us closer to the realization of the promise of behavior therapy: empirical clinical practice.

REFERENCES

American Psychiatric Association. (1980). *Diagnostic and statistical manual of mental disorders* (3rd ed.). Washington, DC: Author.

Angle, H. V., Hay, L. R., Hay, W. M., & Ellinwood, E. H. (1977). Computer assisted behavioral assessment. In J. D. Cone & R. P. Hawkins (Eds.), *Behavioral assessment: New directions in clinical psychology* (pp. 369–380). New York: Brunner/Mazel.

Barlow, D. H. (1980). Behavior therapy: The next decade. *Behavior Therapy, 11,* 315–328.

Barlow, D. H. (Ed.). (1981). *Behavioral assessment of adult disorders.* New York: Guilford Press.

Barlow, D. H. (Ed.). (1985). *Clinical handbook of psychological disorders.* New York: Guilford Press.

Barlow, D. H., & Hersen, M. (1984). *Single case experimental designs: Strategies for studying behavior change* (2nd ed.). New York: Pergamon.

Barlow, D. H., & Seidner, A. L. (1983). Treatment of adolescent agoraphobia: Effects on parent-adolescent relations. *Behavior Research and Therapy, 21,* 519–526.

Barrett, B. H., Johnston, J. M., & Pennypacker, H. S. (1986). Behavior: Its units, dimensions, and measurement. In R. O. Nelson & S. C. Hayes (Eds.), *Conceptual foundation of behavioral assessment* (pp. 156–200). New York: Guilford Press.

Barrios, B. A., & Hartmann, D. P. (1986). The contributions of traditional assessment: Concepts, issues, and methodologies. In R. O. Nelson & S. C. Hayes (Eds.), *Conceptual foundations of behavioral assessment* (pp. 81–110). New York: Guilford Press.

Barrios, B. A., & Hartmann, D. P. (in press-a). Fears and anxieties in children. In E. J. Mash & L. G. Terdal (Eds.), *Behavioral assessment of childhood disorders* (2nd ed.). New York: Guilford Press.

Barrios, B. A., & Hartmann, D. P. (in press-b). Recent developments in single-subject methodology. In M. Hersen, R. Eisler, & P. M. Miller (Eds.). *Progress in behavior modification*. Beverly Hills, CA: Sage Press.

Barrios, B. A., Hartmann, D. P., & Shigetomi, C. (1981). Fears and anxieties in children. In E. J. Mash & L. G. Tergal (Eds.), *Behavioral assessment of childhood disorders* (pp. 259–304). New York: Guilford Press.

Barrios, B. A., Replogle, W., & Anderson-Tisdelle, D. (1983, December). *Multisystem-unimethod analyses of children's fears*. Paper presented at the meeting of the Association for Advancement of Behavior Therapy, Washington, DC.

Barrios, B. A., & Shigetomi, C. C. (1985). Assessment of children's fears: A critical review. In T. R. Kratochwill (Ed.), *Advances in school psychology* (Vol. 4, pp. 89–132). New York: Erlbaum.

Bellack, A. S., Hersen, M., & Kazdin, A. E. (Eds.). (1982). *International handbook of behavior modification and therapy*. New York: Plenum Press.

Borkovec, T. D. (1976). Physiological and cognitive processes in the regulation of anxiety. In G. E. Schwartz & D. Shapiro (Eds.), *Consciousness and self-regulation* (Vol. 1, pp. 261–312). New York: Plenum Press.

Bornstein, P. H., Bornstein, M. T., & Dawson, B. (1984). Integrated assessment and treatment. In T. H. Ollendick & M. Hersen (Eds.), *Child behavioral assessment: Principles and procedures* (pp. 223–243). New York: Pergamon.

Campbell, D. T., & Stanley, J. C. (1966). *Experimental and quasi-experimental designs for research*. Chicago: Rand McNally.

Ciminero, A. R. (1977). Behavioral assessment: An overview. In A. K. Ciminero, K. S. Calhoun, & H. E. Adams (Eds.), *Handbook of behavioral assessment* (pp. 3–13). New York: John Wiley & Sons.

Ciminero, A. R., Calhoun, K. S., & Adams, H. E. (Eds.). (1977). *Handbook of behavioral assessment*. New York: John Wiley & Sons.

Cone, J. D. (1977). The relevance of reliability and validity for behavioral assessment. *Behavior Therapy, 8*, 411–426.

Cone, J. D. (1978). The behavioral assessment grid (BAG): A conceptual framework and a taxonomy. *Behavior Therapy, 9*, 882–888.

Cone, J. D. (1981). Psychometric considerations. In M. Hersen & A. S. Bellack (Eds.), *Behavioral assessment: A practical handbook* (2nd ed., pp. 36–68). New York: Pergamon Press.

Cone, J. D., & Hawkins, R. P. (Eds.). (1977a). *Behavioral assessment: New directions in clinical psychology*. New York: Brunner/Mazel.

Cone, J. D., & Hawkins, R. P. (1977b). Current status and future directions in behavioral assessment. In J. D. Cone & R. P. Hawkins (Eds.), *Behavioral assessment: New directions in clinical psychology*. New York: Brunner/Mazel.

Cook, T. D., & Campbell, D. T. (1979). *Quasi-experimentation: Design and analysis issues for field settings*. Chicago: Rand McNally.

Cronbach, L. J., Gleser, G., Nanda, H., & Rajaratnam, N. (1972). *The dependability of behavioral measurement: Theory of generalizability for scores and profiles*. New York: John Wiley & Sons.

Drabman, R. S., Hammer, D., & Rosenbaum, M. S. (1979). Assessing generalization in behavior modification with children: The generalization map. *Behavioral Assessment, 1*, 203–219.

Ebel, R. L. (1972). Some limitations of criterion-referenced measurement. In G. H. Bracht, K. D. Hopkins, & J. C. Stanley (Eds.), *Perspectives in educational and psychological measurement*. Englewood Cliffs, NJ: Prentice-Hall.

Endler, N. S., & Magnusson, D. (1976). Toward an interactional psychology of personality. *Psychological Bulletin, 33*, 956–974.

Esveldt-Dawson, K., Wisner, K. L., Unis, A. S., Matson, J. L., & Kazdin, A. E. (1982). Treatment of phobias in a hospitalized child. *Journal of Behavior Therapy and Experimental Psychiatry, 11*, 77–83.

Evans, I. M. (1985). Building systems models as a strategy for target behavior selection in clinical assessment. *Behavioral Assessment, 7*, 21–32.

Evans, I. M. (1986). Response structure and the triple-response-mode concept. In R. O. Nelson & S. C. Hayes (Eds.), *Conceptual foundations of behavioral assessment* (pp. 131–155). New York: Guilford Press.

Evans, I. M., & Nelson, R. O. (1977). Assessment of child behavior problems. In A. R. Ciminero, K. S. Calhoun, & H. E. Adams (Eds.), *Handbook of behavioral assessment* (pp. 603–681). New York: John Wiley & Sons.

Evans, I. M., & Wilson, F. E. (1983). Behavioral assessment as decision making: A theoretical analysis. In M. Rosenbaum, C. M. Franks, & Y. Jaffe (Eds.), *Perspectives on behavior therapy in the eighties* (pp. 35–53). New York: Springer.

Foster, S. L., & Ritchey, W. L. (1979). Issues in the assessment of the social competence of children. *Journal of Applied Behavior Analysis, 12*, 625–638.

Fox, J. E., & Houston, B. K. (1983). Distinguishing between cognitive and somatic trait and state anxiety in children. *Journal of Personality and Social Psychology, 45*, 862–870.

Gelfand, D. M., & Hartmann, D. P. (1984). *Child behavior: Analysis and therapy* (2nd ed.). Elmsford, NY: Pergamon Press.

Giebenhain, J. E. (1985). *Multi-channel assessment of children's fear of the dark.* Unpublished doctoral dissertation, University of Mississippi, Oxford, MS.

Goldfried, M. R., & D'Zurilla, T. J. (1969). A behavior-analytic model for assessing competence. In C. D. Spielberger (Ed.), *Current topics in clinical and community psychology* (Vol. 1, pp. 151–196). New York: Academic Press.

Goldfried, M. R., & Kent, R. N. (1972). Traditional versus behavioral assessment: A comparison of methodological and theoretical assumptions. *Psychological Bulletin, 77*, 409–420.

Goldfried, M. R., & Sprafkin, J. N. (1976). Behavioral personality assessment. In J. T. Spence, R. C. Carson, & J. W. Thibaut (Eds.), *Behavioral approaches to therapy* (pp. 295–321). Morristown, NJ: General Learning Press.

Graziano, A. M., & Mooney, K. C. (1980). Family self-control instruction for children's nighttime fear reduction. *Journal of Consulting and Clinical Psychology, 48*, 206–213.

Green, B. F. (1981). A primer of testing. *American Psychologist, 36*, 1001–1011.

Guion, R. M. (1980). On the trinitarian doctrines of validity. *Professional Psychology, 11*, 385–398.

Harris, F. C., & Lahey, B. B. (1982a). Subject reactivity in direct observational assessment: A review and critical analysis. *Clinical Psychology Review, 2*, 523–538.

Harris, F. C., & Lahey, B. B. (1982b). Recording system bias in direct observational methodology: A review and critical analysis of factors causing inaccurate coding behavior. *Clinical Psychology Review, 2*, 539–556.

Hartmann, D. P., Roper, B. L., & Bradford, D. C. (1979). Some relationships between behavioral and traditional assessment. *Journal of Behavioral Assessment, 1*, 3–21.

Hawkins, R. P. (1979). The functions of assessment: Implications for selection and development of devices for assessing repertoires in clinical, educational, and other settings. *Journal of Applied Behavior Analysis, 12*, 501–516.

Hayes, S. C., Nelson, R. O., & Jarrett, R. B. (1986). Evaluating the quality of behavioral assessment. In R. O. Nelson & S. C. Hayes (Eds.), *Conceptual foundations of behavioral assessment* (pp. 463–504). New York: Guilford Press.

Haynes, S. N. (1986). The design of intervention programs. In R. O. Nelson & S. C. Hayes (Eds.), *Conceptual foundations of behavioral assessment* (pp. 386–427). New York: Guilford Press.

Haynes, S. N., & Horn, W. F. (1982). Reactivity in behavioral observations: A methodological and conceptual critique. *Behavioral Assessment, 4*, 369–385.

Hersen, M. (1981). Complex problems require complex solutions. *Behavior Therapy, 12*, 15–29.

Hersen, M. (Ed.). (1983). *Outpatient behavior therapy. A clinical guide.* New York: Grune & Stratton.

Hersen, M. (Ed.). (1985). *Practice of inpatient behavior therapy: A clinical guide.* New York: Grune & Stratton.

Hersen, M., & Barlow, D. H. (1976). *Single case experimental designs: Strategies for studying behavior change.* New York: Pergamon Press.

Himadi, W. G., Boice, R., & Barlow, D. H. (1985). *Assessment of agoraphobia: Measurement of clinical change.* Unpublished manuscript, Center for Stress and Anxiety Disorders, Albany, NY.

Jacobson, N. S. (1985a). The role of observational measures in behavior therapy outcome research. *Behavioral Assessment, 7*, 297–308.

Jacobson, N. S. (1985b). Uses versus abuses of observational measures. *Behavioral Assessment, 7*, 323–330.

Kanfer, F. H. (1985). Target selection for clinical change programs. *Behavioral Assessment, 7*, 7–20.

Kanfer, F. H., & Saslow, G. (1969). Behavioral diagnosis. In C. M. Franks (Ed.), *Behavior therapy: Appraisal and status* (pp. 417–444). New York: McGraw-Hill.

Kazdin, A. E. (1977). Assessing the clinical or applied importance of behavior change through social validation. *Behavior Modification, 1*, 427–452.

Kazdin, A. E. (1979). Fictions, factions, and functions of behavior therapy. *Behavior Therapy, 10*, 629–654.

Kazdin, A. E. (1980). *Research design in clinical psychology.* New York: Harper & Row.

Kazdin, A. E. (1983). Psychiatric diagnosis, dimensions of dysfunction, and child behavior therapy. *Behavior Therapy, 14*, 73–99.

Kazdin, A. E. (1985). Selection of target behaviors: The relationship of the treatment focus to clinical dysfunction. *Behavioral Assessment, 7*, 33–47.

Kazdin, A. E., & Wilson, G. T. (1978). *Evaluation of behavior therapy: Issues, evidence and research strategies.* Cambridge, MA: Ballinger, 1973.

Krantz, S. (Ed.). (1984). Special mini-series on the generalization and maintenance of change. *The Cognitive Behaviorist, 6*, 1–24.

Kratochwill, T. R. (1978). Foundations of time-series research. In T. R. Kratochwill (Ed.), *Single-subject research: Strategies for evaluating change* (pp. 1–101). New York: Academic Press.

Kratochwill, T. R. (1985). Selection of target behaviors in behavioral consultation. *Behavioral Assessment, 7*, 49–62.

Lang, P. J. (1968). Fear reduction and fear behavior: Problems in treating a construct. In J. M. Shlien (Ed.), *Research in psychotherapy* (Vol. 3, pp. 90–103). Washington, DC: American Psychological Association.

Lang, P. J. (1971). The application of psychophysiological methods in the study of psychotherapy and behavior modification. In A. E. Bergin & S. L. Garfield (Eds.),

Handbook of psychotherapy and behavior change: An empirical analysis (pp. 75–125). New York: John Wiley & Sons.

Lang, P. J. (1984). Cognition in emotion: Concept and action. In C. E. Izard, J. Kagan, & R. B. Zajonc (Eds.), *Emotions, cognition, and behavior* (pp. 192–226). New York: Cambridge University Press.

Lindsley, O. R. (1964). Direct measurement and prosthesis of retarded behavior. *Journal of Education, 147*, 62–81.

Magnusson, D., & Endler, N. S. (Eds.). (1977). *Personality at the crossroads: Current issues in interactional psychology.* Hillsdale, NJ: Lawrence Erlbaum.

Mash, E. J. (1979). What is behavioral assessment? *Behavioral Assessment, 1*, 23–30.

Mash, E. J. (1985). Some comments on target selection in behavior therapy. *Behavioral Assessment, 7*, 63–78.

Mash, E. J., & Terdal, L. G. (1976). Behavior therapy assessment: Diagnosis, design and evaluation. In E. J. Mash & L. G. Terdal (Eds.), *Behavior therapy assessment* (pp. 15–31). New York: Springer.

Mash, E. J., & Terdal, L. G. (Eds.). (in press). *Behavioral assessment of childhood disorders* (2nd ed.). New York: Guilford Press.

Matson, J. L. (1981). Assessment and treatment of clinical fears in mentally retarded children. *Journal of Applied Behavior Analysis, 14*, 287–294.

McGlynn, F. D., & McNeil, D. W. (in press). Test-retest reliability and internal consistency of the dental fear survey. *Behavioral Assessment.*

Messick, S. (1980). Test validity and the ethics of assessment. *American Psychologist, 35*, 1012–1027.

Mooney, K. C. (1985). Children's nighttime fears: Ratings of content and coping behaviors. *Cognitive Therapy and Research, 9*, 309–319.

Nathan, P. E. (1981). Symptomatic diagnosis and behavioral assessment. In D. H. Barlow (Ed.), *Behavioral assessment of adult disorders* (pp. 1–11). New York: Guilford.

Nelson, R. O. (1983). Behavioral assessment: Past, present, and future. *Behavioral Assessment, 5*, 195–206.

Nelson, R. O., & Barlow, D. H. (1981). An overview of behavioral assessment with adult clients: Basic strategies and initial procedures. In D. H. Barlow (Ed.), *Behavioral assessment of adult disorders* (pp. 13–43). New York: Guilford.

Nelson, R. O., & Hayes, S. C. (1979). Some current dimensions of behavioral assessment. *Behavioral Assessment, 1*, 1–16.

Nelson, R. O., & Hayes, S. C. (1981). Nature of behavioral assessment. In M. Hersen, & A. S. Bellack (Eds.), *Behavioral assessment: A practical handbook* (2nd ed., pp. 3–37). New York: Pergamon Press.

Nelson, R. O., & Hayes, S. C. (1986). The nature of behavioral assessment. In R. O. Nelson & S. C. Hayes (Eds.), *Conceptual foundations of behavioral assessment* (pp. 3–41). New York: Guilford Press.

Nunnally, J. (1978). *Psychometric theory* (2nd ed.). New York: McGraw-Hill.

Ollendick, T. H. (1983). Reliability and validity of the Revised Fear Survey Schedule for Children. *Behavior Research and Therapy, 21*, 685–692.

Ollendick, T. H., & Hersen, M. (Eds.). (1984). *Child behavioral assessment: Principles and procedures.* New York: Pergamon.

O'Leary, K. D. (1972). The assessment of psychopathology in children. In H. C. Quay & J. S. Werry (Eds.), *Psychopathological disorders of childhood* (pp. 234–272). New York: Wiley.

Paul, G. L., & Bernstein, D. A. (1973). *Anxiety and clinical problems: Systematic desensitization and related techniques.* New York: General Learning Press.

Rachman, S., & Wilson, G. T. (1980). *The effects of psychological therapy*. Oxford: Pergamon.

Rimm, D. C., & Masters, J. C. (1979). *Behavior therapy: Techniques and empirical findings* (2nd ed.). New York: Academic Press.

Ross, A. O. (1985). To form a more perfect union: It is time to stop standing still. *Behavior Therapy, 16*, 195–204.

Ryall, M. R., & Dietikar, K. E. (1979). Reliability and clinical validity of the Children's Fear Survey Schedule. *Journal of Behavior Therapy and Experimental Psychiatry, 10*, 303–310.

Stokes, T. F., & Baer, D. M. (1977). An implicit technology of generalization. *Journal of Applied Behavior Analysis, 10*, 349–367.

Taylor, C. B. (1983). DSM-III and behavioral assessment. *Behavioral Assessment, 5*, 5–14.

Tharp, R. G., & Wetzel, R. J. (1969). *Behavior modification in the natural environment*. New York: Academic Press.

Wiggins, J. S. (1973). *Personality and prediction: Principles of personality assessment*. Reading, MA: Addison-Wesley.

Wilson, G. T. (1978). On the much discussed nature of behavior therapy. *Behavior Therapy, 9*, 89–98.

Wilson, G. T. (1982). Psychotherapy process and procedure: The behavioral mandate. *Behavior Therapy, 13*, 291–312.

Wolf, M. M. (1978). Social validity: The case for subjective measurement or how behavior analysis is finding its heart. *Journal of Applied Behavior Analysis, 11*, 203–214.

Wolpe, J. (1982). *The practice of behavior therapy* (3rd ed.). New York: Pergamon.

Yates, A. J. (1981). Behavior therapy: Past, present, future — imperfect? *Clinical Psychology Review, 1*, 269–291.

Yates, B. T. (1985). Cost-effectiveness analysis and cost-benefit analysis: An introduction. *Behavioral Assessment, 7*, 207–234.

Zatz, S., & Chassin, L. (1983). Cognitions of test-anxious children. *Journal of Consulting and Clinical Psychology, 51*, 526–534.

2
Psychometric Considerations and the Multiple Models of Behavioral Assessment

John D. Cone

Science . . . differs from less promising, noncumulative, and personalistic enterprises . . . in part because of its skeptical insistence on reliable (intersubjective, replicable) protocols that describe observations. (Meehl, 1978, p. 813).

The Physicist's scientific power comes from . . . the immense deductive fertility of the formalism and the accuracy of the measuring instruments. (Meehl, 1978, p. 825).

In the second edition of this handbook an earlier version of this chapter (Cone, 1981) began with a brief section that, like Meehl's quotes, emphasized the basis for concern with measurement adequacy. It is certainly beyond argument that the building of all science rests on a foundation of accurate measurement. It can be argued similarly that responsible intervention, whether at the individual or larger community levels, rests squarely on adequate assessment. Incomplete or inaccurate information can lead to erroneous decisions about a client that can result in harm whether the client is an individual or a larger system. Less extreme, erroneous, or incomplete information can lead to inappropriately chosen and/or unnecessarily prolonged treatment at unwarranted cost to the client or a third-party payer. Recognition of this possibility is one of the bases for quality assurance programs designed to monitor the expenditure of behavioral health monies. The increasing levels of accountability represented by professional standards review organizations (PSROs) and the requirement by third-party payers (such as CHAMPUS: Claiborne & Zaro, 1979) for service providers to furnish client progress reports both underscore the value of adequate assessment procedures. It is conceivable that providers producing the most documented change in the shortest period of time will eventually survive future accountability "shakeouts."

Thus, the development of science, the provision of high quality service, and the representation of the quality of this service to clients and others all require adequate assessment. This chapter looks at just what it means for assessment to be considered adequate. It will be shown that adequacy is relative, varying with the model of assessment that has been adopted. A review of numerous extant models of behavioral assessment reveals the heterogeneity of the enterprise. It is likely that some of the bases for adequate measures mentioned above, especially forces for increased accountability, will narrow the options somewhat in the future. In the meanwhile, any chapter on the psychometric adequacy of assessment procedures should represent the catholicism that exists today.

After reviewing various assessment models and calling attention to model-relevant differences in evaluative criteria, the need for idiographic assessment methodologies will be articulated. The basic inappropriateness of nomothetically derived measures for planning and evaluating intervention programs for individuals will be discussed. After describing several approaches to the development of idiographic instruments, attention will be directed to the minimal criteria needed to establish their adequacy. Finally, the need for developing and evaluating concepts and methodologics in the area of single-subject psychometrics will be argued. Such a discipline would be a logical complement to that which has focused on developing single-subject research design for evaluating the impact of independent variables.

MODELS OF BEHAVIORAL ASSESSMENT

While it is discomfitting to write a chapter without defining early on the subject matter of that chapter, it is, unfortunately, necessary in the present case. There is no single agreed-upon definition of behavioral assessment. Nor is there a consistent repertoire manifested by behavioral assessment professionals that could lead one to abstract an operational definition in terms of their activities. As readers of other chapters in this and similar collections (e.g., Barlow, 1981; Ciminero, Calhoun, & Adams, 1966; Hersen & Bellack, 1976, 1981; Mash & Terdal, 1980) will discover, there is a great deal of diversity among researchers in terms of what they label behavioral assessment.

Recently a description of 32 different approaches to the enterprise was generated via the simultaneous consideration of subject matter (e.g., traits or behavior), focus of assessment (e.g., idiographic or nomothetic), approach to science (deductive or inductive), primary source of variability (inter- or intra-subject), and environmental emphasis (interactive or noninteractive)

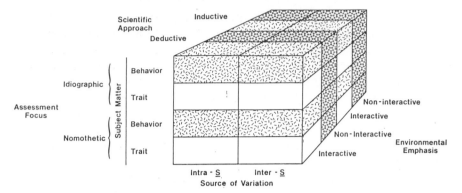

FIGURE 2.1. Models of Behavioral Assessment Research. From "Idiographic, Nomothetic, and Other Perspectives in Behavioral Assessment by J.D. Cone, in *Conceptual Foundations in Behavioral Assessment*, S.C. Hayes and R.O. Nelsons, Eds., in press, New York – Guilford Press. Copywright by Guilford Press. Reprinted by permission.

(Cone, 1986). Figure 2.1 shows the models resulting from crossing only two values on each of these dimensions. Space does not permit a duplication of the detailed description of the 32 approaches. One or two examples will provide a sense of the general scheme, however, and show its basis in contemporary practice of behavioral assessment.

In the previous edition of this handbook, Arkowitz (1981) provided an example of the assessment of a case of "social inadequacy." Among the measures used were the Social Avoidance and Distress Scale (SADS, Watson & Friend, 1969), the Social Anxiety Inventory (SAI, Richardson & Tasto, 1981), and the Beck Depression Inventory (BDI, Beck, 1972). Each of these measures was developed to assess a trait, and the curators as well as other researchers have devoted considerable energy to evaluating a measure's effectiveness. For example, Watson and Friend (1969) stated that "one of the major goals was to foster scale homogeneity" and they examined correlations between individual items and total scale scores as one way of assessing this. As has been pointed out before, concern with internal consistency can reflect the authors' interest in assessing a homogeneous trait rather than multiple independent or partially independent responses (Cone & Hawkins, 1977; Rich & Schroeder, 1976).

The focus of assessment for the authors of the SADS, SAI, and BDI was, furthermore, nomothetic. That is, they studied a particular variable of interest to them, rather than a specific individual client. In addition, their definitions of the variables led to a deductive development of the measures. Thus, they started with a general conception of social avoidance, social anxiety, and depression, and reasoned from that to the particular behavior representing it. Research supporting the initial utility of each measure examined variability in scores of multiple subjects. Finally, while different contexts (e.g., social, occupational) were considered in developing the initial items, actual use of the scales does not require simultaneous consideration of the environment in which the person is functioning. Thus, in terms of *development*, all three of the scales can be classified in the second cell from the front on the bottom right hand side of the model in Figure 2.1. While these instruments are widely used and reported in the behavioral assessment literature, it can be seen from this classification that they are fundamentally no different in concept from the self-report measures of traditional clinical assessment.

Of course, the development of an instrument can be considered somewhat apart from its subsequent uses. Thus, regardless of their origins, their use by Arkowitz (1981) might lead to a different categorization in terms of Figure 2.1. While it is a bit risky interpreting one's conceptualization of a problem from a written case description, it appears reasonably clear in the present case that Arkowitz was coming at it, at least partially, from a trait-based perspective. This is supported by interpretation of results from other measures, for example, a behavioral performance test involving interactions with confederates which showed "considerable anxiety and a skill deficit based on both self- and observer ratings." (p. 321). Further, "treatment was multi-faceted including a psychodynamic approach to help her define her problems . . ." (pp. 321–323).

The focus of Arkowitz's (1981) assessment appears to have been the client. I say "appears" because while it is a case presentation, it is unclear whether the client came to Arkowitz as a client primarily or as a potential participant in research on social skills. If the referral were for the latter reason, it could be said that his primary focus was on the social skills variable as reflected through the medium of this particular client. This is certainly a perfectly proper focus and it is more likely to lead to different assessment tactics than if the concern were solely with the needs of the client. For example, social skills issues might be of lower priority than a number of others or they might be defined differently for this client than would be revealed on standardized measures developed in a variable-focused research tradition.

With respect to scientific approach, it appears a deductive stance was taken in the Arkowitz assessment. The client was referred to Arkowitz because "it was felt that her social difficulties needed attention" (p. 320). In the course of his assessment interview with her, Arkowitz also found her to be concerned about depression and obesity. Following up on these identified areas, the SADS, SAI, and BDI were administered. Additional procedures included the Adult Self-Expression Scale (Gay, Hollandsworth, & Galassi, 1975), self-monitoring of six aspects of social interaction, and self and observer ratings of social anxiety and social skills during separate 10-minute interactions with a male and female confederate.

The selection of these formal procedures appears to have been based on the major problem areas identified in interviews with the client and in referral information. Guided by general terms such as *social anxiety* and *depression*, instruments were selected to assess particular component behavior and to establish whether any were problematic for the client. The overall approach can be characterized as a deductive one. That is, starting with general concepts, Arkowitz, assisted by formal instruments, reasoned to the particulars. An intervention program developed from the assessment data was evaluated in terms of pre/post differences on the instruments. For some of them, normative means were provided as reference points. Thus, the source of variability for examining differences in assessment data as related to the intervention was within the client. An interactive approach was taken with regard to environmental characteristics, at least for social anxiety and skill, by having the client assessed during social contact with confederates.

In the previous version of this chapter (Cone, 1981) it was concluded that classical psychometric concepts, based as they are on differences between persons, are irrelevant to an assessment enterprise concerned with behavior and its variation within individuals. As Figure 2.1 and the example just given show, however, such a conclusion would have to be based on the presumed value of a particular type of behavioral assessment. To reject psychometric concepts entirely is to risk an assumption of uniformity within the general discipline that is unwarranted at the present time. Although it might be tempting to go through Figure 2.1 crossing out those cells that are not truly considered within the purview of behavioral assessment, this would be a somewhat arbitrary exercise at worst, and at best it would not represent what researchers and practitioners often call behavioral assessment.

Acknowledging this pluralism presents problems for someone charged with the task of writing about psychometric considerations for behavioral assessment. The very request belies an unwarranted assumption of uniformity. Issues of measurement adequacy vary considerably depending on the type of behavioral assessment one is pursuing. Given the large number of types, comprehensive discussion of the psychometric issues of each would far exceed the space constraints of a single chapter. Nonetheless it might be instructive to consider major psychometric concepts as they apply or do not apply to two radically different approaches to behavioral assessment. It is toward this exercise that the following section is devoted.

TWO CONTRASTING MODELS OF BEHAVIORAL ASSESSMENT

Because the assessment approach illustrated by Arkowitz (1981) is rather typical among behavioral assessors, it will be chosen and referred to as the *nomothetic-trait approach*. It can be characterized as selecting traits or syndromes (e.g., social anxiety, depression agoraphobia) as its subject matter, developing instruments to assess them deductively, and establishing the adequacy of such instruments in terms of variation in instrument scores between individuals. The instruments are then used to evaluate the effects of independent variables in formal research with groups of subjects or to evaluate interventions applied to individuals.

The contrasting strategy will be referred to as the *idiographic-behavior approach*. It can be characterized as selecting specific behavior as its subject matter, developing procedures to assess it inductively, and establishing the adequacy of such procedures in terms of variation in scores within individuals.

Traditional psychometric concepts as they apply to each approach are listed in Table 2.1. In addition to classical psychometric concepts of reliability and validity, the newer concept of accuracy (Cone, 1981) has been included in the table. It can be seen that the various types of accuracy are relevant only to the idiographic-behavior approach. When behavior is the subject matter of a discipline (as it is in this case), its existence can be more or less objectively verified. An instrument can be said to be accurate to the extent that the data it produces are controlled by the phenomenon being tacted (Skinner, 1945). When traits are the subject matter of a discipline, their existence cannot be objectively verified. They are proposed or supposed when no universally agreed-upon definition exists.

As noted in the earlier exposition (Cone, 1981), an instrument should be accurate or sensitive to revealing five facts about behavior: (a) its occurrence, (b) its repeated occurrence, (c) its occurrence in more than one setting, (d) its susceptibility to being assessed in multiple ways, and (e) its relationship to other behavior. Prerequisite to establishing accuracy are a set of rules/procedures for using the instrument, and an incontrovertible index against which to compare scores generated from the instrument. The index tells us what is really there in nature. If the instrument, when used according to the rules/procedures provided by its developers, reveals the same picture as the incontrovertible index, it can be said to be accurate. To the extent that there is less than perfect agreement between instrument and index, error or noise exists and must be accounted for. This situation is common in the physical sciences where the inclusion of signal to noise ratios, power and resolution, and so on reflect the less than completely accurate or perfect reproduction of what is really there in nature by the instruments being used.

Accuracy must be established *before* the instrument is used to answer questions about behavior. Within the nomothetic-trait approach it is usually the case that the process of instrument validation and elaborating the nomological network (Cronbach & Meehl, 1955) involving the trait or construct occur concurrently. When behavior is the subject matter of interest, however, facts about it are more less objectively determinable. The

Table 2.1. Psychometric Concepts as they Apply to Two Different Approaches to
Behavioral Assessment

CONCEPT	NOMOTHETIC-TRAIT APPROACH	IDIOGRAPHIC-BEHAVIOR APPROACH
Accuracy		
occurrence	Not relevant; subject matter inherently incapable of independent verification	Most important characteristic of any instrument; without known sensitivity to behavior occurrence the instrument is useless for other purposes.
temporal	Not relevant; subject matter inherently incapable of independent verification	Important since multiple occurrences are necessary to study the meaning of any behavior; instruments should be sensitive to repeated occurrences within a restricted time frame (e,g., over days at 8 am) as well as to occurrences at different times (e.g., 8 am vs. 2 pm vs. 8 pm, etc.)
setting	Not relevant; subject matter inherently incapable of independent verification	Important for behavior assumed to occur under different stimulus conditions, whether molecular described (e.g., green vs. red key) or described in more molar terms (e.g., clinic vs. home)
convergent	Not relevant; subject matter inherently incapable of independent verification	Necessary for studying relationships between behaviors. Multiple methods must yield accurate information about behaviors being related in order to establish contributions to the relationship due to method alone.
Reliability		
scorer	Most important in the sense of most fundamental; without reliable scoring, remaining reliability and many of the validity issues cannot be established.	Of comparable importance as in nomothetic-trait approach; without it, accuracy, other forms of reliability, and validity cannot be established.
temporal	Basic requirement of instruments designed to assess most traits, since assumption of their relative permanence over time fundamental to their definition.	Scores on an instrument might or might not show consistency over time; not assumed that behavior is stable.
internal	Basic requirement of instruments designed to assess most (if not all) traits since it is assumed that a unitary underlying construct determines test performance.	Scores on an instrument might or might not be expected to show this depending on the nature of the response class being assessed.
Validity		
content	Of minor importance; survey of instrument content provides minimal information about its adequacy as a measure of the construct underlying the construct.	Important; survey of content indicates extent to which behavior of interest is adequately represented by the sample included.
construct	Very important since it is the construct that is assumed to drive performance on the instrument; without it it is unclear what the instrument is assessing.	Of no importance in nomothetic-trait sense because underlying constructs are not the subject matter; if behavior seen as construct, then instruments should "make sense" in terms of the particular view of the behavior they are tapping.

convergent	Basic requirement to show that trait is more than the measure of it; necessary to establishing construct validity.	See convergent accuracy; scores on multiple ways of assessing the same behavior will correlate if the separate instruments have occurrence accuracy; not necessary in defining behavior but useful in establishing how much control over scores is the result of the instrument and how much is the result of the behavior itself and other non-instrument variables.
criterion-related	Useful but not necessary; more important when trait significance depends on relationships with practical criteria.	Useful but not necessary; of less importance than content validity.
discriminant	Important and probably necessary to show that an instrument is not simply another way of assessing something for which there are already adequate instruments; also to show that the trait being assessed is independent of variables of which it is supposed to be independent.	Not relevant; an accurate instrument, by definition, taps the behavior of interest and not something else.
treatment	Important to extent that data from instrument being used to plan and evaluate instrument.	Important to extent that data from instrument being used to plan and evaluate intervention.

prior requirement of accuracy exists because without it one cannot be sure of the facts about behavior. That is, without knowing that an instrument *can* detect repeated occurrences of behavior before it is used to do so, it is impossible to interpret any information it produces. For example, the instrument might reveal that the behavior does not occur repeatedly or that it occurs at a rate of four times per minute. If the instrument's limits, with respect to temporal accuracy, are unknown, it is uncertain whether the behavior really did fail to recur or whether its repeated occurrences were simply not detected by the inaccurate instrument.

Similarly, the discovery that the behavior occurs at a rate of four times per minute is difficult to interpret since the instrument might be only partially accurate. It might, for example, consistently under- or over-detect, with the result that the obtained rate is systematically lower or higher than what is actually true about the behavior. With previously established and reported accuracy information, adjustments can be made to instrument readings to compensate for systematic error in instrument sensitivity within all or certain specified ranges, just as is done in the physical sciences.

The requirement for the prior establishment of accuracy has not had much effect on the activities of behavioral assessors regardless of the overall approach they have taken. This might be due, in part, to the relative newness of the concept. Its importance and implications might not have reached a wide enough audience at this point in their development. Another reason might be the still widely held view that agreement between independent users of an instrument is enough to certify its appropriateness for assessing a behavior of interest. Despite the fallacious logic underlying this view (Johnston & Pennypacker, 1980) and the repeated recognition that such agreement guarantees nothing about accuracy (Gewirtz & Gewirtz, 1969; Johnson & Bolstad, 1973; Kazdin, 1973), nearly all articles appearing in behavioral journals report inter-user agreement data for the instruments employed without reporting whether either user is actually tacting the events being described!

Another difficulty with widespread use of accuracy concepts is the problem of establishing an incontrovertible index for many assessment purposes. There are two aspects of this problem. One is the infinite regress issue concerning incontrovertibility. It is pointed out that we can never know what is *really* there in any Platonic, real-truth sense because we can never separate what we know from how we know it. Imagine applying this same logic in pursuit of the molecular structure of a certain enzyme. Since it can never be known for certain just how much the structure we see is influenced by the microscope used for seeing it or by the scientist using the microscope, there is no point in establishing the accuracy of the microscope. Instead, we will have several scientists view the enzyme through the scope and use their consensus as the description of the molecular structure.

This is not that unreasonable on its face, and the analogy can apparently be used to support the continued reliance on interuser agreement by behavioral assessors. After all, consensus (i.e., replicability) establishes potential value in the physical sciences as it does in the behavior sciences. If only one scientist had described the molecular structure in a certain way and others had failed to do so in spite of numerous attempts, the single scientist's description would be questioned rather seriously.

What is problematic about the analogy is the relative complexity of the phenomena being studied in the social sciences, on the one hand, and the physical sciences, on the other. Related to this complexity is the diversity of influences on its observation and reporting. As Meehl (1978) has observed, phenomena in the physical sciences are relatively less complex than those studied by the social sciences. In the former it is more likely that observations and reports of them will be controlled by the phenomenon being observed. In the latter, epiphenomena are more likely to influence observations and reports. It is well known that the behavior of observers is affected by the complexity of the events being observed (Mash & McElwee, 1974), the structure of the observation system (Powell, Martindale, Kulp, Martindale, & Bauman, 1977; Powell & Rockinson, 1978), and knowledge that they, in turn, are being observed (Romanczyk, Kent, Diament, & O'Leary, 1973), among other factors. The point is that the requirement for replication in the physical sciences cannot be argued forcefully to support a requirement for inter-observer agreement in the social sciences because agreement in the physical sciences is much more likely to be controlled by the phenomenon being observed than is agreement in the social sciences.

In a related manner, even if a single scientist were to report a particular molecular structure, the implications of the reported structure would be subject to relatively immediate and grave danger of refutation. Given the scientist's description, certain related facts would typically be expected. If they were not forthcoming, the description would be in serious jeopardy. The situation is not the same in the social sciences as Meehl (1978) has very clearly acknowledged. Our deductivism is not so finely developed that observations can be subjected to grave danger of refutation in a relatively short period of time. As a result, we cannot rely on the function or scientific utility of our observations as a substitute for their accuracy in the first place.

The second aspect of the problem of establishing incontrovertible indices is less philosophical than practical. It is difficult to come up with such an index for all but the most trivial of behaviors. This is, in part, because we have not spent much time and energy on the problem. While we would agree that scripting and cueing a person to be in or out of his seat with a certain frequency (e.g., Powell et al., 1977) would provide a reasonably incontrovertible standard against which to compare results obtained from different measures, we are less comfortable with developing standards for instruments designed to assess complex interactions in dyadic relationships. The logic is the same, however, and so, perhaps, is the technology. Developing scripted dyadic interchanges, training actors/actresses to perform under the control of the script, and using their performances as the incontrovertible index does not seem far fetched nor particularly difficult. Incontrovertible indices for other assessment problems should prove to be no more challenging than these.

To summarize briefly, when behavior is the subject matter of interest (as in the right-hand column of Table 2.1), the accuracy of one's assessment instruments is paramount. Accuracy must be established by comparing the results produced by the instrument with what is known to be the case about some behavior as represented by an incontrovertible index of that behavior. Only *after* the limits of an instrument's accuracy have been established can it be used to answer questions about a behavior of interest in an application context. Periodic recalibration of the instrument would be necessary for its continued use.

The remaining psychometric concepts outlined in Table 2.1 will not be discussed in detail here. Their application to nomothetic-trait approaches to behavioral assessment is generally well known. Their application to idiographic-behavior approaches is less well known and will be discussed in some detail in the remaining sections of the chapter.

THE NEED FOR IDIOGRAPHIC ASSESSMENT METHODOLOGY

As noted by Paul (1969) and Kiesler (1971) among others, the ultimate question to be answered by psychologists interested in behavior change is what intervention, administered by whom, is most effective for a given individual, with a specific problem, under what circumstances, and how is that effectiveness produced. Given the highly complex nature of this question it has been customary to assume that its answer could come only from the use of complex factorial designs with multiple groups of subjects and random assignment of subjects to groups (Paul, 1969). As Cronbach (1975) has observed, however, such an approach has "only limited ability to detect interactions . . . but sizable interactions are likely to be suppressed just because any interaction that does not produce a significant F ratio is treated as non-existent" (pp. 123–124). Barlow, Hayes, and Nelson (1984) have gone so far as to state that the ultimate question "cannot be answered using traditional research methodology. The complexity of the human condition will preclude any attempt at experimentally establishing generalization" (p. 58). Later they went on to say that "group-comparison designs have inherent limitations in the ability of practitioners to apply their results to individuals" (p. 66).

What is needed, according to these researchers, is intensive study of the individual case. Only through an accumulation of such studies can we ever hope to establish the generalizability of our procedures. In pursuit of this logic, Barlow et al. (1984) present a number of examples of research designs that can be used with single cases to establish cause–effect relationships between relatively specific variables. Others (e.g., Barlow & Hersen, 1984; Jayaratne & Levy, 1979; Kazdin, 1982; Kratochwill, 1978; Sidman, 1960) have provided similar expositions. The result is that we now have an extensive, relatively sophisticated armamentarium of research designs that can be applied to evaluating the effects of various independent variables or intervention techniques when applied in the individual case.

Unfortunately, and somewhat paradoxically, we do not have a similarly well-developed technology for producing the dependent variables that will provide evidence for any change brought about by the independent ones. To date we have not developed a comprehensive, coherent approach to (a) selecting relevant dimensions for assessing individual clients, (b) developing usable instruments to assess these dimensions, (c) applying these in identifying targets for intervention, (d) evaluating the adequacy of such instruments, or (e) using them to evaluate intervention effects.

There are practical, aesthetic, and scientific reasons for arguing the need for an idiographic assessment methodology. From a practical perspective, instruments developed within a deductive, nomothetic tradition that has relied on interindividual differences as its source of variation are of minimal use to persons involved in behavior change efforts.

In general, the behavior change specialist is concerned with the five issues mentioned as they apply to individuals. When an instrument such as the SADS or BDI has been developed within the deductive, nomothetic tradition and its adequacy has been established via analyses of differences between individuals, it is, by definition, too general to be optimally useful in the single case. This is easy to appreciate when the process of developing the instrument is considered. First, the originators were concerned with a particular variable (e.g., social anxiety or depression), *not* with a particular individual. They reasoned from a general theoretical understanding of the variable to the specific content to be included in the instrument. They did not develop the content from an analysis of the specific behavior of most relevance to a particular individual. Finally, they relied on differences among individuals to establish the reliability and validity of the instrument. Moreover, these differences were crucial to the validation enterprise. Thus, not only was it important to construct the instrument in such a way as to produce differences among individuals in terms of the scores obtained, but it was also necessary to examine the stability of these differences in establishing the reliability and validity characteristics outlined in Table 2.1.

All of these features — the focus on a variable, the deductive reasoning, and the examination of differences among individuals — highlight the general remoteness of the approach from the individual case. A person faced with developing appropriate intervention strategies for individuals will focus on the individual, will reason inductively from cumulated observations of the individual, and will examine differences in the individual over time as they are related to intervention procedures.

The information produced by the deductively driven, nomothetic, interindividual difference-based researcher will seem of minimal generalizability to the person dealing with the individual case. After all, that case was not included among the subjects on whom the instruments were originally developed. Nor was the case among the groups for which reliability and validity were established. The interventionist will be appropriately perplexed at how to make use of information concerning means, standard deviations, and correlation coefficients when they have been based on persons other than the individual being confronted. This is especially problematic since rarely is enough information presented to enable a detailed comparison of the individual with those persons included in the research so that the appropriateness and extent of generalizability can be established.

In addition to the practical difficulties just mentioned, there is a certain pull exerted by the aesthetics of science toward establishing a dependent variable methodology that parallels the methodology already developed to examine the effects of independent variables in the individual case. There is something disquieting about using dependent measures developed in one scientific tradition to evaluate the effects of independent variables in another. A single case experimental research discipline simply ought to have a single case assessment discipline to go along with it.

As it turns out, there are good, scientifically logical bases for the discomfort experienced in trying to force the dependent measures of one tradition to fit the requirements for evaluating independent variables in another. The concern of the behavior change specialist is to produce differences in the behavior of individuals. The amount of difference to be effected requires an agreement between the specialist and the individual as to a satisfactory criterion level of behavior to be pursued. This criterion is almost always stated in relatively concrete terms, such as "I want to be more successful in my work," "I want to be able to go outside my house without feeling anxious," and so on. Thus, an intervention is judged successful if it produces these effects.

Logically, an instrument used to establish intervention effectiveness in such a context should be one that is sensitive to individual behavior change. Moreover, the instrument will be used to document an individual's initial and subsequent behavior viz the criterion levels initially agreed upon. It will not suffice for the instrument to report the individual's behavior viz that represented by the mean and standard deviation of some reference group. After all, the agreement was not to become average, more than average, or less than average with respect to occupational success or anxiety experienced upon leaving one's house.

Understood in this way it can be seen that dependent measures in an idiographic context will be criterion-referenced (Glaser, 1963). Those developed in a nomothetic, variable-focused, interindividual difference context will be norm-referenced. Scores on the former get their meaning from comparisons with an absolute level of behavior, usually one characterizing effective performance in a given situation. Scores on the latter get their meaning from comparisons with the levels of behavior manifested by other persons, usually those included in a norm or standardization sample. Interested readers should consult Fewell and Cone (1983), Livingston (1977), and Wilcox (1979) for comparisons of norm-referenced and criterion-referenced approaches to assessment.

It has been pointed out that norm-referenced measures are inappropriate for uses that involve repeated assessment over time for purposes of evaluating the effectiveness of intervention procedures (Barrett, Johnston, & Pennypacker, 1986). As Messick (1983) has noted, norm-referenced tests are constructed "to yield scores that optimally discriminate among individuals" (p. 483). Score distributions are not required for criterion-referenced tests, however. "Indeed, score distributions are often quite constrained or truncated . . ." (p. 484). Messick goes on to point out that a

> criterion-referenced test may be used for norm-referenced measurement but it has the disadvantage that it was not constructed to maximize score variability ... Similarly, a norm-referenced test may be used for criterion-referenced interpretations, but it is unlikely to provide adequate coverage for assessing performance changes because many relevant items that were either too easy or too hard at a particular level of development or training will have been left out since they did not discriminate among individuals. (p. 484)

Thus, norm-referenced instruments, useful as they are for describing differences among individuals, are, by their very nature, not sensitive enough to be used to evaluate the intervention programs typical of behavior change specialists. Items failing to discriminate among individuals are deliberately deleted from such measures. These items are prevalent in criterion-referenced instruments designed to assess progress toward a priori performance standards. One has only to think of a hierarchy of skills in a carefully sequenced task analysis to appreciate that items (or steps) close together in the hierarchy are likely not to discriminate among individuals, whereas those far apart will produce such discriminations. To render the measure useful for norm-referenced purposes would be to emasculate it for criterion-referenced ones, since items sensitive to small differences in performance would be eliminated.

To summarize, an idiographic assessment methodology is needed by behavior change specialists for practical, aesthetic, and scientific reasons. A methodology based on individuals will have inherent practical advantages compared to a methodology based on variables and groups of people. Such a methodology will, from an aesthetic standpoint, parallel and complement the single-case experimental strategies already developed to evaluate the effects of independent variables. Finally, norm-referenced instruments developed within the nomothetic, interindividual-difference-based tradition are scientifically unsuited for evaluating intervention effects in repeated assessments of individuals. They are constructed in ways that render them insensitive to the kinds of changes likely to be produced by individual intervention programs.

CHARACTERISTICS OF AN IDIOGRAPHIC BEHAVIORAL ASSESSMENT METHODOLOGY

The value of an idiographic approach to psychology has been debated extensively (e.g., Allport, 1937, 1962; Barlow & Hersen, 1984; Beck, 1953; Chassan, 1967; Harris, 1980; Lamiell, 1982; Lewin, 1935; Marceil, 1977; Pervin, 1984). Recently, there appears to have been a "revival of interest in idiographics and the study of the individual" (Pervin, 1984, p. 269). Despite the long history of the debate and the recent revival of interest there are still "no established criteria for what constitutes an idiographic method" (Pervin, 1984, p. 270).

As a basis for discussing an idiographic approach to behavioral assessment, the following characteristics (criteria) are offered. Their eventual necessity and/or value can be determined empirically in future research. They are proposed here as a starting point to stimulate discussion and guide early research efforts. In producing idiographic behavioral assessment procedures, practitioners and researchers would be wise to (a) develop the procedure inductively; (b) specify objective rules for deriving item (behavior) content; (c) develop the procedure from a behavior-environment interactionist perspective; (d) use empirical procedures for combining discrete behaviors into larger categories; (e) specify objective rules for using the procedure; (f) provide data showing the generalizability of the procedure; and (g) develop generalizability data in a series of single-case studies.

An historical overview of idiographic assessment approaches shows that all have met some of these criteria, and none has met all of them. Space does not permit analysis of the examples available in the literature, and interested readers should consult them directly (e.g., Baldwin, 1942; Nunnally, 1955; Pervin, 1983; Shapiro, 1961; Shontz, 1965; Spotts & Shontz, 1980).

Recent work by the author and colleagues (cf. Cone, Bourland, & Wood-Shuman, 1986; Cone & Hoier, 1986) has involved the development of idiographic behavioral assessment techniques based on earlier work with template matching by Bem and colleagues (Bem, 1982; Bem & Funder, 1978; Bem & Lord, 1979). The approach has been described more completely elsewhere (Cone & Hoier, 1986) and will be summarized here only briefly.

Starting with a particular problem area of concern to the client, attention is first directed toward the environmental context in which the problem is experienced. If, for example, a person is experiencing difficulties in interpersonal interactions, the kinds of interactions important to the person are identified. More specifically, persons with whom the client would like to interact more successfully are enumerated. These people are then asked to identify friends with whom they enjoy interacting. Descriptions of the behavior of these friends are obtained, and consistently used descriptors compiled into a template or instrument that can be considered to describe exemplary performers in that particular environmental (i.e., interpersonal) context. This template can then be used to assess the client. Differences between the client's repertoire and template behaviors then become potential targets for clinical intervention.

With respect to the criteria enumerated above, the procedure can be said to be inductive. The persons with whom the client has expressed interest in interacting are presented a comprehensive list of behaviors to use in describing their friends. Various objective rules can be specified for deriving template content, such as requiring that a behavior be used to describe all three of three friends identified by the person(s) with whom the client wished to interact effectively. The procedure is clearly interactive in that the source of assessment content comes from the environment of relevance to the client. If a large number of discrepancies exist between template behaviors and the client's actual repertoire, various empirical approaches to grouping them can be used, including cluster and factor analysis or p technique (Cattell, 1952). Objective rules for using the procedure exist, such that consistency between assessors can be assured.

Some data as to the generalizability of the procedure are available, and more are currently being generated. Thus far it has been used in assessing socially rejected elementary school-aged children (Cone & Hoier, 1986) and in providing objective descriptions of the behavioral requirements of less restrictive residential placements for institutionalized persons (Cone, Bourland, & Wood-Shuman, 1986).

SINGLE-SUBJECT PSYCHOMETRICS AND THE ADEQUACY OF IDIOGRAPHIC ASSESSMENT PROCEDURES

Regardless of how one arrives at an idiographic assessment instrument, whether from using the template-matching approach just described or one of the methods of Baldwin (1942), Shapiro (1961), Pervin (1984), or others, the adequacy of that instrument from a measurement perspective must be established. The general requirements in this regard were presented in Table 2.1 and have been articulated by others (e.g., Kiesler, 1971). It should be emphasized that all of the characteristics in Table 2.1 need not be met by every instrument developed for use with individual clients. Their relevance will depend on the use(s) to be made of the device.

Regardless of which characteristics are identified as relevant, however, some way of establishing them for idiographically developed instruments must be proposed. To date, instruments have been judged as psychometrically fit for use with *individuals* based on data obtained from *groups*. How can such fitness be judged from data obtained from individuals? A complete answer to this question is not available and will not be available until we have a fully developed technology of single-subject psychometrics to parallel the single-case methodology already available for evaluating the effects of intervention efforts. Some preliminary suggestions can be offered, however, and will be offered in the remaining pages of this chapter.

If behavior is the subject matter of our assessment endeavors, it will be important to know whether our instrument is sensitive to facts about that behavior. While absolutely incontrovertible indices might not be available to establish accuracy, various different sources of information external to the assessment context might converge to give the assessor some confidence in the instrument's being controlled by the behavior of interest and not by something else. For example, an agoraphobic client's report of performance on a behavior walk (Agras, Leitenberg, & Barlow, 1968; Barlow & Waddell, 1985) could be corroborated by a spouse. An alcoholic's self-report of alcohol ingestion could be corroborated by a spouse or by others (e.g., Sobell, Sobell, & VanderSpek, 1979).

With respect to reliability, scorer reliability can be determined relatively easily by having someone else in the clinician's office score the instrument independently and compare results. Temporal reliability can be evaluated by comparing the client's responses across several occasions. For example, in assessing verbal interactions in couples, a 10-minute structured problem-solving task might be observed. Comparing data for the same behavior categories obtained during even-numbered minutes (e.g., 2nd, 4th, 6th, etc.) with those obtained during odd-numbered minutes would allow within-session temporal stability to be determined. Doing this for odd and even days of baseline direct observation assessment in the home (e.g., Jones, Reid, & Patterson, 1975) would establish such stability over a longer period.

Internal consistency could be evaluated by comparing the client's scores on two halves of an assessment instrument. This could be done for data obtained in a single session. For example, an idiographically produced self-report measure of urges to drink alcohol might include 20 items describing times and places where the client does and does not experience such urges. Assuming these items were randomly assigned to positions in the instrument, the client's scores on both 10-item halves (odd vs. even items) should be comparable. Repeated use of the instrument over time would allow the calculation of correlations between items and the use of more sophisticated internal consistency measures such as the Kuder-Richardson formulas or coefficient alpha.

Validity issues can be addressed for individual client assessment procedures as well. In single-subject psychometrics, content and face validity are essentially synonymous. The expert for judging both is the individual client. Surveying the content of the assessment instrument to determine its relevance to the client's problem will be undertaken jointly by the practitioner and client. Irrelevant content will be identified and removed. The resulting instrument will have face validity by definition, since its content will have been judged relevant by the client. Incidentally, the content validation process, when carried out in this way, can help clarify the specific behavior of concern to the client and the stimulus conditions under which it occurs. Further, the process helps to assure that the ultimate goals of intervention are appropriately chosen, since these goals, and/or components thereof, will comprise the content of the instrument.

Construct validity will be of no concern to behavioral assessors, in one sense since constructs are not the subject of interest, behavior is; in another sense, behavior can be seen as a construct itself, in which case the instrument will have construct validity to the extent that it "makes sense" in terms of the behavior as the client and the assessor understand it. Viewed in this way, construct validity is very closely related to content and face validity, and for all practical purposes, the three occur simultaneously.

Convergent validity can be an important characteristic of idiographic assessment procedures, especially if relationships between behaviors are being examined. Before behavior–behavior relationships can be established, alternative ways of assessing each of them must be available and their convergence known (Cone, 1979). This is so because relationships between behaviors studied with only a single method might be produced by the method itself. Thus, concluding that the behaviors are related might be overlooking the possibility that method variance produced the relationship. Likewise, concluding that one behavior is not related to another, when different methods have been used with each, might be overlooking the possibility that method differences produced the low correlation.

Convergent validity is a prerequisite to studying synchrony (Rachman & Hodgson, 1974) or the relationship between behaviors from different content areas. Synchrony is important for client problems for which there is no single, completely satisfactory operational definition. For example, sexual arousal is denoted differently by different people. Self-reports of arousal while viewing erotic films correlated differently with various physiological responses and with the same physiological response at different times (Henson, Rubin, & Henson, 1979). Approach/avoidance behavior and heart rate differed in their relationship from client to client in a study of phobic behavior (Leitenberg, Agras, Butz, & Wincze, 1971). When intervention effectiveness is being judged on reductions in sexual arousal or phobic responding, it obviously makes a difference which response is being assessed.

The search for synchrony in behavioral assessment, especially in the areas of sexual arousal and phobic responding, raises some interesting issues. From a purely practical standpoint the issue might be moot. Individual clients know when they are sexually aroused and when they are not, and their subjective ratings of arousal can serve as a satisfactory dependent measure for evaluating intervention effectiveness. Of course, in the case of court-referred sexual deviants there might be good reasons to doubt their subjective rating and focus instead on motor and physiological responses. Motor behavior probably should be given more weight than it has been given since the court does not want the referred person to engage in deviant sexual behavior whether he feels aroused and has an erection or not.

Likewise, careful assessment can discover whether cognitive, motor, or physiological responses are primarily implicated in a given client's phobic behavior. Reductions in the implicated responses would establish intervention effectiveness, regardless of correspondence or synchrony with nonimplicated responses. Indeed, there is some reason to expect lack of synchrony between implicated and nonimplicated responses, since the latter might show minimal variation over the course of intervention and the former might at least eventually show reduced variation.

Thus, the issue of correspondence or synchrony among different responses might be of minimal significance from a practical perspective. In building a science of human behavior from cumulative studies of individuals, however, synchrony will be of much more importance. Given the reservations just mentioned concerning reduced variability in nonimplicated responses, such an enterprise might be difficult. Synchrony or the lack of it has not been studied extensively within individuals, so it is probably premature to be concerned with this problem here.

A related issue of great practical import has to do with the level of analysis to use when monitoring the progress of individual clients. A molecular analysis of the client's problem might produce several very specific behaviors, changes in which will provide sensitive indices of therapeutic effectiveness. Unfortunately, "they may not present a meaningful measure of the presenting problem" (Barlow et al., 1984, p. 83). Conversely, molar behaviors might be better representative of the problem behavior, but they will lack the sensitivity needed to evaluate intervention effectiveness on a day-to-day basis.

The best approach to avoiding the molecular–molar disparity might be to develop higher-order systems (e.g., Paul, 1979). That is, through careful analysis of contributors to molar scores, molecular behaviors can be discovered. The molecular responses to track over time will be those shown to have the highest correlations with scores on the molar instrument. In a single-case assessment context, relationships between molecular and molar responses could be obtained through repeated assessment of both during a preintervention period. Correlations between measures across sessions would reveal which molecular responses are most closely associated with the more "meaningful" molar ones. These could be selected for frequent monitoring throughout therapy. For example, ratings by a wife of her husband's level of "involvement" in their relationship could be obtained over a 2-week baseline period. Simultaneously, the husband might monitor the frequency of his compliments, initiations of conversations about her feelings, and so on. He might also monitor the frequency of certain instrumental acts, e.g., washing dishes and taking care of the children. Correlating the husband's self-monitored molecular behaviors with his wife's molar ratings of "involvement" would reveal which molecular behaviors to monitor over the course of an intervention program designed to increase marital involvement.

Criterion-related validity can be useful for idiographically developed assessment devices, but it is not an essential characteristic. The most important criterion being predicted by such instruments is the accomplishment of intervention goals. To the extent that these goals have been represented in the content of the instrument as it was developed, it should have inherent validity for predicting them. Thus, content validity and criterion-related validity are quite closely related.

Discriminant validity, as reflected in Table 2.1, is not relevant to an assessment enterprise that is built on the accuracy of its instruments. By definition, an accurate instrument taps the behavior of interest and not something else.

Treatment or intervention validity is an important characteristic of idiographic instruments since their data should be useful for planning, implementing, and evaluating an intervention program. By itself, this form of validity is difficult, if not impossible, to establish in the individual case. Again, however, as with criterion-related and construct validity, there is considerable overlap with content validity such that a content-valid instrument should possess a high degree of inherent treatment validity. This is because an instrument's content should reflect the ultimate and instrumental outcomes (Rosen & Proctor, 1981) anticipated for the intervention. If it does, then using it to plan, implement, and monitor intervention effectiveness should result in the delivery of more effective services than not using it, hence establishing its intervention validity.

SUMMARY AND CONCLUSIONS

It has been acknowledged in this chapter that there are multiple ways of approaching the behavioral assessment enterprise. The simultaneous consideration of focus (individual vs. variable), subject matter (behavior vs. trait), scientific approach (inductive vs. deductive), source of variability (within vs. between cases), and influence of the environment (interactive vs. noninteractive) leads to the identification of 32 different models.

Psychometric considerations depend on the model one has adopted, with accuracy, reliability, and validity concepts varying accordingly. Two radically different models (nomothetic-trait and idiographic-behavior) were contrasted in terms of these concepts. It was shown that accuracy concepts are relevant only to the idiographic-behavior approach. Reliability and validity concepts apply to both, but with widely varying degrees, depending on the particular type of each that is being considered. For example, content validity was shown to have minor relevance to the nomothetic-trait approach, but great relevance to the idiographic-behavior approach.

The logical necessity of an idiographic approach to dependent variable assessment paralleling the single-case experimental methodology available for independent variable evaluation was argued. It was shown that nomothetic, norm-referenced instruments are practically, aesthetically, and scientifically inappropriate for practitioners concerned with the single case. Characteristics of an idiographic assessment methodology were suggested, and issues of concern to a discipline of single-subject psychometrics were discussed.

It is hoped that the foregoing will stimulate others to develop assessment procedures specifically for use with individual clients. While specific instruments themselves might not be subjected to extensive validity studies, the procedures for developing them could be. Thus, a template produced for a specific individual might be shown to have adequate psychometric characteristics for that individual, but it would not be examined for the same features with other persons because of the very nature of the idiographic enterprise. Nonetheless, the template-matching *procedure* could be validated across multiple individuals and its scientific adequacy thus established.

It is time to take seriously the task of studying the behavior of individuals using appropriate methodologies. The development of idiographic assessment instruments and their validation via single-subject psychometrics should be accelerated.

REFERENCES

Agras, W. S., Leitenberg, H., & Barlow, D. H. (1968). Social reinforcement in the modification of agoraphobia. *Archives of General Psychiatry, 19*, 423–427.

Allport, G. W. (1937). *Personality: A psychological interpretation*. New York: Holt.

Allport, G. W. (1962). The general and the unique in psychological science. *Journal of Personality, 34*, 405–422.

Arkowitz, H. (1981). Assessment of social skills. In M. Hersen & A. S. Bellack (Eds.), *Behavioral assessment: A practical handbook* (2nd ed., pp. 296–327). New York: Pergamon.

Baldwin, A. L. (1942). Personal structure analysis: A statistical method for investigation of the single personality. *Journal of Abnormal and Social Psychology, 37*, 163–183.

Barlow, D. H. (Ed.). (1981). *Behavioral assessment of adult disorders*. New York: Guilford.

Barlow, D. H., Hayes, S. C., & Nelson, R. O. (1984). *The scientist practitioner*. New York: Pergamon.

Barlow, D. H., & Hersen, M. (1984). *Single-case experimental designs: Strategies for studying behavior change.* (2nd ed.). New York: Pergamon.

Barlow, D. H., & Waddell, M. T. (1985). Agoraphobia. In D. H. Barlow (Ed.), *Clinical handbook of psychological disorders* (pp. 1–68). New York: Guilford.

Barrett, B. H., Johnston, J. M., & Pennypacker, H. S. (1986). Behavior: Its units, dimensions, and measurement. In R. O. Nelson & S. C. Hayes (Eds.), *The conceptual foundations of behavioral assessment* (pp. 156–200). New York: Guilford.

Beck, A. T. (1972). *Depression: Causes and treatment.* Philadelphia: University of Pennsylvania Press.

Beck, S. J. (1953). The science of personality: Nomothetic or idiographic. *Psychological Review, 60*, 353–359.

Bem, D. J. (1982). Assessing situations by assessing persons. In D. Magnusson (Ed.), *Toward a psychology of situations: An interactional perspective.* Hillsdale, NJ: Erlbaum.

Bem, D. J., & Funder, D. C. (1978). Predicting more of the people more of the time: Assessing the personality of situations. *Psychological Review, 85*, 485–501.

Bem, D. J., & Lord, C. G. (1979). Template matching: A proposal for probing the ecological validity of experimental settings in social psychology. *Journal of Personality and Social Psychology, 37*, 833–846.

Cattell, R. B. (1952). The three basic factors — analytic research designs — their interrelations and derivatives. *Psychological Bulletin, 49*, 499–520.

Chassan, J. B. (1967). *Research design in clinical psychology and psychiatry.* New York: Appleton-Century-Crofts.

Ciminero, A. R., Calhoun, K. S., & Adams, H. E. (Eds.). (1986). *Handbook of behavioral assessment* (2nd ed.). New York: John Wiley.

Claiborne, W. L., & Zaro, J. S. (1979). A development of a peer review system: The APA-CHAMPUS contract. In C. A. Kiesler, N. A. Cummings, & G. R. VandenBos (Eds.), *Psychology and national health insurance.* Washington, D.C.: American Psychological Association.

Cone, J. D. (1979). Confounded comparisons in triple response mode assessment research. *Behavioral Assessment, 1*, 85–95.

Cone, J. D. (1981). Psychometric considerations. In M. Hersen & A. S. Bellack (Eds.), *Behavioral assessment: A practical handbook* (2nd ed.). (pp. 38–68). New York: Pergamon.

Cone, J. D. (1986). Idiographic, nomothetic, and related perspectives in behavioral assessment. In R. O. Nelson & S. C. Hayes (Eds.). *Conceptual foundations in behavioral assessment.* (pp. 111–128). New York: Guilford.

Cone, J. D., & Hawkins, R. P. (1977). *Behavioral assessment: New directions in clinical psychology.* New York: Brunner/Mazel.

Cronbach, L. J. (1975). Beyond the two disciplines of scientific psychology. *American Psychologist, 30*, 116–127.

Cronbach, L. J., & Meehl, P. E. (1955). Construct validity in psychological tests. *Psychological Bulletin, 52*, 281–302.

Fewell, R. R., & Cone, J. D. (1983). Identification and placement of severely handicapped children. In M. E. Snell (Ed.), *Systematic instruction of the moderately and severely handicapped* (2nd ed.) (pp. 46–73). Columbus, OH: Charles E. Merrill.

Gay, M., Hollandsworth, J., & Galassi, J. (1975). An assertiveness inventory for adults. *Journal of Counseling Psychology, 22*, 340–344.

Gewirtz, H. N., & Gewirtz, J. L. (1969). Caretaking settings, background events and childrearing environments: Some preliminary trends. In B. M. Foss (Ed.), *Determinants of infant behaviour,* Vol. IV. London: Methuen & Co.

Glaser, R. (1963). Instructional technology and the measurement of learning outcomes. *American Psychologist, 18,* 519–521.

Harris, J. G., Jr. (1980). Nomovalidation and idiovalidation: A quest for the true personality profile. *American Psychologist, 35,* 729–744.

Henson, D. E., Rubin, H. B., & Henson, C. (1979). Analysis of the consistency of objective measures of sexual arousal. *Journal of Applied Behavior Analysis, 12,* 701–711.

Hersen, M., & Bellack, A. S. (1976). *Behavioral assessment: A practical handbook.* New York: Pergamon Press.

Hersen, M., & Bellack, A. S. (1981). *Behavioral assessment: A practical handbook* (2nd ed.). New York: Pergamon.

Jayaratne, S., & Levy, R. L. (1979). *Empirical clinical practice.* New York: Columbia University Press.

Johnson, S. M., & Bolstad, O. D. (1973). Methodological issues in naturalistic observation: Some problems and solutions for field research. In L. A. Hamerlynck, L. C. Handy, & E. J. Mash (Eds.), *Behavior change: Methodology, concepts, and practice* (pp. 7–67). Champaign, IL: Research Press.

Johnston, J. M., & Pennypacker, H. S. (1980). *Strategies and tactics of human behavior research.* Hillsdale, NJ: Lawrence Erlbaum Associates.

Jones, R. R., Reid, J. B., & Patterson, G. R. (1975). Naturalistic observation in clinical assessment. In P. McReynolds (Ed.), *Advances in psychological assessment* (Vol. 3). San Francisco: Jossey-Bass, Inc.

Kazdin, A. E. (1973). Methodological and assessment considerations in evaluating reinforcement programs in applied settings. *Journal of Applied Behavior Analysis, 6,* 517–531.

Kazdin, A. E. (1982). *Single-case research designs: Methods for clinical and applied settings.* New York: Oxford University Press.

Kiesler, D. J. (1971). Experimental designs in psychotherapy research. In A. E. Bergin & S. L. Garfield (Eds.), *Handbook of psychotherapy and behavior change: An empirical analysis* (pp. 36–74). New York: Wiley.

Kratochwill, T. R. (Ed.) (1978). *Single subject research: Strategies for evaluating change.* New York: Academic Press.

Lamiell, J. T. (1982). The case for an idiothetic psychology of personality: A conceptual and empirical foundation. *Progress in Experimental Personality Research, 11,* 1–62.

Leitenberg, H., Agras, W. S., Butz, R., & Wincze, J. (1971). Relationship between heart rate and behavioral change during the treatment of phobias. *Journal of Abnormal Psychology, 78,* 59–68.

Lewin, K. (1935). *A dynamic theory of personality.* New York: McGraw-Hill.

Livingston, S. A. (1977). Psychometric techniques for criterion-referenced testing and behavioral assessment. In J. D. Cone & R. P. Hawkins (Eds.), *Behavioral assessment: New directions in clinical psychology* (pp. 308–329). New York: Brunner/Mazel.

Marceil, J. C. (1977). Implicit dimensions of idiography and nomothesis: A reformulation. *American Psychologist, 32,* 1046–1055.

Mash, E. J., & McElwee, J. D. (1974). Situational effects on observer accuracy: Behavioral predictability, prior experience, complexity of coding categories. *Child Development, 45,* 367–377.

Mash, E., & Terdal, L. (Eds.) (1980). *Behavioral assessment of childhood disorders*. New York: Guilford Press.

Meehl, P. E. (1978). Theoretical risks and tabular asterisks: Sir Karl, Sir Ronald and the slow progress of soft psychology. *Journal of Consulting and Clinical Psychology, 46*, 806–835.

Messick, S. (1983). Assessment of children. In P. H. Mussen (Ed.), *Handbook of child psychology* (4th ed.) (pp. 477–526). New York: Wiley.

Nunnally, J. C. (1955). An investigation of some propositions of self-conception: The case of Miss Sun. *Journal of Abnormal and Social Psychology, 50*, 87–92.

Paul, G. L. (1969). Behavior modification research: Design and tactics. In C. M. Franks, (Ed.), *Behavior therapy: Appraisal and status* (pp. 29–62). New York: McGraw-Hill.

Paul, G. L. (1979). New assessment systems for residential treatment, management, research, and evaluation: A symposium. *Journal of Behavioral Assessment, 1*, 181–184.

Pervin, L. A. (1983). The status and flow of behavior: Toward a theory of goals. In M. M. Page (Ed.), *Personality: Current theory and research*. Lincoln, NE: University of Nebraska Press.

Pervin, L. A. (1984). Idiographic approaches to personality. In N. S. Endler & J. McV. Hunt (Eds.), *Personality and the behavioral disorders*. (pp. 261–282). New York: Wiley.

Powell, J., Martindale, B., Kulp, S., Martindale, A., & Bauman, R. (1977). Taking a closer look: Time sampling and measurement error. *Journal of Applied Behavior Analysis, 10*, 325–332.

Powell, J., & Rockinson, R. (1978). On the inability of interval time sampling to reflect frequency of occurrence data. *Journal of Applied Behavior Analysis, 11*, 531–532.

Rachman, S., & Hodgson, R. (1974). Synchrony and de-synchrony in fear and avoidance. *Behaviour Research and Therapy, 12*, 311–318.

Rich, A. R., & Schroeder, A. E. (1976). Research issues in assertiveness training. *Psychological Bulletin, 83*, 1081–1096.

Richardson, F. C., & Tasto, D. L. (1981). Development and factor analysis of a social anxiety inventory. *Behavior Therapy, 7*, 453–462.

Romanczyk, R. G., Kent, R. N., Diament, C., & O'Leary, K. D. (1973). Measuring the reliability of observational data: A reactive process. *Journal of Applied Behavior Analysis, 6*, 175–186.

Rosen, A., & Proctor, E. K. (1981). Distinctions between treatment outcomes and their implications for treatment evaluation. *Journal of Consulting and Clinical Psychology, 49*, 418–425.

Shapiro, M. B. (1961). A method of measuring psychological changes specific to the individual psychiatric patient. *British Journal of Medical Psychology, 34*, 151–155.

Shontz, F. C. (1965). *Research methods in personality*. New York: Appleton-Century-Crofts.

Sidman, M. (1960). *Tactics of scientific research: Evaluating experimental data in psychology*. New York: Basic Books.

Skinner, B. F. (1945). The operational analysis of psychological terms. *Psychological Review, 52*, 270–277.

Sobell, M. B., Sobell, L. C., & VanderSpek, R. (1979). Relationships among clinical judgment, self-report, and breath analysis measures of intoxication in alcoholics. *Journal of Consulting and Clinical Psychology, 47*, 204–206.

Spotts, J. V., & Shontz, F. C. (1980). *Cocaine users: A representative case approach.* New York: Free Press.

Watson, D., & Friend, R. (1969). Measurement of social-evaluative anxiety. *Journal of Consulting and Clinical Psychology, 33*, 448–457.

Wilcox, B. (1979). Severe/profound handicapping conditions: Instructional considerations. In M. S. Lilly (Ed.), *Children with exceptional needs.* New York: Holt, Rinehart, & Winston.

3
DSM-III and Behavioral Assessment

Michel Hersen
Alan S. Bellack

More so than any other time in its relatively brief history, behavioral assessment is at its crossroads as a methodology for evaluating behavior. The rumblings of currents and cross-currents from both within (McFall, 1986) and outside of the behavioral field (APA, 1980) pose unique challenges to the behavioral assessors operating in the late 1980s. Gone now is the bravura of the 1970s and early 1980s (see Hersen & Bellack, 1976, 1981) when behavioral assessors professed the scientific superiority of their strategies over the indirect approach of the projective testers and the apparent unreliability of the DSM-I and DSM-II systems of psychiatric classification. Moreover, the logic of selecting simple behavioral targets for modification and documenting therapeutic control over their rates of emission has proven to be somewhat illusory. The diagnosis and treatment of clinical entities are far more complex than hitherto believed (Hersen, 1981), given the complicating factors of etiologic differences, developmental considerations, severity and breadth of disturbance, and the intricate relationships of outcome measures seen throughout the course of therapeutic evaluation (see Kazdin, 1983, 1985).

The formal emergence of DSM-III (APA, 1980) clearly questioned the scientific edge of behavioral assessment. Even before the early description of DSM-III categories and the attendant improvement of interrater diagnostic reliability (Spitzer, Forman, & Nee, 1979; Spitzer, Williams, & Skodol, 1980), development of research diagnostic criteria (Spitzer, Endicott, & Robins, 1978) yielded more operationally-based descriptors, thus setting the stage for obtaining vastly improved reliability in the field trials subsequently carried out. Indeed, behavioral assessors no longer could claim that they had cornered the market on empiricism.

But the emergence of DSM-III certainly was not the only challenge to behavioral assessment as practiced in the 1970s. To the contrary, with decreasing insularity within behavioral assessment and a greater openness to the work of other empirical disciplines, the scope of behavioral assessment today has widened considerably. For example, there now is an increased interest in the global evaluation of behavior (e.g., Patterson & Bank, 1986), there is concern with how developmental factors impact on behavior (Harris & Ferrari, 1983), there is interest in the biological underpinnings of behavior (Hersen, 1986; Rebec & Anderson, 1986), and the role of intelligence testing and neuropsychological evaluation in behavioral assessment now has been acknowledged (Goldstein, 1979; Nelson, 1980).

Perhaps the increased scope of behavioral assessment is symbolically best represented by the change of the title of one of two journals specializing in articles on behavioral assessment. First published in 1979, the *Journal of Behavioral Assessment* effective in June of 1985 changed its title to the *Journal of Psychopathology and Behavioral Assessment*. As noted by Adams (1984), one of the editors, this change was necessitated to reflect both the increased breadth of the subject matter of assessment and the improvements of the psychiatric nosological scheme (i.e., DSM-III).

In this chapter we endeavor to examine the aforementioned issues by first considering the importance of classification and the behavioral assessors' initial objections to formal psychiatric diagnosis. We then examine the structure of DSM-III, the politics surrounding its birth, and the numerous criticisms directed toward its conception. Next we look at the possible complementarity of DSM-III and behavioral assessment, and we conclude with an evaluation of the broadening role that behavioral assessment undoubtedly will play in the future.

THE IMPORTANCE OF CLASSIFICATION

Alternatives to formal psychiatric classification have been proposed on a number of occasions by our behavioral colleagues (Adams, Doster, & Calhoun, 1977; Goldfried & Sprafkin, 1977; Kanfer & Saslow, 1965; McLemore & Benjamin, 1979). However, few empirical data are provided to justify their potential widespread use or possible superiority. It should not be surprising, then, that these systems have yielded little in the way of specific application. Formulation of such alternatives undoubtedly has sharpened the theoretical thinking of their proponents and perhaps even have had some influence on improving the DSM system of diagnosis.

Although behavioral assessers historically have been critical of DSM (see Hersen, 1976), even the most ardent critics of psychiatric diagnosis and classification recognize the value of the classification of abnormal behavior. Indeed, Adams et al. (1977) note that the first and fundamental step in the study of behavior, including abnormal behavior, is the grouping of observations into an organized scheme so as to make sense of the bewildering array of response patterns. Classification is the basis of any science because it is the process of identification of a phenomenon so that events can be measured and communication can occur between scientists and professionals. (p. 47)

In reviewing the importance of classification, Sprock and Blashfield (1983) have identified five of its primary purposes: The first, of course, is that it provides a consistent set of descriptors for diagnosticians, thus enhancing the reliability of observation; the second relates to information recovery for statistical, documentary, clinical, and research purposes; the third concerns the clear description of similarities and differences across psychiatric patients so that formal diagnosis will yield knowledge of particular symptom patterns in particular categories and subcategories; the fourth is to enhance prediction of the outcome (i.e., prognosis); and the fifth has greater theoretical import in that it should "provide basic concepts to allow formulations about adequate theories of psychopathology" (p. 290).

Aside from its scientific objectives, the DSM system, or any other nosological scheme for that matter, has political, professional, and financial implications. The political and professional issues, which are discussed further in this chapter, tend to highlight the behavioral-psychiatric split as to the theories of etiology and methods of treatment, in addition to underscoring questions of professional hegemony. With respect to financial considerations, only the most naive of observers could fail to see how DSM-III impacts on the way third-party payers (the insurance companies) reimburse psychiatrists, psychologists, and other mental health professionals for their diagnostic and treatment services. But as previously argued by Hersen and Turner (1984), "at the practical level if reimbursement by third-party payers for clinical services is to occur, some type of categorization is necessary such that a decision can be made as to what types of disorders will be covered for reimbursement and which ones will not. The need for classification exists at the philosophical, scientific, professional, and practical levels" (p. 497).

CRITICISMS OF FORMAL PSYCHIATRIC DIAGNOSIS

Criticism of formal psychiatric diagnosis has emanated from many directions, including the behavioral camp (see Hersen, 1976, for a review of the issues). Historically, when referring to DSM-I and DSM-II, behavioral assessors have been concerned with three major problems inherent in the nosological scheme: (a) poor reliability, (b) poor validity, and (c) unclear relationship between formal diagnostic labeling and subsequent treatment.

In looking at these three deficiencies in the diagnostic schemes, we will focus on DSM-I and DSM-II but also briefly note how these relate to DSM-III.

First, DSM-I and DSM-II, given the absence of clear criteria included in DSM-III, were notoriously *unreliable* (Frank, 1975). With the exception of a few of the major diagnostic categories, interrater reliability (either based on the same interview or on two independent interviews conducted by two clinicians) failed to achieve scientifically acceptable levels. By contrast, the clear criteria presented in DSM-III and the development of standardized interview schedules for a widening variety of disorders have given us "the first robust evidence that such clinician-to-clinician diagnoses have now attained remarkably high levels of reliability" (Matarazzo, 1983, p. 103). But even now, where structured interview schedules have not been developed for a given disorder or where others have been poorly adapted, the reliability across clinicians is somewhat diminished (Mattison, Cantwell, Russell, & Will, 1979; Spitzer et al., 1979). The important difference, however, is that the operationalization of criteria presented in DSM-III allows for the construction of specific interview schedules, either for children or adults (Costello, 1985; DiNardo, O'Brien, Barlow, Waddell, & Blanchard, 1983).

Second, in Hersen's (1976) earlier review of the issues, little evidence for the *validity* of the DSM-I and DSM-II was noted. Indeed, it appeared that there was no relationship between specific life stressors and specific diagnoses, nor was there a pronounced relationship between psychiatric diagnosis and patients' stated treatment expectations. Moreover, commenting on the results obtained from a long series of studies evaluating the ability of signs and symptoms to differentiate across categories, Nathan, Gould, Zare, and Roth (1969) pointed out that their studies of "the diagnostic process revealed only limited differential diagnostic validity for many of the most common signs and symptoms of psychopathology" (p. 370).

Although increased reliability, clear criteria, and structured interview schedules undoubtedly should enhance the likelihood of validity of the categories in DSM-III, almost all of the studies concerned with this issue have been conducted after the publication of the manual (e.g., Barlow, Blanchard, Vermilyea, Vermilyea, & DiNardo, 1986; Kovacs, Feinberg, Crouse-Novak, Paulauskas, & Finkelstein, 1984; Kovacs, Feinberg, Crouse-Novak, Paulauskas, Pollock, & Finkelstein, 1984; Last, Hersen, & Kazdin, 1986), and considerable overlap across diagnostic categories generally has been observed. However, such overlap across categories is not necessarily an indictment of DSM-III but is perhaps more a reflection of how psychopathology actually clusters in some individuals. In short, we argue that "pure" diagnoses are more a function of the diagnostician's needs than a reflection of clinical reality.

A third major criticism of formal psychiatric diagnosis is that it frequently bears little relationship to the selection of treatment and ultimate prognosis of the patient. This was especially true in DSM-I and DSM-II with regard to implementation of psychotherapeutic techniques, but somewhat less so for the pharmacological approach. The situation has improved somewhat with DSM-III, particularly with respect to application of certain drug treatments for particular diagnoses. As argued by Nathan (1981)

> . . . utility of symptomatic diagnoses is greatest with the psychotic disorders for which drug treatment is the treatment of choice; drugs like the phenothiazines, the tricyclic antidepressants, and lithium carbonate are effective more or less indiscriminately across a given diagnostic category's symptomatology. By contrast, the greater individual specificity of behavioral assessment proves most useful when applied to the nonpsychotic disorders for which a clear treatment of choice does not exist; in such cases a behavioral assessment can provide direction to treatment that a descriptive label by symptomatic diagnosis cannot. (p. 10)

In short, the summary statements of diagnosis provided by DSM-III, with only some exceptions, still do not yield the isomorphic relationship between assessment and treatment that has been the hallmark of the behavioral approach. The situation is parallel for nonbehavioral psychotherapy (see Chodoff, 1986; Hadley & Autry, 1984; Schacht, Henry, & Strupp, in press), with the exception of those psychotherapies specifically designed for treating a given diagnostic entity, such as interpersonal psychotherapy (IPT) for depression (Weissman, 1979).

In addition to the three basic scientific criticisms of formal psychiatric diagnosis, there are a number of negative consequences of psychiatric labeling that have been documented over the years (see Hersen & Turner, 1984). One, of course, is that once a psychiatric label has been affixed to an individual, this label remains irrespective of the individual's subsequent behavior. Thus, the social stigma of the psychiatric diagnosis appears to be permanent. A second negative consequence of the diagnostic process is that it often enables people so labeled to excuse all subsequent actions as products of their diagnosis. In short, such individuals are no longer deemed "responsible" for their actions (see Szasz, 1966). And finally, there is evidence in the literature that diagnosis frequently is not based solely on presenting symptoms but is affected by social and cultural factors (Kahn, 1973), the socioeconomic level of the person (Maracek & Kravitz, 1977), and his or her race (Adebimpe, 1982).

THE STRUCTURE OF DSM-III

In spite of the past (e.g., Rutter & Shaffer, 1980) and current (e.g., Schacht, 1985) criticisms of DSM-III, it probably represents the best psychiatric diagnostic scheme that has yet to be devised. We take this position for a number of reasons, even in light of our full awareness of DSM-III's obvious shortcomings. To begin with, DSM-III, although not entirely empirical, was conceived in a spirit of empiricism, with input from both psychiatrists and psychologists of differing theoretical persuasions. The system includes relatively clear criteria for the specific diagnoses. The incorporation of a multiaxial system is a definite aid to the diagnostic process and provides information above and beyond the formal diagnostic label. A portion of the original draft of DSM-III was evaluated in extensive field trials, yielding acceptable levels of interclinician reliability. And, on an overall basis, DSM-III has been able to provide a viable definition of mental disorder, consistent with the input of critics of its earlier drafts (Schacht & Nathan, 1977).

The structure of DSM-III is best described in the Manual (APA, 1980) and in Spitzer et al.'s (1980) review of its major achievements. But from our perspective, two of the most critical advances are the more comprehensive categories of childhood diagnoses (both in number and detail) and the multiaxial system. Let us briefly consider the multiaxial system since, as we shall see in our later section "Complementarity of DSM-III and Behavioral Assessment," this innovation has bearing on the possible contribution from the work in behavioral assessment. As outlined by Spitzer et al. (1980),

> A multiaxial system for psychiatric evaluation provides for the systematic evaluation of an individual's condition in terms of several variables, or axes, that are conceptualized and rated as quasi-independent of each other. The potential advantages of such a system include comprehensiveness and the recording of non-diagnostic data that are valuable in understanding possible etiological factors and in treatment planning and prognosis. Although many multiaxial systems have been proposed . . . , none has come into widespread use. (p. 154)

In the present system, and in the draft of DSM-III-R as well (APA, 1985), there are five axes. The first three contribute to the formal diagnostic labeling of the patient. Axis I is concerned with identification of the clinical syndromes (e.g., schizophrenic disorders, anxiety disorders, substance use disorders). In Axis II the patient's personality disorder, if any (e.g., histrionic personality disorder, antisocial personality disorder), is listed. These disorders are coded in Axis II "to ensure that they will not be overlooked in the presence of a more florid Axis I disorder" (Spitzer et al., 1979, p. 161). Thus, a patient, under DSM-III, can have both Axis I and Axis II diagnoses. In Axis III the patient's medical condition, if any, is documented (e.g., "soft neurological signs"). Axis IV is reserved for the clinician to rate the severity of psychosocial stressors on a seven-point scale, from none to catastrophic (e.g., accident, death of a loved one). Thus, an attempt has been made to relate *possible* precipitants to the formal diagnosis. And finally, on Axis V, the clinician is asked to rate the patient's highest level of adaptive functioning in the preceding year. This is done on a 1 (= superior) to 5 (= poor) scale. "Thus, with the multiaxial system, a more complete biological, psychosocial, and psychiatric picture of the patient emerges. This, of course, should facilitate identification of appropriate targets for treatment" (Hersen & Turner, 1984, p. 490).

POLITICS OF DSM-III

Throughout its relatively short history, DSM-III has been fraught with political controversy. Even before it was published, there was considerable dispute over: (a) the definition of mental disorder (cf. Schacht & Nathan, 1977; Spitzer et al., 1980), (b) which categories should be included or excluded, and (c) whether the concept of "neurosis" should be retained. The most heated conflict centered on the definition of mental disorder and the apparent intent of the American Psychiatric Association to subsume all categories under the long arm of the medical umbrella. As documented by Spitzer et al. (1980):

> This led to a bitter exchange of letters with the American Psychological Association, which challenged the basis for designating the DSM-III disorders as "medical." The American Psychiatric Association responded by noting that it had never attempted to tell the American Psychological Association what constituted a psychological disorder, and therefore . . . after much soul searching, the task force concluded that the purpose of DSM-III was to classify and describe mental disorders and not to clarify the relationship between psychiatry and medicine . . .. With the removal of this statement . . . , the American Psychological Association liaison committee on DSM-III was able to evaluate DSM-III as a scientific document and concluded that DSM-III represents "substantive advances in the state of the art of psychopathologic diagnosis." (p. 152)

The final definition of mental disorder, apparently acceptable to all, follows (Spitzer et al., 1980):

> In DSM-III, a mental disorder is conceptualized as a clinically significant behavioral or psychologic syndrome or pattern that occurs in an individual and that is typically associated with either a painful symptom (distress) or impairment in one or more important areas of functioning (disability). In addition, there is an inference that there is a behavioral, psychologic, or biologic dysfunction and that the disturbance is not only in the relationship between the individual and society. When the disturbance is limited to a conflict between an individual and society, this may represent social deviance

which may or may not be commendable, but is not by itself a mental disorder. (p. 153)

Other areas of controversy were resolved through the help of "advisory committees of psychiatrists," discussion with professional groups such as the American Psychosomatic Society, consensus of so-called "experts" in a given area, and in other instances through data generated through the field trials that began in 1976 and involved over 800 clinicians in more than 120 facilities across the nation. In addition, about 80 clinicians in private practice were involved in these field trials.

We already have indicated that the birth of DSM-III was prolonged and difficult. However, as recently as 1985, controversy about DSM-III still prevails (Spitzer, 1985; Schacht, 1985). In brief, Schacht (1985) has accused Spitzer and his colleagues of developing a document (i.e., DSM-III) that: (a) "serves to validate and reinforce the mechanisms by which we draw politically important distinctions between persons," (b) "participates in the social regulation of both clients' and professionals' access to social resources," and (c) "helps to establish and validate boundaries for professional guilds" (p. 514). As might be expected, in a retort in *American Psychologist*, the primary official publication of the American Psychological Association, Spitzer (1985) defended himself and the American Psychiatric Association by arguing that "Schacht's definition of politics is so broad that no one could deny that there are political dimensions of scientific activities" (p. 522).

The final word is not yet in, and we sincerely doubt that full resolution of this controversy is likely in the near future. Indeed, we suspect that it will continue through publication of DSM-III-R and DSM-IV. So far, however, the working draft of DSM-III-R (APA, 1985) has not generated such heated debate, although the proposal to include the defensive structure of the patient in the Glossary of Technical Terms is likely to be met with serious question by some behaviorists and pharmacologists. There also has been an initial outcry from feminist groups in reaction to three new proposed categories (masochistic personality disorder, paraphilic rapism, and premenstrual dysphoric disorder), particularly with regard to the wording of the categories (see Fisher, 1986). Although the wording apparently has been modified, everyone is not fully satisfied with the categories as they now stand.

Perhaps even more important than the political controversy over DSM-III are the scientific criticisms that have been leveled against it. It is to these, then, that we turn our attention next.

CRITICISMS OF DSM-III

The primary criticism of DSM-III has been most directly articulated by McReynolds (1979) in his assertion that "the process whereby new categories of disturbances are introduced into psychiatric nosology clearly is not a scientific one. No recognizable process of scientific discovery is evident with regard to the names of new disorders in DSM-III'' (p. 125). In a similar vein, but looking at DSM-III as to how it has impacted child psychiatric diagnosis, Rutter and Shaffer (1980) note that "unvalidated diagnostic categories" have "proliferated" and that operational criteria have been included in an attempt to "justify them."

The basic problem with DSM-III, which is unfortunately likely to extend to DSM-III-R albeit to a lesser extent, is that many of the new categories were determined through committee or as a consequence of experts coming to a consensus. Note, for example, Spitzer et al.'s (1980) comment on how Borderline Personality Disorder was distinguished from Schizotypical Personality Disorder. "That an impressive degree of consensus was reached in our field on this difficult category is attested to by the fact that such major investigators in this area as Drs. John Gunderson and Otto Kernberg are relatively satisifed with the way in which DSM-III defines Borderline Personality Disorder" (p. 153).

Obviously, if a science of psychiatric classification is to be achieved, much more than "satisfaction" by two authorities in the field is required. Indeed, it is critical to document the empirical foundation of the categories with respect to: (a) reliability, (b) validity, (c) prognosis, (d) family aggregation, and (e) utility as to selection of a given treatment. There are many research strategies to establish the requisite empirical underpinnings, and many of these have been outlined in an excellent survey article by Grove, Andreason, McDonald-Scott, Keller, and Shapiro (1981). But irrespective of the specific strategies, we argue here against the notion of the "cart being placed before the horse." That is, the empirical basis should help establish the nature of the diagnosis (e.g., which symptoms aggregate together in individuals) rather than have the research be carried out post-hoc to see if diagnostic labels selected have any empirical justification. To date, however, the trend is to "shoot first and ask questions later." Perhaps if the questions were to be posed first and answered adequately, the necessity for "shooting" would be removed. Presently the designers of DSM-III are rushing to emerge with its revision (DSM-III-R) to meet the publication deadlines set by the American Psychiatric Association. We question whether a revision is in order so soon, since much of the research to validate or invalidate the categories originally selected in DSM-III simply has not been carried out. For example, only recently has there been an attempt to examine the empirical basis of two of the anxiety diagnoses in children: Overanxious Disorder and Separation Anxiety Disorder (Last, Hersen, & Kazdin, 1986). More such studies are obviously warranted if the pitfalls of DSM-III are to be avoided in DSM-III-R (scheduled to appear in 1987) and DSM-IV (scheduled to appear in the 1990s). Otherwise, there will be a proliferation of the repetition compulsion by committee sanctioned by

TABLE 3.1. Statements Relating DSM-III to Behavioral Assessment

SOURCE	QUOTE
Hersen & Turner (1984)	"Finally, by working from within the system, the likelihood for behaviorists having impact on future revisions of DSM can only be enhanced" (p. 496).
Kazdin (1983)	"Failure to recognize or actively use DSM-III may make it difficult to integrate findings from child behavior therapy into clinical work in psychiatry where the potential impact could and perhaps should be the greatest" (p. 94).
Maser (1984)	"There seems to be no a priori reason why the criteria symptoms in the DSM-III should not include direct measures of behavior. Behavioral testing has been used so little either for reaching a DSM-III diagnosis or for validating existing diagnoses that it can hardly be known if it has value for these purposes at all" (p. 404).
Nathan (1981)	"Do the diagnostician and the behavioral assessor have things to teach each other? In our judgment — and at this point in time — yes, indeed!" (p. 10).
Nelson & Barlow (1981)	"The first is that behavioral assessors live in a larger world in which we are badly outnumbered. Thus, in order to communicate with others, it is important to share their terminology" (p. 27).
Taylor (1983)	"And a behaviorally based assessment system could be developed which allowed for categories to include symptomatic diagnoses without burdening all target behaviors within a DSM-III type diagnostic system" (p. 13).

the American Psychiatric Association.

COMPLEMENTARITY OF DSM-III AND BEHAVIORAL ASSESSMENT

As can be readily seen from the quotations presented in Table 3.1, there is general consensus among the behaviorists that the complementarity of DSM-III and behavioral assessment is an area that merits further study. The bases for such complementarity are twofold: one being *political* and the other being *empirical*. Throughout this chapter we have noted the political implications of psychiatric diagnosis for behavioral assessors and other psychologists and the role of politics in the realm of science in general (cf. Schacht, 1985; Spitzer, 1985). Therefore there is no point in belaboring the issue any further, other than underscoring the importance of the behavioral assessors remaining in good communication with their nonbehavioral colleagues, who still predominate the field.

The *empirical* contribution of behavioral assessors to psychiatric diagnosticians, of course, has considerable scientific import, perhaps resulting in some practical clinical gains. The general research question in this area has, in our opinion, been most clearly stated by Maser (1984), who notes that

> "The absence of any generally recognized utility in using behavioral testing to produce a DSM-III diagnosis is unfortunate, since that system of classification is, for the first time, based on observable signs and symptoms. That no one has attempted to connect an objective scheme of classification and an objective method of recording symptomatic behaviors is probably due to prejudices established during training rather than any realistic obstruction in the task. Behavioral testing might bring with it less subjectivity than the most standardized clinical interview, self-report, or rating scale and also serve to enhance the health of assessment." (p. 407)

Although Maser's position is certainly supported by the clinical researchers quoted in Table 3.1, only one formal proposal to link DSM-III and behavioral assessment has come to our attention. Indeed, in a detailed and careful analysis of the issues, Tryon (1986) has shown, for both children and adults, how motor activity measurements (i.e., the motoric sphere of behavioral assessment) can be used to enhance the precision of the diagnostic criteria listed for the various categories in DSM-III. Tryon first points out how the diagnosis is often related to the patient's accelerated or decelerated motor activity. For example, the Attention Deficit Disorder with Hyperactivity (314.01) lists five hyperactivity behaviors (APA, 1980, p. 44): 1. runs about or climbs on things excessively; 2. has difficulty sitting still or fidgets excessively; 3. has difficulty staying seated; 4. moves about excessively during sleep; 5. is always "on the go or acts as if driven by a motor." Another pertinent example is found in the diagnosis of Manic Episode. Four of the criteria for that diagnosis clearly reflect increases in motor activity (APA, 1980, p. 208): 1. increase in activity (either socially, at work or sexually) or physical restlessness; 2. more talkative than usual or pressure to keep talking; 5. decreased need for sleep; 7. excessive involvement in activities that have a high potential for painful consequences which are not recognized. Conversely, in Major Depressive Disorder there may be *decreased* motor activity.

All of the aforementioned criteria have obvious behavioral referents. However, words such as "increase," "more," "excessive," "decrease," or "slowed down" are most imprecise in and of themselves. Through the use of observational coding schemes to evaluate such behaviors, greater precision will allow for a more reliable diagnostic appraisal, particularly if activity norms are established. As argued cogently by Tryon (1986),

In short, behavioral physics will need to be seen as a subspecialty within the broader area of behavioral assessment. This will happen when journals that publish research in behavioral assessment begin accepting articles reporting activity data on interesting groups for its descriptive value rather than for its ability to test one theoretical hypothesis or position against another. We need bench marks and ultimately norms for patient and normal populations if we are to develop an empirical basis for rendering diagnoses using activity measurements. (pp. 64–65)

Yet another way to view the complementarity of behavioral assessment and DSM-III is to conceptualize behavioral assessment as the *idiographic* approach within the broader *nomothetic* system encompassed by DSM-III. Thus, the strength of behavioral assessment is to identify specific targets (e.g., activity levels) that can be evaluated during the course of a treatment (pharmacologic or behavioral). And, using behavioral analytic strategies (Barlow & Hersen, 1984), experimental control over these targets can be documented scientifically. On the other hand, it is the specific targets (or criteria) in a particular pattern that contribute to the diagnostic label. How such specific criteria aggregate in common patterns across individuals has never been a strength of behavioral assessment. As a matter of fact, until recently behavioral assessors (see Kazdin, 1983; Nathan, 1981; Nelson & Barlow, 1981) have given short shrift to such conceptualizations. In this connection we must fully concur with Nathan's evaluation that "it is when behavior therapists and 'traditional' diagnosticians attempt summary statements, however, that the latter may now have an edge in reliability they did not have before" (p. 6). Particularly telling is that, given the enhanced reliability in the DSM-III system, there is now at least some relationship between specific diagnoses and specific treatments (e.g., use of lithium for manic episodes or use of imipramine for panic attacks). But irrespective of the improved reliability of DSM, behavioral assessors no longer can simply focus solely on individual targets, nor can they ignore the patterns of covariation of criteria that differentiate one group of patients from another. They cannot divorce themselves from the process of psychiatric diagnosis.

Earlier we mentioned that the multiaxial system is one of the most innovative features of DSM-III. However, despite such innovation, reliability across clinicians for two of the axes (Axis IV — Severity of Psychosocial Stressors; Axis V — Highest Level of Adaptive Functioning in the Past Year) has not been documented at acceptable levels (Taylor, 1983). Although we applaud the development of these two axes, insufficient empirical work has been carried out to establish anchor points and operational criteria to enhance reliable assessment. In this connection, there exists a vast literature on both psychosocial stressors (e.g., Depue & Monroe, 1986) and adaptive living skills (e.g., Bellack & Hersen, 1979) that could readily be used to operationalize the two axes. Clear behavioral referents incorporated within a structured interview format are probably warranted.

This most certainly is a task that behavioral assessors should tackle with great relish, especially if applied to Axis II disorders where reliability has been poorer than that obtained for Axis I disorders.

BROADENING ROLE OF BEHAVIORAL ASSESSMENT

By implication, at the very least, we foresee a much broader role for behavioral assessment in the future. With this, some of the role functions of behavioral assessors are likely to be blurred; but even though this undoubtedly will cause discomfort for some, we contend that the field must move on. We are convinced that the unique perspectives that behavioral assessors hold can yield only an improved nosological scheme, especially if the contributions of behavioral assessors become integrated into mainstream diagnoses and classifications.

In addition to the potential input of behavioral assessment to the DSM process, we need to examine with care those important aspects of assessment that generally have been overlooked. We are all obviously familiar with the extensive literature from developmental psychology. But it is amazing how few of the findings have found their way into the behavioral literature. Indeed, as do Harris and Ferrari (1983), we contend that there is much to be gained for both behaviorists and developmentalists in carrying on a more extensive discourse. Developmental psychologists have the concepts, but behavioral assessors possess the methodology to pinpoint and codify behaviors at relevant developmental levels from infancy to the adulthood of senior citizens. Development of such behavioral coding schemes (based on naturalistic observation or staged situations that can be videotaped) will allow for the much-needed generation of norms. If behaviors can be coded both across age groups and across normal and pathological populations, behavioral assessment will have a developmental context from which it can operate. Moreover, establishment of normative behaviors should facilitate the clinician's job in modifying aberrant behavior to the point where we truly have a referent for whether "social validation" (Kazdin, 1977) has been achieved.

Consistent with the several criteria listed for each of the diagnoses in DSM-III, behavioral assessors now need to look at multiple targets when evaluating patients. As noted by Kazdin (1985):

> Assumptions about the clinical relevance of the target foci in behavior therapy need to be examined empirically given the evidence attesting to the complexity of clinical change, the varied interrelationships among alternative outcome measures, and the possibility that change in the target behavior may not accomplish many of the concurrent and long-term goals of treatment." (p. 33)

The simplistic selection of singular target measures for purposes of documenting experimental control of treatment strategies, although of scientific interest, does not capture the complete diagnostic picture. Clinical realities warrant a much more comprehensive approach. Not only is the evaluation of multiple targets indicated, but a careful simultaneous assessment of three response channels (motoric, cognitive, physiological) can prove to be of considerable importance (e.g., Van Hasselt, Hersen, Bellack, Rosenblum, & Lamparski, 1979). An important unresolved question that needs to be tackled is whether all three response channels require modification to bring about lasting change.

In addition, it is clear that behavioral assessors can no longer deny the critical biological underpinnings of behavior either from an etiological (see Rebec & Anderson, 1986) or treatment perspective (see Hersen, 1986). In the future, behavioral assessors will have to examine in great detail the relevant biochemical–behavioral relationships in their patients in addition to their traditional pursuit of examining antecedent and consequent behavioral events.

Finally, there exists a large body of literature in the realm of intellectual and neuropsychological evaluation (see Goldstein & Hersen, 1984) that has received virtually no integration with behavioral assessment. Such complementarity surely can only further enhance the comprehensiveness of the diagnostic assessment. As cogently stated by Goldstein (1979):

> There are practical and empirical considerations that suggest that neuropsychological tests are currently the best tools available for behavioral assessment of brain-damaged patients. However, the results of these tests can be used not only diagnostically but also to identify target behavioral deficits that may be rehabilitated through systematic retraining efforts. Such rehabilitation efforts can be optimally planned, implemented, and evaluated through an alliance between the neuropsychologist, who identifies the ability and deficit pattern, and the behavior therapist, who devises and evaluates the retraining program. (p. 23)

SUMMARY

In this chapter we have considered the broadening role of behavioral assessment within the context of improvements in the DSM system and in the context of other empirical directions in our field. In so doing, we have looked at the importance of classification in general; criticism of formal psychiatric diagnosis; the structure of DSM-III; the politics before, during, and after the emergence of DSM-III; criticism of DSM-III; the possible complementarity of DSM-III and behavioral assessment; and the broadening role of behavioral assessment. The underlying theme throughout the chapter has been that behavioral assessment is at a scientific and political crossroads. Some purists will probably object to our conclusions concerning the enhanced role of behavioral assessment vis-à-vis DSM and other empirical systems of evaluation. However, in anticipation of such criticism we argue that as behavioral assessors we should not follow the donkey's tail, but perhaps should steer the donkey onto the right path.

REFERENCES

Adams, H. E. (1984). Editorial. *Journal of Behavioral Assessment, 16*, 261–262.

Adams, H. E., Doster, J. A., & Calhoun, K. S. (1977). A psychologically based system of response classification. In A. R. Ciminero, K. S. Calhoun, & H. E. Adams (Eds.), *Handbook of behavioral assessment* (pp. 47–48). New York: John Wiley & Sons.

Adebimpe, V. R. (1982). Psychiatric symptoms in black patients. In S. M. Turner & R. T. Jones (Eds.), *Behavior modification in black populations: Psychosocial issues and empirical findings*. New York: Plenum Press.

American Psychiatric Association (1980). *Diagnostic and statistical manual of mental disorders*. (Third Edition). Washington, D.C.: Author.

American Psychiatric Association (1985). *Draft: DSM-III-R in development*. Washington, D.C.: Author.

Barlow, D. II., Blanchard, E. B., Vermilyea, J. A., Vermilyea, B. B., & DiNardo, P. A. (1986). Generalized anxiety and generalized anxiety disorder: Description and reconceptualization. *American Journal of Psychiatry, 143*, 40–44.

Barlow, D. H., & Hersen, M. (1984). *Single case experimental designs: Strategies for studying behavior change* (Second Edition). New York: Pergamon Press.

Bellack, A. S., & Hersen, M. (Eds.). (1979). *Research and practice in social skills training*. New York: Plenum Press.

Chodoff, P. (1986). DSM-III and psychotherapy. *American Journal of Psychiatry, 143*, 201–203.

Costello, A. J. (1985). Assessment of children and adolescents: An overview. *Psychiatric Annals, 15*, 15–24.

Depue, R. A., & Monroe, S. M. (1986). Conceptualization and measurement of human disorders in life stress research: The problem. *Psychological Bulletin, 90*, 66–77.

Di Nardo, P. A., O'Brien, G. T., Barlow, D. H., Waddell, M. T., & Blanchard, E. B. (1983). Reliability of DSM-III anxiety disorder categories using a new structured interview. *Archives of General Psychiatry, 40*, 1070–1074.

Fisher, B. (1986). DSM-III-R amendment process frustrates non-MDs. *American Psychological Association Monitor, 17*, 18–19, 24.

Frank, G. (1975). *Psychiatric diagnosis*. Oxford: Pergamon Press.

Goldfried, M. R., & Sprafkin, J. M. (1976). Behavioral personality assessment. In J. T. Spence, R. C. Corron, & J. W. Thibaut (Eds.), *Behavioral approaches to therapy*. Morristown, New Jersey: General Learning Press.

Goldstein, G. R. (1979). Methodological and theoretical issues in neuropsychological assessment. *Journal of Behavioral Assessment, 1*, 23–41.

Goldstein, G. R., & Hersen, M. (Eds.). (1984). *Handbook of psychological assessment*. New York: Pergamon Press.

Grove, W. M., Andreasen, N. C., McDonald-Scott, P., Keller, M. B., & Shapiro,

R. W. (1981). Reliability studies of psychiatric diagnosis: Theory and practice. *Archives of General Psychiatry, 38*, 408–413.

Hadley, S. W., & Autry, J. H. (1984). DSM-III and psychotherapy. In S. M. Turner & M. Hersen (Eds.), *Adult psychopathology and diagnosis* (pp. 465–484). New York: John Wiley & Sons.

Harris, S. L., & Ferrari, M. (1983). Developmental factors in child behavior therapy. *Behavior Therapy, 14*, 54–72.

Hersen, M. (1976). Historical perspectives in behavioral assessment. In M. Hersen & A. S. Bellack (Eds.), *Behavioral assessment: A practical handbook* (pp. 3–22). New York: Pergamon Press.

Hersen, M. (1981). Complex problems require complex solutions. *Behavior Therapy, 12*, 15–29.

Hersen, M. (Ed.). (1986). *Pharmacological and behavioral treatment: An integrative approach.* New York: John Wiley & Sons.

Hersen, M., & Bellack, A. S. (Eds.). (1976). *Behavioral assessment: A practical handbook.* New York: Pergamon Press.

Hersen, M., & Bellack, A. S. (Eds.). (1981). *Behavioral assessment: A practical handbook* (2nd ed.) New York: Pergamon Press.

Hersen, M., & Turner, S. M. (1984). DSM-III and behavior therapy. In S. M. Turner & Michel Hersen (Eds.), *Adult psychopathology and diagnosis* (pp. 485–502). New York: John Wiley & Sons.

Kahn, M. L. (1973). Social class and schizophrenia: A critical review and reformulation. *Schizophrenia Bulletin, 1*, 60–79.

Kanfer, F. H., & Saslow, G. (1965). Behavioral diagnosis. *Archives of General Psychiatry, 12*, 529–538.

Kazdin, A. E. (1977). Assessing the clinical or applied importance of behavior change through social validation. *Behavior Modification, 1*, 427–452.

Kazdin, A. E. (1983). Psychiatric diagnosis, dimensions of dysfunction, and child behavior therapy. *Behavior Therapy, 14*, 73–99.

Kazdin, A. E. (1985). Selection of target behaviors: The relationship of the treatment focus to clinical dysfunction. *Behavioral Assessment, 7*, 33–47.

Kovacs, M., Feinberg, T. L., Crouse-Novak, A., Paulauskas, S. L., & Finkelstein, R. (1984). Depressive disorders in childhood: I. A longitudinal prospective study of characteristics and recovery. *Archives of General Psychiatry, 41*, 229–237.

Kovacs, M., Feinberg, T. L., Crouse-Novak, A., Paulauskas, S. L., Pollock, M., & Finkelstein, R. (1984). Depressive disorders in childhood: II. A longitudinal study of the risk for a subsequent major depression. *Archives of General Psychiatry, 41*, 643–649.

Last, C. G., Hersen, M., & Kazdkin, A. E. (1986). Unpublished data.

Maracek, J., & Kravitz, D. (1977). Women and mental health. A review of feminist change efforts. *Psychiatry, 40*, 323–328.

Maser, J. D. (1984). Behavioral testing of anxiety: Issues, diagnosis, and practice. *Journal of Behavioral Assessment, 6*, 397–409.

Matarazzo. J. D. (1983). The reliability of psychiatric and psychological diagnosis. *Clinical Psychology Review, 3*, 103–145.

Mattison, R., Cantwell, D. P., Russell, A. T., & Will, L. (1979). A comparison of DSM-II and DSM-III in the diagnosis of childhood psychiatric disorders: II. Interrater agreement. *Archives of General Psychiatry, 36*, 1217–1222.

McFall, R. M. (1986). Theory and method in assessment: The vital link. *Behavioral Assessment, 8*, 3–10.

McLemore, C. W., & Benjamin, L. S. (1979). Whatever happened to interpersonal diagnosis: A psychological alternative to DSM-III. *American Psychologist, 34*, 17–33.

McReynolds, W. T. (1979). DSM-III and the future of applied science. *Professional Psychology, 10*, 123–132.

Nathan, P. E. (1981). Symptomatic diagnosis and behavioral assessment: A synthesis. In D. H. Barlow (Ed.), *Behavioral assessment of adult disorders* (pp. 1–11). New York: Guilford Press.

Nathan, P. E., Gould, C. F., Zare, N. C., & Roth, M. (1969). A systems analysis of diagnosis: VI. Improved diagnostic validity from median data. *Journal of Clinical Psychology, 25*, 370–375.

Nelson, R. O. (1980). The use of intelligence tests within behavioral assessment. *Behavioral Assessment, 2*, 417–423.

Nelson, R. O., & Barlow, D. H. (1981). Behavioral assessment: Basic strategies and initial procedures. In D. H. Barlow (Ed.), *Behavioral assessment of adult disorders* (pp. 13–43). New York: Guilford Press.

Patterson, G. R., & Bank, L. (1986). Bootstrapping your way in the nomological thicket. *Behavioral Assessment, 8*, 49–73.

Rebec, G. V., & Anderson, G. D. (1986). Regional neuropharmacology of the antipsychotic drugs. Implications for the dopamine hypothesis of schizophrenia. *Behavioral Assessment, 8*, 11–29.

Rutter, M., & Shaffer, D. (1980). DSM-III: A step forward or back in terms of the classification of child psychiatric disorders. *Journal of the Academy of Child Psychiatry, 19*, 371–394.

Schacht, T. E. (1985). DSM-III and the politics of truth. *American Psychologist, 40*, 513–521.

Schacht, T. E., Henry, W. P., & Strupp, H. H. (in press). Psychotherapy. In C. G. Last & M. Hersen (Eds.), *Handbook of anxiety disorders*. New York: Pergamon Press.

Schacht, T. E., & Nathan, P. E. (1977). But is it good for psychologists? Appraisal and status of DSM-III. *American Psychologist, 32*, 1017–1025.

Spitzer, R. L. (1985). DSM-III and the politics-science dichotomy syndrome: A response to Thomas E. Schacht's "DSM-III and the politics of truth." *American Psychologist, 40*, 522–526.

Spitzer, R. L., Endicott, J., & Robins (1978). Research diagnostic criteria: Rationale and reliability. *Archives of General Psychiatry, 35*, 773–782.

Spitzer, R. L., Forman, J. B. W., & Nee, J. (1979. DSM-III field trials: I. Initial interrater diagnostic reliability. *American Journal of Psychiatry, 136*, 815–817.

Spitzer, R. L., Williams, J. B. W., & Skodol, A. E. (1980). DSM-III: The major achievements and an overview. *American Journal of Psychiatry, 137*, 151–164.

Sprock, J., & Blashfield, R. K. (1983). Classification and nosology. In M. Hersen, A. E. Kazdin, & A. E. Bellack (Eds.), *The clinical psychology handbook* (pp. 289–307). New York: Pergamon Press.

Szasz, T. S. (1966). The psychiatric classification of behavior. A strategy of personal constraint. In L. D. Eron (Ed.), *The classification of behavior disorders*. Chicago: Aldine.

Taylor, C. B. (1983). DSM-III and behavioral assessment. *Behavioral Assessment, 5*, 5–14.

Tryon, W. W. (1986). Motor activity measurements and DSM-III. In M. Hersen, R. M. Eisler, & P. M. Miller (Eds.), *Progress in behavior modification,* Volume 20 (pp. 35–66). Orlando: Academic Press.

Van Hasselt, V. B., Hersen, M., Bellack, A. S., Rosenblum, N., & Lamparksi, D.

(1979). Tripartite assessment of the effects of systematic desensitization in a multiphobic child. *Journal of Behavior Therapy and Experimental Psychiatry*, *10*, 51–56.

Weissman, M. M. (1979). The psychological treatment of depression: Evidence for the efficacy of psychotherapy alone and in combination with pharmacotherapy. *Archives of General Psychiatry*, *36*, 1261–1269.

PART 2

ASSESSMENT STRATEGIES

4
Behavioral Interviewing

Kenneth P. Morganstern

Behavioral interviewing has always been an integral part of the entire behavioral assessment and therapy process. It is within such interviews that the therapeutic relationship is established, essential preliminary clinical decisions are made, and the therapist begins to gather the information with which ultimate treatment goals and priorities are established. Despite the remarkable surge of interest and the increasing specificity of the behavioral assessment literature over the last decade, the *manner* in which the necessary information is obtained, i.e., how the interview is conducted, is often unclear. Moreover, there is a growing acknowledgement that the practice of behavior therapy is considerably more complex than the "experimental" behavioral literature has implied (Bellack & Hersen, 1985; Evans, 1985; Fishman & Lubetkin, 1983; Goldfried, 1983; Hersen, 1981, 1983b; Kanfer, 1985; Kazdin, 1985; Kratochwill, 1985a; Mash, 1985). As behaviorists examine the reasons for treatment failure (Foa & Emmelkamp, 1983), respond to the practical and ethical demands of clinical practice, and question both the conceptualization and traditional methodology of "target behavior" selection within behavior therapy, the importance of skillful, broad-based behavioral interviewing is further underscored. The purpose of this chapter is to provide a framework for clinicians during the initial stages of assessment and to elaborate upon a number of practical issues and procedures in behavioral interviewing.

This chapter is divided into two sections. The first part discusses several important conceptual issues in behavioral interviewing. These include goals of assessment, problem identification and target selection issues, ethical considerations, and the role of relationship variables. The second section focuses primarily on a few selected methods and procedures employed in the

Grateful acknowledgment is extended to Helen E. Tevlin for her valuable comments and critical reading of the manuscript.

behavioral interview and presents a number of clinical illustrations. Assessment often requires information from a variety of sources, including the client's family, employer, friends, coworkers, etc. Also, there are a number of different purposes for the behavioral interview (Haynes, 1978; Wiens, 1985). The major emphasis of this chapter, however, is on the information provided by the individual client during the therapy process.

One of the major goals of this chapter is to provide some practical suggestions for the beginning or inexperienced clinician. There is a growing trend toward such practical guidelines and handbooks for both assessment (e.g., Barlow, 1981; Hersen & Bellack, 1981) and therapy (e.g., Barlow, 1985; Hersen, 1983a; Hersen & Bellack, 1985). It is essential to note that, in contrast to the considerable empirical support of behavioral treatments, research on the effects of behavioral interview procedures are noticeably absent. The techniques and strategies that are presented in this chapter are theoretically consistent with a behavioral model, but as yet have not been empirically validated.

BEHAVIORAL INTERVIEWING: CONCEPTUAL ISSUES

Goals of Assessment

Behavioral interviewing is intimately tied to the ultimate goals of assessment and behavior therapy. Assessment is a complex, continuing, "recursive" process (Kanfer, 1985), the major goal of which is the accurate identification of a client's problems. The behavioral interview gathers information that enables the clinician to define and fully understand the nature and context of an individual's problematic behavior(s). Such a "functional behavioral analysis" establishes the "precise covariations" between changes in stimulus conditions and changes in selected behaviors (Mishel, 1971); that is, it defines the "ABC's (antecedents, behaviors, and consequences) of behavior control" (O'Leary & Wilson, 1975, p. 25).

Such a behavioral *microanalysis* may be distinguished from a behavioral *macroanalysis*, the latter of which establishes possible relationships between the variety of the client's presenting problems (Emmelkamp, 1982). These analyses are important challenges to the criticisms that behavioral approaches are superficial and narrow. Broad conceptualizations may include the exploration of "behavioral dynamics" and "underlying determinants" of a client's presenting problems, provided the referents are concrete and behavioral (Fishman & Lubetkin, 1983).

A thorough assessment of problematic behavior, therefore, often goes beyond first appearances in therapy (Goldfried, 1977; Goldfried & Davison, 1976; Hersen, 1981, 1983b; Mahoney, Kazdin, & Lesswing, 1974; Wolpe,

1977). The "bridge phobia" described by Lazarus (1971a) is a well known example. In this case, the client originally complained of a fear of crossing bridges. Further exploration revealed considerable anxiety and uncertainty in regard to work, competence, obligations, and achievements. In particular, the client was acutely sensitive to his mother's pejorative statements that "he would never amount to anything." What was actually being avoided was not only a bridge, but also a new work situation across the bridge and, in turn, the potential criticisms of himself and his mother. While desensitization was, in fact, successfully employed, it was directed primarily at the real and imagined critical statements of the client's mother.

Similarly, Hersen (1983b) cautioned against the "tendency to seize the first (or most apparent) 'juicy' behavior that obviously can be measured and operationalized, without considering that behavior within the context of the entire case" since it "could lead to failure in treatment and even tragic consequences" (p. 13). Hersen briefly described two cases in which presenting anxiety problems were prematurely selected for treatment. In both cases, more serious but less apparent depressive behaviors were overlooked. It was only after a suicide attempt in one case and minimal progress in the other that a more thorough behavioral analysis was performed and a more appropriate (and successful) therapeutic plan carried out. Although it is important to avoid the tautology that behavior therapy "successes" are the result of thorough analyses while "failures" are the product of inadequate ones (Kazdin, 1973), most behavior therapists would agree with Lazarus' (1973) statement that "faulty problem identification (inadequate assessment) is probably the greatest impediment to successful therapy" (p. 407).

A final caution is important. In their desire to be thorough, clinicians need not, and should not, move toward the other extreme and attempt to assess everything in the background and present situations of their clients. Often, much of the information gathered by traditional therapists is unnecessary. Peterson (1968), for example, estimated that three-fourths of the material usually covered in traditional interviews could probably be eliminated "with no loss whatever to the patient [since] only rarely do the conventional data have anything to do with treatment" (p. 119). Not only is such practice inefficient, it also raises the ethical question regarding the legitimacy of inquiry into diverse aspects of a client's life, however interesting they may be to the therapist or the client, when such content is probably irrelevant to treatment. In sum, the heuristic answer to the question often asked by students — "What do I need to know about the client?" — is, "Everything that is *relevant* to the development of effective, efficient, and durable treatment interventions." And from an ethical (and economical) consideration, one could add, "And no more."

Problem Identification and Target Selection Issues

Although accurate, complete, and sophisticated problem identification is the most important goal of behavioral interviewing, the task is neither easy nor free of conceptual and methodological controversy. Mash (1985) recently noted the distinction drawn (Evans, 1985; Kanfer, 1985; Nelson, 1983) between the *methods* of assessment and the *process* of synthesizing the information obtained. This dichotomy has variously been referred to as behavioral *assessment* vs. behavioral *analysis* (Barlow, 1981; Barlow & Waddell, 1985; Mash, 1985; Nelson & Barlow, 1981), *microanalysis* vs. *macroanalysis* (Emmelkamp, 1982), and *molecular* vs. *molar* assessment (Bellack & Morrison, 1982). The methods have frequently been characterized as "objective, structured, reliable, and valid," whereas the process has been assumed to be "clinical, subjective, flexible, and changing" (Mash, 1985). The inherent paradox of the behavioral interview is that the interview is expected to be not only reliable and valid (Haynes, 1978; Haynes & Jensen, 1979) but also flexible and sensitive enough for subtle and illusive information to be obtained (Evans & Wilson, 1983). Sophisticated behavior therapists, however, have become increasingly skeptical of the simple, albeit reliable, assessment methods which provide "elegant but trivial set(s) of data" (Bellack & Morrison, 1982, p. 727).

The growing dissatisfaction with single-target behavior measurement as an adequate representation of the complexity of clinical problems (Bellack & Hersen, 1985; Hersen, 1981, 1983a) provided much of the impetus for a recent mini-series devoted to target behavior selection (Mash, 1985) in *Behavioral Assessment* (Hartmann, 1985) that included important and provocative articles by Kanfer, Evans, Kazdin, and Kratochwill as well as a concluding commentary by Mash. The focus of this mini-series was on the problem of defining *what* are acceptable and appropriate "targets" for behavior therapy treatment. In addition, the important questions of *how* the behavioral clinician selects those targets for treatment, what factors influence those decisions, and how those selections are validated were explored. Such issues are of central importance for the behavioral clinician and are discussed throughout this chapter.

Defining Target Behaviors

How does the behavioral clinician accurately and completely identify a client's problems? Although there is no simple answer to this question, it would seem that the variety of existing multifaceted assessment schema provide some useful guidelines. A number of such broad-spectrum assessment strategies have been proposed, the most notable being those of

Goldfried (1982; Goldfried & Pomeranz, 1968; Goldfried & Sprafkin, 1974), Kanfer (Kanfer & Grimm, 1977; Kanfer & Saslow, 1969), and Lazarus (1971b, 1973, 1976, 1981). Despite somewhat different emphases, these assessment schema all suggest gathering extensive information from clients that describe their problems and strengths in terms of the client's affect, cognitions, and behavior (overt and physiological), especially as they relate to the client's interpersonal functioning. (See Morganstern & Tevlin, 1981, for a more extensive review of these multifaceted assessment guidelines.) By using such structured schema, the interviewer may be encouraged to assess modalities of a client's functioning that might, because of the therapist's ignorance or prejudgment, be overlooked or ignored. It is important to note, however, that such comprehensive assessment guidelines, while applicable in many cases, may be unnecessary for some individual situations. Multifaceted behavioral assessment, therefore, must always be guided by the principle of parsimony (Stuart, 1970).

Establishing Treatment Goals and Priorities

Once a client's presenting problems are identified, they must be conceptually integrated, and preliminary treatment goals and priorities must be established. Often the highest treatment priority is *different* from the client's initial complaint (Evans, 1985). The presenting problem may serve as the client's "calling card" (Lazarus, 1981) or convenient focal point to begin (Evans, 1985). Moreover, behaviorists generally recognize (without resorting to a medical model [i.e., symptom–disease] of psychopathology) that an individual's problems are part of larger, integrated systems (Evans, 1985; Kanfer, 1985; Staats, 1978) which may necessitate treatment intervention at a more "basic" level. Consider an example presented by Evans (1985):

> The severe tension headaches of one recent client seemed to be causally related to the stress of contending with extremely disruptive behaviors of her 8-year-old child; the headaches in turn interfered with her ability to initiate some positive strategies for more effective child behavior management and provided an excuse for her nonparticipation in social activities where meeting new potential male friends made her anxious. Her lack of social contacts, however, seemed to be contributing to her loneliness and depression. (p. 24)

Such an interactive model illustrates quite well the inadequacy of the "target" metaphor for behavioral assessment and behavior therapy, since it perpetuates the "monosymptomatic" view of complex client problems which rarely fit into such a framework (Evans, 1985). Tevlin (personal communication, January 1986) criticizes the use of the "target" metaphor on two other grounds: (a) the war-like connotations and "shooting" imagery associated with the term and (b) the dissatisfaction with the implied power relationship between therapist and client, where the client is seen as being the passive "recipient" of clinical interventions. More importantly, the interactive model (which Evans readily concedes is neither particularly mysterious nor original) requires the therapist to "intervene at some point or points of the sequence in the most effective and broadly beneficial manner" (Evans, 1985, p. 24). Unfortunately, there is no empirical model, as yet, within behavioral assessment for formalizing the analytic processes that guide the necessary clinical decision-making (Evans, 1985; Kanfer, 1985; Mash, 1985). How then does the clinician establish preliminary treatment goals and priorities? While Evans (1985) proposes an elegant systems theory model to answer this question, and while Mash (1985) calls for the application of high-speed microprocessors for actuarial analyses, the inexperienced clinician certainly needs a more immediate and pragmatic solution to this problem.

A number of behavioral writers have developed guidelines for establishing such treatment priorities. Nelson and Barlow (1981) suggested four philosophical guidelines influencing target behavior selection. These included the notions that: (a) behavior should be altered if it is dangerous to the client or to others; (b) target behaviors should be altered so that the client's reinforcers are maximized; (c) undesirable behaviors should be decreased, not through punishment, but by substituting desirable behaviors; and (d) target behaviors should maximize the flexibility of the client's skills for achieving long-term individual and social benefits.

Kratochwill (1985b) summarized some of the more explicit criteria for the selection of target behaviors for treatment:

> Conceptual criteria . . . include such factors as physical danger to the client or others, likelihood of being maintained by others, positive valence, importance for the development of other behaviors in a chain or hierarchy of development, maximization of flexibility or adaptation to the environment, and effectiveness in changing existing contingency systems so as to promote long-term positive development. Empirical criteria for selection of target behaviors include consistency with developmental or local norms, relevance to successful performance, positiveness as rated through social validation, capacity for discriminating between skilled and non-skilled performance, and if left untreated, would result in a negative prognosis. (pp. 3–4)

Fishman and Lubetkin (1983), on the basis of their extensive clinical experience, proposed a number of important practical guidelines for establishing treatment priorities. The first of these, consistent with ethical and legal demands of the clinical situation, is the *urgency* of an individual client's problems. That is, are the presenting problems life-threatening or do they have serious legal ramifications? The second consideration explores the client's *expectations* for treatment. Fishman and Lubetkin underscored the importance of determining the particular needs of the individual client, even if the initial focus of therapy is on a less "therapeutically desirable" area (as perceived by the therapist). In this way trust, rather than alienation, is established. Finally, Fishman and Lubetkin believed it essential that clinicians give attention to the "core" problems of a client (e.g., feelings of worthlessness or inadequacy) in order to ensure generalization of treatment success to other problematic areas.

In summary, the establishment of treatment goals and priorities, an integral part of behavioral interviewing, appears to be a highly complex and subjective process involving sequential and hierarchical decision-making by the clinician. Although most writers agree that serious or dangerous problems warrant high priority (Fishman & Lubetkin, 1983; Mash & Terdal, 1981; Millard & Evans, 1983; Nelson & Barlow, 1981), the selection process of other target behaviors for treatment is far less straightforward.

Validating Target Behavior Selection

One of the hallmarks of behavior therapy has been its insistence on experimentally derived and empirically validated procedures. With regard to the behavioral interview (and the identification and selection of problem behaviors for treatment), a number of writers (cf. Haynes, 1978; Haynes & Jensen, 1979; Mash, 1985) view behavioral assessment as conceptually no different than any other behavioral method. Accordingly, behavioral assessment must identify and select treatment targets that are objectively and reliably measured, as well as generate agreed-upon treatment criteria against which the selection can be validated (Mash, 1985; Strupp, 1978).

In contrast to this view, however, is the growing appreciation of the complexity of behavior therapy and the need, therefore, for greater flexibility, particularly in regard to the formulation of a client's problems and treatment focus. Behavioral interviewing and assessment, in this way, is seen as a process (Evans, 1985; Evans & Wilson, 1983; Kanfer, 1985) which generates *working hypotheses* for problem identification and treatment rather than *static* treatment choices (Mash, 1985). Such an approach, although broader in scope and more sensitive to the day-to-day clinical realities, makes validation more difficult. Addressing this need, Kazdin (1985) suggested a number of ways in which target selections may be concurrently and predictively validated. Finally, the consensus within the behavioral community emphasizes that positive treatment results provide the best validation for behavioral assessment, although such validation procedures are not without confounds. In sum, it is only with the appreciation of more long-term indices of validity (such as treatment success and "consumer satisfaction," Kratochwill, 1985b) that the evaluation of behavior therapy will be able to adequately reflect the complex realities of clinical practice.

Ethical Issues

Behavior therapy, characterized by empirically validated procedures for *client-stated* objectives, has considerably tempered Halleck's (1971) observation that therapists are never politically or ethically neutral. Nevertheless, several critical ethical issues remain, particularly during behavioral interviewing and the initial stages of assessment. These include: the determination of the client's goals; the degree of therapist influence on the selection of these objectives; and the decision of whether to accept the goals of the client and intervene or to refuse treatment when it is ethically necessary to do so. The ethical issue regarding the client's right to minimal intrusion has previously been discussed. In general, the arguments presented here assume the individual to be an adult volunteer in an outpatient setting; however, many of the remarks may be equally applicable to clients not sharing these criteria. Questions concerning children or institutionalized individuals, while important, are beyond the scope of this chapter (see Feldman & Peay, 1982; McNamara, 1978; Sheldon-Wildgen & Risley, 1982; Wexler, 1974).

For many years, behaviorists have emphasized that behavior therapy "is a system of principles and not a system of ethics" (Bandura, 1969, p. 87). In addition, clinicians have underscored the client's — not the therapist's — goals as the focus of treatment. Rarely, however, do clients who refer themselves to therapy have their problems and future objectives crystallized. Far more often, clients' needs and wants become clearer as they talk to the practitioner (Halleck, 1971), and thus the goals, desires, and values of the therapist are an inescapable reality in influencing both the interview process and the end product of assessment — the identification and selection of problem behavior for treatment. With regard to the selection of target behaviors within behavior therapy, there is a growing acknowledgement (Evans, 1985; Franks, 1983; Kanfer, 1985; Kazdin, 1985; MacDonald, 1984) that the assessment process "reflects the individual clinician's experiential base, theoretical predilections, knowledge base in psychology, skill and competence, and social and personal norms" (Mash, 1985, p. 70).

Previously, behaviorists were criticized for the kinds of target behaviors they selected for "powerless" populations such as institutionalized clients (Wexler, 1974) and school children (Winett & Winkler, 1972). Similar issues are relevant to adult clients in voluntary, outpatient settings. The case of homosexuality provides an excellent example of the therapist's implicit (and often explicit) value judgments, which influence the determination of the client's goals. Despite the fact that homosexuality is no longer included in the

Diagnostic and statistical manual of mental disorders (DSM-III, APA, 1980), many therapists, including behavioral clinicians, "regard homosexual behavior and attitudes to be undesirable, sometimes pathological, and at any rate in need of change towards a heterosexual orientation" (Davison, 1974, p. 4). It is difficult to imagine such biases not entering into the assessment process. Consider, for example, the decision made by Fensterheim (1972) to offer behavior therapy to a client who was homosexual but who emphatically stated that he did not desire to change his sexual orientation:

> I do agree to confine the treatment to the specific target symptoms as best I can. However, I also state that I will present for their consideration a plan for the treatment of homosexuality. All I ask is that I be permitted a brief time to present a possible treatment plan and that the client listen to it. (pp. 25–26)

Although Fensterheim goes on to emphasize that no attempt is made to "sell" treatment of homosexuality to the client, there is the implicit assumption in the therapeutic suggestion that the individual *should*, in fact, change. Whereas Fensterheim's decision to accept the client's original objective for treatment is a highly commendable one, it should be clear that additional suggestions on the part of the therapist to modify these objectives may constitute very powerful influences on the client.

Ethical issues become more complicated when the therapist must decide whether it is responsible to *accept* the client's initially stated goals. The choice to "deny" particular treatment requests may be obvious in certain stereotypic examples (e.g., the abused housewife who requests anxiety reduction to reduce her discomfort when anticipating or receiving her husband's beatings). Similarly, it is unlikely that practitioners would immediately accept a client's request to stop him or her from masturbating and proceed to treat the "problem." The therapist would almost certainly offer information about masturbation and sexuality to the client or use desensitization or cognitive restructuring procedures to reduce the anxiety associated with masturbation.

More often, however, the ethical implications are considerably more subtle, as in the case of homosexuality, when therapists are far more likely to consider the behavior as problematic and to intervene accordingly. The very existence of a variety of techniques to change sexual orientation not only encourages their use, but may condone the current societal prejudice concerning such behavior (Davison, 1974, 1977; Silverstein, 1977). Although the resolution of such ethical problems may be exceedingly difficult, therapists need to be aware of the implications of accepting the client's goals when to do so explicitly reinforces the social status quo and may, in fact, impede social change. Winett and Winkler (1972) emphasized this point in their criticism of target behaviors that have often been selected for disruptive school children. In a similar fashion, Davison (1974) suggested a critical examination of the target behaviors involved in *any* anxiety reduction procedure:

> Should we reduce anxiety, or should we perhaps address ourselves to the problematic education system which can contribute to the kind of test anxiety we desensitize? . . . Why do we engage in assertion training for people who are taken advantage of by an unfeeling society rather than attempt to persuade the offenders that their sometimes unkind actions cause others grief? (p. 3)

More recently, MacDonald (1984) and Hunter and Kelso (1985) underscored the importance of gender bias in assessment and psychotherapy. Although MacDonald criticized behavioral assessment for having evaluated women within the context of a male-dominated culture (which may presume, for example, a fundamental superiority of one gender relative to the other), she does view behavioral assessment as having more potential (than do traditional approaches) to be responsive to feminist concerns. MacDonald (1984) recommended that information gathered in behavioral assessment be interpreted from a "feminist perspective." Further, "particularly when working with women, for whom culturally supported behaviors may be personally damaging, target selection must proceed with considerable reflection" (p. 76). Hunter and Kelso (1985) noted the importance of assessing a client's sex-role history and ethnic background. In addition, they suggested that therapists also look at the interaction of gender with age, socioeconomic status, sexual orientation, and geographical location. They showed, for example, how certain behaviors can be tolerated quite differently, depending on what part of the country they are evaluated in. Such biases are, of course, subsets of the clinician's general cultural bias and framework that influence the selection of target behaviors and treatment goals, as has been previously discussed.

It would seem apparent that behaviors cannot separate themselves from the important ethical and societal implications that are involved in any assessment and treatment intervention. The behavior therapist must also wrestle with a number of difficult, value-laden questions recently posed by Feldman and Peay (1982): For example, how does behavior therapy decide what is the "good life" or "what is happiness"? Further, Feldman and Peay questioned whether clinicians have the right to, for example, guide the "unliberated housewife" toward a better job or a different way of life: "Is it desirable for therapists to take on the role of leading clients in directions that go well beyond the problem they present"? (p. 237)

Feldman and Peay (1982) urged that the overriding consideration be the right of the client to seek his or her preferred goal "by the most effective and efficient available method that he or she finds acceptable" (p. 239). In this regard, they disagree with Davison's (1974, 1977) and Silverstein's (1977) admonition to clinicians not to treat homosexuals who desire change in their sexual orientation. Feldman and Peay proposed that such ethical questions ideally be resolved by some neutral consumer agency or arbitration group. In the absence of such organizations, they suggest that clinicians refer to other therapists those clients who present themselves with problems or treatment goals that are "unacceptable." Such a decision is, of course, itself a value judgment. Because it appears that behavior therapy cannot be ethically neutral, it may be desirable for behaviorists to make clear (and to justify) just what those value judgments are (Franks, 1983).

Related ethical questions involve situations when the client insists on a technique that the practitioner has evidence is ineffective, when a specific "problem" may be beyond the realm of therapy, or when a thorough assessment reveals that the person is unable or unwilling to change the contingencies that control certain problem behaviors. It is the responsible clinician who, after careful assessment, concludes that he or she cannot effectively treat the individual *unless* certain environmental conditions are considered, whether that means including the spouse in treatment or involves the extensive rearrangement of contingencies. Kanfer (personal communication, University of Oregon, June 1975) eloquently remarked that behavior therapy need not adopt a "Statue of Liberty" ("Give me your tired, your poor . . .") philosophy. In other words, behaviorists need to accept their limitations and realize they cannot treat everybody, whether this is because effective procedures do not exist for a specific problem or because the environmental "realities" of an individual client contraindicate therapeutic efficacy for a given treatment goal.

This does not mean that certain problems, for which there is *currently* no behavioral framework, are *inherently* beyond the scope of behavior therapy. Thompson and Williams (1985) noted, for example, a variety of "existential" problems, which include apathy, lethargy, general discontent, and lack of direction and meaning. These "disorders of the 80s" are concerns that "behavior therapy *must* learn to treat because they will become the dominant problems for clinical psychology in the coming years" (p. 49).

Regardless of the theoretical orientation of the clinician, individuals come to therapy with a variety of expectations about what treatment will be like. Many request specific techniques such as hypnosis, bioenergetics, dream interpretations, past-life regressions, and a host of other treatments. Although it is probably sound clinical practice to incorporate some of those procedures that the client *believes* will be most helpful (because expectancy of therapeutic gain undoubtedly accounts for some portion of outcome variance [Lick & Bootzin, 1975]), the ethically responsible therapist must assess and communicate to the client the likelihood of success with any of these procedures. In many cases, the practitioner will refuse to adopt a particular method, either because he or she is unfamiliar with the technique or because there is no evidence that such a procedure is effective (especially when other, empirically validated, treatments are available). In situations in which the client is in complete agreement with the therapist (with respect to both the assessment of the problem and the intervention planned), it is still the responsibility of the therapist to communicate to the individual the probabilities of success with a given technique, the "emotional cost" of such a procedure (Morganstern, 1973), and the availability of alternative treatments. Finally, even when *potentially* successful therapeutic strategies exist (e.g., weight loss methodology), the clinician must still question whether treatment might be worse than "benign neglect" (Thompson & Williams, 1985).

In sum, behaviorists need to examine and be acutely aware of the ethical considerations and value judgments that are continually made within clinical practice. Whereas social learning principles may be relatively free of such biases, the interview and assessment process is not. In the final analysis, behavior therapy has little to apologize for, particularly when compared to other schools of therapy. The emphasis given to functional behavioral analyses, specification of goals, and objective measurement of process and outcome fosters accountability on the part of behavioral practitioners (Davison, 1974).

Interviewer–Client Relationship Variables

The image of the behaviorist as a cold, mechanistic, uncaring technician with little regard for the therapeutic relationship has, unfortunately, not been limited to the lay public. Graduate-level students as well as professionals have entered the clinical setting with a variety of misconceptions about how skilled behavioral clinicians work (Fishman & Lubetkin, 1983; Last & Hersen, 1985). Apparently, the stereotype of the "misanthropic behaviorist" has been popular enough to compel some authors to caution the "would-be practitioner who chooses to be a behavior therapist because he finds it difficult to put clients at ease through using a more traditional approach . . . to rethink his professional goals" (Rimm & Masters, 1974, p. 35). Similarly, Lazarus (1971a) suggested

> If a person does not possess genuine compassion for the plight of his patients and have a strong desire to diminish their suffering, it would be a boon to psychotherapy if he would enter some other field of endeavor. (p. 56)

Despite the recent criticism of Lambert (1983) that behaviorists have viewed the therapeutic relationship as merely an "administrative function" of therapy rather than an integral part of treatment, behavioral clinicians have increasingly underscored the importance of the therapist–client relationship (e.g., Beck, Rush, Shaw, & Emery, 1979; Bellack & Hersen, 1985; Evans & Nelson, 1977; Fishman & Lubetkin, 1983; Goldfried & Davison, 1976; Hersen, 1983b; La Greca, 1983; Last & Hersen, 1985; Lazarus, 1971a; G. T. Wilson, 1982, 1983, 1984; Wilson & Evans, 1976, 1977; Wolpe, 1982). Bellack and Hersen (1985), in fact, concluded that "of all the extant therapeutic schools it is in behavior therapy that the therapeutic alliance with the patient is most critical" (p. 14).

In contrast to public and professional stereotypes of behavior therapists, it is interesting to note that behavioral clinicians have been described as "experienced clinicians" who are confident and skillful and make "very effective use of the patient–therapist relationship to establish a context in which the specific behavioral techniques can be utilized most effectively" (Klein, Dittman, Parloff, & Gill, 1969, p. 265). Similarly, a number of studies have reported that behavior therapists are rated by clients as significantly more empathic, congruent, and supportive than their nonbehavioral counterparts (e.g., Bruninck & Shroeder, 1979; Greenwald, Kornblith, Hersen, Bellack, & Himmelhoch, 1981; Sloane, Staples, Cristol, Yorkston, & Whipple, 1975). It would seem, therefore, that the myth of behaviorists as mechanistic and uncaring is clearly inaccurate. How relationship variables and therapist characteristics relate, however, to the completeness and accuracy of information obtained during the interview (and ultimately to treatment outcome) is, at present, not entirely clear.

Within traditional psychotherapy research, there has been considerable agreement that a variety of therapist behaviors relate to the openness, accuracy, and content of interviews (cf. Carkhuff, 1969a, 1969b; Cormier & Cormier, 1979; Goldstein, 1975; Goldstein & Myers, 1986; Gordon, 1970; Kanfer, 1968; Krasner, 1962; Marsden, 1971; Matarazzo, 1965; Salzinger, 1959; Truax & Carkhuff, 1967; Truax & Mitchell, 1971; Wiens, 1985). Within the behavioral literature, Peterson (1968) remarked:

> The nature of the transaction . . . between interviewer and client [is] of utmost importance in determining the amount and quality of information gained [and] a sense of [the interviewer's] interest on the part of the client probably has much to do with the extent and the accuracy of the information he provides. (p. 123)

Rimm and Masters (1974) reported that an atmosphere of warmth and acceptance will facilitate the goal of assessment (i.e., to obtain considerable information from the client). And recently, Foa, Steketee, Grayson, and

Doppelt (1983) emphasized the importance of the interaction between therapist and client during the assessment stage, despite their belief that relationship variables have less impact on more "technical" procedures. In their discussion of why treatment may fail for obsessive-compulsive clients, for example, Foa et al. (1983) suggested that therapist personality qualities might determine whether adequate assessment information is obtained and, thus, whether treatment will succeed or fail. More generally, G. T. Wilson (1984) concluded that the establishment of a good therapeutic relationship is vital to the assessment and treatment process, regardless of how specific or "potent" a particular technique might be (cf. Foa & Emmelkamp, 1983).

Whereas such variables as empathy, warmth, genuineness, and honesty may be important components of assessment and intervention, it is essential to note that the accumulated evidence relating these variables to therapy outcome has shown that those factors *by themselves* are simply not enough (Rachman & Wilson, 1980). Moreover, any relationship variable may, under certain circumstances with certain clients, have a *negative* impact. Beck et al. (1979) described how such variables might be frustrating or misinterpreted by a particular individual. Even Truax (Truax & Mitchell, 1971), who concluded that "the personality of the therapist is more important than his techniques" (p. 341), cautioned that high levels of warmth or accurate empathy could be totally inappropriate with certain clients. In this regard, it is interesting to consider Bandura's (1969) challenge to the distinction made between *specific* and *nonspecific* influences in therapy:

> It is difficult to conceive of nonspecific influences in social interchanges. Each expression by one person elicits some type of response from the other participant, which inevitably creates a specific reinforcement contingency that has a specific effect on the immediately preceding behavior. (p. 77)

In sum, effective treatment outcome depends on thorough and accurate assessment, continuance in therapy, and compliance with therapeutic suggestions in addition to the treatment methods themselves. How client–therapist relationship variables affect each of these factors is, as yet, an unanswered but empirical question. It is encouraging, as G. T. Wilson (1984) noted, to see the increasing number of researchers addressing this issue.

BEHAVIORAL INTERVIEWING: METHODS AND PROCEDURES

Within traditional psychotherapy, the interview has been the most important (if not the only) source of information about the client. Not surprisingly, a wealth of material about the interview is available, much of it quite valuable to the behavioral clinician. The reader is referred to the classic texts of Menninger (1952) and Sullivan (1954) and, more recently, the works of Gorden (1969), Cormier and Cormier (1979), Pope (1979), and Johnson (1981). Practical resources within the behavioral literature, however, have been limited. A few sources provide examples of behavioral interviews, particularly the initial session (Fensterheim, 1972; Goldfried & Davison, 1976; Haynes, 1978; Lazarus, 1971a, 1976; Meyer, Liddel, & Lyons, 1977; Rimm & Masters, 1974; Wolpe, 1970, 1982).

As previously discussed, the ultimate goal of assessment is an accurate and thorough analysis of the problematic behaviors as well as an understanding of the environmental contingencies of those behaviors, the resources available to the individual, and any other information that is necessary in arriving at effective treatment decisions. With this objective as a focal point of interviewing, the remainder of this section outlines a number of procedures, questions, and problems encountered in this process. Needless to say, there are many avenues one can take to obtain the same end product. Thus, one might view the following techniques and issues as only a few of the many conceivable strategies that may be employed. In addition, it should not be inferred that all of these procedures are always applicable or that any particular sequence must be rigidly followed.

Starting the Interview

The first session is often of critical importance. Several decisions need to be made, not the least of which concerns whether or not the client (and the therapist) wishes to continue. Both the client and the therapist will be (and should be) asking the questions: Does the therapist understand what the problem is? What can be gained from therapy? What are the probabilities that such outcomes will be reached? Are there alternative procedures that are as effective, more efficient, less risky, and so on? In addition, the client will undoubtedly be concerned about the therapeutic relationship (i.e., Does the therapist care about me? Will treatment be a pleasant or unpleasant process? Does the therapist like me?)

Students awaiting their first contact with clients ask numerous questions about getting the interview started. They are often concerned with introductions; seating arrangements; whether it is better to remain silent until the client has spoken or if it is better to make some opening statements, and if so, what they should say. While anything but the most nondirective approach will shape and bias the interview to some degree, there are a number of advantages in having the therapist make some introductory remarks. Such an opening statement is likely to reduce some of the client's initial anxiety about what to say and expect. In almost every case, something is already known about the client. Often, the person has already been through one or more intake evaluations, has been referred with some accompanying statement, or has communicated by telephone something about the nature of the problem when setting up an appointment. Therefore, some introduction briefly summarizing what is already known about the client is usually desirable. For example:

> *Therapist:* Dr. Gordon, whom you spoke with last week, has told me that you are having some difficulties since your recent divorce. From what I understand, you said that you are depressed much of the time and are finding it hard to make some career decisions. Apart from that, I don't know much more about you. What I would like to do today is to explore more fully what your problems and concerns are and what has brought you to seek therapy at this particular time. Can you tell me how you see the problem?

This brief summary statement communicates to the client that the therapist has taken the time to speak to the referral source, read the case material that is available, or simply remembers the initial telephone conversation. In addition, the simple invitation to elaborate upon the problems provides the client with a framework from which to start and some initial expectations about the purpose of the interview. The latter is not as obvious as it sounds, considering the many myths and misconceptions about psychotherapy. Some individuals, for example, may expect to be tested, answer long questionnaires, start talking about his childhood, or lie on a couch and free associate. Still others may enter the first session with little notion of what will be expected of them and may experience considerable anxiety in response to ambiguous clues about where to begin.

With such a minimal stimulus as this opening statement, a great many clients will begin to relate, often in very specific detail, the reasons they seek treatment. Others, however, have considerable difficulty getting started (e.g., they become tearful, stammer, or wring their hands in silence), apparently inhibited by the interview situation itself. Clients may be embarrassed about sharing intimate feelings with a stranger, worry that their problems are not important enough to merit therapy or "the doctor's time," or, in contrast, are afraid that once they reveal their true concerns, they will be labelled "crazy" or even be institutionalized. Some intervention to reduce the client's current anxiety may be necessary before a meaningful assessment of the presenting problem can proceed. Often, encouraging clients to discuss their fears about the interview, reassuring them that other people also find it hard to begin, or providing them information about confidentiality will enable the client to continue with more comfort. For those clients who are unresponsive and distracted by high levels of anxiety, breathing or brief relaxation exercises may be helpful. Finally, therapeutic attention to the client's initial distress communicates caring and respect for his or her feelings and can enhance therapeutic expectancy.

When clients begin to describe the reasons why they seek treatment, it is useful, within limits, to simply listen and allow them to "tell their story." The decision to seek professional counseling is rarely an immediate, spur-of-the-moment step. Clients have most likely considered their problems over and over, with facts, thoughts, and feelings weighed and ordered. Just as it is often unsettling to have prepared at length for an important exam and not be tested as expected, so it is probably quite frustrating for clients to have carefully thought out their present difficulties and then not have a chance to share them. This is not to imply that the therapist adopt a nondirective attitude, following clients wherever, and for as long as, they lead. Certainly, carefully considered questions are essential to both direct and clarify what is being said. Just listening to clients present their "autobiography" session after session is unnecessary, inefficient, and ineffectual.

Listening, then, would seem to be an essential skill of the interviewer. Interrupting with premature questions or clarifications of misconceptions may inhibit the client from relating certain information. It is possible for the therapist to distort what the client is saying since the therapist may actually prompt and shape inaccurate or partially accurate verbal statements by the client to coincide with the interviewer's initial perception of the problem. Annon (1976) provided some excellent examples of how this may occur in the assessment of sexual problems. For example, a client's statements, "I've been a homosexual for 10 years" or "I'm not easily aroused" might immediately elicit reassuring comments or detailed inquiry on the part of the therapist when the problems may lie elsewhere. Listening focuses on the problems of the client, not the preconceptions of the therapist.

During these first stages of behavioral assessment (and to a lesser extent throughout the course of therapy), a case can be made for the *selective* use of empathic statements, such as reflection and paraphrasing. One does not have to accept Rogers' deterministic notion of "self-actualization" or believe in the need or utility of "unconditional positive regard" to effectively make use of reflective procedures. A number of behavior therapists have explicitly suggested such techniques (e.g., Lazarus, 1971a; Peterson, 1968; Rimm & Masters, 1979), and the general use of reflective statements is apparent in most behavioral assessments. When reflecting, the therapist communicates to the client that he or she has heard and understood the message. Needless to say, behavioral clinicians cannot effectively intervene until they understand fully and accurately what the problem is. Training in reflection and paraphrasing, therefore, helps the therapist to listen and focus on what the client is saying. These techniques, in combination with direct questioning, probes, and provisional restatements (Peterson, 1968), may facilitate assessment in a number of ways. First, the experience of being heard and understood may be extremely positive for many individuals, encouraging them to continue in further detail. While good questions serve this purpose to some degree, reflective statements frequently communicate this message better. In addition, the therapist who is perceived as understanding may be a potent source of social reinforcement for the client. Finally, reflective remarks and restatements are often necessary to validate for the interviewer what is being said. In the following example, a number of these techniques are illustrated:

Therapist: You say that you are very jealous a lot of the time and this upsets you a great deal.

Client: Well, I know it's stupid for me to feel that way, but I am hurt when I even *think* of Mike with another woman.

Therapist: You don't want to feel jealous but you do.

Client: I know that's not the way a "liberated" woman should be.

Therapist: Can you give me your idea of how a liberated woman "should" feel?

Client: I don't know. In many ways I feel I've changed so much in the last year. I really don't believe you have the right to own another person — and yet, when it happens to me, I really feel hurt. I'm such a hypocrite!

Therapist: You're unhappy with yourself because you're not responding the way you would like to.

Client: I'm not sure of the person I want to be. Or I can't be her!

Therapist: There's really "double jeopardy." When Mike is with someone else you feel hurt. But when you feel jealous, you criticize yourself for being that way.

Client: Yes. I guess I lose either way.

In the above example, the reflective statements communicated to the client that she was being understood and helped her specify what she was experiencing. The final synthesis integrated the various feelings she was expressing, and the validation at the end indicated that the therapist was, indeed, accurate. Quite often, however, the process is not as straightforward. In the following scenarios, the reflections and questions are, at first, somewhat off track. The therapist eventually narrows in on what the client is saying:

Client: Whenever my boss asks to see me, I almost start shaking, wondering what I've done wrong.

Therapist: The anticipation of criticism makes you anxious.

Client: Well, it's not really that. I'm scared of what might happen.

Therapist: What do you anticipate might happen?

Client:	I don't know what will happen; that's it.
Therapist:	It's the suspense that makes you feel uncomfortable.
Client:	No, not the suspense — I keep saying to myself that if she starts chewing me out I'm going to let her have it.
Therapist:	How would you let her have it?
Client:	Well, what I *think* I'm going to do is argue right back — or even quit right there.
Therapist:	And what *do* you do?
Client:	Nothing!
Therapist:	Nothing . . .
Client:	I never do anything. I just stand there while she's talking and never say a word.
Therapist:	What really makes you shake, as you say, is feeling a great deal of anger and not being able to express it.
Client:	Yeah. And the one I'm really mad at is myself for being such a patsy all the time.
Therapist:	What do you think would happen if you really expressed your anger to your boss?
Client:	She'd probably respect me a lot more than someone who's too scared to defend himself.
Therapist:	You're afraid to challenge your boss's criticism. But when you think about it, you become angry at yourself for not being assertive.
Client:	Yes.

It should be evident that reflective comments are not novel techniques. In most conversations, there is a continual exchange of information with feedback that the information has been received and understood. The intention here is not to suggest that reflection be the therapist's sole — or even major — assessment procedure. Often reflection is useful to keep assessment flowing smoothly, to validate the conclusions of the therapist, or simply to acknowledge that the client is being understood. However, it must be emphasized that the goals of assessment are quite clear, underscoring the need, frequently, for specific questions and direct behavioral measures. Thus, the *extensive* use of nondirective procedures may be, at best, inappropriate for behavioral interviewing (Suinn, 1974). At worst, it can be "an extremely hostile act to refuse to answer a direct and reasonable request or to withhold information from patients" (Marquis, 1974, p. 44). Finally, suggesting the selective use of reflective methods during the initial stages of the interview does not imply that such a procedure is advocated as the sole treatment technique. Reflection is probably insufficient for the vast majority of target behaviors for which the individual desires change. Noteworthy in this regard is Haley's (1969) inclusion of "Be reflective" in his satirical article outlining "The Five B's Which Guarantee Dynamic Failure."

Preparing the Client for Assessment

Whereas the goals of assessment may be clear to the therapist, clients are not always aware that "an assessment" is taking place, what this process entails, or that such information will influence later treatment decisions. In contrast to many traditional forms of psychotherapy where there is no assessment, or where assessment is indistinguishable from therapy, behaviorists take for granted that their interventions *depend* upon the information obtained in the interview and assessment process. This is not to say that behavior therapists are unresponsive to clients' needs during assessment. Therapy often begins during the initial interview, during which time the sensitive clinician may need to offer hope and reassurance to the client (Lazarus, 1981; Wolpe, 1982), allow time for "catharsis" (Last & Hersen, 1985), or address a client's "full-blown" panic (Barlow & Waddell, 1985). Nonetheless, behavioral clinicians must frequently complete at least their initial assessment and analyses before comprehensive treatment plans can be instituted. Such a "delay" may be surprising or frustrating to the client, who expects "full-scale" treatment to begin in the initial session (especially in situations when baseline data are necessary). A brief introduction, therefore, *preparing* the client for the continued assessment process, is useful in the early stages of assessment. For example:

> *Therapist:* Now that I understand more of the reasons that you are coming for therapy, we will be exploring in the next session(s) these concerns in more detail. I need to learn as much as possible about each of your concerns and how you'd like things to be different so that together we can make some decisions about how therapy will proceed. How does this sound to you?

This introduction communicates to clients that more complete information about their problems is required. It communicates that therapy, rather than a magical elixir dispensed to a passive client irrespective of his or her individual needs and desires, will be a cooperative process requiring the client's active participation in providing assessment information and, eventually, treatment planning. Finally, the invitation to the client to react to the therapist's overview introduces the notion that therapy, even at the initial stages of assessment, will be of a contractual nature.

Specification of the Problem

Quite often clients can specify in explicit detail the nature of their problems and, with the help of the therapist, provide the necessary data concerning both antecedent and consequent conditions. Many times, however, the client is unable to explain what is wrong. It is in these cases that the inexperienced therapist may encounter much difficulty. There are several ways to facilitate the delineation process. Since the decision to seek professional services is frequently related to some events that have recently occurred in the client's life, questions centering around the reasons that brought the client to treatment can be extremely useful. Often there have been recent changes such as a new job, marriage, divorce, moving, or other situations that have taken place. In addition, the client may have recently had a number of unfortunate experiences such as being fired, rejected at a party, a fight with a spouse, or a death in the family. Finally, in many cases, the "problem" may have been defined by someone else. That is, the recommendation to go for treatment may have come from the client's spouse, parents, or friends, and information regarding the reasons for such referrals may be quite helpful. Such an analysis of the labeling process may provide valuable information, although the questions "Who is the client?" and "To whom is the problem disturbing?" must always be considered.

Once the problem area has been broadly defined, a thorough behavioral analysis is derived, including a careful description of the behavior itself, as well as the antecedent and consequent variables. Even in situations where clients report that they are depressed *all* of the time, or are *always* anxious, or are a failure at *everything*, careful questions may delimit the problem considerably. A person who reports that he or she is depressed all the time almost certainly can think of circumstances when he or she is less depressed than others. Detailing certain activities, certain places, and certain people also serve to specify the problems more clearly. The client may also be able to relate experiences in the past or imagine future situations in which the depression may be better or worse. Similarly, the individual who reports a global, undifferentiated fear of traveling, for example, will almost certainly be able to identify situations in which the fear is somewhat attenuated because of the time of day, number of people present, presence of companions, familiarity with the route, type of transportation, and so on.

In many cases, the interview material may be supplemented with observation in the natural setting or with behavioral measurement during the interview process. Tracking the frequency of certain behaviors may help clients define more precisely the problem behavior and the circumstances surrounding it even when they have previously been unable to specify those variables. Behavior therapists, therefore, often ask their clients to carry around a diary in which frequency, duration, time, and other circumstances surrounding the target behaviors are carefully recorded. As O'Leary and Wilson (1975) noted, most clients present themselves as "trait theorists" with descriptions such as "uptight," "lazy," "passive-aggressive," etcetera. A focused functional analysis with behavioral referents of the problem (using both the client's self-report during the interview and the record of the tracked behavior) is probably one of the most essential activities of behavioral assessment. It is quite likely that the behavioral monitoring *itself* may be therapeutic, communicating to the client that he or she does not suffer from a deep-seated disease or some enduring underlying personality trait. Rather, the emphasis is on specific behaviors experienced at specific times with certain frequencies and intensities.

A behavioral analysis also minimizes the possibility that certain self-reported feelings will be misinterpreted. Literally hundreds of commonly used words may imply very different meanings for different people. It is, therefore, a mistake for the therapist to assume that he or she knows what the client is talking about without any operational referents. It is quite illuminating, for example, to ask a class of students to define in one sentence what they mean by the words *anxiety* or *depression* or *assertive*. Even in a group of professional counselors there is often a diversity of meaning attached to these feelings or states. In sum, it is sound advice for clinicians to be "ignorant" when it comes to understanding what a client means by such words as *uptight, heavy, angry, together, spaced-out, freaky, dependent, mellow, passive*, etcetera. The following examples illustrate, first, the acceptance without further exploration of several poorly defined terms used by the client, and second, a more careful analysis of these self-reported feelings:

Client:	When I'm in such heavy situations, I just get real uptight.
Therapist:	What makes you uptight?
Client:	Well, the whole thing. Everybody kind of hanging out and running around. I can't seem to get it together with anybody, so I guess I freak out.
Therapist:	And then what happens?
Client:	I usually go home and go to sleep. But I'm usually pretty bummed out.
Therapist:	Are you saying that you don't fit in with these people and that's what makes you feel bummed out?
Client:	Well, I don't know. These are my friends, I guess — but it never seems to work out.

In this example, the therapist may have no idea what the client is talking about. Furthermore, there is certainly no way of knowing whether any inferences are accurate or not. While at first glance it may appear that the therapist who does not understand such terminology is hopelessly naive, such "naivete" is probably essential in order to understand exactly what the client is saying:

Client:	When I'm in such heavy situations, I just get real uptight. You know, I just can't make it, so I kind of drop out.

Therapist: When you say that you're uptight in these situations, what does that mean for you?

Client: Well, uptight, you know. Tense.

Therapist: You mean your muscles get tense?

Client: My neck gets very sore — and I get a headache lots of times.

Therapist: What else happens?

Client: Well, either because of my neck or my headache, I start sweating a lot.

Therapist: When you say you're uptight, then, you seem to be experiencing it physically. What are you thinking when this happens? What thoughts are going through your head?

Client: I'm thinking, man, you really are paranoid. You just can't relax in any situation. You really are a loser. And then I want to get out of there fast . . .

In this example, the interviewer has clarified the word "uptight." Although we all have some idea of what this word means, there is much variation in its usage depending upon the individual. The client in this case was able to point to some very definite physiological changes that accompany this feeling. In addition, there were a number of self-verbalizations (which would have required further elaboration and behavioral reference) as well as resultant avoidance behaviors. The therapist then would have proceeded to formulate a good behavioral analysis of what the "heavy" situations were in the client's life and to what he was referring when he said he "couldn't make it." Although such questions may initially seem to the client to be evidence of a lack of therapist understanding, it is quickly communicated to the client that this inquiry is essential for maximal understanding of the problem. Care must be taken, however, to elicit the necessary information without insulting or punishing clients for using their own words.

The need for specific, operational terminology is especially well illustrated in the assessment of sexual concerns, particularly because discussion of this material may be associated with a great deal of discomfort and embarrassment for the client and even for the therapist. Annon (1976) discussed the merits of using technical descriptions versus the "street" language that is commonly used, and indicated that a compromise between the two is sometimes the best strategy. Whatever the language, an exact understanding on the part of both the therapist and the client is important. Thus, the expressions "doing it" or "down there" may be so vague as to provide very little information to the therapist. Even the use of precisely defined terms must be validated to insure that both individuals understand what is being communicated. Annon noted that some clients did not know what the word circumcision meant, or exactly where the clitoris was located; intervention in these cases might be doomed to fail unless such terms are clarified. In dealing with very sensitive topics, therapists as well as clients may be prone to use vague explanations and descriptions, depending on their own comfort with such terminology. The direct, straightforward discussion and questioning on the part of the interviewer communicates to the client that it is quite acceptable to talk about such issues. The therapist who models vague and euphemistic language may reinforce the client's belief that such topics should not be discussed and that it is better not to deal openly with these problems.

Redefinition of Problems

In a sense, the assessment process, with its demand for a functional behavioral analysis and clear, operationalized behavioral referents, is a reinterpretation of the client's problems in a social-learning framework. An important question is whether the same ethical objections that are raised about such redefinitions in insight-oriented therapies (Bandura, 1969) cannot also be raised concerning behavioral assessment. It is important to note, however, that behavioral assessment, unlike insight-oriented approaches, redefines neither the client's problems nor the client's goals in terms of *unmeasurable* hypothetical constructs.

Within a behavioral assessment, it may be quite useful and ethically responsible for the interviewer to explicitly redefine the client's statements within a behavioral framework. This is not to suggest that clinicians attack or antagonize clients by demanding well-thought-out "operational definitions" for everything the client says. Rather, a delicate balance needs to be achieved between listening to what clients have to say in their own words, and providing clients with alternative ways of conceptualizing their problems. Considerable care must be taken not to prematurely "reassure" clients, because that process may actually inhibit what information clients will reveal about themselves. When appropriate, however, therapists may model and shape the use of a social-learning language. Such a reformulation may communicate to clients that they need not label themselves as "crazy," "paranoid," or "lazy," and the reformulation may be therapeutic in its own right. Ideally, clients will eventually see their problems as specific behaviors observed in specific circumstances, with understandable psychological principles to explain the development and maintenance of those problems. The example below illustrates a few ways in which a client's statements may be formulated:

Client: I know I must be pretty neurotic.

Therapist: Can you tell me what you mean by neurotic?

Client: Someone who panics everytime she's alone and even cries when her husband leaves for work must be pretty crazy. Isn't that neurotic?

Therapist:	Practically everything we do is based on experiences that we have had. Apparently at some time you learned to feel very anxious when you were alone. That fear now is very disruptive in your life and you'd like to change how you react.
Client:	But most people don't act that way. Why is that?
Therapist:	More than likely, most people have not had the same experiences with being alone as you describe; but if they had, they would probably feel much the same way as you.
Client:	But if I know this, why don't things change? I keep saying to myself that I'll be okay if I'm alone and that nothing bad is going to happen. But when my husband starts to leave, I panic and burst into tears.
Therapist:	And then . . .
Client:	I feel terrible. I feel like a helpless little girl.
Therapist:	And then what happens?
Client:	My husband is very understanding. I don't know how he puts up with me, but he is so considerate. When I've really been panicked he takes off from work and sits and talks with me until I've calmed down.
Therapist:	Even though it is really painful for you, when you feel so intensely, it's comforting to have your husband home with you.

The therapist in this case redefined the client's self-labels of crazy or neurotic. In addition, in very simple terms, the interviewer pointed out how the intense reactions might be reinforced. Finally, the brief explanation of the client's problems in terms of learning theory should be noted. Although the interviewer's attitudes and orientation are implicitly communicated to the client via the types of questions asked, the explanations offered, and the areas explored, an *explicit* restatement of the problem in social-learning terms at some time early in assessment may also be desirable. It should be emphasized, however, that the presentation of a social-learning model may be quite unexpected by the client. It is useful, therefore, to continually assess the reactions that the client may have to any analysis, interpretation, or conceptualization that the interviewer offers. Lazarus (1971a) suggested that every comment made by the therapist be followed with the question "What do you think about (or how do you feel about) what I have just said?" (p. 61) Although it is unnecessary to follow each statement with such a question, it is important to gauge whether or not the client understands or agrees with what is being communicated.

Toward a Broad Assessment

Although the possession of certain professional credentials does not give a therapist license to explore everything in a client's life, the need for a thorough analysis is obvious. Not only must the therapist assess in great detail the specific presenting problems, he or she must also gain an understanding of how these problems have generalized and affected other areas in the client's life. In addition, a complete assessment forestalls the introduction of treatment strategies that are inappropriate or likely to fail. Thus, modifying a child's behavior in therapy without intervening in the home environment may be pointless. Similarly, assessing a client's aggressive behaviors and providing techniques to reduce or eliminate them without also assessing whether or not the client has other behaviors in his repertoire that can be equally reinforced is, at best, a sloppy and inefficient method of treatment.

A good analysis of the problematic behavior not only allows the therapist to get a very specific understanding of the client's presenting difficulties but also provides information about other problem areas. Explorations into the client's social relationships and the social, cultural, and physical environment may all be important, not only in defining the problem (and all the controlling variables) but also in assessing both the resources available to the client and what limitations must be considered in treatment (Kanfer & Saslow, 1969). A variety of multifaceted assessment outlines have already been cited and the reader is referred to those sources for more-detailed guidelines. It should be noted that a behavioral assessment rarely includes a complete life history of the client, since the past is considered relevant *only to the extent* that it affects or helps us to understand the present. Some demographic data, of course, is essential to evaluate much of what the client reports. For example, career indecision may be viewed quite differently by both the therapist and the client depending upon whether the individual is 19 or 39 years of age. Similarly, lack of employment may be related to an entirely different set of circumstances for the uneducated, unskilled client than for the person with a college degree.

Closing the Interview

A sufficient amount of time at the end of the initial interview(s) should be allowed for the therapist to provide the client with a summary of the information that has already been obtained, an explanation of additional information that is needed, and a reasonable estimate of the likelihood of successful intervention. A good summary communicates to clients that they have been understood and provides them with a behavioral framework for their problems. Although the therapist may have offered such "redefinitions" before, it is desirable to reiterate many of these statements at the end of the session, integrating all of the material that has been covered. Caution must be taken to insure that this explanation is neither condescending nor too technical for the client to comprehend.

Quite often, additional information is necessary before any treatment decisions can be made, and the client should know what areas need further delineation and what he or she can do to facilitate the process. Sometimes they may be asked to track certain behaviors, seek out information from others, or simply spend some time thinking about problems that they have had difficulty clarifying.

Even though assessment may be incomplete at this stage, clients should be provided with information concerning possible intervention strategies, length of treatment, and the financial and emotional cost of therapy. Most importantly, it should be clearly communicated to clients that they have a choice in every decision that is made.

While the majority of clients may feel reassured that mutual treatment decisions will be based on a thorough assessment, others may have entirely different expectations and hopes for therapy or for the roles of client and therapist. A discussion of the client's expectations can help clarify the wishes of the client, correct certain misconceptions, and even enhance positive expectancy about therapy. It is crucial at this point that clinicians be able to respond to the variety of criticisms and ethical challenges that have been directed toward behavior therapy. The behaviorist must be comfortable answering questions about the issues, e.g., freedom, control, superficiality, etc. that are commonly raised (see Bandura, 1969; Davison & Stuart, 1975; Mahoney et al., 1974, for good summaries of these answers). Such an invitation to the client to openly air objections and doubts will more likely lead to the establishment of trust and increase the client's initial receptivity and motivation for therapy.

At the end of the initial interview(s), the therapist (or client) may conclude that behavior therapy is inappropriate. The client may present problems and goals for which there is no available treatment, the client may not accept a behavioral explanation or treatment plan, or the objectives may be unacceptable to the therapist because of certain ethical or practical reasons. In such instances, the clinician may decide that an appropriate referral is in the client's best interests.

Finally, when the joint decision is made to continue therapy, the client should be offered as much encouragement as is reasonably possible. As obvious as this may appear, trainees often neglect to communicate any hope to the individual, or they take the other extreme and make unrealistic promises that are doomed to fail. Unlike most traditional approaches, behavior therapy has considerable empirical support for a variety of treatments. Both therapist and client have a legitimate basis for optimism.

SUMMARY

Behavioral interviewing is an integral part of the entire assessment and therapy process. The growing awareness of the complexity of clinical behavior therapy has further underscored the importance of skillful, broad-based assessment. This chapter has elaborated on a number of issues and procedures in behavioral interviewing in order to provide a framework for clinicians during the initial stages of assessment.

Four major issues, interrelated to some degree, were discussed in the first section of this chapter. First, the goals of assessment were specified, since the interview process is ultimately tied to such objectives. The basic task for the clinician is to obtain as complete an understanding as possible of the client's problems (i.e., a behavioral analysis) in order to develop effective, efficient, and durable treatment interventions. At the same time, gathering information that is unnecessary for such a task and that may overstep the ethical boundaries of legitimate inquiry is avoided.

Second, a number of issues related to problem identification and target selection were described. These included methodological and conceptual considerations in defining target behaviors; guidelines for establishing treatment priorities and goals; and issues related to the validity of target selection. Noteworthy is the current dissatisfaction with the selection of single-target behaviors as representative of the complexity of clinical practice.

Third, several ethical considerations were described. The influence of therapist (and cultural) biases on the determination of the client's problems and objectives was discussed. In addition, the ethical responsibilities inherent in deciding whether or not to accept client goals for treatment were highlighted.

The fourth issue concerned the interviewer–client relationship in behavioral interviewing. Despite the myths about behavior therapy, there is a general and growing consensus that relationship factors are critical (albeit insufficient) to the entire behavioral assessment and therapy process. Research and interest in this area is noteworthy and encouraging.

The second section of this chapter outlined a number of procedures and strategies available to the clinician during the early stages of assessment. Methods were proposed for starting the initial interview, preparing the client for the assessment process, specifying target behaviors, redefining problems, and finally, closing the interview.

REFERENCES

Annon, J. S. (1976). *The behavioral treatment of sexual problems: Brief therapy.* New York: Harper & Row.

American Psychiatric Association. (1980). *Diagnostic and statistical manual of mental disorders* (3rd ed.). Washington, DC: Author.

Bandura, A. (1969). *Principles of behavior modification.* New York: Holt, Rinehart & Winston.

Barlow, D. H. (Ed.). (1981). *Behavioral assessment of adult disorders.* New York: Guilford.

Barlow, D. H. (Ed.). (1985). *Clinical handbook of psychological disorders.* New York: Guilford.

Barlow, D. H., & Waddell, M. T. (1985). Agoraphobia. In D. T. Barlow (Ed.), *Clinical handbook of psychological disorders.* New York: Guilford.

Beck, A. T., Rush, A. J., Shaw, B. F., & Emery, G. (1979). *Cognitive therapy of depression.* New York: Guilford.

Bellack, A. S., & Hersen, M. (1985). General considerations. In M. Hersen & A.S. Bellack (Eds.), *Handbook of clinical behavior therapy with adults.* (pp. 3-19). New York: Plenum.

Bellack, A. S. & Morrison, R. L. (1982). Interpersonal dysfunction. In A. S. Bellack, M. Hersen, & A. E. Kazdin (Eds.), *International handbook of behavior modification and therapy.* (pp. 717-747). New York: Plenum.

Brunink, S., & Schroeder, H. E. (1979). Verbal therapeutic behavior of expert psychoanalytically oriented, gestalt, and behavior therapists. *Journal of Consulting and Clinical Psychology*, *47*, 567-574.

Carkhuff, R. (1969a). *Helping and human relations: Vol. 1. Selection and training.* New York: Holt, Rinehart & Winston.

Carkhuff, R. (1969b). *Helping and human relations: Vol. 2. Practice and research.* New York: Holt, Rinehart & Winston.

Cormier, W. H., & Cormier, L. S. (1979). *Interviewing strategies for helpers: A guide to assessment, treatment, and evaluation.* Monterey: Brooks/Cole.

Davison, G. C. (1974, November). *Homosexuality: The ethical challenge.* Presidential address presented at the meeting of the Association for Advancement of Behavior Therapy, Chicago.

Davison, G. C. (1977). Homosexuality, the ethical challenge. *Journal of Homosexuality*, *2*, 195-204.

Davison, G. C., & Stuart, R. B. (1975). Behavior therapy and civil liberties. *American Psychologist*, *30*, 755-763.

Emmelkamp, P. M. G. (1982). *Phobic and obsessive-compulsive disorders: Theory, research and practice.* New York: Plenum.

Evans, I. M. (1985). Building systems models as a strategy for target behavior selection in clinical assessment. *Behavioral Assessment*, *7*, 21-32.

Evans, I. M., & Nelson, R. O. (1977). Assessment of child behavior problems. In A. R. Ciminero, H. E. Adams, & K. S. Calhoun (Eds.), *Handbook of behavioral assessment.* (pp. 603-681). New York: Wiley.

Evans, I. M., & Wilson, F. E. (1983). Behavioral assessment as decision making: A theoretical analysis. In M. Rosenbaum, C. M. Franks, & Y. Jaffe (Eds.), *Perspectives on behavior therapy in the eighties.* (pp. 35-51). New York: Springer.

Feldman, M. P., & Peay, J. (1982). Ethical and legal issues. In A. S. Bellack, M. Hersen, & A. E. Kazdin (Eds.), *International handbook of behavior modification and therapy.* (pp. 231-261). New York: Plenum.

Fensterheim, H. The initial interview. (1972). In A.A. Lazarus (Ed.), *Clinical behavior therapy.* (pp. 22-40). New York: Brunner/Mazel.

Fishman, S. T., & Lubetkin, B. S. (1983). Office practice of behavior therapy. In M. Hersen (Ed.), *Outpatient behavior therapy: A clinical guide.* (pp. 21-41). New York: Grune & Stratton.

Foa, E. B., & Emmelkamp, P. M. G. (Eds.). (1983). *Failures in behavior therapy.* New York: Wiley.

Foa, E. B., Steketee, G., Grayson, J. B., & Doppelt, H. G. (1983). Treatment of obsessive-compulsives: When do we fail? In E. B. Foa & P. M. G. Emmelkamp (Eds.), *Failures in behavior therapy.* (pp. 10-34). New York: Wiley.

Franks, C. M. (1983). Behavior therapy: An overview. In C. M. Franks, G. T. Wilson, K. D. Brownell, & P. C. Kendall (Eds.), *Annual review of behavior therapy: Theory and practice.* (Vol. 9, pp. 1–38). New York: Brunner/Mazel.

Goldfried, M. R. (1977). *Behavioral assessment: New directions in clinical psychology.* New York: Brunner/Mazel.

Goldfried, M.R. (1982). Behavioral assessment: An overview. In A. S. Bellack, M. Hersen, & A. E. Kazdin (Eds.), *International handbook of behavior modification and therapy.* (pp. 81–107). New York: Plenum.

Goldfried, M. R. (1983). The behavior therapist in clinical practice. *The Behavior Therapist, 6,* 45–56.

Goldfried, M. R., & Davison, G. C. (1976). *Clinical behavior therapy.* New York: Holt, Rinehart & Winston.

Goldfried, M. R., & Pomeranz, D. M. (1968). Role of assessment in behavior modification. *Psychological Reports, 23,* 75–87.

Goldfried, M. R., & Sprafkin, J. N. (1974). *Behavioral personality assessment.* Morristown, NJ: General Learning Press.

Goldstein, A. P. (1975). Relationship-enchantment methods. In F. H. Kanfer & A. P. Goldstein (Eds.), *Helping people change.* (pp. 15–49). New York: Pergamon.

Goldstein, A. P., & Meyers, C. R. (1986). Relationship-enhancement methods. In F. H. Kanfer & A. P. Goldstein (Eds.), *Helping people change: A textbook of methods* (3rd ed.) (pp. 19–65). New York: Pergamon.

Gorden, R. L. (1969). *Interviewing: Strategies, techniques, and tactics.* Homewood, IL: Dorsey.

Gordon, T. (1970). *Parent effectiveness training.* New York: Wyden.

Greenwald, D. P., Kornblith, S. J., Hersen, M., Bellack, A. S., & Himmelhoch, J. M. (1981). Differences between social skills therapists and psychotherapists in treating depression. *Journal of Consulting and Clinical Psychology, 49,* 757–759.

Haley, J. (1969). The art of being a failure as a therapist. *American Journal of Orthopsychiatry, 39,* 691–695.

Halleck, S. L. (1971). *The politics of therapy.* New York: Science House.

Hartmann, D. (Ed.). (1985). Target behavior selection [Special mini-series]. *Behavioral Assessment, 7,* 1–78.

Haynes, S. N. (1978). *Principles of behavioral assessment.* New York: Gardner.

Haynes, S. N., & Jensen, B. J. (1979). The interview as a behavioral assessment instrument. *Behavioral Assessment, 1,* 97–106.

Hersen, M. (1981). Complex problems require complex solutions. *Behavior Therapy, 12,* 15–29.

Hersen, M. (Ed.). (1983a). *Outpatient behavior therapy: A clinical guide.* New York: Grune & Stratton.

Hersen, M. (1983b). Perspective on the practice of outpatient behavior therapy. In M. Hersen (Ed.), *Outpatient behavior therapy: A clinical guide.* (pp. 3–20). New York: Grune & Stratton.

Hersen, M. & Bellack, A. S. (Eds.). (1981). *Behavioral assessment: A practical handbook* (2nd ed.). New York: Pergamon.

Hersen, M., & Bellack, A. S. (Eds.). (1985). *Handbook of clinical behavior therapy with adults.* New York: Plenum.

Hunter, P., & Kelso, E. N. (1985). Feminist behavior therapy. *The Behavior Therapist, 10,* 201–204.

Johnson, W. R. (1981). Basic interviewing skills. In C. E. Walker (Ed.), *Clinical practice of psychology.* New York: Pergamon.

Kanfer, F. H. (1968). Verbal conditioning: A review on its current status. In T. R.

Dixon & D. L. Norton (Eds.), *Verbal behavior and general behavior theory* (pp. 254–290). Englewood Cliffs, NJ: Prentice-Hall.

Kanfer, F. H. (1985). Target selection for clinical change programs. *Behavioral Assessment, 7,* 7–20.

Kanfer, F. H., & Grimm, L. G. (1977). Behavioral analysis: Selecting target behaviors in the interview. *Behavior Modification, 4,* 419–444.

Kanfer, F. H., & Saslow, G. (1969). Behavioral diagnosis. In C. M. Franks (Ed.), *Behavior therapy: Appraisal and status.* (pp. 417–444). New York: McGraw-Hill.

Kazdin, A. E. (1973). The failure of some patients to respond to token programs. *Journal of Behavior Therapy and Experimental Psychiatry, 4,* 7–14.

Kazdin, A. E. (1985). Selection of target behaviors: The relationship of the treatment focus to clinical dysfunction. *Behavioral Assessment, 7,* 33–47.

Klein, M. H., Dittman, A. T., Parloff, M. B., & Gill, M. M. (1969). Behavior therapy: Observations and reflections. *Journal of Consulting and Clinical Psychology, 33,* 259–266.

Krasner, L. (1962). The psychotherapist as a social reinforcement machine. In H. H. Strupp & L. Luborsky (Eds.), *Research in psychotherapy* (Vol. 2, pp. 61–94). Washington, DC: American Psychological Association.

Kratochwill, T. R. (1985a). Selection of target behaviors in behavioral consultation. *Behvioral Assessment, 7,* 49–61.

Kratochwill, T. R. (1985b). Selection of target behaviors: Issues and directions. *Behavioral Assessment, 7,* 3–5.

LaGreca, A. M. (1983). Interviewing and behavioral observations. In C. E. Walker & M. C. Roberts (Eds.), *Handbook of clinical child psychology.* (pp. 109–131). New York: Wiley.

Last, C. G., & Hersen, M. (1985). Introduction: Clinical practice of behavior therapy. In M. Hersen & C. G. Last (Eds.), *Behavior therapy casebook.* (pp. 3–15). New York: Springer.

Lazarus, A. A. (1971a). *Behavior therapy and beyond.* New York: McGraw-Hill.

Lazarus, A. A. (1971b). Notes on behavior therapy, the problem of relapse and some tentative solutions. *Psychotherapy, 8,* 192–196.

Lazarus, A. A. (1973). Multimodal behavior therapy: Treating the "BASIC ID." *The Journal of Nervous and Mental Disease, 156,* 404–411.

Lazarus, A. A. (1976), *Multimodal behavior therapy.* New York: Springer.

Lazarus, A. A. (1981). *The practice of multimodal therapy.* New York: McGraw-Hill.

Lick, J. R., & Bootzin, R. R. (1975). Expectancy factors in the treatment of fear: Methodological and theoretical issues. *Psychological Bulletin, 82,* 917–981.

MacDonald, M. L. (1984). Behavioral assessment of women clients. In E. A. Blechman (Ed.), *Behavior modification with women.* (pp. 60–93). New York: Guilford.

Mahoney, M. J., Kazdin, A. E. & Lesswing, N. J. (1974). Behavior modification: Delusion or deliverance. In C. M. Franks & G. T. Wilson (Eds.), *Annual review of behavior therapy: Theory and practice* (Vol. 2, pp. 11–40). New York: Brunner/Mazel.

Marquis, J. N. (1972). An expedient model for behavior therapy. In A. A. Lazarus (Ed.), *Clinical behavior therapy.* New York: Brunner/Mazel.

Marsden, G. (1971). Content analysis studies of psychotherapy: 1954 through 1968. In A. E. Bergin & S. L. Garfield (Eds.), *Handbook of psychotherapy and behavior change: An empirical analysis.* (pp. 345–407). New York: Wiley.

Mash, E. J. (1985). Some comments on target selection in behavior therapy, *Behavioral Assessment*, *7*, 63–78.

Mash, E. J., & Terdal, L. G. (1981). Behavioral assessment of childhood disturbance. In E. J. Mash & L. G. Terdal (Eds.), *Behavioral assessment of childhood disorders*. (pp. 3–78). New York: Guilford.

Matarazzo, J. D. (1965). The interview. In B. B. Wolman (Ed.), *Handbook of clinical psychology*. (pp. 403–450). New York: McGraw-Hill.

McNamara, J. R. (1978). Socioethical considerations in behavior therapy research and practice. *Behavior Modification*, *2*, 3–23.

Menninger, K. A. (1952). *A manual for psychiatric case study*. New York: Grune & Stratton.

Meyer, V., Liddel, A., & Lyons, M. (1977). Behavioral interviews. In A. R. Ciminero, K. S. Calhoun, & H. E. Adams (Eds.), *Handbook of behavioral assessment*. (pp. 117–152). New York: Wiley.

Millard, R. W., & Evans, I. M. (1983). Clinical decision processes and criteria for social validity. *Psychological Reports*, *53*, 775–778.

Mischel, W. (1971). *Introduction to personality*. New York: Holt, Rinehart & Winston.

Morganstern, K. P. (1973). Implosive therapy and flooding procedures: A critical review. *Psychological Bulletin*, *79*, 318–334.

Morganstern, K. P., & Tevlin, H. E. (1981). Behavioral interviewing. In M. Hersen & A. S. Bellack (Eds.), *Behavioral assessment: A practical handbook*. (2nd ed.) (pp. 71–100). New York: Pergamon.

Nelson, R. O. (1983). Behavioral assessment: Past, present, and future. *Behavioral Assessment*, *5*, 195–206.

Nelson, R. O., & Barlow, D. H. (1981). Behavioral assessment: Basic strategies and initial procedures. In D. H. Barlow (Ed.), *Behavioral assessment of adult disorders*. (pp. 13–43). New York: Guilford.

O'Leary, K. D., & Wilson, G. T. (1975), *Behavior therapy: Application and outcome*. Englewood Cliffs, NJ: Prentice-Hall.

Peterson, D. R. (1968). *The clinical study of social behavior*. New York: Appleton-Century-Crofts.

Pope, B. (1979). *The mental health interview: Research and application*. New York: Pergamon.

Rachman, S., & Wilson, G. T. (1980). *The effects of psychological therapy*. Oxford: Pergamon.

Rimm, D. C., & Masters, J. C. (1974). *Behavior therapy: Techniques and empirical findings*. New York: Academic Press.

Rimm, D. C., & Masters, J. C. (1979). *Behavior therapy: Techniques and empirical findings* (2nd ed.). New York: Academic Press.

Salzinger, K. (1959). Experimental manipulation of verbal behavior: A review. *Journal of General Psychology*, *61*, 65–94.

Sheldon-Wildgen, J., & Risley, T. R. (1982). Balancing clients' rights: The establishment of human rights and peer review committees. In A. S. Bellack, M. Hersen, & A.E. Kazdin (Eds.), *International handbook of behavior modification and therapy*. New York: Plenum.

Silverstein, G. (1977). Homosexuality and the ethics of behavioral interventions. *Journal of Homosexuality*, *2*, 205–211.

Sloane, R. B., Staples, F. R., Cristol, A. H., Yorkston, N. J., & Whipple, K. (1975). *Psychotherapy versus behavior therapy*. Cambridge: Harvard University Press.

Staats, A. W. (1978). *Social behaviorism*. Homewood, IL: Dorsey.

Strupp, H. H. (1978). Psychotherapy research and practice: An overview. In S. L. Garfield & A. E. Bergin (Eds.), *Handbook of psychotherapy and behavior change: An empirical analysis* (2nd ed.). (pp. 3–22). New York: Wiley.

Suinn, R. M. (1974). Training undergraduate students as community behavior modification consultants. *Journal of Counseling Psychology, 21*, 71–77.

Sullivan, H. S. (1954). *The psychiatric interview*. New York: Norton.

Thompson, J. K., & Williams, D.E. (1985). Behavior therapy in the 80's: Evolution, exploitation, and the existential issues. *the Behavior Therapist, 8*, 47–50.

Truax, C. B., & Carkhuff, R. (1967). *Toward effective counseling and psychotherapy: Training and practice*. Chicago: Aldine.

Truax, C. B., & Mitchell, K. M. (1971). Research on certain therapist interpersonal skills in relation to process and outcome. In A. E. Bergin & S. L. Garfield (Eds.), *Handbook of psychotherapy and behavior change: An empirical analysis*. (pp. 299–344). New York: Wiley.

Wexler, D. B. (1974). Token and taboo: Behavior modification, token economies, and the law. In C. M. Franks & G. T. Wilson (Eds.), *Annual review of behavior therapy: Theory and practice* (Vol. 2). (pp. 279–309). New York: Brunner/Mazel. (Reprinted from *California Law Review, 1973, 61.)*

Wiens, A. N. (1985). The assessment interview. In I. B. Weiner (Ed.), *Clinical methods in psychology* (2nd ed.). (pp. 3–57). New York: Wiley.

Wilson, T. E., & Evans, I. M. (1983). The reliability of target behavior selection in behavioral assessment. *Behavioral Assessment, 5*, 33–54.

Wilson, G. T. (1982). Clinical issues and strategies in the practices of behavior therapy. In C. M. Franks, G. T. Wilson, P. C. Kendall, & K. D. Brownell (Eds.), *Annual review of behavior therapy: Theory and practice, 8* 305–345. New York: Guilford.

Wilson, G. T. (1983). Clinical issues and strategies in the practice of behavior therapy. In C. M. Franks, G. T. Wilson, K. D. Brownell, & P. C. Kendall (Eds.), *Annual review of behavior therapy: Theory and practice, 9*, 309–343. New York: Guilford.

Wilson, G. T. (1984). Clinical issues and strategies in the practice of behavior therapy. In C. M. Franks, G. T. Wilson, P. C. Kendall, & K. D. Brownell (Eds.), *Annual review of behavior therapy: Theory and practice, 10*, 291–309. New York: Guilford.

Wilson, G. T., & Evans, I. M. (1976). Adult behavior therapy and the therapist–client relationship. In C.M. Franks & G. T. Wilson (Eds.), *Annual review of behavior therapy: Theory and practice, 4*, 771–792. New York: Brunner/Mazel.

Wilson, G. T., & Evans, I. M. (1977). The therapist-client relationship in behavior therapy. In A. S. Gurman & A. S. Razin (Eds.), *The therapist's contribution to effective psychotherapy: An empirical approach*. (pp. 544–565). New York: Pergamon.

Winett, R. A., & Winkler, R. C. (1972). Current behavior modification in the classroom: Be still, be quiet, be docile. *Journal of Applied Behavior Analysis, 5*, 499–504.

Wolpe, J. (1970). Transcript of initial interview in a case of depression. *Journal of Behavior Therapy and Experimental Psychiatry, 1*, 71–78.

Wolpe, J. (1977). Inadequate behavior analysis: The achilles heel of outcome research in behavior therapy. *Journal of Behavior Therapy and Experimental Psychiatry, 3*, 1–3.

Wolpe, J. (1982). *The practice of behavior therapy* (2nd ed.). New York: Pergamon.

5
Behavioral Observation

Sharon L. Foster
Debora J. Bell-Dolan
Donald A. Burge

Direct observation of behavior has traditionally been a mainstay of behavioral assessment. At least in early years, behavioral assessment typically focused on the assessment of overt behavior while at the same time asserting the importance of studying behavior as a phenomenon of interest in its own right rather than solely as a surrogate of some more interesting underlying property of the person (e.g., a trait). Because self-report methods were seen both as providing only indirect measures of observable behavior and as being beset by potential biases such as social desirability and susceptibility to "faking," direct observation came to be almost a requirement for publication of studies claiming a "behavioral" emphasis.

Recent years have witnessed a disenchantment with direct observation as an inherently superior and unbiased assessment strategy. Part of this disenchantment springs from an increasing body of literature showing that direct observation data, like self-report measures, can under certain conditions be susceptible to biases that jeopardize the quality and interpretation of the information generated by the method. A second criticism attacks the uses of direct observation for evaluating treatment outcome rather than the treatment method per se and argues that behaviors targeted in treatment and assessed by direct observation may lack social validity. In other words, it may be of limited importance in a client's day-to-day environment and functioning (Kazdin, 1977b; Wolf, 1978). A final concern about direct observation lies in the increasing recognition that cognitive and affective events may play important roles in client problems and that direct observation cannot directly assess these private events (see, for example, Jacobson, 1985a, 1985b).

Concerns about social validity and the relevance of direct observation for assessing private events point out the importance of (a) selecting meaningful behaviors to observe, (b) letting the nature of a target behavior (selected for its importance to the issue at hand) dictate the method for its assessment, rather than preselecting a method and constraining the target, and (c) interpreting the results of direct observation appropriately without inferring that they represent response domains other than those assessed. Despite these concerns, direct observation and its cousin, self-observation, are still the strategies of choice for assessing publicly observable behavior whenever such behavior is the focus of interest and observation is feasible.

This chapter describes considerations relevant to designing and using direct observation systems, with particular emphasis on practical implications of research evaluating how the characteristics and implementation of direct observation systems can influence data quality. Early sections focus on developing a behavior code, selecting a sampling strategy, and training observers. Later sections highlight factors that can influence observer performance and methods of evaluating that performance. The final section discusses problems encountered in using direct observation in applied nonresearch settings and suggests some methods for circumventing these difficulties.

DESIGNING A CODE

Selecting Target Behaviors

The first step in designing an observation code is to select the behavior(s) of interest. Several factors must be considered when choosing behaviors for an observation code. One important factor is the person targeted for observation. Are one or more children the target, or is the teacher the target, or both? A related consideration is whether to observe a single response or an interactive unit. Although it can be more difficult, observing and coding interactive units is useful for determining functional relations, identifying alternatives to the target response, and evaluating interventions (Cone & Foster, 1982). Finally, when direct observation is used for research purposes, target behaviors should be closely related to the research question; when the purpose is to evaluate treatment effects in clinical settings, the behavior should be related in some meaningful way to the client's presenting problems and most pervasive life difficulties (cf. Kazdin, 1985).

Another point the code developer needs to consider is the breadth of information desired and the molarity of the categories (Hartmann & Wood, 1982). Observation codes that include a broad range of behavior may be most appropriate for preliminary assessment and screening, but hypothesis testing and evaluation of intervention probably require more narrow-band behavior categories. Similarly, Hartmann and Wood (1982) suggest that molar categories of behavior (e.g., grouped by topographical or functional similarities) may be psychologically meaningful, but are likely to require inferences on the part of observers. Furthermore, molar categories require demonstration of their content validity — in other words, empirical evidence that the category *exhaustively* and *appropriately* samples the designated response class. This is particularly important when evaluative labels like "positive" and "negative" are used, since individuals may evaluate the quality of specific behaviors differently (Stouthamer-Loeber & Peters, 1984). Molecular categories, although sometimes more difficult to interpret, may be easier for observers to use since behavioral units are defined more discreetly.

The way molecular behaviors are grouped into response classes is also important to consider. Topographical response classes group together behaviors that have similar form whereas functional response classes may group topographically dissimilar behaviors that function in the same way. When functional similarities are assumed a priori by investigators rather than assessed empirically, however, data on so-called "functional" response classes can misrepresent behavior–environment relations (Johnston & Pennypacker, 1980).

An additional consideration is how many behaviors to record. While some investigators suggest that no more than 8 categories can be reliably coded (Mash & McElwcc, 1974), others have set this limit higher (e.g., 14; Frame, 1979). The actual limit probably depends on the complexity of the observation code and the situations in which it is being used. Situations in which the limit is being approached can be dealt with by simplifying the observation (e.g., combining or excluding categories) or the recording procedures (e.g., by using electromechanical keyboards, audio- or video-taping).

Preliminary narrative and ABC (antecedent, behavior, consequence) recordings (Bijou, Peterson, Harris, Allen, & Johnston, 1969) are often useful in making decisions about what to observe. Narrative observations can be transformed into ABC tables to suggest possible relationships between the behaviors of interest and environmental events; from these records, behaviors can be selected and definitions and recording procedures refined.

Defining Behaviors

Once target behaviors have been selected, the second step in designing a code involves constructing and evaluating definitions of the behaviors. Definitions permit both within and between laboratory replication; thus, a definition should be constructed to minimize both idiosyncratic interpretations and the discrepancies between the explicit written definition and the implicit working definitions used by observers. According to Hawkins and Dobes (1977), adequate response definitions are objective, clear, and complete. An objective definition refers to observable characteristics; inferential terms (e.g., happy, disinterested, etc.) are translated into more objective terms. A clear definition is readable, unambiguous, and can be summarized by an experienced observer. A complete definition includes a descriptive name, a general dictionary-like definition, an elaboration — which points out differences from other response categories, and both typical and borderline examples and nonexamples along with rationales for their inclusion and exclusion. Fabry (1983), borrowing from the concept-formation literature (cf., Markle & Tiemann, 1972), also suggests including lists of critical and unnecessary attributes of examples.

Hawkins and Dobes (1977) recommend that the adequacy of definitions be tested by having several experienced observers who are unfamiliar with the definition read it and independently record the behavior using the definition. By discovering and correcting inadequacies in definitions early, considerable time can be saved at the observer training stage. For example, Hawkins, Berler, and DeLawyer (1984) gave observers a training manual containing extensive definitions of verbal behavior created according to the above guidelines, from which the observers were to learn to code audiotapes of parent–adolescent verbal interactions. Following approximately 1 hour of reading the manual and completing practice exercises, observers coded transcripts with at least 80% accuracy.

Dimensions of Behavior

Another major decision in designing an observation system involves choosing which dimension(s) of behavior to observe. An observation code can focus on the quantity or quality of the behavior, or on some by-product of the behavior. *Frequency* data involve counting the number of times a behavior occurs during an observation period. Rates per minute, per hour, or per day can be derived from frequency data, allowing comparisons across observation periods differing in duration. Frequency and rate measures are relatively easy to obtain, and thus are particularly well-suited for participant observers who have some role in the observation setting besides observing. Nonetheless, frequency measures obviously do not yield information on duration, intensity, and quality of behavior (Cone & Foster, 1982). In addition, Baer (1982) has argued that pure rate measures are inappropriate for opportunity-bound responses such as compliance with instructions. Finally, frequency is difficult to code reliably for behaviors that do not have easily discriminable starting and stopping points.

Duration measures can include (a) latency, the time between a specific stimulus and the response; (b) response duration, the time between the initiation and cessation of the response; and (c) interresponse time, the time between successive responses. Response duration data can be transformed into frequency data, percent of total time, and average response duration measures. The choice of a particular duration measure depends on whether the behavior dimension of interest is duration per response (average response duration), total time (percent), or some temporal relationship between occurrences of the behavior (interresponse time) or between the behavior and environmental stimuli (latency). Measuring duration requires that the behavior have clear starting and stopping points and also that the observer be able to measure and record the passage of time. Because this requires access to a timing device as well as attention to both onset and offset of the behavior, duration recording is not always feasible, especially with participant observers. In addition, in at least some cases, percent of total time and frequency data are very similar (Gaines, 1973), although it is not clear in which situations these measures are and are not comparable.

Qualitative aspects of behavior can also be assessed. Magnitude, accuracy, and acceptability are qualitative aspects of how behavior relates to some continuum or standard. These dimensions of behavior are useful to incorporate into a direct observation system when value judgments are routinely made about the behavior. For example, verbal statements made by schizophenic patients could be coded as "appropriate" or "inappropriate," and speech dysfluencies of anxious individuals could be recorded along with the degree of dysfluency. It is important to distinguish between qualitative appraisals of behavior per se (e.g., appropriateness of conversational statements) and global appraisals of overall performance (e.g., rating of social skill), and to recall that the latter — while presumably based on behavior — provide no information about the specific response displayed by the observed individual.

When qualitative appraisals of specific responses are desired, the code developer can either incorporate observers' subjective evaluations into the system or explicitly define the points along an evaluation continuum to provide evaluation guidelines and thus minimize subjectivity. As will be described in more detail later, ratings have more often been associated with biased recording as a function of information given to observers than have rate measures of behavior (e.g., Kent, O'Leary, Diament, & Dietz, 1974), so special precautions should be taken when using global ratings to prevent biasing influences. The likelihood of observer bias can also be decreased when an observer records some aspect of behavior that has no apparent relation to a quality standard (such as frequency), but the investigator has access to prior information that allows a qualitative judgment to be made about the data after they are gathered. Such might be the case, for example, if a normative range of on-task behavior in the classroom had been previously shown to be generally acceptable to most teachers. Rates of on-task behavior for a particular child could then be compared with these norms to determine the "appropriateness" of a particular child's behavior, relative to his or her peers (Kazdin, 1981).

In some instances, an observation code may not target actual behavior at all, but instead may measure a *by-product* of behavior. This is useful when the behavior itself is not readily accessible to an observer but regularly leaves some residue or product that is easily detectable. For example, counting cigarette butts may be a more efficient measure of smoking at a party than direct observation. Measuring by-products is also useful when the outcome produced by the behavior is more important its topography (e.g., the number of toys returned to the toybox may be more important than how they got there). Measuring by-products presents some difficulties, though. As Cone and Foster (1982) and Johnston and Pennypacker (1980) discuss, measuring the product provides no information about the producer or the form of the behavior. Thus, the observer cannot necessarily guarantee that the target person actually emitted the behavior responsible for the product, nor that the assumed behavior actually produced the effect (e.g., the child may have talked a playmate into putting the toys away). Although measuring by-products of behavior is often useful, it cannot provide the same kind of information about specific behaviors as would direct observation of those responses per se.

Data Recording Systems

The next step in designing an observation code is selecting among several types of recording systems. The simplest is *event recording*. With this system, the observer simply records the relevant dimension (usually frequency, but sometimes duration or quality) of the target behavior each time it occurs. Since event recording is so simple, it is practical for use by participant observers. However, because this observation system usually involves recording only one dimension of behavior, other types of information are lost. Since the time of occurrence is not usually recorded, temporal patterns cannot be determined and the source of disagreements between observers cannot be pinpointed (Cone & Foster, 1982). However, if a rough index of behavior is all that is needed, event recording is an efficient system.

To improve the information yield of event recording, environmental events can be recorded along with the target behavior to produce an ABC record. The occurrence of behavior can also be recorded in *real time*, which involves recording an event as it occurs in uninterrupted time, along with some indication of the time elapsed both during and between responses. Real-time recording is a flexible recording system (Hartmann & Wood, 1982). It can be used to collect both frequency and duration measures as well as rate and conditional probability data. Real-time recording also permits precise pinpointing of disagreements between observers (Hawkins, 1982). Unfortunately, real-time recording usually requires an electromechanical recording device, such as a computerized, hand-held data entry mechanism that automatically records the time between category entries.

Observations can also be recorded in terms of any of several interval recording systems which approximate real-time recording. With interval recording, the observation period is divided into (usually brief) blocks of time and observers use a cuing device (stopwatch, tape-recorded beeps, etc.) to signal each interval. Intervals may be contiguous, in which case observers observe and record simultaneously, or may be interspersed with breaks during which the observers stop observing to record behavior. In *whole interval* recording, the behavior is recorded only if it occurs throughout the entire interval. *Partial-interval* recording requires that the behavior occur only during a portion of the interval. A minimum duration may be specified (e.g., "half of the interval" or "2 seconds"; Powell, Martindale, & Kulp, 1975) or any duration may be acceptable. Specifying a minimum duration can cause problems, though, because observers may not be able to estimate accurately the passage of the required amount of time. *Frequency-within-interval* recording involves counting each instance of the behavior within each interval. Frequency-within-interval resembles event recording of frequency, with the added advantages of allowing closer pinpointing of observer disagreements and examination of rate changes over time. With a *momentary time-sampling* system, the behavior is recorded if it is observed at a specific moment within the interval, such as the beginning or end.

The advantages of interval-recording systems include (a) the division of time into units, which allows observer disagreements to be pinpointed; (b) the ability to estimate both frequency and duration (Hawkins, 1982), (c) applicability (with the exception of frequency within interval) for assessing behaviors without readily identifiable onsets and offsets, and (d) practical utility for observing several behaviors at the same time. The different interval recording systems have limitations, however. One limitation of all interval-recording systems is that they require more observer attention than the simple forms of event recording and thus ordinarily are not as useful to participant observers (Cone & Foster, 1982). Second, the concentration required with interval recording can generate considerable observer fatigue over long periods of recording low-frequency behaviors (Sulzer-Azaroff & Mayer, 1977). Third, while most interval recording systems can be used to derive estimates of both frequency and duration, these estimates are frequently biased (Green, McCoy, Burns, & Smith, 1982). Several researchers (Green & Alverson, 1978; Green et al., 1982; Powell, Martindale, Kulp, Martindale, & Bauman, 1977) have found that, in general, accuracy of both frequency and duration estimates (compared with real-time recording) obtained with interval recording is related to interval size. Interval recording with short intervals overestimates frequency, whereas using longer interval leads to underestimation. Duration is overestimated unless the interval size is small in comparison to the mean duration of behavior. Whole- and partial-interval and momentary time sampling also differ from one another in terms of accuracy. Powell et al. (1977) found that whole-interval sampling became increasingly inaccurate as interval duration increased over 5 seconds, partial-interval sampling was fairly accurate for up to 10 seconds, and momentary time sampling was accurate through 1-minute interval durations. Green et al. (1982) also found that partial-interval sampling produced lower observer accuracy than momentary time sampling.

Ary (1984) integrates many of these findings by producing mathematical formulae that estimate the error produced by partial-interval, whole-interval, and momentary time-sampling procedures when used to estimate duration. Ary argues that if human error is disregarded, all three sampling methods will be subject to error only if a behavior changes (i.e., starts or stops) during an interval, since intervals during which behavior occurs continuously will be recorded, no matter which method is used. Ary goes on to show how sampling error can be estimated based on the total number of intervals scored, the number of intervals containing changes in a target behavior, and the number of intervals where the target behavior occurs during the entire interval. Although it may be difficult to obtain accurate figures for actual duration and onset/offset of behavior prior to designing an observation system, Ary's formulae permit evaluation of the likelihood of sampling error with different interval durations if probable values are available. Unfortunately, similar models for error when interval methods are used to estimate frequency (rather than duration) have not been developed.

Data Recording Methods

The final step in designing an observation code is to decide on a data recording method. As Johnston and Pennypacker (1980) note, "the permanent record that remains after defining, observing, and recording have taken place is the only evidence that measurement actually occurred, and the quality of the entire process cannot exceed the characteristics of that record" (p. 170). Thus, this decision is an important one.

One simple method of recording data is *paper-and-pencil* recording. Written records are cheap, flexible, and mobile (Bijou et al., 1969). However, to allow efficient and accurate recording, they must be well-designed (see Gelfand & Hartmann, 1984, and Barton & Ascione, 1984, for descriptions of recording form design). Critical information for an observation recording form includes the date, the name of observer and target subject(s), and — for interval-based systems — numbered observation intervals. Explanations of symbols and spaces for comments may also be included. For participant observers in clinical settings, it is often helpful to record the names, definitions, and recording rules for the behavior on the data sheet. With nonparticipant observers conducting live observations, forms can be designed to minimize the number of times observers break visual contact with subjects by requiring a minimum of writing and providing auditory cues rather than a clock or stopwatch. For example, transitions from one interval to another can be announced on an audiotape that the observer listens to through an earphone. In addition, it is sometimes helpful to intersperse observation intervals with recording intervals so that the observer does not have to observe and record simultaneously.

Another simple data-recording method employs *clocks* or *counters*. These are useful when information about the pattern of occurrence over time is not required and only one response (or a few infrequent, mutually exclusive behaviors) are being observed. The observer either pushes a button each time a behavior occurs or holds down a button while the behavior is occurring (Holm, 1978). The product of observation is a summary frequency or duration score. Clocks and counters are readily available (e.g., stopwatches golf counters) and are especially useful for participant observers.

Electromechanical devices, such as event recorders and keyboards, are gaining popularity as data-collection aids. Event recorders and keyboards often consist of a number of buttons on a control board which are electrically connected to pens. The buttons correspond to behavior categories. The observer depresses a button when the behavior begins and holds it down until the behavior terminates. The pens mark on continuous paper and provide a permanent record of the behaviors over time. Some devices store the information in computer memory rather than transferring it to paper. Built-in duration timers, in which a button automatically stays depressed until another button is pressed, are features of some keyboards. The advantages of these devices include enabling observers to record greater numbers of behaviors with less distraction from the recording procedure, increasing ease in recording duration, increasing opportunity to assess sequential or temporal relations, and (with computerized devices) automatically summarizing data (Bijou et al., 1969; Holm, 1978; Barton & Ascione, 1984). In addition, with some devices, data can be read directly into a computer (Holm, 1978). Electromechanical devices are commercially available, but these are often expensive. Holm suggests that if an electronics shop and computer programming are available, a recording device can be custom-made for about $600 using a microprocessor. Besides expense, another limitation of electromechanical devices lies in the possibility of equipment failure. To prepare for this, a second device and/or pencil-and-paper recording forms should be considered as backups.

Audio- and video-recording can also be used to record behavior for later coding. This is useful if the behaviors of interest are too many or too complex to record accurately in vivo, since a taped session can be replayed several times (Hawkins, 1982). It is also useful if the presence of observers would be more reactive than that of the camera or tape recorder (Hartmann & Wood, 1982). The investigator/practitioner must be prepared for equipment failure and must also consider fidelity of equipment, length of time required to prepare tapes for coding (e.g., dubbing time markers onto tapes), and time required to code and transcribe tapes, which can take 10 to 15 times the original observation time (Holm, 1978). Ethical issues should also be addressed. For example, Hartmann and Wood (1982) suggest that subjects give informed consent and be allowed to edit the tapes if they so choose. As with all observations, observers should be informed of their responsibility to keep the identity of subjects and information about the observation sessions confidential.

Establishing System Accuracy

Accuracy refers to the ability of a measurement procedure to yield data that reflect the domain under investigation without distortion. Therefore, for a direct observation system to be accurate, it must be sensitive to the aspects of behavior it is intended to reflect, such as occurrence, change, and covariation with other responses. Good interobserver agreement does not guarantee accuracy, as it is possible for observers to show consensus after training with a highly inaccurate system or when the accuracy of a system has deteriorated over time through consensual shifts in application of category definitions.

Establishing accuracy requires that the data generated by a direct observation system under conditions typical of its future use match data generated by an incontrovertible concurrent measure of the same behavior. The difficulty in establishing such accuracy lies in determining an incontrovertible alternative measure, which will be de facto treated as establishing the truth about the behavior being observed. With some behaviors, mechanical means of assessing behavior in real time serve as criteria, as when observations of in-seat behavior in the classroom are compared with results generated by pressure-sensitive mechanical devices placed underneath a chair. Interval recording systems can be assessed for accuracy against real-time recordings. Scripts can be used to produce videotapes that contain particular behaviors, and the system's accuracy in reflecting those responses can be assessed. The problem with the last strategy, however, lies in the tautology of independently verifying that the behavior occurred as scripted using direct observation, and then claiming that the direct observation system is accurate because it reflects the scripted behavior.

Because incontrovertible indices of behavior are not always readily available, some users of direct observation systems create a series of videotapes which they score using the observation system, creating criterion protocols for each videotape. As Cone and Foster (1982) point out, use of such criterion protocols does not guarantee accuracy, since the protocols are created using the newly designed observation system and thus are not independent of it. Nonetheless, creating a series of criterion protocols assists greatly in training observers to observe consistently and in maintaining consistent use of a system over time (DeMaster, Reid, & Twentyman, 1977). Consistency of system use over time, like good interobserver agreement, is necessary but not sufficient for system accuracy (see Cone & Foster, 1982, and Foster & Cone, 1986, for more in-depth discussions of establishing system accuracy).

PLANNING A SAMPLING STRATEGY

Selecting an Environmental Setting

The environmental settings that can be used for conducting direct behavior observations are almost unlimited, even though in reality most observational data are collected in schools, clinics or hospitals, homes, and laboratories. The factors that typically dictate the choice of the observation environment include location and number of persons to be observed, personnel and resources, number of observations to be scheduled, and degree of situational specificity of the target behavior.

One important dimension to consider in selecting the observation setting is the degree of experimental control that can be exercised over the events of interest within a particular environment. Setting control ranges from completely uncontrolled "natural" settings (e.g., an individual's primary living environment) to highly controlled laboratory or clinic settings. In this section, in vivo and analog observational assessment procedures are discussed in terms of clinical application, advantages, and disadvantages.

In Vivo Observation

In vivo observations involve collecting data on target behaviors and behavior–environment interactions as they occur in natural settings. In vivo observation is a particularly powerful method for evaluating the effects, maintenance, and generalization of interventions, and has been used to this end with a broad range of target behaviors and settings including compliance behaviors in parent–child interactions in the home (Hawkins, Peterson, Schweid, & Bijou, 1966), institutional behaviors of psychiatric patients in day-treatment (Alevizos, DeRisi, Liberman, Eckman, & Callahan, 1978), marital interaction in the home (Haynes, Follingstad, & Sullivan, 1979), and work behaviors of mentally retarded adolescents in a halfway house (Johnson & Bailey, 1977). In the actual environment that the target individual is reported to emit behavior of interest (e.g., classroom, office, playground, shopping mall, or dining room), the nonparticipant observer typically has little or no direct control over the behavior to be observed. For this reason, in vivo observation techniques are usually considered to be those that achieve realism at the expense of environmental control.

In vivo procedures are especially warranted when a target behavior occurs only in the presence of other events or in settings which cannot be feasibly duplicated via an analog. Nonetheless, there are several disadvantages associated with in vivo observation. For example, there are circumscribed situations where the behavior of interest may occur only in the absence of others (e.g., stealing, fire-setting, binge eating) and may therefore render direct observation impossible. Ethical and legal restrictions may also preclude the use of in vivo procedures under some conditions (e.g., child abuse or illicit drug use). Assessment alternatives in these cases include the use of reliable by-products, self-monitoring, or self-report.

Despite the utility and ecological validity of observing behavior in vivo, it can be labor-intensive and costly. The consent and cooperation of several persons are usually required, session scheduling is vulnerable to disruptions, and the physical parameters of some environments may prohibit the use of electromechanical recording devices due to lack of light, space, or supply of electrical power. Finally, a major practical disadvantage of using in vivo procedures is the observation time and subsequent expense sometimes expended to obtain a sufficient sampling of target behaviors. This is a particularly relevant issue when the behavior of interest occurs at low or variable rates across settings.

One method of increasing the efficiency (i.e., cost per unit of observed behavior) of in vivo observation is to impose some degree of structure within natural settings that results in a higher probability that the target behavior will occur during observations. The amount of structure can range from presumably minor restrictions in the movement or activities of those observed to complete specification of the activity or interaction of certain persons for a prescribed duration (Hayne, 1978). Between these points, there are various levels and types of structure that can be employed (see McFall, 1977; Nay, 1979, for reviews). The obvious questions here involve the functional similarity between *natural* and *modified* environments, and how that similarity diverges as a result of various types of structure. Unfortunately, these issues have not been systematically studied.

Analog Observation

As in vivo observation incorporates more and more environmental restrictions, it approaches analog observation — the direct observation of behavior in environments that are structured for the express purpose of maximizing observational efficiency. Analog observation procedures are often used to increase the probability of directly observing behavior–environment interactions by structuring situational and stimulus elements thought to elicit target responses into the observation environment. Since these types of structural manipulation, if effective, increase the number of significant interactions per unit of observation time, they are particularly useful in reducing the time needed for the observation of low-rate behaviors.

A common sort of structural control has been over physical settings, in which a target individual's social behavior is observed in an artificial environment such as a clinic interview room or playroom. Here, as with the term *natural*, the term *artificial* can be misleading since it does not indicate the absence of functional relationships between environmental factors and behaviors of interest, but rather that these functional elements may not ordinarily be present in the subject's routine environment. Instructions to subjects (such as telling a mother to give a series of commands to her child or instructing a couple to attempt to solve a specific marital problem) further restrict the sample of behavior to be observed. At an even more molecular level, a particular set of stimuli are provided to subjects, as in role-played responses to videotaped conflict situations. Of course, any of these types of controls can be used in combination for even further environmental structure.

Analog procedures are particularly useful when data are impractical or impossible to collect in the natural environment, as, for example, when a client refuses to serve as a participant observer or does not comply with self-monitoring instructions. The primary concern with analog procedures is the degree of generalizability or external validity. Because behavior varies in response to situational factors, highly structured and novel environments may affect whether performance is typical of the targeted response class (Foster & Cone, 1980). Some researchers have suggested that behavior emitted in analog situations may not be generalizable to behavior in the natural environment (e.g., Bellack, Hersen, & Turner, 1979). Others (Reisinger & Ora, 1977) have found satisfactory relationships between observations collected in structured versus natural environments.

Ensuring Sufficient Sampling

Once the observation code, method to record data, and environment to observe are selected, questions of how long to observe and over how many sessions arise. Although there are no hard and fast answers to these questions, a few guidelines exist. To the extent that a behavior occurs in limited situations with relatively stable frequencies, less observation time will be needed to establish reliable estimates of targeted events. Conversely, when behavior rates are low, variable, and/or show a sloping trend (either increasing or decreasing) when events occasioning the target behaviors vary substantially over either time or setting, or when topographical features of the target events are complex, then the minimum amount of sampling required to achieve stability is less certain (Haynes, 1978).

One way to assess these parameters is to pilot observational procedures in the settings in which the target behavior is reported to occur and then evaluate the subsequent data to plan a sampling strategy. With single-subject research that is in progress, one empirical way to demonstrate stability of observed behavior calls for collecting data until the slope of plotted data for the last *n* data points approximates zero. A variation on this stability criterion, which is less conservative and perhaps more realistically obtained, involves accepting less than plus or minus 5% variability around a trend line across some number of consecutive observations as stable. In group design research, split-half reliability coefficients can also be computed to determine the number of observations required to yield stable estimates of behavior for the group as a whole.

SELECTING AND TRAINING OBSERVERS

Selecting Observers

One factor to consider when selecting observers is whether to use participant or nonparticipant observers (see Cone & Foster, 1982). Participant observers, who take part in the activities in the setting while collecting data, have the advantage of being part of the natural environment whereas nonparticipant observers, who are not naturally part of the setting, must be scheduled and are often more costly to employ. Since they are not strangers, participant observers may cause less reactivity than nonparticipant observers. Participant observers are also more likely to be able to collect data over longer periods of time and are particularly useful for observing low-frequency behaviors. Using participant observers requires that observation be compatible with the observer's normal routine. For this reason, nonparticipant observers are more appropriate when continuous observation is required, such as when high-rate behaviors or long sequences of behavior are under investigation.

It is unclear whether participant and nonparticipant observation yield similar results. While acceptable (80–100%) levels of agreement among participant and nonparticipant observers have often been reported, Hay, Nelson, and Hay (1977), observing student and teacher behaviors in the classroom, found reactive changes in both teacher and student behavior following introduction of participant observation by the teachers. Several studies in the marital area comparing participant and nonparticipant observers have also yielded mixed results. Robinson and Price (1980) found only moderate correlations in the .4–.5 range between nonparticipant observers' and spouses' observations of frequency of pleasurable behaviors.

It is not clear, however, how these correlations would translate to interobserver agreement scores. Margolin, Hattem, John, and Yost (1985) compared nonparticipant observers' and spouses' observations but found very little agreement (average weighted kappa = .057). A major problem in interpreting the results of both studies stems from the difference in levels of sophistication with observation between participant and nonparticipant observers. Nonparticipant observers are routinely trained on some observation code, whereas participant observers rarely receive much training on how or what to observe. Floyd and Markman (1983) attempted to equate the amount of guidance given to participant and nonparticipant observers. They, too, found little correspondence between spouses' and nonparticipant observers' evaluations of the positiveness of the partners' comments. However, one major limitation of this study was the failure to assess interobserver agreement among nonparticipant observers, thus limiting the comparability to other observation studies. More studies examining the comparability of participant and nonparticipant observation are needed.

Other characteristics are also important to consider when selecting observers. It is important to recruit observers who can handle the many responsibilities involved in data collection (i.e., prompt and dependable attendance, honest and accurate observation, maintaining a good relationship with those in the observation setting, and keeping the data confidential). Several researchers have suggested that important observer attributes may include maturity and professionalism (Rosenthal, 1966), motivation (Dancer et al., 1987), verbal skill (Skindrud, 1973), and personal appearance and manner (Haynes, 1978). Ability to attend to detail for long periods of time, to manage high levels of environmental stimulation without becoming confused, and to remain detached may also be important (Yarrow & Waxler, 1979).

Introduction to Observation

Once observers have been selected, several steps should be taken before formal training begins. If observers are naive with regard to the purpose of observation, it is useful to provide a rationale for systematic direct observation. This can be done by (a) providing observers with introductory readings on direct observation, (b) having observers try to make justifiable decisions about interventions or predict behavior patterns without the aid of observation data, and/or (c) having observers attempt to record behaviors without a coding system (Hartmann & Wood, 1982). These procedures may help to demonstrate to observers the value of direct observation per se, a formal coding system, and training.

Responsibilities of observers should be presented and the importance of their naiveté regarding the purpose and hypotheses of the investigation should be explained. Observers should also be warned against attempting to guess the experimental hypothesis (Hartmann & Wood, 1982). Observers should be informed about appropriate dress and manner (e.g., remaining inconspicuous, not interacting with subjects, etc.), since these can affect both the relationship with those in the observation setting and possibly the reactivity of the observed subjects (Grimm, Parsons, & Bijou, 1972). Confidentiality of subjects' data should be addressed and observers should read *Ethical Principles in the Conduct of Research with Human Participants* (1982). Finally, the importance of accurate, objective data should be stressed and the consequences of cheating explained. Observers should be instructed *not* to (a) *share* their data with one another, (b) watch how another observer records, or (c) discuss disagreements with another observer unless the trainer is present and uses this as a method of instruction. Providing reasons for all of these instructions by showing how they can jeopardize the quality of the data can help observers understand their key role in the scientific process.

Training Observers

Several researchers have described various training procedures (e.g., Barton & Ascione, 1984; Bijou et al., 1969; Hartmann & Wood, 1982; Hawkins & Dobes, 1977; Reid, 1982; Rojahn & Wool, 1979). Although these descriptions differ in the number of steps and particular components they emphasize, most contain similar general features. The initial step in training observers involves introduction of the observation categories, usually via a coding manual which includes definitions of the behaviors under investigation and decision rules for coding. Observers can learn the observation categories through the use of written study objectives, discussions with the trainer, quizzes, and feedback on performance. Barton and Ascione (1984) recommend that observers reach 100% mastery on memorization of the code before moving to the next step of observer training. Following mastery on the observation manual, observers should practice using the observation tools (e.g., recording forms, stopwatches, tape recorders, electromechanical recording devices, etc.) and learn the specific recording system they will employ (e.g., frequency, interval, and momentary time sampling).

Once observers have learned the observation code and are familiar with the observation tools, they can begin to practice observing behavior. Initial observations should involve analog situations, preferably on videotapes to permit replays and discussion when observers make errors. To shape complex, fast discriminations among categories, trainers should present slow, simple sequences of behavior initially and gradually move to more complex sequences that span the range of circumstances observers are likely to encounter. Behavior sequences should be short at the beginning of training, to avoid observer fatigue and allow maximal opportunity for trainer feedback, and gradually approach the length of observation to be used in the target setting. If videotapes are used, the trainer should code the videotapes prior to using them with observers so that observers' performance can be compared to a criterion. The trainer should also make numerous training tapes so that observers do not see the same behavior sequence over and over. This is important since predictability of behavior during training sequences can lead to decreased interobserver agreement in novel observation situations (Mash & Makohoniuk, 1975; Mash & McElwee, 1974). It is also important that practice tapes represent the full range of behavior and settings likely to be encountered during data collection to ensure that observers learn to perform well in a variety of circumstances. Barton and Ascione (1984) recommend a minimum of 85% accuracy (agreement with criterion) before observers advance in training.

Following coding in analog settings, observers should practice in the target setting or a similar setting. Initially, it may be useful for the trainer to accompany the observers and observe with them, stopping frequently to provide feedback about agreement and to discuss disagreements. When observers reliably agree with the trainer, they can begin to observe with each other. They should be reminded of the importance of observing independently and avoiding discussions of disagreements in the absence of the trainer. Feedback on interobserver agreement should be provided to observers at the end of each observation session. Again, Barton and Ascione (1984) suggest a criterion of 85% agreement before observers begin actual data collection. Although agreement scores of less than 85% may be acceptable during data collection, overtraining may help to minimize the impact of a decrease in agreement which often occurs following training (Reid, 1982; Taplin & Reid, 1973).

Retraining During Data Collection

Once data collection begins, there may be some decay in observers' performance. Reid and DeMaster (1972) and Taplin and Reid (1973) have demonstrated that interobserver agreement can drop as much as 15% when training ends and data collection begins. Another source of error in observational data is observer "drift," where observer consistency and accuracy decrease as a function of idiosyncratic modifications made by observers following training. Observer error can be compounded when observers drift systematically and together across trials. This form of "consensual observer drift" (Johnson & Bolstad, 1973) is characterized by good interobserver agreement but declining observer accuracy across observations. Unclear definitions and/or recording procedures can lead to changes in the use of the observation system. Drift can also result from observers altering their coding to accommodate unexpected changes in target behaviors.

Observer drift and its effects have been repeatedly demonstrated in the behavior assessment literature (e.g., Kent et al., 1974; Romanczyk, Kent, Diament, & O'Leary, 1973; Wildman, Erickson, & Kent, 1975). The results of these studies suggest that, because drift develops after training, interobserver agreement estimates based only on training sessions may be inflated. Similarly, interobserver agreement data from observer pairs working together during lengthy data collection periods may show good agreement despite considerable drift.

O'Leary and Kent (1973) described how observer drift can affect internal validity. In between-subjects designs, the effects of observer drift may be confounded with experimental manipulations if different pairs of observers are assigned to different treatment groups. In within-subjects designs, differences among conditions may be a function of drift and not experimental manipulations if a single pair of observers is used in all conditions.

Observer drift that affects some but not all members of an observation team can be detected by having routine assessments of interobserver agreement in which all observers record behavior simultaneously; agreement is then computed among all possible pairs to see if any pairs routinely agree with each other but not with other observers. Frequent checks of covert interobserver agreement during data collection among different observer pairs can also be used to examine whether certain pairs of observers show poor agreement. This would indicate that these individuals may be using the observation system differently. When drift is consensual, accuracy and/or consistency checks against criterion measures are required to detect observer drift, since interobserver agreement is insensitive to consensual observer drift.

Fortunately, DeMaster, Reid, and Twentyman (1977) provide data showing that observer drift can be prevented, at least with observations of videotapes of behavior, via continued practice during data collection together with feedback from the trainer on interobserver agreement and accuracy (relative to criterion protocols). Several authors have suggested additional ways for preventing observer drift and for minimizing the chances that any drift that occurs be confounded with changes in experimental conditions. These include (a) rotating observer pairs frequently (Haynes, 1978), (b) videotaping observation sessions which will then be scored by coders in random sequences (Kazdin, 1977a), (c) using independent reliability assessors (Kent et al., 1974), and (d) discussing the observation code only in the presence of the trainer and including all observers in any discussions that occur (Kazdin, 1977a).

Despite precautions to avoid observer drift, some observers' performance may still decay during data collection. In this case, the cause of the problem should be explored. Merely discussing the problem with the observer may correct it, by influencing motivation, for example. It may also be necessary to provide remedial training. This can include any or all of the steps of initial observer training.

DATA COLLECTION PROCEDURES

Once a code has been designed and observers have been trained, data collection can begin. Several aspects of the data-collection process can influence the information obtained by direct observation. Here we examine subject reactivity to observation, then turn to an examination of factors that can influence the accuracy and consistency with which a coding system can be used.

Reactivity

Introduction of observers and/or recording devices into an environment to collect data may present a threat to external (Haynes & Horn, 1982) or ecological validity (Rogers-Warren & Warren, 1977) and to internal validity (Nelson, Kapust, & Dorsey, 1978) of the data. If the process of observing behavior alters — either permanently or temporarily — the characteristics being assessed, it cannot be assumed that the derived data validly represent behavior when it is not being observed. Similarly, behavior change that is actually the result of reactivity may be erroneously attributed to a covarying intervention. Johnson and Bolstad (1973) identified four potential sources of reactivity: (a) conspicuousness of the observer and/or recording equipment, (b) interaction of physical characteristics (e.g., age, gender) of observer and subject, (c) personal attributes of the observer which may determine changes in the subjects' behavior, and (d) the rationale provided for observation.

Although as Baum, Forehand, and Zegiob (1979) noted, direct observation is not always associated with reactivity, it does occur under some conditions, and its effects can be statistically and clinically significant. Research examining reactive effects associated with direct observation by outside observers has generally focused on increases and decreases in rates of behaviors, with some studies finding reactive effects for some behaviors and some subjects, and others not (see Haynes & Horn, 1982, for a complete review). Studies examining reactivity associated with participant observation have located two potential types of reactivity: changes in subjects' behavior when they are observed and changes in participant observers' behavior when they are conducting the observations. Reactive effects in both of these domains have been shown to occur with some observers and with some behaviors (Ciminero, Graham, & Jackson, 1977; Hay, Nelson, & Hay, 1977, 1980).

Unfortunately, dimensions of behavior other than rate, such as variability and sequencing, have received little empirical attention. Haynes and Horn (1982) argue that variability may be particularly sensitive to reactive effects since changes in environmental stimuli often produce increased variability in animal behavior (see Sidman, 1960).

Detecting Reactivity

Several ways have been suggested for detecting reactive effects. One involves inspecting plotted data points for increasing or decreasing slope, which — if found — is attributed to habituation to observation. A major change in behavior between the first observation and subsequent sessions is also sometimes used as evidence that habituation has occurred. Of course, this type of analysis requires that a sufficient number of observation samples be collected to detect systematic changes in behavior. In addition, the assumption of habituation assumes that behavior changes in a way that makes it increasingly *less* reactive over time — an assumption that may not be valid and cannot be tested without comparing data collected under observer-absent and observer-present conditions.

Thus, a more powerful way of detecting reactivity is to compare behavior in conditions where subjects are and are not aware of being observed, with differences in behavior between the two conditions assumed to indicate reactivity. This generally is accomplished by collecting data throughout a study by some inconspicuous means (e.g., a permanent camera built into the environment or observers placed behind a one-way mirror), while leading subjects to believe that observations will take place only at certain times, by either (a) informing subjects that data are or are not being collected, or (b) having observers enter and leave the observation setting to create observer-present and observer-absent conditions (see Baum et al., 1979, and Hayes & Horn, 1982, for reviews of these studies). Collecting these kinds of overt and covert observations over extended time periods permits assessment of habituation by examining the extent to which behavior in observer-absent conditions approximates that in observer-present circumstances over time.

Despite the utility of this method of assessing reactive effects, it presents both practical and ethical problems. In the practical domain, a means of surreptitious observation must be available throughout the study. It is important that the medium used to collect information (e.g., video camera, one-way mirror, etc.) be consistent throughout the study, since observations of the same events with different media may yield different data (Kent, O'Leary, Dietz, & Diament, 1979). From an ethical point of view, comparisons of observation during subject-aware versus subject-unaware intervals entail risks to human subjects of privacy invasion, absence of informed consent, and negative reactions to deception. While these difficulties can be dealt with technically and ethically (e.g., Christensen &

Hazzard, 1983), they certainly must be addressed by researchers who choose to evaluate their procedures in this manner.

A final way to evaluate the degree to which observation affects the behavior of target subjects involves asking them or others in their environment who have first-hand experience with the target individual's preobservation rates of behavior (e.g., parents, spouses, teachers, etc.) whether and how the subject's behavior had changed during observations. In the absence of other data, such subjective reports can yield useful information about potential reactive effects, although they should be interpreted cautiously and not be taken automatically at face value as valid indicators of actual behavior. It is worth noting that the process of soliciting information from target subjects about their observed behavior may itself present demand characteristics that alter future behavior. A researcher should be aware of this source of reactivity so that the content and timing of probe questions can be designed to avoid influencing subsequent observation sessions.

Precautions Against Reactivity

Practically speaking, demonstrating the complete absence of subject reactivity may be technically impossible. However, even though evidence on the effects of reactivity is still tentative, several authors (Haynes & Horn, 1982; Haynes & Wilson, 1979; Hartmann & Wood, 1982; Kent & Foster, 1977) have proposed methods designed to reduce the likelihood of reactive effects. One set of recommendations is aimed at approximating the subject's everyday environment by minimizing the intrusiveness of extraneous cues that signal the collection of data. Using observation procedures where observers and equipment are invisible obviously minimizes their visual impact. When covert observation is possible, subjects can be asked to agree to being observed without being told specifically when observations will occur; thus they know they will be observed but are unaware of the exact times of observations. Using participant observers also minimizes changes in the subjects' environment, although — as previously stated — participant observation can have reactive effects on both the observers and the observed. When outside observers must be present to collect data, their obtrusiveness can be minimized by having them dress in a manner that does not call attention to their presence, asking them to avoid subject–observer interaction and eye contact during observation sessions and placing them where they can see and hear but are not in the way of ongoing activities.

Other recommendations for dealing with possible reactivity involve permitting subjects to get used to observation procedures by extending the number of observations until data are stable and/or discarding data from early observations. Instructing subjects to act naturally, providing an acceptable and nonthreatening rationale for the observation, and assuring subjects that their performance during observation sessions will have no important consequences for them may minimize possible demand characteristics of direct observation. As Foster and Cone (1986) have noted, however, these suggestions have more intuitive appeal than empirical backing at this point.

Sources of Observer Error

Observer errors are potentially significant sources of distortion in direct observation data. When error is idiosyncratic, it can often be detected through lowered interobserver agreement coefficients. A more dangerous situation occurs when all observers are similarly affected by a biasing factor, and interobserver agreement figures remain high while data become increasingly distorted. One source of error, observer drift, has already been described. Other sources of observer error include information, instructions, and feedback provided by experimenters to observers; observer cheating; and characteristics of the behavior being observed, such as complexity, predictability, rate, and context.

Interactions Between the Experimenter and Observers

Concern that observers who are explicitly told experimental hypotheses might produce biased data stems from the work of Rosenthal and colleagues (Rosenthal & Fode, 1963; Rosenthal & Jacobsen, 1966). These studies found that experimenters informed of experimental hypotheses produced data that were biased in the direction of those hypotheses. Similarly, two other early studies (Kass & O'Leary, 1970; Scott, Burton, & Yarrow, 1967) found that information about predicted experimental outcomes produced biased observational data.

Unfortunately, these studies were beset by methodological problems (see Kent & Foster, 1977, for a review). Later attempts to replicate these results with well-trained observers and improved methodologies failed to find evidence of observer bias. Skindrud manipulated information about subjects that was provided to groups of observers who recorded family interactions in videotapes (Skindrud, 1972) and in home settings (Skindrud, 1973). In both studies, all groups showed good agreement with criterion protocols, and there was no evidence of observer bias. Similarly, Kent et al. (1974) varied treatment outcome expectancy across two groups of trained observers who recorded videotaped interactions that actually showed no change in target behavior from baseline to treatment. Their findings showed that even though observers produced biased global ratings on a postexperimental questionnaire, observers' actual recordings did not show evidence of bias. Shuller and McNamara (1976, 1980) later replicated these results.

Despite these encouraging findings, information about expected outcomes coupled with contingent positive and negative experimenter feedback to observers when data match and do not match expectations can produce data aligned with the expected experimental outcome (O'Leary, Kent, & Kanowitz, 1975). Thus, although feedback regarding observer conduct, accuracy, and interobserver agreement should be provided during a study, researchers should carefully refrain from commenting on the findings of the study in the presence of observers while the investigation is in progress.

Although these studies indicated that trained observers using systematic observation codes did not produce biased data in the absence of feedback despite differing expectations, global ratings were influenced by expectations. Subsequent studies examining the effects of information related to experimental hypotheses on global ratings based on videotaped behavior samples have shown mixed findings. Ernst, Bornstein, and Weltzien (1984) found that ratings of overall effectiveness and of specific behaviors were significantly higher for a group of raters told that videotaped individuals had participated in a speech anxiety treatment program than for a group of raters given no information. In contrast, Wessberg, Coyne, Curran, Monti, and Corriveau (1982) found that ratings of anxiety and social skills based on videotapes of role-played performance did not differ for groups of raters told that some subjects were "competent" and "incompetent," as compared to groups of raters who received no information. Interestingly, the Wessberg et al. (1982) study differed from all others that found biases in ratings in that it was the only study to include extensive observer training (8 hours) for use of the rating scale, suggesting that training in how to use the scale consistently may help overcome the potential effects of information about predicted results.

Besides extended training, writers have suggested a variety of precautions to minimize the possibility of biases due to implicit or explicit expectations. These include the use of (a) precise, low-inference operational definitions (Haynes, 1978); (b) stringent training criteria (Redfield & Paul, 1976); (c) professional or expert observers (Rosenthal, 1966); (d) video- or audio-taped behaviors for coding by observers blind to experimental hypotheses and the experimental conditions under which the taped interactions occurred (Johnson & Bolstad, 1973); and (e) a newly-trained and uninformed observer to serve as a "calibrator" against which to evaluate knowledge of experimental hypotheses or expectations of the usual observer (Skindrud, 1973).

Cheating

In addition to observer biases and drift, another source of error which can inflate levels of interobserver agreement artificially and lead to inaccurate data is cheating (Kent & Foster, 1977; O'Leary & Kent, 1973). Cheating may be intentional or unintentional and may include copying, discussing data, recording what the observer's partner does, changing data entries, and miscalculating interobserver agreement coefficients. O'Leary and Kent (1973) found a systematic tendency for agreement levels to be higher when observers were left unsupervised than when the experimenter was in the room with observers as they calculated their agreement. Kent, Kanowitz, O'Leary, and Cheiken (1977) and Boykin and Nelson (1981) similarly reported that mathematical errors made by the observers inflated their actual agreement when observers calculated their own agreement scores.

Precautions against observer cheating include using random and unannounced reliability spot-checks, collecting data forms immediately following observation sessions, restricting data analysis and reliability calculations to individuals who did not collect the data, having observers stand so that they cannot see when and what the other observers record, and providing raters with pens rather than pencils so that alterations may be evaluated as an indirect measure of cheating (Hartmann & Wood, 1982). In addition, trainers should describe specific forms of cheating and discuss the ramifications of these behaviors for data quality with the observers. Providing retraining options when interobserver agreement drops rather than providing more adverse consequences or automatically dismissing an observer may reduce the incentive to falsify observation records intentionally.

Characteristics of Behaviors and Settings

Early investigations of the general issue of the types of circumstances that produced observer errors were prompted by the hypothesis that frequent, rapid shifts in behavior should be more difficult to observe than behavior that changes at a slower pace. Results supporting this hypothesis came from studies showing that greater levels of behavior complexity (computer based on the diversity of discriminations made by observers using multicategory coding systems) were negatively related to interobserver agreement (House & House, 1979; Jones, Reid, & Patterson, 1975). Unfortunately, increases in complexity in these studies were confounded with increases in use of categories of behavior that occur very infrequently and tend to be recorded unreliably (House & House, 1979). Thus, whether increasingly complex situations or the occurrence of infrequent, unreliable behavior categories accounted for lower interobserver agreement cannot be determined (Foster & Cone, 1986). Kapust and Nelson (1984), however, provided less confounded data relevant to this issue by manipulating the rate of behavior displayed by an experimental confederate, finding that low rates of the behavior observed (touching metal touchplates) yielded higher accuracy and interobserver agreement figures than higher rates of the behavior.

Variations in contextual features of the observation environment can also influence what observers record. Cues from the environment that have repeatedly occurred with the behavior in the past or are assumed to covary with the behavior can lead to errors in criterion scoring and to decreased interobserver agreement figures, with some observers recording behavior that would be expected given the cues despite the fact that the behavior actually does not occur (Harris & Ciminero, 1978; Mash & Makohoniuk, 1975).

A second environmental variation that has been examined involves the contrast between the behavior of the target individual and that of others in the setting. Cunningham and Tharp (1981) varied the off-task behavior of two boys interacting with a third (target) boy. Observations of the on-task behavior of the target boy using a time-sampling procedure showed no effects as a function of variations in off-task behavior of the nontarget boys and only minor deviations from criterion observations. Global estimates of the percentage of time spent on task were much more susceptible to biasing effects of the nontarget boys' behavior, in some cases deviating substantially from criterion observations. Klonoff, Revis, and Tice (1985) reported similar findings for global ratings of anxiety, with ratings of videotapes of one individual showing systematic bias as a function of the behavior of a second individual shown just previously on a separate videotape. Klonoff et al. (1985) also found that stimulus videotapes arranged to display ascending rates of anxiety-related behaviors generated generally higher ratings of anxiety than randomly ordered videotapes, which in turn resulted in significantly higher ratings than videotapes arranged to show descending rates of anxious behavior.

Together these studies imply that researchers using global ratings should be particularly sensitive to methodological variations that can bias their ratings. In addition, since variations in behavior rates and complexity may alter observer performance, observers should be trained to criterion levels of interobserver agreement across the ranges of complexity, behavior rates, and situational variability they might encounter, thus systematic and/or idiosyncratic biases can be detected and corrected before data collection begins.

EVALUATING DATA QUALITY

Collecting Interobserver Agreement Data

The most common way of demonstrating the acceptability of observational data is to report interobserver agreement, assessed by arranging for two or more observers to conduct observations on the same individual(s) simultaneously. Unfortunately, certain arrangements for checking interobserver agreement appear to produce misleadingly high agreement figures, resulting in the conclusion that data quality is acceptable when in fact it is not. It is even more unfortunate that these conditions are those easiest to arrange — assessment of an announced agreement check with a known assessor under conditions unsupervised by the experimenter.

Several studies compared interobserver agreement assessed with versus without the observers knowing an agreement check would take place; they consistently showed that agreement was higher when checks were announced (Kent et al., 1977; Romanczyk et al., 1973; Taplin & Reid, 1973). Knowledge of the person performing the assessment further increased interobserver agreement scores, particularly if the agreement checkers and observers had worked together previously (Kent et al., 1977) and if in these previous encounters different checkers had used the observation categories in different ways (Romanczyk et al., 1973). The magnitude of these effects was sometimes large, with agreement figures occasionally being as many as 70 percentage points higher during overt agreement assessment than when an agreement check was not announced (Romanczyk et al., 1973).

Because of these findings, researchers have offered numerous suggestions for making conditions similar when agreement is assessed and when it is not. Cone and Foster (1982) suggest that, when data are stored on videotape or audiotape, experimenters can inform observers that agreement will be checked, but observers will not be told which tapes will be assessed or by whom. Tapes can then be scored independently, with a percentage assigned to two or more observers. With live observations, covert agreement checks may be more difficult to arrange but can be engineered by always using two observers who generally observe different people and/or behaviors during part of the session but occasionally conduct overlapping observations. The two observers would not be informed of when they will observe simultaneously. Alternatively, interobserver agreement can be continuously assessed.

In scheduling interobserver agreement checks, agreement should be sampled during the full range of conditions encountered by observers. This both permits the investigator to demonstrate that interobserver agreement figures are high across experimental conditions and to locate possible sources of lowered agreement while the study is progressing. Thus, agreement should be assessed periodically during each experimental condition, for each subject, in all settings where observations take place, for a variety of observer pairs, etcetera. At a minimum, the investigator should compute and report interobserver agreement for each experimental group, condition, and phase to be used in statistical analyses to ensure that experimental conditions are not confounded with observational measures differing markedly in reliability. Further, interobserver agreement should be computed for each category (or combination of categories) that will be analyzed, with the goal of ensuring that data quality is examined at the level of statistical analysis and interpretation. Thus, an investigator who compares the praise and criticism rates of distressed and nondistressed husbands and wives discussing high-

and low-conflict issues would compute and report 16 agreement figures, representing agreement on praise and criticism in each of the 8 cells of the design.

Clearly, then, a sufficient amount of interobserver agreement data should be obtained to ensure a representative sample for each experimental condition. Although no firmly established rule exists, collecting agreement on 20% of the data as a minimum could be used as a working guideline, with larger numbers of agreement checks being required if circumstances changed radically during the course of a study or if a particular phase were very brief.

Statistics for Computing Agreement

Interobserver agreement statistics estimate numerically the extent to which two or more observers using the same observation system to observe the same individual at the same time agree that the individual behaved in a particular fashion. Two general sorts of interobserver agreement statistics are available: those based on comparisons of recordings within intervals and those based on session totals. Here we summarize the most widely used of these statistics. Berk (1979); Hartmann (1982); and A.E. House, B.J. House, and Campbell (1981) discuss many others, and formulae for many common statistics are provided by Hartmann (1982) and Foster and Cone (1986).

Interval-Based Statistics

Interval-based statistics rely on comparisons of observers' records on an interval-by-interval basis. Within each interval, these records may either agree that a behavior occurred, agree that it failed to occur, or be discrepant (i.e., one observer indicates that the behavior occurred, the other does not).

The most common agreement statistic, usually called *percent agreement*, involves computing the number of agreements on occurrence and on nonoccurrence and dividing by the number of agreements plus disagreements. This statistic is simple to understand and quick to compute. It is particularly useful during observer training because intervals where disagreements occur can be easily spotted and discussed. Percent agreement, however, is grossly influenced by chance agreement when behaviors occur very frequently or very infrequently. That is, when behavior occurs often, its occurrence is more likely to be recorded by two observers solely as a function of chance than when occurrence is occasional; when behavior occurs infrequently, agreement on nonoccurrence will be similarly inflated. Therefore, modifications of the percent-agreement formula compute agreements based only on occurrence when a behavior is very infrequent (thus ignoring agreements on nonoccurrence, which are inflated by chance). A variation computes agreements based only on nonoccurrence when a behavior occurs often. Neither of these methods eliminates the influence of chance agreement when a behavior fluctuates in frequency, however, as it could over the course of a treatment program. Further, multicategory observation systems often assess both infrequent and frequent behaviors, and calculating different interobserver agreement statistics for different categories is cumbersome and conceptually unappealing.

Perhaps because of these problems, statistics that adjust for chance agreement have been developed and are applicable across a range of observation circumstances. Probably the most widely used statistic that takes change agreement between two observers into account is *kappa* (Cohen, 1960). In essence, the formula for kappa subtracts a numerical estimate of chance agreement from the numerator and denominator of the occurrence–nonoccurrence agreement formula described for percent agreement. Thus, the occurrence–nonoccurrence agreement figure represents the upper limit of the value of kappa. Despite its conceptual appeal, kappa has several drawbacks. First, it is impossible to calculate when both observers agree perfectly that a behavior always occurred or never occurred. Second, Brennan and Prediger (1981) argue that the formula used to compute chance agreement for kappa is overly stringent because its computational procedures are based on the assumption that the experimenter knows the degree of agreement and disagreement between observers in advance (i.e., that these values are fixed rather than free to vary) — an assumption that is clearly not true with observational data. Although different methods of computing chance agreement are available (see Hartmann, 1977; Brennan & Prediger, 1981), little discussion of this issue has found its way into the direct observation literature.

Recommendations for the minimum level of acceptable values of interobserver agreement scores vary with the computational method used. For percent agreement, recommended lower limits range from .80–.90; for kappa and other chance-corrected statistics, from .60–.75 (Hartmann, 1982). When interobserver agreement data are collected under circumstances known to inflate agreement, minimum acceptable agreement levels should be increased to compensate for the probable effects of these circumstances. Similarly, Hartmann (1982) points out that agreement scores should always be interpreted in light of an overriding research issue — the ability of the data to detect experimental effects. Examining this issue requires evaluation of the experimental design, statistics employed, number of subjects, etcetera, as well as consideration of interobserver agreement levels.

Session-Based Statistics

When data are scored such that interval-by-interval comparisons are impossible (e.g., frequency counts, duration recording, qualitative ratings of behavior without indication of the time the recording occurred, etc.), measures of interobserver agreement based on summaries for observation sessions, or session-based statistics, are required. The simplest of these bears a close resemblance to percent agreement and involves dividing the smaller session total by the larger. Like percent agreement, this measure can be inflated by chance agreement (Hartmann, 1977).

Other session-based measures are correlational in nature. The *Pearson product-moment correlation* (*r*), familiar to most, is one such measure. Its advantages lie in its familiarity, its ties to psychometric theory, and its relatively easy calculation. A major disadvantage involves its insensitivity to consistent bias across observers. For example, a consistent difference of +2 between the observations of two observers (which otherwise showed identically rank-ordered scores) would still yield a perfect correlation.

Other correlational statistics are based on generalizability analyses. *Generalizability analyses* use analysis of variance models to apportion variance due to various aspects of the procedure (called facets). When observers are included as one facet of the analysis, the relative variance accounted for by observer differences, both alone and in combination with other facets, such as settings, observation sessions, persons observed, etcetera, can be estimated.

One asset of this approach is that it allows the investigator to examine more than just interobserver agreement. For example, Hartmann and Wood (1982) suggest that generalizability analyses be used for estimating how many sessions are necessary to obtain stable estimates of behavior. The difficulty with such studies is that they require fairly large samples of data simultaneously collected by both observers before stable correlations can be computed. This in turn means that a substantial amount of data may be wasted if interobserver agreement turns out to be unacceptably low. Further, no correlation-based statistics allow the investigator to locate precisely the instances on which observers disagree. Thus, for studies with tight time schedules, even if session scores will be used for formal presentation of interobserver agreement, it is wise to build time markers into the observation system so that simpler, more immediate computations of interval-based interobserver agreement statistics can be calculated to check interobserver agreement on an ongoing basis and to locate sources of disagreement for discussion during training.

Limits of Interobserver Agreement

Interobserver agreement is only one way of assessing data quality. In fact, as already indicated, it is possible for interobserver agreement figures to be high when the observation system is being used neither consistently nor accurately. Although accuracy can be estimated by establishing criteria against which the performance of observers can be compared, and consistency can be demonstrated by having the same observer code the same stimulus material (e.g., videotapes) at different points in time, these properties of observation systems are rarely examined during investigations. Even less often do investigators provide evidence that they have sampled sufficient durations and numbers of observation sessions despite the importance of adequate sampling for establishing representative estimates of behavior (Hartmann & Wood, 1982). Finally, it goes without saying that interobserver agreement says nothing about the validity of an observation system. Thus, acceptable interobserver agreement should be seen only as one of several indicators of data quality — not as the sole method for determining that observational data can be trusted.

USING DIRECT OBSERVATION FOR CLINICAL PURPOSES

To this point, we have described considerations involved in designing and using direct-observation systems without considering the purpose of the observations. Yet clinical and research purposes vary, and these variations influence the way direct observation will be used. The goal of most research is to develop generalizable knowledge based on data acceptable to the scientific community. Thus, direct observation is generally used in research to describe the behavior of individuals or groups, how that behavior changes over time (e.g., as a function of treatment or experimental manipulations), and/or how the behavior covaries with environmental characteristics. Reliability, accuracy, and validity are of paramount importance. In contrast, in clinical settings, the major goals of service providers are to determine the difficulties experienced by the individual client and to effect some change in those difficulties. This in turn requires identifying target behaviors, hypothesizing controlling variables, selecting a treatment strategy, and monitoring the effects of treatment (Nelson & Hayes, 1981). Direct observation is only one of several procedures (e.g., interviews, questionnaires, self-observation, etc.) relevant to these endeavors. The utility of direct observation data (i.e., its information yield measured against the cost of the procedure) is of primary concern: Accurate, valid, reliable systems that yield little useful data will not be used, regardless of their sophistication.[1]

The resources generally available in clinical and research settings also

---

[1]The utility of direct-observation data will generally (but not always) depend on their ability to reflect accurately and reliability variations in the behavior of interest, and thus accuracy, reliability, and validity are ordinarily prerequisites for useful data. Exceptions occur when the clinician finds that data are biased, and in exploring why this has occurred, develops new hypotheses about characteristic ways the client reacts to the environment.

differ. While researchers can schedule time for code development into their research plans, clinicians confronted with a client may need to develop an observation system that fits the client's unique problems on the spot. Time to try out, revise, and validate an observation system may be a luxury to the clinician whose job is to help the client as quickly as possible. These problems are compounded for the clinician who sees clients with a variety of problems and would frequently need to develop new observation systems. Nonparticipant observers, audiovisual equipment, etcetera, may also be in short supply in applied settings. Unfortunately, the resources that are likely to be absent in service delivery settings — time, personnel, equipment — are precisely those that are recommended for developing an accurate, bias-free observation system. Taken in this light, Wade, Baker, and Hartmann's (1979) findings — that 43.8% of the 257 behaviorally oriented professionals surveyed reported that a major disadvantage of behavioral assessment procedures is their impracticality in applied settings — are not surprising.

It would be easy to reject direct observation as a clinical assessment tool on the grounds that good observation systems are either impossible or too impractical to use in service delivery settings. It may in fact be true that the kinds of multicategory interval and sequential recording observation systems often used in academic settings are not widely applicable to practicing clinicians because of their nomothetic focus and resource requirements. Nonetheless, direct observation and its cousin, self-observation, still offer the best ways to assess overt behavior directly. To discard direct observation in favor of more indirect methods of collecting information about a client's behavior is clearly premature.

Using direct observation in clinical settings therefore requires a translation of research-based coding systems and recommendations for practical solutions that permit direct observation to be fitted into service delivery practices. Unfortunately, little attention has been directed toward (a) evaluating direct observation under conditions typically encountered by the practitioner, (b) developing practical direct-observation procedures, and (c) providing guidelines for interpreting direct-observation data when observations are one of several sources of sometimes conflicting information. Here we offer suggestions for making direct observation more practical, recognizing that most of these suggestions require future empirical scrutiny. We then speculate on how a clinician might interpret information based on direct observation, and we estimate the quality of those observations.

Making Direct Observation Practical

Direct-observation procedures need not be time-consuming nor need they require small armies of data-collection personnel. The following six suggestions are aimed at making direct-observation data both easier to collect and more useful.

1. Arrange a job setting to make observation easier. Decreasing the response cost associated with direct observation is one way to increase the likelihood that it will be used. Frequently this can involve rearranging one's schedule, work requirements, and physical environment to facilitate collecting observational data. For example, systematically using the first portion of a session to review a client's observational data provides time to examine the data as well as reinforces the client's compliance with data collection. The clinician may also want to schedule specific times for processing direct-observation data (e.g., to review audiotapes or videotapes of client behavior). When service delivery requirements in a setting leave no time for this, negotiations with a supervisor to reduce other responsibilities to create time for systematically processing assessment information may be in order. Alternatively, it may be possible to arrange for "therapy aides" to act as observers. People already employed in the setting are one source of assistance, as are students, trainees, and volunteers. In using this strategy, though, it is important both to select an individual who appreciates and is committed to the goal of obtaining information systematically, and to build in time to train, supervise, and recalibrate the individual's performance.

The physical environment can also be arranged to facilitate use of observation. Keeping all-purpose ABC charts and recording forms in a desk drawer assures that these will be ready when they are needed to send home with a client. Having a tape recorder and unused audiotapes handy allows the clinician to tape sessions, role-played performance, and samples of interaction (e.g., in couples therapy). Setting up a room appropriate for analog observations facilitates on-the-spot decisions to observe client behavior, as, for example, when a playroom is available for observing parent–child interaction.

2. Systematically observe in-session behavior. For many target problems in outpatient settings, the client's behavior in the session provides a rich source of direct-observation data. The behavior of clients with interpersonal difficulties and of families and couples with interaction problems may be readily observed and systematically noted during the session on a continuous or time-sampled basis (e.g., first, middle, and last 10 minutes). Alternatively, sessions can be audiotaped or videotaped and later systematically scored. Observation of in-session interaction is also an excellent way of pinpointing rapport or session-management difficulties. Interestingly, very little empirical attention has been directed toward how to observe behavior systematically in session, with the notable exception of Chamberlain, Patterson, Reid, Kavanagh, and Forgatch's (1984) work on assessing resistant client behavior.

3. Integrate direct observation with other assessment methods. Especially during the initial assessment phase of intervention, the therapist's major goals are to distill formulations of the client's problems and to design treatment plans based on a wide variety of data from multiple sources collected via multiple methods. Thus, creating situations that allow the clinician both to observe the client's behavior and to sample other sorts of information increase the information yield associated with the assessment endeavor. Observing client behavior in sessions while listening to self-report during an interview is one way to collect information from two sources simultaneously. Another is to videotape or audiotape the client's behavior in an analog situation, then review the tape while instructing the client to reconstruct his or her thoughts and feelings during the situation (see Gottman & Levenson, 1985, for an example). Finally, it is possible to check a client's self-report against the clinician's direct observation of the same events to see how well the client's perceptions of what happened correspond with direct observation. If similar checks under various conditions show good correspondence, then the clinician can have a certain amount of faith in the client's verbal portrayal of events.

4. Design the observational system to suit its purpose. To have maximum utility, a direct observation strategy should be used with a specific purpose in mind. If the information is to be used to specify targets for intervention, coding the occurrence of many different behaviors may be useful. Thus, for example, after the initial session, parents might be asked to record any behavior their child displayed that made them angry, or a clinician might listen to a distressed couple's discussion and screen it for a variety of positive and negative communication habits. If observation information is to be used in formulating hypotheses about controlling variables, the system need not assess a variety of responses but should include some way of examining the antecedents and consequences of the specific target(s) that have been selected. If observations are used to demonstrate the acquisition of new skills, a system that directly assesses those skills is needed, and observations in analog settings can be employed. If the purpose is to assess performance in the natural environment, however, observations of the target behavior conducted in vivo — either continuously or periodically — are preferable.

Of course, direct observation may not be the assessment method of choice for all of these purposes, or even for all clients. If cognitions are the target of intervention, for example, self-observation and self-report may be preferable to direct observation. It is important to avoid the automatic assumption that direct observation is preferable to other assessment procedures (cf. Jacobson, 1985a, 1985b). Rather, the purpose of gathering information, the nature of the phenomenon to be assessed, and the directness of the assessment method should be jointly considered in selecting an assessment procedure.

5. Borrow from preexisting systems when relevant. A number of

BA—F

multicategory observation systems have been developed for research purposes. While many of these are too complex to be used without extensive resources, the behavior categories employed in these codes can be adapted when relevant for specific clients. Furthermore, various research studies specifying how specific categories differ in clinic and nonclinic populations provides clues as to the kinds of behaviors the clinician can expect to see, at least in a certain percentage of cases. In borrowing from the published literature, however, it is important to avoid the tendency to ignore idiosyncratic client behaviors simply because no published study has described them. Similarly, the client's concerns should not be translated into irrelevant target behaviors simply because the clinician knows how to observe those behaviors (see Kazdin, 1985).

6. *Use participant observers.* Despite research indicating that participant observers may not always agree with nonparticipant observers (Floyd & Markman, 1983) or with other participant observers (e.g., Christensen, Sullaway, & King, 1983; Jacobson & Moore, 1981), participant observers often are the best way of gathering observational data in the natural environment. Since interobserver agreement among couples observing whether spouse behaviors did or did not occur each day correlates positively with ratings of the specificity and objectivity of the behaviors being rated (Christensen et al., 1983; Jacobson & Moore, 1981), presumably data quality can be enhanced by working out with the client specific working definitions of what will and will not be observed.

Compliance can be a problem with participant-observation data, particularly over lengthy time periods. Shelton and Levy (1981) offer several suggestions for increasing therapeutic compliance that are relevant here. These include explaining the task clearly, getting a commitment to comply, training the client in how to perform the task, reducing the response cost associated with the task, monitoring whether the task is being completed, and cueing and reinforcing compliance. In our experience, and in line with these guidelines, it is especially important to design a task that is within the client's capabilities. An uneducated client told to time-sample 10 behaviors on a daily basis will quickly find the observations too difficult. It may also be helpful, especially during initial stages of therapy, to telephone the client during the week to obtain the data, thus providing both a prompt for data collection and an opportunity to reinforce compliance. Finally, direct observation can sometimes become an integral part of treatment, as when a parent records each chore a child completes as part of a reinforcement program. When noncompliance with observation persists despite attempts to use these strategies, the clinician must decide whether to press the issue or to rely on a more indirect method (e.g., self-report) for obtaining the required information.

Estimating the Quality of Direct Observation in Clinical Settings

Just as limited resources hamper the use of direct observation, they also make the common procedures for assessing and protecting the quality of direct-observation data more difficult to implement. Secondary observers may not be readily available to check interobserver agreement; accuracy assessments may be impossible. Reactivity of both participant observers and those observed may be difficult to assess. Both clinicians and clients are obviously aware of and have a vested interest in the outcome of treatment, and a clinician ordinarily praises a client for behaviors that lead to improved observational data. These conditions recall O'Leary et al.'s (1975) findings that feedback for data conforming to experimental hypotheses led nonparticipant observers to record data that reflected change when no change had actually occurred, implying that conditions promoting biased observations by clients may be present frequently in the therapy environment.

Thus, the quality of direct-observation data should not automatically be assumed to be high. The best ways to assess data quality are to approximate the ways data are used in research studies. For example, interobserver agreement can be assessed by having a second, independent observer record data without the primary observer's awareness to assess interobserver agreement. When practical difficulties make this impossible on a regular basis, interobserver agreement can be spot checked. For example, a mother who records child noncompliance at home can be asked to record the same behavior during an interaction in the clinic playroom, where the clinician can also observe and record. Observer drift can be informally assessed by asking observers to describe in more detail incidents that they did and did not record, in order to see if recording criteria seem to be shifting over time. Clinicians who double as observers can check themselves for drift by keeping previously coded audiotapes or videotapes on hand and recoding them occasionally. Reactivity can sometimes be detected by asking the client or other individuals who are familiar with the client's behavior whether they see differences in target behaviors when the client is being observed.

At a more general level, one of the best ways to assess the quality of the information obtained via direct observation is to compare the results of different methods assessing similar behaviors. Thus, a client's self-report, the report of others who know the client, and direct observation by the clinician could be compared. When information sources agree, the likelihood of accurate information is increased. When the information generated by one procedure differs from that generated by another, the source of the discrepancy can be explored. For example, if a client's behavior in analog situations shows dramatic increases in appropriate assertion but the client reports not behaving assertively on an assertiveness questionnaire, the client may be failing to perform the newly learned assertive responses in appropriate situations in daily life or may be mislabeling or misperceiving his or her behavior. Alternatively, the analog situations created for observation may not match those encountered regularly by the client. Similarly, if a mother reports that her child's behavior is much improved but her daily data show no change in the child's behavior, perhaps the mother has shifted her definition of the behavior she is recording, is indicating the presence of change to obtain praise from the therapist, or bases global statements of improvement on something other than the behaviors she is recording. Exploring why two data sources fail to converge, rather than simply designating one as inferior and dismissing it, can lead to valuable insights into the factors controlling the client's report of their own and others' behavior, which in turn can be used to interpret future information obtained from or about the client via different assessment methods.

SUMMARY

In this chapter we have surveyed with broad brush strokes various guidelines for the design and use of direct observation. In so doing, several areas emerge that warrant further conceptual and empirical scrutiny. Sampling issues warrant further attention, as do methods of observer training. Content validity issues, when inclusive (molar) coding categories are used, are important but rarely discussed, either at a conceptual or at a pragmatic level. Social validity, too, is important, particularly when a generic coding system is used to monitor change in group design studies with individuals with a variety of presenting problems. In such cases, unless the coding categories are known exemplars of the factors that brought people to therapy, change should not be assumed to reflect changes in clients' presenting problems (see Jacobson, 1985a, 1985b).

Equally important are concerns related to the clinical use of direct observation as only one aspect of the overall assessment process. In-session behavior is a good source of direct observation data, but the generalizability of this information warrants clarification. Decision rules for using direct observation as part of an overall assessment strategy would be helpful for the practicing clinician. Perhaps more important, the correspondence between direct observation and other, less direct methods of assessing behavior, such as self-report, should be examined, with the goal of developing indicators of the circumstances under which indirect methods reasonably reproduce the information that would be obtained via direct observation. Such indicators might include client characteristics and cognitive style; types, frequency, and salience of behaviors being reported; and setting characteristics of the behavior. Wahler and Afton's (1980) work on the differences in the ways disadvantaged, isolated mothers describe their children relative to the descriptions of mothers from better social and economic environments provides one example of how these efforts might proceed. In conducting comparisons between direct observation and less direct measures, it will be important to assess equivalent content with the different methods to avoid confounding content with method differences (Cone & Foster, 1982).

Investigations of practical ways a clinician might assess the quality of observational data under conditions typically encountered in service delivery could encourage critical examination of information gathered in the assessment process. If, as is likely, the biases that hamper direct observation in research also affect clinical use of direct observation, it will be important to provide cost-effective methods of reducing those biases, or at least of assessing and compensating for them when interpreting assessment information. As Barlow (1981) has indicated, attempting to devise new and creative ways to make systematic study of clinical phenomena available to the practitioner can narrow the scientist–practitioner gap and facilitate the development of new knowledge truly generalizable to the problems encountered by service delivery providers on a daily basis.

REFERENCES

Alevizos, P., DeRisi, W., Liberman, R., Eckman, T., & Callahan, E. (1978). The behavior observation instrument: A method of direct observation for program evaluation. *Journal of Applied Behavior Analysis, 11*, 243–257.

Ary, D. (1984). Mathematical explanation of error in duration recording using partial interval, whole interval, and momentary time sampling. *Behavioral Assessment, 6*, 221–228.

Baer, D. M. (1982, May). *Some recommendations for a modest reduction in the rate of current recommendations for an immodest increase in the rate of exclusive usages of rate as a dependent measure.* Paper presented at the Eighth Annual Convention of the Association for Behavior Analysis, Milwaukee.

Barlow, D. H. (1981). On the relation of clinical research to clinical practice: Current issues, new directions. *Journal of Consulting and Clinical Psychology, 49*, 147–155.

Barton, E. J., & Ascione, F. R. (1984). Direct observation. In T. H. Ollendick & M. Hersen (Eds.), *Child behavioral assessment.* New York: Pergamon.

Baum, C. G., Forehand, R., & Zegiob, L. E. (1979). A review of observer reactivity in adult–child interactions. *Journal of Behavioral Assessment, 1*, 167–178.

Bellack, A. S., Hersen, M., & Turner, S. M. (1979). Relationship of role playing and knowledge of appropriate behavior to assertion in the natural environment. *Journal of Consulting and Clinical Psychology, 47*, 670–678.

Berk, R. (1979). Generalizability of behavior observations: A clarification of interobserver agreement and interobserver reliability. *American Journal of Mental Deficiency, 83*, 460–472.

Bijou, S. W., Peterson, R. F., Harris, F. R., Allen, K. E., & Johnston, M. S. (1969). Methodology for experimental studies of young children in natural settings. *The Psychological Record, 19*, 177–210.

Boykin, R. A., & Nelson, R. O. (1981). The effects of instructions and calculation

156   *Behavioral Assessment*

procedures on observer's accuracy, agreement, and calculation correctness. *Journal of Applied Behavior Analysis, 14*, 479-489.

Brennan, R. L., & Prediger, D. J. (1981). Coefficient kappa: Some uses, misuses, and alternatives. *Educational and Psychological Measurement, 41*, 687-699.

Chamberlain, P., Patterson, G., Reid, J., Kavanagh, K., & Forgatch, M. (1984). Observation of client resistance. *Behavior Therapy, 15*, 144-155.

Christensen, A., & Hazzard, A. (1983). Reactive effects during naturalistic observations of families. *Behavioral Assessment, 5*, 349-362.

Christensen, A., Sullaway, M., & King, C. E. (1983). Systematic error in behavioral reports of dyadic interaction: Egocentric bias and content effects. *Behavioral Assessment, 5*, 129-140.

Ciminero, A. R., Graham, L. E., & Jackson, J. L. (1977). Reciprocal reactivity: Response-specific changes in independent observers. *Behavior Therapy, 8*, 48-56.

Cohen, J. (1960). A coefficient of agreement for nominal scales. *Educational and Psychological Measurement, 20*, 37-46.

Cone, J. D., & Foster, S. L. (1982). Direct observation in clinical psychology. In P. C. Kendall & J. N. Butcher (Eds.), *Handbook of research methods in clinical psychology*. New York: Wiley.

Cunningham, T. R., & Tharp, R. G. (1981). The influence of settings on accuracy and reliability of behavioral observation. *Behavioral Assessment, 3*, 67-78.

Dancer, D. D., Braukmann, C. J., Shumaker, J. B., Kirigin, K. A., Willner, A. G., & Wolf, M. M. (1978). The training and validation of behavioral observation and description skills. *Behavior Modification, 12*, 113-134.

DeMaster, B., Reid, J., & Twentyman, C. (1977). The effects of different amounts of feedback on observer's reliability. *Behavior Therapy, 8*, 317-329.

Ernst, J., Bornstein, P. H., & Weltzien, R. T. (1984). Initial considerations in subjective evaluation research: Does knowledge of treatment affect performance ratings! *Behavioral Assessment, 6*, 121-128.

Ethical principles in the conduct of research with human participants. (1982). Washington, DC: American Psychological Association.

Fabry, B. D. (1983). *Effects of definition characteristics and training procedures on the generalizability of direct observation data*. Unpublished doctoral dissertation, West Virginia University.

Floyd, F. J., & Markman, H. J. (1983). Observational biases in spouse observation: Toward a cognitive/behavioral model of marriage. *Journal of Consulting and Clinical Psychology, 51*, 450-457.

Foster, S. L., & Cone, J. D. (1980). Current issues in direct observation. *Behavioral Assessment, 2*, 313-338.

Foster, S. L., & Cone, J. D. (1986). Design and use of direct observation procedures. In A. Ciminero, K. S. Calhoun, & H. E. Adams (Eds.), *Handbook of behavioral assessment* (2nd ed.). New York: Wiley.

Frame, R. E. (1979). Interobserver agreement as a function of the number of behaviors recorded simultaneously. *The Psychological Record, 29*, 287-296.

Gaines, D. M. (1973, September). *A comparison of two observation methods: Percent vs. frequency*. Paper presented at the Annual Meeting of the American Psychological Association, Montreal.

Gelfand, D. M., & Hartmann, D. P. (1984). *Child behavior analysis and therapy* (2nd ed.). New York: Pergamon.

Gottman, J. M., & Levenson, R. W. (1985). A valid procedure for obtaining self-report of affect in marital interaction. *Journal of Consulting and Clinical Psychology, 53*, 151-160.

Green, S. B., & Alverson, L. G. (1978). *A comparison of indirect measures for long duration behaviors. Journal of Applied Behavior Analysis, 11*, 530.

Green, S. B., McCoy, J. F., Burns, K. P., & Smith, A. C. (1982). Accuracy of observation data with whole interval, partial interval, and momentary time sampling recording techniques. *Journal of Behavioral Assessment, 4*, 103–118.

Grimm, J. A., Parsons, J. A., & Bijou, S. W. (1972). A technique for minimizing subject–observer looking interactions in field settings. *Journal of Experimental Child Psychology, 14*, 500–505.

Harris, F. C., & Ciminero, A. R. (1978). The effect of witnessing consequences on the behavioral recordings of experimental observers. *Journal of Applied Behavior Analysis, 11*, 513–522.

Hartmann, D. P. (1977). Considerations in the use of interobserver reliability estimates. *Journal of Applied Behavior Analysis, 10*, 103–116.

Hartmann, D. P. (1982). Assessing the dependability of observational data. In D. P. Hartmann (Ed.), *New directions for methodology of social and behavioral science: Using observers to study behavior.* San Francisco: Jossey-Bass.

Hartmann, D. P., & Wood, D. D. (1982). Observational methods. In A. S. Bellack, M. Hersen, & A. E. Kazdin (Eds.), *International handbook of behavior modification and therapy.* New York: Plenum.

Hawkins, R. P. (1982). Developing a behavior code. In D. P. Hartmann (Ed.), *New directions for methodology of social and behavioral science: Using observers to study behavior.* San Francisco: Jossey-Bass.

Hawkins, R. P., Berler, E. S., & DeLawyer, D. D. (1984, May). *Defining units of verbal behavior for applied behavior analytic research.* Paper presented at the Tenth Annual Convention of the Association for Behavior Analysis, Nashville.

Hawkins, R. P., & Dobes, R. W. (1977). Behavioral definitions in applied behavior analysis: Explicit or implicit? In B. C. Etzel, J. M. LeBlanc, & D. M. Baer (Eds.), *New developments in behavioral research: Theory, method, and application. In honor of Sidney W. Bijou.* Hillsdale, NJ: Lawrence Erlbaum.

Hawkins, R. P., Peterson, R. F., Schweid, E., & Bijou, S. W. (1966). Behavior therapy in the home: Amelioration of problem parent-child relations with the parent in a therapeutic role. *Journal of Experimental Child Psychology, 4*, 99–107.

Hay, L. R., Nelson, R. O., & Hay, W. M. (1977). The use of teachers as behavioral observers. *Journal of Applied Behavior Analysis, 10*, 345–349.

Hay, L. R., Nelson, R. O., & Hay, W. M. (1980). Methodological problems in the use of participant observers. *Journal of Applied Behavior Analysis, 13*, 501–504.

Haynes, S. N. (1978). *Principles of behavioral assessment.* New York: Gardner Press.

Haynes, S. N., Follingstad, D. R., & Sullivan, J. (1979). Assessment of marital interaction and satisfaction. *Journal of Consulting and Clinical Psychology, 47*, 789–791.

Haynes, S. N., & Horn, W. F. (1982). Reactivity in behavioral observation: A review. *Behavioral Assessment, 4*, 369–386.

Haynes, S. N., & Wilson, C. C. (1979). *Behavioral assessment: Recent advances in concepts, methodology, and outcome.* San Francisco: Jossey-Bass.

Holm, R. A. (1978). Techniques of recording observational data. In G.P. Sackett (Ed.), *Observing behavior, vol. 2: Data collection and analysis methods.* Baltimore: University Park Press.

House, A. E., House, B. J., & Campbell, M. D. (1981). Measures of interobserver agreement: Calculation formulas and distribution effects. *Journal of Behavioral Assessment, 3*, 37–57.

House, B. J., & House, A. E. (1979). Frequency, complexity, and clarity as covariates

Of observer reliability. *Journal of Behavioral Assessment*, *1*, 149–166.

Jacobson, N. S. (1985a). The role of observational measures in behavior therapy outcome research. *Behavioral Assessment*, *7*, 297–308.

Jacobson, N. S. (1985b). Uses versus abuses of observational measures. *Behavioral Assessment*, *7*, 323–330.

Jacobson, N. S., & Moore, D. (1981). Spouses as observers of the events in their relationship. *Journal of Consulting and Clinical Psychology*, *40*, 269–277.

Johnson, M. S., & Bailey, J. S. (1977). The modification of leisure behavior in a halfway house for retarded women. *Journal of Applied Behavior Analysis*, *10*, 273–282.

Johnson, S. M., & Bolstad, O. D. (1973). Methodological issues in naturalistic observation: Some problems and solutions for field research. In L. A. Hamerlynck, L. C. Handy, & E. J. Mash (Eds.), *Behavior change: Methodology, concepts, and practice*. Champaign, IL: Research Press.

Johnston, J. M., & Pennypacker, H. S. (1980). *Strategies and tactics of human behavioral research*. Hillsdale, NJ: Lawrence Erlbaum.

Jones, R. R., Reid, J. B., & Patterson, G. R. (1975). Naturalistic observation in clinical assessment. In P. McReynolds (Ed.), *Advances in psychological assessment*. San Francisco: Jossey-Bass.

Kapust, J. A., & Nelson, R. O. (1984). Effects of the rate and spatial separation of target behaviors on observer accuracy and interobserver agreement. *Behavioral Assessment*, *6*, 253–262.

Kass, R. E., & O'Leary, K. D. (1970). *The effects of observer bias in field-experimental settings*. Paper presented at the Behavior Analysis in Education Symposium, University of Kansas.

Kazdin, A. E. (1977a). Artifact, bias, and complexity of assessment: The ABCs of reliability. *Journal of Applied Behavior Analysis*, *10*, 141–150.

Kazdin, A. E. (1977b). Assessing the clinical or applied importance of behavior change through social validation. *Behavior Modification*, *1*, 427–451.

Kazdin, A. E. (1981). Behavioral observation. In M. Hersen & A. S. Bellack (Eds.), *Behavioral assessment: A practical handbook* (2nd ed.). New York: Pergamon.

Kazdin, A. E. (1985). Selection of target behaviors: The relationship of the treatment focus to clinical dysfunction. *Behavioral Assessment*, *7*, 33–48.

Kent, R. N., & Foster, S. L. (1977). Direct observation procedures: Methodological issues in applied settings. In A. Ciminero, K. S. Calhoun, & H. E. Adams (Eds.), *Handbook of behavioral assessment* (1st ed.). New York: Wiley.

Kent, R. N., Kanowitz, J., O'Leary, K. D., & Cheiken, M. (1977). Observer reliability as a function of circumstances of assessment. *Journal of Applied Behavior Analysis*, *10*, 317–324.

Kent, R. N., O'Leary, K. D., Diament, C., & Dietz, A. (1974). Expectation biases in observational evaluation of therapeutic change. *Journal of Consulting and Clinical Psychology*, *42*, 774–780.

Kent, R. N., O'Leary, K. D., Dietz, A. & Diament, C. (1979). Comparisons of observational recordings in vivo, via mirror, and via television. *Journal of Applied Behavior Analysis*, *12*, 517–522.

Klonoff, E. A., Revis, E. S., & Tice, D. M. (1985). The effect of stimulus presentation order and observational method on ratings of performance anxiety. *Behavioral Assessment*, *7*, 185–196.

Margolin, G., Hattem, D., John, R. S., & Yost, K. (1985). Perceptual agreement between spouses and outside observers when coding themselves and a stranger dyad. *Behavioral Assessment*, *7*, 235–247.

Markle, S. M., & Tieman, P. W. (1972). Some principles of instructional design at higher cognitive levels. In U. T. Stachnik & J. Mabry (Eds.), *Control of human behavior* (Vol. 3). Glenview, IL: Scott, Foresman.

Mash, E. J., & Makohoniuk, G. (1975). The effects of prior information and behavioral predictability on observer accuracy. *Child Development, 46,* 513-519.

Mash, E. J., & McElwee, J. D. (1974). Situational effects on observer accuracy: Behavioral predictability, prior experience, and complexity of coding categories. *Child Development, 45,* 367-377.

McFall, R. M. (1977). Analogue methods in behavioral assessment: Issues and prospects. In J. D. Cone & R. P. Hawkins (Eds.), *Behavioral assessment: New directions in clinical psychology.* New York: Brunner/Mazel.

Nay, W. R. (1979). *Multimethod clinical assessment.* New York: Gardner Press.

Nelson, R. O., & Hayes, S. C. (1981). Nature of behavioral assessment. In M. Hersen & A. S. Bellack (Eds.), *Behavioral assessment: A practical handbook* (2nd ed.). New York: Pergamon.

Nelson, R. O., Kapust, J. A., & Dorsey, B. L. (1978). Minimal reactivity of overt classroom observations in student and teacher behaviors. *Behavior Therapy, 9,* 695-702.

O'Leary, K. D., & Kent, R. N. (1973). Behavior modification for social action: Research tactics and problems. In L. A. Hammerlynck, L. C. Handy, & E. J. Mash (Eds.), *Behavior change: Methodology, concepts, and practice.* Champaign, IL: Research Press.

O'Leary, K. D., Kent, R. N., & Kanowitz, J. (1975). Shaping data collection congruent with experimental hypotheses. *Journal of Applied Behavior Analysis, 8,* 463-469.

Powell, J., Martindale, A., & Kulp, S. (1975). An evaluation of time-sample measures of behavior. *Journal of Applied Behavior Analysis, 8,* 463-469.

Powell, J., Martindale, A., Kulp, S., Martindale, A., & Bauman, R. (1977). Taking a closer look: Time sampling and measurement error. *Journal of Applied Behavior Analysis, 10,* 325-332.

Reid, J. B. (1982). Observer training in naturalistic research. In D. P. Hartmann (Ed.), *New directions for methodology of social and behavioral science: Using observers to study behavior.* San Francisco: Jossey-Bass.

Reid, J. B., & DeMaster, B. (1972). The efficacy of the spot-check procedures in maintaining the reliability of data collected by observers in quasi-natural settings. Two pilot studies. *ORI Research Bulletin, 12.*

Reisinger, J. J., & Ora, J. P. (1977). Parent–child and home interaction during toddler management training. *Behavior Therapy, 8,* 771-786.

Redfield, J. P., & Paul, G. L. (1976). Bias in behavioral observation as a function of observer familiarity with subjects and typicality of behavior. *Journal of Consulting and Clinical Psychology, 44,* 156.

Robinson, E. A., & Price, M. G. (1980). Pleasurable behavior in marital interaction: An observational study. *Journal of Consulting and Clinical Psychology, 48,* 117-118.

Rogers-Warren, A., & Warren, S. F. (1977). *Ecological perspectives in behavior analysis.* Baltimore: University Park Press.

Rojahn, J., & Wool, R. (1979). Inter- and intra-observer agreement as a function of explicit behavior definitions in direct observation. *Behavioral Analysis and Modification, 3,* 211-228.

Romancyzk, R. G., Kent, R. N., Diament, C., & O'Leary, K. D. (1973). Measuring the reliability of observational data: A reactive process. *Journal of Applied*

Behavior Analysis, *6*, 175–186.

Rosenthal, R. (1966). *Experimenter effects in behavior research.* New York: Appleton-Century-Crofts.

Rosenthal, R., & Fode, K. L. (1963). The effect of experimenter bias on the performance of the albino rat. *Behavior Science, 8,* 183–189.

Rosenthal, R., & Jacobsen, L. (1966). Teacher's expectancies: Determinants of pupils' IQ gains. *Psychological Reports, 19,* 115–118.

Scott, P. M., Burton, R. V., & Yarrow, M. R. (1967). Social reinforcement under natural conditions. *Child Development, 38,* 53–63.

Shuller, D. Y., & McNamara, J. R. (1976). Expectancy factors in behavioral observation. *Behavior Therapy, 7,* 519–527.

Shuller, D. Y., & McNamara, J. R. (1980). The use of information derived from norms and from a credible source to counter expectancy effects in behavioral assessment. *Behavioral Assessment, 2,* 183–196.

Shelton, J. L., & Levy, R. L. (1981). *Behavioral assignments and treatment compliance.* Champaign, IL: Research Press.

Sidman, M. (1960). *Tactics of scientific research.* New York: Basic Books.

Skindrud, K. (1972). *An evaluation of observer bias in experimental-field studies of social interaction.* Unpublished doctoral dissertation, University of Oregon.

Skindrud, K. (1973). Field evaluation of observer bias under covert and overt monitoring. In L. A. Hamerlynch, L. C. Handy, & E. J. Mash (Eds.), *Behavior change: Methodology, concepts, and practice.* Champaign, IL: Research Press.

Stouthamer-Loeber, M., & Peters, R. DeV. (1984). A priori classification systems of observation data: The eye of the beholder. *Behavioral Assessment, 6,* 275–282.

Sulzer-Azaroff, B., & Mayer, G. R. (1977). *Applying behavior analysis procedures with children and youth.* NY: Holt, Rinehart, & Winston.

Taplin, P. S., & Reid, J. B. (1973). Effects of instructional set and experimental influence on observer reliability. *Child Development, 44,* 547–554.

Wade, T. C., Baker, T. B., & Hartmann, D. P. (1979). Behavior therapists' self-reported views and practices. *The Behavior Therapist, 2,* 3–6.

Wahler, R. G., & Afton, A. D. (1980). Attentional processes in insular and noninsular mothers: Some differences in their summary reports about child problem behavior. *Child Behavior Therapy, 2,* 25–41.

Wessberg, H. W., Coyne, N. A., Curran, J. P., Monti, P. M., & Corriveau, D. P. (1982). Two studies of observers' ratings of social anxiety and skill. *Behavioral Assessment, 4,* 299–306.

Wildman, B. G., Erickson, M. T., & Kent, R. N. (1975). The effect of two training procedures on observer agreement and variability of behavioral ratings. *Child Development, 46,* 520–524.

Wolf, M. M. (1978). Social validation: The case for subjective measurement or how applied behavioral analysis is finding its heart. *Journal of Applied Behavior Analysis, 11,* 203–214.

Yarrow, M. R., & Waxler, C. Z. (1979). Observing interactions: A confrontation with methodology. In R. B. Cairns (Ed.), *The analysis of social interactions: Methods, issues, and illustrations.* Hillsdale, NJ: Erlbaum.

6
Cognitive Assessment

Carlton W. Parks, Jr.
Steven D. Hollon

Interest in cognitive processes within behavior therapy has been renewed over the last 2 decades. Once relegated to the status of a mentalistic epiphenomenon, consideration of cognition and information processing in both psychopathology and behavior change has again begun to receive serious attention. As Mahoney (1977) has described, it is not unscientific to entertain constructs not directly observable by others so long as those phenomena are themselves directly tied to observables.

This is what modern efforts at cognitive assessment attempt to do. As suggested by recent major texts in the area (e.g., Kendall & Hollon, 1981a; Merluzzi, Glass, & Genest, 1981), modern efforts at cognitive assessment have gone far beyond the earlier emphasis on subjective introspection by heavily trained subjects as the primary method of exploration. As Ericsson and Simon (1980) have described, a thorough understanding of the principles governing information processing and memory can be used to construct assessment procedures that yield reliable and accurate information.

Clearly, there are limits to what can be expected. As Nisbett and Wilson (1977) have demonstrated, subjects may be quite unable to accurately describe the processes they have followed to arrive at a judgment. While people can often describe the products of their information processing, the actual processes followed may need to be inferred on the basis of carefully structured assessment paradigms. In addition, some critical aspects of information processing may occur outside of conscious awareness (Shevrin & Dickman, 1980). Memory retrieval appears to be a largely reconstructive process (cf. Loftus & Loftus, 1980), meaning that each successive instance of retrieval may result in a modification of the existing trace. These basic issues and others are discussed in greater detail in a chapter in the second edition of this text (Hollon & Bemis, 1981).

Kendall and Korgeski (1979) have outlined some of the purposes to be served by cognitive assessment. In brief, these include: (a) an interest in the processes and contents of the phenomenon itself; (b) an interest in clarifying what role, if any, such cognitions play in the etiology or maintenance of psychopathology; (c) an interest in ascertaining whether those change strategies that allegedly work by means of altering cognitive content and process actually do so by changing those contents and processes; and (d) an interest in determining whether those procedures seen as involving the manipulation of cognition are adequately implemented. Thus, accurate cognitive assessment is necessary whether one is interested in cognition as a phenomenon in and of itself (dependent variable), as a mechanism mediating change in other phenomena of interest (intervening variable), or as a manipulation check for an experimental or clinical intervention (independent variable). In any of these cases, interest may extend to either basic psychopathological research or treatment outcome research. As shall be described, the purposes for which assessment is intended may help guide the selection of the means.

In this chapter we first provide an overview of the kinds of methods developed to assess cognitive content, structure, and process; the field is probably better developed in the first respect than in the latter two, but some encouraging new methodologies are evident. We then provide an overview of the major instruments and systems in those areas (depression, anxiety disorders, assertion problems, and behavioral medicine) that have received the greatest attention in the empirical literature. Again, different problem areas have received different degrees of attention, with depression clearly having received the greatest. We begin with a description of the various approaches to cognitive assessment.

HOW DO WE ASSESS COGNITION?

A number of methods and procedures that currently exist are designed specifically for the measurement of cognitive functioning. These approaches vary in the types of assumptions inherent in each technique. Similarly, each technique varies with respect to the advantages and disadvantages associated with its use.

Verbal Ruminative Processes

Recording Methods

Think aloud. In the "think aloud" procedure, the client is instructed to verbalize whatever comes to mind, typically for a period 5–10 minutes. Hopefully, the client will not be inclined to edit any of the ongoing cognitions which come to mind. The think-aloud method has a number of disadvantages. First, the request to think out loud continuously for a specified period of time often places clients in a rather unnatural situation. Consequently, efforts to verbalize more than the main verbal stream of thought (e.g., two or more thoughts may occur simultaneously) may result in interference with the subject's natural stream of consciousness (Klinger, 1978). It is likely that the subjects reveal only a fraction of what is going on inside since there is some delay between the thought and its verbalization. The major advantage associated with this approach involves the subject's increased ability to report the content and sequences of his or her inner mental activity, given the close temporal contiguity between occurrence and report. Pope (1978) found that think-aloud subjects shifted the content of their thoughts onto new topics about every 30 seconds, whereas subjects not participating in thinking out loud made shifts to new content topics about every 5 or 6 seconds. These findings suggest that more detailed accounts of content topics may be attainable with this approach. One assumes, with this or any other immediate self-report procedure, that topics of interest will occur during the sampling period. Given this reality, it becomes important that the circumstances surrounding the sampling of cognitions does not promote dishonesty or other forms of subject biases (Bowers, 1967).

Private speech. Several cognitive assessment procedures currently exist that resemble, in many respects, the think-aloud procedure and provide data on cognitive phenomena of interest to clinicians. The first procedure is used frequently in child research and involves the measurement of private speech. Private speech is barely audible speech that does not appear to serve a communicative function but is considered to be closely aligned with thinking (Behrend, Rosengren, & Perlmutter, 1986; Flavell, Beach, & Chinsky, 1966; Meichenbaum & Goodman, 1971; Rosengren, Behrend, & Perlmutter, 1985).

Vygotsky (1962) and Piaget (1926) have speculated about the connections between private speech and thinking. Unfortunately, there are numerous limitations associated with the collection of private speech. First, the recording of barely audible speech is difficult at best. Subjects rarely articulate and enunciate words clearly since they are not meant to serve a communicative function. More often than not, the only visual sign that private speech may be occurring is the slight movement of the lips. Unless the situation is contained, it is difficult to control the content of the verbalizations (Genest & Turk, 1981).

Roberts and Tharp (1980) documented the presence of private speech in a representative sample of school-aged children engaged in academic problem-solving tasks. Almost three-fourths of the private speech that occurred in this context preceded a motoric response. Not surprisingly, several cognitive variables (e.g., reading test scores and intelligence test scores) influenced the patterning of private speech. For example, less competent readers were more likely to have difficulty performing the academic problem-solving tasks. Likewise, they evaluated their performance, with respect to those tasks, in a more negative manner. Similarly, high-IQ children were found to increase their self-directed speech (phonemes) during the harder tasks, especially following the completion of the task. These results are suggestive of the ecological validity of private self-speech as a self-instructional strategy (for a more detailed discussion of self-referent speech see Kendall & Hollon, 1981b).

Free association. An allied methodology to the think-aloud and private-speech approaches is the free-association technique that was developed within the framework of psychoanalysis. With this approach, the patient is requested to relate out loud everything that comes to mind in the order and form which it occurs. It is assumed that the patient will be willing to openly reveal intimate details of his or her life to the psychoanalyst without editing (Kubie, 1950). Free-association technique is vulnerable to some of the same limitations and strengths as the think-aloud procedure. There is less reliance on retrospective memory than in some other methods, with the verbal data emitted during free associations being minimally affected by the patient's distortions and causal inferences (Genest & Turk, 1981).

The verbalization of thought flow has the potential of being an anxiety-provoking task. The patient may feel compelled to provide comprehensive background data in a form that an outside observer can fully comprehend. Likewise, the monitoring and expression of spontaneous thoughts can be overwhelming. This is especially the case when several thoughts occur simultaneously or the thoughts in question relate to more nearly automatic processes. Pope (1978) has documented that with normal populations, posture, solitude, and physical surroundings affect the nature of stream of thought. Other types of techniques have also been developed to assess cognitions in the natural environment.

Articulated thoughts. Davison, Robins, and Johnson (1983) proposed an in vivo cognitive assessment procedure referred to as Articulated Thoughts during Simulated Situations (ATSS). With this procedure, an audiotape of a conversation is made and subjects are instructed to pretend that they are a part of the event as it is actually occurring. A brief 15–25-second portion of the tape is played, followed by 30 seconds of silence. During this period, subjects are to report what they are thinking or feeling. This process is repeated continuously, and the subject's verbal remarks are recorded for later analysis. Davison and colleagues found that subjects' evaluative remarks varied as a function of the situation or context. Perceived personal involvement affected the way subjects thought. Subjects reported fewer rational thoughts when confronted with stressful social-evaluative situations than when dealing with situations not involving criticism of themselves (Davison, Feldman, & Osborn, 1984; Davison et al., 1983). The valence of the subjects' remarks also varied as a function of the target of the speaker's criticism (Davison et al., 1983). This procedure permits the assessment of cognitive content and process in a number of contexts. The underlying assumption inherent in this procedure is that there are relationships between people's thought patterns and the situations in which they find themselves. Thus, by structuring hypothetical situations within the clinical context, the therapist or researcher can tailor the structured situation to assess whatever thought patterns are desired.

Endorsement Methods

Endorsement methods typically involve presenting the subject with a predetermined set of items. The subject's task is to make some type of rating (e.g., frequency of occurrence, degree of belief, or how characteristic or descriptive each cognition is for the subject). Two different strategies currently exist in relation to the development of items. Items are either developed rationally, by some type of expert or judge, or items are selected empirically, on the basis of the item's ability to successfully discriminate among specific relevant groups. The endorsement method is a widely used assessment method which typically involves several different strategies. For instance, some endorsement procedures are designed to assess a client's cognitive processes while completing a specific task; others are much more general.

Such an approach lends itself nicely to the exploration of contextual influences. In addition, cognitive processing styles can also be monitored using such a strategy. However, the endorsement method is not without its limitations. Since the method relies heavily on the client's recall, questions are often raised concerning the completeness and accuracy of these recollections. Likewise, this methodology is particularly vulnerable to situational variables such as social desirability and demand characteristics (Mitchell & Richman, 1980; Richman, Mitchell, & Reznick, 1979). Implicit in the use of an endorsement method is the tacit acceptance of the notion that the cognitions under examination are within the conscious awarenes of the client.

Production Methods

In recent years there has been a marked development of in vivo self-report procedures that permit the naturalistic assessment of cognitive processes (Hollon & Kendall, 1981; Klinger, 1978). Production methods lend themselves particularly nicely to applied clinical settings, in which the need for flexibility in specification offsets the complexities raised in scoring uniformly.

Thought listing. The collection of cognitive data through the listing or verbalization of thoughts is one of the most common strategies in the cognitive assessment literature (Cacioppo & Petty, 1981). Thought samples have been obtained from subjects using several different prompts, among them: (a) thoughts elicited by the stimulus (e.g., Roberts & Maccoby, 1973), (b) general thoughts focusing on a given topic or problem (Greenwald, 1968), and (c) all thoughts that occurred while anticipating or attending to a stimulus (Petty & Cacioppo, 1977). The type of instruction given appears to affect the type of listing produced (Petty & Cacioppo, 1977). When subjects are instructed to "try to record only those ideas that you were thinking during the last few minutes," the thoughts listed tend to be either unfavorable or unrelated to the topic or problem. In contrast, when subjects are asked to list their thoughts on a particular topic or issue, they tend to list more favorable and fewer neutral or irrelevant thoughts. Similarly, the time interval for listing thought responses has proven to be an important variable, with brief intervals (i.e., 2–3 minutes) producing the most salient thoughts (Petty & Cacioppo, 1981).

Thought sampling. Yet another type of production method is called thought sampling. With this procedure, the experimenter interrupts the client at random intervals either in a laboratory setting or through some type of portable stimulus generator, such as an electronic beeper or random-tone generator (Hurlburt, 1976, 1979, 1980).

Whatever the prompting stimulus, whenever the client receives a prompt, he or she makes a record of the cognitions immediately prior to the interruption. The development of such a technique enables researchers to assess cognitive phenomena in as close a temporal proximity to their occurrence as possible. Two kinds of data collection strategies have been developed in connection with the thought-sampling procedure: descriptive data and ratings. With the descriptive procedure, the experimenter requests from clients a narrative description of their stream of thought just prior to the interruption. A narrative description typically consists of several thoughts expressed in the form of sentences. Such a procedure is particularly useful in the exploration of properties of stream of thought expressed during a thought-sampling session as well as the nature of thought dimensions. One example of the descriptive-data approach is a study by Klinger, Barta, and Glass (1981), which used a thought-sampling procedure to sample the thoughts of basketball players during a collegiate game. With the ratings procedure, subjects are asked to rate their inner experience along a number of dimensions (e.g., vividness, controllability, etc.; Klinger, 1978).

Thought-sampling data provide the client with the opportunity to reconstruct just what was occurring prior to the interruption (Klinger, 1978). Thus, the procedure draws upon retrospective memory to a limited extent, but certainly less so than is the case with questionnaires (Klinger, 1978; Sheehan, Ashton, & White, 1983). Participants report that the thought segments which occur prior to the interruption generally last about 5 seconds (Klinger, 1978). This estimate fits well within most cognitive researchers' estimates of short-term memory. Given the fleeting nature of short-term memory, it is important that the thought sampling descriptive process be performed as efficiently as possible. It is therefore often helpful for the clinician to provide clients with some prior knowledge of the variables of interest so that clients can focus their attention on those aspects of their inner experience. In a related vein, Klinger and colleagues have attempted to systematically examine the effect of motivational influences on the content of waking thought: the current concerns construct (Klinger, Barta, & Maxeiner, 1981). One outgrowth of this line of research has been the development of a line of assessment instruments designed to assess current concerns (i.e., the state of the organism between the commitment to a goal and either the attainment of the goal or the disengagement from pursuit of it; Klinger, 1977).

Event recording. The event-recording procedure, a form of self-monitoring, involves the sampling of targeted behaviors or events (see Hollon & Kendall, 1981, for a review). Within such a context, the client can be asked to perform a number of activities. For example, one task might be to attend closely to when specific events occur and to describe the thoughts occurring during the event. Another task might be to describe in detail the situation or sequence of events that occurred immediately prior to or following the event in question. Since most maladaptive thought-behavior sequences of clinical interest occur rather infrequently, it becomes even more important to collect systematic data on these low-frequency events, especially if the eventual goal is the modification of the maladaptive behaviors in question. Such an approach requires that the client has a clear understanding of the phenomena of interest. It is likely that such an intensive approach will result as an increased reactivity. Putting all these limitations aside (see Ciminero, Nelson, & Lipinski, 1977), event recording provides rich information in close temporal proximity to events in a manner that can provide insights into the thought processes surrounding maladaptive behaviors. This technique has become an integral component in the cognitive-behavioral treatment of depression (Beck, Rush, Shaw, & Emery,

1979), anxiety (Beck & Emery, 1985; Goldfried, 1979; Goldfried, Decenteceo, & Weinberg, 1974; Goldfried & Goldfried, 1980), anger (Novaco, 1979), and alcoholism (Marlatt & Gordon, 1979, 1985).

Inferential Methods

A major trend in recent years has involved the utilization of a variety of tasks drawn from basic cognitive research to study the cognitive organizations (or structures) of clinically relevant populations. Typically, this has involved studies of cognitive organizations/structures in various psychopathological groups (see, for example, Goldfried & Robins, 1982, 1983; Hollon & Kriss, 1984; Turk & Salovey, 1984a; Turk & Speers, 1983), but interesting examples also exist for studying the clinical judgment process (e.g., Cantor, Smith, French, & Mezzich, 1980; Horowitz, Post, French, Wallis, & Siegelman, 1981).

Frequently, but not invariably, these efforts are directed at uncovering various aspects of schematic processing. The concept of cognitive schema has come to play an increasingly central role in recent cognitive theorizing. First introduced by Bartlett (1932), and subsequently propounded by Neisser (1967, 1976), schemata are seen as internal associative organizations, largely acquired through prior experience, which guide the way in which an individual searches for information, the ways in which certain features are selected out of the larger display of information available in any given context, the credibility assigned to that information, the ways in which that new information is combined with prior information already stored in memory, the inferences that are generated under conditions of ambiguity and uncertainty, and subsequent information storage and retrieval (Alba & Hasher, 1983; Kihlstrom & Nasby, 1981; Neisser, 1967, 1976; Nisbett & Ross, 1980; Taylor & Crocker, 1981). Clearly, any interest in cognitive processes must include a parallel interest in more than just a specific cognition in a specific situation (although such discrete observations are important in their own right). Efforts at assessing such phenomena as personal constructs, prototypes, and — at the highest level of abstraction — schemata, reflect a desire to capture those presumed higher levels of cognitive organization.

Several of the assessment paradigms to be described below have the propensity of being rather indirect in nature; that is, the purpose of the assessment is not readily discernible from the procedure, making them less subject to response bias, dissimulation, and demand characteristics than other major approaches. Virtually all depend on inference; investigators do not ask subjects to report their operating self-schemata, personal constructs, etcetera. Rather, these cognitive structures are inferred from subjects' performances on a variety of cognitive and/or behavioral tasks, typically developed and validated in the basic cognitive psychology literature. In the following discussion, we describe several of the more prominent procedures that have been employed in the clinical literature and that may be of interest to behaviorally and cognitive-behaviorally oriented researchers and clinicians. This discussion draws heavily on a fine review by Kihlstrom and Nasby (1981), from whom we have drawn the basic categories.

Features of social categories. One major set of procedures involves efforts to identify the personal constructs by which people organize information, usually by inducing subjects to generate the features ascribed to some target category. For example, Cantor (1980a, 1980b; Cantor & Mischel, 1979) has adapted a procedure first developed by Rosch (1978) in which subjects are asked to list the attributes of a target category; common features are then used to define a consensual prototype. Such methodologies appear likely to supplement the older, more cumbersome, Role Construct Reperatory Test (Bonarius, 1965; Kelly, 1955).

Category judgments. If the essence of the features analysis involves presenting subjects with a general category and asking them to provide its attributes or features (instantations), then the essence of the category judgment approach involves presenting subjects with specific features or attributes (instantations) and then asking subjects to determine whether or not these features belong to a general category. An example of this approach has been provided by Horowitz et al. (1981). Several types of measures have been applied to such category judgments, including simple endorsement (Markus, 1977), latency (there appears to be a curvilinear relationship between prototypicality and categorization latency; Fazio, Sanbonmatsu, Powell, & Kardes, 1986; Kuiper & Derry, 1981), and the utilization of false recognition (Cantor & Mischel, 1977; Dodge & Frame, 1982; Rogers, Rogers, & Kuiper, 1979; Tsujimoto, 1978).

One of the more interesting paradigms in the psychopathology literature has involved the use of an incidental recall task following the processing of various adjectival instantations under conditions varying in depth. The basic logic behind this paradigm is that the depth of associative context at which a target instantation is processed plays a major role in determining the probability of its subsequent recall (Craik & Lockhart, 1972; Craik & Tulving, 1975). Utilization of incidental recall as the test task means that subjects are not informed that they will be asked to recall the specific instantations; this prevents any idiosyncratic rehearsal strategies from confounding the results. It also makes the paradigm unsuitable as a repeated measure, an important limitation for investigators interested in studying change over time. As applied to the study of self-schema (see, for example, Rogers, Kuiper, & Kirker, 1977), subjects are first asked to evaluate a set of words (typically adjectives) under one of several conditions: structural ("Is

the word capitalized or not capitalized?''); phonemic (''Does it sound like
_____?''); semantic (''Does it mean the same thing as . . . ?''); and self-
referent (''Does it describe you?''). Typically, the larger target word list is
divided into equally sized sublists, which are equated for important
characteristics such as word frequency, positivity-negativity, and
associativity, with different sublists counterbalanced across the conditions
noted above. After completing these tasks, subjects are asked to recall as
many of the adjectives as possible in a limited period of time: the incidental
recall component. Under the depth of processing model (Craik & Tulving,
1975), words processed affirmatively under the self-referent condition would
be expected to appear more frequently in the incidental recall. This appears to
be precisely what happens, with several investigators finding, for example,
that depressed subjects appear to have negative self-referential schema (cf.
Hammen, Marks, Mayol, & deMayo, 1985; Kuiper & Derry, 1981). Several
other groups have failed to note schematic processing in depressed groups
(Davis, 1979b; Ingram, Smith, & Brehm, 1983), but may not have employed
target stimuli appropriate to such schema (see Kuiper & Derry, 1981, for a
discussion of their ''content-specificity'' model and a critique of those
studies with negative findings).

The specific studies utilizing the depth of processing incidental recall
paradigm as applied to psychopathology and clinical judgment will be
discussed in greater detail in a later section. It is of interest to note that
virtually all of these studies are found in the depression literature. Given the
negative self-perceptions common to that disorder, this is not surprising.
However, it should be noted that nothing in the paradigm restricts its usage to
self-schema. As it stands, the paradigm appears to provide an interesting
approach not readily subject to demand characteristics or dissimulation. Its
unsuitability as a repeated measure, however, remains a major limitation.

Organization in free recall. Yet a third approach to the assessment of
cognitive schemata and personal constructs involves the detection of patterns
of subjective organization imposed on the recall of specific targets learned as
part of random stimulus patterns. Based on work by Sternberg and Tulving
(1977), this paradigm typically involves having subjects learn lists of
randomly assorted target words, then providing those subjects with multiple
trials in which they are asked to recall as many of the words as possible, with
no imposed constraints on order of recovery. Over successive trials, subjects
can be shown to cluster words in recall that are associatively connected for
them; that is, subjective organization occurs along schematic lines. Specific
use of the multiple-trial, free-recall paradigm has been made by Davis and
colleagues (Davis, 1979a; Davis & Unruh, 1981) in the area of depressive self-
schema (no such schema were evident, but this may have been an artifact of
target word choice; Kuiper & Derry, 1981).

Autobiographical memory and prediction. Yet another category involves the ascertainment of recollections regarding personal experiences. Following Bartlett (1932) and Neisser (1967, 1976), it is assumed that schemata guide the recall process, an assumption that appears to have been borne out in the empirical literature (Alba & Hasher, 1983). Recent studies by Hammen, Marks, Mayol, and deMayo (1985; using a procedure adapted from Bower, 1981; Markus, 1977; and Teasdale, Taylor, & Fogarty, 1980) and Markus (1977) have demonstrated the utility of this approach.

Mapping psychological space. Finally, interesting recent work has utilized multidimensional scaling to map the perceived relationships among the features of categories or objects of interest (Landau & Goldfried, 1981). For example, Landau (1980) found that dog phobics, relative to nonphobic controls, were much more likely to emphasize the ferocity of a breed rather than its size. Clearly, such a procedure could have great merit for exploring cognitive differentiation between groups of interest.

Clinical Imagery Assessment

On occasion, clients' fantasies and daydreams may provide clues to the presenting problem (Beck, 1970; Tower & Singer, 1981). Some fantasy themes are useful as diagnostic aids since various themes are associated with nosological categories. For instance, themes of failure or self-debasement are associated with depression; personal danger is associated with anxiety or phobic disorders (Beck, Laude, & Bohnert, 1974); persecution is associated with paranoid disorders (Beck, 1970). There also appear to be linkages between daydreams, dreaming states, verbal cognitions, and psychopathology (Beck, 1967). Likewise, clinical research data suggest rehearsals of fantasy material has been found to produce cognitive restructuring (Beck, 1970).

The vast majority of instruments designed to measure imagery measure, in actuality, imagery ability (Sheehan et al., 1983). Performance tests have been created where imagery ability is inferred from the mental manipulating of spatial relationships (e.g., Minnesota Paper Form Board: Likert & Quasha, 1970). Most imagery ability tests are questionnaires or self-report measures where subjects report on characteristics of imagery behavior (e.g., vividness or controllability). One of the most widely used imagery questionnaires is the Imaginal Processes Inventory (Singer & Antrobus, 1972). Another measure focuses on the in vivo assessment of inner mental activity. Immediate self-report techniques attempt to capture inner experience as it occurs. Some examples of immediate self-report procedures include the thinking-out-loud procedure (Hurlburt, 1976, 1979, 1980; Klinger, 1974; Pope, 1978) and thought-sampling procedures (Hurlburt, Lech, & Saltzman, 1984; Klinger,

1978; Klos & Singer, 1981). Other types of imagery assessments (e.g., projectives, physiological measures) fit somewhere in between the global groupings.

There are obvious advantages and limitations inherent in the use of each of these three approaches. The assessment of imagery in laboratory settings may not generalize to other situations. Self-report measures rely heavily on recall and assume that individuals are consciously aware of their inner experience (Klinger, 1978). Most immediate self-report techniques are rather novel procedures for most individuals. Consequently, the ecological validity of these procedures needs to be periodically monitored. One major advantage of all of these procedures is their ability to obtain data about the thoughts and inner experience associated with stream of consciousness in the visual domain (Singer, 1984).

One current, pressing research issue is whether existing self-report measures of imagery ability are capable of assessing clinically relevant dimensions of imagery capacity (Strosahl & Ascough, 1981). It comes as no surprise that experimental and clinical imagery may actually involve different cognitive processes. Indeed, what is surprising is that many of the self-report measures used currently in clinical imagery research are designed for use in experimental laboratory research (Stroshal & Ascough, 1981). Thus, there is a need for a research program geared toward the development of assessment tools designed to assess imagery within the therapeutic context.

The frontiers within clinical imagery research over the next decade will certainly be focused on topics like the multidimensional nature of the imagery construct (Parks, 1982), the relationship between waking and nonwaking states of cognitive activity (e.g., Cartwright, 1986; Cartwright, Lloyd, Knight, & Trenholme, 1984; Hoelscher, Klinger, & Barta, 1981; Melstrom & Cartwright, 1983), and the role of conscious and unconscious processes on mental processes and cognitive structures (Horowitz, 1985). Major progress has been made in clinical imagery research over the past 15 years, but considerable work is still needed, particularly in relation to the cognitive assessment of clinical imagery.

SPECIFIC CONTENT AREAS

Depression

A diverse array of assessment procedures has been developed to assess the relationship between cognition and depression. While the bulk of these devices are endorsement-type instruments, some use has been made of both production-type and inferential-type approaches. We next review the major instruments and procedures in this domain.

Automatic Thoughts Questionnaire (ATQ)

The Automatic Thoughts Questionnaire (ATQ: Hollon & Kendall, 1980) is a 30-item, endorsement-type inventory designed to assess surface level depressotypic cognitions: the relatively accessible thoughts passing through the sensorium. Items were developed by asking normal college students to recall recent situations in which they had felt sad and to report the thoughts "running through their heads" as they recalled those situations. Thirty items that discriminated between psychometrically identified depressed and nondepressed college students, both in an initial sample and a cross-validation sample, were retained for the final scale. All items are presented in a 1–5 format, anchored by "not-at-all" (1) to "all-the-time" (5), with subjects asked to recall how frequently they had experienced the thought in the last week.

Empirical evaluations have indicated that the ATQ possesses reasonable psychometric properties, both in terms of internal consistency (e.g., coefficient alphas of .96 and .95 were reported by Dobson & Breiter, 1983, and by Harrell & Ryon, 1983) and in terms of covariation with syndrome measures of depression (e.g., Dobson & Breiter, 1983, reported a correlation with Beck Depression Inventory [BDI] of .64, higher than comparable correlations for other cognitive measures). The instrument appears to readily discriminate depressed from nondepressed psychopathological and normal controls (Dobson & Shaw, 1986; Eaves & Rush, 1984; Harrell & Ryon, 1983; Hollon, Kendall, & Lumry, 1986; Ross, Gottfredson, Christensen, & Weaver, 1986), demonstrating both covariation and specificity.

It appears that the construct measured by the ATQ is largely state dependent (DeRubeis, Hollon, Evans, & Tuason, 1985; Eaves & Rush, 1984; Hollon et al., 1986; Simons, Garfield, & Murphy, 1984), normalizing as depression normalizes. Change on the ATQ appears to be nonspecific; change following interventions specifically targeted at changing beliefs (such as cognitive therapy) is no greater than change following tricyclic pharmacotherapy (DeRubeis et al., 1985; Simons et al., 1984). Furthermore, there is little reason to believe that levels of endorsement of the ATQ in euthymic populations are predictive of subsequent levels of depression (Evans et al., 1985; Rush, Weissenburger, & Eaves, 1986). It should be noted, however, that asking subjects to rate the degree to which they believe, as opposed to how frequently they experience, those thoughts did predict subsequent relapse in Evans et al. (1985). Whether assessing degree of belief as opposed to frequency of occurrence identifies a conceptually more interesting aspect of the construct of automatic thoughts remains to be determined. Curiously, there have been virtually no efforts to validate the ATQ against other types of cognitive assessment methods (e.g., thought listing, production methods, etc.) other than other paper-and-pencil endorsement measures. In the lone exception to this observation, Dobson and Shaw (1986) found only modest covariation ($r = .38$) between the ATQ and the production method Cognitive Response Test (CRT: Watkins & Rush,

1983). In general, it would appear that the ATQ is probably a reasonably good index of what it purports to measure: the frequency with which stream-of-consciousness surface-level cognitions typical of depression are experienced. That construct, however, does not appear to play a central role in either the etiology or maintenance of depression.

Dysfunctional Attitudes Scale (DAS)

The Dysfunctional Attitudes Scale (DAS: Weissman & Beck, 1978) consists of a pair of parallel-form, 40-item inventories designed to identify attitudes and beliefs held by individuals prone to depression. In keeping with Beck's cognitive theory of depression (Beck, 1963, 1967, 1976; Kovacs & Beck, 1978), it is presumed that individuals adhering to certain beliefs may be at greater risk in becoming depressed in the face of life stresses. Whether adherence to such beliefs ought to be a stable (and measurable) propensity remains a point of theoretical contention (see Beck, 1984; Hollon, DeRubeis, & Evans, 1987; Simons, 1984). What is clear is that the DAS was intended to capture attitudes and beliefs associated with depression that are more generic and less immediately evocative of dysphoria than scales directed at "stream-of-consciousness" material such as the ATQ (Hollon & Kendall, 1980). In this sense, the DAS can be seen as a more depression-specific corollary of Jones's (1969) Irrational Beliefs Test (see the following section on anxiety disorders).

Items for the DAS were selected by its authors, guided by their rather extensive familiarity with depressed populations. Examples include statements such as "If others dislike you, you cannot be happy" (positively keyed), and "One can get pleasure from an activity regardles of the end result" (negatively keyed), which are responded to on a 1-7 metric ranging from "do not agree" (1) to "totally agree" (7). Subsets of items are negatively keyed so as to minimize response bias.

Psychometric properties appear adequate (Oliver & Baumgart, 1985), with high internal consistency (alpha = .90) and reasonable stability (r = .73 over 6 weeks). In general, the DAS has held up well in studies differentiating depressed from normal subjects (Eaves & Rush, 1984; Hamilton & Abramson, 1983; Silverman, Silverman, & Eardley, 1984). That is, scores on the DAS are typically elevated for depressed subjects currently in episode compared to scores obtained from normal or nondepressed psychopathological controls. The correlation between the DAS and syndrome depression measures (r = .36) is typically lower than comparable correlations involving the ATQ (r = .64; Dobson & Breiter, 1983), but given the apparent state dependency of the ATQ, that may be to the credit of the DAS. Such a finding would be particularly consistent with underlying theory if the bulk of the noncovariation was accounted for by normal subjects, evidencing high DAS scores, who could be shown to have either prior histories of depression or to be at greater risk for subsequent episodes. Such studies remain to be done. Conversely, finding some depressives who do not exhibit such elevations would also be consistent with theory since most cognitive models claim only that cognitive abnormalities are sufficient (when combined with life stress) to produce depression but are not necessary (Abramson, Metalsky, & Alloy, 1986). The existing studies, however, tend to suggest that most subtypes of depression evaluated evidence elevations on the DAS, including both endogenous unipolar (Eaves & Rush, 1984; Giles & Rush, 1982; Zimmerman & Coryell, 1986) and bipolar depressives (Hollon et al., 1986), the most likely candidates for noncognitive mediation of depressive onset. Zimmerman and Coryell (1986) did note that inpatients with abnormal DST scores, a biological parameter, evidenced lower DAS scores than those without abnormal DST scores.

There is also some evidence to suggest greater heterogeneity in inpatient populations than is typically found in outpatients (Hamilton & Abramson, 1983). Given a similar pattern on other measures (Miller & Norman, 1986), it may well prove that different subtypes of depression are likely to be found in different settings. In general, scores decline as depression remits. Whether scores decline to normal levels (Hamilton & Abramson, 1983; Silverman et al., 1984) versus remaining somewhat elevated (DeRubeis et al., 1985; Dobson & Shaw, 1986; Eaves & Rush, 1984; Rush et al., 1986) remains controversial. Resolution of this issue may require more careful attention to the precise nature of the subpopulations sampled, the intervals selected between assessments, and the nature of the intervening treatments provided.

There is also some disagreement as to whether the DAS is differentially affected by different forms of treatment. Simons and colleagues (Simons et al., 1984) found no differential change over 12 weeks of cognitive therapy versus tricyclic pharmacotherapy, while DeRubeis and colleagues did so (DeRubeis et al., 1985), albeit not as great as for a measure of attributional styles described in a following section. DAS scores have been found to be predictive of response to cognitive therapy in one analog trial (Keller, 1983), but with higher scores predicting *poorer* response, a finding that may not be robust (Garvey, Hollon, DeRubeis, Evans, & Tuason, 1986; Simons, Lustman, Wetzel, & Murphy, 1985). There is evidence that the instrument may be predictive of relapse following treatment (Evans et al., 1985; Rush et al., 1986), a finding more directly called for by the cognitive model. In a nonclinical population, the DAS was found to interact with recent life stress to predict level of depression, whereas both DAS levels and recent life events evidenced main effects but no interaction in a clinical population (Wise & Barnes, 1986). Both sets of data were, however, cross-sectional rather than longitudinal. Wilbert and Rupert (1986) found that scores on the DAS covaried with rated loneliness, even when depression levels were covaried out. Finally, there is at least some evidence that the DAS may not be as fully specific to depression as might be desired. In a study contrasting several depressed groups with various nondepressed psychopathological control groups, the DAS was found to be appropriately nonelevated in neurotic and alcoholic patients, but inappropriately elevated in nondepressed schizophrenics (Hollon et al., 1986).

Again, as for the ATQ, there has been a curious absence of efforts to test the validity of the DAS as a measure of cognition associated with depression by virtue of relating it to other than paper-and-pencil endorsement measures of cognition. Although the instrument has been rapidly adopted in studies assessing differences between known groups and in projects looking for differential change over time, a more complete explication of the construct(s) it actually measures would appear desirable.

Attributional Styles Questionnaire (ASQ) and Other Attributional Assessment Systems

The Attributional Styles Questionnaire (ASQ: Seligman, Abramson, Semmel, & von Baeyer, 1979) appears to be a somewhat psychometrically troubled measure of a conceptually interesting construct. The original impetus for the construction of the ASQ was derived from the attributional reformulation of the learned helplessness theory of depression (Abramson, Seligman, & Teasdale, 1978). Whereas the original helplessness theory had postulated that it was the experience of uncontrollability which produced helplessness and depression (Seligman, 1975), reformulated helplessness argues that the nature of the explanation (causal attribution) generated to account for negative events plays a major role in determining who becomes depressed in the face of life stress.

The ASQ consists of 12 vignettes, 6 describing generally positive outcomes and 6 describing generally negative ones. Vignettes are further subdivided into those dealing with interpersonal versus achievement-related themes. For each vignette, respondents are asked to identify the one major cause (a free-response *production* method), then to rate that cause on four 7-point dimensions: internality-externality, globality-specificity, stability-instability, and importance. According to the reformulated helplessness model, causal attributions that are internal, global, and stable for important negative outcomes tend to contribute to the generation of depression.

In general, the scale has performed well in empirical trials despite the fact that its complexity and language elicit frequent complaints from subjects and researchers alike. Scores on the instrument tend to covary only moderately with measures of syndrome depression (Peterson & Seligman, 1984), but, as with the DAS, that is to be expected in a measure that is purported to lead to, not simply covary with, depression. Psychometric indices are generally adequate (Peterson et al., 1982), although subscale reliability is not overly strong. The instrument appears to discriminate depressed from nondepressed psychiatric controls (Eaves & Rush, 1984; Hamilton & Abramson, 1983; Persons & Rao, 1985; Raps, Peterson, Reinhard, Abramson, & Seligman, 1982; but see Miller, Klee, & Norman, 1982, for a null finding). In all these studies, only a subset of the depressed inpatients were found to exhibit the purported depressogenic attributional style, whereas few of the nondepressed controls did so. That is, the scale appeared to be less *sensitive* than it was *specific*. Given the earlier cited argument that the etiologic status of cognitive factors in depression has never been claimed to be *necessary* (Abramson et al., 1986), such a finding is not embarrassing to the reformulated helplessness model. In a particularly important study, Metalsky, Abramson, Seligman, Semmel, and Peterson (1982) found that prior levels of attributional styles interacted with a subsequent negative life event (poor performance on a college exam) to predict subsequent distress. DeRubeis et al. (1985) found evidence of both partial nonnormalization following treatment and differential treatment impact (drug-treated patients improved symptomatically, but did not decrease in their proclivity for depressotypic causal explanations), while posttreatment scores on the ASQ proved to be a particularly powerful predictor of relapse in that same sample (Evans et al., 1985). However, Rush et al. (1986) found little evidence that remission ASQs could predict subsequent relapses. The ASQ's ability to predict postpartum depression remains controversial, as it has done so in some studies (Cutrona, 1983; O'Hara, Rehm, & Campbell, 1982), but not others (Manly, McMahon, Bradley & Davidson, 1982; O'Hara, Neunaber, & Zekoski, 1984). In a wholly different context, Seligman and Schulman (1986) found the ASQ predictive of sales and subsequent on-the-job longevity for insurance salesmen.

Unlike the other paper-and-pencil measures reviewed, the ASQ has been systematically contrasted with alternative measurement methodologies. In one study, Peterson, Bettes, and Seligman (1985) had subjects write a 250–300 word vignette describing the two worst events happening to them in the previous year. No mention was made by the researchers of causal explanations. Subjects then completed the ASQ. The transcripts were subsequently scored by independent judges (see Peterson, Luborsky, & Seligman, 1983, for a description of the scoring system used). Good correspondence was observed between the spontaneously generated explanatory statements embedded in the transcripts and scores on the ASQ. In a second study, Castellon, Ollove, and Seligman (1982) evaluated explanatory statements regarding patients' reasons for seeking treatment and the origin of those patients' symptoms, based on verbal statements again generated with no reference to causal explanations. Once again, explanatory style based on free verbalizations converged nicely with scores on the ASQ.

A major problem in the attributional-style literature appears to involve non-robustness when measures other than the ASQ are used to provide the primary cognitive assessment. Thus, several studies (e.g., Barthe & Hammen, 1981; Gong-Guy & Hammen, 1980; Hammen & Cochrane, 1981; Hammen & deMayo, 1982; Hammen, Krantz, & Cochran, 1981; Harvey, 1981; Lewinsohn, Steinmetz, Larson, & Franklin, 1981) have measured subjects' causal attributions for various negative life events and found them to have little predictive utility in accounting for subsequent depression. Although this observation has led some to question the utility of the attribution construct (see, for example, Coyne & Gotlib, 1983), Peterson, Villanova, and Raps (1985) have argued that one important distinction is whether one asks for causal explanations for only a single event versus requesting comparable explanations for multiple events. The nonconfirmatory studies, they argue, do assess attributions for a specific event, but do not necessarily assess attributional *style*. On the other hand, there is some tendency for supportive studies to involve hypothetical rather than real-life situations (Coyne & Gotlib, 1983). Nonetheless, a recent meta-analysis by Sweeney, Anderson, and Bailey (1986) found that depressotypic explanatory style was significantly related to depression and predictive of distress, regardless of how that style was measured or in which population it was explored.

The other major problem with the ASQ has been its complexity and the relative inappropriateness of a specific vignette's contents for adult patient populations. Recently, Abramson and colleagues sought to remedy these problems with a modification of the ASQ called the Hospital Attributional Styles Questionnaire (HASQ). This instrument follows the same general format as the ASQ, but utilizes vignette themes selected on the basis of extensive pretesting with adult psychiatric populations. In addition, wording and instructions have been streamlined, making comprehension easier. Whether the HASQ will solve the practical problems inherent in the ASQ remains to be seen, but preliminary pilot data have been promising.

On the whole, although considerable controversy still exists, the various attributional style strategies remain as some of the more conceptually interesting and empirically successful ones for evaluating cognition in depression. The ASQ is virtually the only measure that "primes" subjects by providing hypothetical negative life events to which to respond. As we discuss elsewhere, we think the issue of schema activation and accessibility will prove quite critical (see Riskind & Rholes, 1984, for an extended discussion). Some of the apparent success of the ASQ as a predictive agent (cf. DeRubeis et al., 1985; Metalsky et al., 1982) is, we think, a consequence of the fact that it primes subjects for depressotypic thinking.

Cognitive Response Test (CRT)

Watkins and Rush (1983) developed the CRT for assessing cognition in depression. The CRT essentially involves a production-type format in response to structured prompts, utilizing an open-ended, sentence-completion format in which subjects respond to 1 of 25 vignettes by writing down the first thought that comes into their minds. For example, one representative item reads: "My employer says he will be making some major staff changes. I immediately think: _____." Vignettes were generated to focus on occupational, family, marital, and friendship themes. An initial pool of 72 items was narrowed to 50 nonredundant items that were further screened on an empirical basis to yield the final 25 vignettes. A detailed coding manual and training program have been developed, with responses sorted on the basis of rational/irrational process and depressed/nondepressed content. Interrater agreement was found to be an acceptable 88% (Watkins & Rush, 1983).

In an initial trial of the system, Watkins and Rush (1983) found that depressed outpatients evidenced higher "irrational-depressed" (CRT-ID) scores and fewer "rational" (CRT-R) responses than subjects in either normal, nondepressed-psychiatric, or nondepressed-medical outpatient control groups. Dobson and Shaw (1986) similarly found adequate interrater agreement (average $r = .75$) in a study contrasting depressed inpatients, nondepressed psychiatric inpatients, and a nonpsychiatric control. Once again, the depressed group evidenced significantly higher scores on the "depressed-irrational" scale, but no other. Correlations in this sample between the CRT-ID scale and two depression scales were moderate ($r = .47$ with the Hamilton Rating Scale (HRS) and $r = .52$ with the BDI), but only modest with the ATQ ($r = .38$) and DAS ($r = .34$). The instrument further demonstrated reasonable stability over a 60-day test-retest interval (as did the DAS but not the ATQ), despite reductions in levels of syndrome depression. Simons et al. (1984) did note reductions in CRT-ID scores over time for patients in treatment, but change was not as fully state dependent as for the ATQ. Such changes as were observed were clearly nonspecific with respect to type of treatment, as change was as great in tricyclic pharmacotherapy as for cognitive therapy. Similarly, Wilkinson and Blackburn (1981) found no evidence that CRT scores evidenced any residual elevation in recovered depressives who were considered to be at risk for subsequent depression.

Overall, the CRT appears to provide an alternative means of assessing depressotypic thinking to the more numerous endorsement methods such as the ATQ or DAS. If there is a valid distinction to be made between surface-level "stream-of-consciousness' self-statements (e.g., the ATQ) versus deeper, more generic underlying assumptions (e.g., the DAS), it is not clear precisely which level the CRT is intended to tap. On the one hand, it would seem that the CRT asks for surface-level cognitions, hence that it should correspond most closely to the ATQ. On the other hand, in the Dobson and Shaw (1986) study, the CRT-ID's performance most clearly paralleled the DAS. Clearly, further research is needed to resolve these issues.

Expectations

Probably no potentially important area of cognition in depression has been less adequately explored than that of expectations. Most major cognitive models accord the generation of negative expectations a central role in depression. For example, Beck lists negative views of the future as one of the three legs of his negative cognitive triad (Beck, 1967) and helplessness theorists consider negative expectations regarding control and/or outcomes to be the proximal precursor of depression (Abramson et al., 1978, 1986; Peterson & Seligman, 1984). However, few if any serviceable systems for assessing expectations exist.

One existing paper-and-pencil measure, the Hopelessness Scale (HS: Beck, Weissman, Lester, & Trexler, 1974), was developed to assess general pessimism. The HS is a 20-item true–false inventory that appears to correlate strongly with measures of depression but seems to be an even better predictor of propensity for suicide than are those measures of depression (Beck, Kovacs, & Weissman, 1975; Kovacs, Beck, & Weissman, 1975; Minkoff, Bergman, Beck, & Beck, 1973; Wetzel, 1976; Wetzel, Margulies, Davis, & Karam, 1980; but see also Linehan & Nielsen, 1983, for a critique; and Nevid, 1983, and Petrie & Chamberlain, 1983, for a response). Although it appears to be heavily state dependent (DeRubeis et al., 1985; Wilkinson & Blackburn, 1981), Rush, Beck, Kovacs, Weissenberger, and Hollon (1982) found evidence of differential change over time in cognitive therapy relative to pharmacotherapy for depressives, at least early in therapy. Kazdin and colleagues (Kazdin, Rodgers, & Colbus, 1986) have developed a comparable scale for child and adolescent populations, which, as for adults, is a better predictor of suicidality than of depression per se (Kazdin, French, Unis, Esveldt-Dawson, & Sherick, 1983). One major problem with the HS is that we really don't know the extent to which it actually measures expectations (criterion validity) as opposed to more broadly defined cognition. Concurrent studies evaluating the HS against other cognitive assessment procedures would appear warranted. A second major problem is that it simply may not prove sufficiently situation-specific for some purposes. Another approach involves the examination of differential expectancy change in chance versus skill situations. Based on a social-learning theory perspective (Rotter, 1954, 1966; Phares, 1973), it is presumed that expectations for subsequent success will change more in a manner consistent with previous outcomes on tasks requiring skilled performance than on tasks based largely on chance. Several studies have demonstrated precisely such a phenomenon in normal populations (e.g., Phares, 1957; Rotter, Liverant & Crowne, 1961). With regard to depression, early formulations of helplessness theory (cf. Seligman, 1975) have suggested that depressives are less likely than nondepressives to evidence expectancy shifts in skilled task situations, largely because depresives were seen to view such outcomes as being independent of their own efforts. A variety of studies have evidenced precisely such differences between psychometrically depressed and nondepressed college students (Garber & Hollon, 1980; Klein & Seligman, 1976; Miller & Seligman, 1973, 1976; Miller, Seligman, & Kurlander, 1975) and clinical populations (Abramson, Garber, Edwards, & Seligman, 1978). Both Miller and Seligman (1976) and Klein and Seligman (1976) were able to induce nondepressed college students to behave in the fashion predicted for depressives by exposing the nondepressed college students to inescapable noise, and Klein and Seligman (1976) were further able to reverse this pattern in depressives by exposing them to escapable stress. Miller et al. (1975) found the phenomenon specific to depression, as opposed to anxiety, in a college student population, and Abramson et al. (1978) found the phenomenon specific to schizophrenia in an inpatient psychiatric sample. Several other investigators have noted similar patterns using other related paradigms (cf., Golin, Terrell, Weitz, & Drost, 1979; Lobitz & Post, 1979; but see Smolen, 1978, for a null finding). Garber and Hollon (1980) demonstrated that psychometrically identified college students did not exhibit reduced expectancy change in the skilled task when generating predictions for others, indicating that the locus of the phenomenon resides in depressives' views of themselves, not their view of the task.

Although relatively consistent in its findings, the paradigm has proven quite difficult to interpret. In a careful replication, plus extension in a normal population, Woollert (1979) demonstrated that the observed pattern was more directly attributable to differential confidence in one's expectations rather than differential expectations for control. If valid, such an *expectancy-confidence* hypothesis would force different interpretations of the existing studies than had previously been made under the older *control-perception* hypothesis. Largely for this reason, the paradigm appears to have lost favor with researchers. Nonetheless, large differences between depressives and nondepressives have been observed in relation to expectational processes, regardless of how the data are interpreted. It is not entirely clear why this line of research appears to have been abandoned.

Overall, then, there remains a clear need for greater clarity in the area of the assessment of expectations by depressed individuals. The existing measurement operations all appear inadequate to the task, yet the importance of the endeavor is undeniable.

Self-Schema

Beck's cognitive model of depression (Beck, 1963, 1967, 1976; Kovacs & Beck, 1978) accords a central role to negative self-schemata. Schemata have been variously defined (Kihlstrom & Nasby, 1981; Markus, 1977; Neisser, 1967, 1976; Nisbett & Ross, 1980; Taylor & Crocker, 1981), but a general definition involves the notion that schemata represent internal principles that serve to organize some stimulus domain, guide subsequent information search, color the way in which new organization is interpreted, and provide default inferences when information is ambiguous or absent. Scripts, closely related to schemata, may guide actual behavioral sequences (Abelson, 1981). A variety of recent articles have attempted to relate the schema concept to psychopathology, clinical change, and clinical inference (Goldfried & Robins, 1982, 1983; Hollon & Kriss, 1984; Landau & Goldfried, 1981; Turk & Salovey, 1985a, 1985b; Turk & Speers, 1983; Wachtel, 1981).

As noted earlier, the schema construct has been operationalized in a variety of ways in studies of depression. Davis (1979a) utilized a multitrial free recall paradigm to examine the subjective organization imposed on personally relevant adjectives by depressed versus nondepressed college students. Clustering during free recall is taken as an indication of schematic processing. Nondepressives were found to evidence such clustering, while psychometrically identified depressives did not. However, as Kulper and Derry (1981) have noted, schematic processing would be expected to follow a content-specificity model. Since all of Davis's stimulus words were evaluatively positive adjectives, they should have elicited schematic clustering only from nondepressives and aschematic nonclustering from depressives. Similar logic can be applied to trials by Ingram et al. (1983), in which nondepressives exhibited schematic recall for positive adjectives following manipulated success whereas psychometrically identified depressives did not (again, no negative content adjectives were utilized). Davis (1979b) evaluated incidental recall in a depth-of-processing task (Craik & Lockhart, 1972; Craik & Tulving, 1975). This paradigm has been previously described. Davis (1979b) found that depressives differed from nondepressives only for adjectives processed under the self-referent condition. Duration, but not severity, was related to strength of recall. In a subsequent study, Davis and Unruh (1981) found evidence for stronger subjective organization in either long-term depressives or nondepressives than for short-term depressives. In general, the absence of any negative content in Davis's adjective set makes it difficult to evaluate the presence of any negative self-schema in depression.

Kuiper and colleagues (Derry & Kuiper, 1981; Kuiper & Derry, 1982; Kuiper & MacDonald, 1982; MacDonald & Kuiper, 1982) have conducted a particularly solid series of investigations of the role of self- (and other) schemata in depression. Building on a model first put forward by Rogers et al. (1977), the authors consider the self to be a cognitive organization that can be defined in terms of both its structure and its process: that is, a schema. As a structure, the self-schema represents a hierarchically organized body of knowledge stored in long-term memory. In terms of process, the self-schema can be shown to both facilitate processing of novel information and to impart biasing effects on the resultant products. Schematic processing can be revealed by virtue of meaningful clustering in recall, differential retrieval during incidental recall following different levels of initial processing (depth of processing), and on "inverted-U" reaction time effect, in which stimuli both high and low in self-reference are processed more rapidly than stimuli intermediate in relevance (Kuiper, Derry, & MacDonald, 1982).

A major advance in the paradigm used to test for schematic processing was the delineation of stimulus adjectives consisting of both positive and negative content. In keeping with their content-specific schemata model (Kuiper & Derry, 1981), Kuiper and colleagues argued that not all prompts ought to elicit evidence of schematic processing. Rather, only those prompts for which a given individual was schematic should do so. Kuiper and colleagues have found rather consistent evidence of schematic processing in depressed populations in studies involving both psychometrically identified (Kuiper & Derry, 1982; Kuiper & MacDonald, 1982) and bona fide clinical depressives (Derry & Kuiper, 1981; MacDonald & Kuiper, 1982) with procedures including the evaluation of clustering during free recall, incidental recall (depth-of-processing), and examination of reaction times.

As Ruehlman, West, and Pasahow (1985) have observed in a recent review, the general pattern appears to be one of overly positive self-evaluations (optimistic schemata) for nondepressives and overly negative self-schemata (pessimistic schemata) for clinical depressives, with no clear schematic processing evident for mild or newly depressed individuals. These authors have advanced the notion that such individuals "in transition" may be between schemata, no longer certain of previous nondepressive organizations, but not yet crystallized into depressive patterns. The episodic nature of depression makes it a particularly interesting process to study with regard to cognitive organizations. If, as appears to be the case, clinical depressives are schematic in a pessimistic sense, how stable are those self-structures? The major cognitive models talk about a propensity to think in certain depressogenic ways when confronted by stressful life events (cf. Abramson et al., 1978; Kovacs & Beck, 1978) rather than focusing on stable ongoing beliefs that dominate the sensorium. If depressotypic schemata are latent, then once developed, how are they best measured? Simple cross-sectional assessment, even contrasting subjects with histories of depression versus those with no such history, should fail to detect underlying differences in cognitive structure. The issue of the differential measurement of potentially latent propensities is one of the major assessment procedures, adequate though they may be for detecting differences in cognitive organization between those currently depressed and those currently not depressed, will likely prove inadequate to the task of identifying differential propensities in the absence of the appropriate stresses. Riskind and Rholes (1984) have discussed this at some length, noting that the issue is one of the accessibility of those purportedly latent cognitive structures (see also discussions by Higgins & King, 1980; Tversky & Kahneman, 1973). In the social cognitive literature, this issue has been largely addressed by use of "priming" strategies (cf. Higgins, Rholes, & Jones, 1977; Srull & Wyer, 1979, 1980; Wyer & Srull, 1981). In the psychopathology literature, except for the inadvertent priming provided by the ASQ, the only instance of priming of latent structures of which we are aware was contributed by Southwick, Steele, and Lindell (1986) in a study of expectancies about alcohol.

A second major issue that needs to be resolved involves the role of affect in either activating or totally superseding differential schematic processes. Since existing studies have typically evaluated information-processing in individuals differing in affective state, and since different mood states have been shown to alter information-processing (Bower, 1981; Clark & Teasdale, 1982; Ingram, 1984a; Teasdale, 1983), it remains entirely possible that what appears to be a between-subject difference in cognitive organization will prove to be merely the consequence of within-subject variability in mood (see Coyne & Gotlib, 1983, and Zajonc, 1980, for major critiques of the cognitive model; and Blaney, 1986, and Brewin, 1985, for a discussion of reciprocal causal processes).

In a particularly compelling study, Hammen, Marks, deMayo, and Mayol (1985) followed a sample of college students over a 4-month interval. Nondepressed schematic individuals at intake proved to be at no greater risk for subsequent dysphoria than did the nondepressed nonschematic subjects, arguing against any etiologic role for the depressive schema. Initial level of depression, regardless of schematic status, was strongly predictive of subsequent depression. Although the occurrence of negative life events did increase the risk for subsequent depression, there was no indication of any preexistent schema by negative life events interaction in predicting subsequent dysphoria. Subjects confronted by negative life events were as likely to become depressed if non-schematic as if schematic for depression. In a companion study in the same article, schematic individuals were no more likely to evidence differential memorial recall than were aschematic individuals, although mood state, regardless of schematic status, was strongly predictive. In general, although current mood state typically predicted information-processing, previous information-processing did not do so. These findings were strongly supportive of a mood-congruency hypothesis in which mood is a more powerful predictor of concurrent cognition than previous cognition is a predictor of subsequent mood or information-processing. Thus, the two studies yielded little support for the notion that depressotypic self-schemas (as measured) are causal determinants of subsequent depression.

Several comments are in order. First, it must be remembered that the particular type of schematic assessment paradigm in Hammen, Marks, deMayo, and Mayol (1985) utilized relied on adjectival trait self-descriptions. While this type of cognitive organization evidenced little indication of subsequent depression, it is far from the only type of cognitive organization possible. Kuiper and colleagues (Kuiper, Olinger, & MacDonald, in press) have recently distinguished between episodic and vulnerability schemata, with the kind of negative self-schema evidenced by the type of adjectival descriptors used in the typical depth of processing/incidental recall task representing the former category. Episodic schema are seen as being largely, but not wholly, state dependent, occurring after the onset of depression (if they were wholly state dependent, we could not account for Hammen, Marks, deMayo, and Mayol's (1985) finding of depressed nonschematics or nondepressed schematics). While they may exacerbate or prolong the episode, they are not seen as causing it. Vulnerability schemata, on the other hand, may play a role in episode onset, probably in conjunction with life events. Potential candidates might include beliefs about the meaning, importance, or consequences of various types of life events or propositions about one's self-worth (see Hammen, Marks, deMayo, & Mayol, 1985; Kuiper et al., in press; Olinger, Kuiper, & Shaw, in press, for discussions of this issue). In a separate design, Hammen, Marks, Mayol, and deMayo (1985) found evidence that stable recall-based self-schema which assessed specific themes (e.g., affiliativeness vs. achievement schemata) differentially predicted dysphoria after negative life events in the relevant life phase. Neither schema was negative, per se, in the sense of being isomorphic with the kind of thinking we have come to regard as being depressotypic. Rather, individuals schematic for affiliative issues tended to become depressed if they experienced a disappointment in the interpersonal sphere, whereas individuals schematic for achievement issues tended to become depressed if they experienced a disappointment in the interpersonal sphere, whereas individuals schematic for achievement issues tended to become depressed if they experienced a disappointment in the achievement-related sphere. Thus, the collective suggestion emerging from the work of Kuiper and colleagues and Hammen and colleagues is that those schematic processes most *isomorphic* with the way diagnosable depressed patients think may be largely state dependent, noncausal concomitants of being depressed, whereas other types of cognitions less isomorphic, with clear-cut depressotypic cognitive content, may play a larger role in initial etiology, especially in conjunction with particular kinds of negative life events.

Second, although Hammen, Marks, deMayo, and Mayol (1985) provided one of the most powerful efforts to integrate cognitive and life-event variables yet found in the literature, their effort fell short of capturing the essence of a cognitive diathesis-stress model in which the cognitive diathesis lies dormant until activated by life stresses. There are at least three versions of a cognitive psychopathology model possible. In the first, the *cognitive trait model*, stable cognitive processes can, by themselves, produce dysphoria. Clearly, the Hammen, Marks, deMayo, and Mayol (1985) data are not consistent with such a model. In the second, the *stable cognitive diathesis-stress model*, both a stable, preexistent cognitive predisposition and a subsequent negative life event are necessary to produce subsequent depression. Given that Hammen and colleagues first assessed schematic processing, then followed subjects longitudinally, assessing both life events and eventual depression status, it was this model that they tested and rejected with a series of regression analyses. The third model, the *latent cognitive diathesis-stress model*, in which a preexistent cognitive predisposition is present but inactive until activated by triggering life events, was not tested. In this model, latent cognitive structures would be seen as accounting for variability in affective response to the same negative event, but not necessarily as being activated prior to the occurrence of those negative events. Anyone who has taken on a clear-cut social role (e.g., parent, teacher, employer, etc.) knows what it is like to think in a manner consistent with that role, yet also knows that one does not always think in such a fashion. The issue is one of the triggering or priming of latent cognitive organizations, organizations that may be relatively inaccessible prior to the priming but that are not universally present in all people. This last point is critical, since it may represent the only way to avoid the risk of devolving into unacceptable metaphor and untestable tautology. In this sense, Hammen, Marks, deMayo, and Mayol (1985) tested a stable trait diathesis-stress model, but not the latent trait diathesis-stress model closer to the processes typically put forward by theorists in this area (e.g., Beck, 1976; Kovacs & Beck, 1978).

Irrationality in Process.

Given the interest in cognition in depression, it is striking that so much literature has focused on the *content* of what depressives think and the larger structures they possess (*schemata*) while so little has focused on the actual processes they follow. Beck (1963, 1967, 1976) has long specified certain irrational processes he believes to operate in depression, including *arbitrary inference,* the propensity to draw inferences without substantiating evidence, *selective abstraction,* the tendency to base a judgment on a minor aspect of the larger stimulus complex, *overgeneralization,* the inclination to extrapolate in an unjustified fashion from a single event, and *magnification/ minimization,* the tendency to overemphasize the consequences of negative events and underestimate the consequences of positive events.

Hammen and colleagues (Hammen & Krantz, 1976; Krantz & Hammen, 1979) have developed an endorsement-type inventory designed to assess the propensity for distorted thinking. The specific instrument, the Cognitive Bias Questionnaire (CBQ), consists of a series of vignettes each followed by an array of responses crossing depressed/nondepressed with distorted/

nondistorted options. In general, depressed populations typically endorse more depressotypic, but not nondepressotypic, distortions (Hammen, 1978; Hammen & Krantz, 1976; Krantz & Hammen, 1979; Michael & Funabiki, 1985; but see Blaney, Behar, & Head, 1980, for a contrary finding). Norman, Miller, and Klee (1983) and Miller and Norman (1986) have typically found evidence of *specificity* of elevations in psychiatric samples, but with considerable heterogeneity within the depressed groups (as did Hamilton & Abramson, 1983, on the ASQ in inpatients). CBQ scores do appear to change as depression remits, but little is known about the specificity of such change (Krantz & Hammen, 1979; Miller & Norman, 1986). Finally, Haley, Fine, Marriage, Moretti, and Freeman (1985) have modified the CBQ for use with child populations, with results similar to those observed for adults. In general, although the effort to assess process rather than simple content is laudable, it would appear that greater sophistication in specifying the nature of the processes involved will prove necessary.

In the only other study that directly assesses cognitive process in depression (the attributional literature, of course, infers style from specific content), Cook and Peterson (1986) asked depressed and nondepressed college students to list (a) up to three recent negative events and (b) their perceptions of the single most important cause for each event. Subjects were further asked to provide the evidence they had for believing that the specified cause had indeed produced the event. These evidential justifications were then scored by blind, independent judges in accordance with a coding system based on Beck's taxonomy of distortions in information-processing. Depressed subjects were found to be far more likely to present one or more of the distortions in the evidence they put forward (although arbitrary inferences could be reliably distinguished from the other categories, selective abstraction, overgeneralization, and magnification/minimization could not be discriminated from one another, and were combined into a single index). Depressives were less likely than normals to utilize a nondistorted process, covariation information, but did not differ with regard to the use of evidence. We find this investigation most interesting and look forward to subsequent studies of this kind.

Miscellaneous Measures

A variety of other measures have received at least some limited use in the depression literature. Lewinsohn and colleagues (Lewinsohn, Larson & Munoz, 1982) developed a battery of endorsement-type measures focused on expectations, cognitive contents (automatic thoughts), and more generic beliefs that appear to have at least some adequate psychometric properties. They do not, however, appear to be differentially sensitive to treatment variations (Zeiss, Lewinsohn, & Munoz, 1979) or to be either predictive of or stable following episodes of depression (Lewinsohn et al., 1981). Perhaps for these and other reasons, the measures have not been adopted by other investigators. Several investigators have utilized Jones's Irrational Belief Test (IBT: Jones, 1969; cf. Cook & Peterson, 1986; Nelson, 1977). This endorsement-type measure of generic beliefs typically separates depressed from nondepressed samples, but appears to have been largely superseded by the more focused DAS. Harrell, Chambless, and Calhoun (1981) developed a self-statement inventory with rather adequate properties. This measure, too, has been largely superseded by the ATQ.

Conclusions

Overall, there appears to be a rather large number of potential instruments and systems developed to assess cognition in depression. Most, but by no means all, are endorsement-type devices. While many appear to function adequately in terms of distinguishing depressed from nondepressed samples, little effort has been directed to assessing their construct validity against alternative measurement procedures. The bulk of the efforts have involved the utilization of these instruments to test substantive theory (e.g., that cognition causes depression). The results of these efforts have been quite mixed. The development of methods for inferring the presences of cognitive structures is quite noteworthy, and some of the resultant designs are quite sophisticated (e.g., Hammen, Marks, deMayo, & Mayol, 1985; Hammen, Marks, Mayol, & deMayo, 1985). Nonetheless, even greater sophistication in dealing with issues of construct accessibility when euthymic (cf. Riskind & Rholes, 1984) and the nature of the causal relationships between cognition and affect (see Brewin, 1985; Teasdale, 1983) are clearly in order. Activity in this area has been extensive, with simpler cognition-affect models clearly not holding up. Even more clarity will be required in subsequent empirical efforts.

Anxiety Disorders

There have been fewer efforts to develop cognitive assessment systems for anxiety disorders than there have been for depression (Cerny, Himadi, & Barlow, 1984; Last, Barlow, & O'Brien, 1985). Clearly, this is not due to any lack of cognitive theories of anxiety or stress reactivity (e.g., Beck 1970, 1976; Beck & Emery, 1985; Dember, 1974; Goldfried, 1979; Holyrod & Lazarus, 1982; Lazarus, 1966; Miller, 1981). Similarly, cognitive and cognitive-behavioral interventions have shown real promise in the treatment of anxiety disorders (cf. Beck & Emery, 1985; Hollon & Beck, 1986; Holyrod, 1979; Meichenbaum, 1977; Meichenbaum & Jaremko, 1982). This lack of instrument development may in part be coincidental since the last period of major focus on anxiety disorders occurred during the 1960s, the period of ascendancy for radical behaviorism. It may also reflect the nonconcordance between the cognitive, behavioral, and physiological components of the syndrome itself (cf. Hodgson & Rachman, 1974; Lang, 1968, 1984; Maser, 1984; Rachman & Hodgson, 1974; Vermilyea, Boice, & Barlow, 1984). Nonetheless, it is clear that as major attention has again become focused on anxiety disorders in the 1980s (Tuma & Maser, 1986), renewed interest has become evident in the role of cognition in its etiology and maintenance. In the sections to follow, some of the instruments and assessment paradigms that have been utilized are described.

General Neuroticism

The determinants of emotional arousal is a topic of long-standing interest within theoretical and treatment circles. The ability of symbolic activities or covert verbalizations to elicit emotional reactivity has been documented in a number of studies (e.g., Goldfried & Sobocinski, 1975; May & Johnson, 1973; Rimm & Litvak, 1969; Russell & Brandsma, 1974; Velten, 1968). As we shall see, many of the assessment systems developed in this regard have involved general endorsement-type instruments drawing heavily on Ellis's (1962) theories about the nature of dysfunctional cognition.

One of the most frequently utilized measures is the Irrational Beliefs Test (IBT: Jones, 1969). This endorsement-type instrument consists of 100 items selected to identify various irrational beliefs. The scale is designed to assess 10 different "irrational beliefs," with some evidence supportive of this internal structure, but not overwhelmingly so (Lohr & Bonge, 1982a). Psychometric characteristics have generally been adequate, although subscale reliabilities leave something to be desired (Lohr & Bonge, 1982a), and the IBT has generally been found to covary with distress (Nelson, 1977) or predict arousal in response to real or fantasized provocations (Goldfried & Sobocinski, 1975). Lohr and Bonge (1980, 1981, 1982a) have pursued a program of research designed to enhance the psychometric properties and construct validity of the IBT with some apparent success. Overall, the instrument appears to have some utility, although the specific psychometric adequacies and construct validities of the respective subscales and the specificity of the overall instrument's relationship to specific problematic emotions remains relatively weak.

Several other endorsement-type instruments have been developed that appear to parallel the IBT in nature and function. Shorkey, Reyes, and Whiteman (1977) developed a 70-item Rational Behavior Inventory (RBI), with factorially derived subscales, that appears to have held up well in empirical trials (Himle, Thyer, & Papsdorf, 1982; Whiteman & Shorkey, 1978). Other similar measures include Hartman's (1968) Personal Beliefs Inventory (PBI; see Tosi & Eshbaugh, 1976, for an empirical evaluation) and Bessai's (1976) Common Beliefs Survey-III (CBS-III; see Tosi, Forman, Rudy, & Murphy, 1986, for an empirical evaluation).

Although there is some evidence that different types of irrational beliefs may indeed be related to different types of fears (Deffenbacher, Zwemer, Whisman, Hill, & Sloan, 1986), other studies have pointed to nondifferentiation of internal structure for these inventories (e.g., Smith, 1983). On the whole, these various inventories appear to provide an adequate, if rather cumbersome, assessment of general irrationality. Whether such instruments provide sufficiently divergent internal structures to be of use in fine-grained research investigstions remains an open question.

Simple Phobias

The simple phobia literature and, in particular, the test anxiety literature has been the subject of several comparisons highlighting the differences and similarities between various immediate self-report techniques. For example, Galassi, Frierson, and Sharer (1981) examined whether concurrent assessment (during an exam) versus retrospective assessment (after an exam) yields comparable findings with regard to the role of cognition. Galassi et al. (1981) found that both concurrent and retrospective assessment groups did not differ in the frequency of positive and negative thoughts emitted during the examination or on self-reports of anxiety or even on test performance. Under either assessment condition, the more anxious students differed from less anxious students by virtue of exhibiting fewer positive and more negative thoughts. Similarly, Blackwell, Galassi, Galassi, and Watson (1985) compared two immediate self-report procedures, a think-aloud procedure and a thought-listing procedure, with a sample of undergraduates participating in a mathematical problem-solving session. Blackwell et al. (1985) revealed that in terms of both frequency and proportions of cognitions, the think-aloud procedure produced more cognitions overall and more specific types of cognitions (e.g., problem-solving thoughts) than did the thought-listing procedure. Blackwell et al. (1985) argued that the thought-listing procedure might be best suited to the examination of problem-solving thought. Surprisingly, the thought-listing procedure was found to be associated with higher levels of anxiety among undergraduate subjects than was the think-aloud procedure.

Several empirical examples of the utility of using cognitive assessment can be drawn from this literature. For example, Arnkoff (1986) used a thought-listing technique in a study comparing coping self-statement versus cognitive restructuring components of a cognitive-behavioral intervention for test anxiety. Deffenbacher and Hazaleus (1985) used a posttask questionnaire to determine that cognitive "worry" was a primary source of performance disruption for test-anxious students. High test-anxious fifth and sixth graders reported more negative self-evaluations and off-task thoughts on the Children's Cognitive Assessment Questionnaire (CCAQ), a 40-item endorsement-type instrument, than did moderate or low test-anxious children (Zatz & Chassin, 1983, 1985). On the other hand, Klinger (1984), utilizing an ongoing thought-sampling procedure, found little support for the notion that cognitive interference suppresses test performance in those prone to test anxiety. Cognitive content during the examination was only weakly related to performance (unlike prior preparation, which was strongly predictive), although retrospective cognitive recall was quite consistent with performance difficulties. It is quite possible that different types of cognitive assessments will yield quite different patterns of substantive findings. Finally, Bruch, Kaflowitz, and Kuethe (1986) have demonstrated the importance of looking not only at the occurrence/nonoccurrence of particular cognitions, but at the degree of belief ascribed to those beliefs when they occur. Clearly, although cognitive processes appear to be quite central to the experience of test anxiety, the exact nature of this relationship may prove more complex than was once believed.

Several interesting studies have focused on other types of simple phobias. For example, Huber and Altmaier (1983) used a thought-listing paradigm to evaluate self-statements during a behavioral avoidance task. Interestingly, phobics differed from nonphobics more on the degree of salience of the perceived threat than on the actual perception of threat. Sutton-Simon and Goldfried (1979) found general social anxiety to be more directly related to general irrational beliefs on the IBT while specific acrophobia was related to both general irrationality and specific negative self-statements. As mentioned earlier, Landau (1980) used multidimensional scaling to determine that dog phobics organized information about dogs differently than did normal controls, emphasizing ferocity over breed. These examples point to some of the uses to which cognitive assessment can be put in addressing substantive issues.

Social Phobias

Social anxiety, as a diagnostic category, is an area of research in which there is increasing emphasis on the exploration of the role that cognition plays in the etiology, maintenance, and treatment-induced reduction of anxiety (Goldfried, Padawer, & Robins, 1984). For example, Sewitch and Kirsch (1984), using a thought-sampling technique modeled after Hurlburt and Sipprelle (1978), found the perception of interpersonal threat to be the dominant content of cognition preceding anxiety in an interpersonal context. This was particularly striking since they had led one set of their subjects to expect themes of interpersonal loss to predominate. Lake and Arkin (1985) found that individuals high in social anxiety were particularly likely to rate favorable interpersonal feedback as being inaccurate and unfavorable and to devalue "judges" who had evaluated them positively.

Social anxiety has received considerable attention, perhaps due to the prevalence of these problems among late adolescents and young adults found in most university settings (Cacioppo, Glass, & Merluzzi, 1979). Increasingly, more attention is being focused on the role of cognitive distortions and dysfunctional thoughts in social anxiety. In a recent review, Galassi and Galassi (1979) concluded that cognitive deficits play a greater role than social skills deficits in the generation of such disorders. Relative to low-anxious subjects, high-anxious individuals recall more negative information, interpret ambiguous feedback more negatively, underestimate their own performance, and expect more negative evaluations from others (Smith & Sarason, 1975). Goldfried and Sobocinski (1975), using the IBT (Jones, 1969), found that individuals high in "need for approval" (as well as general irrationality) became particularly aroused as a consequence of imagining themselves in a social rejection situation.

Three types of assessment paradigms have predominated. Several investigators have utilized various thought-listing production methods. Glass, Gottman, and Shmurak (1976) found that successful modification of cognitive self-statements, assessed via production methods, led to improved (and generalized) social interaction performances in shy college students. Cacioppo et al. (1979), also using a thought-listing approach, similarly observed that high socially anxious subjects were more likely to emit negative self-statements prior to a social interaction. Glass and Arnkoff (1983), again using a thought-listing procedure, observed different patterns of problematic cognitions in different types of threatening situations. Heterosexual social interaction situations elicited fewer self-referent thoughts than did the test-taking situation and elicited more facilitative thoughts and fewer debilitating thoughts than did the prospect of giving a speech. Subjects most troubled by the interpersonal interaction evidenced a pattern of "internal dialogue of conflict" similar to that described for assertion problems by Schwartz and Gottman (1976) in which both positive and negative self-statements were evident.

Glass, Merluzzi, Biever, and Larsen (1982) developed what appears to be the major endorsement-type instrument in this literature: the 30-item Social Interaction Self-Statement Test (SISST). The SISST appears to have strong psychometric properties and to possess reasonable construct validity. Merluzzi, Burgio, and Glass (1984) found strong evidence of concurrent validity with respect to social introversion on standard personality measures in an adult clinical sample. Zweig and Brown (1985) developed an alternative format for the SISST which includes a series of hypothetical vignettes. Once again, psychometric properties appear strong. Overall, the SISST appears to provide a strong, endorsement-type measure of problematic cognition in a social interaction situation.

Finally, Goldfried et al. (1984) have applied multidimensional scaling techniques to the mapping of psychological constructs regarding interpersonal situations for individuals rated high and low in social anxiety.

Relative to low-anxious subjects, high-anxious subjects viewed such situations as being particularly high on the dimension of "chance of being evaluated" and gave little consideration to the dimension of intimacy. In general, it would appear that assessment procedures drawn from a variety of methodological domains hold real promise in the study of the role of cognition in social anxiety.

Agoraphobia

As for other anxiety disorders, there has been a recent surge of interest in the role of cognition in agoraphobia. Various researchers (e.g., Beck, 1976; Beck & Emery, 1985; Chambless, Gallagher, & Bright, 1981; Goldstein & Chambless, 1978; Raimy, 1975) have conceptualized agoraphobia as a cognitively mediated phenomenon which has at its core a basic "phrenaphobia," or fear of fear. Beck, Laude, and Bohnert (1974) found that catastrophic cognitions involving incipient physical illness (heart attack) or mental infirmity (psychotic decompensation) dominated the sensorium of patients seeking emergency-room consultations for panic attacks. On the other hand, Last, Barlow, and O'Brien (1985) found only minimal covariation between in vivo cognitive assessment, imaginal cognitive assessment, and a thought-listing procedure (see also Last, O'Brien, & Barlow, 1985).

Chambless, Caputo, Bright, and Gallagher (1984) have provided what appears to be the most promising of the endorsement-type instruments in this literature, the Agoraphobic Cognitions Questionnaire (ACQ). The ACQ consists of 14 statements reflecting consequences expected in a typical anxiety-eliciting situation. The ACQ has been shown to clearly discriminate between agoraphobics and normal control samples.

Although work in this area is still in its preliminary stages, it appears quite promising. Clearly, important substantive issues require the further development of cognitive assessment procedures if they are to be explored fully.

Assertion Problems

Research on assertion problems has been markedly influenced by cognitive theories and assessment procedures. Fiedler and Beach (1978), for example, found that the decision to act in assertion situations was largely determined by the consequences that an individual expected to follow from that action. Alden and Safran (1978), utilizing an endorsement-type Irrational Beliefs Quesionnaire (IBQ), found that low assertive subjects endorsed higher levels of irrational beliefs. Lohr and Bonge (1982b) have observed only modest correlations between such general irrationality endorsement-type inventories and assertion problems.

Perhaps the best known endorsement-type instrument in this literature is Schwartz and Gottman's (1976) Assertiveness Self-Statement Test (ASST). In an initial study, low-assertion subjects were found to endorse fewer positive and more negative self-statements in assertion situations than high-assertion subjects. It was this study that gave rise to the hypothesized "dialogue of conflict," marked by a balance between positive and negative cognitions, held to be central to assertion problems. Heimberg, Chiauzzi, Becker, and Modrazo-Peterson (1983) extended the Schwartz and Gottman findings to a fully clinical sample. While they found little evidence for a "dialogue of conflict" phenomenon, they did observe significant differences in the level of negative self-statements in the low-assertion subjects. Bruch, Haase, and Purcell (1984) conducted a factor analysis of the ASST (both alone and in combination with measures of expected consequences in assertion situations, the Subjective Probability of Consequences Inventory, or SPCI). The ASST was found to consist of two primary dimensions: (a) apprehension over negative interpersonal consequences and (b) preoccupation with moral standards involving responsibility to others. It would appear that the ASST can play an important role in the exploration of the role of cognition in assertion problems.

Finally, Rudy, Merluzzi, and Henahan (1982) have utilized multidimensional scaling to investigate differential schemata regarding assertion situations. These analyses indicated important distinctions between differing levels of formality and situations, as well as intimate/nonintimate and status level of target dimensions. Although such efforts are relatively recent, it would appear that the application of inferential methods may facilitate understanding of the nature of assertion problems.

Behavioral Medicine

Within the domain of behavioral medicine, the assessment of beliefs related to medical problems has recently attracted the attention of behavioral theorists. With regard to children, assessment devices have been developed to assess children's fears concerning hospitalization (Vernon, Foley, & Schulman, 1967), surgery (Melamed & Siegel, 1975), and dental treatment (Hermecz & Melamed, 1984; Melamed, Yurchenson, Hawes, Heiby, & Glick, 1975).

In the adult literature, Smith, Follick, Ahern, and Adams (1986) have developed an endorsement-type inventory, the Cognitive Error Questionnaire (CEQ), designed to assess beliefs related to low back pain. The CEQ consists of 48 separate vignettes, each followed by a potential cognitive distortion. Disability status was found to be strongly predicted by scores on the CEQ.

Kendall et al. (1979) developed a 20-item Self-Statement Inventory (SSI) designed to assess beliefs found in patients about to undergo cardiac catheterization. Negative self-statements predicted greater arousal over and poorer coping with this medical procedure.

Finally, Kleinknecht and colleagues (Brandon & Kleinknecht, 1982; Early & Kleinknecht, 1982; Klenknecht & Berstein, 1978; Richardson & Kleinknecht, 1984) have utilized dental fear analog situations to evaluate the relationship between cognition and arousal in a medical intervention situation. In general, high-anxiety subjects report more nearly catastrophic cognitions regarding these situations than do low-anxiety subjects.

Clearly, efforts to assess beliefs in behavioral medicine contexts are just beginning. Nonetheless, the initial efforts thus far have been quite promising. Further work in this area is indicated.

SUMMARY

Despite the rather rich array of cognitive assessment strategies, questions may still arise concerning the clinical utility of including such instruments in the clinician's existing assessment battery. Mental health practitioners are constrained by institutional demands that involve heavy patients loads, third-party payments, and time pressures. Consequently, the introduction of any new procedure that requires additional time and attention on the part of the clinician needs to be carefully considered.

Such issues have been raised within the context of behavioral assessment (Mash & Terdal, 1982). Many of the those procedures, typically involving direct observtion, are time-consuming and result in high personnel costs. Moreover, such strategies provide information that consumers may find readily apparent given the low level of inference required to interpret the data (Goldfried & Kent, 1972). In contrast, the interpretation of data yielded from cognitive assessment techniques tends to necessitate a higher level of inferential processes on the part of the clinician. Conversely, the time investment with respect to data collection as well as data coding is lower than for many of the behavioral assessment strategies. Consequently, adoption of cognitive assessment strategies has the potential of providing the clinician with a systematic assessment of inner mental activity not previously available while requiring only a minimal increase in the clinician's time and effort. Nonetheless, the need to confront such constraints is made evident by reports that behavioral assessors often continue to use more traditional assessment strategies (e.g., projectives) rather than procedures (e.g., direct observation) specific to behavioral assessment (e.g., Swan & MacDonald, 1978; Wade, Baker, & Hartmann, 1979).

The central issue is the extent to which there is a benefit from incorporating cognitive assessment measures into the existing assessment battery. Cognitive assessment, as a process, has the capability of addressing diagnostic and treatment evaluation questions. Certainly, such ongoing assessment has a major role to play in any of the newer cognitive and cognitive-behavioral interventions. Given the increasing interest in basic belief structures and information processing in both dynamic (cf. Goldfried, 1982; Wachtel, 1981) and humanistic approaches (Rice, 1974; Wexler, 1974) (see Goldfried & Robins, 1982, for an extended discussion), such assessment can be seen to serve a variety of general functions that transcend any single theoretical system (Hollon & Kriss, 1984).

As we have seen, the available systems run the gamut from simple endorsement-type checklists and in vivo self-monitoring systems to complex inferential paradigms based on findings derived from basic cognitive science. As Kihlstrom and Nasby (1981) describe, many of the latter require the availability of computerized testing laboratories before they can become widely available to the practicing clinician, but such widespread availability is already developing in conjunction with some of the more traditional assessment devices. Clearly, most clinical practitioners already possess the means to integrate the bulk of the methods described in this chapter into their ongoing practice, should they choose to do so.

REFERENCES

Abelson, R. P. (1981). Psychological status of the script concept. *American Psychologist, 36*, 715–729.

Abramson, L. Y., Garber, J., Edwards, N. B., & Seligman, M. E. P. (1978). Expectancy changes in depression and schizophrenia. *Journal of Abnormal Psychology, 87*, 102–109.

Abramson, L. Y., Metalsky, G. I., & Alloy, L. B. (1986). *The hopelessness theory of depression: A metatheoretical analysis with implications for psychopathology research*. Unpublished manuscript, University of Wisconsin, Madison, WI.

Abramson, L. Y., Seligman, M. E. P., & Teasdale, J. (1978). Learned helplessness in humans: Critique and reformulation. *Journal of Abnormal Psychology, 87*, 49–74.

Alba, J. W., & Hasher, L. (1983). Is memory schematic? *Psychological Bulletin, 93*, 203–231.

Alden, L., & Safran, J. (1978). Irrational beliefs and nonassertive behavior. *Cognitive Therapy and Research, 2*, 357–364.

Arnkoff, D. B. (1986). A comparison of the coping and restructuring components of cognitive restructuring. *Cognitive Therapy and Research, 10*, 147–158.

Barthe, D. G., & Hammen, C. L. (1981). The attributional model of depression: A naturalistic extension. *Personality and Social Psychology Bulletin, 7*, 53–58.

Bartlett, F. C. (1932). *Remembering: A study in experimental and social psychology*. London: Cambridge University Press.

Beck, A. T. (1963). Thinking and depression: I. Idiosyncratic content and cognitive distortions. *Archives of General Psychiatry, 9*, 324–333.

Beck, A. T. (1967). *Depression: Clinical, experimental, and theoretical aspects*. New York: Harper & Row.

Beck, A. T. (1970). Role of fantasies in psychotherapy and psychopathology. *Journal of Nervous and Mental Diseases, 150*, 3–17.

Beck, A. T. (1976). *Cognitive therapy and the emotional disorders.* New York: International Universities Pres.

Beck, A. T. (1984). Cognition and therapy. *Archives of General Psychiatry, 41,* 1112–1114.

Beck, A. T., & Emery, G. (1985). *Anxiety disorders and phobias.* New York: Basis Books.

Beck, A. T., Kovacs, M., & Weissman, A. (1975). Hopelessness and suicidal behaviors: An overview. *Journal of the American Medical Association, 234,* 1146–1149.

Beck, A. T., Laude, R., & Bohnert, M. (1974). Ideational components of anxiety neurosis. *Archives of General Psychiatry, 31,* 319–325.

Beck, A. T., Rush, A. J., Shaw, B. F., & Emery, G. (1979). *Cognitive therapy of depression.* New York: Guilford Press.

Beck, A. T., Weissman, A., Lester, D., & Trexler, L. (1974). The measurement of pessimism: The Hopelessness Scale. *Journal of Consulting and Clinical Psychology, 42,* 861–865.

Behrend, D., Rosengren, K., & Perlmutter, M. (1986). *Private speech in preschool children's problem-solving alone and with their mother.* Manuscript submitted for publication.

Blackwell, R. T., Galassi, J. P., Galassi, M. D., & Watson, T. E. (1985). Are cognitive assessment methods equal? A comparison of think aloud and thought listing. *Cognitive Therapy and Research, 9,* 399–413.

Blaney, P. H. (1986). Affect and memory: A review. *Psychological Bulletin, 99,* 229–246.

Blaney, P. H., Behar, V., & Head, R. (1980). Two measures of depressive cognitions: Their association with depression and with each other. *Journal of Abnormal Psychology, 89,* 678–682.

Bonarius, J.C.J. (1965). Research in the personal construct theory of George A. Kelly. In B. A. Mather (Ed.), *Progress in experimental personality research* (Vol. 2, pp. 1–46). New York: Academic Press.

Bower, G. (1981). Mood and memory. *American Psychologist, 36,* 129–148.

Bowers, K. S. (1967). The effect of demands for honesty on reports of visual and auditory hallucinations. *International Journal of Clinical and Experimental Hypnosis, 15,* 31–36.

Brandon, R. K., & Kleinknecht, R. A. (1982). Fear assessment in a dental analog setting. *Journal of Behavioral Assessment, 4,* 317–325.

Brewin, C. R. (1985). Depression and causal attributions: What is their relation? *Psychological Bulletin, 98,* 297–309.

Bruch, M. A., Haase, R. F., & Purcell, M. J. (1984). Content dimensions of self-statements in assertive situations: A factor analysis of two measures. *Cognitive Therapy and Research, 8,* 173–186.

Bruch, M. A., Kaflowitz, N. G., & Kuethe, M. (1986). Beliefs and the subjective meaning of thoughts: Analysis of the role of self-statements in academic test performance. *Cognitive Therapy and Research, 10,* 51–69.

Cacioppo, J. T., Glass, C. R., & Merluzzi, T. V. (1979). Self-statements and self-evaluations: A cognitive response analysis of heterosocial anxiety. *Cognitive Therapy and Research, 3,* 249–262.

Cacioppo, J. T., & Petty, R. E. (1981). Social psychological procedures for cognitive response assessment: The thought-listing technique. In T. V. Merluzzi, C. R. Glass & M. Genest (Eds.), *Cognitive Assessment* (pp. 309–342). New York: Guilford Press.

Cantor, N. (1980a). A cognitive-social analysis of personality. In N. Cantor & J. F. Kihlstrom (Eds.), *Personality, cognition, and social interaction* (pp. 23–44). Hillsdale, New Jersey: Erlbaum.

Cantor, N. (1980b). Perceptions of situations: Situation prototypes and person-situation prototypes. In D. Magnusson (Ed.), *The situation: An interactional perspective* (pp. 229–244). Hillsdale: NJ: Erlbaum.

Cantor, N., & Mischel, W. (1977). Traits as prototypes: Effects on recognition memory. *Journal of Personality and Social Psychology, 35,* 38–48.

Cantor, N., & Mischel, W. (1979). Prototypes in person perception. In L. Berkowitz (Ed.), *Advances in experimental social psychology* (Vol. 12, pp. 32–59). New York: Academic Press.

Cantor, N., Smith, E., French, R. deS., & Mezzich, J. (1980). Psychiatric diagnosis as prototype categorization. *Journal of Abnormal Psychology, 89,* 181–193.

Cartwright, R. D. (1986). Affect and dream work from an information-processing point of view. *Journal of Mind and Behavior, 7,* 411–428.

Cartwright, R. D. (in press). Dream work from the emotional information processing point of view. *Journal of Mind and Behavior.*

Cartwright, R. D., Lloyd, S., Knight, S., & Trenholme, I. (1984). Broken dreams: A study of the effects of divorce and depression on dream content. *Psychiatry, 47,* 251–259.

Castellon, C., Ollove, M., & Seligman, M. E. P. (1982). Unpublished data, University of Pennsylvania (cited in Peterson & Seligman, 1984).

Cerny, J. A., Himadi, W. G., & Barlow, D. H. (1984). Issues in diagnosing anxiety disorders. *Journal of Behavioral Assessment, 6,* 301–329.

Chambless, D. L., Caputo, G. C., Bright, P., & Gallagher, R. (1984). Assessment of fear of fear in agoraphobics: The Body Sensations Questionnaire and the Agoraphobic Cognitions Questionnaire. *Journal of Consulting and Clinical Psychology, 52,* 1090–1097.

Chambless, D. L., Gallagher, R., & Bright, P. (1981). *The measurement of fear of fear in agoraphobics.* Paper presented at the Proceedings of the Association for the Advancement of Behavior Therapy, Toronto, Canada.

Ciminero, A. R., Nelson, R. O., & Lipinski, D.P. (1977). Self-monitoring procedures. In A. R. Ciminero, K. S. Calhoun, & H. E. Adams (Eds.), *Handbook of behavioral assessment* (pp. 195–232). New York: Wiley.

Clark, D. M., & Teasdale, J. D. (1982). Diurnal variation in clinical depression and accessibility of memories of positive and negative experiences. *Journal of Abnormal Psychology, 91,* 87–95.

Cook, M. L., & Peterson, C. (1986). Depressive irrationality. *Cognitive Therapy and Research, 10,* 293–298.

Coyne, J. C., & Gotlib, I. H. (1983). The role of cognition in depression: A critical appraisal. *Psychological Bulletin, 94,* 472–505.

Craik, F. I. M., & Lockhart, R. S. (1972). Level of processing: A framework for memory research. *Journal of Verbal Learning and Verbal Behavior, 11,* 671–684.

Craik, F. I. M., & Tulving, E. (1975). Depth of processing and the retention of words in episodic memory. *Journal of Experimental Psychology: General, 104,* 268–294.

Cutrona, C. E. (1983). Causal attributions and perinatal depression. *Journal of Abnormal Psychology, 92,* 161–172.

Davis, H. (1979a). The self-schema and subjective organization of personal information in depression. *Cognitive Therapy and Research, 3,* 415–425.

Davis, H. (1979b). Self-reference and the encoding of personal information in depression. *Cognitive Therapy and Research, 3,* 97–110.

Davis, H., & Unruh, W. R. (1981). Development of self-schema in adult depression. *Journal of Abnormal Psychology*, *90*, 125-133.

Davison, G. C., Feldman, P. M., & Osborn, C. E. (1984). Articulated thoughts, irrational beliefs and fear of negative evaluation. *Cognitive Therapy and Research*, *8*, 349-362.

Davison, G. C., Robins, C., & Johnson, M. K. (1983). Articulated thoughts during simulated situations: A paradigm for studying cognition in emotion and behavior. *Cognitive Therapy and Research*, *7*, 17-40.

Deffenbacher, J. L., & Hazaleus, S. L. (1985). Cognitive, emotional, and physiological components of test anxiety. *Cognitive Therapy and Research*, *9*, 169-180.

Deffenbacher, J. L., Zwemer, W. A., Whisman, M.A., Hill, R. A., & Sloan, R. D. (1986). Irrational beliefs and anxiety. *Cognitive Therapy and Research*, *10*, 281-291.

Dember, W. N. (1974). Motivation and the cognitive revolution. *American Psychologist*, *29*, 161-168.

Derry, P. A., & Kuiper, N. A. (1981). Schematic processing and self-reference in clinical depression. *Journal of Abnormal Psychology*, *90*, 286-297.

DeRubeis, R. J., Hollon, S. D., Evans, M. D., & Tuason, V. B. (1985). *Components and mechanisms in cognitive therapy and pharmacotherapy for depression: III. Processes of change in the CPT project.* Unpublished manuscript, University of Minnesota and the St. Paul-Ramsey Medical Center, Minneapolis – St. Paul, Minnesota.

Dobson, K. S., & Breiter, H. J. (1983). Cognitive assessment of depression: Reliability and validity of three measures. *Journal of Abnormal Psychology*, *92*, 107-109.

Dobson, K. S., & Shaw, B. F. (1986). Cognitive assessment with major depressive disorders. *Cognitive Therapy and Research*, *10*, 13-29.

Dodge, K. A., & Frame, C. L. (1982). Social cognitive biases and deficits in aggressive boys. *Child Development*, *53*, 620-635.

Early, C. E., & Kleinknecht, R. A. (1978). The palmer sweat index as a function of repression-sensitization and fear of dentistry. *Journal of Consulting and Clinical Psychology*, *46*, 184-185.

Eaves, G., & Rush, A. J. (1984). Cognitive patterns in symptomatic and remitted unipolar major depression. *Journal of Abnormal Psychology*, *93*, 31-40.

Ellis, A. (1962). *Reason and emotion in psychotherapy*. New York: Lyle Stuart.

Ericsson, K. A., & Simon, H. A. (1980). Verbal reports as data. *Psychological Review*, *87*, 215-251.

Evans, M. D., Hollon, S. D., DeRubeis, R. J., Piasecki, J. M., Tuason, V. B., & Garvey, M. J. (1985). *Relapse/recurrence following cognitive therapy and pharmacotherapy for depression: IV. Two-year follow-up in the CPT project.* Unpublished manuscript, University of Minnesota and the St. Paul-Ramsey Medical Center, Minneapolis – St. Paul, Minnesota.

Fazio, R. H., Sanbonmatsu, D. M., Powell, M. C., & Kardes, F. R. (1986). On the automatic activation of attitudes. *Journal of Personality and Social Psychology*, *50*, 229-238.

Fiedler, D., & Beach, L. R. (1978). On the decision to be assertive. *Journal of Consulting and Clinical Psychology*, *46*, 537-546.

Flavell, J., Beach, D., & Chinsky, J. (1966). Spontaneous verbal rehearsal in a memory task as a function of age. *Child Development*, *37*, 283-289.

Galassi, J. P., Frierson, H. T., & Sharer, R. (1981). Concurrent versus retrospective assessment in test anxiety research. *Journal of Consulting and Clinical Psychology*, *49*, 614-615.

Galassi, J. P., & Galassi, M. D. (1979). Modification of heterosocial skills deficits. In A. S. Bellack & M. Hersen (Eds.), *Research and practice in social skills training* (pp. 131-187). New York: Plenum Press.

Garber, J., & Hollon, S. D. (1980). Universal versus personal helplessness in depression: Belief in uncontrollability or incompetence? *Journal of Abnormal Psychology, 89*, 56-66.

Garvey, M. J., Hollon, S. D., DeRubeis, R. J., Evans, M. D., & Tuason, V. B. (1986). *Prediction of response to pharmacotherapy, cognitive therapy, and combined cognitive pharmacotherapy: II. Predicting response in the CPT project.* Unpublished manuscript, University of Minnesota and the St. Paul-Ramsey Medical Center, Minneapolis – St. Paul, Minnesota.

Genest, M., & Turk, D. C. (1981). Think-aloud approaches to cognitive assessment. In T. V. Merluzzi, C. R. Glass & M. Genest (Eds.), *Cognitive assessment* (pp. 233-269). New York: Guilford Press.

Giles, D. E., & Rush, A. J. (1982). Relationship of dysfunctional attitudes and dexamethasone in endogenous and nonendogenous depression. *Biological Psychiatry, 17*, 1303-1314.

Glass, C. R., & Arnkoff, D. B. (1983). Cognitive set and level of anxiety: Effects on thinking processes in problematic situations. *Cognitive Therapy and Research, 7*, 529-542.

Glass, C., Gottman, M., & Shmurak, S. H. (1976). Response-acquisition and cognitive self-statement modification approaches to dating-skills training. *Journal of Counseling Psychology, 23*, 520-526.

Glass, C. R., Merluzzi, T. V., Biever, J. L., & Larsen, K. H. (1982). Cognitive assessment of social anxiety: Development and validation of a self-statement questionnaire. *Cognitive Therapy and Research, 6*, 37-55.

Goldfried, M. R. (1979). Anxiety reduction through cognitive-behavioral intervention. In P. C. Kendall & S. D. Hollon (Eds.), *Cognitive-behavioral interventions: Theory, research, and procedures* (pp. 117-152). New York: Academic Press.

Goldfried, M. R. (1982). Resistance and clinical behavior therapy. In P. L. Wachtel (Ed.), *Resistance: Psychodynamics and behavioral approaches* (pp. 95-113). New York: Plenum Press.

Goldfried, M. R., Decenteceo, E. T., & Weinberg, L. (1974). Systematic rational restructuring as a self-control technique. *Behavior Therapy, 5*, 247-254.

Goldfried, M. R., & Goldfried, A. (1980). Cognitive change methods. In F. H. Kanfer & A. P. Goldstein (Eds.), *Helping people change* (pp. 97-130). New York: Pergamon Press.

Goldfried, M. R., & Kent, R. N. (1972). Traditional versus behavioral assessment: A comparison of methodological and theoretical assumptions. *Psychological Bulletin, 77*, 409-420.

Goldfried, M. R., Padawer, W., & Robins, C. (1984). Social anxiety and the semantic structure of heterosocial interactions. *Journal of Abnormal Psychology, 93*, 87-97.

Goldfried, M. R., & Robins, C. (1982). On the facilitation of self-efficacy. *Cognitive Therapy and Research, 6*, 361-380.

Goldfried, M. R., & Robins, C. (1983). Self-schema, cognitive bias, and the processing of therapeutic experiences. In P. C. Kendall (Ed.), *Advances in cognitive-behavioral research and therapy* (Vol. II, pp. 33-80). New York: Academic Press.

Goldfried, M., & Sobocinski, D. (1975). Effects of irrational beliefs on emotional arousal. *Journal of Consulting and Clinical Psychology, 43*, 504–510.

Goldstein, A. J., & Chambless, D. J. (1978). A reanalysis of agoraphobia. *Behavior Therapy, 9*, 47–59.

Golin, S., Terrell, F., Weitz, J., & Drost, P. L. (1979). The illusion of control among depressed patients. *Journal of Abnormal Psychology, 88*, 454–457.

Golin, S., Terrell, F., Weitz, J., & Drost, P. L. (1979). The illusion of control among depressed patients. *Journal of Abnormal Psychology, 88*, 454–457.

Gong-Guy, E., & Hammen, C. (1980). Causal perceptions of stressful life events in depressed and nondepressed clinic outpatients. *Journal of Abnormal Psychology, 89*, 662–669.

Greenwald, A. G. (1968). Cognitive learning, cognitive response to persuasion and attitude change. In A. G. Greenwald, T. C. Brock, & T. M. Ostrom (Eds.), *Psychological foundations of attitudes* (pp. 147–170). New York: Academic Press.

Haley, G. M. T., Fine, S., Marriage, K., Moretti, M. M., & Freeman, R. J. (1985). Cognitive bias and depression in psychiatrically disturbed children and adolescents. *Journal of Consulting and Clinical Psychology, 53*, 535–537.

Hamilton, E. W., & Abramson, L. Y. (1983). Cognitive patterns and major depressive disorders: A longitudinal study in a hospital setting. *Journal of Abnormal Psychology, 92*, 173–184.

Hammen, C. L. (1978). Depression, distortion, and life stress in college students. *Cognitive Therapy and Research, 2*, 189–192.

Hammen, C., & Cochrane, S. (1981). Cognitive correlates of life stress and depression in college students. *Journal of Abnormal Psychology, 90*, 23–27.

Hammen, C., & deMayo, R. (1982). Cognitive correlates of teacher stress and depressive symptoms: Implications for attributional models of depression. *Journal of Abnormal Psychology, 91*, 96–101.

Hammen, C. L., & Krantz, S. (1976). Effect of success and failure on depressive cognitions. *Journal of Abnormal Psychology, 85*, 577–586.

Hammen, C., Krantz, S. E., & Cochran, S. D. (1981). Relationships between depression and causal attributions about stressful life events. *Cognitive Therapy and Research, 5*, 351–358.

Hammen, C., Marks, T., deMayo, R., & Mayol, A. (1985). Self-schemas and risk for depression: A prospective study. *Journal of Personality and Social Psychology, 49*, 1147–1159.

Hammen, C., Marks, T., Mayol, A., & deMayo, R. (1985). Depressive self-schemas, life stress, and vulnerability to depression. *Journal of Abnormal Psychology, 94*, 308–319.

Harrell, T. H., Chambless, D. L., & Calhoun, J. F. (1981). Correlational relationships between self-statements and affective states. *Cognitive Therapy and Research, 5*, 159–173.

Harrell, T. H., & Ryon, N. B. (1983). Cognitive behavioral assessment of depression: Clinical validation of the Automatic Thoughts Questionnaire. *Journal of Consulting and Clinical Psychology, 51*, 721–725.

Hartman, G. J. (1968). Sixty revealing questions for 20 minutes. *Rational Living, 6*, 7–8.

Harvey, D. (1981). Depression and attributional style: Interpretations of important personal events. *Journal of Abnormal Psychology, 90*, 134–142.

Heimberg, R. G., Chiauzzi, E. J., Becker, R. E., & Modrazo-Peterson, R. (1983). Cognitive mediation of assertive behavior: An analysis of the self-statement patterns. *Cognitive Therapy and Research, 7*, 455–464.

Hermecz, D. A., & Melamed, B. G. (1984). The assessment of emotional imagery training in fearful children. *Behavior Therapy, 15,* 156–172.

Higgins, E. T., & King, G. (1980). Accessibility of social constructs: Information processing consequences of individual and contextual variability. In N. Cantor & J. F. Kihlstrom (Eds.), *Cognition, social interaction, and personality* (pp. 69–121). Hillsdale, NJ: Erlbaum.

Higgins, E. T., Rholes, C. R., & Jones, C. R. (1977). Category accessibility and impression formation. *Journal of Experimental Social Psychology, 13,* 141–154.

Himle, D. P., Thyer, B. A., & Papsdorf, J. D. (1982). Relationships between rationale beliefs and anxiety. *Cognitive Therapy and Research, 6,* 219–223.

Hodgson, R., & Rachman, S. (1974). Desynchrony in measures of fear. *Behavior Research and Therapy, 12,* 319–326.

Hoelscher, T. J., Klinger, E., & Barta, S. G. (1981). Incorporation of concern- and nonconcern-related verbal stimuli into dream content. *Journal of Abnormal Psychology, 90,* 88–91.

Hollon, S. D., & Beck, A. T. (1986). Cognitive and cognitive-behavioral interventions. In S. L. Garfield & A. E. Bergin (Eds.), *Handbook of psychotherapy and behavior change: An empirical analysis* (3rd ed., pp. 443–482). New York: Wiley.

Hollon, S. D., & Bemis, K. M. (1981). Self-report and the assessment of cognitive functions. In M. Hersen & A. S. Bellack (Eds.), *Behavioral assessment: A practical handbook* (2nd ed., pp. 216–252). New York: Pergamon Press.

Hollon, S. D., DeRubeis, R. J., & Evans, M. D. (1987). Causal mediation of change in treatment for depression: Discriminating between nonspecificity and noncausality. *Psychological Bulletin, 102,* 139–149.

Hollon, S. D., & Kendall, P. C. (1980). Cognitive self-statements in depression: Development of an automatic thoughts questionnaire. *Cognitive Therapy and Research, 4,* 383–395.

Hollon, S. D., & Kendall, P. C. (1981). In vivo assessment techniques for cognitive-behavioral processes. In P. C. Kendall and S. D. Hollon (Eds.), *Assessment strategies for cognitive-behavioral interventions* (pp. 21–35). New York: Academic Press.

Hollon, S. D., Kendall, P. C., & Lumry, A. (1986). Specificity of depressotypic cognitions in clinical depression. *Journal of Abnormal Psychology, 95,* 52–59.

Hollon, S. D., & Kriss, M. R. (1984). Cognitive factors in clinical research and practice. *Clinical Psychology Review, 4,* 38–78.

Holroyd, K. A. (1979). Stress, coping, and the treatment of stress related illnes. In J. R. McNamara (Ed.), *Behavioral approaches in medicine: Application analysis* (pp. 191–226). New York: Plenum Press.

Holroyd, K. A., & Lazarus, R. S. (1982). Stress, coping, and somatic adaptation. In L. Goldberger & S. Breznitz (Eds.), *Handbook of stress: Theoretical and clinical aspects* (pp. 21–35). New York: Free Press.

Horowitz, L. M., Post, D. L., French, R., Wallis, K. D., & Siegleman, E. Y. (1981). The prototype as a construct in abnormal psychology: 2. Clarifying disagreements in psychiatric judgments. *Journal of Abnormal Psychology, 90,* 575–585.

Horowitz, M. J. (1985). *Report of the program on conscious and unconscious mental processes of the John D. and Catherine T. Macarthur Foundation.* UC, San Francisco, California.

Huber, J. W., & Altmaier, E. M. (1983). An investigation of the self-statement systems of phobic and nonphobic individuals. *Cognitive Therapy and Research, 7,* 355–362.

Hurlburt, R. T. (1976). *Self-observation and self-control*. Unpublished doctoral dissertation, University of South Dakota.

Hurlburt, R. T. (1979). Random sampling of cognitions and behavior. *Journal of Research in Personality*, *13*, 103–111.

Hurlburt, R. T. (1980). Validation and correlation of thought sampling with retrospective measures. *Cognitive Therapy and Research*, *4*, 235–238.

Hurlburt, R. T., Lech, B. C., & Saltman, S. (1984). Random sampling of thought and mood. *Cognitive Therapy and Research*, *8*, 262–275.

Hurlburt, R. T., & Sipprelle, C. N. (1978). Random sampling of cognitions in alleviating anxiety attacks. *Cognitive Therapy and Research*, *2*, 165–169.

Ingram, R. E. (1984a). Information processing and feedback. Effects of mood and information favorability on the cognitive processing of personality relevant information. *Cognitive Therapy and Research*, *8*, 371–386.

Ingram, R. E. (1984b). Toward an information processing analysis of depression. *Cognitive Therapy and Research*, *8*, 443–447.

Ingram, R. E., Smith, T. W., & Brehm, S. S. (1983). Depression and information processing: Self-schemata and the encoding of self-referent information. *Journal of Personality and Social Psychology*, *45*, 412–420.

Jones, R. G. (1969). A factored measure of Ellis's Irrational Belief System. *Dissertation Abstracts International*, *29*, 4379B–4380B. (University Microfilms No. 69-64,43).

Kazdin, A. E., French, N. H., Unis, A. S., Esveldt-Dawson, K., & Sherick, R. B. (1983). Hopelessness, depression, and suicidal intent among psychiatrically disturbed inpatient children. *Journal of Consulting and Clinical Psychology*, *51*, 504–510.

Kazdin, A. E., Rodgers, A., & Colbus, D. (1986). The Hopelessness Scale for Children: Psychometric characteristics and concurrent validity. *Journal of Consulting and Clinical Psychology*, *54*, 241–245.

Keller, K. E. (1983). Dysfunctional attitudes and the cognitive therapy for depression. *Cognitive Therapy and Research*, *7*, 437–444.

Kelly, G. A. (1955). *The psychology of personal constructs*. New York: Norton.

Kendall, P. C., & Hollon, S. D. (Eds.). (1981a). *Assessment strategies for cognitive-behavioral interventions*. New York: Academic Press.

Kendall, P. C., & Hollon, S. D. (1981b). Assessing self-referent speech: Methods in the measurement of self-statements. In P. C. Kendall & S. D. Hollon (Eds.), *Assessment strategies for cognitive-behavioral interventions* (pp. 85–118). New York: Academic Press.

Kendall, P. C., & Korgeski, G. P. (1979). Assessment and cognitive-behavioral interventions. *Cognitive Therapy and Research*, *3*, 1–21.

Kendall, P. C., Williams, L., Pechacek, T. F., Graham, L. E., Shisslak, & Herzoff, N. (1979). Cognitive-behavioral and patient education interventions in cardiac catheterization procedures. *Journal of Consulting and Clinical Psychology*, *47*, 49–58.

Kihlstrom, J. F., & Nasby, W. (1981). Cognitive tasks in clinical assessment: An exercise in applied psychology. In P. C. Kendall & S. D. Hollon (Eds.), *Assessment strategies for cognitive-behavioral interventions* (pp. 287–317). New York: Academic Press.

Klein, D. C., & Seligman, M. E. P. (1976). Reversal of performance deficits in learned helplessness and depression. *Journal of Abnormal Psychology*, *85*, 11–26.

Kleinknecht, R. A., & Bernstein, D. A. (1978). Assessment of dental fear. *Behavior Therapy*, *9*, 626–634.

Klinger, E. (1974). Utterances to evaluate steps and control attention distinguish operant from respondent thought while thinking out loud. *Bulletin of the Psychonomic Society, 4*, 4-45.

Klinger, E. (1977). *Meaning and void*. Minneapolis: University of Minnesota.

Klinger, E. (1978). Modes of normal conscious flow. In K. S. Pope & J. L. Singer (Eds.), *The stream of consciousness: Scientific investigations into the flow of human experience* (pp. 225-258). New York: Plenum Press.

Klinger, E. (1984). A consciousness-sampling analysis of test anxiety and performance. *Journal of Personality and Social Psychology, 47*, 1376-1390.

Klinger, E., Barta, S. G., & Glass, R. A. (1981). Thought content and gap time in basketball. *Cognitive Therapy and Research, 5*, 109-114.

Klinger, E., Barta, S. G., & Maxeiner, M. E. (1981). Current concerns: Assessing therapeutically relevant motivations. In P. C. Kendall & S. D. Hollon (Eds.), *Assessment strategies for cognitive-behavioral interventions* (pp. 161-196). New York: Academic Press.

Klos, D. S., & Singer, J. L. (1981). Determinants of the adolescent's ongoing thought following simulated parental confrontations. *Journal of Personality and Social Psychology, 41*, 975-987.

Kovacs, M., & Beck, A. T. (1978). Maladaptive cognitive structures in depression. *American Journal of Psychiatry, 135*, 525-533.

Kovacs, M., Beck, A. T., & Weissman, A. (1975). Hopelessness: An indicator of suicidal risk. *Suicide, 5*, 98-103.

Krantz, S., & Hammen, C. L. (1979). Assessment of cognitive bias in depression. *Journal of Abnormal Psychology, 88*, 611-619.

Kubie, L. S. (1950). *Practical and theoretical aspects of psychoanalysis*. New York: International University Press.

Kuiper, N. A., & Derry, P. A. (1981). The self as a cognitive prototype: An application to person perception and depression. In N. Cantor & J. Kihlstrom (Eds.), *Personality, social interaction, and cognition* (pp. 215-232). Hillsdale, N. J.: Erlbaum.

Kuiper, N. A., & Derry, P. A. (1982). Depressed and nondepressed content self-reference in mild depressives. *Journal of Personality, 50*, 67-79.

Kuiper, N. A., Derry, P. A., & MacDonald, M. R. (1982). Self-reference and person perception in depression: A social cognition perspective. In G. Weary & H. L. Mirels (Eds.), *Integrations of clinical and social psychology* (pp. 79-103). New York: Oxford University Press.

Kuiper, N. A., & MacDonald, M. R. (1982). Self and other perception in mild depression. *Social Cognition, 1*, 223-229.

Kuiper, N. A., Olinger, L., & MacDonald, M. (in press). Depressive schemata and the processing of personal and social information. In L. Alloy (Ed.), *Cognitive processes in depression*. New York: Guilford.

Lake, E. A., & Arkin, R. M. (1985). Reactions to objective and subjective interpersonal evaluation: The influence of social anxiety. *Journal of Social and Clinical Psychology, 3*, 143-160.

Landau, R. J. (1980). The role of semantic schemata in phobic word interpretation. *Cognitive Therapy and Research, 4*, 427-434.

Landau, R. J., & Goldfried, M. R. (1981). The assessment of schemata: A unifying framework for cognitive, behavioral, and traditional assessment. In P. C. Kendall & S. D. Hollon (Eds.), *Assessment strategies for cognitive-behavioral interventions* (pp. 363-399). New York: Academic Press.

Lang, P. J. (1968). Fear reduction and fear behavior: Problems in treating a construct. In J. M. Shlien (Ed.), *Research in Psychotherapy* (Vol. 3, pp. 90–102). Washington, D.C.: American Psychological Association.

Lang, P. J. (1984). Affective information processing and the assessment of anxiety. *Journal of Behavioral Assessment, 6,* 369–395.

Last, C. G., Barlow, D. H., & O'Brien, G. T. (1985). Assessing cognitive aspects of anxiety: Stability over time and agreement between several methods. *Behavior Modification, 9,* 72–93.

Last, C. G., O'Brien, G. T., & Barlow, D. H. (1985). The relationship between cognitions and anxiety: A preliminary report. *Behavior Modification, 9,* 235–241.

Lazarus, R. S. (1966). *Psychological stress and the coping process.* New York: McGraw-Hill.

Lewinsohn, P. M., Larson, D. W., & Munoz, R. F. (1982). The measurement of expectancies and other cognitions in depressed individuals. *Cognitive Therapy and Research, 6,* 437–446.

Lewinsohn, P. M., Steinmetz, J. L., Larson, D. W., & Franklin, J. (1981). Depression-related cognitions: Antecedent or consequences? *Journal of Abnormal Psychology, 90,* 213–219.

Likert, R., & Quasha, W. H. (1970). *Revised Minnesota Paper From Board Test.* New York: The Psychological Corporation.

Linehan, M. M., & Nielson, S. L. (1983). Social desirability: Its relevance to the measurement of hopelessness and suicidal behavior. *Journal of Consulting and Clinical Psychology, 51,* 141–143.

Lobitz, W. C., & Post, R. D. (1979). Parameters of self-reinforcement and depression. *Journal of Abnormal Psychology, 88,* 33–41.

Loftus, E. F., & Loftus, G. R. (1980). On the permanence of stored information in the human brain. *American Psychologist, 35,* 409–420.

Lohr, J. M., & Bonge, D. (1980). Retest reliability of the Irrational Beliefs Test. *Psychological Reports, 47,* 1314.

Lohr, J. M., & Bonge, D. (1981). On the distinction between illogical and irrational beliefs and their relationship to anxiety. *Psychological Reports, 48,* 191–194.

Lohr, J. M., & Bonge, D. (1982a). The factorial validity of the Irrational Beliefs Test: A psychometric investigation. *Cognitive Therapy and Research, 6,* 225–230.

Lohr, J. M., & Bonge, D. (1982b). Relationships between assertiveness and factorially validated measures of irrational beliefs. *Cognitive Therapy and Research, 6,* 353–356.

Mahoney, M. J. (1977). Reflections on the cognitive learning trend in psychotherapy. *American Psychologist, 32,* 5–13.

MacDonald, M. R., & Kuiper, N. A. (1982). *Self-schema processing: Decision consistency and automaticity in clinical depression.* Submitted for publication.

Manly, P. C., McMahon, R. B., Bradley, C. F., & Davidson, P. O. (1982). Depressive attributional style and depression following childbirth. *Journal of Abnormal Psychology, 91,* 245–254.

Markus, H. (1977). Self-schemata and processing information about the self. *Journal of Personality and Social Psychology, 35,* 63–78.

Marlatt, G. A., & Gordon, J. R. (1979). Determinants of relapse: Implications for the maintenance of behavior change. In P. O. Davidson (Ed.), *Behavioral medicine: Changing health lifestyles.* (pp. 410–452). New York: Brunner/Mazel.

Marlatt, G. A., & Gordon, J. R. (Eds.). (1985). *Relapse prevention.* New York: Guilford Press.

Maser, J. D. (1984). Behavioral testing of anxiety: Issues, diagnosis, and practice. *Journal of Behavioral Assessment, 6,* 397–409.

Mash, E. J., & Terdal, L. G. (1982). Behavioral assessment of childhood disturbance. In E. J. Mash and L. G. Terdal (Eds.), *Behavioral assessment of childhood disorders* (pp. 3–78). New York: Guilford Press.

May, J. R., & Johnson, H. J. (1973). Physiological activity to internally elicited arousal and inhibitory thoughts. *Journal of Abnormal Psychology, 82*, 239–245.

Meichenbaum, D. (1977). *Cognitive-behavior modification: An integrative approach.* New York: Plenum Press.

Meichenbaum, D., & Goodman, J. (1971). Training impulsive children to talk to themselves: A means of developing self-control. *Journal of Abnormal Psychology, 77*, 115–120.

Meichenbaum, D., & Jaremko, M. (Eds.) (1982). *Stress prevention and management: A cognitive-behavioral approach.* New York: Plenum Press.

Melamed, B. G., & Siegel, L. J. (1975). Reduction of anxiety in children facing hospitalization and surgery by use of filmed modeling. *Journal of Consulting and Clinical Psychology, 43*, 511–521.

Melamed, B. G., Yurchenson, A. T., Hawes, R., Heiby, E., & Glick, J. (1975). The use of filmed modeling to reduce uncooperative behavior of children during dental treatment. *Journal of Dental Research, 54*, 797–801.

Melstrom, M. A., & Cartwright, R. D. (1983). Effects of successful vs. unsuccessful psychotherapy outcome on some dream dimensions. *Psychiatry, 46*, 51–65.

Merluzzi, T. V., Burgio, K. L., & Glass, C. R. (1984). Cognition and psychopathology: An analysis of social introversion and self-statements. *Journal of Consulting and Clinical Psychology, 52*, 1102–1103.

Merluzzi, T. V., Glass, C. R., & Genest, M. (Eds.) (1981). *Cognitive assessment.* New York: Guilford Press.

Metalsky, G. I., Abramson, L. Y., Seligman, M. E. P., Semmel, A., & Peterson, C. (1982). Attributional styles and life events in the classroom: Vulnerability and invulnerability to depressive mood reactions. *Journal of Personality and Social Psychology, 43*, 612–617.

Michael, C. C., & Funabiki, D. (1985). Depression, distortion, and life stress: Extended findings. *Cognitive Therapy and Research, 9*, 659–666.

Miller, I. W., Klee, S. H., & Norman, W. H. (1982). Depressed and nondepressed inpatients' cognitions of hypothetical events, experimental tasks, and stressful life events. *Journal of Abnormal Psychology, 91*, 78–81.

Miller, I. W., III, & Norman, W. H. (1986). Persistence of depressive cognitions within a subgroup of depressed inpatients. *Cognitive Therapy and Research, 10*, 211–224.

Miller, S. M. (1981). Predictability and human stress: Toward a classification of evidence and theory. In L. Berkowitz (Ed.), *Advances in experimental social psychology* (Vol. 14, pp. 204–256). New York: Academic Press.

Miller, W. R., & Seligman, M. E. P. (1973). Depression and the perception of reinforcement. *Journal of Abnormal Psychology, 82*, 62–73.

Miller, W. R., & Seligman, M. E. P. (1976). Learned helplessness, depression and the perception of reinforcement. *Behavior Research and Therapy, 14*, 7–17.

Miller, W. R., Seligman, M. E. P., & Kurlander, H. (1975). Learned helplessness, depression, and anxiety. *Journal of Nervous and Mental Disease, 161*, 347–357.

Minkoff, K., Bergman, E., Beck, A. T., & Beck, R. (1973). Hopelessness, depression, and attempted suicide. *American Journal of Psychiatry, 130*, 455–459.

Mitchell, D. B., & Richman, C. L. (1980). Confirmed reservations: Mental travel. *Journal of Experimental Psychology: Human Perception and Performance, 6*, 58–66.

Neisser, U. (1967). *Cognitive psychology*. New York: Appleton-Century-Croft.

Neisser, U. (1976). *Cognition and reality: Principles and implications of cognitive psychology*. San Francisco: Freeman.

Nelson, R. E. (1977). Irrational beliefs in depression. *Journal of Consulting and Clinical Psychology*, *45*, 1190–1191.

Nevid, J. S. (1983). Hopelessness, social desirability, and construct validity. *Journal of Consulting and Clinical Psychology*, *51*, 139–140.

Nisbett, R. E., & Ross, L. (1980). *Human inference: Strategies and shortcomings of social judgment*. Englewood Cliffs, N.J.: Prentice-Hall.

Nisbett, R. E., & Wilson, T. D. (1977). Telling more than we can know: Verbal reports on mental processes. *Psychological Review*, *84*, 231–259.

Norman, W. H., Miller, I. W., III, & Klee, S. H. (1983). Assessment of cognitive distortion in a clinically depressed population. *Cognitive Therapy and Research*, *7*, 133–140.

Novaco, R. W. (1979). The cognitive regulation of anger and stress. In P. C. Kendall & S. D. Hollon (Eds.), *Cognitive-behavioral interventions: Theory, research, and procedures* (pp. 241–285). New York: Academic Press.

O'Hara, M. W., Neunaber, D. J., & Zekoski, E. M. (1984). Prospective study of postpartum depression: Prevalence, course, and predictive factors. *Journal of Abnormal Psychology*, *93*, 158–171.

O'Hara, M. W., Rehm, L. P., & Campbell, S. B. (1982). Predicting depressive symptomatology: Cognitive-behavioral models and postpartum depression. *Journal of Abnormal Psychology*, *91*, 457–461.

Olinger, L., Kuiper, N., & Shaw, B. (in press). Dysfunctional attitudes and negative life events: A cognitive vulnerability to depression. *Cognitive Therapy and Research*.

Oliver, J. M., & Basumgart, E. P. (1985). The Dysfunctional Attitudes Scale: Psychometric properties and relation to depression in a unselected adult population. *Cognitive Therapy and Research*, *9*, 161–167.

Parks, C. W., Jr. (1982). *A multidimensional view of the imagery construct: Issues of definition and assessment*. Unpublished manuscript.

Persons, J. B., & Rao, P. A. (1985). Longitudinal studies of cognitions, life events, and depression in psychiatric inpatients. *Journal of Abnormal Psychology*, *94*, 51–63.

Peterson, C., Bettes, B. A., & Seligman, M. E. P. (1985). Depressive symptoms and unprompted causal attributions: Content analysis. *Behavior Research and Therapy*, *23*, 379–382.

Peterson, C., Luborsky, L., & Seligman, M. E. P. (1983). Attributions and depressive mood shifts: A case study using the symptom-context method. *Journal of Abnormal Psychology*, *92*, 96–103.

Peterson, C., & Seligman, M. E. P. (1984). Explanatory style and depression: Theory and evidence. *Psychological Review*, *91*, 188–204.

Peterson, C., Semmel, A., von Baeyer, C., Abramson, L. Y., Metalsky, G. I., & Seligman, M. E. P. (1982). The Attributional Style Questionnaire. *Cognitive Therapy and Research*, *6*, 287–299.

Peterson, C., Villanova, P., & Raps, C. S. (1985). Depression and attributions: Factors responsible for inconsistent results in the published literature. *Journal of Abnormal Psychology*, *94*, 165–168.

Petrie, K., & Chamberlain, K. (1983). Hopelessness and social desirability as mediator variables in predicting suicidal behavior. *Journal of Consulting and Clinical Psychology*, *51*, 485–487.

Petty, R. E., & Cacioppo, J. T. (1977). Forewarning, cognitive responding, and resistance to persuasion. *Journal of Personality and Social Personality*, *35*, 645–655.

Petty, R. E., & Cacioppo, J. T. (1981). *Attitudes and persuasion: Classic and contemporary approaches*. Dubuque, Ia.: Wm C. Brown.

Phares, E. J. (1957). Expectancy change in chance and skill situations. *Journal of Abnormal and Social Psychology*, *54*, 339–342.

Phares, E. J. (1973). *Locus of control: A personality determinant of behavior*. Morristown, NJ: General Learning Press.

Piaget, J. (1926). *The language and thought of the child* (M. Gabain, trans.). New York: Meridian, 1955. (Originally published, 1923).

Pope, K. S. (1978). How gender, solitude, and posture influence the stream of consciousness. In K. S. Pope & J. L. Singer (Eds.), *The stream of consciousness: Scientific investigation into the flow of human experience* (pp. 259–299). New York: Plenum Press.

Rachman, S., & Hodgson, R. (1974). Synchrony and desynchrony in fear and avoidance. *Behavior Research and Therapy*, *12*, 311–318.

Raimy, V. (1975). *Misunderstandings of the self: Cognitive psychotherapy and the misconception hypothesis*. San Francisco: Jossey-Bass.

Raps, C. S., Peterson, C., Reinhard, K. E., Abramson, L. Y., & Seligman, M. E. P. (1982). Attributional style among depressed patients. *Journal of Abnormal Psychology*, *91*, 102–108.

Rice, L. N. (1974). The evocative function of the therapist. In D. A. Wexler & L. N. Rice (Eds.), *Innovation in client-centered therapy* (pp. 284–311). New York: Wiley-Interscience.

Richardson, S. S., & Kleinknecht, R. A. (1984). Expectancy effects on anxiety and self-generated cognitive strategies in high and low dental-anxious females. *Journal of Behavior Therapy and Experimental Psychiatry*, *15*, 241–247.

Richman, C. L., Mitchell, D. B., & Reznick, J. S. (1979). Mental travel: Some reservations. *Journal of Experimental Psychology: Human Perception and Performance*, *5*, 13–18.

Rimm, D. C., & Litvak, S. B. (1969). Self-verbalization and emotional arousal. *Journal of Abnormal Psychology*, *74*, 181–187.

Riskind, J. H., & Rholes, W. S. (1984). Cognitive accessibility and the capacity of cognitions to predict future depression: A theoretical note. *Cognitive Therapy and Research*, *8*, 1–12.

Roberts, D. F., & Maccoby, N. (1973). Information processing and persuasion: Counterarguing behavior. In P. Clarke (Ed.), *New models for mass communication*. Beverly Hills, Calif.: Sage Publications.

Roberts, R. N., & Tharp, R. G. (1980). A naturalistic study of school children's private speech in an academic problem-solving task. *Cognitive Therapy and Research*, *4*, 341–352.

Rogers, T., Kuiper, N., & Kirker, W. (1977). Self-reference and the encoding of personal information. *Journal of Personality and Social Psychology*, *35*, 677–688.

Rogers, T. B., Rogers, P. J., & Kuiper, N. A. (1979). Evidence for the self as a cognitive prototype: The "false alarms effect." *Personality and Social Psychology Bulletin*, *5*, 53–56.

Rosch, E. (1978). Principles of categorization. In E. Rosch & R. B. Lloyd (Eds.), *Cognition and categorization*. Hillsdale, NJ: Erlbaum.

Rosengren, K., Behrend, D., & Perlmutter, M. (1985, July). *Parent and child speech during puzzle solving*. Paper presented at the biennial meeting of the Society for

Research in Child Development, Toronto, Canada.

Ross, S. M., Gottfredson, D. K., Christensen, P., & Weaver, R. (1986). Cognitive self-statements in depression: Findings across clinical populations. *Cognitive Therapy and Research, 10,* 159–165.

Rotter, J. B. (1954). *Social learning and clinical psychology,* New York: Prentice-Hall.

Rotter, J. B. (1966). Generalized expectancies for internal versus external control of reinforcement. *Psychological Monographs, 80* (1, Whole No. 609).

Rotter, J. B., Liverant, S., & Crowne, D. P. (1961). The growth and extinction of expectancies in chance-controlled and skilled tasks. *Journal of Psychology, 52,* 161–177.

Rudy, T. W., Merluzzi, T. V., & Henahan, P. T. (1982). Construal of complex assertion situations: A multidimensional analysis. *Journal of Consulting and Clinical Psychology, 50,* 125–137.

Ruehlman, L. S., West, S. G., & Pasahow, R. J. (1985). Depression and evaluative schemata. *Journal of Personality, 53,* 46–92.

Rush, A. J., Beck, A. T., Kovacs, M., Weissenberger, J., & Hollon, S. D. (1982). Comparison of the effects of cognitive therapy on helplessness and self concept. *American Journal of Psychiatry, 139,* 862–866.

Rush, A. J., Weissenberger, J., & Eaves, G. (1986). Do thinking patterns predict depressive symptoms? *Cognitive Therapy and Research, 10,* 225–235.

Russell, P. C., & Brandsma, J. M. (1974). Theoretical and empirical integration of the rational-emotive and classical conditioning theories. *Journal of Consulting and Clinical Psychology, 42,* 389–397.

Schwartz, R. M., & Gottman, J. (1976). Toward a task analysis of assertive behavior. *Journal of Consulting and Clinical Psychology, 44,* 910–920.

Seligman, M. E. P. (1975). *Helplessness: On depression, development, and death.* San Francisco: Freeman.

Seligman, M. E. P., Abramson, L. Y., Semmel, A., & von Baeyer, C. (1979). Depressive attributional style. *Journal of Abnormal Psychology, 88,* 242–247.

Seligman, M. E. P., & Schulman, P. (1986). Explanatory style as a predictor of productivity and quitting among life insurance sales agents. *Journal of Personality and Social Psychology, 50,* 832–838.

Sewitch, T., & Kirsch, I. (1984). The cognitive content of anxiety: Naturalistic evidence for the predominance of threat-related thoughts. *Cognitive Therapy and Research, 8,* 49–58.

Sheehan, P. W., Ashton, R., & White, K. (1983). Assessment of mental imagery. In A. A. Sheikh (Ed.), *Imagery: Current theory, research, and application* (pp. 189–221). New York: Wiley.

Shevrin, H., & Dickman, S. (1980). The psychological unconscious: A necessary assumption for all psychological theory? *American Psychologist, 35,* 421–434.

Shorkey, C. L., Reyes, E., & Whiteman, V. L. (1977). Development of the rational behavior inventory: Initial validity and reliability. *Educational and Psychological Measurement, 37,* 527–534.

Silverman, J. S., Silverman, J. A., & Eardley, D. A. (1984). Do maladaptive attitudes cause depression? *Archives of General Psychiatry, 41,* 28–30.

Simons, A. D. (1984). Cognition and therapy. *Archives of General Psychiatry, 41,* 1114–1115.

Simons, A. D., Garfield, S. L., & Murphy, G.E. (1984). The process of change in cognitive therapy and pharmacotherapy for depression. *Archives of General Psychiatry, 41,* 45–51.

Simons, A. D., Lustman, P. J., Wetzel, R. D., & Murphy, G. E. (1985). Predicting response to cognitive therapy of depression: The role of learned resourcefulness. *Cognitive Therapy and Research, 9*, 79–90.

Singer, J. L. (1984). The private personality. *Personality and Social Psychology Bulletin, 10*, 7–30.

Singer, J. L., & Antrobus, J. S. (1972). Daydreaming, imaginal processes, and personality: A normative study. In P. W. Sheehan (Ed.), *The function and nature of imagery* (pp. 175–202). New York: Academic Press.

Smith, R. E., & Sarason, I. G. (1975). Social anxiety and the evaluation of negative interpersonal feedback. *Journal of Consulting and Clinical Psychology, 43*, 429.

Smith, T. W. (1983). Change in irrational beliefs and the outcome of rational-emotive psychotherapy. *Journal of Consulting and Clinical Psychology, 51*, 156–157.

Smith, T. W., Follick, M. J., Ahern, D. K., & Adams, A. (1986). Cognitive distortion and disability in chronic low back pain. *Cognitive Therapy and Research, 10*, 201–210.

Smolen, R. C. (1978). Expectancies, mood, and performance of depressed and nondepressed psychiatric inpatients on chance and skill tasks. *Journal of Abnormal Psychology, 87*, 91–101.

Southwick, L., Steele, C., & Lindell, M. (1986). The roles of historical experience and construct accessibility in judgments about alcoholism. *Cognitive Therapy and Research, 10*, 167–185.

Srull, T. K., & Wyer, R. S. (1979). The role of category accessibility in the interpretations of information about persons: Some determinants and implications. *Journal of Personality and Social Psychology, 37*, 1660–1672.

Srull, T. K., & Wyer, R. S. (1980). Category accessibility and social perception: Some implications for the study of person memory and interpersonal judgments. *Journal of Personality and Social Psychology, 38*, 841–856.

Sternberg, R. J., & Tulving, E. (1977). The measurement of subjective organization in free recall. *Psychological Bulletin, 84*, 539–557.

Strosahl, K. D., & Ascough, J. C. (1981). Clinical uses of mental imagery: Experimental foundations, theoretical misconceptions, and research issues. *Psychological Bulletin, 89*, 422–438.

Sutton-Simon, K., & Goldfried, M. R. (1979). Faculty thinking patterns in two types of anxiety. *Cognitive Therapy and Research, 3*, 193–203.

Swan, G. E., & MacDonald, M. L. (1978). Behavior therapy in practice: A national survey of behavior therapists. *Behavior Therapy, 9*, 799–807.

Sweeney, P. D., Anderson, K., & Bailey, S. (1986). Attributional style in depression: A meta-analytic review. *Journal of Personality and Social Psychology, 50*, 974–991.

Taylor, S. E., & Crocker, J. (1981). Schematic basis of information processing. In E. T. Higgins, C. P., Herman, & M. P. Zanna (Eds.), *Social cognition: The Ontario symposium* (Vol. 1, pp. 89–134). Hillsdale, NJ: Erlbaum.

Teasdale, J. D. (1983). Negative thinking in depression: Cause, effect, or reciprocal relationship? *Advances in Behavior Research and Therapy, 5*, 3–25.

Teasdale, J. D., Taylor, R., & Fogarty, F. J. (1980). Effects of induced elation-depression on the accessibility of memories of happy and unhappy experiences. *Behavior Research and Therapy, 18*, 339–346.

Tosi, D. J., & Eshbaugh, D. M. (1976). The Personal Beliefs Inventory: A factor analytic study. *Journal of Clinical Psychology, 32*, 322–327.

Tosi, D. J., Forman, M. A., Rudy, D. R., & Murphy, M. A. (1986). Factor analysis of the Common Beliefs Survey III: A replication study. *Journal of Consulting and*

Clinical Psychology, 54, 404–405.
Tower, R. B., & Singer, J. L. (1981). The measurement of imagery: How can it be clinically useful? In P. C. Kendall & S. D. Hollon (Eds.), *Assessment strategies for cognition-behavioral interventions* (pp. 119–159). New York: Academic Press.
Tsujimoto, R. N. (1978). Memory bias toward normative and novel trait prototypes. *Journal of Personality and Social Psychology, 36,* 1391–1401.
Tuma, A. H., & Maser, J. D. (Eds.). (1986). *Anxiety and the anxiety disorders.* Hillsdale: N.J.: Erlbaum.
Turk, D. C., & Salovey, P. (1985a). Cognitive structures, cognitive processes, and cognitive-behavior modification: I. Client issues. *Cognitive Therapy and Research, 9,* 1–18.
Turk, D. C., & Salovey, P. (1985b). Cognition structures, cognitive processes, and cognitive-behavior modification: II. Judgments and inferences of the clinician. *Cognition Therapy and Research, 9,* 19–33.
Turk, D. C., & Speers, M. A. (1983). Cognitive schemata and cognitive processes in cognitive-behavioral interventions: Going beyond the information given. In P. C. Kendall (Ed.), *Advances in cognitive-behavioral research and therapy* (Vol. II, pp. 1–32). New York: Academic Press.
Tversky, A., & Kahneman, D. (1973). Availability: A heuristic for judging frequency and probability. *Cognitive Psychology, 5,* 207–232.
Velten, E. (1968). A laboratory task for induction of mood states. *Behavior Research and Therapy, 6,* 473–482.
Vermilyea, J. A., Boice, R., & Barlow, D. H. (1984). Rachman and Hodgson (1974) a decade later: How do desynchronous response systems relate to the treatment of agoraphobia? *Behavior Research and Therapy, 22,* 615–621.
Vernon, D. T. A., Foley, J. M., & Schulman, J. L. (1967). Effect of mother–child separation and birth order on young children's responses to two potentially stressful experiences. *Journal of Personality and Social Psychology, 5,* 162–174.
Vygotsky, L. (1962). *Thought and language.* In I. E. Hanfinswn & G. Vakar (Eds. and trans.). Cambridge, Mass: Massachusetts Institute of Technology Press. (Originally published, 1934).
Wachtel, P. L. (1981). Transference, schema, and assimilation: The relevance of Piaget to the psychoanalytic theory of transference. In Chicago Institute for Psychoanalysis (Eds.), *Annual of psychoanalysis* (Vol. 8, pp. 227–254). New York: International Universities Press.
Wade, T. C., Baker, T. B., & Hartmann, D. P. (1979). Behavior therapists' self-reported views and practices. *The Behavior Therapist, 2,* 3–6.
Watkins, J. T., & Rush, A. J. (1983). Cognitive response test. *Cognitive Therapy and Research, 7,* 425–435.
Weissman, A., & Beck, A. T. (1978, November). *Development and validation of the Dysfunctional Attitude Scale (DAS).* Paper presented at the 12th annual meeting of the Association for the Advancement of Behavior Therapy, Chicago.
Wetzel, R. D. (1976). Hopelessness, depression, and suicide intent. *Archives of General Psychiatry, 33,* 1069–1073.
Wetzel, R. D., Margulies, T., Davis, R., & Karam, E. (1980). Hopelessness, depression, and suicidal intent. *Journal of Clinical Psychiatry, 41,* 159–160.
Wexler, D. A. (1974). A cognitive theory of experiencing, self-actualization, and therapeutic process. In D. A. Wexler & L. N. Rice (Eds.), *Innovations in client-centered therapy.* (pp. 49–116). New York: Wiley-Interscience.
Whiteman, V., & Shorkey, C. (1978). Validation testing of the rational behavior inventory. *Educational and Psychological Measurement, 38,* 1143–1149.

Wilbert, J. R., & Rupert, P. A. (1986). Dysfunctional attitudes, loneliness, and depression. *Cognitive Therapy and Research, 10*, 71–77.

Wilkinson, I. M., & Blackburn, I. M. (1981). Cognitive style in depressed and recovered patients. *British Journal of Clinical Psychology, 20*, 283–292.

Wise, E. H., & Barnes, D. R. (1986). The relationship among life events, dysfunctional attitudes, and depression. *Cognitive Therapy and Research, 10,* 257–266.

Wollert, R. W. (1979). Expectancy shifts and the expectancy confidence hypothesis. *Journal of Personality and Social Psychology, 37*, 1888–1901.

Wyer, R. S., Jr., & Srull, T. K. (1981). Category accessibility: Some theoretical and empirical issues concerning the processing of social stimulus information. In E. T. Higgins, C. P. Herman, & M. P. Zanna (Eds.), *Social Cognition: The Ontario Symposium* (Vol. 1, pp. 161–197). Hillsdale, NJ: Erlbaum.

Zajonc, R. (1980). Feeling and thinking: Preferences need no inferences. *American Psychologist, 35*, 151–175.

Zatz, S., & Chassin, L. (1983). Cognitions of test-anxious children. *Journal of Consulting and Clinical Psychology, 51*, 526–534.

Zatz, S., & Chassin, L. (1985). Cognitions of test-anxious children under naturalistic test-taking conditions. *Journal of Consulting and Clinical Psychology, 53*, 393–401.

Zeiss, A. M., Lewinsohn, P. M., & Munoz, R. F. (1979). Nonspecific improvement effects in depression using interpersonal skills training, pleasant activities schedules, or cognitive training. *Journal of Consulting and Clinical Psychology, 74*, 427–439.

Zimmerman, M., & Coryell, W. (1986). Dysfunctional attitudes in endogenous and nonendogenous depressed inpatients. *Cognitive Therapy and Research, 10*, 339–346.

Zweig, D. R., & Brown, S. D. (1985). Psychometric evaluation of a written stimulus presentation format for the social interaction self-statement test. *Cognitive Therapy and Research, 9*, 285–295.

7
Psychophysiological Assessment

Ellie T. Sturgis
Sandra Gramling

Psychophysiological responses have been of interest to behavioral psychologists since the early days of the behavior therapy movement. Several factors contribute to this interest including (a) progress in electronics and instrumentation resulting from the space program, (b) the discovery that humans and animals could learn to voluntarily control physiological responses formerly regarded as involuntary, (c) the increased awareness of physiological and neurochemical components of behavior, and (d) the development of the field of behavioral medicine. Indeed, Lang's (1971) classic article emphasizing a tripartite model of behavior — measurement of physiological activity, overt motor behavior, and subjective experience — has become the standard design for studies investigating the nature of psychological dysfunction and the efficacy of psychotherapy. Early research involving psychophysiological assessment was often simplistic and responses considered to be independent from one another. The ready availability of biofeedback and simple physiological recording devices made it relatively easy for investigators to include psychophysiological responses as dependent variables in studies, but there often was little understanding of what the measures actually assessed or what factors affected the validity of the measures. More recently, however, the quality of research has generally improved, partly as a function of the interest of basic psychophysiologists in educating the applied researcher about the field of psychophysiology. This chapter discusses basic issues in the measurement of psychophysiological responses, the more commonly assessed responses, and issues threatening the validity of psychophysiological measurements. In the discussion of the measures, the anatomy and physiology of the responses are discussed in addition to the ways in which the response is measured. Of necessity, the discussions will be brief and somewhat superficial. For further information the reader is directed to several basic texts on psychophysiological assessment including Andreassi (1980); Coles, Donchin, and Porges (1986); Greenfield and Sternbach (1972); Hassett (1978); Martin and Venables (1980); and Stern, Ray, and Davis (1980).

MEASUREMENT ISSUES

The goals of psychophysiological assessment are to quantify and interpret the results obtained from recording the various biological responses under a specific set of conditions. As is the case with all aspects of human behavior, there are factors that affect the specified response in predictable ways which must be considered in the interpretation of the recorded data. The principles or laws of applicability to psychophysiological response are discussed in this section and include concepts of autonomic balance, homeostasis, the law of initial value, habituation, and orienting and defensive responses.

Autonomic Balance

Individuals show differing patterns of responsivity to varied types of stimulation. The responses of certain persons largely reflect sympathetic activation whereas the responses of others reflect more predominant parasympathetic responsivity. The particular impact of this difference remains unclear but has been the subject of investigation for many years. Eppinger and Hess (1917) first classified responders as vagotonic (parasympathetic responders) and sympatonic (sympathetic responders). Later research by Gellhorn, Cortell, and Feldman (1941) and Darrow (1943) investigated the role of personality style and response pattern. Wenger (1966) created an autonomic balance score using a composite of electrodermal activity, heart rate, diastolic blood pressure, and salivation. Scores were found to be normally distributed, with low scores indicative of sympathetic dominance and higher scores reflecting parasympathetic dominance. Studies examining autonomic balance have found (a) patients with a diagnosis of an anxiety disorder demonstrate autonomic balance scores skewed in the sympathetic direction, (b) unmedicated schizophrenic patients show sympathetic dominance, and (c) persons diagnosed as antisocial personalities show parasympathetic dominance (Porges, 1976; Wenger, 1966).

Homeostasis

Homeostasis is defined as the tendency of the organism to maintain constant conditions or a state of equilibrium between different but interdependent elements of the organism. The state is usually maintained by a negative feedback loop that provides the CNS and PNS with information if levels of activity of a given response are higher or lower than normal. The body then activates mechanisms designed to restore the resting state of balance. The homeostatic mechanism functions to protect the integrity of the organism and to insure proper operation of the varied response systems. The principle of homeostasis applies to most physiological response systems but has been demonstrated most consistently in the control of the cardiovascular and respiratory response systems (Kaufman & Schneiderman, 1986; Obrist, 1981).

Law of Initial Values

The *law of initial value* states that the magnitude of a particular physiological response to a given stimulus or situation depends on the prestimulus level of the system being measured (Wilder, 1950). The higher the prestimulus level of the response, the smaller the increase in the response following stimulation generally designed to increase the response; conversely, the higher the prestimulus level, the greater the decrease in a response following a stimulation generally designed to decrease that response. Wilder (1967) considered the law of initial value to apply to all physiological variables, and a number of early studies seemed to support this view (Lacey, 1956). However, although the law has been found to apply to most of the cardiovascular and vasomotor responses (Hord, Johnson, & Lubin, 1964; Lovallo & Zeiner, 1975), it has not been found to hold true in the measurement of salivation, electrodermal responses, and vaginal pressure pulse (Andreassi, 1980; Rothenberg & Geer, 1980; Stock & Geer, 1982; White, 1977). Further research is needed to determine the extent to which the law is operative across different physiological systems. The law of initial value presents particular problems for data analysis since it means that responses are not independent of one another. The power of an analysis of data using the change-score measure is markedly reduced by the law of initial values. Usually investigators deal with the problem by using covariance analyses and the autonomic lability score (Coles, Gratton, Kramer, & Miller, 1986).

Habituation

Habituation refers to the process in which the magnitude of a physiological response diminishes with continued presentation of a stimulus. Habituation has been demonstrated to affect a number of levels of behavior, including neuronal firing, physiological responsivity, subjective awareness, and gross motor activity (O'Gorman, 1983). Research has shown the process of habituation to be slower the greater the intensity, the more unique, or the more complex the stimulus. Physiologically, habituation does not occur equally across systems. For example, O'Gorman (1983) found finger-pulse

BA—H

volume and blood volume to decrease across trials among anxious subjects but found no change in electrodermal phenomena in these individuals. The habituation response is intimately related to the orienting and defensive responses next described.

Orienting and Defensive Responses

The *orienting response* refers to a reflexive response in humans and animals that occurs immediately after the slightest change in the environment. The response occurs when an event does not match what is expected by the individual. The orienting response involves a series of physiological changes (increased muscle tone, activation of electroencephalogram [EEG], peripheral vasoconstriction, cephalic vasodilation, decreased then increased respiration depth, decreased heart rate, and increased sensitivity of sense organs) that alert the body to the presence of a new or unexpected stimulus and prepare it to deal with the situation. The "what is it?" response leads to improved perceptual abilities. Habituation of the orienting response is rapid (Sokolov, 1963). Analyses investigating responses to novel stimuli must consider the role of the orienting response in the response profile.

The defensive response is a reflexive response in humans and animals that occurs immediately after the occurrence of threatening stimuli in the environment. The defensive response involves a series of physiological changes (increased muscle tone, activation of EEG, peripheral vasoconstriction, cephalic vasoconstriction, decreased then increased respiration depth, increased heart rate, and increased sensitivity of sense organs) that represent the turning away from threatening or painful stimuli. Habituation of the defensive response is slow. The defensive response is often examined in the evaluation of clinical patients. Phobic patients often show a marked defensive response to anxiety-provoking slides (Lang, Melamed, & Hart, 1970; Fredrikson, 1981; Hare & Blevings, 1975). As is usually the case, the effect is not always consistent (Zahn, 1986). Over time, the repetition of fear-inducing slides can lead to a decrease in the magnitude of the defensive response as habituation occurs (Klorman, Weissberg, & Wiesenfeld, 1977).

INSTRUMENTATION

The measurement of human behavior always requires an assessment instrument. Just as observational recording sheets and self-report inventories are commonly used in the assessment of motor and cognitive behavior, respectively, the physiograph (polygraph) is a commonly used instrument in psychophysiological assessment. The electronic complexity of a physiograph may create an illusion of precision, yet use of a physiograph is limited by the same constraints and is subject to the same problems as other forms of behavioral assessment. Specifically, the issues of reliability, validity, experimental design, appropriate data analysis, etcetera, are important issues in all assessment procedures and should not be minimized by the apparent complexity of the assessment instrument.

An intact sensory system would be an adequate assessment instrument if one were interested in detecting gross changes in psychophysiological functioning (e.g., the increase in perspiration often associated with the application of a stressor). However, if precise measurement and quantification of less obvious psychophysiological events is sought, a more sensitive instrument is required. The physiograph has become an essential instrument in psychophysiological assessment because it permits the detection of otherwise covert physiological events and, through proper filtering and amplification, permits the meaningful display and quantification of these events. For example, the magnitude of some of the electrical events of interest in psychophysiological research are in the microvolt range (e.g., electroencephalography) and cannot be detected without the aid of sensitive equipment. The equipment of interest in psychophysiological assessment typically includes (a) electrodes or transducers which detect the signal; (b) the physiograph proper, which includes preamplifiers and amplifiers to filter and amplify the signal; (c) output devices including penwriters and oscilloscopes; and (d) integrators, magnetic tape, analog-to-digital (ACD) converters, and computers to quantify the output.

Signal Detection

In psychophysiological assessment, signal detection is usually accomplished by use of electrodes or transducers. When the physiological process of interest manifests itself as a bioelectrical signal (e.g., electroencephalogram), electrodes are typically used to detect that signal. When the physiological process of interest manifests itself as a mechanical or physical response (e.g., respiration), a transducer of some type may be used to convert the response into an electrical signal. In both cases, the final product is an electrical signal which is then made available to the physiograph for further conditioning and amplification.

Electrodes

There are two basic types of electrodes generally used to detect the physiological processes of interest to the psychophysiologist, surface electrodes and, less frequently, needle electrodes. Surface electrodes are typically constructed of silver/silver chloride metal disks encased in plastic housing. Surface electrodes are commonly used in the measurement of electromyography (EMG), electrocardiography (ECG), electrooculography

(EOG), electroencephalography (EEG), and electrodermal (ED) responses. The placement and exact type of electrode depends on the nature of the response being measured. For example, the signal generated by the contraction of the heart muscle in the ECG recording is relatively large and easily detected with little concern about artifact obscuring the signal. Other response systems produce much smaller signals and, consequently, more attention must be paid to skin preparation, type of electrode, and electrode placement in order to provide a clear signal for the physiograph. For several response systems (e.g., EEG, ED), recordings can be made with unipolar or bipolar electrode placements. For example, in measuring EEG, one electrode can be placed on the scalp over the area of the brain that is of interest while a second electrode is placed on a neutral or reference site, such as an earlobe (monopolar). Alternatively, both electrodes can be placed on the scalp and the potential difference between the two electrodes can be measured (bipolar).

The use of needle electrodes is a far more invasive technique and, consequently, is less frequently used in psychophysiological assessment. Basically, these electrodes are sharp needle-like pieces of metal inserted through the skin to the recording site of interest. The electrodes are most commonly used in EMG recordings. Unlike surface electrodes, these electrodes provide a more direct method of measurement and allow the evaluation of discrete units of muscle fiber.

Transducers

Transducers are used in psychophysiological assessment when the response of interest is not a bioelectrical signal, but rather is a form of physical or mechanical energy that must be converted into an electrical signal to be input into the physiograph. A common example of a transducer is the strain gauge which can be strapped around the chest. Physical changes in chest size that occur with inspiration or expiration are converted to an electrical signal suitable for input into the preamplifier of the physiograph.

Signal Filtering and Amplification

Once detected, the electrical signal must be input into an appropriate preamplifier which in turn boosts (amplifies) the signal before it is sent to the driver amplifier. The amplitude (measured in volts) and frequency (measured in Hz or cycles/sec) of the electrical signal being studied will largely determine the type of preamplifier used. The preamplifier must have an appropriate bandwidth to process signals within the frequency range being studied. That is, the frequency at which a preamplifier can operate with maximum amplification and minimum signal distortion should match the frequency characteristics of the electrical signal of interest. Similarly, signals of very low amplitude must be input into preamplifiers with very low "noise" (any electrical signal not part of the signal of interest) in order to prevent the true signal of interest from being obscured. Electrical noise can creep into the signal from many sources, including faulty placement of electrodes, improper skin preparation, undesirable movement of the subject, and operation of other devices without proper electrical shielding. Interference should always be minimized; however, with relatively high amplitude signals, internally generated amplifier noise is not a major concern.

The type of preamplifier input coupling will also determine the characteristics of the signal received by the preamplifier. In direct-coupling (DC) input, the actual potential difference between two points of the body is the measure of interest. Consequently, only unidirectional electrical signals are passed to the preamplifier, thus permitting the measurement of these slow biological responses. In capacitor-coupled (AC) input, the slow DC portion of the signal is filtered out, and the rapidly changing bidirectional aspects of the signal are passed. Thus, preamplifiers are sometimes referred to as DC or AC preamps and are often so labeled on the front panel.

Finally, the various filters provided with many amplifiers partly determines the characteristics of the observed output signal. The most common types of filters include high-pass filters (where high frequency signals are selectively passed) and 60 Hz notch filters (which selectively suppress the 60 Hz signals from wall outlets, for example, from being included in the recording). The use of filters permits adjustment of the bandwidth of the amplifier to encompass only the relevant frequencies of the potentials being recorded, thus excluding noise and artifact frequencies that fall above and below the adjusted bandwidth limits. Finally, the signal is input from the preamplifier to the driver amplifier, which further boosts the signal to a level sufficient to drive or power an external output device.

Displaying the Signal

The driver amplifier powers an external output device so that the data can be displayed in a meaningful fashion. A penwriter, which typically accompanies the physiograph, is the most common output device. The penwriter produces a tracing of the physiological signal on paper, thus providing a permanent record of the recording. The oscilloscope is another output device typically used when recording high-frequency signals. Signals that occur at frequencies higher than 75 Hz exceed the mechanical limitations of most penwriters and therefore require a different output display.

Quantifying the Data

Quantifying the recordings produced by the penwriter is a tedious and time-consuming task. Integrators are often used to simplify the quantification process. Essentially, an integrator condenses the raw data by providing a measure of total electrical activity (recorded from a given channel) as a function of time. For example, a resetting integrator continuously stores the "buildup" of voltage reflected in the raw data. When a predetermined amount of charge has accumulated, the integrator resets and the discharge triggers a brief deflection of the penwriter. The amount of electrical activity is reflected by the number of deflections per unit of time. Other types of integrators include contour-following and computer-controlled integrators. Though integrator units make the quantification of EMG a much easier task, two points of caution should be noted. First, artifact that is not excluded from the record prior to the intregation will be integrated as if it were a true signal. That is, visual inspection of an integrated EMG record will not permit the detection of artifact as would be the case in visually inspecting the "raw," unintegrated signal. Second, the integrated potentials from one channel cannot be directly compared with the integrated potentials from another channel.

The growing availability of computers has greatly aided the quantification of psychophysiological data as well as reduced the time involved in data acquisition, reduction, and analysis. For example, a signal such as EMG that had been filtered and amplified would traditionally be output to a penwriter and the record would then be scored by hand. With a relatively inexpensive computer system, including a real-time clock, an analog-to-digital converter (ACD), a disk drive, and appropriate software, the analog EMG signal can be sampled at fixed time intervals, digitized, stored on a diskette, and later analyzed with speed and objectivity. With analog multiplexing and the sample-and-hold routine, multiple channels can be recorded virtually simultaneously. Another advantage of computerization is that sampling can occur at a much quicker rate, yielding close to continuous data. Data scored by hand are usually sampled no more frequently than once every 5 seconds. The data acquisition software can include routines that can act as filters and exclude data that do not fall within the desired frequencies. The computer can also be used to control the presentation of stimuli. Powerful computer statistical packages are readily available which can facilitate the analysis and interpretations of psychophysiological data.

Depending upon the needs and interests of the psychophysiologist, a laboratory computer system can be instrumented to perform some to virtually all of the signal conditioning, display, quantification, storage, and data analysis. There are many considerations to be taken into account when equipping a laboratory. Many are discussed by McGuigan (1979) and Rugg, Fletcher, and Lykken (1980). The most important step in equipping a psychophysiological laboratory is the careful consideration of what is to be measured, how the measurements will be made, and why the measurements are being made.

RESPONSE SYSTEMS

The measurement of psychophysiological activity involves knowledges of electronics, anatomy, and physiology as well as a familiarity with the response system being measured and the questions being asked. While any physiological response can be measured given appropriate instrumentation and a cooperative subject, behavioral scientists have largely concentrated upon the cardiovascular, musculoskeletal, central nervous system, respiratory, and electrodermal activity. More recently, the ocular and gastrointestinal systems have been investigated. This section covers each system, emphasizing the anatomy and physiology of the system as well as discussing pertinent measurement issues.

Cardiovascular System

The cardiovascular system has several functions, including the distribution of oxygen and other nutrients to the body, the return of carbon dioxide from the body to the lungs, the return of other products of metabolism to the kidneys, the regulation of body temperature, and the transport of hormones and other chemicals to target organs. The functions of the heart are dynamic and complex and change as a function of demands of the tissues and the release of hormones. Some of these changes are subject to autoregulation, some are centrally innervated, and some vary as a function of the blood flowing into the heart (Larsen, Schneiderman, & Pasin, 1986). Measurement of the varied activities of the cardiovascular system is accomplished using a number of different techniques, each reflective of the varied functions of this critical system. The measures which are of most interest to the behavioral scientist include the electrocardiogram, blood pressure, and vasomotor activity. The measurement of each is discussed in this section.

Anatomy and Physiology

The cardiovascular system consists of the heart, a series of distributing arteries and arterioles, a system of collecting venules and veins, and a connection system of thin-walled capillaries. The heart is a four-chambered muscular organ which essentially consists of two pumps. Each of the pumps has two chambers, an atrium and a ventricle. As each chamber or pump fills, the cardiac muscles relax. During the emptying period, the cardiac muscles are activated and contract. The blood flow is unidirectional and is maintained by a series of one-way valves sensitive to pressure changes. The right ventricle sends unoxygenated blood to the lungs for oxygenation through the pulmonary valve into the pulmonary artery. The oxygenated blood returns to the left atrium via the pulmonary vein. The left ventricle is a pressure pump that sends oxygenated blood throughout the circulatory system.

Control of the heartbeat involves mechanisms internal and external to the heart. The efficiency of the heart as a pumping system is a function of the sequential pattern of excitation and contraction coordinated by four internal structures, namely, the sinoatrial node (SA), the atrioventricular node (AV), the bundle of His, and the Purkinje system. The SA node is located in the right atrium and its electrical discharge produces the normal rhythmic contraction of the heart. The impulses are transmitted through atrial muscle to the AV node where they are slightly delayed, and are subsequently transmitted to the bundle of His and Purkinje system which conduct the impulse for contraction to all parts of the ventricles. The contraction phase of the heart is termed *systole*, while the relaxation phase is termed *diastole*. These internal structures are affected by external factors from the central and autonomic nervous systems. The regulation of cardiovascular activity requires coordination of local, reflexive, and central nervous system activities. Impulses initiated in the visceral receptors are relayed to the CNS, integrated within the system at various levels of the neuroaxis, and transmitted to the cardiovascular effectors. CNS activity is both neuronal and hormonal and is determined by CNS regulatory activities, negative feedback systems, and cellular metabolism.

Autonomic activation occurs via the sympathetic and parasympathetic divisions of the peripheral nervous system. The parasympathetic system works primarily through acetylcholine with the sympathetic system (adrenergic system) working through epinephrine and norepinephrine. The adrenergic influences are further subdivided on the basis of receptor groups with alpha-adrenergic receptors mediating vasoconstriction and beta-adrenergic receptors mediating such actions as increases in cardiac rate and the strength of cardiac contractions (Larsen et al., 1986). The rate and contractile force of the heart are under control of both sympathetic and parasympathetic divisions. In adults the normal heart rate (HR) is about 70 beats per minute. The parasympathetic system influences heart rate through stimulation of the vagus nerve which subsequently influences the SA node. Increased parasympathetic activation results in a slowing of the heart rate (Guyton, 1981). The sympathetic system increases heart rate by decreasing vagal activity. This activation increases the rate of SA discharge, increases excitability of heart tissue, and increases the force of contraction of both the atrial and ventricular musculature.

Baroreceptors (pressure-sensitive receptors) function to insure an adequate blood supply to the brain and are located in the carotid sinus, which is supplied by fibers from the ninth cranial nerve. Decreases in blood pressure cause pressure on the walls of the carotid sinus which sends a signal the medulla. The medulla then activates the sympathetic nervous system, causing an increased heart rate, thus returning the pressure of the carotid sinus to an acceptable level (Andreassi, 1980).

Measurement of Heart Activity

The electrocardiogram is used to trace the electrical impulse that passes through the heart during contraction. Electrodes are placed on the skin and a wave-form is recorded. The electrodes may be made of stainless steel or silver and typically measure $\frac{1}{2}$-2 inches across. They are attached to the individual in a variety of ways, including the use of rubber straps, suction cups, surgical tape, or plastic adhesive strips. When possible, the electrodes should be attached to hairless sites. The area of application is cleaned and lightly abraded and electrode jelly and electrodes applied. There are standard configurations of electrode placement (Andreassi, 1980). Following the application of the electrodes, the wave form resulting from the depolarization of the heart can be recorded using a physiograph. This wave-form reflects the pattern of activation, including activation at the SA node, which results in the contraction of the atrium and the ventricles, producing a characteristic spike.

In addition to the use of physiographs, telemetry or portable recorders may be used. The miniature recorders enable ECGs to be obtained from subjects as they go through their daily routines and are often used to record ECG activity over a 24-hour period (Gunn, Wolf, Block, & Person, 1972). There are three ways to interpret the heartbeat data. An analysis of the configuration of the waveform is used to diagnose a variety of cardiac dysfunctions. Heartbeat data can be measured by counting the heart rate or measuring the interbeat interval, the time between successive heart beats.

Blood pressure is another common measure of cardiovascular function and can be measured using a host of invasive and noninvasive techniques (Steptoe, 1980). Blood pressure describes the force built up in the arteries as blood encounters resistance in the peripheral circulation and is usually measured in terms of systolic pressure and diastolic pressure. Systolic pressure is the force that results as muscles contract and blood leaves the heart. Diastolic pressure is the force with which blood flows back to the heart and represents the residual pressure present in the vascular system when the cardiac muscle relaxes between contractions (Kallman & Feuerstein, 1986). The pressures are reported as systolic/diastolic and are expressed in terms of millimeters of mercury (mmHg). Factors affecting blood pressure include heart rate; muscular contractility; stroke volume; elasticity of the arteries, veins, and capillaries; viscosity of the blood; and volume of the blood supply (Hassett, 1978). Blood pressure can be measured using a sphygmomanometer and stethoscope, use of a physiograph and a microphone designed to pick up the sound of blood flowing through and being occluded by the pressure cuff, use of intra-arterial cannulas which are inserted into the vessel and coupled with a pressure transducer, and the use of indirect measures that estimate pressure by measuring the rate of propagation of a pulse-wave through the arterial system (Sturgis & Arena, 1984). To date, the most commonly used methods to assess blood pressure are the sphygmomanometer, the physiograph and microphone system, and the physiograph and pulse-wave velocity systems.

Vasomotor activity refers to processes reflective of blood flow through a given body part (Jennings, Tahmoush, & Redmond, 1980). The two most commonly recorded measures of vasomotor activity are blood volume and pulse volume. Blood volume reflects the slowly changing absolute amount of blood in a vascular bed at a particular point in time; pulse volume reflects the blood flow through the tissue with each cardiac contraction and represents the combined blood volume and pulse volume (Brown, 1967). Both measures reflect the volume of blood present in the system, the strength of cardiac contraction, and the diameters of the vessels under examination (Kallman & Feuerstein, 1986). The measures are commonly recorded using photosensitive plethysmography, a technique that measures the amount of light transmitted through or reflected from a section of tissue. The blood volume is measured using a DC amplifier, whereas an AC amplifier is needed to measure the more rapidly changing pulse volume.

Skin temperature is largely a function of peripheral circulation. Vasoconstriction, resulting from sympathetic activation, lowers skin temperature. Vasodilation, caused by parasympathetic activation, increases skin temperature. Thus, skin temperature measures are often used as indirect indices of the vasomotor response. Skin temperature is measured by attaching a thermistor to the part of the body to be monitored, with the voltage of the thermistor changing systematically with changes in temperature. Artifacts affecting skin temperature include climatic variables, room temperature, air currents, and respiration, making the measure a difficult one to evaluate. More recently, sophisticated radiometric devices have been developed that can measure heat radiation without touching the skin, and the product can be photographed and analyzed. Thermography, the measurement of temperature by radiographic analysis, has become an important diagnostic tool in the assessment of skin temperature and pain complaints (Chucker, Fowler, Motomiya, Singh, & Hurley, 1971).

Applications

Measures of cardiovascular activity are quite common in the psychophysiological assessment and treatment literature. Because of the volume of research in this area, only major applications for each measure are discussed in this section.

Abnormal ECG recordings provide evidence concerning the presence of a myocardial infarction, myocardial ischemia, and cardiac arrhythmias. Myocardial infarctions (MIs) typically result in some scarring of the muscle tissue which can be detected by an examination of the ECG wave-form, particularly the QRS complex. The early phase of an MI or a reversible ischemia resulting from angina pectoris will often cause a deviation of the ST segment. However, abnormal ECGs may not always be present with cases of coronary heart disease, particularly in the early phases, thus other measures such as blood analyses and cardiac catheterization are commonly used (Blumenthal, 1982). Early biofeedback efforts attempted to use instrumental conditioning paradigms to train heart-rate speeding and slowing (Shearn, 1962; Hnatiow & Lang, 1974). Early studies often showed a contamination of respiration and heart rate. While the research has shown that cardiac activity can be brought under some control, the changes are minimal. Increases in heart rate are more easily attained than are decreases. The physiological mechanisms underlying the changes are not clear, but in some studies they have been found to involve the respiratory and musculoskeletal systems (Andreassi, 1980).

Blood pressure responses have been found to be important in studies examining cardiac activity and emotional arousal and to be of direct interest to behavioral medicine researchers. Interest in responses increased markedly in the late 1970s, following the discovery that biofeedback and relaxation procedures could yield decreases in blood pressure (Blanchard, Miller, Abel, Haynes, & Wicker, 1979; Jacob, Kraemer, & Agras, 1977). More recently, Blanchard et al. (1984) found thermal biofeedback to be more effective than relaxation training in yielding significant decreases in hypertension. Unfortunately, in most cases the results were somewhat disappointing for decreases were often of questionable clinical significance, with diastolic pressures showing less of a decrease than systolic pressures. More robust changes were documented when the behavioral techniques were combined with pharmacotherapy (Orton, Beiman, & Ciminero, 1982; Hatch et al., 1985). The use of behavioral techniques appears most promising in individuals with borderline hypertension or in the treatment of more resistant cases (Jacob et al., 1977). In the latter case, the procedures are considered an adjunctive form of treatment.

The finger blood volume and blood volume pulse measures have been used primarily in the study of sexual responsiveness and headache activity. Sintchak and Geer (1975) have developed a vaginal photometer measuring the blood volume and pulse volume which is used in the evaluation of sexual responsiveness. Several investigators have found the vaginal pulse amplitude to be sensitive to erotic stimulation and related to the subjective experience of arousal (Heiman, 1977; Rothenberg & Geer, 1980). The applicability of these findings to the evaluation and treatment of sexual dysfunction is currently under investigation. Numerous investigators have evaluated the cephalic blood-volume pulse of individuals with vascular headaches. The role of the cephalic vasomotor response as measured from the surface in the development and maintenance of a headache is somewhat unclear, with some studies yielding no physiological differences in headache groups and normals, while others found marked differences (Andrasik, Blanchard, Arena, Saunders, & Baron, 1982). The clinical treatment picture, is somewhat different, however. Numerous investigators have found blood volume pulse feedback effective in the treatment of vascular headaches (Bild & Adams, 1980; Friar & Beatty, 1976; Gauthier, Lacroix, Coté, Doyon, & Drolet, 1985; Sturgis, Tollison, & Adams, 1978). Unfortunately, given the discrepancy between the assessment data and treatment outcome, the mechanism of action of blood volume pulse feedback is not yet understood.

Skin temperature responses have been used frequently in psychophysiological assessment. Thermal biofeedback is a relatively simple technique which is easily learned by an individual. There are also a number of inexpensive devices which can be used by patients at home to improve generalizability of the responses. Thermal biofeedback has been used in the successful treatment of Raynaud's syndrome (Blanchard & Haynes, 1975; Surwit, Pilon, & Fenton, 1978), migraine headache (Blanchard, Theobald, Williamson, Silver, & Brown, 1978; Gauthier et al., 1985; Sargeant, Green, & Walter, 1972), and essential hypertension (Blanchard et al., 1984). While the technique appears widely used in the clinical literature, as is the case in the headache research, the mechanism of the treatment response is not clear.

Electromyography (EMG)

The EMG is most commonly used to assess the activity of the musculoskeletal system. An EMG recording reflects the electrical activity (action potentials) of stimulated muscle fibers which eventuate muscle contraction. The EMG is typically measured with surface electrodes placed on the skin over the muscle group of interest. Psychophysiologists have used the EMG to study basic constructs such as emotion and arousal (Hassett, 1978). EMG has also been used in applied research to assess and treat muscular disorders such as muscle contraction headaches (Blanchard, Andrasik, Evans, Neff, Appelbaum, & Rodichok, 1985) and in muscular rehabilitation (Middaugh, 1982; Agras, 1984).

Anatomy and Physiology

There are two types of muscle fibers, extrafusal and intrafusal, but only the activity of the extrafusal fibers is recorded in the EMG. These thread-like fibers measure about 0.1 mm in width and up to 30 mm in length. The functional unit of the striated muscle is the motor unit, which is comprised of an alpha motor neuron, its axon, and associated muscle fibers (the number of muscle fibers in a motor unit ranges from 10 to over 1,000). A single muscle is comprised of many interrelated motor units (Carlson, 1981).

In the resting state, the muscle fibers maintain a negative intracellular potential of 50–100 mv. When stimulated, the motor neuron "fires" (initiates an action potential) and a wave of depolarization passes along the associated muscle fibers causing them to contract. The number of motor units activated and the frequency of firing determines both the total amount of contraction observed and the strength of the signal detected at the EMG recording site (Carlson, 1981). An EMG recording detects the depolarization of the muscle fiber membrane rather than the contraction per se (Goldstein, 1972). If the question of interest requires measurement of the electrical activity of a single motor unit, then needle electrodes must be used.

Measurement

There are a number of considerations that should be noted in the signal detection phase of EMG measurement. First, proper skin preparation is essential in EMG recording. Ideally, the skin should be shaved and then cleaned with alcohol and acetone. The skin should then be abraded with fine sandpaper or another abrasive material to remove the high-impedance dead surface layer of the skin. The electrodes are then prepared by coating or filling them with electrode jelly. Attachment of the electrodes to the skin is possible using adhesive collars or suction cups. The electrical impedance between the electrodes should be less than 5,000 ohms. Higher impedance reduces the amplitude of the signal input into the preamplifier. If impedance exceeds 5,000 ohms, the electrodes should be removed and the preparation repeated (Stern, Ray, & Davis, 1980). Whenever possible, the electrodes should be placed in a line parallel with the muscle fiber. Generally, increasing the distance between the electrodes increases the number of motor units included in the recording. Conversely, the closer the electrode placement, the more specific and localized the recording. Finally, in the use of frontalis EMG recording, there has been some debate regarding proper recording methods. Traditionally, the method suggested by J.F. Davis (1952) using bipolar recording techniques with electrodes placed above the eyebrows has been used. The convention of placing the electrodes over each eyebrow (and consequently over two different frontalis muscles) has been questioned (C.M. Davis, Brikette, Stern, & Kimball, 1978). However, other investigations of bilateral versus unilateral electrode placement in frontalis EMG recording suggests that for many applications (e.g., evaluating changes in EMG levels for individual subjects within sessions) electrode placement per se is of little importance (Williamson, Epstein, & Lombardo, 1980; van Boxtel, Goudswaard, & Schomaker, 1984). Ultimately, the choice of electrode placement site should be determined by thoughtful consideration of the question being asked and a careful review of the relevant literature.

Signal filtering and amplification depends on similar considerations. The amplitude and frequency of the EMG signal will vary depending on the activity being measured. In general, the amplitude and frequency of the EMG signal will increase as the amount of force or exertion of the muscle group increases (Wilcott & Beenken, 1957). The magnitude of the EMG detected from surface electrodes may range from as low as 1 microvolt through the millivolt range, and the frequency may range from 2-3 Hz to over 10,000 Hz (Goldstein, 1972). The signal to be detected may be relatively small, as when one imagines engaging in an activity, or may be relatively large, as when one actually contracts the muscle. Therefore, the preamplifier should be adjusted with high-pass and low-pass filters to a bandwidth that will encompass the range of frequencies of interest, thus excluding noise and artifact frequencies that fall above or below the bandwidth limits. The use of bandpass filters has become commonplace because, in most applications, the range 10-70 Hz is representative of the larger frequency spectrum (Wilcott & Beenken, 1957). The reader should note, however, that restricting the frequency bandwidth with high- and low-pass filters has been reported to result in biased estimates of proportional changes in overall integrated EMG (van Boxtel, Goudswaard, van der Molen, & van den Bosch, 1983; van Boxtel & Schomaker, 1984; van Boxtel et al., 1984). The use of bandpass filters always reflects a compromise between rejecting artifact while including as much of the EMG signal as possible. A 60 Hz notch filter (or a low-pass filter) is often used in EMG recording to exclude the electrical noise generated by appliances using standard AC electrical outlets. The pen tracings of the EMG recording constitute the raw data of the session, although an integrator unit and/or computer controlled data acquisition and reduction techniques are frequently employed in EMG measurement.

Applications

The EMG has been used to assess a variety of behavioral phenomena. Only a few of the major applications are discussed here. Hassett (1978) and Goldstein (1972) provide additional information. The EMG has been used extensively in applied settings in the assessment and treatment of muscle contraction headache (MCH), in muscle rehabilitation and training, and in more basic research in the study of facial expressions and emotion.

The pathophysiology of the MCH has traditionally been assumed to be the result of excessive levels of muscle tension (Wolff, 1963). Consequently, EMG biofeedback aimed at reducing muscle tension in the head, neck, and shoulder muscles has been a frequently employed treatment modality for MCHs (e.g., Budzynski, Stoyva, Adler, & Mullaney, 1973). Two recent reviews of the treatment outcome literature indicate that EMG biofeedback is effective in reducing reported MCH pain in some patients (Holroyd & Penzien, in press; Blanchard et al., 1985). However, a number of well-controlled assessment studies (e.g., Anderson & Franks, 1981; Andrasik, Blanchard, Arena, Saunders, & Baron, 1982) have failed to observe significant differences in EMG levels between MCH sufferers and controls; these results seem to compromise the validity and specificity of EMG biofeedback in the treatment of MCHs (e.g., Holmes & Burish, 1983; Silver & Blanchard, 1978). Yet assessment and treatment are interdependent and therefore researchers have begun to use more discerning methods to assess physiological differences in MCH sufferers compared to controls (e.g., assessing across multiple-response systems; Cohen et al., 1983) and to identify critical variables which account for the therapeutic effects of EMG biofeedback in the treatment of MCHs (e.g., client variables; Holroyd & Penzien, in press). These studies seem to reaffirm the utility of EMG biofeedback in the assessment and treatment of MCHs.

Agras (1984) suggests that in the long run, the primary use of biofeedback may be in the area of muscular rehabilitation and training. Electromyographic biofeedback has been reported to decrease muscle spasms, strengthen damaged muscles, and increase range of motion and control of paretic muscles (Inglis, Campbell, & Donald, 1976). Similarly, clinically significant improvement has been reported with EMG biofeedback for patients with neurological disorders such as cerebral palsy (Wooldridge & Russell, 1976) and Parkinsonism (Hand, Burns, & Ireland, 1979). Musculoskeletal disorders such as temporomandibular joint pain (Carlsson & Gale, 1977) have been reported to improve with masseter EMG biofeedback. Excellent reviews of this literature can be found in Middaugh (1982) and Agras (1984).

In a more basic research application, facial EMG recordings have been used to study overt facial displays and covert affective states (e.g., Fridlund & Izard, 1983; Fridlund, Schwartz, & Fowler, 1984). Studies in this area demonstrate the usefulness of examining patterns of psychophysiological responses as well as the increasing utility of multivariate statistics in psychophysiological research. The trend toward response patterning and multivariate analysis of those multiple response systems is likely to be a continuing trend in future EMG research.

Electroencephalography

The measurement of electrical activity in the brain by psychophysiologists has steadily accelerated (Johnson, 1980). The rapid rise in EEG analysis has been attributed to many factors, but two of the most frequently cited are the increased mathematical sophistication of data analysis and the more readily available computer technology (Haimi-Cohen & Cohen, 1984; Hunt, 1985; Johnson, 1980; McGuigan, 1979; O'Conner, 1980; Picton, 1980).

Anatomy and Physiology

The brain is composed of over 1 billion neurons. Each individual neuron is capable of two basic types of electrical responses: graded potentials and action potentials. Graded potentials are small, gradual changes in the neuronal membrane potential resulting from inhibitory and excitatory synaptic activity. When the sum of the graded potentials exceeds the critical threshold, the neuron initiates an action potential. The action potential is an all-or-none digital electrical pulse which originates at the axon hillock, propagates down the axon, and results in the release of neurotransmitter substances in the synaptic cleft. The EEG includes both types of electrical activity in its record; however, the graded potentials make up a proportionately larger part of the record (Groves & Schlesinger, 1982).

The spontaneous EEG consists of many signals of various frequencies and amplitudes. Traditionally, the wave-forms which comprise the EEG record have been classified along the frequency dimension into four, and sometimes five, bandwidths of a specified frequency range. The frequency bands have been thought to reflect levels of arousal; however, this remains a controversial issue. Frequencies of less than 4 Hz are classified as *delta waves* and are associated with sleep. Delta waves are not present in the normal, awake adult. *Theta waves* refer to EEG signals in the 4–8 Hz range, are associated with drowsiness, and are found primarily in children. *Alpha waves* fall in the 8–13 Hz range and are associated with relaxation. *Beta waves* include all the signals in the EEG with frequencies greater than 13 Hz and are associated with an awake, alert state (Groves & Schlesinger, 1982). A further classification, *gamma waves*, is sometimes used to describe brain activity of very high (30–50 Hz) frequencies.

Measurement

The EEG is a measure of the electrical potential difference between any two electrodes placed on the scalp (using bipolar measurement). Since the EEG reflects the combined electrical activity of millions of neurons, the changes in voltage that characterize the EEG are relatively large. Therefore, surface electrodes placed on the scalp are suitable signal detectors, even though the scalp is several millimeters from the surface of the brain. However, the scalp area where the electrodes are to be placed must be thoroughly cleaned and abraded in order to obtain a clear signal. Electrode placement has been standardized by the International Federation of Societies for Electroencephalography and Clinical Neurophysiology with the "10-20" system of electrode placement (Jasper, 1958). The 10-20 system of electrode placement allows for individual differences in skull size by specifying that electrodes be placed on the scalp either 10 or 20% of the distance from common cranial landmarks (Hassett, 1978; Jasper, 1958; Margerison, St. John-Loe, & Binnie, 1967).

After the signal is detected, it must be amplified and filtered before being displayed by the penwriter. The amplitude of the normal EEG signal ranges from 5 to over 100 microvolts, whereas during a convulsive (e.g., epileptic) seizure the amplitude may increase to 1 millivolt (Shagass, 1972). The EEG ranges in frequency from 1 to 100 Hz. In general, the higher frequency signals are of a lower amplitude. Most of the useful information in the spontaneous EEG lies below 45 Hz and, therefore, a low-pass filter can be used to exclude both 60-cycle noise and muscle artifact. An overall pattern of electrical activity can be obtained when several channels of EEG are recorded at one time and bandpass filters are used to include only a small band of the frequency spectrum on each channel. The electrooculogram (EOG) is often recorded on another channel so that artifact caused by eye movements can be excluded from the record. Additional channels may also be used to monitor other possible sources of artifact or other response systems (e.g., EMG, respiration, ECG, etc.). In a sleep laboratory where numerous measures are recorded in addition to EEG, the use of a physiograph with 12–18 channels is not unusual.

While clinical interpretations are often made based on the visual analysis and hand-scoring of an EEG record, the volume of data resulting from the EEG recording and the complexity of the analysis usually necessitates the use of computer technology in the interpretation of EEG recordings, particularly when recording event-related potentials. Specifics regarding laboratory configurations and appropriate data analysis can be found in Coles, Gratton, Kramer, and Miller (1986); Hunt (1985); Johnson (1980); O'Connor (1980); and Picton (1980).

Applications

The EEG has been used most frequently by the medical profession to diagnose convulsive disorders and other forms of cerebral dysfunction. The EEG reveals a pattern of sharp, spike-like changes in voltage alternating with large, slow dome-shaped fluctuations in voltage during an epileptic seizure (Groves & Schlesinger, 1982). The EEG is also used in the medical setting to assess the course of recovery after brain trauma, to locate brain lesions, and to diagnose sleep disorders (Kolb & Whishaw, 1980). The clinical use of the EEG has slowed somewhat in recent years as a result of new CNS imaging techniques such as computerized transaxial tomography (CT scan) and positron emission tomography (PET scan; Neidermeyer, 1985).

The use of the EEG by psychophysiologists continues to increase, particularly the use of two measures of cortical activity which can be derived from the spontaneous EEG record. The first of these measures is the event-related potential (ERP), sometimes referred to as the averaged evoked potential, or simply the evoked potential (EP). An ERP is measured by repeatedly presenting a sensory stimulus (visual, auditory, etc.), recording the EEG, and then averaging the post-stimulus EEGs in a time-locked fashion to obtain the average cortical response to the stimulus. Averaging in this case filters out the random noise of the spontaneous EEG (which, of course, continues to occur but is unrelated to the stimulus presentation and therefore will cancel itself out over many trials) to reveal a small but reliable cortical response to the stimulus (Picton, 1980). Further information on recording techniques can be found in Hassett (1978) and Picton (1980). Recent reviews of clinical applications of visual-evoked potentials (VEP), auditory-evoked potentials (AEP), and brainstem auditory evoked potentials can be found in Celesia and Cone (1985), Hughes (1985), and Boston and Moller (1985), respectively. These techniques have been found to be useful in mapping sensory pathways and localizing sensory deficits when used in a medical context.

From a psychophysiological point of view, the ERP is of interest because the size and shape of the obtained ERP does not depend solely on the physical characteristics of the stimulus. The ERP is also influenced by the state of the organism and therefore has been used to study a variety of psychological variables, including information processing. The P300 potential is an ERP that is considered one of the more important tools in understanding information processing in humans (Duncan-Johnson, 1981; Papanicolaou, Loring, Raz, & Eisenberg, 1985). The P300 potential is a large, positive potential that occurs approximately 300 milliseconds after stimulus presentation. In the frequently used "oddball" paradigm, a subject's task is to count the number of times a low-frequency stimulus occurs when its presentation is interspersed in a series of high-frequency stimuli. The P300 potential seems to reflect the resolution of uncertainty in that the magnitude of the P300 potential varies monotonically with the probability of a task-relevant (low frequency) stimulus occurring. That is, the P300 potential is much larger following the presentation of a stimulus that occurs infrequently. The P300 has been used to study information processing efficiency in both normal (e.g., McCarthy & Donchin, 1981) and clinical (e.g., Hansch et al., 1982) populations. Picton (1980) provides more information on both applications and measurement of the ERP.

A second measure frequently derived from the EEG record and used in psychophysiological research is the contingent negative variation response (CNV). The CNV is a slow, negative potential that occurs in subjects who expect something to happen. In the typical CNV paradigm, the onset of a warning stimulus precedes the onset of an imperative stimulus. The imperative stimulus signals the subject to make some predetermined response. The CNV occurs in the time period between the two stimuli or before the subject makes a response. O'Connor (1980) notes that in subjective terms, the CNV is an anticipatory response. Decreasing the expectancy (probability) of the imperative stimulus reduces the amplitude of the CNV. However, the effects of motivation, meaning, expectancy, and anticipation cannot be separated from the CNV. By measuring other response systems concurrently with the CNV, researchers may be able to specify more accurately the critical variables associated with the response (Backs & Grings, 1985).

Electrodermal Activity

Measurement of electrodermal activity is the foundation upon which the field of psychophysiology was built. Use of the measure has a long history. Féré (1888) passed a small current between two electrodes on the skin surface and noted changes in the response when the subject was exposed to a variety of stimuli. Similarly, Tarchanoff (1890) found differences in electrical potential between two skin areas which changed when the individual was exposed to differing stimuli. Because of the relationship of the measures to differing stimuli, the electrodermal responses were considered to be a possible window into the psychological state of the organism, and for years this measure was considered a key assessment tool (Stern, Ray, & Davis, 1980). Use of electrodermal measures fell into some disrepute in the mid-1960s. Tursky and O'Connell (1966) published a survey showing an alarming range in the techniques used by investigators and subsequently a lack of standardization of the measure. As a result, basic psychophysiologists became active in the development of appropriate standards and guides to measurement (Fowles et al., 1981). The measures now are considered to be more valid, and the electrodermal response is again receiving increased attention as a valuable assessment tool.

There are several different measures of electrodermal activity. Skin resistance (SR), the most frequently used response in early research, represents the measure that results when an external source of voltage is passed through the skin and changes in electrical resistance are recorded. Skin conductance (SC) is the reciprocal of skin resistance and is more easily analyzed in statistical manipulations since it is more likely to conform to the normal distribution required for many analyses. The conductance response also increases with higher levels of arousal and decreases with lower levels of arousal, a relationship that makes more sense to most individuals (Andreassi, 1980). Skin potential (SP) measures electrical activity at the surface of the skin with no current passed through it. This measure usually yields a biphasic response curve with an initial negative component followed by a positive phase. Each of the electrodermal measures can be expressed as responses or as levels. Levels represent basal or tonic levels of the response whereas responses represent phasic or temporary changes in activity that result from exposure to specific stimuli. Investigators also discuss spontaneous activity which represents responses that occur in the absence of any known stimulation (Andreassi, 1980; Stern, Ray, & Davis, 1980).

Anatomy and Physiology

The electrodermal measures are recorded from the surface of the skin. The function of the skin is to (a) form a protective barrier for the organism against bacteria, parasites, and chemicals; (b) to keep fluids inside the body; and (c) to carry out the process of temperature regulation by increasing blood vessel dilation and sweating when the individual is hot and by constricting the blood vessels and decreasing sweat gland activity when the temperature is lower (Andreassi, 1980). The skin is composed of two layers, the epidermis, or outer layer, and the dermis, or inner layer. There are two types of sweat glands, one of which is the eccrine gland, used in electrodermal measurement. The eccrine gland is a tubular structure opening onto the skin surface and extending from the dermis to the epidermis. The gland is innervated by acetylcholine, not the norepinephrine normally produced by the sympathetic nervous system (Stern, Ray, & Davis, 1980). This difference in innervation limits the generalizability of electrodermal response to other sympathetically mediated psychophysiological measures. With increased sympathetic nervous system innervation, sweat rises toward the surface of the skin in varying amounts and in varying numbers of sweat glands. The greater the rise of sweat in a given gland, the lower the resistance and the higher the conductance. Overflow of the sweat to the surface of the skin increases not only skin conductance, but also skin potential. It was previously thought that electrodermal activity was solely determined by the amount of sweat on the surface of the skin, but this is not true. The gland operates as a variable resistor and is affected by hydration inside the tubules as well as moisture external to the gland (Fowles, 1986; Stern, Ray, & Davis, 1980).

Generally, the SC and SR are indices of the amount of neural activity reaching the sweat gland through the sympathetic nervous system. However, the system represents a "noisy" transducer to the central nervous system. The extent of hydration of the skin also influences the magnitude of the responses. While the SC measures are generally preferred to SR measures because the recordings do not have to be corrected for basal levels (Stern, Ray, & Davis, 1980), the SC is more drastically affected by changes in hydration (Fowles, 1986).

Measurement

Two types of circuits are used to measure the SC and SR response: constant voltage and constant current circuits. As would be expected, the constant voltage measure holds the voltage across the surface constant, and the current varies through the skin with changes in resistance or conductance. With the current held constant, the voltage or potential differences between the two electrodes placed on the skin surface vary with changes in resistance or conductance (Stern, Ray, & Davis, 1980). Lykken and Venables (1971) recommend the use of constant voltage recording with voltage limited to .50 V while Edelberg (1972) recommends a constant voltage of .75–1.0 V across sites.

Electrodes should be constructed of a nonpolarizing metal, typically with a salt of that metal adhered to the surface. The most commonly used electrodes are silver/silver chloride and zinc/zinc sulfate. Most investigators recommend that the electrode paste contain a potassium chloride or sodium chloride electrolyte. Electrode placement sites vary as a function of the response being measured. In the measurement of the SC or SR response, use of the palms, fingertips, and soles of the feet are preferred. This choice maximizes the observed activity since it sums across two sites. Edelberg (1972) recommends recording from the medial phalanx of the second and third fingers of one hand. Another common choice for SC/SR recording is from the thenar and hypothenar eminences of the palm (Hassett, 1978). Skin potential recordings reflect a potential difference between the sweat glands and internal body tissues, thus a monopolar placement is most common. For best recording, one electrode is placed on an "emotionally active" site (such as the thenar eminence) while the other electrode is placed over a small hole drilled in the skin, usually on the forearm.

Signal filtering and amplification is more difficult for the electrodermal responses. The SCL typically ranges from 2 to 100 micromhos/cm^2, the SRL from 10 to 500 kilohms/cm^2, and the SPL from $+10$ to -70 mv. One frequent annoyance for the EDA investigator is the fact that, for many subjects, the level changes may be of a relatively large magnitude compared to the responses, necessitating a change in the baseline scale. One way to avoid this is to filter out the level changes that have a slower frequency through the use of a high-pass filter of 3 Hz. While this procedure assists in finding a detectable range for change, level information and the data about response topography are lost, and information on the true response amplitude is not available (Hassett, 1978). Another way to cope with the problem is to use dual recording, with one channel of the physiograph measuring levels and the second with the gain set high so that small changes in the response are noted. Further procedures for the scoring of the EDR may be found in Andreassi (1980), Fowles et al. (1981), and Hassett (1978).

Applications

Electrodermal activity has one of its greatest uses in the study of anxiety. Early research, as mentioned earlier, found electrical changes in the skin as a result of exposure to emotionally charged situations. Generally, there is increased palmar sweat-gland activity in anxiety neurotics compared to normal controls; anxiety neurotics show an increased frequency of SCRs, high SCL, slow habituation of the orienting response, and slower decline of the SCL during baseline periods (Zahn, 1986). Lader (1967) compared SC responses of five groups (anxiety with depression, anxiety state, agoraphobia, social phobia, and specific phobia) and found the first four groups to show similar response patterns (frequent spontaneous skin conductance responses with slow habituation), while the specific phobic group showed normal activity except when exposed to the phobic stimulus.

Use of electrodermal responses for assessment and as indices of treatment effectiveness is common.

Respiratory Activity

Early psychophysiologists were interested in respiratory activity as a way of evaluating the psychological state of the individual. This most likely resulted from the relative ease with which the measure could be detected as well as the importance of the response to the survival and functioning of the individual. These researchers found that subjects showed rapid, deep breathing when exposed to emotional stimuli. However, as with most of the other measures, researchers were not able to differentiate emotions on the basis of respiratory activity (Stern, Ray, & Davis, 1980).

In current research, respiration is seldom investigated as a response in its own right but is evaluated as a check on artifact in other measures. Deep breathing causes changes in a number of autonomic responses: digital vasoconstriction, an initial increase then decrease in heart rate, decreased skin resistance, and increased skin conductance. Recently, Kaufman and Schneiderman (1986) have proposed several reasons for the investigation of respiratory activity: (a) major respiratory changes are associated with a number of behaviors such as emotions, exercise, talking, and laughing; (b) respiratory integrity can influence behavioral performance; (c) respiration is under voluntary and involuntary control; and (d) respiratory function is of importance in the field of behavioral medicine.

Anatomy and Physiology

The primary role of the respiratory system is to maintain proper concentrations of oxygen, carbon dioxide, and hydrogen in the body fluids. The respiratory system consists of the nose, mouth, pharynx, larynx, trachea, and lungs. The trachea subdivides into smaller and less cartilaginous structures that eventually terminate into alveolar ducts which are involved in the exchange of gases. Muscles of the chest wall and diaphragm control the respiratory process by expanding and contracting the lungs. While it is possible to control inspiration and expiration within normal and safe limits, the primary respiratory center is located in the medulla and operated by assessing concentrations of CO_2 in the blood. When CO_2 concentration is too high or serum pH is too low, the neurons of the ventrolateral medulla increase ventilation. Decreased concentrations of oxygen in the arterial blood supply can stimulate ventilation peripherally through sensors located in the carotid sinus, which transmit messages to the medulla to increase ventilation (Kaufman & Schneiderman, 1986). It is likely, however, that CO_2 is more important in the regulation of respiration than is oxygen. The air that flows into the lungs during inspiration is passed on to the blood through the alveolar ducts. The CO_2 from the blood is passed through the alveolar ducts and then expired.

Measurement

Several methods are used to measure respiration rate and volume. The volume of air inhaled and exhaled can be determined using a spirometer which measures the rise and fall of a floating drum as a function of breathing. A pneumotachograph is a device for measuring airflow and can be used to provide a breath-by-breath record of tidal volume and respiratory rate. More common measures involve respiratory rates and may use a thermistor taped near the nose to detect differences in air temperature. Other investigators use strain gauges which are placed around the chest and measure changes in girth of the chest with each breath. These last two measures do not provide absolute measures of air flow, but can measure rates. The major problem with most of the respiratory measures is that they cannot be calibrated, thus comparisons cannot be made across subjects nor sessions. In addition, the measures have not been compared with spirometric data. More recently, investigators have begun to use more direct measures for O_2 and CO_2 concentrations with the utilization of indwelling electrodes. Finally, there has been some use of a gas analyzer to measure tidal CO_2. In this procedure, the subject wears a plastic face mask through which air is drawn by a blower on a flexible hose. The unit maintains a flow of air directly proportional to the oxygen consumption, allowing a more accurate determination of respiratory activity.

Applications

Measurement of respiratory activity is used primarily to control for artifact in the response being measured. Coughs, sneezes, and breaths can increase EMG activity, cause a sweat-gland response to occur, and alter heart rate. Indeed, early biofeedback research designed to investigate the feasibility of heart-rate control was affected by the breathing patterns of the patient. Subsequently, respiration has been measured with the response of interest and the subject told to try a different strategy if he or she uses breathing patterns as a method for changing activity. This response is also of interest in the evaluation of anxiety disorders, since hyperventilation is a common symptom of this disorder.

Electroocular Response

The electrooculogram has been used by psychophysiologists to infer cognitive processing and to examine sleep patterns. Through use of this response, investigators have examined differences between good and poor readers (Oster & Stern, 1980), the presence of dreams and fantasy (Dement &

Kleitman, 1957), and differential processing between the two cerebral hemispheres (Ehrlichman & Weinberger, 1978). More recently, research has focused upon difficulties in ocular tracking as a genetic marker of schizophrenia (Holzman, 1984; Spohn, 1983; Zahn, 1986).

Anatomy and Physiology

The purpose of eye movements is to direct images of objects so they stimulate the foveal area of the eye, the area of greatest acuity (Andreassi, 1980). Movement of the eyes is controlled by six muscles which are innervated by the third, fourth, and sixth cranial nerves. These muscles coordinate movement of both eyes in horizontal, vertical, and circular directions by innervating three separate pairs of eye muscles (Stern, Ray, & Davis, 1980). The three sets of muscles are reciprocally innervated to allow one pair to relax while another pair contracts. Fixation movements of the eyes are controlled by two different neural mechanisms. Voluntary fixations of the convergence of the eyes on an object of choice is controlled by an area in the premotor cortex of the frontal lobes. Involuntary fixations are controlled by the occipital cortex (Guyton, 1981). There are three types of eye movements. Saccadic movements refer to the movement of the eyes from one fixation point to the next and account for 10% of the time spent in eye movements; fixations account for 90% of the time. Smooth pursuit refers to the eye movement that occurs when a moving object is fixated and followed by the eyes, such as watching a softball move through the air. Perception can occur while the eye is in motion (Andreassi, 1980). Nystagmoid movements are oscillations of the eyes which can be elicited by a moving pattern containing repeated patterns, by a head movement that stimulates the semicircular canals, and by spontaneous nystagmus which is an anomaly of the eye related to certain neurological disorders.

Measurement

The direction of gaze and the movement of the eye can be measured using a number of procedures. One method is to watch the eyes or record their movement with a movie camera. The intrusiveness of this approach and the volume of data to be scored make observational analyses difficult. Alternate methods are the contact-lens method, the corneal reflection method, and the recording of the EOG. The EOG is the most popular method and is based upon the 1 mV potential that exists between the cornea and retina, with the retina being electrically negative and the cornea electrically positive. When the eyes are fixed straight ahead, recording electrodes register a steady potential. With eye movements, the potential changes and a deflection occurs on the recorder. The electrode pairs placed horizontally on the skin surface at the corners of the eyes detect horizontal movements. Electrodes placed above and below the eyes detect vertical movements. Typically, a binocular placement with the electrodes on the outside of both eyes is used (Andreassi, 1980). Electrodes are small disc or cup electrodes similar to those used in EEG recording. The electrodes should be nonpolarizing, small, and light enough to permit placement with surgical tape or electrode collars. Skin resistance between the electrodes with the eyes straight forward should be less than 2,000 ohms.

Signal detection should occur through a device suitable for DC recordings and capable of reproducing voltages in the range of 15 to 200 microvolts (Stern, Ray, & Davis, 1980). The head should remain in a stable position. Some researchers use a chin rest to do this, yet others have the person position his or her mouth on a bite board before each trial. The system can be calibrated by having the person fixate a series of points at a known angle of eye rotation, with gain adjusted so that one division on the paper equals 1 or 2 degrees of eye movement (Andreassi, 1980).

The analysis and quantification of eye movement varies with the purpose of the study. If the recording is used as a control for artifact, one simply looks at the record to determine whether movement occurred during a given time. One can also analyze the record for the occurrence of saccadic movements. If early calibrations have been done by standardizing gazes to objects at known distances which are straight ahead, up, down, left, and right, it is possible to combine outputs of vertical and horizontal movements and display the results on an oscilloscope or X-Y plotter to determine where the eyes are at a given point in time. Computer analysis can also be used for pattern recognition and will yield information about the presence, duration, and direction of saccades. Oster and Stern (1980) may be consulted for a more comprehensive discussion of the EOG response.

Applications

The EOG has been used in the assessment of cerebral hemisphericity, schizophrenia, learning disorders, and sleep-related phenomena. Its importance in evaluating sleep patterns and dreaming is substantial. Aserinsky and Kleitman (1953) were the first investigators to document the importance of rapid eye movements (REM) as an index of dreaming. Snyder and Scott (1972) found that dreams are present during REM activity 74% of the time and only 12% of the time during non-REM (NREM) activity. In addition to the value of the EOG as a tool in the investigation of dreaming, the response is also of interest in the study of narcolepsy, idiopathic insomnia, and depression (Hyde & Pegram, 1982; Kaplan & Sadock, 1985).

Electrogastric Response

The measurement of gastrointestinal activity is of interest to the psychophysiologist since (a) much human behavior involves the appetite, thirst, food-seeking, food preparation, and fasting; (b) the functioning of all other bodily responses is affected by what is and is not consumed; (c) the GI system has so many neural afferents; and (d) behavioral medicine is increasingly becoming involved in the treatment of eating and gastrointestinal (GI) disorders. However, the measure is difficult to record because the electrical charges are difficult to detect and many of the subjective experiences attributed to the GI system are a function of changes in chemical concentrations in the GI tract.

Anatomy and Physiology

The GI system is composed of a hollow tube inside of which are a number of layers termed the *mucosa*. The mucosa includes supportive and secretory cells. There is also a thin muscular level arranged so that the contractions of the muscles adjust the secretory levels and may influence the secretions of digestive juices. The muscular layers are on the outside of the mucosa. The smooth muscle fibers of the GI system are organized in bundles. Some of the muscles show a periodic variation in transmembrane electrical activity, termed *electrical control activity* (ECA). Local and CNS influences affect the frequency, rhythm, and size of the ECAs. In the stomach, the ECA originates high on the greater curvature of the structure and moves downward in a caudal direction. When the depolarization exceeds the threshold, the action potential spreads over the entire surface of the cell and to other cells, leading to contraction of the entire bundle. The smooth muscle of the gut is innervated by the CNS; parasympathetic activation by way of the vagus nerve increases stomach motility.

Measurement

The electrogastrogram (EGG) is recorded using silver/silver chloride electrodes with the inactive reference electrode located on the arm or leg. The active electrode is placed on the skin at the intersection of the midline and epigastric line. Measurement is done using a DC preamplifier which can record in the millivolt range. Ideally, the channel used should allow a 6-inch pen deflection to allow the recording of the DC potential and be accurate enough to record the muscular contractions. The general frequency of the EGG is 3/min, with an amplitude ranging from 0.1 to 1 mV. A common problem in the EGG is the artifact caused by the ECG and respiration, so simultaneous measures of those responses is recommended. The measure can be analyzed by examining the amplitude and frequency of the response, a measure of slow-level changes, and more recently through the use of spectral analysis.

Applications

The use of the EGG by behavioral scientists is relatively rare. Stunkard

(1959) first used the measure to determine whether subjective sensations of hunger were associated with increases in EGG activity. EGG has potential as a measure to be incorporated in the evaluation of eating disorders. Given the marked increase in such disorders during the past few years, we are likely to see increasing emphasis on this measure. The response also has potential utility in the evaluation and management of irritable bowel syndrome, a gastrointestinal disorder thought to have a psychological component.

GENERAL ISSUES

In the general field of assessment, there are several variables of importance which may affect the responses provided by the individual being evaluated. Such variables include evaluator, subject, and session factors. The primary components of each are discussed in this section.

Evaluator Variables

No studies have concentrated on the effect of the evaluator's behavior upon the psychophysiological responses of the individual that is being assessed. However, biofeedback research has examined the effect of therapist variables on biofeedback training. A study by Blanchard ct al. (1984) found no systematic relationship between perceived warmth, competence, and helpfulness in outcome of biofeedback training. However, in a single session, the appearance of incompetence or disinterest would intuitively seem likely to change baseline physiological activity of the individual. It seems desirable, therefore, to balance evaluators across different groups or conditions in psychophysiological assessment. Borgeat, Hade, Larouche, and Bedwani (1980) have shown EMG levels to be higher when the evaluator is physically present in the room. This effect is greater the more intrusive the evaluator is in interacting with the individual (Hamberger & Lohr, 1981). No systematic trend has been found for the interaction between evaluator expectancy and response pattern (Sturgis & Arena, 1984).

Subject Variables

Internal factors can affect the response pattern in addition to the operation of external factors. Age has been found to influence the level of responding for at least some psychophysiological functions. By the time a person is 60 years of age, there are usually declines in the speed of conduction of neural impulses, cardiac output, basal metabolism, vital capacity, maximum breathing capacity, gonadal endocrine secretion, muscular strength, and speed of motion, and there are increases in cerebrovascular resistance, blood pressure, and peripheral resistance. To confuse the picture, however, age does not affect all systems in all situations in the same way. Since most responses are mediated in part by the central nervous system, any aging effects that affect the CNS will likely affect other psychophysiological responses (Porges & Fox, 1986). Few studies have attempted to determine how and when these changes occur. In addition, there appears to be an increase in patterns of response specificity to a variety of stressors as the individual ages (Garwood & Engel, 1981). Whether this is correlated with the increased incidence of psychophysiological disorders in an aging population is not clear.

The sex of the individual being evaluated also needs to be considered. There are conflicting data on the presence of sex differences in the electrodermal response (Kopacz & Smith, 1971). Schwartz, Brown, and Ahern (1980) have documented sex differences in the facial EMG responses during baseline and imaging conditions. Liberson and Liberson (1975) have documented sex differences in blood pressure and respiration rates during stressful stimulation, with males showing increased BP and females increased RR. The data are sketchy, however, thus more information is needed on sexual norms for the varied responses.

The importance of racial differences in psychophysiological measures has been investigated primarily in regard to electrodermal phenomena. Blacks generally show higher skin resistance levels than do caucasians (Bernstein, 1965; Fisher & Kotses, 1973; Janes, Worland, & Stern, 1976). Blacks also show different patterns of digital vasomotor responding, an obvious finding given the fact that the measure is recorded using a photosensitive device (Janes et al., 1976). Epidemiological research indicates that blacks show higher levels of blood pressure than do whites. Given these data, it appears that additional normals are needed for the interpretation of racial effects in psychophysiological assessment.

Cyclical variables also affect psychophysiological variables, and it is recommended that time of day, day of the week, and phase of the menstrual cycle be considered when interpreting psychophysiological responding. Wineman (1971) examined phases of the menstrual cycle on sublingual temperature, diastolic BP, HR, three measures of EDR activity, and salivary output. During menstruation, follicular, and ovulatory phases, parasympathetic activity dominated, while during the luteal phase, sympathetic activation was dominant. Temperature appeared to be the most robust measure. These results, however, are based on a small number of subjects, thus further research is needed here.

Session Variables

A sufficient adaptation period is critical if meaningful data are to be gathered. The adaptation period is the duration of time the participant spends in the session before baseline and experimental data are collected. The purpose of the period is to allow the participant to familiarize himself with the novel conditions and to allow the psychophysiological responses being measured to stabilize. Stabilization is critical if changes in the response following stimulation are to be interpreted. Several studies have examined the adaptation period (Meyers & Craighead, 1978; Sallis & Lichstein, 1979). The time needed for stabilization ranges from 5 to 13 minutes. A conservative approach would allow a 13-minute period or the finding of "no change" in the response to be measured over a 3-minute period.

The environment of the session can also affect responses. The electrodermal response is markedly affected by changes in ambient temperature and humidity. Changes in room temperature, outdoor temperature, and humidity increase skin conduction (Andrasik et al., 1982; Taub & School, 1978; Venables, 1955).

One of the problems of experimenter, subject, and session variables is that variation in each of them affects the reliability and, consequently, the validity of psychophysiological assessment. This has not been a well-researched area, for the most part. Early EMG studies found good reliability of the response. Sturgis (1980) found intersession reliability measures, frontalis EMG, and bilateral cephalic and digital vasomotor responses to be .31 across sessions, with the EMG being more stable than the vascular responses in a population of normals, migraine, and muscle-contraction headache sufferers. Measures were taken at the same time of day and on the same day of the week. Menstrual cycles were not controlled. Arena et al. (1983) examined this issue for EMG, hand temperature, heart rate, SRL, and cephalic vasomotor responses in a group of six subjects. Measures were recorded on days 1, 2, 8, and 28. There were no significant differences for basal measures of the responses across sessions; however, reliability estimates indicated that only the EMG response was consistently reliable across sessions. Heart rate, skin resistance, and vasomotor responding were not found to be reliable. Reasons for the poor reliability can include operation of the variables already specified, differences in electrode or transducer placement, differential level of arousal of the individual as a function of internal or external factors, electrical noise, etcetera. Because of this problem, most statistical analyses of psychophysiological activity do not compare absolute levels of responses across sessions. Further discussion of the statistical management of psychophysiological data can be found in Coles, Grafton, Kramer, and Miller (1986).

SUMMARY

Psychophysiological assessment has added an important dimension to the evaluation of behavior. Physiology is indeed a level of behavior which interacts with other levels of behavior, affecting them and being affected by them. Psychophysiology was early regarded as a way of objectifying previously unquantifiable and unmeasureable responses such as cognition or emotional lability. To some extent, the measures have allowed experimenters to study such concepts. However, the machines and transducers present their own problems (e.g., intrusiveness, lack of generalizability, etc.) and are subject to other factors that limit their reliability or validity. However, knowledge in the field is advancing rapidly, and with increasing computerization, improved instrumentation, and increasing statistical sophistication, the utility of psychophysiology in the understanding and control of behavior is likely to become increasingly significant.

REFERENCES

Agras, W. S. (1984). The behavioral treatment of somatic disorders. In W. D. Gentry (Ed.), *Handbook of behavioral medicine* (pp. 479–530). New York: Guilford.

Anderson, C. B., & Franks, R. D. (1981). Migraine and tension headache: Is there a physiological difference. *Headache*, *21*, 63–71.

Andreassi, J. L. (1980). *Psychophysiology: Human behavior and physiological response*. New York: Oxford University Press.

Andrasik, F., Blanchard, E. B., Arena, J. G., Saunders, N. L., & Baron, K. D. (1982). Psychophysiology of recurrent headache: Methodological issues and new empirical findings. *Behavior Therapy*, *13*, 407–429.

Arena, J. G., Blanchard, E. B., Andrasik, F., Crotch, P. A., & Meyers, P. E. (1983). Reliability of psychophysiological assessment. *Behavior Research and Therapy*, *21*, 447–460.

Aserinsky, E., & Kleitman, N. (1953). Regularly occurring periods of eye motility, and concomitant phenomena, during sleep. *Science*, *118*, 273–274.

Backs, R., & Grings, W. W. (1985). Effects of UCS probability on the contingent negative variation and electrodermal response during long ISI conditioning. *Psychophysiology*, *22*, 268–275.

Bernstein, A. (1965). Race and examiner as significant influences on basal skin impedance. *Journal of Personality and Social Psychology*, *1*, 346–349.

Bild, R., & Adams, H. E. (1980). Modification of migraine headaches by cephalic blood volume pulse and EMG biofeedback. *Journal of Consulting and Clinical Psychology*, *48*, 51–57.

Blanchard, E. B., Andrasik, F., Evans, D. D., Neff, D. F., Appelbaum, D. A., & Rodichok, L.D. (1985). Behavioral treatment of 250 chronic headache patients: A clinical replication series. *Behavior Therapy*, *16*, 308–327.

Blanchard, E. B., & Haynes, M. R. (1975). Biofeedback treatment of a case of Raynaud's disease. *Journal of Behavior Therapy and Experimental Psychiatry*, *6*, 230–234.

Blanchard, E. B., McCoy, G. C., Andrasik, F., Acerra, M., Pallmeyer, T. P., Gerardi, R., Halpern, M., & Musso, A. (1984). Preliminary results from a controlled evaluation of thermal biofeedback as a treatment for essential hypertension. *Biofeedback and Self-Regulation*, *9*, 471–495.

Blanchard, E. B., Miller, S. T., Abel, G. G., Haynes, M. R., & Wicker, R. (1979). Evaluation of biofeedback in the treatment of borderline essential hypertension. *Journal of Applied Behavior Analysis*, *12*, 99–109.

Blanchard, E. B., Theobald, D. E., Williamson, D. A., Silver, B. V., & Brown, D. A. (1978). Temperature biofeedback in the treatment of migraine headaches: A controlled evaluation. *Archives of General Psychiatry, 35*, 581–588.

Blumenthal, J. A. (1982). Assessment of patients with coronary heart disease. In F. J. Keefe & J. A. Blumenthal (Eds.), *Assessment strategies in behavioral medicine* (pp. 37–97). New York: Grune & Stratton.

Borgeat, F., Hade, B., Larouche, L. M., & Bedwani, C. N. (1980). Effects of therapist's active presence on EMG biofeedback training of headache patients. *Biofeedback and Self-Regulation, 5*, 275–282.

Boston, J. R., & Moller, A. R. (1985). Brainstem auditory-evoked potentials. *Critical Reviews in Biomedical Engineering, 13*, 97–123.

Brown, C. C. (1967). The technique of plethysmography. In C. C. Brown (Ed.), *Methods of psychophysiology* (pp. 54–74). Baltimore, MD: Williams and Wilkins.

Budzynski, T. H., Stoyva, J. M., Adler, C. S., & Mullaney, D. J. (1973). EMG biofeedback and tension headache: A controlled outcome study. *Psychosomatic Medicine, 35*, 484–496.

Carlson, M. R. (1981). *Physiology of behavior* (2nd ed.). Boston: Allyn and Bacon.

Carlsson, S. G., & Gale, E. N. (1977). Biofeedback in the treatment of long-term temporomandibular joint pain. *Biofeedback and Self-Regulation, 2*, 161–171.

Celesia, G. C., & Cone, S. (1985). Visual evoked potentials: A practical approach within the guidelines for clinical evoked potential studies. *American Journal of EEG Technology, 25*, 93–113.

Chucker, R., Fowler, R., Motomiya, T., Singh, B., & Hurley, W. (1971). Induced temperature transients in Raynaud's disease measured by thermography. *Angiology, 24*, 612–618.

Cohen, R. A., Williamson, D. A., Monguillot, J. E., Hutchinson, P. C., Gottlieb, J., & Waters, W. F. (1983). Psychophysiological response patterns in vascular and muscle-contraction and headaches. *Journal of Behavioral Medicine, 6*, 93–107.

Coles, M. H., Donchin, E., & Porges, S. W. (1986). *Psychophysiology: Systems, processes, and applications*. New York: Guilford.

Coles, M. H., Grafton, G., Kramer, A. G., & Miller, G. A. (1986). Principles of signal acquisition and analysis. In M. G. H. Coles, E. Donchin, & S. W. Porges (Eds.), *Psychophysiology: Systems, processes, and applications* (pp. 183–226). New York: Guilford.

Darrow, C. W. (1943). Physiological and clinical tests of autonomic function and autonomic balance. *Physiological Review, 23*, 1–36.

Davis, C. M., Brickett, P., Stern, R. M., & Kimball, W. H. (1978). Tension in the two frontales: Electrode placement and artifact in the recording of forehead EMG. *Psychophysiology, 15*, 591–593.

Davis, J. F. (1952). *Manual of electromyography*. Montreal: Laboratory for Psychological Studies, Allan Memorial Institute of Psychiatry.

Dement, W., & Kleitman, N. (1957). Relation of eye movement during sleep to dream activity: Objective method for the study of dreaming. *Journal of the Optical Society of America, 53*, 339–346.

Duncan-Johnson, C. C. (1981). P300 latency: A new metric of information processing. *Psychophysiology, 18*, 207–215.

Edelberg, R. (1972). Electrical activity of the skin: Its measurement and uses in psychophysiology. In N. S. Greenfield & R. A. Sternbach (Eds.), *Handbook of psychophysiology* (pp. 367–418). New York: Holt, Rinehart & Winston.

Eppinger, H., & Hess, L. (1917). *Vagotonia*. New York: Nervous and Mental Disease Publishing Company.

Erlichman, H., & Weinberger, A. (1978). Lateral eye movements and hemispheric asymmetry: A critical review. *Psychological Bulletin, 85*, 1080–1101.

Féré, C. (1988). Note sur les modifications de la résistance électrique sous l'influence des excitations sensorielles et des émotions. *Compte Rendus des Sánces de la Société de Biologies, 5*, 217–219.

Fisher, L. E., & Kotses, H. (1973). Race differences and experimenter race effects in galvanic skin response. *Psychophysiology, 10*, 578–582.

Fowles, D. C. (1986). The eccrine system and electrodermal activity. In M. G. H. Coles, E. Donchin, & S. W. Porges (Eds.), *Psychophysiology: Systems, processes, and applications* (pp. 51–96). New York: Guilford.

Fowles, D. C., Christie, M. J., Edelberg, R., Grings, W. W., Lykken, D. T., & Venables, P. H. (1981). Committee report: Publication recommendations for electrodermal measurements. *Psychophysiology, 18*, 232–239.

Fredrikson, M. (1981). Orienting and defensive reactions to phobic and conditioned fear stimuli in phobics and normals. *Psychophysiology, 18*, 456–465.

Friar, L. R., & Beatty, J. (1976). Migraine: Management by trained control of vasoconstriction. *Journal of Consulting and Clinical Psychology, 44*, 46–53.

Fridlund, A. J., & Izard, C. E. (1983). Electromyographic studies of facial expressions of emotions and patterns of emotions. In J. T. Cacioppo & R. E. Petty (Eds.), *Social psychophysiology: A sourcebook* (pp. 243–256). New York: Guilford Press.

Fridlund, A. J., Schwarz, G. E., & Fowler, S. C. (1984). Pattern recognition of self-reported emotional state from multiple site facial EMG activity during affective imagery. *Psychophysiology, 21*, 622–637.

Garwood, M., & Engel, B. T. (1981). Age differences in individual specificity. *Psychophysiology, 18*, 139.

Gauthier, J., Lacroix, R., Coté, A., Doyon, J., & Drolet, M. (1985). Biofeedback control of migraine headaches. *Biofeedback and Self-Regulation, 10*, 139–159.

Gellhorn, E., Cortell, L., & Feldman, J. (1941). The effect of emotion, sham rage, and hypothalamic stimulation on the vago-insulin system. *American Journal of Physiology, 133*, 532–541.

Goldstein, I. B. (1972). Electromyography: A measure of skeletal muscle response. In N.S. Greenfield & R. A. Sternbach (Eds.), *Handbook of psychophysiology* (pp. 329–365). New York: Holt, Rinehart, & Winston.

Greenfield, N. S., & Sternbach, R. A. (Eds.). (1972). *Handbook of psychophysiology*. New York: Holt, Rinehart, & Winston.

Grovs, P. M., & Schlesinger, K. (1982). *Biological psychology* (2nd ed.). Dubuque, Iowa: Wm. C. Brown Company.

Gunn, C. G., Wolf, S., Block, R. T., & Person, R. J. (1972). Psychophysiology of the cardiovascular system. In N.S. Greenfield & R. A. Sternbach (Eds.), *Handbook of psychophysiology* (pp. 457–489). New York: Holt, Rinehart, & Winston.

Guyton, A. C. (1981). *Textbook of medical physiology* (6th ed.). Philadelphia: Saunders.

Haimi-Cohen, R., & Cohen, A. (1984). A microcomputer-controlled system for stimulation and acquisition of evoked potentials. *Computers and Biomedical Research, 17*, 399–408.

Hamberger, L. K., & Lohr, J. M. (1981). Effects of trainer's presence and response-contingent feedback in biofeedback-relaxation training. *Perceptual and Motor Skills, 53*, 15–24.

Hand, C. R., Burns, M. O., & Ireland, E. (1979). Treatment of hypertonicity of muscles of lip retraction. *Biofeedback and Self-Regulation, 4*, 171–181.

Hansch, E. C., Syndulko, K., Cohen, S. N., Goldberg, I. Z. I., Potvin, A. R., & Tourtellotte, W. W. (1982). Cognition in Parkinson's disease: An event-related potential perspective. *Annals of Neurology, 11*, 599–607.

Hare, R. D., & Blevings, G. (1975). Defensive responses to phobic stimuli. *Biological Psychology, 3*, 1–13.

Hassett, J. (1978). *A printer of psychophsiology*. San Francisco: W. H. Freeman and Company.

Heiman, J. A. (1977). A psychological exploration of sexual arousal patterns in females and males. *Psychophysiology, 14*, 266–273.

Hnatiow, W., & Lang, P. J. (1965). Learned stabilization of cardiac rate. *Psychophysiology, 1*, 330–336.

Holmes, D. S., & Burish, T. G. (1983). Effectiveness of biofeedback for treating migraine and tension headaches: A review of the evidence. *Journal of Psychosomatic Research, 27*, 515–532.

Holroyd, K. A., & Penzien, D. B. (in press). Client variables and the behavioral treatment of recurrent tension headache: A meta-analytic review. *Journal of Behavioral Medicine*.

Holzman, P. S. (1984). Pursuit eye movement dysfunctions in schizophrenia. Family evidence for specificity. *Archives of General Psychiatry, 41*, 136–139.

Hord, D. J., Johnson, D. C., & Lubin, A. (1964). Differential effect of the law of initial value (LIV) on autonomic variables. *Psychophysiology, 1*, 79–87.

Hughes, J. R. (1985). A review of the auditory system and its evoked potentials. *American Journal of EEG Technology, 25*, 115–158.

Hunt, E. (1985). Mathematical models of the event related potential. *Psychophysiology, 22*, 395–402.

Hyde, P., & Pegram, V. (1982). Sleep, sleep disorders, and some behavioral approaches to treatment of insomnia. In D. M. Doleys, R. L. Meredith, & A. R. Ciminero (Eds.), *Behavioral medicine: Assessment and treatment strategies* (pp. 447–470). New York: Plenum.

Inglis, J., Campbell, D., & Donald, M. (1976). Electromyographic biofeedback and neuromuscular rehabilitation. *Canadian Journal of Behavioral Science, 8*, 299–323.

Jacob, R. G., Kraemer, H. C., & Agras, W.S. (1977). Relaxation training in the treatment of hypertension: A review. *Archives of General Psychiatry, 34*, 1417–1427.

Janes, C. L., Worland, J., & Stern, J. A. (1976). Skin potential and vasomotor responsiveness of black and white children. *Psychophysiology, 13*, 523–527.

Jasper, H. H. (1958). Report of committee on methods of clinical examination in EEG: Appendix: The ten-twenty electrode system of the International Federation. *Electroencephalography and Clinical Neurophysiology, 10*, 371–375.

Jennings, J. R., Tahmoush, A. J., & Redmond, D. P. (1980). Non-invasive measurement of peripheral vascular activity. In I. Martin & P. H. Venables (Eds.), *Techniques in psychophysiology* (pp. 60–137). New York: Wiley.

Johnson, L. C. (1980). Measurement, quantification, and analysis of cortical activity. In I. Martin & P. H. Venables (Eds.), *Techniques in psychophysiology* (pp. 329–357). New York: John Wiley & Sons.

Johnson, R., & Donchin, E. (1985). Second thoughts: Multiple P300s elicited by a single stimulus. *Psychophysiology, 22*, 182–194.

Kaplan, H. I., & Sadock, B. J. (1985). *Modern synopsis of comprehensive textbook of psychiatry/IV* (4th ed.). Baltimore: Williams & Wilkins.

Kaufman, M. P., & Schneiderman, N. (1986). Physiological bases of respiratory psychophysiology. In M. G. H. Coles, E. Donchin, & S. W. Porges (Eds.), *Psychophysiology: Systems, processes, and applications* (pp. 107–121). New York: Guilford.

Kallman, W. M., & Feuerstein, M. (1986). Psychophysiological procedures. In A. R. Ciminero, K. S. Calhoun, & H. E. Adams (Eds.), *Handbook of behavioral assessment* (2nd edition) (pp. 329–364). New York: Wiley.

Klorman, R., Weissberg, R. P., & Wiesenfeld, A. R. (1977). Individual differences in fear and autonomic reactions to affective stimulation. *Psychophysiology, 16*, 23–29.

Kopacz, F. M., & Smith, B. D. (1971). Sex differences in skin conductance measures as a function of shock threat. *Psychophysiology, 8*, 293–303.

Kolb, B., & Whishaw, I. Q. (1980). *Fundamentals of human neuropsychology*. San Francisco: W. H. Freeman and Company.

Lacey, J. I. (1956). The evaluation of autonomic responses: Towards a general solution. *Annals of the New York Academy of Science, 67*, 123–163.

Lader, M. H. (1967). Palmar skin conductance measures in anxiety and phobic states. *Journal of Psychosomatic Research, 11*, 271–281.

Lang, P. (1971). The application of psychophysiological methods in the study of psychotherapy and behavior modification. In A. E. Bergin & S. S. Garfield (Eds.), *Handbook of psychotherapy and behavior change: An experimental analysis* (pp. 75–125). New York: Wiley.

Lang, P. J., Melamed, B. G., & Hart, J. (1970). A psychophysiological analysis of fear modification using an automated desensitization procedure. *Journal of Abnormal Psychology, 76*, 220–234.

Larsen, P. B., Schneiderman, N., & Pasin, R. D. (1986). Physiological bases of cardiovascular psychophysiology. In M. G. H. Coles, E. Donchin, & S. W. Porges (Eds.), *Psychophysiology: Systems, processes, and applications* (pp. 122–165). New York: Guilford.

Liberson, C. W., & Liberson, W. T. (1975). Sex differences in autonomic responses to electric shock. *Psychophysiology, 12*, 182–186.

Lovallo, W., & Zeiner, A. R. (1975). Some factors influencing the vasomotor response to cold pressure stimulation. *Psychophysiology, 12*, 499–505.

Lykken, D. T., & Venables, P. H. (1971). Direct measurement of skin conductance: A proposal for standardization. *Psychophysiology, 8*, 656–672.

Margerison, J. H., St. John-Loe, P., & Binnie, C. D. (1967). Electroencephalography. In P. H. Venables & I. Martin (Eds.), *A manual of psychophysiological methods* (pp. 351–402). North-Holland: Amsterdam.

Martin, I., & Venables, P. H. (Ed.) (1980). *Techniques in psychophysiology*. New York: John Wiley & Sons.

McCarthy, G., & Donchin, E. (1981). A metric for thought: A comparison of P300 latency and reaction time. *Science, 211*, 77–80.

McGuigan, F. J. (1979). *Psychophysiological measurement of covert behavior: A guide for the laboratory*. Hillsdale, NJ: Lawrence Erlbaum.

Meyers, A. W., & Craighead, W. E. (1978). Adaptation periods in clinical psychophysiological research: A recommendation. *Behavior Therapy, 9*, 355–362.

Middaugh, S. J. (1982). Muscle training. In D. M. Doleys, R. L. Merideth, & A. R. Ciminero (Eds.), *Behavioral medicine* (pp. 145–171). New York: Plenum.

Niedermeyer, E. (1985). Electroencephalography — A prospective: Past, present, and future. *American Journal of EEG Technology, 25*, 3–12.

Obrist, P. A. (1981). *Cardiovascular psychophysiology: A perspective*. New York: Plenum.

O'Conner, K. P. (1980). Application of the contingent variation in psychophysiology. In I. Martin & P. H. Venables (Eds.), *Techniques in psychophysiology* (pp. 263–328). New York: Holt, Rinehart, & Winston.

O'Gorman, J. G. (1983). Habituation and personality. In A. Gale & J. Edwards (Eds.), *Physiological correlates of human behavior, Volume 3, Individual differences and psychopathology*. London, Academic.

Orton, I. Keith, Beiman, I., & Ciminero, A. R. (1982). The behavioral assessment of treatment of essential hypertension. In D. M. Doleys, R. L. Meredith, & A. R. Ciminero (Eds.), *Behavioral medicine: Assessment and treatment strategies* (pp. 175–198). New York: Plenum.

Oster, P. J., & Stern, J. A. (1980). Electrooculography. In I. Martin & P. H. Venables (Eds.), *Techniques in psychophysiology* (pp. 275–308). New York: John Wiley.

Papanicolaou, A. C., Loring, D. W., Raz, N., & Eisenberg, H. M. (1985). Relationship between stimulus intensity and the P330. *Psychophysiology, 22,* 326–329.

Picton, T. W. (1980). The use of human event-related potentials in psychology. In I. Martin & P. H. Venables (Eds.), *Techniques in psychophysiology* (pp. 357–395). New York: John Wiley.

Porges, S. W., & Fox, N. A. (1986). Developmental psychophysiology. In M. G. H. Coles, E. Donchin, & S. W. Porges (Eds.), *Psychophysiology: Systems, processes, and applications* (pp. 611–626). New York: Guilford.

Rothenberg, G. S., & Geer, J. H. (1980). *Induced mood and sexual arousal: Some negative findings*. Paper presented at the annual meeting of the Eastern Psychological Association, Hartford, Conn.

Rugg, M. D., Fletcher, R. P., & Lykken, D. T. (1980). Computers in psychophysiological research. In I. Martin & P. H. Venables (Eds.), *Techniques in psychophysiology* (pp. 583–595). New York: John Wiley.

Sallis, J. F., & Lichstein, K. L. (1979). The frontal electromyographic adaptation response: A potential source of confounding. *Biofeedback and Self-Regulation, 4,* 337–339.

Sargent, J., Green, E. E., & Walters, E. D. (1973). Preliminary report on the use of aurogenic feedback training in the treatment of migraine and tension headaches. *Psychosomatic Medicine, 35,* 129–135.

Schwartz, G. E., Brown, S., & Ahern, G. L. (1980). Facial muscle patterning and subjective experience during affective imagery: Sex differences. *Psychophysiology, 17,* 75–82.

Shagass, C. (1972). Electrical activity of the brain. In N. S. Greenfield & R. A. Sternbach (Eds.), *Handbook of psychophysiology* (pp. 263–328). New York: Holt, Rinehart, & Winston.

Shearn, D. N. (1962). Operant conditioning of heart rate. *Science, 137,* 530–531.

Silver, B. V., & Blanchard, E. B. (1978). Biofeedback and relaxation training in the treatment of psychophysiological disorders: Or are the machines really necessary? *Journal of Behavioral Medicine, 1,* 217–239.

Sintchak, G., & Geer, J. H. (1975). A vaginal plethysmograph system. *Psychophysiology, 12,* 113–115.

Sokolov, Y. N. (1963). *Perception and the conditioned reflex*. New York: McMillan.

Snyder, F., & Scott, J. (1972). The psychophysiology of sleep. In N. S. Greenfield & R. A. Sternbach (Eds.), *Handbook of psychophysiology* (pp. 645–708). New York: Holt, Rinehart, & Winston.

Spohn, H. E. (1983). Is eye-tracking dysfunction specific to schizophrenia? *Schizophrenia Bulletin, 9,* 13–72.

Steptoe, A. (1980). Blood pressure: In I. Martin & P. H. Venables (Eds.), *Techniques in psychophysiology* (pp. 247–274). New York: Wiley.

Stern, R. M., Ray, W. J., & Davis, C. M. (1980). *Psychophysiological recording.* New York: Oxford Press.

Stock, W. E., & Geer, J. H. (1982). A study of fantasy-based sexual arousal in women. *Archives of Sexual Behavior, 1,* 33–47.

Stunkard, A. J. (1959). Obesity and the denial of hunger. *Psychosomatic Medicine, 21,* 281–289.

Sturgis, E. T. (1980). *Physiological lability and reactivity in headache activity.* Paper presented at the annual meeting of the Association for Advancement of Behavior Therapy, New York.

Sturgis, E. T., & Arena, J. G. (1984). Psychophysiological assessment. In Hersen, M., Bellack, A. S., & Miller, P. M. (Eds.), *Progress in behavior modification.* (Vol. 17, pp. 1–30). Orlando, FL: Academic.

Sturgis, E. T., Tollison, C. D., & Adams, H. E. (1978). Modification of combined migraine-muscle contraction headaches using BVP and EMG feedback. *Journal of Applied Behavioral Analysis, 11,* 215–233.

Surwit, R., Pilon, R., & Fenton, C. (1978). Behavioral treatment of Raynaud's disease and phenomenon. *Annals of Internal Medicine, 72,* 17–27.

Tarchanoff, J. (1890). Über die galvanischen erscheinungen an der haut des menschen bei reizung der sinnesorgane und bei verschiedenen formen der psychischen tatigkeit. *Pflüger's Archiv Psycholischen, 46,* 46–55.

Taub, E., & School, P. J. (1978). Some methodological considerations in thermal biofeedback training. *Behavior Research Methods and Instrumentation, 10,* 617–622.

Tursky, B., & O'Connell, D. N. (1966). Survey of practice in electrodermal measurement. *Psychophysiology, 2,* 237–240.

van Boxtel, A., Goudswaard, P., & Schomaker, L. R. B. (1984). Amplitude and bandwidth of the frontalis surface EMG: Effects of electrode parameters. *Psychophysiology, 21,* 699–707.

van Boxtel, A., Goudswaard, P., van den Molen, G. M., & van der Bosch, W. (1983). Changes in EMG power spectra of facial and jaw-elevator muscles during fatigue. *Journal of Applied Physiology, 54,* 51–58.

van Boxtel, A., & Schomaker, L. (1984). Influence of motor unit firing statistics on the median frequency of the EMG power spectrum. *European Journal of Applied Physiology and Occupational Physiology, 52,* 207–213.

Venables, P. H. (1955). The relationship between PGR scores and temperature and humidity. *Quarterly Journal of Experimental Psychology, 11,* 548–558.

Wenger, M. A. (1966). Studies of autonomic balance: A summary. *Psychophysiology, 2,* 173–186.

White, K. D. (1977). Salivation and the law of initial value. *Psychosomatic Medicine, 14,* 560–562.

Wilcott, R. C., & Beenken, H. G. (1957). Relation of integrated surface electromyography and muscle tension. *Perceptual and Motor Skills, 7,* 295–298.

Wilder, J. (1950). The law of initial value. *Psychosomatic Medicine, 12,* 392–400.

Wilder, J. (1967). *Stimulus and response: The law of initial value.* Bristol: Wright.

Williamson, D. A., Epstein, L. H., & Lombardo, T. W. (1980). EMG measurement as a function of electrode placement and level of EMG. *Psychophysiology, 17,* 279–282.

Wineman, E. W. (1971). Autonomic balance changes during the human menstrual cycle. *Psychophysiology, 8,* 1–6.

Wolff, J. G. (1963). *Headache and other head pain.* New York: Oxford University Press.

Wooldridge, C. P., & Russell, G. (1976). Head positioning training with the cerebral palsied child: An application of biofeedback techniques. *Archives of Physical Medicine and Rehabilitation, 57,* 407–414.

Zahn, T. P. (1986). Psychophysiological approaches to psychopathology. In M. G. H. Coles, E. Donchin, & S. W. Porges (Eds.), *Psychophysiology: Systems, processes, and applications* (pp. 508–610). New York: Guilford.

8
Structured Interviews and Rating Scales

Randall L. Morrison

Structured psychiatric interviews and rating scales have proliferated during the past decade. Indeed, the number of instruments currently available far exceeds that which could be discussed in the space allotted for this chapter. The rapid development of structured diagnostic interviews and rating scales has occurred concomitantly with the development and refinement of more objective diagnostic criteria for psychiatric disorders. In fact, each of the primary structured diagnostic interviews in use today is closely tied to a particular system of diagnostic classification.

It could be argued that although standardized[1] psychiatric interviews were not initially identified or developed as behavioral assessment instruments per se, the use of these measures, along with the further refinement of rating scales and behavioral checklists regarding psychiatric functioning, represents one of the primary advancements within behavioral assessment during the past decade. It is noteworthy that among the leading behavioral assessment texts, chapters on standardized interview measures have been conspicuously absent. Of course, the use of psychiatric diagnoses was considered to be little short of heresy by early behavior therapists, who placed emphasis on describing behavioral phenomena as opposed to labeling. However, empirical research has produced diagnostic categories that are much more

---

[1]Throughout this chapter, the terms *structured* and standardized interviews are used synonymously. As outlined by Helzer (1983), "standardized" implies that the interview follows a specific format that dictates: (a) the symptoms or clinical information to be obtained; (b) the manner in which information is to be elicited; (c) the order of questions; (d) the wording of, or definitions for, symptom questions; and, (e) guidelines or verbatum wording for probing of initial responses in order to obtain a codable response.

reliable and valid than previous classification systems. Earlier furor over the detrimental effects of labeling has been tempered by demonstrations of the heuristic value of diagnoses and syndrome classification schemas. As a result, structured interviews, as well as rating scales, have become critical components of behavioral assessment technology. The use of these measures is requisite for selection and description of subject samples for research activity and permits careful evaluation of response to treatment.

This chapter will review the principal structured diagnostic interviews and rating scales for the evaluation of psychiatric symptomatology. The development of standardized interview measures, and the diagnostic criteria associated with each, will be discussed. Data regarding the psychometric properties of each instrument will be evaluated and future directions considered.

STRUCTURED DIAGNOSTIC INTERVIEWS

The derivation of increasingly valid and systematic criteria for psychiatric disorders has been one of the most significant developments relating to the treatment of mental disorders. The history of the use of verbal report and observational data in order to classify and diagnose illness dates to the earliest records of the human race. This history is closely related to progress in the field of medicine in general, and psychiatry and psychology (Matarazzo, 1983). Records exist from a system of psychiatric classification and diagnosis which was in use as early as 2600 B.C. The diagnostic schemes of the classic Greek period from the 5th and 4th century B.C., including the works of Hippocrates and Plato, have been praised for their descriptive rigor (Zilboorg, 1941). In fact, as Matarazzo (1983) has pointed out, "most of the diagnostic names themselves (namely epilepsy, alcoholism, senility, hysteria and other neuroses, and mental retardation) and the description of their clinical features have changed little during the last 2500 years" (p. 104).

What has changed, albeit only recently, is the degree of empirical rigor with which the process diagnosis has been approached. While this process still relies on the use of verbal and observational data, the way in which these data are obtained has been changing rapidly.[2] Emphasis has recently been placed on establishing the reliability (stability and reproducibility) of these data. In part, this emphasis has resulted from the empiricism accompanying behavioral psychology during the past several decades. Early data from

---

[2]Progress in biological psychiatry has included the development of biological markers of mental illness, and specific somatic therapies that often result in marked response for particular diagnostic groups, but these factors have yet to be routinely incorporated into diagnostic practice.

studies conducted between 1930 and 1965 indicated that there was little interrater agreement using existing diagnostic classification systems, even between two experienced clinicians interviewing the same patient (see Matarazzo, 1983 for a review of these data).

Two problems have been identified as contributing to the lack of diagnostic reliability: criterion variance and information variance. *Criterion variance* refers to differences in the inclusion and exclusion criteria that clinicians use to summarize patient data into psychiatric diagnoses (Endicott & Spitzer, 1978; Spitzer, Endicott, & Robins, 1978). The standard diagnostic classificatory systems, including the first and second editions of the *Diagnostic and Statistical Manual of Mental Disorders* (American Psychiatric Association, 1952, 1968), did not contain explicit criteria for psychiatric diagnoses. Rather, the clinician or research investigator was forced to select the diagnostic category which most closely resembled the symptomatology of the patient being diagnosed. In actuality, then, the diagnostician would rely on his/her own conceptual interpretation of the disorder in the absence of specific, objective criteria. Studies showed that professionals of comparable experience disagreed on the particulars required for any given diagnosis. Disagreements of this sort indicated the need for a commonly held and objective set of criteria. *Information variance* refers to differences in the amount and kind of information obtained from patients by clinicians during the diagnostic interview. Without specific objective criteria to evaluate, clinicians were asking patients different questions in order to derive diagnoses, often guided by their own theoretical orientation about personality functioning.

In order to reduce both criterion and information variance in diagnosing subjects, a number of research groups began to develop their own explicit criteria and classification schemes as well as structured interviews involving standardized questions to elicit data from patients. These efforts began most earnestly in this country in St. Louis at the Washington University School of Medicine. The St. Louis group ultimately developed explicitly enumerated clinical criteria for 16 psychiatric disorders in DSM-II (Feighner et al., 1972). The Feighner criteria were published in a book by Woodruff, Goodwin, and Guze (1974), and research conducted by Helzer et al. (1977) demonstrated that they resulted in an immediate, dramatic improvement in clinician–clinician diagnostic reliability. Helzer and colleagues at Washington University soon developed an interview constructed around the Feighner criteria called the Renard Diagnostic Inverview (RDI: Helzer, Robins, Croughan, & Welner, 1981).

Shortly after the publication of the Feighner criteria, a second set of research diagnostic criteria were developed. The Research Diagnostic Criteria (RDC) (Spitzer, Endicott, & Robins, 1978) provided a modification and elaboration of some of the Feighner criteria, and included additional diagnoses (e.g., the schizoaffective disorders). Concomitant with the development of RDC, Endicott and Spitzer (1978) published the Schedule for Affective Disorders and Schizophrenia (SADS), a structured interview designed to elicit information necessary for making RDC diagnoses. The SADS and the RDI (which later was modified and expanded to become the Diagnostic Interview Schedule; Robins, Helzer, Croughan, & Ratcliff, 1981) have remained the two primary structured diagnostic interview measures in use today.

The Schedule for Affective Disorders and Schizophrenia

The SADS was first employed as a diagnostic instrument in a large, NIMH-sponsored collaborative study of depression. There are actually three versions of the SADS: the regular version (SADS), the lifetime version (SADS-L), and the version for measuring change (SADS-C). The SADS and SADS-L are most widely used.

The SADS is organized into two parts. Part 1 is designed to obtain a detailed description of the current episode and of the subject's functioning during the week prior to the interview. Part 2 is concerned primarily with information regarding past psychiatric disturbance. The SADS-L is similar to Part 2 of the SADS, with the exception that the time period is not limited to the past and includes any current disturbance. Therefore, the SADS is most suitable for interviewing patients during a current episode of illness, whereas SDAS-L is more appropriate for use with persons who are not experiencing a current episode (e.g., relatives of patients) (Endicott & Spitzer, 1978).

Part 1 of the SADS assesses features of the current episode when they were at their most severe, and, as noted, during the week preceding the interview. The organization of the SADS and SADS-L provide for a progression of questions, items, and criteria that systematically rule in or rule out RDC diagnoses. More than 20 diagnostic categories are covered by the SADS and RDC, some of which contain subcategories or specific syndromes (see Table 8.1).

Each question is rated on a Likert scale with anchor points that define different levels of severity for the symptom in question (see Table 8.2). Instructions for the SADS direct the interviewer to use all available sources of information (including chart notes and information from significant others) and as many general or specific questions which are required to accurately score the items. SADS items typically refer to symptoms, duration, or course of illness, or to severity of impairment. Several questions are suggested for each item to guide the interviewer in probing for information (see Figure 8.1). The interview typically takes 1 1/2 to 2 hours depending on the degree of pathology exhibited by the patient or subject. Endicott and Spitzer (1978) suggest that because the types of judgments called for require knowledge of

TABLE 8.1. Research Diagnostic Criteria Diagnoses Covered by the Schedule for Affective Disorders and Schizophrenia Interview

Schizophrenia
    Acute — chronic   Catatonic
    Paranoid   Mixed (undifferentiated)
    Disorganized   Residual

Schizo-affective disorder — manic
    Acute — chronic   Mainly affective
    Mainly schizophrenic

Schizo-affective disorder — depressed
    Acute — chronic   Mainly affective
    Mainly schizophrenic

Depressive syndrome superimposed on residual schizophrenia

Manic disorder

Hypomanic disorder

Bipolar with mania (biopolar I)*

Bipolar with hypomania (bipolar II)*

Major depressive disorder
    Primary   Agitated
    Secondary   Retarded
    Recurrent unipolar*   Situational
    Psychotic   Simple
    Incapacitating   Predominant mood
    Endogenous

Minor depressive disorder with significant anxiety

Intermittent depressive disorder*

Panic disorder

Generalized anxiety disorder with significant depression

Cyclothymic personality*

Labile personality*

Briquet's disorder (somatization disorder)*

Antisocial personality*

Alcoholism

Drug use disorder

Obsessive compulsive disorder

Phobic disorder

Unspecified functional disorder

Other psychiatric disorder

Schitzotypal features*

Currently not mentally ill

Never mentally ill*

---

* These conditions are diagnosed on a longitudinal or lifetime basis. All other conditions are diagnosed on the basis of current or past episodes of psychopathology.

Note: Adapted from "A Diagnostic Interview: The Schedule for Affective Disorders and Schizophrenia" by J. Endicott and and R.L. Spitzer, 1978, *Archives of General Psychiatry, 35,* 838. Copyright 1981 by the American Medical Association.

TABLE 8.2. Screening Items for Manic Syndrome

The next 5 items are screening items to determine the presence of manic-like behavior. If any of the items are judged present, inquire in a general way to determine how the patient was behaving at that time with such questions as: "When you were this way, what kinds of things were you doing? How did you spend your time?" Do not include behavior which is clearly explainable by alcohol or drug intoxication.

If the subject has only described dysphoric mood, the following questions regarding the manic syndrome should be introduced with a statement such as: "I know you have been feeling (depressed). However, many people have other feelings mixed in or at different times, so it is important that I ask you about those feelings also."

Elevated mood and/or optimistic attitude toward the future which lasted at least several hours and was out of proportion to the circumstances.	0 No information 1 Not at all: normal or depressed
Have (there been times when) you felt very good or too cheerful or high — not just your normal self?	2 Slight: e.g., good spirits, more cheerful than most people in these circumstances, but of only possible clinical significance
If unclear: When you felt on top of the world as if there was nothing you couldn't do?	3 Mild: e.g., definitely elevated mood and optimistic outlook that is somewhat out of proportion to circumstances
(Have you felt that everything would work out just the way you wanted?)	4 Moderate: e.g., mood and outlook are clearly out of proportion to circumstances
If people saw you would they think you were just in a good mood or something more than that?	5 Severe: e.g., quality of euphoric mood
	6 Extreme: e.g., clearly elated, exalted expression and says "Everything is beautiful, I feel so good"
(What about during the past week?)	PAST WEEK 0 1 2 3 4 5 6
Less need for sleep than usual to feel rested (average for several days when needed less sleep).	0 No information 1 No change or more sleep needed
Have you needed less sleep than usual to feel rested? (How much sleep do you ordinarily need?) (How much when you were/are/high?)	2 Up to 1 hour less than usual 3 Up to 2 hours less than usual 4 Up to 3 hours less than usual 5 Up to 4 hours less than usual 6 4 or more hours less than usual
(What about during the past week?)	PAST WEEK 0 1 2 3 4 5 6
Unusually energetic, more active than usual level without expected fatigue.	0 No information 1 No different than usual or less energetic
Have you had more energy than usual to do things?	2 Slightly more energetic but of questionable significance
(More than just a return to normal or usual level?)	3 Little change in activity level but less fatigued than usual
(Did it seem like too much energy?)	4 Somewhat more active than usual with little or no fatigue
	5 Much more active than usual with little or no fatigue
	6 Usually active all day long with little or no fatigue
(What about during the past week?)	PAST WEEK 0 1 2 3 4 5

Note: Adapted from "A Diagnostic Interview: The Schedule for Affective Disorders and Schizophrenia" by J. Endicott and R.L. Spitzer, 1978. *Archives of General Psychiatry, 35,* 839. Copyright 1981 by the American Medical Association.

psychiatric concepts, the interview should only be conducted by psychiatrists, clinical psychologists, and psychiatric social workers.

Reliability

Endicott and Spitzer (1978) initially reported intraclass correlation coefficients of interrater reliability for the individually scaled items of the current section of the SADS and for summary scale scores (these scores are essentially summarized diagnostic categories; see Table 8.1). These coefficients were based on data from 210 newly admitted inpatients who were neither jointly evaluated by pairs of raters or who were independently interviewed twice within 72 hours. For all individual items and summary scale scores with the exception of the Formal Thought Disorder Scale (FTDS) under test-retest conditions, the reliabilities were quite high. Endicott and Spitzer (1978) examined the ratings of FTDS and found that the low reliability was due to a lack of variability or ratings within this dimension (none of the subjects exhibited markedly disordered thought).

Spitzer et al. (1978) further examined joint-interview and test-retest reliability coefficients for specific subtypes of major depressive disorder identified in the RDC (see Table 8.1). Their findings indicate that, although these coefficients are smaller than those for the major diagnostic categories, "for the most part, they are quite satisfactory for research use, and much higher than generally reported" (p. 780). A later study by Andreasen and her colleagues (Andreasen et al., 1981) found that the lifetime version of the SADS generally had good reliability as well, although coefficients for the 10 specific items which operationally define the global diagnosis of anxiety disorder were smaller than those for other disorders.

The SADS is currently the most widely utilized structured diagnostic interview in clinical research investigations. It is, of course, used most frequently in studies pertaining to schizophrenic and depressed patients, but has been used in investigations of other disorders including alcoholism (Jacob, Dunn, & Leonard, 1983). While it was specifically developed in relation to the RDC criteria, it can be used to systematically gather information about symptoms which can then be applied to other diagnostic classificatory systems. The format of the SADS requires the interviewer to essentially make diagnostic decisions while conducting the interview, but results in a level of considerable detail in the subtyping of affective disorders and schizophrenia. This degree of detail has been one of the reasons for the instrument's popularity among clinical researchers. For example, included among the differential diagnoses provided by the SADS-RDC are a number of subtypes of schizoaffective disorder. This category has been relatively neglected in DSM-III. However, revisions to DSM-III will incorporate specific criteria for schizoaffective disorders and will make modifications to other diagnostic categories. Already, investigators have begun work on structured interviews based on DSM-III-R criteria, which will undoubtedly reduce use of the SADS interview (Spitzer & Williams, 1985a).

The Diagnostic Interview Schedule

The Diagnostic Interview Schedule (DIS) (Robins et al., 1981) is unique in that it was specifically developed to permit administration by a lay interviewer. The particular feature of the DIS which facilitates its use by lay persons is its highly structured format. The verbatim wording to be used in all questions and probes is clearly specified for the interviewer, as is the progression or flow within the interview from one question to the next.

The DIS was developed at the request of the Division of Biometry and Epidemiology of the National Institute of Mental Health (NIMH) for use in a series of epidemiological studies (Robins et al., 1981). NIMH requested that the St. Louis group design the interview based on the format contained in the Renard Diagnostic Interview. In addition, the interview was to be structured so that it could provide current as well as lifetime diagnoses, diagnoses by DSM-III and RDC criteria and diagnoses by Feighner criteria.

Diagnoses are made by the DIS on a lifetime basis first, and then the interviewer inquires as to how recently the last symptom was experienced (Robins et al., 1981). Disorders classified as "current" are further subdivided into those occurring within the past 2 weeks, within the past month, within the past 6 months, or within the past year. The pattern of probes used to determine the clinical significance of a patient's endorsement of a symptom is specified and is the same for each item. Thus, the amount of discretion that the interviewer is to exercise, either in wording questions or in deciding when to probe, is reduced to a minimum. Training for interviewers typically requires about 1 week. The actual diagnosis based on the interview can be made by computer using a scoring program developed for the DIS. As noted, diagnoses can be made for all three diagnostic systems. For most patients, the DIS can be completed within 60–75 minutes.

Reliability

The psychometric properties of the DIS have been evaluated in a series of studies by Robins and her colleagues. Robins et al. (1981) present data regarding the concordance of lay interviews' and psychiatrists' diagnoses, as well as the sensitivity (percentage of cases correctly identified) and specificity (percentage of noncases correctly identified) of the lay interviews' diagnoses, using the psychiatrists' interviews as a yardstick. Subjects included 118 psychiatric inpatients, 39 psychiatric outpatients, 24 nonpatient controls, 10 members of Gamblers Anonymous, and 26 ex-patients. Subjects were interviewed using the DIS twice, once by a lay interviewer and once by a psychiatrist. The order in which the two interviews were conducted was randomized. For DSM-III diagnoses, the mean kappa value (as the measure of concordance between lay persons' and psychiatrists' diagnoses) was .69. Mean sensitivity was 75% and the mean specificity was 94%. It should be noted here that the specific meaning of these data has been debated. Essentially, Robins et al. (1981) suggested that their findings may relate to either the reliability of the DIS, or its validity, or both. However, this interpretation was strongly contested by Endicott (1981), in a debate that has yet to be adequately resolved. Indeed, the issue of *how* to evaluate the validity of a diagnostic interview is quite complex. This issue will be discussed separately in a later section of this chapter. Given the lack of consensus on this issue, the data reported by Robins et al. (1981) in support of the DIS are perhaps best interpreted as a measure of the test-retest reliability of the instrument.

More detailed examination of the DIS interviews with the same 216 patients was provided by Robins, Helzer, Ratcliff, and Seyfried (1982). Their data indicate that disorders in remission or borderline conditions are diagnosed less accurately than current and severe disorders. However, this finding presumably would hold true for any interview measure.

Finally, a recent study by Helzer et al. (1985) examined the level of agreement between lay interviewers using the DIS and clinical diagnoses made by psychiatrists. Data were collected as part of a general population survey. Overall percent agreement between the lay DIS and the clinical impression of psychiatrists ranged from 79% to 96%. The chance-corrected concordance between lay DIS and psychiatrists' clinical diagnoses was .60 or greater for 8 of the 11 diagnostic categories. Specificity was 90% or better for each diagnostic category. While sensitivity was lower, lay interview results indicated a bias for only 2 diagnoses. Major depression was significantly underdiagnosed by lay interviewers, and obsessive-compulsive illness was overdiagnosed.

In general, the results of lay DIS interviews appear to agree with psychiatrists' judgments for most diagnostic categories. These data suggest that the DIS is a useful instrument for use by lay interviewers to derive a psychiatric diagnosis. There, its use is appropriate in those situations in which a psychiatrist or psychologist or other professional trained diagnostician is unavailable. Robins and her colleagues are continuing to refine the DIS and to make additions to it that deal with a broader range of DSM-III diagnoses. For example, while earlier versions of the DIS did not include questions pertaining to social phobia (DiNardo et al., 1983), this category is included in the most recent version (Helzer et al., 1985).

Other Adult Structured Diagnostic Interviews

While the DIS is intended to cover a selected group of diagnoses by DSM-III (Axis I) criteria, and the SADS has as its primary purpose the differential diagnosis of schizophrenic and affective disorders, other investigators have recently developed interviews to focus on specific diagnostic categories. DiNardo, O'Brien, Barlow, and Waddel (1983) developed the Anxiety Disorders Interview Schedule (ADIS) as an instrument that would (a) permit differential diagnosis among the DSM-III anxiety disorder categories and (b) provide adequate information to rule out psychosis, substance abuse, and major affective disorders. Thus, the interview is not intended as a general diagnostic instrument and is perhaps best suited for use with patients for whom there is reason to suspect an anxiety disorder prior to the interview. The ADIS creators note that since depression is frequently associated with anxiety, the ADIS also includes within it questions from the Hamilton Depression Scale (Hamilton, 1960) in order to provide a more detailed description of depressive symptoms and their relationship to anxiety symptoms. The ADIS requires some clinical judgment on the part of the interviewer with regard to evaluating the patient's responses and deciding upon further questioning. Therefore, the ADIS should only be administered by clinicians with experience in interviewing and familiarity with the DSM-III. Average time for administration is 90 minutes. DiNardo et al. (1983) report psychometric findings from test-retest interviews by two different interviewers on 60 consecutive outpatients at an anxiety disorders clinic. The findings indicate good agreement for anxiety, affective, and adjustment disorders as well as for the specific anxiety disorder categories of agoraphobia, panic, social phobia, and obsessive-compulsive disorder. Agreement for generalized anxiety disorder failed to reach acceptable levels.

Other interviews have been developed which specifically focus on Axis II diagnoses. They include measures that are concerned with a specific personality disorder as well as instruments developed to improve diagnostic reliability for all DSM-III Axis II diagnoses. Of these, the Diagnostic Interview for Borderline Patients ([DIBP] Gunderson, Kolb, & Austin, 1981) has been used most widely. Acceptable test-retest reliability, sensitivity, and specificity have been noted in a series of studies with the DIBP (Frances, Clarkin, Gilmore, Hurt, & Brown, 1984; Gunderson et al., 1981; Hurt, Hyler, Frances, Clarkin, & Brent, 1984).

Baron, Asnis, and Gruen (1981) have recently developed the Schedule for Schizotypal Personalities (SSP). Test-retest interrater reliabilities of the SSP have generally been high, although agreement for individual items has often been far less than that for scaled scores or overall diagnoses (Baron et al., 1981; Perry, O'Connell, & Drake, 1984). Sensitivity and specificity (as regards clinical concensus) data revealed marked variations depending upon which cutoff scores (from 5-point Likert scales of symptom severity) were used to declare an item as positive or significant.

Finally, Stangl, Pfohl, Zimmerman, Bowers, and Corenthal (1985) recently undertook the ambitious task of developing the Structured Interview for DSM-III Personality Disorders (SIDP), a measure intended to improve diagnostic reliability across Axis II diagnoses. Data were gathered on 63 subjects who were independently rated by two interviewers using the SIDP. Coefficients for interrater agreement were .70 or higher for histrionic, borderline, and dependent personalities, whereas coefficients for other disorders were lower and suggest that refinement of sections of the interview is needed.

A further issue regarding each of these measures is the validity of the information that is derived from them. Clearly, the validity of DSM-III Axis II diagnoses has been questioned. For example, there is no evidence that borderline personality patients differ from histrionic personality patients with respect to phenomenology (Pope, Jonas, Hudson, Cohen, & Genderson, 1983), etiology, family history, treatment response, or other parameters (Stangl et al. 1985). As mentioned earlier, the difficulty in validating any structured diagnostic interview for psychiatric illnesses involves finding an appropriate standard against which to validate results. This difficulty has spawned enthusiastic debates in the literature and led investigators to amend some traditional concepts of psychometrics. During the next several years, as revisions to diagnostic classification systems and related structured interviews continue, it is likely that even greater attention will be placed on validity issues. Separate issues apply to the interviews and classification systems themselves, as will be discussed in the next section.

The Validity of Psychiatric Diagnoses: Methodologic Issues in Interview Development

As already noted, the St. Louis group's development of the RDI and the DIS sparked many other efforts relating to the development of structured psychiatric interview measures. Their work has served as a methodological model for interview development and has also generated a number of issues as to *how* one evaluates a new interview measure. Some of these issues have yet to be resolved. Basic among them is the issue of validity.

In one of their earliest papers in this area, Robins et al. (1981) raised the issue of, with regard to psychometric evaluation, exactly *what* the DIS was evaluating:

> Finally, we need to ask just what we are studying with the test-retest design we have described. Is it the reliability of the DIS, or the validity? Ideally, to study the validity of an instrument, one would like to have an absolute standard to compare it against .. our use of specificity and sensitivity shows that we are assuming that the psychiatrists' interview (using the DIS) is the correct one against which the lay interviewers' work is to be judged. In short, like many prior efforts to establish validity, our work is a bootstrapping

operation. We are using an imperfect yardstick against which to measure (the instrument). (p. 389)

This issue was further discussed in a series of spirited letters to the editor between Endicott (1981) and Helzer and Robins (1981) in which the difficulty of establishing the validity of a diagnostic interview was again highlighted.

The procedure used by Robins et al. (1981) of comparing the results of an interview administered by a lay interviewer to the results of an interview administered by a psychiatrist independently and blindly to the same respondent has subsequently been termed *procedural validity* (Spitzer & Williams, 1985b). Robins et al.'s (1981) methodology does not involve a precise repetition with the same instrument under the same circumstances, which is the ordinary method used to evaluate reliability, because the professional training of the interviewers being compared differs systematically. On the other hand, as Robins et al. (1982) point out, it is not a measure of the DIS against a different, validated instrument, which is the preferred manner to demonstrate validity.

According to Spitzer and Williams (1985b), procedural validity refers only to the issue of the validity of the evaluation procedure and not to the validity of the diagnostic categories per se. An instrument can be evaluated and found to have adequate procedural validity by comparing the results obtained with it to the results of an established diagnostic procedure that is used as a criterion. However, there exist no diagnostic interview measures for which the validity has been unequivocally demonstrated. Indeed, as the discussion of the history of the development of structured interviews illustrated, the impetus for the development of such interviews was the absence of psychometrically sound diagnostic measures to begin with. Therefore, attempts to validate such measures will almost by definition remain inconclusive. Assuredly, diagnostic criteria for psychiatric disorders continue to be better specified, thus producing more accurate clinical diagnoses. As a result, comparisons of the results of diagnoses derived from structured interviews and those derived from strictly clinical assessments may be more meaningful now than they would otherwise have been prior to the development of DSM-III. Nevertheless, there is still considerable variance in such a validation strategy, including both information variance and criterion variance. Indeed, DSM-III is already under revision in order to (hopefully) derive more valid diagnostic categories.

The reader should keep in mind two critical points. First, diagnostic criteria for different disorders continue to be refined, and the *validity* of structured psychiatric interviews based on these criteria is limited by the validity of the criteria themselves. Second, at present, only the procedural validity of interview measures can be demonstrated. No absolute validational criteria can be applied to an interview measure. The best support for any one measure will consist of repeated demonstrations of predicted relationships between diagnoses derived on the basis of what measure and other diagnostic procedures or measures. These other measures would include predicted outcome or response to treatment, indices of specific biochemical or neuropathological abnormality, and concordant ratings of behavioral symptomatology. Pertaining to this issue, Hesselbrock, Stabenau, Hesselbrock, Mirken, and Meyer (1982) compared diagnostic concordance between the SADS-L and the DIS and found high levels of agreement between the two. Additional studies addressing these issues are needed as existing interviews undergo refinement and new measures are developed. The Structured Clinical Interview for DS-III (SCID), being developed by Spitzer and Williams (1985a), is intended to provide reliable assessments of DSM-III-R diagnostic categories.

Structured Psychiatric Interviews for Children: An Overview

Until quite recently, child psychiatric assessment typically did not involve systematic symptom evaluation based on interview of the child. Rather, the two primary sources of diagnostic information have been (a) data on the child's developmental history, familial functioning, behavior, and school functioning provided by parents and teachers, and (b) observations based on the play interview with the child (Chambers et al., 1985). Rutter and Graham (1968) were among the first to demonstrate that symptom-oriented interviews can be reliably conducted with children. Their findings triggered interest in the development of clinical research interviews for use with children. Currently, there are three primary structured child diagnostic interview measures in use. These are the Diagnostic Interview for Children and Adolescents (Herjanic, Herjanic, Brown, & Wheatt, 1975), the Schedule for Affective Disorders and Schizophrenia for School Age Children (Chambers et al., 1985), and the Diagnostic Interview for Children (Costello, Edelbock, Dulcan, & Kales, 1984).

The Diagnostic Interview for Children and Adolescents (DICA)

Researchers at Washington University once again pioneered the development of a structured diagnostic interview for clinical research with children and adolescents. Herjanic and colleagues (Herjanic & Campbell, 1977; Herjanic et al., 1975) patterned both the Washington University DICA and the corresponding parent interview on the RDI described by Helzer et al. (1981). Revisions to the DICA were based upon the DSM-III and the adult DIS. DICA is for use with children aged 6–17 and typically requires 60–90 minutes to complete. Like the DIS, DICA is highly structured and intended to be administered by trained lay interviewers.

DICA contains three parts. Initially, a joint interview is conducted with parent and child in order to obtain relevant chronological and baseline data. Next, parent and child are separately interviewed. In this stage of the interview the parent is questioned about the child using the same questions that are simultaneously being asked of the child. Questions provide coverage of 18 DSM-III child diagnostic categories. Finally, Part 3 of the DICA-P — the Parent Questionnaire — contains information about developmental and medical history as well as several diagnoses which are not covered in the child interview.

While psychometric studies of the DICA are pending, Reich, Herjanic, Welner, and Gandh (1982) and Herjanic and Reich (1982) have reported data from a similar interview measure that they describe as a predecessor to the DICA. In these reports, interviews were conducted by different interviewers with 307 mother–child pairs. Children in the study ranged from age 6–16, and most were recruited from referrals for outpatient psychiatric evaluation. Results indicated that there was generally good agreement between mothers and their children on items concerning symptoms that are concrete, observable, severe, and unambiguous. Mothers tended to report more behavioral symptoms and children tended to report more subjective symptoms. Comparisons of diagnoses on mother–child interviews revealed agreement based solely on separate, but similar, interviews with children and their mothers. Older children tended to agree more with their mothers. Eneuresis and depression were reliably reported throughout the age range.

The Schedule for Affective Disorders and Schizophrenia for School-Age Children [Present Episode] (Kiddie-SADS-P, K-SADS-P)

Research by Puig-Antich and co-workers established the existence of major depressive disorders in prepubertal children (Chambers, Puig-Antich, Tabrizi, & Davies, 1982; Puig-Antich, 1982; Puig-Antich, Blau, Marx, Greenhill, & Chambers, 1978). As a result, these same investigators began development of K-SADS-P as a means to reduce information variance with this population (Chambers et al., 1985; Puig-Antich, Chambers & Fabrizi, 1973). The K-SADS-P is based on the format used in the SADS and was originally designed for use in a study of major depression in prepuberty. It provides for the semistructured assessment of an ongoing episode of psychiatric disorder in children and adolescents 6–17 years of age. Similar to the current episode version of the SADS, the K-SADS-P addresses symptom severity during two time periods: when the current episode was at its worst, and during the past week. Four major categories of child and adolescent psychiatric disorders are assessed: affective, anxiety, conduct, and psychotic. The authors suggest that the parent should be interviewed first in order to establish a chronology for onset and course for the episode. The parent interview begins with an unstructured overview of the specifics of the present episode, including onset, duration, and a description of all presenting problems. Then the interviewer proceeds to the structured portion of the interview, including a review of salient symptoms of most child psychiatric disturbances.

The interview with the child follows the interview with the parent, and is conducted according to the same format (unstructured/semistructured). The child is typically alone with the interviewer, who asks questions in the most simple language possible so that the child can understand. Chambers et al. (1985) indicate that the interview with parents and children over 8 years old each generally requires one hour; younger children require longer periods.

Test-retest reliability data based on interviews of 52 children aged 6–17 years referred to an outpatient clinic and indicated that depressive and conduct disorders and related symptoms can be assessed with good reliability. However, test-retest coefficients for anxiety disorders were unacceptably low. Overall, the reliability of assessments was generally less than that obtained in studies with adults using the SADS. Puig-Antich and colleagues are currently working on further refinements of the K-SADS-P, especially of the anxiety disorder items (Chambers et al., 1985).

The Diagnostic Interview Schedule for Children (DISC)

A third major child diagnostic interview has been developed by Costello and his colleagues at the University of Pittsburgh (Costello et al., 1984). The DISC was developed under contract with the National Institute of Mental Health in order to make DSM-III diagnoses in large scale epidemiologic studies of children aged 6–17. It contains parallel interviews for the child (DISC-C) and the parent (DISC-P) that can be administered by trained lay interviewers or persons with professional clinical training. The DISC differs from the DICA and K-SADS in that questions are ordered according to areas of functioning and activity such as school, peer relationships, home relationships, and community life (as opposed to organizations around particular symptom clusters that define specific disorders). A computer program has been developed that picks out of the different sections of the interview information about the symptoms needed to make DSM-III diagnoses. Questions are precoded and administered verbatim. The DISC takes between 45 and 60 minutes to administer.

Test-retest reliability data on a sample of 316 children aged 6–18 who were referred for psychiatric evaluation indicate that the interview yields reliable symptom scores and DSM-III diagnoses (Edelbrock, Costello, Dulcan,

Kalas, & Conover, 1985). Test-retest reliability of total symptom scores was .84 for parent interviews and .75 for child interviews. However, test-retest reliability coefficients indicated an opposite age pattern for parent and child. The reliability of children's reports increased with 'age and was lower for children aged 6–9 than those aged 10–13 and 14–18. The reliability of the parent reports decreased with age of the child. Edelbrock et al. (1985) predicted the increase in reliability of the child reports based on age, and attribute it to children's improving cognitive, memory, and language skills. They attribute the unexpected relationship between the child's age and the reliability of the parent's report to decreasing exposure to children's behavior' and shifting behavioral norms. In an attempt to evaluate the validity of the DISC, Costello, Edelbrook, and Costello (1985) compared interviews of 40 psychiatric referrals aged 7–11 and 40 matched pediatric referrals (and parents of children in each group). The psychiatric referrals had more psychiatric diagnoses and higher symptom scores than the pediatric referrals. Results of parent interviews better discriminated between the two groups than child reports. The authors conclude that their results provide support for the validity of the DISC-P, and to a lesser extent the DISC-C, in discriminating psychiatric from pediatric referrals, "at the level of both symptoms and severe diagnoses, but not at the mild/moderate level of diagnosis" (p. 580).

Concluding Comments

Despite the recent proliferation of child interview measures, much further work is needed. Efforts to establish the validity of these measures have only reached preliminary stages. As is the case for adult measures, the task of establishing validity is interrelated with the validity of diagnostic classificatory schemas, and so is a difficult one. A major issue specific to the childhood measures is the extent to which alternative sources of information about a child's symptomatology correspond. Further investigation of this issue, as it applies to children of different ages, is needed.

RATING SCALES

It would be a trite understatement to report that there are numerous rating scales in existence for the evaluation of psychopathology and related behaviors. A rating instrument has been devised to evaluate seemingly every behavior that is even conceivably of interest to mental health professionals. Of course, the quality of these instruments varies tremendously in terms of their psychometric properties. However, there is a trend for the development of new instruments to be conducted using stringent empirical evaluation techniques, and many of the older instruments continue to be the subject of psychometric evaluations.

Psychiatric rating scales are being increasingly used to complement the psychiatric diagnostic process by providing a measure of the *severity* of the disturbance and/or subcategorization of the symptomatology. Specification of subject samples, as well as evaluation of clinical outcome, can be greatly enhanced through the use of validated, quantifiable measures of symptom severity. Therefore, these instruments can be useful for the clinician and researcher alike.

This section is concerned with two types of rating scales. First, scales of general psychiatric adjustment which are scored on the basis of a structured or semi-structured interview with the patient will be discussed. Second, instruments which are specific to schizophrenic symptomatology will be reviewed. These latter measures will be presented here since there is no chapter on the assessment of schizophrenia in this book. However, other rating scales that are limited in focus to a specific subset of psychiatric symptomatology will be reviewed in other chapters. Such measures include the Beck Depression Inventory (Beck, Ward, Mendelson, Mock, & Erbaugh, 1961), the Hamilton Rating Scale for Depression (Hamilton, 1960), the Child Behavior Checklist (Achenbach, 1978; Achenbach & Edelbrock, 1979), and the State-Trait Anxiety Inventory (Spielberger, Gorsuch, & Lushene, 1970).

Brief Psychiatric Rating Scales (BPRS)

The BPRS was developed by Overall and Gorham (1962) as an easily administered interview measure of psychiatric symptoms. It was originally intended to be used to evaluate change in symptomatology over time. The BPRS was derived from factor-analytic evaluation of two earlier scales: the Lorr Multidimensional Scale for Rating Psychiatric Patients, (Lorr, Jenkins, & Holsopple, 1953) and the Lorr Inpatient Multidimensional Psychiatric Scale (Lorr, McNair, Klett, & Lasky, 1960). Eighteen symptom areas are rated on 7-point scales following a brief, unstructured interview. The symptom areas are: somatic concern, anxiety, emotional withdrawal, conceptual disorganization, guilt feelings, tension, mannerisms and posturing, grandiosity, depressive mood, hostility, suspiciousness, hallucinatory behavior, motor retardation, uncooperativeness, unusual thought content, blunted affect, excitement, and disorientation. The BPRS is intended for use by a trained clinician who makes ratings based upon observation of the patient and the patient's verbal report. The 18 ratings of distinct symptom areas are summed to yield a "total pathology" score. Four composite "syndrome factor" scores can also be derived: thought disturbance, withdrawal-retardation, hostility-suspiciousness, and anxiety-depression (Overall & Klett, 1972). Brief descriptions of each symptom are are provided on the BPRS rating form, and more detailed definitions are available in the original publication by Overall and Gorham (1962). Since its original development, the BPRS has undergone a number of revisions. Earlier versions contained 14 and 16 items.

Overall and Gorham (1962) report interrater reliability coefficients ranging from .56 to .87, with an average of .78. The validity of the BPRS is also quite acceptable. In a study with 149 psychiatric patients by Zimmerman, Vestre, and Hunter (1975), the 16-item BPRS showed a canonical correlation of .65 with the Katz Adjustment Scales, .71 with the MMPI scales, .54 with global ratings of pathology by nurses, .61 with ratings by psychiatric residents, and .51 with patients' self-ratings. The BPRS is sensitive to clinical change. In a pharmacological outcome study with newly admitted schizophrenic patients, Hollister, Overall, Bennett, Kimbell, and Shelton (1965) reported significant treatment effects on 13 of the scales on the 16-scale version of the BPRS and on all four syndrome factors. Also, the mean improvement of 28 points on the total pathology score reported by these authors represented "highly significant change" in the functioning of their patient sample.

Katz Adjustment Scale-Relative Form (KAS-R)

Although the use of trained, blind raters to obtain observations of patient or subject behavior is recommended in order to maximize the objectivity of observational data, other methods of gathering independent ratings may sometimes be desirable. Significant others in the patient's life (e.g., husband, mother, roommate, etc.) can sometimes provide observations that draw upon these persons' more intimate knowledge of the patient's behavior. The KAS-R (Katz & Lyerly, 1963) is an objectively scored multiple choice paper-and-pencil questionnaire which is completed by a significant other of the patient. It contains 205 items which are completed by the significant other either independently or with the aid of a trained examiner. The informant rates the frequency and/or expected level of the patient's behavior on a 4-point scale. Eighteen separate scale scores covering symptomatology and social behavior are derived by summing the ratings of individual items. The 18 scales have been derived through cluster analysis and include belligerence, verbal expansiveness, negativism, helplessness, suspiciousness, anxiety, withdrawal and retardation, general psychopathology, nervousness, confusion, bizarreness, hyperactivity, emotional stability, performance of socially expected activities, relative's expectations of performance, performance of free-time activities, satisfaction with free-time activities, and satisfaction with performance of socially expected activities. The KAS-R is applicable for diverse ages, ranging from adolescents through geriatric patients. The time frame assessed is the past 3 weeks.

There have been no reports of test-retest reliability data with the KAS-R. The results of various studies have revealed significant relationships between

KAS-R scores and post-discharge criterion measures including relapse and probability of rehospitalization (Lyerly, 1973; Michaux, Katz, Kurland, & Gansereit, 1969). Zimmerman et al. (1975) reported correlations between KAS-R scores and scores on the MMPI, BPRS, Psychotic Reaction Profile, and Interpersonal Checklist (Family Form) which ranged between .53 and .87. However, KAS-R scores did not significantly correlate with global pathology ratings by nurses or psychiatry residents or self-ratings by patients. An early study by Hogarty, Katz, and Lowery (1967) reported that all but 1 of the 18 KAS-R scales differentiated between normal subjects and psychiatric day hospital patients. The KAS-R is sensitive to change. A number of studies have reported significant changes in scale scores from pretreatment to follow-up (Lyerly, 1973; Michaux et al., 1969).

Unfortunately, there has been little effort to establish norms for particular patient groups, so the clinical significance of change scores may be difficult to determine. It is also unclear whether the results from self-report, relative informant, and interviewer-assisted administration are comparable. The scale may provide clinicians with useful information regarding the family's perceptions of attitudes toward the patient.

Global Adjustment Scale (GAS)

The GAS is a 100-point rating scale of overall functioning (Endicott, Spitzer, Fleiss, & Cohen, 1976). Descriptive anchors are provided at 10-point intervals. The observer is asked to rate the subject's lowest level of functioning during the past week by selecting the lowest range that describes functioning. Ratings can be based on direct observation, interview, or information provided by significant others. Outpatients typically attain scores between 31 and 70; inpatients typically score between 1 and 40. Scores above 70 are usually not obtained by persons who are receiving treatment (Endicott et al., 1976). Endicott et al. (1976) report interrater reliability coefficients ranging from .61 to .91 on interview ratings of inpatient and aftercare patients, and ratings based on case notes. In a second study with a diagnostically heterogeneous inpatient sample, interrater reliability coefficients ranged from .80 to .90 (Newman, 1980).

Evidence for the validity of GAS scores has been reported in a number of studies. In their original article regarding the GAS, Endicott et al. (1976) reported moderate correlations between GAS scores and overall severity of illness scores from several other assessment measures, and between GAS scores and symptom dimensions on other measures. These correlations were typically higher at 6 months postadmission than at admission. Also, increases in GAS scores 3 months after the target admission were associated with decreasing readmission rates over the next 6 months. The GAS has been shown to be sensitive to treatment gains in schizophrenic (Meyer & King,

1980) and depressed patients (Van Putten & May, 1978).

The GAS is applicable to a wide range of patients and levels of functioning. However, only a portion of the scale is likely to be used by raters within any one study, or with any one type of patient. Within such a small range, the differentiation provided by the GAS may not be adequate for documenting differences between groups and/or changes over time. The GAS is simple for clinicians to use, and results in easy data-recording and statistical analysis.

Rating Scales of Schizophrenic Symptomatology

In considering the content areas covered by the other chapters in this book, it seems appropriate to add here a brief discussion of two instruments which specifically pertain to schizophrenic symptomatology. While the BPRS and GAS are widely used as symptom rating scales with schizophrenic subjects, and a wide array of measures of social functioning have been applied with this population, there has been considerable recent interest in subcategorizing schizophrenic patients based on specific constellations of psychiatric symptoms. Two relatively recent rating scales developed for this purpose are the Maine Scale of Paranoid and Nonparanoid Schizophrenia (Vojtisek, 1976), and the Scale for Assessing Negative Symptoms (SANS) (Andreasen, 1982; Andreasen & Olsen, 1982).

The Maine scale was developed by Vojtisek and was subsequently discussed by Magaro, Abrams, and Cantrell (1981). It includes five paranoid subscale items and three nonparanoid subscale items adapted from the Venables and O'Connor (1959) Short Scale for Rating Paranoid Schizophrenia, as well as from two additional items based on symptoms assessed by Overall and Gorham's (1962) Brief Psychiatric Rating Scale. The paranoid items are concerned with delusions of control, reference, persecution, grandeur, and overt expressions of hostility. Nonparanoid items refer to incongruous emotion, unusual posture, disorientation, cognitive disorganization, and hallucinations. Ratings on each scale are summed to produce total scores for paranoid and nonparanoid schizophrenia. The Maine scale can be completed by a trained rater after a brief interview. It has acceptable test-retest reliability, and initial validity studies indicate that it measures meaningful differences between patient subtypes (Magaro et al., 1981).

The SANS was developed by Andreasen to provide an objective measure of the "negative" or deficit symptoms of schizophrenia. As discussed by Andreasen and others, negative schizophrenia is characterized by prominent affective flattening, alogia, avolition, anhedonia, and attentional impairment. Positive schizophrenia involves prominent delusions, hallucinations, formal thought disorder, and persistently bizarre behavior. The SANS contains 30 specific items, each rated on a 6-point scale. There are also five global scores representing the major negative symptom complexes: alogia, affective flattening, avolition, apathy, anhedonia-asociality, and attentional impairment. Although an initial interview with the patient and observation of his or her behavior are intended as the primary bases upon which SANS ratings are made, other sources of information should be considered, including observations by nurses and ward personnel and reports from significant others. Initial psychometric evaluation of the SANS suggests that it has adequate reliability and that it is useful for distinguishing a poor prognostic group of schizophrenic patients.

SUMMARY AND FUTURE DIRECTIONS

Clearly, the use of structured diagnostic interviews and rating scales has resulted in marked improvements in the information-gathering process that is central to the diagnosis and description of patients for both clinical and research activity. As diagnostic criteria for the psychiatric disorders continue to be refined, the specific content areas covered by interviews and rating scales will continue to change. As indicated, the DIS has already gone through a number of revisions and will presumably undergo substantial modification as the result of the publication of DSM-III-R. Similarly, the development of new rating scales and revisions to existing rating scales may be expected based on changing interests and emphasis on different symptom clusters or syndromes. For example, Andreasen's SANS was developed as the result of a rejuvenation of interest in the concept of deficit symptoms in schizophrenia.

Other changes might further increase the usefulness of these types of measures. With specific regard to structured diagnostic interviews, questions regarding family history of psychiatric disorder could be incorporated as an additional content area. Detail regarding family history is increasingly being collected as part of initial interviewing in both clinical and research settings. This information can be quite useful, both as an aid to the diagnostic process (especially in the cases of difficult differentials), and from an epidemiological perspective. Although the RDI did contain questions regarding family history, these questions were dropped from the DIS and are not yet part of other standardized diagnostic interviews.

A major issue pertaining to standardized diagnostic interviews is the fact that an increasingly diverse number of interviews exist. There is overlap among some of these measures. For example, the most recent, expanded version of the DIS incorporates sections which pertain to several of the anxiety disorders. However, these same disorders are addressed in an extremely similar fashion in the ADIS. Guidelines should be established which identify the most appropriate interview to be used under different circumstances. Also, some integration of interviews may be possible and desirable. The various personality disorder measures might conceivably be combined to form a single Axis II disorder interview and/or might be integrated with other measures to form an all-inclusive, DSM-III structured diagnostic interview measure.

The use of separate interviews that focus only on the symptoms of certain specific disorders raises the possibility that concomitant, multiple diagnoses may be missed. For example, several DSM-III personality disorders may be present simultaneously. Or, an Axis I disorder and a personality disorder may be present in the same subject. Certainly, the presence of concomitant illnesses could have marked implications for both clinical treatment and research. Yet, existing interviews do not provide complete coverage of the range of psychiatric disorders. However, an all-inclusive interview may prove to be cumbersome or too time consuming for certain applications.

Computerized scoring of interviews and rating scales has been conducted and holds promise for the future. This may be especially valuable when lay interviewers are used, so that they can be totally removed from the process of interpreting the information used to classify patients. Additionally, it may be possible to utilize computer-administered measures with certain patient groups. The use of computer-administered tests is becoming more and more commonplace in the area of cognitive and neuropsychological assessment. However, such an assessment procedure will only be suitable for relatively high-functioning persons who are motivated to provide valid responses in the absence of the support and rapport provided by a trained interviewer.

As refinements of existing measures continue, additional attention should be directed toward furthering the comparability of child and adult interview and rating-scale measures. Recent data have confirmed the existence of similar psychiatric syndromes in both child and adult populations, especially affective and anxiety disorders. Comparability of child and adult assessment measures will facilitate examination of the relationships between childhood psychopathology and adult psychiatric illness.

Finally, there is a need for greater international agreement on diagnoses and the related use of structured interviews and rating scales. While the DIS and the SADS are the primary diagnostic interviews used in this country, the Present State Examination (Wing, Birley, & Cooper, 1967) and the International Classification of Diseases of the World Health Organization have been more widely used in Europe. In order to facilitate greater international collaboration on epidemiological and clinical outcome studies, efforts are needed to develop classificatory systems and interview measures which are international in scope.

REFERENCES

Achenbach, T. M. (1978). The Child Behavior Profile: I. Boys aged 6 through 11. *Journal of Consulting and Clinical Psychology, 46*, 478–488.

Achenbach, T. M., & Edelbrock, C. S. (1979). The Child Behavior Profile: II. Boys aged 12–16 and girls aged 6–11 and 12–16. *Journal of Consulting and Clinical Psychology, 47*, 223–233.

American Psychiatric Association (1952). *Diagnostic and statistical manual of mental disorders.* Washington, D.C.: Author.

American Psychiatric Association (1968). *DSM-II. Diagnostic and statistical manual of mental disorders* (2nd ed.) Washington, D.C.: Author.

Andreasen, N. C. (1982). Negative symptoms in schizophrenia. *Archives of General Psychiatry, 39*, 784–788.

Andreasen, N. C., Grove, W. M., Shapiro, R. W., Keller, M. B., Hirschfeld, R. M., & McDonald-Scott, P. (1981). Reliability of lifetime diagnosis. *Archives of General Psychiatry, 38*, 400–405.

Andreasen, N. C., & Olsen, S. (1982). Negative vs. positive schizophrenia: Definition and validation. *Archives of General Psychiatry, 39*, 788–794.

Baron, M., Asnis, L., & Gruen, R. (1981). The Schedule for Schizotypal Personalities (SSP): A diagnostic interview for schizotypal features. *Psychiatry Research, 4*, 213–228.

Beck, A. T., Ward, C. H., Mendelson, M., Mock, J., & Erbaugh, J. (1961). An inventory for measuring depression. *Archives of General Psychiatry, 4*, 561–571.

Chambers, W. J., Puig-Antich, J., Tabrizi, M. A., & Davies, M. (1982). Psychotic symptoms in prepubertal major depressive disorder. *Archives of General Psychiatry, 39*, 921–927.

Chambers, W. J., Puig-Antich, J., Hirsch, M., Paez, P., Ambrosini, P. J., Tabrizi, M. A., & Davies, M. (1985). The assessment of affective disorders in children and adolescents by semistructured interview: Test-retest reliability of the Schedule for Affective Disorders and Schizophrenia for School Age Children, Present Episode Version. *Archives of General Psychiatry, 42*, 696–702.

Costello, E. J., Edelbrock, C. S., Dulcan, M. K., & Kalas, R. (1984). *Testing of the NIMH Diagnostic Interview Schedule for Children (DISC) in a clinical population. Final report to the Center for Epidemiological Studies, National Institute for Mental Health.* Pittsburgh: University of Pittsburgh.

Costello, E. J., Edelbrock, C. S., & Costello, A. J. (1985). Validity of the NIMH Diagnostic Interview Schedule for Children: A comparison between psychiatric and pediatric referrals. *Journal of Abnormal and Child Psychology, 13*, 579–595.

DiNardo, P. A., O'Brien, G. T., Barlow, D. H., Waddel, M. T., & Blanchard, E. B. (1983). Reliability of DSM — III anxiety disorder categories using a new structured interview. *Archives of General Psychiatry, 40*, 1070–1074.

Edelbrock, C., Costello, A. J., Dulcan, M. K., Kales, R., & Conover, N. C. (1985). Age differences in the reliability of the psychiatric interview of the child. *Child Development, 56*, 265–275.

Endicott, J. (1981). Diagnostic Interview Schedule: Reliability and validity, [Letter to the editor]. *Archives of General Psychiatry, 38*, 1300.

Endicott, J., & Spitzer, R. L. (1978). A diagnostic interview: The Schedule for Affective Disorders and Schizophrenia. *Archives of General Psychiatry, 35*, 837–844.

Endicott, J., Spitzer, R. L., Fleiss, J. L., & Cohen, J. (1976). The Global Assessment Scale: A procedure for measuring overall severity of psychiatric disturbance. *Archives of General Psychiatry, 33*, 766–771.

Feighner, J. P., Robins, E., Guze, S. B., Woodruff, R. A., Winokur, G., & Munoz, R. (1972). Diagnostic criteria for use in psychiatric research. *Archives of General Psychiatry, 26*, 57–63.

Frances, A., Clarkin, J. F., Gilmore, M., Hurt, S. W., & Brown, R. (1984). Reliability of criteria for borderline personality disorder: A comparison of DSM-III and the Diagnostic Interview for Borderline Patients. *American Journal of Psychiatry, 141*, 1080-1083.

Gunderson, J. G., Kolb, J. E., & Austin, V. (1981). The Diagnostic Interview for Borderline Patients. *American Journal of Psychiatry, 138*, 896-903.

Hamilton, M. (1960). A rating scale for depression. *Journal of Neurology, Neurosurgery and Psychiatry, 23*, 56-61.

Helzer, J. E. (1983). Standardized interviews in psychiatry. *Psychiatric Developments, 2*, 161-178.

Helzer, J. E., & Robins, L. N. (1981). Diagnostic Interview Schedule: Reliability and Validity. In Reply [Letter to the editor]. *Archives of General Psychiatry, 38*, 1300-1301.

Helzer, J. E., Robins, L. N., Croughan, J. L., & Welner, A. (1981). Renard Diagnostic Interview: Its reliability and procedural validity with physicians and lay interviewers. *Archives of General Psychiatry, 38*, 393-398.

Helzer, J. E., Robins, L. N., McEvoy, L. F., Spitznagel, E. L., Stolzman, R. K., Farmer, A., & Brockington, I. F. (1985). A comparison of clinical and Diagnostic Interview Schedule diagnoses: Physician reexamination of lay-interviewed cases in the general population. *Archives of General Psychiatry, 42*, 657-666.

Helzer, J. E., Robins, L. N., Taibleson, M., Woodson, R. A., Reich, T., & Wish, E. D. (1977). Reliability of psychiatric diagnosis: I. A methodological review. *Archives of General Psychiatry, 34*, 129-133.

Herjanic, B., & Campbell, W. (1977). Differentiating psychiatrically disturbed children on the basis of a structured interview. *Journal of Abnormal Child Psychology, 51*, 127-134.

Herjanic, B., Herjanic, M., Brown, F., & Wheatt, T. (1975). Are children reliable reporters? *Journal of Abnormal Child Psychology, 3*, 41-48.

Herjanic, B., & Reich, W. (1982). Development of a structured psychiatric interview for children: Agreement between child and parent on individual symptoms. *Journal of Abnormal Child Psychology, 10*, 307-324.

Hesselbrock, V., Stabenau, J., Hesselbrock, M., Mirkin, P., & Meyer, R. (1982). A comparison of two interview schedules. The Schedule for Affective Disorders and Schizophrenia-Lifetime and the National Institute for Mental Health Diagnostic Interview Schedule. *Archives of General Psychiatry, 39*, 674-677.

Hogarty, G. E., Katz, M. M., & Lowery, H. A. (1967). Identifying candidates from a normal population for a community mental health program. In R. R. Monroe, G. D. Klee, & E. B. Brody (Eds.), *Psychiatric epidemiology and mental health planning*. Washington, D.C.: American Psychiatric Association.

Hollister, L. E., Overall, J. E., Bennett, J. L., Kimbell, I., & Shelton, J. (1965). Triperidol in newly admitted schizophrenics. *American Journal of Psychiatry, 122*, 96-98.

Hurt, S. M., Hyler, S .E., Frances, A., Clarkin, J. F., & Brent, R. (1984). Assessing borderline personality disorder with self-report, clinical interview, or semistructured interview. *American Journal of Psychiatry, 141*, 1228-1231.

Jacob, T., Dunn, N. J., & Leonard, K. (1983). Patterns of alcohol abuse and family stability. *Alcoholism: Clinical & Experimental Research, 7*, 382-385.

Katz, M. M., & Lyerly, S. B. (1963). Methods for measuring adjustment and social behavior in the community: I. Rationale, description, discriminative validity and scale development. *Psychological Reports, 13*, 503-535. (Monograph supplement 4-V13).

Lorr, M., Jenkins, R. L., & Holsopple, J. L. (1953). Multidimensional Scale for Rating Psychiatric Patients. *Veterans Administration Technical Bulletin, 10*, 507.

Lorr, M., McNair, D. M., Klett, C. J., & Lasky, J. J. (1960). A confirmation of nine postulated psychotic syndromes. *American Psychologist, 15*, 495.

Lyerly, S. B. (1973). *Handbook of psychiatric rating scales* (2nd ed.). Rockville, Maryland: National Institute of Mental Health.

Magaro, P., Abrams, L., & Cantrell, P. (1981). The Maine Scale of Paranoid and Nonparanoid Schizophrenia: Reliability and validity. *Journal of Consulting and Clinical Psychology, 49*, 438–447.

Matarazzo, J. D. (1983). The reliability of psychiatric and psychological diagnosis. *Clinical Psychology Review, 3*, 103–145.

Meyer, J., & King, D. (1980, July). *Studying the reliability of clinician assessments of client mental health related problems.* Paper presented at the Region I Evaluation Conference, Durham, New Hampshire.

Michaux, W. W., Katz, M. M., Kurland, A. A., & Gansereit, K. H. (1969). *The first years out: Mental patients after hospitalization.* Baltimore: Johns Hopkins Press.

McGlashan, R. H. (1984). Testing four diagnostic systems for schizophrenia. *Archives of General Psychiatry, 41*, 141–144.

Newman, F. L. (1980). Global scales: Strengths, uses and problems of global scales as an evaluation instrument. *Evaluation and Program Planning, 3*, 257–268.

Overall, J. E., & Gorham, D.R. (1962). The Brief Psychiatric Rating Scale. *Psychological Reports, 10*, 799–812.

Overall, J. E., & Klett, C. J. (1972). *Applied multivariate analysis.* New York: McGraw-Hill.

Perry, J. C., O'Connell, M. E., & Drake, R. (1984). An assessment of the Schedule for Schizotypal Personalities and the DSM-III criteria for diagnosing schizotypal personality disorder. *The Journal of Nervous and Mental Disease, 192*, 674–680.

Pope, H. G., Jonas, J. M., Hudson, J. L., Cohen, B. M., & Gunderson, J. G. (1983). The validity of DSM-III borderline personality disorder. *Archives of General Psychiatry, 40*, 23–30.

Puig-Antich, J. (1982). Major depression and conduct disorder in prepuberty. *Journal of the American Academy of Child Psychiatry, 21*, 118–128.

Puig-Antich, J., Blau, S., Marx, N., Greenhill, L. L., & Chambers, W. (1978). Prepubertal major depressive disorder: A pilot study. *Journal of the American Academy of Child Psychiatry, 17*, 695–707.

Puig-Antich, J., Chambers, W. J., & Fabrizi, M. A. (1983). The clinical assessment of current depressive episodes in children and adolescents: Interviews with parents and children. In D. Cantrell & G. Carlson (Eds.), *Childhood depression* (pp. 157–179). New York: Spectrum Publications.

Reich, W., Herjanic, B., Welner, Z., & Gandh, P. R. (1982). Development of a structured psychiatric interview for children: Agreement on diagnosis comparing child and parent interviews. *Journal of Abnormal Child Psychology, 10*, 325–336.

Robins, L. N., Helzer, J. E., Ratcliff, K. S., & Seyfried, W. (1982). Validity of the Diagnostic Interview Schedule, version II: DSM-III diagnoses. *Psychological Medicine, 12*, 855–870.

Robins, L. N., Helzer, J. E., Croughan, J., & Ratcliff, K. S. (1981). National Institute of Mental Health Diagnostic Interview Schedule: Its history, characteristics, and validity. *Archives of General Psychiatry, 38*, 381–389.

Rutter, M., & Graham, P. (1968). The reliability of validity of the psychiatric assessment of the child: I. Interview with the child. *British Journal of Psychiatry, 114*, 563–579.

Spielberger, C. D., Gorsuch, R. L., & Lushene, R. E. (1970). *Manual for the State-Trait Anxiety Inventory*. Palo Alto, California: Counseling Psychologist Press.

Spitzer, R. L., Endicott, J., & Robins, E. (1978). Research diagnostic criteria. *Archives of General Psychiatry, 35,* 773–782.

Spitzer, R. L., & Williams, J. B. W. (1985a). *Structured Clinical Interview for DSM-III — Psychotic Disorders Version.* New York: Biometrics Research Department, New York State Psychiatric Institute.

Spitzer, R. L., & Williams, J. B. M. (1985b). Classification of mental disorders. In H. I. Kaplan & B. J. Sadock (Eds.), *Comprehensive textbook of psychiatry: Vol. 1.* Baltimore: Williams & Wilkens.

Stangl, D., Pfohl, B., Zimmerman, M., Bowers, W., & Corenthal, C. (1985). A structured interview for the DSM-III personality disorders. *Archives of General Psychiatry, 42,* 591–596.

Van Putten, T., & May, P. R. (1978). Subjective response as a predictor of outcome in psychotherapy: The consumer has a point. *Archives of General Psychiatry, 35,* 477–480.

Venables, P. H., & O'Connor, N. A. (1959). A short scale for rating paranoid schizophrenia. *Journal of Mental Science, 105,* 815–818.

Vojtisek, J. E. (1976). Signal detection and size estimation in schizophrenia. *Dissertation Abstracts International, 36,* 5290B-5291B.

Wing, J. K., Birley, J. L. T., & Cooper, J. E. (1967). Reliability of a procedure for measuring and classifying "present psychiatric state." *British Journal of Psychiatry, 113,* 449–515.

Woodruff, R. A., Jr., Goodwin, D. W., & Guze, S. B. (1974). *Psychiatric diagnosis.* New York: Oxford University Press.

Zilboorg, G. (1941). *A history of medical psychology.* New York: Norton.

Zimmerman, R. L., Vestre, N. D., & Hunter, S. H. (1975). Validity of family informants' ratings of psychiatric patients: General validity. *Psychological Reports, 37,* 619–630.

PART 3

EVALUATION FOR TREATMENT PLANNING

9
Assessment of Anxiety and Fear

Michael T. Nietzel
Douglas A. Bernstein
Robert L. Russell

Anxiety is one of psychology's central concepts. It has been reliably related to perception, performance, affiliation, learning, memory, cognition, and sexual responsiveness. Every major theory of personality and psychopathology has used anxiety as an important explanatory concept, and anxiety disorders are among the most prevalent clinical phenomena treated by modern therapists. Anxiety and fear are emotions that all persons — from the heroic to the meek — experience throughout their lives. For example, the noted psychoanalyst, Wilhelm Stekel (1923), listed several great persons who suffered from intense anxieties:

> Augustus Caesar's whole body trembled when it began to thunder . . . Erasmus was horrified if he saw a fish, and Pascal was afraid of a thousand and one things. Frederick the Great had an aversion for all new clothing or new uniforms . . . Mozart ran away at the sound of a trumpet or hunting horn. Schopenhauer trembled at the sight of a razor. Edgar Allen Poe, Musset, Schumann, and Chopin were all afraid of the dark. . . . Finally, Maupassant had a fear and horror of open doors. (p. 11)

In this chapter, we make no distinction between the terms *anxiety* and *fear*. We are aware of several differentiations such as defining anxiety as "generalized emotional distress" and fear as "an aversive emotion elicited by a particular stimulus" (e.g., Stekel, 1923, referred to anxiety as the "neurotic sister" of fear). Fear has also been described as the cognitive appraisal of danger and anxiety as the unpleasant emotions experienced when fear is evoked (Beck & Emery, 1985). However, these distinctions have not played any important role in existing behavioral approaches to assessing anxiety or fear, and for that reason we do not emphasize them.

The origin of the term *anxiety* comes from the Latin *anxius*, referred to in German as *angst*, "a word [Freud] used to describe the negative affect and physiological arousal that is analogous to the consequences of having food stuck in one's throat . . . " (Borkovec, Weerts, & Bernstein, 1977, p. 367). Over the past 50 years, research on the construct of anxiety has been prolific. Prior to the ascendency of behavioral approaches in recent years, Cattell and Scheier (1961) identified over 120 instruments that measure some aspect of anxiety. The advent of behavioral approaches to clinical research and practice resulted in a host of new anxiety measures, many of which we will discuss later. Behavioral theorists also contributed new approaches which were responsive to criticisms that anxiety had become a vague, poorly defined concept that had failed to promote satisfying theoretical or practical advances.

A prior version of this chapter (Nietzel & Bernstein, 1981) identified four principles that distinguished behavioral conceptualizations of anxiety from other perspectives. Because these four principles continue to be influential, sometimes in modified form, they are reviewed again here, along with three more recent principles that have guided behavioral assessment of anxiety in the past 5 years.

1. *Anxiety is not a trait or personality characteristic which is internal to an individual.* Because of this notion, behavioral approaches to anxiety measurement place a premium on identifying the conditions in which a person responds fearfully and on quantifying these responses. Behaviorists tend to employ self-report instruments, but the use of psychological tests to measure a global, generalized personality construct is minimized. As with behavioral assessment of any clinical target, three tasks are essential in anxiety assessment: first, description of the phenomenon as accurately, reliably, and validly as possible; second, specification of the external and cognitive stimuli that prompt distress; and third, identification of the contingencies that maintain the distress. Consistent with this perspective, evaluations of interventions for anxiety-based problems concentrate on reliably measured changes in the targeted components of anxiety assessed before and after an intervention.

2. *Anxiety can be acquired through numerous learning mechanisms.* Traditionally, behaviorists have suggested that anxiety is developed through associative learning in which formerly neutral stimuli take on stressful properties because of conditioning based on their association with aversive stimuli. In recent years conditioning explanations of anxiety have been subjected to a host of criticisms (Rachman, 1977; Öhman, 1979; Eysenck, 1982) and are now regarded as inadequate accounts of how many fears develop.

Currently, it appears that fears can be acquired by at least four different pathways including, first, the well-known classical conditioning mechanisms described by Mowrer (1939) and Eysenck and Rachman (1965). Second, anxiety can develop as a result of real dangers or behavioral deficits. This type of anxiety is a realistic reaction to objective stressors, and for that reason is sometimes called *reactive* (as opposed to *conditioned*) anxiety. Reactive anxiety is common in interpersonal-evaluative situations where persons with minimal social skills may suffer rejection and become fearful of social encounters as a consequence. Third, anxiety may develop vicariously, a mechanism inferred primarily from the success of vicarious anxiety-reduction techniques. Finally, and related to vicarious mechanisms, instructional processes can transmit fear-inducing information to individuals who subsequently become fearful of stimuli to which they have never been directly exposed.

In addition to these pathways, biological factors may play a substantial role in potentiating the acquisition of some fears and dampening the development of others. Eysenck (1986) describes a model of anxiety that emphasizes genetically transmitted differences in the personality dimensions of neuroticism and extraversion-introversion. Seligman's (1971) concept of *preparedness* refers to underlying physiological differences (tied to evolutionary development) that make certain fears more or less difficult to learn. Perhaps not all fears are equally learnable; this lack of equipotentiality poses a problem for strictly associational explanations of anxiety acquisition.

Manifestations of anxiety are likely to be similar regardless of etiological mechanisms (e.g., Öst & Hugdahl, 1985); however, it remains particularly important to discriminate reactive anxiety from other types. Interviews and role-played interactions are often useful in differentiating reactive from conditioned anxiety. When reactive anxiety is present, training in requisite social, sexual, study, or other skills is the necessary intervention prior to or in association with anxiety-reduction procedures such as flooding or desensitization. In the absence of reactive anxiety, skills training becomes a less essential component of treatment.

3. *Anxiety consists of complex, multiple response components that occur in relation to anxiety-eliciting cues.* Anxious behavior is usually manifest in three *response* channels. The first is the self-report or *subjective channel*. On this dimension, an individual reports the amount of distress felt. Although behaviorists have often criticized self-report measures, subjective reports are very important for two reasons: First, they are the only access to the feelings of dread, vulnerability, and helplessness which clients suffer; and second, they are very efficient assessment instruments. Both of these characteristics account for the increasing use of self-report measures of anxiety, which are described later in this chapter.

The second anxiety measurement channel is the *physiological* (also termed *visceral* or *somatic*), which focuses on the responsiveness of the sympathetic portion of the autonomic nervous system. Anxiety in this channel is revealed by changes in such indices as galvanic skin response, blood pressure, heart rate, muscular tension, respiration rate, and temperature. Physiological assessments of anxiety are plagued by many technical problems that make accurate, unbiased measurement difficult. Body movement, temperature and weight, diet, cognitive activity, and drug use are just a few of the factors that can affect physiological measures. Characteristics of the physical environment (lighting, temperature, humidity), attachment of electrodes, habituation, and a variety of procedural variations also influence electrophysiological assessments. Furthermore, it is advisable to measure anxiety through more than one index of physiological activity since arousal for each individual can appear on different measures and at different temporal rates. This is part of the reason that different physiological measures often correlate poorly with one another (see principle number 4).

The third response channel involves *motor* or *overt behavior*. Paul and Bernstein (1974) subdivided this channel into direct and indirect measures. *Direct assessments* involve measures of overt, behavioral consequences of physiological arousal. The frequency and intensity of behavioral disruptions (e.g., stuttering, trembling, pacing, tremors) during stressful activities, such as giving a speech, are examples of direct behavioral measures. *Indirect assessments* involve observation of escape and/or avoidance of anxiety-eliciting stimuli. Direct and indirect observations are usually quantified on some type of rating scale. Behavioral measures have been emphasized in evaluations of treatments for anxiety disorders even though both subtypes are subject to artifactual influences (Bernstein & Nietzel, 1977).

4. *Anxiety response channels are not highly correlated.* Problems in measuring anxiety are complicated by the common finding that the three anxiety channels do not correlate well with one another (Lacey, 1967; Lang, 1977). An individual who is anxious in a particular stimulus setting may show strong reactivity in only one channel (for example, in self-report but not in physiological or motor activity). This characteristic of anxiety indices has been called *response fractionation* (Haynes, 1978), *asynchrony* (Lick & Katkin, 1976), or *desynchrony* (Hodgson & Rachman, 1974), and is a reliable finding in the anxiety assessment literature.

Response desynchrony is due, in part, to the fact that the display of anxiety in each channel is a function not only of the eliciting stimulus but of many other variables as well. A male college student may experience extreme physiological arousal and behavioral disruption whenever he interacts with a female but, because he does not want to appear foolish, he denies any discomfort. On the other hand, a person may report strong anxiety on visiting the dentist, and show clear autonomic responses when in a dentist's chair, but reveal little overt avoidance behavior because of the anticipated relief from the pain of a toothache (Kleinknecht & Bernstein, 1978).

When anxiety becomes a clinical problem, the client's presenting complaints may involve clearly recognized and defined symptoms in one or more of the three anxiety response systems. Desynchrony of anxiety channels requires not only multi-method assessment but also suggests the need for multiple-component treatments. Lang (1977) has proposed in this regard that:

> The behavior therapeutic enterprise should be a vigorous multi-system program. That is to say, the patient who shows social performance deficits, the physiology of anxiety and also reports a feeling of dread or helplessness would most likely respond to a program which included the direct modification of each of these behavior sets. (p. 181)

In the 6 years since the first version of this chapter appeared, three additional trends in behavioral conceptualizations of anxiety have been observed. All are associated with important developments in assessment. Because many of the recent anxiety-assessment instruments, which are reviewed later, reflect these trends, these guiding principles are summarized later.

5. *Recent conceptualizations of anxiety have attempted to account for the patterning and organization of anxiety's triple response channels while explaining the desynchrony among the channels.* A common feature of these explanations is that anxiety involves a network of responses structured by certain central processes such as cognitive encoding (Hamilton, 1986), cognitive distortions involving the exaggeration of vulnerability and the underestimation of coping capacities (Beck & Emery, 1985), excesses in meta-cognitive activity (Hartmann, 1983), or affect-relevant information organized in images (Lang, 1977, 1979, 1985).

Of these theories, Lang's bio-informational model has received the most experimental attention and has exerted the greatest influence. Lang's theory attempts to interrelate current work in psychophysiology, cognitive information processing, and behavior therapy so as to be able "to describe the conditions under which affective reactions are evoked by symbolic stimuli, to show how differences in the structure of image networks and the subject's capacity for image generation could be related to psychopathology, and to suggest how emotional imagery may be a vehicle for emotional behavior change" (Lang, 1979, p. 495). To accomplish these goals, Lang views images as principally comprised of information, coded like any other cognitive information, into networks of propositions. In other words, the image is constructed by a set of internally related propositions that form a perceptual description. There are three types of propositions which define the emotional image: (a) stimulus propositions which concern the semantic content of the image, (b) response propositions which concern the efferent outflow appropriate to the image content, and (c) relational propositions which connect stimulus and response propositions. The efferent outflow coded as response propositions consists of verbal responses, behavioral acts, and patterns of somatic arousal, which together give the image its emotional character.

From this framework, Lang and associates have begun to unravel the relationship between physiological responses accompanying instructionally evoked imagery and emotional behavior. For example, they have shown that subjects trained to report their images principally in terms of response propositions undergo the largest and most consistent physiological changes (Lang, Levin, Miller, & Kozak, 1983). Based on physiological pattern identity (i.e., the identity of the perceptual-affective response in reality to the perceptual-affective response during imagery), modification of the physiological pattern in either context is hypothesized to have a reciprocal effect on the other. Thus, imagery therapies that help subjects access response propositions and undergo faithful physiological responses to feared objects can be expected to be particularly successful (Foa & Kozak, 1986). Consistent with this view is recent evidence that clients with more synchronized anxiety respond better to certain treatments than do "desynchronizers" (Michelson & Mavissakalian, 1985).

6. *DSM-III's partitioning of the anxiety disorders into ten subcategories* (see Table 9.1) *has encouraged investigators to search for differences and similarities in the etiology, phenomenology, psychophysiology, and course of anxiety problems.* As a result, the literature contains increasingly sophisticated analyses of possible subtypes of anxiety that may parallel or underlie DSM-III distinctions. One of the more interesting examples of this work involves the differentiation of panic attacks from other anxiety disorders on the basis of symptoms, cognition, and physiology (e.g., Barlow et al., 1984). A common discovery of these studies is that panic disorder involves greater somatic responsivity and sensitivity to physiological changes than other anxiety states. These differences may have important implications for the etiology and treatment of panic. Social anxiety also appears to have subclusters that involve different patterns of cognitive and somatic responses (Turner & Beidel, 1985). A third syndrome frequently investigated for possible differential psychology and physiology relative to other anxiety problems is agoraphobia (e.g., Fisher & Wilson, 1985).

One also finds attempts to extract commonalities among anxiety-related syndromes with distinct symptomatology. A prime example is Heide and Borkovec's (1984) integration of relaxation-induced anxiety, generalized anxiety, and agoraphobia by speculating that intermediate anxieties, such as fear of somatic arousal and loss of control which these problems share, themselves stem from a basic core fear of rejection, abandonment, and being alone.

TABLE 9.1. DSM-III Anxiety Disorders

I.	Phobic Disorders
	A. Agoraphobia*
	1. with panic attacks (300.21)
	2. without panic attacks (300.22)
	B. Social Phobia (300.23)
	C. Simple Phobia (300.29)
II.	Anxiety States
	A. Panic Disorder (300.01)
	B. Generalized Anxiety Disorder (300.02)
	C. Obsessive Compulsive Disorder (300.03)
	D. Posttraumatic Stress Disorder
	1. Acute (308.30)
	2. Chronic or Delayed (309.8)
	E. Atypical Anxiety Disorder (300.00)**

* Early working drafts of DSM-III-R categorize agoraphobia as a subtype of panic disorders (for a review of other proposed revisions in the DSM-III criteria for anxiety disorders, see Cerny et al., 1984).

** The necessity of this category is questionable. In almost 200 consecutive cases at the Albany Phobia and Anxiety Disorders Clinic, not a single patient was diagnosed with this classification (Cerny et al., 1984).

7. *DSM-III's emphasis on specific, operational criteria for the diagnosis of psychological disorders has exerted several influences on behavioral approaches to the assessment of anxiety.* A host of new paper-and-pencil instruments and structured interviews have been developed to assess the criteria and/or associated symptoms of the DSM-III anxiety disorders. Several of these instruments are described in the following sections (see also Cerny, Himadi, & Barlow, 1984; Roberts, Aronoff, Jensen, & Lambert, 1983; Turner & Michelson, 1984).

PSYCHOPHYSIOLOGICAL MEASURES

Psychologists have long struggled with the relationships among patterns of visceral, subjective, and behavioral responsiveness. For example, William James (1890) proposed that verbal accounts of the emotions were determined by initial reactivity in the physiological and behavioral channels. Cannon's (1915) formulation was more physiological and stressed lower brain structures as a common activating agent for the other parameters of emotional responding. More recently, Schachter (1964) emphasized visceral arousal as a substrate of emotion, with the subjective nature of affect determined by subjects' interpretations of the environmental cues present during the arousal.

Psychophysiological measurements can serve important diagnostic functions when applied as part of a comprehensive, preintervention assessment. They may pinpoint etiological factors, suggest the most appropriate treatments to be applied to a given problem (Lehrer, Woolfolk,

Rooney, McCann, & Carrington, 1983) and predict treatment responsiveness (Vermilyea, Boice, & Barlow, 1984). In practice, however, sophisticated psychophysiological measurement has been more characteristic of the laboratory researcher than the working clinician. Reasons for this imbalance include the expense of the measurement technology, inconvenience, the need to be skilled in principles of electronics and physiology, and the realization that physiological measures are very sensitive to instrument errors and artifactual contamination.

Although physiological measures are often included in comprehensive assessments of anxiety, there has been surprisingly little investigation of their basic properties. In particular, the reliability of psychophysiological measures has not been documented, in part because investigators have simply assumed that a person's autonomic responsiveness is reliable over time. However, a study by Arena, Blanchard, Andrasik, Cotch, and Myers (1983) found that with the exception of frontal electromyography (EMG) the physiological responsiveness (heart rate, skin resistance level, hand temperature, and vasomotor response) of normal subjects measured under different conditions on four occasions across 28 days was not consistently reliable. Holden and Barlow's (1986) study of 10 agoraphobics found that the test-retest reliability of heart rate measures was quite low. These results remind us that investigators are obligated to assess the reliability of *any* measure before including it in their assessment/evaluation batteries.

Although recent technological advances (e.g., Holden & Barlow, 1986) have allowed physiological recordings to be made in the natural environment, laboratory settings are still the most common location for psychophysiological assessment. Haynes (1978) describes the usual physiological measurement procedure as follows:

> Typically, a client is seated in an environmentally controlled room and electrodes and transducers are attached. An adaptation period usually precedes measurement. This period allows the subject to adjust to the new surroundings and is associated with decreases in the level of arousal and variability of psychophysiological measures. Following the adaptation period, the client is usually presented with audio or visual stimuli, exposed to intervention procedures or instructed to engage in various activities. The client's physiological responses to these stimuli and procedures are monitored. In some cases, the client may be presented with intervention manipulations prior to or between test stimuli (e.g., desensitization or relaxation training prior to presentation of feared stimuli). (p. 346)

For our present purposes, we discuss only those methods most often used as indices of fear and anxiety: electromyographic, cardiovascular, and electrodermal measures. Newer methods involving blood or urine assays of stress-relayed substances such as epinephrine, norepinephrine, cortisol, or uric acid (Singer, 1986) are not described because of their still-limited utilization.

Electromyography

Technique

When skeletal muscles contract, electrical activity is generated. The measurement of this activity is called electromyography (EMG). It is possible to infer the level of muscular tension by measuring electrical activity in a contracting muscle or muscle group. EMG levels are usually recorded from electrodes placed on a carefully prepared skin surface at the site of a muscle group. Signals from the electrodes are then fed to an amplifier, where they are increased until they can be monitored visually on some type of polygraph, meter, or scope. Interpretation of the signal may be further aided by integration techniques that allow the user to grade the raw electrical activity data over a certain period of time. EMG recordings have been taken from several muscle sites, but the most common location is the frontalis muscle (across the forehead) because it is believed to be sensitive to general tension and arousal.

Examples

Frontalis EMG is often monitored in clients suffering from muscle-contraction headaches (Epstein & Abel, 1977) and in clients being treated with biofeedback, desensitization, and relaxation training (Lehrer et al., 1983). To the extent that anxiety is mediated in part by muscular tension, EMG should be responsive to fear-eliciting stimuli.

There are data which indicate the utility of EMG as an index of anxiety. For example, Haynes (1978) reports data on subjects who listened to tape-recorded descriptions of scenes (e.g., being in an accident) they had previously identified as anxiety-arousing. EMG and cardiovascular measures were collected before, during, and after presentations of the scenes, and were also used to assess the effects of relaxation training. Although relaxation training did not affect various cardiovascular measures, it was associated with reduced frontalis EMG response to the stressful stimuli. Other research on EMG as an outcome measure has been mixed. For example, Brandt (1973), Reinking and Kohl (1975), and Schandler and Grings (1976) found that EMG measures differentiated progressive relaxation from a variety of control conditions in reducing EMG, but Israel and Beiman (1977) and Russell, Sipich, and Knipe (1976) did not.

Of course, EMG can also be monitored as subjects confront in vivo fear stimuli, behavioral avoidance tests, or role-playing tasks, or as they engage in fear imagery. This type of assessment has both diagnostic and outcome implications since it can be conducted before, during, and after treatment.

Issues in Interpretation

Although EMG levels are sensitive to general arousal, they are particularly subject to both measurement artifact (Katkin & Hastrup, 1982) and the fractionation problem mentioned earlier. EMG not only demonstrates low correlations with other physiological measures, but frontalis EMG levels often do not correlate well with EMG monitored at other sites. For this reason, reliance on single-site EMG as a measure of physiological activation can be hazardous.

Cardiovascular Measures

Technique

Cardiovascular measures are the most frequently utilized index of physiological arousal in anxiety research. Among the several indicators available, measures of heart rate, blood pressure, and peripheral blood flow are the most popular.

Heart rate has been the most frequently selected cardiovascular index of fear. It is often measured by a cardiotachometer, which can track the time interval between successive heartbeats before, during, and after presentations of aversive stimuli. Although heart rate data are subject to nonthreat parameters of fear stimuli and therefore require appropriate control procedures, heart rate is less sensitive than most other visceral responses to measurement artifacts and is monitored relatively easily. It also correlates fairly well with muscular tension. While it is generally assumed that exposure to a stressor produces heart rate acceleration, this is an overly simplified view (Lacey, 1967). Some subjects may show heart rate *deceleration* (indicating an orienting response) to certain stimuli they fear, or even a *diphasic* pattern in which heart rate first increases and then sharply decreases (Öst, Sterner, & Lindahl, 1984).

Systolic and diastolic blood pressure are additional cardiovascular activities measured in anxiety research. Although several factors influence blood pressure, its utility as a measure of fear is based on its involvement in sympathetic activity in the autonomic system. Because systolic blood pressure is more sensitive to short-term environmental changes, it is usually a better measure than diastolic blood pressure for detecting reactivity to stressful stimuli. One difficulty with blood pressure as a measure of arousal is that unless sophisticated equipment is available, a rather long interval between measures is required (see Katkin & Hastrup, 1982).

Reactions to stress may also be revealed by changes in blood flow through peripheral arterioles since such changes are a result of sympathetic reactivity. Measures of this type include strain gauges and plethysmography that assess blood volume of tissue and monitoring of skin surface temperatures through the use of various temperature sensors. Blood volume is often measured as part of an overall assessment of sexual preferences and performance. Skin temperature is a useful indicator for conditions such as Raynaud's disease. Although peripheral blood flow is responsive to environmental changes, it has not been used frequently as a fear index (see Kaloupek & Levis, 1983, for a rare example).

Examples

Early examples of heart rate assessments in the anxiety treatment literature are provided by Paul's (1966) classic study on fear of public speaking and Lang, Melamed, and Hart's (1970) investigation of automated desensitization. An interesting investigation of heart rate and blood pressure changes in fearful subjects is provided by Öst et al. (1984). Blood phobics (n = 18) watched a 30-minute film of four thoracic surgeries in which large quantities of blood were shown and had their heart rate and blood pressure measured before, during, and after watching the film. As a group, these phobics showed an unusual response pattern. Like most phobics, they showed an increase in heart rate and blood pressure at the beginning of the film. Then, however, 5 of these subjects showed a sharp decrease in heart rate and blood pressure that is associated with fainting or near-fainting. When the film was turned off, subjects showed another increase in both heart rate and blood pressure. It remains to be seen whether this disphasic response is unique to blood phobics or characteristic of any person exposed to blood stimuli.

Issues in Interpretation

Heart rate appears to be the cardiovascular index of choice within the research literature on anxiety. This preference is primarily justified by its capacity to be monitored continuously and by the fact that it is, relative to other physiological measures, reasonably error-free. However, caution in the use of heart rate as a measure of anxiety is warranted on two counts. First, it is sensitive to motor and perceptual activities, which are often confounded with stress in many assessment tasks (motion sensors can now be used to assess and then covary out activity data; see Michelson, Mavissakalian, & Marchione, 1985). Second, the direction of heart rate change will not be identical for all subjects, thereby requiring the researcher to consider individual differences in the response tendencies of the participants.

Electrodermal Measures

Techniques

Electrodermal activity is measured by placing electrodes on the skin and passing a slight electric current between them. Several types of electrodermal response measures are available. The most common in fear research are skin conductance and its reciprocal, skin resistance. Changes in conductance and resistance can then be displayed on a polygraph or meter (see Edelberg, 1973; Katkin, 1975; Prokasy & Raskin, 1973).

Conductance and resistance are influenced by sweat glands innervated by the sympathetic nervous system. Increases in sweating will be reflected by decreased resistance (increased conductance) to the electrical flow between the skin electrodes. A typical procedure for assessing skin-conductance changes as a stress response would involve the following steps: (a) determine the basal or resting level of skin conductance (often measured from the palm of the hand); (b) present the fear stimulus either live, pictorially, or through imagery; (c) measure the maximal increase in palmer skin conductance following stimulus presentation; and (d) compute the difference in conductance before and after stimulation.

Changes that occur after presentation of a stimulus are called *elicited* or *evoked responses*. Changes in skin conductance may also occur without any specific stimulus presentations. These changes are known as *spontaneous* or *nonspecific fluctuations*, and although they are usually less pronounced than evoked responses, they are believed to be a relatively valid measure of anxiety (Taché & Selye, 1986). In an extensive research program, Katkin (1966, 1975; Lick & Katkin, 1976) has shown that spontaneous electrodermal fluctuations are related to induced stress.

Examples

Electrodermal measures have been used extensively in laboratory evaluations of behavioral treatments such as desensitization (Katkin & Deitz, 1973). Several studies (e.g., Falkowski & Steptoe, 1983; Lehrer, 1977) have found greater electrodermal changes associated with relaxation training and/ or biofeedback than with control procedures; others (e.g., Lehrer, Schoicket, Carrington, & Woolfolk, 1980) have not found relaxation training effects on skin conductance measures.

Several studies have demonstrated that electrodermal activity can differentiate phobics' responses to feared objects from their responses to nonfeared objects, and that phobics can be discriminated from nonphobics on the basis of skin conductance or resistance changes (Katkin & Hastrup, 1982). Electrodermal measures have also shown a concurrent relationship with other measures of arousal, although this relationship is not as replicable as one would hope (see Haynes, 1978).

Issues in Interpretation

Electrodermal measures can be recommended as a component of a comprehensive clinical assessment of anxiety. Lick and Katkin (1976) endorse the use of spontaneous electrodermal activity on the grounds that it is easily scored, technically undemanding, and economical. Electrodermal measures are influenced by procedural variations and environmental intrusions and are therefore not free of artifact. However, for the clinican seeking a middle ground between the burdens of psychophysiological techniques and the disadvantages of omitting such measures altogether, electrodermal assessment may provide an acceptable compromise.

BEHAVIORAL MEASURES

The preference for overt behavioral measures of anxiety by social learning theorists is illustrated by several themes in the literature. One sign is that discrepancies among the three assessment channels are often resolved by concentrating on the behavioral data as the "real" phenomena and demoting self-report and physiological data to secondary roles. Accompanying this seeing-is-believing attitude is the conviction that samples of behavior represent the most direct, error-free assessment channel available. This confidence in the reliability and validity of behavioral observation is difficult to reconcile with some of the data on observation (e.g., Cone & Foster, 1982) and has been challenged by clinicians who are less sanguine about a behavioral emphasis (e.g., Korchin, 1976).

Direct Measures

The clinician interested in direct behavioral measures may either observe the overt effects of physiological activation and emotional distress on motor functioning or look for the interference effects of arousal on ongoing performance. Examples of the first category include heavy breathing, tremors, moistening/biting of the lips, facial grimaces, pacing, and perspiration. Interference effects might involve stammering, impaired recall, reduced motor dexterity and speech blocks.

One of the best-known illustrations of the observation of overt behavioral manifestations of anxiety is provided in Paul's (1966) Timed Behavioral Checklist (TBCL). The TBCL includes 20 behaviors thought to be directly related to physiological activation (e.g., pacing, extraneous limb movements). Observers using the TBCL are trained to record the occurrence of each of these behaviors during specific time intervals. Occurrences of each behavior can then be summed over all intervals and represented as an index of overt anxiety. Interrater reliabilities on the TBCL can be quite high (Paul, 1966, reported an average of .95), and it has been used in a variety of anxiety studies (e.g., Bernstein & Nietzel, 1974; Borkovec, Stone, O'Brien, & Kaloupek, 1974; Sharp & Forman, 1985).

Several overt behavioral measures concentrate on disruptions of speech as a direct index of anxiety. Perhaps the most widely used of these methods is Mahl's (1956) speech disturbance ratio. This measure is computed by dividing the number of speech dysfluencies (corrections, "ah's," "uh's," mispronunciations, incomplete words, etc.) by the total number of word productions. Percentage of silent time is also computed as a measure of arousal. Mahl's indices show good interrater reliabilities and test-retest stability. Borkovec, Fleischmann, and Caputo (1973) reported that "non-ah" speech disturbances increased in association with stress produced by a social interaction task. Mahl's ratio has also been used to assess anxiety in children (Milos & Reiss, 1982). Anxiety assessment using content analysis of speech has been described by Gottschalk and Gleser (1969).

In the area of social anxiety, Monti et al. (1984) have developed a nine-category system that measures what they call "midi-level" behaviors (midway between measures that are too global or too specific to be clinically useful) that correlate with physiological arousal and global ratings of anxiety. The nine direct behavioral measures were: movements of extremities, self-manipulations, facial expressions, posture, eye and body orientation, gesturing, quality and tone of voice, rate and pressure of speech, and synchrony between verbal and nonverbal behaviors.

Direct behavioral measures may also focus upon the general effectiveness and efficiency of other ongoing behaviors that should be related to anxiety. Monitoring the academic performance of test-anxious clients before and after a clinical intervention and observing the recovery and recuperation efforts of patients undergoing stressful medical procedures illustrate this approach.

There are several reasons why no single, direct behavioral measure of anxiety is an entirely acceptable index. First, because less than maximum degrees of arousal are usually involved, only the effects on an individual's most responsive systems are usually observed. Second, the level of task difficulty and the amount of previous practice at the observed activity will interact in determining the extensiveness of behavioral disruption. Finally, as with any behavior, performance is influenced by many other variables besides affect and physiological responsiveness.

Indirect Measures

Indirect behavioral measures involve observing the secondary behavioral effects of anxiety reactions. They rest on the assumption that escalating anxiety will be accompanied by behaviors that have reduced the anxiety reaction in the past, either by avoiding or escaping arousing stimuli or by being incompatible with anxiety.

Observation in the Natural Environment

Indirect assessment can be conducted in the natural environment. For example, claustrophobics can be watched as they enter and then remain in closed, restrictive places. This approach is akin to "free operant" measurement, where a person's relative frequency of avoidance or interaction with a particular stimulus is monitored.

Other examples of indirect measures of anxiety in natural settings include "behavioral walks," in which the distance agoraphobics can walk from a safe place is measured (Michelson, Mavissakalian, & Marchione, 1985), the number of procedures in a routine dental exam that dental phobics can complete (Öst & Hugdahl, 1985), and the distance up a fire escape that acrophobics can climb (Emmelkamp & Felten, 1985). Indirect assessments in the natural environment are time-consuming and are subject to some special ethical problems. Other difficulties include the fact that the observation itself can affect the person being observed. This quality of observation, known as *reactivity*, can be partly circumvented through the planful use of unobtrusive measures and/or third party informers (Lick & Katkin, 1976).

Behavioral Avoidance Tests

The most common indirect behavioral measure is the behavioral avoidance test (BAT), where a fear-eliciting stimulus is placed in a standardized environment and a person is instructed to approach the stimulus and engage in progressively more intimate or bold interactions with it. The logic of the BAT is that the more intense the anxiety elicited, the earlier in the approach sequence the person will avoid or escape from the provocative stimulus.

Lang and Lazovik (1963) were the first to use a standard BAT in a therapy-outcome study. Their procedure consisted of requesting individuals who feared snakes to enter a room containing a caged, harmless snake. Subjects were informed that the purpose of the test was to assess their feelings toward snakes. While the subject remained at the door of the test room, the experimenter opened the top of the cage, and invited the subject to approach, touch, and hold the snake. The experimenter repeated each invitation once if the subject did not immediately comply. The subject's behavior was scored on a 3-point scale which corresponded to discrete look, touch, hold criteria.

While the Lang and Lazovik procedures served as a prototype for fear researchers, several procedural variations have been introduced into BAT administration. These include type of subject (required subject-pool participants vs. volunteers), mode of instructional presentation (live, taped, or written), timing of instructions (one-shot, pre-BAT presentation vs. progressive presentation augmented by written instructions which the subject takes to the BAT), nature of instructions ("approach as close as you can" versus "do only what is comfortable for you"), criterion behavior (proximity from the target object, touching the object, or holding the object), and experimenter behavior in the test situation (experimenter present versus absent; experimenter-modeled approach versus no modeled approach).

Researchers' interest in the BAT has resulted in a sizable literature on this technique's validity and reliability, and several problems have become apparent. As Paul and Bernstein (1973) note:

> All the problems of the potential lack of validity of self-report measures as a response system under direct voluntary control also apply to the observational assessment of secondary behaviors. Thus, in mild or moderate degrees of anxiety, the situational context of assessment, the level of demand for approach behavior, and the perceived positive or negative consequences for a given degree of approach may be more potent motivating factors in determining secondary motoric behaviors than the degree of anxiety experienced. These motoric behaviors may further interact with other individual characteristics (tolerance for distress, knowledge and experience in interacting with the stimuli involved, prior cultural experience) relatively independently of anxiety level. (p. 9)

While level of anxiety may determine general behavioral tendencies on a BAT, the amount of avoidance displayed within these limits can be viewed as a function of method variance, social cues, demand characteristics, and payoffs transmitted explicitly and implicitly to a subject in the measurement situation (Bernstein, 1974; Bernstein & Nietzel, 1977; Borkovec, 1973; Lick & Unger, 1975; Smith, Diener, & Beaman, 1974). These findings represent an extension and confirmation of results supporting the pervasive influence of situational-demand factors on many clinical phenomena (Bernstein & Nietzel, 1977) and underscore the importance of exploring the degree to which all targets of behavioral assessment are vulnerable to bias via unprogrammed factors.

Role-Playing Tests

Whereas BATS are used primarily to assess fear elicited by some specific stimulus, role-playing tests are employed to measure anxiety generated by various social interactions. They involve the creation of make-believe situations in which the subject is asked to respond in his or her typical way. Role playing has been an element in several types of therapy for many years, but it is only since the late 1960s that it has become part of the clinical assessment of anxiety.

Sometimes the procedures are simple and structured, as in the Situation Test (ST) developed by Rehm and Marston (1968) to explore college males' social skills. In the ST, the client sits with a person of the opposite sex and listens to tape recorded descriptions of scenes to be role played. The woman (an assistant to the clinician) then reads a question or statement, such as "What would you like to do now?" or "I thought that was a lousy movie," and the client is asked to respond as if the situation were real. Another example is provided by Nelson, Hayes, Felton, and Jarrett (1985) who required subjects to respond to interpersonal situations such as the following:

"You have been seeing this man/woman for about 4 months. He/she has been very demanding on you and he/she gets extremely jealous when he/she sees you just talking to another man/woman. He/she says he/she doesn't want to lose you but you want to end this relationship. So you say . . . ."

Role-playing procedures have become a standard ingredient in the assessment of social skills of socially anxious adults (Beidel, Turner, & Dancu, 1985) and unassertiveness in a multitude of different types of people. In most role plays, the subjects' responses are videotaped and then rated by observers on such target criteria as anxiety, appropriateness of content, level of positive and refusal assertiveness, latency to respond, response duration, speech dysfluencies, posture, eye contact, gaze, hand gestures, head movements, and voice loudness. This list is not exhaustive, but it illustrates the wide variability of measures employed (see Bellack, 1983, for a review of the problems associated with these measures).

How valid are role-playing assessments? Do their results generalize to natural, everyday settings? Do they agree with other types of assessment such as self-report or peer evaluation? Are they correlated with physiological measures or important external criteria? In the early days of role-playing assessments their use was based on their assumed face validity. Today, most investigators require proof that results obtained from role-playing are actually related to naturalistic behavior.

Although the results of research on the validity of role-playing methods are mixed, the basic conclusion is that with proper care they can yield useful data (Bellack, 1983; Nelson et al., 1985). A large number of variables influence the way clients and subjects respond to role-playing assessments. For example, instructions to behave as one naturally would versus to behave as an assertive person would can produce very different behavior (Kazdin, Esveldt-Dawson, & Matson, 1983; Rodriguez, Nietzel, & Berzins, 1985), their level of difficulty (Kolotkin, 1980), the responses of the experimenter to the subject (Kirchner & Draguns, 1979), and the social impact of role-played behavior (Kern, Cavell, & Beck, 1985) are other variables that affect role-played responses.

As investigators have learned about the effects of such variables, they have modified role-playing methods to make them more realistic and more specific to the problems of individual clients. For example, the Extended Interaction Test (McFall & Lillesand, 1971) assesses the generality of client's behavior by using a tape that "talks back" to clients who are trying to be assertive. In order to assess the persistence of clients' ability to refuse unreasonable requests, the Extended Interaction Test requires clients to respond to a series of gradually escalating demands made by a taped antagonist. Presumably, a person who withstands repeated requests is more assertive than one who gives in after an initial refusal.

One clinical advantage of role-playing tests is that they permit the simultaneous assessment of reactive and conditioned contributions to an anxiety reaction. The sequential use of different types of role-playing tests can provide information about whether a client has failed to acquire the requisite behaviors for skillful social performance and is anxious as a consequence, or whether the performance of available skills is inhibited by conditioned anxiety or other factors (Nietzel & Bernstein, 1976). Clients displaying performance deficits could then be assigned to treatments designed to remove inhibitions, whereas those with repertoires could be exposed to skill-building experiences instead of, or as a prelude to, techniques aimed at disinhibition.

SELF-REPORT MEASURES

Social learning clinicians have often been critical of self-report measures. Their objections have focused on deficiencies in reliability and validity, contamination by faking and bias, low correlations with concurrent behavioral and physiological measures, and error associated with acquiescence, social desirability, and other response sets. Despite these limitations, self-reports are the only means assessors have to learn about the subjective components of fear experienced by their clients. Behaviorists are realizing that wholesale rejection of self-report instruments is inappropriate and would result in a limited conception of anxiety. As mentioned earlier, DSM-III's operational approach to diagnosis has stimulated the development of new self-report instruments by behaviorally oriented clinicians. In the next section we discuss four categories of self-report measures: questionnaires or surveys about the intensity of certain fears, ratings of elicited anxiety, self-monitoring, and interviews.

Questionnaires and Surveys

There are many self-report instruments requiring respondents to indicate the presence and intensity of their fear in relation to various stimuli. One type of questionnaire asks subjects to rate a wide variety of fear stimuli (e.g., high places, closed places, dogs, snakes, strangers, etc.); others concentrate on a particular stimulus class (e.g., the dentist), but contain several items representing different parameters of the situation. Ratings are usually made on 5- or 7-point Likert scales.

The best known questionnaire that covers a diversity of commonly feared stimuli is the Fear Survey Schedule (FSS). Geer's (1965) version contains 51 items; Wolpe and Lang (1964) developed a 120-item FSS; and Braun and Reynolds (1969) report a 100-item form. There is also a Fear Survey Schedule for Children (Ollendick, 1983). Fear Survey Schedules are generally used either to screen large samples of subjects for inclusion in a study on some shared fear or to monitor changes in fears in addition to the one(s) targeted for clinical intervention.

There are several questionnaires that measure *state anxiety*, as opposed to *trait anxiety*. Measures of state anxiety are often used diagnostically as measures of induced stress and as an evaluation of change following some therapeutic intervention. The most prominent instrument of this type is the state form of the State-Trait Anxiety Inventory (Spielberger, Gorsuch, & Luchene, 1970). Other popular measures of current (state) anxiety are Zuckerman and Lubin's (1965) Multiple Affect Adjective Checklist which yields scores for anxiety, depression, and hostility; Husek and Alexander's (1963) Anxiety Differential; and Endler, Hunt, and Rosenstein's (1962) S-R Inventory of Anxiousness. Table 9.2 summarizes other questionnaires to measure anxiety. Much of this work has been influenced by the triple-response-channel view of anxiety and has sought to construct efficient, psychometrically sound, multidimensional, self-report inventories.

Table 9.2 also contains listings of self-report inventories frequently used for two other purposes: a) assessing the severity of anxiety symptoms in clinical populations, particularly in outpatients suffering from anxiety disorders, somatoform disorders, or personality disorders; and b) contributing to the diagnosis and clinical evaluation of specific DSM-III anxiety disorders. Additional scales of these types are described by Roberts et al. (1983).

Ratings of Elicited Anxiety

Prior and/or immediately following actual or imagined exposure to a feared stimulus, subjects can be asked to rate the degree of their subjective discomfort. Ratings of this sort are actually focused measures of state anxiety. Walk's (1956) Fear Thermometer (FT) and the Wolpe and Lazarus (1966) Subjective Units of Disturbance (SUD) scale are frequently-used examples. The FT usually involves asking a subject to rate on a 10-point scale (1 = completely calm, 10 = absolute terror) the amount of anxiety experienced during approach or exposure to the feared stimulus. The SUD scale ranges from 1–100. The major advantage of such scales is the ease with which they can be applied to virtually any type of fear. Their psychometric properties appear adequate, although they are obviously subject to deliberate distortions by raters.

Husek and Alexander's (1963) Anxiety Differential (AD) and Zuckerman and Lubin's (1966) Multiple Affect Adjective Checklist can also be used as measures of current anxiety.

Self-Monitoring

Self-monitoring, an increasingly popular form of behavioral assessment, involves asking a person to observe certain aspects of his or her own behavior

TABLE 9.2. Frequently Used Self-Report Measures of State Anxiety, Severity of Anxiety Symptoms, and Specific Anxiety Disorders

NAME OF INSTRUMENT	REFERENCE

Measures of State Anxiety
1. State-Trait Anxiety Inventory — Spielberger et al. (1970)
2. Multiple Affect Adjective Checklist — Zuckerman & Lubin (1965)
3. Anxiety Differential — Husek & Alexander (1963)
4. S-R Inventory of Anxiousness — Endler, Hunt, & Rosenstein (1962)
5. Cognitive Somatic Anxiety Questionnaire — Schwartz, Davison, & Goleman (1978)
6. Autonomic Perception Inventory — Mandler, Mandler, & Uviller (1958)
7. Trimodal Anxiety Symptom Inventory — Lehrer & Woolfolk (1982)
8. Anxiety Sensitivity Index* — Reiss, Peterson, Gursky, & McNally (1986)

Measures of the Severity of Anxiety Symptoms
1. Subjective Anxiety Scale — Zung (1971)
2. Hamilton Anxiety Rating Scale (rated by clinician) — Hamilton (1959)
3. The Symptom Checklist 90 — Derogatis (1977)
4. IPAT Anxiety Scale — Krug, Scheier, & Cattell (1976)

Measures of Specific Anxiety Disorders
Agoraphobia
1. Fear Questionnaire (agoraphobia subscale) — Marks & Mathews (1979)
2. Mobility Inventory for Agoraphobia — Chambless, Caputo, Jasin, Gracely, & Williams (1985)
3. Agoraphobic Cognitions Questionnaire — Chambless, Caputo, Bright, & Gallagher (1984)
4. Body Sensations Questionnaire — Chambless et al. (1984)

Social Phobia
1. Social Avoidance and Distress Scale — Watson & Friend (1969)
2. Fear of Negative Evaluation Scale — Watson & Friend (1969)
3. Fear Questionnaire (social phobia subscale) — Marks & Mathews (1979)
4. Social Interaction Self-Statement Test — Glass, Merluzzi, Biever, & Larsen (1982)
5. Social Anxiety Inventory — Richardson & Tasto (1976)
6. Willoughby Personality Schedule — Willoughby (1934)

Simple Phobias
1. Dental Fear Survey — Kleinknecht, Klepak, &Alexander (1973)
2. Mutilation Questionnaire — Hastings (1971)
3. Acrophobia Questionnaire — Baker, Cohen, & Saunders (1973)
4. Snake Anxiety Questionnaire — Lang, Melamed, & Hart (1970)
5. Fear Questionnaire (blood/injury subscale) — Marks & Mathews (1979)
6. Spider Phobia Questionnaire — Watts & Sharrock (1984)
7. Lebanese Fear Inventory — Saigh (1982)
8. Test Anxiety Scale for Children — Sarason, Davidson, Lighthall, Waite, & Ruebush (1960)
9. Multidimensional Fear of Death Scale — Hoelter (1979)
10. Fear Survey Schedules — Lang & Lazovick (1963); Wolpe & Lang (1964); Geer (1965); Braun & Reynolds (1969)

Panic Disorders
1. Anxiety Disorder Interview Schedule
   (structured interview)   Di Nardo et al. (1983)
2. Hillside Acute Panic Inventory   Zitrin, Klein, Woerner, & Ross (1983)

Generalized Anxiety Disorder
1. Anxiety Disorder Interview Schedule
   (structured interview)   Di Nardo et al. (1983)

Obsessive-Compulsive Disorder
1. Maudsley Obsessional-Compulsive
   Inventory   Hodgson & Rachman (1977)
2. Leyton Obsessional Inventory   Cooper (1970)
3. Lynfield Obsessional-Compulsive
   Questionnaire   Allen & Tune (1975)
4. Cues for Urges to Ritualize Inventory   Steketee & Foa (1985)
5. Thought Inventory   Steketee & Foa (1985)

Post-Traumatic Stress Disorder
1. PTSD Scale   Roberts, Penk, Gearing, Robinowitz,
                                            Dolan, & Patterson (1982)
2. Vietnam Veteran Survey   Figley (1977)
3. PTSD Diagnostic Scale   Foy, Sipprelle, Rueger, & Carroll (1984)
4. MMPI PTSD Scale   Keane, Malloy, & Fairbank (1984)

---

*Measures various beliefs about the negative consequences that anxiety will have. It has been conceptualized as a "fear of fear" scale (see also Heide & Borkovec, 1984).

and keep a record of these observations. For example, a client may keep a diary of how often and in what stimulus contexts a problem behavior occurs, how long it lasts, and what the consequences of its occurrence are. Such diaries can later serve as a dependent measure in assessing the success of an intervention.

Reactivity is an important methodological issue in self-monitoring. To what extent does the act of self-observation affect the behavior being monitored? Reactivity is a threat to valid assessment, but it can also serve therapeutic purposes since, in some cases, it accelerates positive behaviors and suppresses negative behaviors.

Although self-monitoring can be used to measure either overt or covert events, it has not been employed to assess fear as often as other targets. Anxiety may be particularly difficult to self-monitor because the crucial behavioral and physiological changes are often fleeting and subtle. In addition, high levels of arousal may disrupt accurate self-observation.

A recent example of self-monitoring of anxiety is provided by Barlow et al. (1984). In that study, patients with panic disorder or generalized anxiety disorder used daily diaries to rate the level of anxiety during morning, afternoon, evening, and bedtime periods as well as the duration and intensity of anxiety attacks. Other clinical populations who have self-monitored level of anxiety or frequency of fear-related behaviors include obsessive-compulsives (Foa, Steketee, Grayson, Turner, & Latimer, 1984), dental phobics (Thrash, Marr, & Boone, 1982), agoraphobics (Arnow, Taylor,

Agras, & Telch, 1985), and socially anxious undergraduates (Twentyman & McFall, 1975).

The value of self-monitoring in a multi-channel approach to anxiety assessment rests on its capacity to focus on specific target events as they occur in the client's daily life. As such, self-monitoring extends the data collection process to the natural flow of problem behavior while providing fine-grain information on the topography, frequency, and consequences of that behavior. Data from self-observation can be used to order the items in a desensitization hierarchy, to highlight skill deficits that may be contributing to social anxiety, to assess characteristics of stimulus settings that are most stressful for a client, to evaluate the immediate effects of therapeutic interventions, and to measure the generalizability and durability of posttreatment reductions in anxiety.

Interviews

For any clinical problem, including anxiety, the interview is an indispensable element in a complete assessment enterprise. A properly conducted interview will enable the clinician to assess the specific manifestations of a client's anxiety; the situations in which it most often occurs; the consequences of its appearance; the circumstances which constrain or exacerbate it; and its history, current intensity, and prognosis. Interviews can be conducted at any time before, during, or after treatment, thereby allowing an up-to-date description and understanding of changes in crucial behaviors.

The emphasis of behavioral interviews is on specifying as many of the functional or controlling dimensions of a problem as possible. Questions usually concentrate on *what* a client does, and *when*, *where*, and under *what circumstances* various activities occur. With respect to anxiety and fear, the clinician will normally inquire about the following factors (Haynes, 1978):

1. What is the client's specific complaint? It is important to determine what a client means by "anxiety" and to distinguish it from other aversive emotional states such as depression and anger. The therapist will try to translate vague concepts into clear behavioral descriptions.
2. What events follow the experience of anxiety? What are the consequences of being anxious? Anxiety can sometimes be reduced by altering maladaptive reinforcement contingencies that may be present.
3. What are the cues that precede anxiety? The therapist will need to know the triggering stimuli for anxiety in order to help the client modify it. Adequate assessment of stimulus-control is important for treatments that will have a generalized effect on targeted fears.
4. What historical and developmental factors have contributed to anxiety? Have there been methods that have previously proven successful in alleviating the client's problem?

5. Are there special client strengths or weaknesses that the therapist must consider in designing a treatment program? It is also important to determine whether the client's customary environment presents special demands that will maintain anxiety reactions unless they are modified in some way.

Structured interviews have substantial importance in the clinical assessment and diagnosis of anxiety disorders. As with other forms of psychopathology, interviews for anxiety disorders have been structured along DSM-III guidelines for diagnosis. For example, Malloy, Fairbank, and Keane (1983) derived a structured interview for posttraumatic stress disorders from DSM-III criteria. The most comprehensive structured interview for anxiety disorders is the Anxiety Disorder Interview Schedule (ADIS) designed by DiNardo, O'Brien, Barlow, Waddell and Blanchard (1983) to facilitate differential diagnosis among DSM-III anxiety disorder categories, while ruling out psychosis, substance abuse, and the major affective disorders. In addition, ADIS provides a data base for the description and investigation of the history, situational and cognitive components, and other clinical characteristics associated with each anxiety disorder category as well as a means of assessing the reliability of the DSM-III classification. The ADIS includes items developed by DiNardo et al. (1983) to relate to DSM-III categories as well as selected items from the SADS (Endicott & Spitzer, 1978) and the Present State Examination (Wing, Cooper, & Sartorius, 1974). In addition, the Hamilton Anxiety Scale (Hamilton, 1959) and Hamilton Depression Scale (Hamilton, 1960) are embedded in the interview, which lasts about 90 minutes.

To assess the reliability of DSM-III anxiety diagnoses with the ADIS, its authors administered it to a sample of 60 mostly self-referred patients at the Phobic and Anxiety Disorders Clinic in Albany, NY, on two separate occasions (3 weeks apart) through independent clinician interviewers. The K coefficient was calculated for exact overall agreements between interviewers on the 14 specific DSM-III category diagnoses included in the study (K = .65), and for the anxiety disorders (K = .68) and affective disorders (K = .82) taken separately. In addition, K coefficients were reported for certain specific anxiety diagnoses: Agoraphobic with Panic Attacks (K = .86), Panic Disorder (K = .69), Generalized Anxiety Disorder (K = .47), Social Phobia (K = .77), and Obsessive-Compulsive Disorder (K = .66). These relatively high K coefficients compare quite favorably to reliabilities reported in other field studies of DSM-III Axis I categories.

A CASE STUDY

Now that we have considered the multichannel nature of anxiety and examined various anxiety assessment techniques, it may be helpful to illustrate the way clinicians integrate assessment and treatment.

A typical example is provided in a case study reported by Kleinknecht and Bernstein (1979). The client was Mr. R., a 38-year-old man whose fear of dentists kept him from dental examination and treatment for 13 years. He experienced extreme distress at the mere thought of making a dental appointment, but he was also preoccupied with worry — quite justified, it turned out — that his avoidance was allowing serious dental problems to go unchecked. Finally, at his wife's urging, Mr. R. attempted to undergo a routine oral examination. That examination was, in his words, "so stressful" that he was unwilling to return for much-needed dental treatment. The dentist recommended a program of behavioral fear reduction. Mr. R. agreed to behavioral treatment but refused to resume dental treatment unless he could learn to be more relaxed about it.

Assessment began by asking the client to complete several questionnaires. Some, such as the Dental Fear Scale and Conceptions of Dentistry (Kleinknecht, Klepac, & Alexander, 1973; Kleinknecht & Bernstein, 1978), focused on Mr. R's reported fear. The Fear Survey Schedule (Geer, 1965) gave a picture of the client's rated fear of other objects and situations. The Eysenck Personality Inventory (Eysenck & Eysenck, 1963) and the Health Locus of Control Scale (Wallston, Wallston, Kaplan, & Maides, 1976) provided a more general picture of the client's personality and of his orientation toward health.

Next came two 2-hour interviews designed to (a) establish rapport; (b) outline the general nature of Mr. R.'s presenting problem; (c) obtain an overview of Mr. R.'s life history and current living situation, his level of psychological and behavioral functioning, and his most prominent strengths and weaknesses; and (d) develop a more detailed picture of his fear. The goal of these interviews was not just to learn about the fear that brought Mr. R. to treatment, but to try to place that fear in some perspective relative to his life in general.

The questions in the therapist's mind during these interviews included the following: Is dental fear the client's only (or main) problem? How does the problem affect those around him? Is the fear central enough to make it the focus of treatment? If not, should it be dealt with anyway as a first step toward tackling more significant problems? To what extent does he receive social or other rewards that maintain his fear? What effect will resolution of the problem have on the client and those with whom he interacts? What personal and environmental assets can the client utilize in dealing with the problem?

During the interviews, Mr. R. described his fear of dentistry as stemming from very unpleasant, often painful childhood treatment experiences at the hands of a "rough, unsympathetic" dentist. His discomfort was made worse when, during a tour of duty in the Army, Mr. R. received what he considered to be inconsiderate and needlessly painful treatment from a military dentist known on the base as "The Butcher." Detailed discussion revealed that Mr. R.'s fear was particularly intense in relation to the pain of having "back teeth" (molars) drilled under inadequate anesthesia, a circumstance he had been forced to face more than once.

More interviewing, along with personality test results, established a picture of the client as a person whose developmental history, current life situation, and general functioning were unremarkable. The history of his fear showed the clear pattern of increasing intensity and growing avoidance indicative of a learning process; there was no reason to suspect that other, more subtle, etiological or maintenance factors were responsible for the presenting problem. Data that might have suggested the need to assess such factors further or to focus on other problems would have included (a) sudden onset of the fear in the absence of a precipitating event, (b) a history of more general maladaptive behavior, (c) evidence of stress in relation to the client's job or family, or (d) observations of verbal or nonverbal behaviors suggesting significant dependency, manipulativeness, or bizarreness.

The next phase of assessment focused on recording the client's subjective, behavioral, and physiological responses during an oral examination at a dentist's office. These measures established pretreatment baselines against which posttreatment changes could be compared. While the client sat in the dental chair prior to the examination, his state anxiety was assessed via the Anxiety Differential (Husek & Alexander, 1963). Before, during, and after the examination, his physiological arousal was measured through the Palmar Sweat Index (a fingerprint technique that allows the number of open sweat glands to be counted), and his overt behavior was monitored through an observational system known as the Dental Operatory Rating Scale (Bernstein & Kleinknecht, 1982).

Following the oral examination, the client participated in several treatment sessions which included symbolic modeling, a variant on systematic desensitization, and practice at remaining relaxed while in a dental operatory. Details of treatment are described by Kleinknecht and Bernstein (1979). Assessment continued during all treatment sessions, particularly while the client was watching videotaped scenes of dental treatment. The therapist obtained verbal reports of state anxiety via the Fear Thermometer (Walk, 1956) and remained sensitive to behavioral displays of discomfort. Both measures were used to pace the presentation of feared stimuli during these sessions. After treatment, the client participated in a second oral examination, during which all pretreatment assessments were repeated.

At the pretreatment oral examination, the client showed considerable physiological arousal through the Palmar Sweat Index and gave reports of clear discomfort on the Anxiety Differential. The posttreatment Anxiety Differential score dropped to a level identical to that given while the client was in a relaxed, nondental setting. Posttreatment PSI was ruined by an error in the assessment procedure, so no change score could be calculated. The client showed no change in motor behavior during post versus pretreatment assessments, but did find it possible to enter a program of dental treatment (including oral surgery) which, at follow-up several months later, was continuing without notable discomfort.

REFERENCES

Allen, J. J., & Tune, G. S. (1975). The Lynfield Obsessional/Compulsive Questionnaire. *Scottish Medical Journal, 20,* (supplement 1), 21–24.

Arena, J. G., Blanchard, E. B., Andrasik, F., Cotch, P. A., & Myers, P. E. (1983). Reliability of psychophysiological assessment. *Behaviour Research and Therapy, 21,* 447–460.

Arnow, B. A., Taylor, C. B., Agras, W. S., & Telch, M. J. (1985). Enhancing agoraphobia treatment outcome by changing couple communication patterns. *Behavior Therapy, 16,* 452–467.

Baker, B. L ., Cohen, D. C., & Saunders, J. T. (1973). Self-directed desensitization for acrophobia. *Behaviour Research and Therapy, 11,* 79–89.

Barlow, D. H., Cohen, A. S., Waddell, M. T., Vermilyea, B. B., Klosko, J. S., Blanchard, E. B., & Di Nardo, P. A. (1984). Panic and generalized anxiety disorders: Nature and treatment. *Behavior Therapy, 15,* 431–449.

Beck, A. T., & Emery, G. (1985). *Anxiety disorders and phobias: A cognitive perspective.* New York: Basic Books.

Beidel, D. C., Turner, S. M., & Dancu, C. V. (1985). Physiological, cognitive, and behavioral aspects of social anxiety. *Behaviour Research and Therapy, 23,* 109–118.

Bellack, A. S. (1983). Recurrent problems in the behavioral assessment of social skill. *Behaviour Research and Therapy, 21,* 29–42.

Bernstein, D. A. (1974). Manipulation of avoidance behavior as a function of increased or decreased demand on repeated behavioral tests. *Journal of Consulting and Clinical Psychology, 42,* 896–900.

Bernstein, D.A., & Kleinknecht, R.A. (1982). Multiple approaches to the reduction of dental fears. *Journal of Behavior Therapy and Experimental Psychiatry, 13,* 287–292.

Bernstein, D. A., & Nietzel, M. T. (1974). Behavioral avoidance tests: The effects of demand characteristics and repeated measures on two types of subjects. *Behavior Therapy, 5,* 183–192.

Bernstein, D. A., & Nietzel, M. T. (1977). Demand characteristics in behavior modification: A natural history of a "nuisance." In M. Hersen, R. M. Eisler, & P. M. Miller (Eds.), *Progress in behavior modification* (Vol. 4). New York: Academic Press.

Borkovec, T. D. (1973). The effects of instructional suggestion and physiological cues on analogue fear. *Behavior Therapy, 4,* 185–192.

Borkovec, T. D., Fleischmann, D. J., & Caputo, J. A. (1973). The measurement of anxiety in an analogue social situation. *Journal of Consulting and Clinical Psychology, 41,* 157–161.

Borkovec, T. D., Stone, N. M., O'Brien, G. T., & Kaloupek, D. G. (1974). Evaluation of a clinically relevant target behavior for analogue outcome research. *Behavior Therapy, 5,* 504–514.

Borkovec, T. D., Weerts, T. C., & Bernstein, D. A. (1977). Assessment of anxiety. In

A. R. Ciminero, K. S. Calhoun, & H. E. Adams (Eds.), *Handbook of behavioral assessment*. New York: Wiley.

Brandt, K. (1973). The effects of relaxation training with analog HR feedback on basal levels of arousal and response to aversive tones in groups selected according to Fear Survey scores. *Psychophysiology, 11*, 242. (Abstract)

Braun, P. R., & Reynolds, D. N. (1969). A factor analysis of a 100-item fear survey inventory. *Behaviour Research and Therapy, 7*, 399–402.

Cannon, W. B. (1915). *Bodily changes in pain, hunger, fear, and rage*. New York: Appleton-Century-Crofts.

Cattell, R. B., & Scheier, I. H. (1961). *The meaning and measurement of neuroticism and anxiety*. New York: Ronald Press.

Chambless, D. L., Caputo, G. L., Bright, P., & Gallagher, R. (1984). Assessment of fear in agoraphobics: The Body Sensations Questionnaire and the Agoraphobic Cognitions Questionnaire. *Journal of Consulting and Clinical Psychology, 52*, 1090–1097.

Chambless, D. L., Caputo, G. C., Jasin, S. E., Gracely, E. J., & Williams, C. (1985). The Mobility Inventory for Agoraphobia, *Behaviour Research and Therapy, 23*, 35–44.

Cerny, J. A., Himadi, W. G., & Barlow, D. H. (1984). Issues in diagnosing anxiety disorders. *Journal of Behavioral Assessment, 6*, 301–329.

Cone, J. D., & Foster, S. L. (1982). Direct observation in clinical psychology. In P. C. Kendall & J. N. Butcher (Eds.), *Handbook of research methods in clinical psychology* (pp. 311–354). New York: John Wiley & Sons.

Cooper, J. (1970). The Leyton Obsessional Inventory. *Psychological Medicine, 1*, 48–64.

Derogatis, L. R. (1977). *SCL-90 Manual-1*, Baltimore, MD: Johns Hopkins University School of Medicine.

Di Nardo, S. A., O'Brien, G. T., Barlow, D. H., Waddell, M. T., & Blanchard, E. B. (1983). Reliability of DSM-III anxiety disorder categories using a new structured interview. *Archives of General Psychiatry, 40*, 1070–1075.

Edelberg, R. (1973). Mechanisms of electrodermal adaptations for locomotion, manipulation or defense. In E. Stellar & J. M. Sprague (Eds.), *Progress in physiological psychology* (Vol. 5). New York: Academic Press.

Emmelkamp, P. M. G., & Felten, M. (1985). The process of exposure *in vivo*: Cognitive and physiological changes during treatment of acrophobia. *Behaviour Research and Therapy, 23*, 219–224.

Endicott, J., & Spitzer, R. L. (1978). A diagnostic interview: The schedule for affective disorders and schizophrenia. *Archives of General Psychiatry, 35*, 837–844.

Endler, N. S., Hunt, J. McV., & Rosenstein, A. J. (1962). An S-R inventory of anxiousness. *Psychological Monographs: General and Applied, 76*, 1–31.

Epstein, L. H., & Abel, G. G. (1977). An analysis of biofeedback training effects for tension headache patients. *Behavior Therapy, 8*, 37–47.

Eysenck, H. J. (1982). Neobehavioristic (S-R) theory. In G. T. Wilson & C. M. Franks (Eds.), *Contemporary behavior therapy: Conceptual and empirical foundations* (pp. 205–276). New York: Guilford Press.

Eysenck, H. J. (1986). A genetic model of anxiety. In C. D. Spielberger & I. G. Sarason (Eds.), *Stress and anxiety. Vol. 10: A sourcebook of theory and research* (pp. 159–199). Washington, DC: Hemisphere Publishing Corporation.

Eysenck, H. J., & Eysenck, S. B. G. (1963). *Eysenck Personality Inventory*. San Diego, CA: Educational and Industrial Testing Service.

Eysenck, H. J., & Rachman, S. (1965). *The causes and cures of neurosis.* London: Routledge & Kegan Paul.

Falkowski, J., & Steptoe, A. (1983). Biofeedback-assisted relaxation in the control of reactions to a challenging task and anxiety provoking film. *Behaviour Research and Therapy, 21,* 161–167.

Figley, C. R. (1977). *The American Legion study of psychological adjustment among Vietnam veterans.* Lafayette, In: Purdue University.

Fisher, L. M., & Wilson, G. T. (1985). A study of the psychology of agoraphobia. *Behaviour Research and Therapy, 23,* 97–108.

Foa, E. B., & Kozak, M. J. (1986). Emotional processing of fear: Exposure to corrective information. *Psychological Bulletin, 99,* 20–35.

Foa, E. B., Steketee, G., Grayson, J. B., Turner, R. M., & Latimer, P. R. (1984). Deliberate exposure and blocking of obsessive-compulsive rituals: Immediate and long-term effects. *Behavior Therapy, 15,* 450–472.

Foy, D. W., Sipprelle, R. C., Rueger, D. B., & Carroll, E. M. (1984). Etiology of posttraumatic stress disorder in Vietnam veterans: Analysis of premilitary, military, and combat exposure influences. *Journal of Consulting and Clinical Psychology, 52,* 79–87.

Geer, J. H. (1965). The development of a scale to measure fear. *Behaviour Research and Therapy, 3,* 45–53.

Glass, C. R., Merluzzi, T. V., Biever, J. L., & Larsen, K. H. (1982). Cognitive assessment of social anxiety: Development and validation of a self-statement questionnaire. *Cognitive Therapy and Research, 6,* 37–55.

Gottschalk, L. A., & Gleser, G. C. (1969). *The measurement of psychological states through the content analysis of verbal behavior.* Berkeley, CA: University of California Press.

Hamilton, M. (1959). The assessment of anxiety states by rating. *British Journal of Medical Psychology, 32,* 50–55.

Hamilton, M. (1960). A rating scale for depression. *Journal of Neurology, Neurosurgery, and Psychiatry, 23,* 56–62.

Hamilton, V. (1986). A cognitive model of anxiety: Implications for theories of personality and motivation. In C. D. Spielberger & I. G. Sarason (Eds.). *Stress and anxiety. Vol 10: A sourcebook of theory and research.* Washington Hemisphere Publishing Corporation.

Hartmann, L. M. (1983). A metacognitive model of social anxiety: Implication for treatment. *Clinical Psychology Review, 3,* 435–456.

Hastings, J. E. (1971). *Cardiac and cortical responses to affective stimuli in a reaction time task.* Unpublished doctoral dissertation. University of Wisconsin at Madison.

Haynes, S. N. (1978). *Principles of behavioral assessment.* New York: Gardner Press, Inc.

Heide, F. J., & Borkovec, T. D. (1984). Relaxation-induced anxiety: Mechanisms and theoretical implications. *Behaviour Research and Therapy, 22,* 1–12.

Hodgson, R., & Rachman, S. (1974). Desynchrony in measures of fear. *Behaviour Research and Therapy, 2,* 319–326.

Hodgson, R. J., & Rachman, S. (1977). Obsessional-compulsive complaints. *Behaviour Research and Therapy, 15,* 389–395.

Hoelter, J. W. (1979). Multidimensional treatment of fear of death. *Journal of Consulting and Clinical Psychology, 47,* 996–999.

Holden, A. E., & Barlow, D. H. (1986). Heart rate and heart rate variability recorded in vivo in agoraphobics and nonphobics. *Behavior Therapy, 17,* 26–42.

Husek, T. R., & Alexander, S. (1963). The effectiveness of the Anxiety Differential in examination stress situations. *Educational and Psychological Measurement*, *23*, 309–318.

Israel, E., & Beiman, I. (1977). Live versus recorded relaxation training: A controlled investigation. *Behavior Therapy*, *8*, 251–254.

James, W. (1980). *The principles of psychology*. New York: Holt.

Kaloupek, D. G., & Levis, D. J. (1983). Issues in the assessment of fear: Response concordance and prediction of avoidance behavior. *Journal of Behavioral Assessment*, *5*, 239–260.

Katkin, E. S. (1966). The relationship between a measure of transitory anxiety and spontaneous autonomic activity. *Journal of Abnormal Psychology*, *71*, 142–146.

Katkin, E. S. (1975). Electrodermal lability: A psychophysiological analysis of individual differences in response to stress. In I. G. Sarason & C. D. Speilberger (Eds.), *Stress and anxiety*. Washington, DC: Hemisphere Publishing Company.

Katkin, E. S., & Deitz, S. R. (1973). Systematic desensitization. In W.F. Prokasy & D. Raskin (Eds.), *Electrodermal activity and psychological research*. New York: Academic Press.

Katkin, E. S., & Hastrup, J. L. (1982). Psychophysiological methods in clinical research. In P. C. Kendall & J. N. Butcher (Eds.). *Handbook of research methods in clinical psychology* (pp. 387–425). New York: John Wiley & Sons.

Kazdin, A. E., Esveldt-Dawson, K., & Matson, J. L. (1983). The effects of instructional set on social skills performance among psychiatric inpatient children. *Behavior Therapy*, *14*, 413–423.

Keane, T. M., Malloy, P. F., & Fairbank, J. A. (1984). Empirical development of an MMPI subscale for the assessment of combat-related posttraumatic stress disorder. *Journal of Consulting and Clinical Psychology*, *52*, 888–891.

Kern, J. M., Cavell, T. A., & Beck, B. (1985). Predicting differential reactions to males' versus females' assertions, empathic-assertions, and non-assertions. *Behavior Therapy*, *16*, 63–75.

Kirchner, E. P., & Draguns, J. G. (1979). Assertion and aggression in adult offenders. *Behavior Therapy*, *10*, 452–471.

Kleinknecht, R. A., & Bernstein, D. A. (1978). The assessment of dental fear. *Behavior Therapy*, *9*, 626–634.

Kleinknecht, R. A., & Bernstein, D. A. (1979). Short-term treatment of dental avoidance. *Journal of Behavior Therapy and Experimental Psychiatry*, *10*, 311–315.

Kleinknecht, R. A., Klepac, R. K., & Alexander, L. D. (1973). Origin and characteristics of fear of dentistry. *Journal of American Dental Association*, *86*, 842–848.

Korchin, S. J. (1976). *Modern clinical psychology: Principles of intervention in the clinic and community*. New York: Basic Books, Inc.

Krug, S. E., Scheier, I. H., & Cattell, R. B. (1976). *Handbook for the IPAT Anxiety Scale*. Champaign, IL: Institute for Personality and Ability Testing.

Lacey, J. I. (1967). Somatic response patterning and stress: Some revisions of activation theory. In M. H. Appley & R. Trumball (Eds.), *Psychological stress*. New York: Appleton-Century-Crofts.

Lang, P. J. (1977). Physiological assessment of anxiety and fear. In J. D. Cone & R. P. Hawkins (Eds.), *Behavioral assessment: New directions in clinical psychology* (pp. 178–195). New York: Brunner/Mazel Publishers.

Lang, P. J. (1979). A bio-informational theory of emotional imagery. *Psychophysiology*, *16*, 495–512.

Lang, P. J. (1985). The cognitive psychophysiology of emotion: Fear and anxiety. In

A. H. Tuma & J. D. Maser (Eds.). *Anxiety and the anxiety disorders* (pp. 131–170). Hillsdale, NJ: Lawrence Erlbaum.

Lang, P. J., & Lazovik, A. D. (1963). Experimental desensitization of a phobia. *Journal of Abnormal and Social Psychology, 66,* 519–525.

Lang, P. J., Levin, D. N., Miller, G. A., & Kozak, M. J. (1983). Fear behavior, fear imagery, and the psychophysiology of emotion: The problem of affective response integration. *Journal of Abnormal Psychology, 92,* 276–306.

Lang, P. J., Melamed, B. G., & Hart, H. (1970). A psychophysiological analysis of fear modification using an automated desensitization procedure. *Journal of Abnormal Psychology, 76,* 220–234.

Lehrer, P. M. (1977). The physiological effects of relaxation in anxiety neurotic patients and the physiology effects of relaxation and alpha feedback in "normal" subjects. *Psychophysiology, 14,* 93. (Abstract)

Lehrer, P. M., Schoicket, S., Carrington, P., & Woolfolk, R. L. (1980). Psychophysiological and cognitive responses to stressful stimuli in subjects practicing progressive relaxation and clinically standardized meditation. *Behaviour Research and Therapy, 18,* 293–303.

Lehrer, P. M., & Woolfolk, R. L. (1982). Self-report assessment of anxiety: Somatic, cognitive, and behavioral modalities. *Behavioral Assessment, 4,* 167–177.

Lehrer, P. M., Woolfolk, R. L., Rooney, A.J ., McCann, B., & Carrington, P. (1983). Progressive relaxation and meditation: A study of psychophysiological and therapeutic differences between two techniques. *Behaviour Research and Therapy, 21,* 651–662.

Lick, J. R., & Katkin, E. S. (1976). Assessment of anxiety and fear. In M. Hersen & A. S. Bellack (Eds.), *Behavioral assessment: A practical handbook.* New York: Pergamon Press.

Lick, J. R., & Unger, T. (1975). External validity of laboratory fear assessment: Implications from two case studies. *Journal of Consulting and Clinical Psychology, 43,* 864–866.

Mahl, G. F. (1956). Disturbances and silences in patient's speech in psychotherapy. *Journal of Abnormal and Social Psychology, 53,* 1–15.

Malloy, P. F., Fairbank, J. A., & Keane, T. M. (1983). Validation of a multimethod assessment of post traumatic stress disorders in Vietnam veterans. *Journal of Consulting and Clinical Psychology, 51,* 488–494.

Mandler, G., Mandler, J. M., & Uviller, E. T. (1958). Autonomic feedback: The perception of autonomic activity. *Journal of Abnormal and Social Psychology, 56,* 367–373.

Marks, I. M., & Mathews, A. M. (1979). Brief standard self-rating for phobic patients. *Behaviour Research and Therapy, 17,* 263–267.

McFall, R. M., & Lillesand, D. B. (1971). Behavior rehearsal with modeling and coaching in assertion training. *Journal of Abnormal Psychology, 77,* 313–323.

Michelson, L., & Mavissakalian, M. (1985). Psychophysiological outcome of behavioral and pharmacological treatment of agoraphobia. *Journal of Consulting and Clinical Psychology, 53,* 229–236.

Michelson, L., Mavissakalian, M., & Marchione, K. (1985). Cognitive and behavioral treatments of agoraphobia: Clinical, behavioral and psychophysiological outcomes. *Journal of Consulting and Clinical Psychology, 53,* 913–925.

Milos, M. E., & Reiss, S. (1982). Effects of three play conditions on separation anxiety in young children. *Journal of Consulting and Clinical Psychology, 50,* 389–395.

Monti, P. M., Boice, R., Fingeret, A. L., Zwick, W. R., Kolko, D., Munroe, S., &

Grunberger, A. (1984). Midi-level measurement of social anxiety in psychiatric and non-psychiatric samples. *Behaviour Research and Therapy, 22*, 651–660.

Mowrer, O. H. (1939). A stimulus-response analysis of anxiety and its role as a reinforcing agent. *Psychological Review, 46*, 553–565.

Nelson, R. O., Hayes, S. C., Felton, J. L., & Jarrett, R. B. (1985). A comparison of data produced by different behavioral assessment techniques with implications for models of social skills inadequacy. *Behaviour Research and Therapy, 23*, 1–12.

Nietzel, M. T., & Bernstein, D. A. (1976). The effects of instructionally mediated demand on the behavioral assessment of assertiveness. *Journal of Consulting and Clinical Psychology, 44*, 500.

Nietzel, M. T., & Bernstein, D. A. (1981). Anxiety and fear. In M. Hersen & A. S. Bellack (Eds.), *Behavioral assessment: A practical handbook* (2nd ed., pp. 215–245). New York: Pergamon Press.

Öhman, A. (1979). Fear relevance, autonomic conditioning, and phobias: A laboratory model. In P. Sjoden, S. Bates, & W. S. Dockens (Eds.). *Trends in behavior therapy*. New York: Academic Press.

Ollendick, T. H. (1983). Reliability and validity of the Revised Fear Survey Schedule for Children (FSSC-R). *Behaviour Research and Therapy, 21*, 685–692.

Öst, L., & Hugdahl, K. (1985). Acquisition of blood and dental phobia and anxiety response patterns in clinical patients. *Behaviour Research and Therapy, 23*, 27–34.

Öst, L., Sterner, U., & Lindahl, I. (1984). Physiological responses in blood phobias. *Behaviour Research and Therapy, 22*, 99–108.

Paul, G. L. (1966). *Insight vs. desensitization in psychotherapy*. Stanford, CA: Stanford University Press.

Paul, G. L., & Bernstein, D. A. (1973). *Anxiety and clinical problems: Systematic desensitization and related techniques*. New York: General Learning Press.

Prokasy, W. F., & Raskin, D. C. (Eds.). (1973). *Electrodermal activity in psychological research*. New York: Academic Press.

Rachman, S. (1977). The conditioning theory of fear acquisition: A critical examination. *Behaviour Research and Therapy, 13*, 375–387.

Rehm, L. P., & Marston, A. R. (1968). Reduction of social anxiety through modification of self-reinforcement: An instigation therapy technique. *Journal of Consulting and Clinical Psychology, 32*, 565–574.

Reinking, R. H., & Kohl, M. L. (1975). Effects of various forms of relaxation training on physiological and self-report measures of relaxation. *Journal of Consulting and Clinical Psychology, 43*, 595–600.

Reiss, S., Peterson, R. A., Gursky, D. M., & McNally, R. J. (1986). Anxiety sensitivity, anxiety frequency, and the prediction of fearfulness. *Behaviour Research and Therapy, 24*, 1–8.

Richardson, F. C., & Tasto, D. L. (1976). Development and factor analysis of a social anxiety inventory. *Behavior Therapy, 7*, 453–462.

Roberts, S., Aronoff, J., Jensen, J., & Lambert, M. J. (1983). Measurement of outcome in anxiety disorders. In M. S. Lambert, E. R. Christensen, & S. S. DeJulio (Eds.), *The assessment of psychotherapy outcome* (pp. 304–355). New York: John Wiley & Sons.

Roberts, W. R., Penk, W. E., Gearing, M. L., Robinowitz, R., Dolan, M. P., & Patterson, E. T. (1982). Interpersonal problems of Vietnam combat veterans with symptoms of post traumatic stress disorder. *Journal of Abnormal Psychology, 91*, 444–450.

Rodriguez, R., Nietzel, M. T., & Berzins, J. I. (1980). Sex role orientation and assertiveness among female college students. *Behavior Therapy, 11*, 353–366.

Russell, R., Sipich, J., & Knipe, J. (1976). Progressive relaxation training: A procedural note. *Behavior Therapy*, *7*, 566–567.

Saigh, P. A. (1982). The Lebanese Fear Inventory: A normative report. *Journal of Clinical Psychology*, *38*, 352–355.

Sarason, S. B., Davidson, K. S., Lighthall, F. F., Waite, R. R., & Ruebush, B. K. (1960). *Anxiety and elementary school children*. New York: Wiley.

Schachter, S. (1964). The interaction of cognitive and physiological determinants of emotional state. In L. Berkowitz (Ed.), *Advances in experimental social psychology* (Vol. 1). New York: Academic Press.

Schandler, S. L., & Grings, W. W. (1976). An examination of methods for producing relaxation during short-term laboratory sessions. *Behaviour Research and Therapy*, *14*, 419–426.

Schwartz, G. E., Davidson, R. J., & Goleman, D. J. (1978). Patterning of cognitive and somatic processes in the self-regulation of anxiety: Effects of medication versus exercise. *Psychosomatic Medicine*, *40*, 321–328.

Seligman, M. P. (1971). Phobias and preparedness. *Behavior Therapy*, *2*, 307–320.

Sharp, J. J., & Forman, S. G. (1985). A comparison of two approaches to anxiety management for teachers. *Behavior Therapy*, *16*, 370–383.

Singer, J. E. (1986). Traditions of stress research: Integrative comments. In C.D. Spielberger & I. G. Sarason (Eds.), *Stress and anxiety. Vol. 10: A sourcebook of theory and research* (pp. 25–33). Washington, DC: Hemisphere Publishing Corporation.

Smith, R. E., Diener, E., & Beaman, A. L. (1974). Demand characteristics and the behavioral avoidance measure of fear in behavior therapy and analogue research. *Behavior Therapy*, *5*, 172–182.

Spielberger, C. D., Gorsuch, R. L., & Lushene, R. E. (1970). *Manual for the State-Trait Anxiety Inventory*. Palo Alto, CA: Consulting Psychologists Press.

Stekel, W. (1923). *Conditions of nervous anxiety and their treatment*. (Translation by Rosalie Gabler.) New York: Dodd, Mead & Co.

Steketee, G., & Foa, E. B. (1985). Obsessive-compulsive disorder. In D. H. Barlow (Ed.), *Clinical handbook of psychological disorders* (pp. 69–144). New York: The Guilford Press.

Tache', J., & Selye, H. (1986). On stress and coping mechanisms. In C. D. Spielberger & I. G. Sarason (Eds.), *Stress and anxiety. Vol. 10: A sourcebook of therapy and research* (pp. 3–24). Washington, DC: Hemisphere Publishing Corporation.

Thrash, W. J., Marr, J. N., & Boone, S. E. (1982). Continuous self-monitoring of discomfort in the dental chair and feedback to the dentist. *Journal of Behavioral Assessment*, *4*, 273–284.

Turner, S. M., & Beidel, D. C. (1985). Empirically derived subtypes of social anxiety. *Behavior Therapy*, *16*, 384–392.

Turner, S. M., & Michelson, L. (1984). Conceptual, methodological, and clinical issues in the assessment of anxiety disorders. *Journal of Behavioral Assessment*, *6*, 265–279.

Twentyman, C. T., & McFall, R. M. (1975). Behavioral training of social skills in shy males. *Journal of Consulting and Clinical Psychology*, *43*, 384–395.

Vermilyea, J. A., Boice, R., & Barlow, D. H. (1984). Rachman and Hodgson (1974) a decade later: How do desynchronous response systems relate to the treatment of agoraphobia? *Behaviour Research and Therapy*, *22*, 615–622.

Walk, R. D. (1956). Self-ratings of fear in a fear-invoking situation. *Journal of Abnormal and Social Psychology*, *52*, 171–178.

Wallston, B. S., Wallston, K. A., Kaplan, G. D., & Maides, S.A. (1976).

Behavioral Assessment

Development and validation of the health locus of control (HLC) scale. *Journal of Consulting and Clinical Psychology*, *44*, 580–585.

Watson, D., & Friend, R. (1969). Measurement of social-evaluative anxiety. *Journal of Consulting and Clinical Psychology*, *33*, 448–457.

Watts, F. N., & Sharrock, R. (1984). Questionnaire dimensions of spider phobia. *Behaviour Research and Therapy*, *22*, 575–580.

Willoughby, R. R. (1934). Norms for the Clark-Thurstone Inventory. *Journal of Social Psychology*, *5*, 91–97.

Wing, J. K., Cooper, J. E., & Sartorius, N. (1974). *The description and classification of psychiatric symptoms*. London, England: Cambridge University Press.

Wolpe, J., & Lang, P. J. (1964). A fear survey schedule for use in behavior therapy. *Behaviour Research and Therapy*, *2*, 27–30.

Wolpe, J., & Lazarus, A. A. (1966). *Behavior therapy techniques*. New York: Pergamon Press.

Zitrin, C. M., Klein, D. F., Woerner, M. G., & Ross, D. C. (1983). Treatment of phobias: Comparison of imipramine hydrochloride and placebo. *Archives of General Psychiatry*, *40*, 125–138.

Zuckerman, M., & Lubin, B. (1965). Normative data for the multiple affect adjective checklist. *Psychological Reports*, *16*, 438.

Zung, W. W. K. (1971). A rating instrument for anxiety disorders. *Psychosomatics*, *12*, 371–379.

10
Assessment of Depression

Lynn P. Rehm

OVERVIEW

Only recently have behaviorally oriented clinicians and researchers turned their attention to the problems of depression. After a delayed start there has been a tremendous growth of interest in the area in recent years. Theoretical models, case reports, outcome studies, and experimental psychopathology studies have proliferated in the journals. A great diversity of approaches to the topic are represented in these published studies.

This diversity reflects some of the basic problems inherent in the conceptualization of depression, especially from a behavioral perspective. Depression is a heterogeneous and amorphous syndrome of complaints. It is generally considered pervasive in its influence, but it is elusive in its identifying signs and symptoms. Many of the models behaviorists found useful in attacking other forms of psychopathology (notably anxiety) do not carry over well when applied to depression. This has forced behaviorists to make a variety of assumptions about the nature of the disorder. Before it is possible even to approach the topic of depression assessment, it will be necessary to address the problems inherent in the construct of depression.

Heterogeneity of the Construct

The disorder of depression is considered a syndrome. While sad affect may also be a symptom of other disorders (see Mendels, 1968), a diagnosis depends on the existence of a correlated constellation of behavioral excesses and deficits. Many symptoms are included in the depressive syndrome. While there is general agreement among clinicians about the nature and existence of the syndrome, the specific symptom lists vary from one authority to another (e.g. APA, 1980; Beck, 1972; Lewinsohn, Biglan, & Zeiss, 1976; Mendels, 1970; Woodruff, Godwin, & Guze, 1974).

Given the lack of consistency of these lists, the question arises as to whether there are necessary or sufficient conditions (symptoms) for a diagnosis of depression. Many of the symptoms in the typical list are not exclusive to depression. For instance, Harrow, Colbert, Detre, and Bakeman (1966) found that only 11 of 24 hypothetically differential symptoms discriminated between depressed and schizophrenic patients in state hospitals. It is also difficult to find single symptoms that are universally ascribed to depression. Even sad affect may not be necessary if one considers the possibility "masked", "smiling," or anhedonic depressions. In a discussion of the problem in the context of assessment, Levitt and Lubin (1975) present a list of 54 symptoms that are each included on at least two of a group of 16 depression scales. Only the symptom "self-devaluation" was represented on all 16 scales. Clinical descriptions of some apathetic depressed patients suggest that this symptom may not be necessary for depression (e.g., Beck, 1972). The problem is further complicated by the fact that some classes of symptoms may be bidirectional. For example, sleep disturbances may include excessive or deficient sleep, and eating disturbances can include weight loss or weight gain. Thus, there may be no single symptom that is either necessary or sufficient. The coexistence of a number of the symptoms in the syndrome is necessary for the diagnosis.

One way of attempting to bring greater homogeneity to the study of depression has been by characterizing subtypes of depression in various ways. Many categorization schemas have been suggested. The American Psychiatric Association's previous *Diagnostic and Statistical Manual of Mental Disorders* (DSM-II: APA, 1968) listed three depressive diagnoses under psychotic disorders (schizophrenia, schizo-affective type, depressed; involutional melancholia; and manic-depressive illness, depressed type), one depressive diagnosis under psychoneurotic disorders (depressive neurosis), and one depressive diagnosis under personality disorders (cyclothymic personality). Involutional melancholia has been dropped from the DSM-III (APA, 1980), with the rationale that it is indistinguishable from other forms of depression except for age of onset. Schizo-affective disorder remains in DSM III, but major depressive disorder can also have psychotic symptoms.

A frequently cited dichotomous typology in the research literature is the distinction between endogenous and reactive depressions (e.g., Mendels & Cochrane, 1968). The typology is based on inferred etiology but also assumes some differences in symptomatology (i.e., a greater predominance of somatic symptoms in depression). While DSM-III does not employ diagnoses based on etiology, major depressive disorder with melancholia is closely related to endogenous depression. Winokur (1973) suggested a classification schema consisting of: (a) normal grief; (b) secondary depression, in which depression occurs with other nonaffective pathology; and (c) primary affective disorders. The latter category is further divided into unipolar and bipolar depressions (Perris, 1966). In bipolar depression, episodes of mania or hypomania alternate with depressive episodes (a broadening of the concept of manic-depressive disorder). In unipolar depressions, only episodes of depression are seen. Some differences in symptomatology differentiate the two. For example, unipolars more frequently show initial insomnia whereas bipolars more frequently show middle-of-the-night or early morning awakening. Bipolars more frequently show retardation while unipolars may be agitated. Differential response to drugs has also been found to support this value of the dichotomy. The unipolar-bipolar distinction has largely supplanted the endogenous-reactive distinction as a focus of research, and it has been incorporated into DSM-III.

It is notable that, with the exception of diagnostic interviews, none of the standardized methods for assessing depression acknowledges subtypes of depression. Standardized methods do not provide differentiating subscales nor specify a subtype of depression for which assessment is targeted.

Behavioral Perspectives

The phenomena of depression have been particularly difficult to account for from a behavioral perspective (cf. Rehm, in press). Some of the problems are highlighted by a comparison with a behavioral approach to the phenomena of anxiety. Behavior therapy made progress with anxiety by assuming that it was a response to relatively specific situations, in that its manifestations are expressed in changes in many response systems. As opposed to the sampling of stimulus situations characteristic of many anxiety assessment techniques, assessment techniques for depression tend to evaluate response systems widely. The pervasiveness of depression also pertains to a temporal dimension, since it is assumed to occur in episodes measurable in weeks or months. While there is considerable evidence for day-to-day variation in mood as a function of concurrent events (Grosscup & Lewinsohn, 1980; Lewinsohn & Graf, 1973; Lewinsohn & Libet, 1972; Rehm, 1978), syndromal depression is an effect over a longer time span. Anxiety quite often occurs in situational attacks measurable in minutes. Intraindividual comparisons in depression are commonly made to premorbid baseline states that are usually not directly observable. Intraindividual comparisons in anxiety can be made by observations of individuals in the presence or absence of anxiety-provoking stimuli. Depression instruments must deal both with the response generality and the time frame of depressive symptoms.

Models of depression, behavioral, or otherwise, have dealt with the heterogeneity and pervasiveness of depression by assuming that it has a central or core symptom, and that all other symptoms follow as consequences or elaborations of the core deficit. The core symptoms tend to be deficits of some generality. This kind of assumption is unusual for behavioral models, where the ideal is to measure directly the behavioral target of the intervention. With depression, the intervention is aimed at a core deficit, which may or may not be directly assessed, and the larger outcome is assessed in terms of the multiple behaviors of syndromal depression.

Many core deficits have been hypothesized. Lowered rate of activity was posed as the primary datum of depression by Ferster (1973). Lewinsohn (1974a, 1976) and his colleagues have developed methods for identifying and increasing mood-related activity. Anhedonia is hypothesized by Lewinsohn, Biglan, and Zeiss (1976) to be based on anxiety, and desensitization is used to increase enjoyment potential. Several cases of treating depression with desensitization or its variants, such as flooding, have been reported (see Rehm & Kornblith, 1979, Rehm & Kaslow, 1984). Social skills in various forms have been hypothesized as the core deficits in depression. Wolpe (1979), arguing that anxiety is the basis for neurotic depression, recommends assertion training for certain cases. Lewinsohn, Weinstein, and Alper (1970) conducted group therapy, focusing on deficits in communications skills of depressed subjects within groups. Several reports of social skill training have appeared in the literature (e.g., Hersen, Bellack, Himmelhoch, & Thase, 1984). Other variations on this theme include problem-solving deficits (e.g., Caple & Blechman, 1976; Shipley & Fazio, 1973) and marital communication problems (e.g., Lewinsohn & Atwood, 1969; McLean & Hakstian, 1979; McLean, Ogston, & Grauer, 1973). Cognitive distortion has been hypothesized by Beck (1972) as the core deficit in depression, and distorted beliefs are cited by Ellis (1962). Seligman's theory (Seligman, 1974, 1975) postulates the construct of learned helplessness as central to depression. Elsewhere, I (Rehm, 1977) have proposed a model postulating deficits in self-control to account for the phenomena of depression. This model differs from the others in that it postulates multiple deficits relating to specific depressive phenomena. One of the recent trends in the assessment of depression has been the development of instruments to measure hypothetical core deficits directly. These instruments will be reviewed briefly below.

Symptom Content

In order to compare and evaluate depression assessment instruments, it is necessary to begin with a standard list of depressive behaviors. It should be clear from the preceding discussion that any such list must necessarily be somewhat arbitrary. A list is necessary, however, in order to compare and assess how instruments cover the relevant dimensions of depression. In order to resolve some of the difficulties inherent in establishing such a list, I have opted for establishing two separate ones. The first list includes broad categories of symptomatology applicable to most forms of psychopathology.

The second is made up of a few specific symptoms most frequently cited as central to a syndrome of depression. The first list is as follows:

Verbal-Cognitive Symptoms of Depression

This label is one that has been used in the behavioral literature (e.g., Lang, 1968) to denote those symptoms expressed primarily through verbalizations or observations of the cognitive processes of the individual. For purposes of discussing the psychopathology of depression, this category can be broken down into three major subcategories: (a) sad affect, (b) cognitive distortions, and (c) changes in cognitive functioning. From a behavioral perspective, affect is a summary report of cognitive, overt-motor, and somatic responses, but it is ordinarily assessed in the response. Sad affect is essentially depression as a symptom. It is that state people describe as depressed, sad, blue, low, down, unhappy, despairing, etc. It might also include the absence of emotions usually believed incompatible with depression: for instance, joy, elation, happiness, etc. The syndrome of depression is sometimes held to include affects which are differentiated from depression, including anxiety, hostility, frustration, and irritability. Cognitive distortion in depression includes a variety of attitudes and beliefs about oneself and the world. Beck (1972) identifies the cognitive triad of a negative view of self, world, and future as essential features of depression. Other symptoms would be pessimism, hopelessness, helplessness, low self-esteem, and guilt. Changes in cognitive functioning, such as reduced ability to concentrate and memory difficulties, are sometimes viewed as symptoms of depression, although the problem may be in the person's perception rather than in their actual performance. Research interest is focusing on qualitative changes in memory retrieval as important in depression as a way of explaining cognitive distortion, but this is not easily assessable as a symptom.

Overt-Motor Behavioral Symptoms of Depression

This category includes those symptoms of depression that are manifest in the individual's observable overt-motor behavior. These may include behavioral excesses which involve an acceleration or increased frequency, and behavioral deficits involving deceleration or decreased frequency. Behavioral excesses in depression include such observables as sad demeanor, hanging of the head, crying, lack of eye contact, wringing of the hands, and, at times, agitation. Suicidal behavior might also be classed as a behavioral excess. Behavioral deficits include psychomotor retardation, decreases in work and recreational activities, and disturbances in sleep, eating behavior, and sexual behavior.

Somatic Symptoms of Depression

Somatic symptoms include those bodily complaints and physical disorders frequently manifest in depression, including such typical complaints as excessive fatigue, constipation, loss of appetite, diffuse pain, and troubled breathing. Also in this category are those somatic symptoms that could be physically assessed. This would include, for example, physiological changes, such as alterations in facial-muscle tension or patterns of electroencephalograph (EEG) sleep recordings associated with depression. Biochemical assays might also be included here.

Interpersonal Symptoms of Depression

Although this category has not been a part of the traditional symptomatology of depression, theory and research evidence is increasingly pointing to the importance of social interactions as a possible locus of depressive disorder. In interpersonal behavior, depressed persons have variously been described as dependent, demanding, manipulative, negative, hostile, complaining, or withdrawn. Research on life situations (e.g., Brown & Harris, 1978), recent life events of major magnitude (e.g., Lloyd, 1980), and minor life events (MacPhillamy & Lewinsohn, 1971) suggests that interpersonal and social stresses may be an important contributor to the onset and maintenance of depression. Alternatively, depression may yield stressful disturbances in interpersonal relationships.

Additional major categories could potentially be added to this list. History and course of the disorder are important in establishing differential diagnosis in depression. The frequency and nature of shifts or swings in mood differentiates between unipolar and bipolar depression and between episodic, intermittent, and chronic forms. Therapy outcome assessment is usually cross-sectional in nature so that these considerations are probably more important for pretest assessment in establishing a diagnosis and prognosis, and more important for follow-up assessment in tracing the course of the disorder after therapy.

Depressive Signs

The depression symptoms mentioned consist of broad categories applicable to psychopathology generally. In depression, certain disturbances in critical areas of life are usually considered necessary and sufficient conditions for a diagnosis. These criterion symptoms include the so-called neurovegetative signs. A working list of these signs would include: (a) sleep disturbances, including difficulty getting to sleep, frequent awakening, early morning awakening, and hypersomnia; (b) eating disturbances, including weight loss or gain and loss of appetite; (c) sexual disturbances, including decreased frequency of sexual behavior, diminished interest, and diminished capacity; (d) work disturbance, including decreased productivity, increased effortfulness, fatigability, and lack of motivation; and (e) suicidal behavior, including attempts, gestures, threats, plans and ruminations.

In reviewing instruments for assessing depression, the contents can be compared as to the relative weight given to verbal-cognitive (affect and cognition), behavioral, somatic, and interpersonal symptomatology. An ideal instrument would include items that would specifically assess each of these areas and each of the salient depressive signs. It is important to note that the neurovegetative signs could be assessed in multiple-symptom categories. For instance, work disturbance could be assessed in terms of cognitive behavior (e.g., a loss of interest), overt behavior (e.g., reduced performance), somatic behavior (e.g., fatigability), or interpersonal behavior (e.g., inability to get along with coworkers). Thus, both lists seem to be essential for evaluating assessment instruments.

ASSESSMENT FORMATS

Several types of assessment modalities will be reviewed in this section. These include self-report, clinician rating scales, direct observational methods, and significant-other evaluations. In addition, methods for assessing core symptoms of depression will also be discussed.

The review will concentrate on the most popular methods employed in research and clinical settings, along with some promising methods that have the potential for filling certain gaps in the assessment armamentarium. Certain instruments that measure constructs related but not central to the concept of depression (e.g., suicidality) have been omitted as beyond the scope of the review. The review will attempt to describe each instrument, including its content, format, and rationale; examine its psychometric properties; and evaluate its potential contribution to clinical and research assessment.

The latter distinction is made since the needs of clinicians and researchers may be different in terms of assessment methods. Both need to categorize individuals, predict future behavior, and measure the severity of the disorder, but clinicians need to categorize clients into classes that help to conceptualize the problem and shape detailed inquiry.

Such categorizations are ideally reliable and communicable to others. The categorization schema should aid in prediction. What will be the natural course of this type of disorder? Will it respond to this or that therapy strategy? Severity may also have treatment implications in addition to being a gauge of therapy progress. Researchers need to categorize subjects reliably in order to enhance the comparability of studies conducted in different settings. Prediction of differential course or response to treatment is an increasingly important focus of research. Valid assessment of severity is essential to any study of variables hypothesized to influence a disorder. Both clinicians and researchers have decisions to make among instruments based on practicality and purpose.

Self-Report Depression Scales

Self-report has been the traditional format for assessing depression. Many instruments have been published and employed in research reports. Levitt and Lubin (1975), for example, list 23 self-report scales. Many of these are not well developed psychometrically and have been used in only a few studies. One of the problems in depression research has been the lack of comparability among studies because so many different scales have been used. Only those scales that have achieved some popularity will be reviewed here.

Beck Depression Inventory (BDI) ˙

Although originally conceived as a clinician-administered scale, the BDI (Beck, Ward, Mendelson, Mock, & Erbaugh, 1961) is now used almost exclusively as a self-report instrument. Its 21 items consist of a series of ordered statements relating to a particular sympton of depression. The subjects indicate which statements describe their current state. Each statement is scaled from 0 to 3. Items and weights were derived logically. A 13-item short form is also available (Beck & Beck, 1972). The intent of the BDI was to cover the symptomatology of depression comprehensively, but it tends to emphasize cognitive content. Two items are devoted to affect (one of these to irritability), 11 to cognition, 2 to overt behavior, 5 to somatic symptoms, and 1 to interpersonal symptoms. All of the major signs are covered.

While no manual exists, considerable psychometric data on the BDI has accumulated. Some standardization data are available in the original report (Beck et al., 1961), and cut-off scores of 13 for screening and 21 for clinical research have been recommended (Beck & Beamesderfer, 1974). While designed for use in clinical populations, it has frequently been used in normal populations such as for college students with cut-off scores in the 7–9 range. The instrument appears to be valid in this range (see Blumberry, Oliver, & McClure, 1978).

The accumulated reliability and validity data on the scale are quite large, and a full review is beyond the scope of this chapter. Only representative data will be cited in an attempt to summarize the findings. Beck (1972) reports Kruskal-Wallis item-total correlations of .31–.68 and a .93 Spearman-Brown corrected split-half reliability. Weckowicz, Muir, and Cropley (1967) report a Kuder-Richardson-20 of .78. Test-retest reliabilities of .75 for 23 undergraduates after 3 months (Miller & Seligman, 1973), and .48 for 59 psychiatric patients after 3 weeks (May, Urquhart, & Tarran, 1969) have been obtained.

Correlations reported with other self-report depression scales are generally fairly good. Although Beck (1972) asserts that the BDI has excellent discriminant validity — differentiating it from self-report of anxiety — this can be questioned. Moderate to high correlations with anxiety have been reported suggesting considerable method variance. Good correlations have been found with clinician rating scales and with a behavioral observation scale (Williams, Barlow, & Agras, 1972). The BDI is sensitive to clinical change as demonstrated in its frequent use as an outcome measure in drug trials (see McNair, 1974) and behavior therapy outcome studies (see Rehm & Kornblith, 1979).

In summary, the BDI is a relatively short and easily administered instrument with a fairly solid psychometric base. While stressing cognitive symptoms, its structure allows for the possibility of systematic item or subscale analyses. It has become a very popular instrument in research and clinical practice.

Center for Epidemiological Studies' Depression Scale (CES-D)

The CES-*D* was developed by the Center for Epidemiological Studies of the National Institute of Mental Health (NIMH). CES-*D* items were derived from other self-report depression inventories and were selected to sample the major components of depressive symptomatology. The purpose of this scale was to measure current level of depressive symptomatology with emphasis on the affective component, depressed mood. Thus, it was intended not as a diagnostic instrument or a severity instrument, but as a survey of depressive symptoms that might be found in psychiatric, medical, or general populations. Although the development of the scale is not described in detail in the major article (Radloff, 1977), reference is made to a series of revisions in which items were refined.

The scale is made up of 20 items, each consisting of a first-person statement of a relatively specific depressive symptom (e.g., "my sleep was restless"; "I felt sad"). Instructions ask the examinee to indicate how often he or she has felt this way during the past week. Ratings are made on a 0–3 scale anchored as follows: 0 = rarely or none of the time (less than one day); 1 = some or a little of the time (1–2 days); 2 = occasionally or a moderate amount of time (3–4 days); 3 = most or all of the time (5–7 days). Sixteen items describe negative symptoms, and 4 are stated in a positive direction to avoid a response bias or set.

The content areas the authors tried to sample were depressed mood, feelings of guilt and worthlessness, feelings of helplessness and hopelessness, psychomotor retardation, loss of appetite, and sleep disturbance (Radloff, 1977). When viewed in terms of affect, verbal-cognitive, behavioral, somatic, and social-interpersonal symptomatology, the scale is heavily weighted in the affective area. Eight items directly tap affect (six depressive, one anxiety, or "bothered"). Four items tap other cognitive symptoms. Four items tap behavioral symptoms, and two items tap both somatic and social symptoms. One item covers each of the specific signs of sleeping, eating, and work disturbances; none refers to sexual disturbance, or suicide.

The CES-*D* was used in a large survey study assessing psychiatric symptoms in two communities. The probability samples yielded 1,173 completed interviews from a Kansas City, Missouri, sample and 1,673 completed interviews from a Washington County, Maryland, sample. Repeat interviews were available on significant groups of subjects to assess test-retest reliability, and samples of psychiatric patients have also been reported in the literature (Craig & VanNatta 1976a, 1976b; Weissman, Sholomskas, Pottenger, Prusoff, & Locke, 1977). Radloff (1977) presented data on the nature of the distributions of CES-*D* scores for the major samples and for subgroups based on various demographic variables. She notes that the scale is skewed for normals, although it appears to be symmetrical for clinical populations.

There is a fair amount of evidence that reliability and validity replicate across various normal and clinical samples (Craig & VanNatta, 1976a; Radloff, 1977; Weissman, Pottenger, Kleber, Ruben, Williams, & Thompson, 1975; Weissman, Prusoff, & Newberry, 1975). Radloff reports that, as expected for this kind of scale, the interitem correlations are relatively low, and item scale correlations are moderate. Internal consistency reliability, however, is very good. Coefficient-alpha, split-half, and Spearman-Brown estimates of internal consistency reliability are relatively uniform. Test-retest reliability data are available on samples with intervals of 2, 4, 6, and 8 weeks and 3, 6, 9, and 12 months. As expected in a scale intended to assess fluctuations in mood, correlations up to 8 weeks are moderate (overall test-retest correlations of .57), and correlations across months taper off to .32 for 1-year test-retest reliability. Test-retest correlations were highest for individuals who had not had intervening major life events (Radloff, 1977).

The CES-*D* is valid in the sense that it discriminates between clinical and normal populations (Craig & VanNatta, 1976a, 1976b; Radloff, 1977; Weissman, Pottenger, Kleber, Ruben, Williams, & Thompson, 1977; Weissman et al., 1975). The scale also differentiates between more acutely depressed subgroups (Craig & VanNatta, 1976a, 1976b; Weissman, Pottenger, Kleber, Ruben, Williams, & Thompson, 1977; Weissman et al., 1975). It does not discriminate, however, between subgroups of depression, such as primary versus secondary depressives (Weissman, Sholomskas, Pottenger, Prusoff, & Locke, 1977). Also, at least some of the items may measure psychopathology generally rather than depression specifically (Craig & VanNatta, 1976a). Concurrent validity with other scales is generally quite good (Craig & VanNatta, 1976b; Radloff, 1977; Weissman, Pottenger, Kleber, Ruben, Williams, & Thompson, 1977; Weissman et al., 1975). Correlations with clinician ratings are acceptable, although there appears to be some method variance differentiating this and other self-report instruments from clinician rating scales (e.g., Weissman, Pottenger, Kleber, Ruben, Williams, & Thompson, 1977; Weissman et al., 1975). Weissman, Pottenger, Kleber, Ruben, Williams, and Thompson (1977) report that the CES-*D* changes with clinical improvement. Evidence for the discriminant validity of the CES-*D* is summarized by Radloff (1977) and Weissman, Sholomskas, Pottenger, Prusoff, and Locke (1977). It is notable that the test does not discriminate between subtypes of depression, nor is there evidence that it adequately discriminates depression from anxiety. This might be particularly important for the scale since it seems to have a fair amount of correlation with other measures of psychopathology.

In summary, this instrument has very good psychometric properties. It tends to stress affective symptomatology per se and is probably best suited for its original purpose: exploring relationships between depressive symptomatology and other characteristics of populations in survey samples (e.g., Radloff, 1975). The 1-week time focus limits the CES-*D*'s value in assessing certain kinds of change that might be expected to occur within short periods (e.g., drug treatment effects). However, this same time focus also may be an advantage in specifying to the patient a particular objective criterion that may increase the objective validity of this self-report instrument. Since the instrument has not been widely used in clinical trials, it is not known how well it operates or relates to other instruments as an outcome measure.

Depression Adjective Checklists (DACL)

The DACL (Lubin, 1965, 1966, 1967) consists of seven alternate forms (A–G). Forms A–D contain 22 positive and 10 negative adjectives from a pool that significantly differentiated 48 depressed female psychiatric patients from 179 normal females. Forms E–G consist of 22 positive and 12 negative adjectives from a pool that differentiated 47 depressed male psychiatric patients from 100 normal males. Each form can be scored from a single template. The scoring system takes the number of positive adjectives minus the negative adjectives for a total score that attempts to minimize the bias introduced by the simple number of adjectives checked. The time frame is "today" or "in general." The content is usually in the nature of affect words, making the scale more one of mood than of syndromal depression.

A manual for the DACL is available (Lubin, 1967), and psychometric development is fairly extensive. Normative data are available for students, senior citizens, adolescent delinquents, depressed and nondepressed psychiatric samples (Lubin, 1967), and a national sample of 3,000 adults (Levitt & Lubin, 1975).

Lubin (1967) reports internal consistency reliabilities for the DACL, ranging from .79 to .88 for males and .85 to .90 for females. Split-half reliabilities ranged from .83 to .92 for normals and from .89 to .92 for patients. Intercorrelations among scales ranged from .82 to .92 for three samples. Comparable alternate form and split-half reliabilities were reported by Lubin and Himmelstein (1976), who also reported 1-week test-retest reliabilities of .19 for form E, .24 for form F, and .22 for form G. These low correlations are reasonable for mood measures. Lubin (1967; Lubin, Dupre, & Lubin, 1967) found no differences among absolute scores for forms E, F, and B.

Each of the seven scales was crossvalidated on samples of 625 normals, 174 nondepressed psychiatric patients, and 128 depressed psychiatric patients. All seven scales significantly differentiated the groups. Concurrent validity in the form of correlations with other depression scales is moderate. Lubin, Horned, and Knapp (1977) report some evidence for the discriminant validity of the DACL in the form of negligible correlations with the Eysenck Personality Inventory, but Lubin (1967) reports fairly substantial correlations between forms E, F, and G and the MMPI clinical scales. Lubin, Hornstra, and Love (1974) and Lubin, Dupre, and Lubin (1967) report changes in DACL scores as a function of therapeutic interventions. The DACL has been used as an outcome measure in a number of behavior therapy outcome studies (see Rehm & Kornblith, 1979). Lewinsohn and colleagues (Grosscup & Lewinsohn, 1980; Lewinsohn & Graf, 1973; Lewinsohn & Libet, 1972) have used the DACL to assess daily fluctuations in mood as a correlate of daily events.

In sum, the DACL is a set of psychometrically sophisticated alternate forms for which excellent normative data are available. While perhaps most useful for assessing fluctuations in mood over brief periods, it also differentiates groups by severity of depression. It has the advantages of alternate forms to aid in frequent retesting, and is quite short and easy to administer.

Minnesota Multiphasic Personality Inventory Depression Scale (MMPI-D)

The MMPI-*D* (Hathaway & McKinley, 1951) is the most widely used psychological assessment instrument in the United States and, therefore, probably the most widely used instrument for assessing depression. Its 60 true-false items consist of 49 selected because they differentiated between a group of normals and a group of hospitalized manic-depressive depressed patients and 11 selected because they distinguished between the depressed group and other psychiatric patients (Hathaway & McKinley, 1942).

The test is available in several formats (group form, step-down page, or card sort) and has been translated into 30 languages. The full test takes between 45 minutes and 2 hours, but the MMPI-*D* alone can be given in 5–10 minutes.

Due to the empirical nature of the scale development, there was no logical attempt to cover depressive symptomatology in a systematic fashion. Harris and Lingoes (1955) grouped the items into five logical subscales which they termed "subjective depression," "psychomotor retardation," "complaints about physical malfunctioning," "mental dullness," and "brooding." From the point of view of the content areas being used in this review, the MMPI-*D* has a fairly good balance between somatic (18 items) and cognitive (17 items) content. In addition, there are 8 affect items (including 2 anxiety and 3 anger items), 6 social-interpersonal items, and 5 behavioral symptom items. Another 5 items are not easily classified. In regard to the standard signs, there are 3 items relating to sleep disturbances, 2 relating to eating disturbances, 1 relating to work disturbances, and none relating to sexual disturbance or suicide.

A 1967 revision of the manual is available, and other books such as Dahlstrom and Welsh's (1960) *An MMPI Handbook* are available as extensive supplements to the manual. Normative data are available on a wide variety of samples.

Dahlstrom and Welsh (1960) summarize a great deal of data on the reliability of the MMPI scales. Split-half reliabilities for the MMPI-*D* range from .35 to .84, the median being in the low .70s. Criticisms regarding heterogeneity have already been mentioned. Test-retest reliabilities are moderate; however, Dahlstrom and Welsh argue that this is due to the scale's sensitivity to mood changes.

Since the test was empirically constructed to differentiate depressed and nondepressed groups, the MMPI-*D* has frequently been used to identify research populations, usually with a standard *T*-score of 70 or greater. Correlations with other depression scales tend to be fairly good. Intercorrelations among MMPI scales, however, suggest that its discriminant validity is less than desirable. The MMPI-*D* has frequently been criticized for its lack of discriminant validity from anxiety (e.g., Comrey, 1957; Costello & Comrey, 1967; Mendels, Weinstein, & Cochrane, 1972). It is sensitive to change and has frequently been used as an outcome measure. McNair (1974) notes that the MMPI-*D* is the most frequently used instrument to assess outcome in studies of anti-depressant drugs, but he criticizes it for its lack of a distinct time frame, which limits its ability to differentiate over short periods of time. It has also frequently been used in behavior therapy outcome studies (see Rehm & Kornblith, 1979).

In summary, the MMPI-*D* is the most frequently used self-report depression instrument and has accumulated a great deal of statistical and normative background data. Despite its empirical derivation, it has fairly good coverage of a range of depressive content. The most serious shortcomings are its heterogeneity and lack of discrimination from anxiety. Its original intent was to distinguish between diagnostic subgroups. Today this is more frequently done with the MMPI by profile analysis, but screening or population definition may be an appropriate use of this instrument.

Self-Rating Depression Scale (SDS)

The SDS was devised by Zung to tap three factors — pervasive affect, physiological equivalence or concomitants, and psychological concomitants — that were extracted from a review of factor analytic studies of depressive symptomatology. Ten items are written in a positive direction and 10 in a negative direction. The examinee is asked to indicate on a 4-point scale how much of the time during the past week the statement was true of him or her. Answers are weighted 1–4 points.

Using these initial general factors, the SDS was written to include four pervasive affect questions, eight physiological disturbance questions, eight psychological disturbance questions, plus two psychomotor disturbance questions. From a comparative perspective, the SDS includes three affect items (including one on irritability), six cognition items, four overt-motor behavior items, six somatic items, and one social-interpersonal item. All five major signs are covered.

Although no manual exists for the SDS, the test booklet (Zung, 1974) partly serves that purpose by supplying scoring instructions and cut-off scores. While no major standardization effort has been made, Blumenthal and Dielman (1975) summarize means for 22 separate samples. These means are generally consistent with Zung's suggested cut-off scores.

In a fairly extensive review of the literature on this instrument, I was unable to find any published reliability data on either internal consistency or test-retest. In general, the SDS has been found to discriminate between depressed and nondepressed samples (e.g., Carroll, Fielding, & Blashki, 1973; Lunghi, 1977; Marone & Lubin, 1968; Schnurr, Hoaken, & Jarrett, 1976; Zung, 1965; 1967). However, two studies (Humphrey, 1967; Zung, Richards, & Short, 1965) found that only subsets of items actually differentiated depressed individuals. In one of the few studies attempting to differentiate subtypes of depression, Raft, Spencer, Toomey, and Brogan (1977) concluded that the SDS does not differentiate well between primary and secondary depressions, nor was it able to discriminate depressive reactions from conversion reactions.

Concurrent validity related to correlations with other depression instruments is good. Evidence for discriminant validity is weak. Zung (1969) reports near-zero correlations with the Eysenck Personality Inventory, but Zung et al. (1965) report a correlation of .68 with the MMPI-*Pt* scale, which is quite close to the .70 correlation with the *D* scale. Burrows, Foenander, Davies, and Scoggins (1976) found a correlation of .58 between SDS and the Taylor Manifest Anxiety Scale (TMAS). It should be noted, however, that both the MMPI-*Pt* and the TMAS may have poor discriminant validity themselves.

The SDS appears to be sensitive to changes in clinical status. In a review of outcome measures in 75 clinical drug trials, McNair (1974) recommends the SDS quite highly as a sensitive instrument.

In summary, while the SDS has gained some popularity, it is not as well developed psychometrically as some of the other self-report instruments. Standardization data have accumulated over studies, but certain kinds of information are still lacking. The content distribution is fairly good, and probably the best feature is that it is relatively short and simple to administer.

Other Self-Report Scales

Several other self-report depression scales deserve mention. In addition to the MMPI-*D*, other depression scales have been derived from the MMPI item pool. The most frequently used of these is the D-30 scale developed by Costello and Comrey (1967). The D-30 was developed along with a new anxiety scale from the MMPI item pool in order to improve item homogeneity, independence of scale scores, and influence of social desirability. In comparison to the MMPI-*D* and the TMAS, the newly developed scales are indeed improved on all of these dimensions according to data in the original report (Costello & Comrey). On the other hand, Mendels, Weinstein, and Cochrane (1972) found a correlation between two scales of .59, which was greater than the correlation between the MMPI-*D* and the TMAS of .40. Thus, the increased discriminant validity that was the intention of the scale was not replicated. Neufeld, Rogers, and Costello (1972) found that the D-30 appeared to be quite sensitive to therapy changes. Little other work has been done with the scale. In general, the possible advantages of the scale are probably significantly outweighed by the loss of the accumulated experience accrued by the MMPI-*D*. This is perhaps all the more true of other derived scales (e.g., Endicott & Jortner's [1966] D-18 scale, made up of the 18 items found to markedly differentiate depressed and mildly depressed groups at the .10 level or better).

The Profile of Mood States (POMS; McNair, Lorr, & Droppleman, 1971) is an empirically developed instrument based on factor analytic studies. It consists of 65 adjectives, each of which is rated on a 5-point scale. Six scales consist of: (1) tension-anxiety, (2) depression-dejection, (3) anger-hostility, (4) vigor, (5) fatigue, and (6) confusion. Affect terms predominate the 15 items on the depression-dejection scale with a few verbal-cognitive symptoms. The standardization and psychometric development of the POMS is sophisticated, and psychometric properties are quite good. The instrument has the advantages of the additional factorially independent scales. Since its content is limited, it has been used very little in the depression literature.

The SCL-90 (Derogatis, 1977) is another well-developed multiple-scale instrument. Its 90 items consist of symptoms rated on a 5-point scale as to how problematic they have been in the last week. Nine scales are derived: (a) somatization, (b) obsessive-compulsive, (c) interpersonal sensitivity, (d) depression, (e) anxiety, (f) hostility, (g) phobic anxiety, (h) paranoid ideation, and (i) psychoticism. The depression scale stresses cognitive and affective content, but the overall SCL-90 has good coverage of depressive symptoms and signs. There is a short form of the instrument (The Brief Symptom Inventory) and parallel rating scales to be used by expert clinicians (Hopkins Psychiatric Rating Scales) and by less expert clinical observers (SCL-90 Analog). The manual (Derogatis, 1977) presents systematic standardization and psychometric data. As yet, the SCL-90 has not been used extensively in the depression literature, but the parallel rating forms make it a good instrument for assessing various other dimensions of pathology along with depression across the assessment perspectives of self-report, clinician, and observer.

The Social Adjustment Scale's (SAS) clinician interview (Weissman & Paykel, 1974) and self-report (Weissman & Bothwell, 1976) forms also deserve mention. While designed to measure social adjustment per se, it was developed in the context of depression research and can probably be considered a measure of the social-interpersonal aspects of depression. The self-report form consists of 42 items, each involving the choice of one of five alternate statements describing social adjustment in various roles. Psychometric properties appear good to date. The scale has the advantages of symptom coverage of social-interpersonal factors, which are only minimally covered on other scales and parallel self-report and clinicians forms.

Finally, the Visual Analog Scale (Aitken, 1969) consists simply of a 100 mm line anchored at one end by "normal mood" and at the other by "extreme depression." The scale takes only a few seconds to fill out and is adaptable to a variety of time frames. Data available suggest that its psychometric properties are comparable to those of the more elaborate scales (e.g., Davies, Burrows, & Poynton, 1975; Zealley & Aitken, 1969). As a global, self-report depression scale, the Visual Analog Scale may be sufficient for many purposes.

Comment on Self-Report Depression Scales

The scales reviewed vary considerably in terms of content coverage. A balance across categories and systematic coverage are both desirable. Most of the more popular self-report depression instruments stress affective and cognitive symptoms. While it is desirable from a behavioral point of view to be able to look separately at affect, verbal-cognitive, somatic, behavioral, and social symptoms, there is some logic to including them all in a self-report measure. Depression involves distortions of experience, and the self-report of a number of specific behaviors has traditionally been seen as a part of depressive behavior. Thus, an individual's endorsement of a BDI item such as "I wake up early every day and can't get more than 5 hours sleep" should not be taken as an index of overt or physiological sleep behavior. It should be taken as an indication of cognitive-verbal concern and complaint about specific aspects of sleep behavior. Mode of assessment should not be confused with mode of symptom manifestation. This cognitive-verbal behavior may or may not be distorted, but in either case it is a component of depression. If overt or physiological sleep behavior is to be a specific target of intervention, it should be assessed more directly and more objectively as well.

The format of the scales also differs considerably. Instruments vary in the abstractness of items, the time frame for evaluation, and the nature of endorsement (e.g., degree of agreement with versus frequency of occurrence of the item). More specific items endorsed for frequency should better correspond to direct observation. A specific and limited time frame is important for comparisons over time (e.g., improvement from one week to the next).

The psychometric properties of the instruments offer relatively little superiority from one to the next. Although they vary in sophistication of development and in amount of accumulated data, no clear superiority emerges from the available data for one versus another.

Those instruments with more accumulated data have the advantage of comparability with prior work. For example, the MMPI has standardization data for many samples, the BDI has been used frequently in psychotherapy outcome studies, and the SDS has been used frequently in drug trials.

Ultimately, a choice among instruments must rest on intended use. For example, global instruments with good symptom coverage (e.g., BDI, SDS, or MMPI-*D*) are probably best for research population definition or clinical diagnosis. The same instruments, with special attention to symptom coverage, may be good for outcome assessment. Frequent, repeated measures of mood variation are probably best measured by simple affect scales such as the DACL or Visual Analog Scale. If social adjustment is important, the SAS should be added to a battery. The CES-*D* may be particularly appropriate in nonpsychiatric samples.

Clinician Rating Scales

Ratings by expert clinicians are frequently used as a measure of severity, extent, and type of disorder in the depression literature. The general rationale for such measures is that they are attempts to quantify and standardize expert clinical judgment.

These instruments vary considerably in format, from simple global ratings, to more complex anchored scales, to structured interviews designed to make diagnostic decisions. Such instruments are not typical of the behavior therapy literature but are often used in the psychiatric literature, especially in evaluations of drug trials.

Clinician rating scales have the advantage of applying expert opinion in determination about depression. The clinician can decide what behavior is most relevant to a rating dimension. Clinical experience can provide a baseline for judging the severity of a particular patient's complaint and, therefore, compensate in some ways for distortion in the self-report. The clinician can evaluate the patient on abstract unfamiliar dimensions and can conduct an inquiry that branches in different directions depending on the nature of the complaints.

The disadvantages of clinician rating scales are that they introduce their own set of potential biases into the rating process. Since most scales are scored in conjunction with an interview, there is a danger in compounding clinician and self-report biases. Items abstract enough to require expert judgment are perhaps too vague to be predictive of specific behavior. More concrete or well-anchored items could probably be answered validly by self-report.

Rating scales of this type mirror a real-world process since, in clinical settings, decisions about diagnoses and severity are made by clinicians. Compared with the perspectives of self-report, direct measurement of behavior, and evaluation by a significant other, this adds a dimension of reality to an assessment battery by paralleling the evaluative perspectives which occur in clinical settings.

Hamilton Rating Scale (HRS)

The HRS was developed by Max Hamilton (1960, 1967) as a method for assessing severity of depression among patients who have already been diagnosed as depressed. It consists of a survey of 17 depressive symptoms, each of which is rated on either a 3-point or a 5-point scale. Four additional symptom items are included but not scored. Minor variations in the scale occur between the published 1960 and 1967 versions. The scale is intended as a means of quantifying expert clinical judgment. Hamilton advised that all available information from interview, history, relatives, charts, observations, etcetera, should be taken into account when arriving at a rating on each item. Hamilton (1960) further suggests that a total score be derived from the sum of two independent ratings; if only one rater is used, the score should be doubled for comparability. No formal manual exists for the scale, but Hamilton (1967) provides a commentary for each item, suggesting general guidelines for making the ratings.

The HRS is intended as a survey of essential symptoms of depression. It tends to be weighted heavily with somatic complaints (eight items), with five items devoted to behavioral complaints, two to cognitive complaints, and two to affect. (One of these latter items refers to anxiety and one to depression.) There are no items referring to social-interpersonal symptomatology, but all of the depressive signs are covered with one item each for eating, sex, work, and suicide, and three items for sleep disturbance.

No normative data nor cut-off scores are published as such. Means for different samples reported in the literature vary somewhat; means reported for psychiatric inpatients are 32.0, 42.6, 43.6 (Schwab, Bialow, & Holzer, 1967) and 29.5 (Carroll, Fielding, & Blashki, 1973). Schnurr, Hoaken, and Jarrett (1976) report a mean of 30.6 for severe depressives and 23.9 for neurotic depressives. Outpatient means of 27.0 and 25.0 (Schwab et al., 1967) and 23.7 (Carroll et al., 1973) have been reported. Snaith, Ahmed, Mehta, and Hamilton (1971) report a mean of 6.2 for 200 normal subjects. Internal consistency is adequate in one report (Rehm & O'Hara, 1985). Schwab et al. (1967) report item-total correlations ranging from .45 to .78. One project at the University of Pittsburgh found item-total correlations ranging from .22 to .67 (Rehm & O'Hara, 1985). Interrater reliabilities have been reported by a number of sources and have generally been excellent (e.g., in the area of .90), though several individual items have rather low interrater reliabilities. Several studies have demonstrated that the HRS differentiates between clinical and normal populations: Snaith et al. (1971) demonstrated a highly significant difference between 200 normals and 100 patients. Schnurr et al. (1976) found that the HRS differentiated well among different depressed and nondepressed psychiatric groups, as found Weissman, Sholomskas, Pottenger, Prusoff, and Locke (1977). Carroll et al. (1973) found that the Hamilton differentiated well between inpatient day-hospital and general practice depressed patients. Rehm and O'Hara (1985) found that the full scale differentiated depressed outpatients from normals although several individual items did not differentiate. Also, bipolar patients scored significantly more depressed than unipolar.

A number of studies have reported concurrent validity of the HRS in terms of correlations with other methods. Correlations with global clinical ratings tend to be high (.84 by Bech et al., 1975; .98 by Knesevich, Biggs, Clayton, & Ziegler, 1977). Correlations with self-report instruments have been reported in numerous sources and tend to be fairly good. For example, most tend to be .60 or better for the BDI and SDS.

Consistent with the original intent of the scale, the HRS appears to be sensitive to clinical change. Knesevich et al. (1977) report a correlation of .68 between Hamilton change scores and changes in a global change score. Green, Gleser, Stone, and Seifert (1975) found different score correlations between the HRS and SCL-90 ($r = .73$) and a psychiatric evaluation form depression scale ($r = .77$). The HRS has been widely used in evaluations of clinical trials of drugs and in psychotherapy outcome studies.

To summarize, the HRS is psychometrically unsophisticated in its original development. Psychometric evidence, however, seems to be accumulating to suggest that the instrument has adequate internal consistency, excellent interrater reliability, and good concurrent validity. There are some questions about the consistency of structure of its application. Its content is heavily weighted toward somatic symptoms, which may be appropriate for its original intent in evaluating symptomatology of depressed inpatients in drug trials. But this, however, should be noted in any application to psychotherapy outcome for outpatients. The scale has extensive prior usage as an outcome measure and appears to be sensitive to change, but normative information for comparison across studies is currently not very good. Nonetheless, this instrument has achieved a central place in depression assessment, particularly as a clinical instrument, and may continue to serve that purpose until a better one is developed.

Schedule for Affective Disorders and Schizophrenia (SADS)

The underlying rationale for the SADS is that diagnostic reliability can be enhanced by the use of operational criteria and standardized information collection. Toward this end, the Research Diagnostic Criteria (RDC; Spitzer, Endicott, & Robins, 1975; 1978) were developed to establish standardized operational criteria. The original purpose of the RDC was for homogeneous subject selection in research, and much of it has been incorporated into DSM-III. The RDC has gone through an evolutionary process of development and refinement as a function of research and clinical experience. The Spitzer, Endicott, and Robins (1978) RDC is itself an expansion from the Feighner criteria (Feighner et al., 1972). The SADS was developed as a structured interview format for collecting standardized information to base RDC diagnostic decisions. As with the RDC, the SADS focuses heavily on schizophrenia and affective disorders but also has sections for closely related diagnostic categories where differential diagnoses and exclusion decisions need to be made. There are three forms of the SADS: the SADS regular form, the SADS-*L* (for life-time) form, and SADS-*C* (for change). The regular SADS is composed of two parts: Part one collects information concerning the current episode and the prior week; part two collects information concerning past episodes. SADS-*L* is similar to part two of the SADS but is organized to be used by patients who are not presently ill or by patient's relatives on the patient's behalf. The SADS-*C* consists of items from part one of the regular SADS collected for the past week. The purpose of the SADS-*C* is to make posttest or follow-up assessments of current status.

The SADS is unusual in that the time frame of part one of the regular form is the present episode. Diagnostic decisions are made on symptoms as they are displayed at the peak of the present episode. Data are also collected within a past-week time frame and a lifetime time frame. In its January 1978 form, the SADS interview is 78 pages long and yields data filling 12 computer cards.

The form includes instructions to the interviewer, suggested phrasing of questions (which can be followed up with other general and specific questions), and rating scales to be filled out during the course of the interview. Many items are filled out on a "yes," "no," or "no information" basis, while others are rated on 3–9-point rating scales. Although the items are intended to be operational and specific, many require a fairly sophisticated knowledge of manifest psychopathology. Because of this, it is suggested that they be filled out only by professionals (psychiatrists, clinical psychologists, or psychiatric social workers). Endicott and Spitzer (1978) have presented information on 8 summary scales derived from the SADS: (1) depressive mood and ideation; (2) endogenous features; (3) depressive-associated features; (4) suicidal ideation and behavior; (5) anxiety; (6) manic syndrome; (7) delusions-hallucinations; and (8) formal thought disorder. Since their presentation, this list of scales has been expanded to 24, including derived Hamilton scales and replications of some of the original 8 factors for current episode and past week. Scales were derived on a logical basis with reference to factor analytic studies and dimensions of importance in research. They contain items scored either as present, absent, or rated on scales of varying lengths. There is much item overlap between the subscales. Reliability and validity data for these subscales comprise the major psychometric development of an instrument that will be reviewed here. No manual exists for the SADS or its subscales, and content coverage is comprehensive by definition. In terms of standard content areas, the SADS subscales could be described as follows: Scale 1, depressive mood and ideation, consists of 5 items; 1 related specifically to affect and 4 that are cognitive. Scale 2, endogenous features, consists of 13 items; 7 of these refer to behavioral symptoms, 4 to cognitive symptoms, 1 to affective symptoms, and 1 questionable item to social interaction symptoms. Scale 3, depressive-associated features, consists of 17 items that are primarily behavioral symptomatology and cognition with one social item. Scale 4, suicidal ideation and behavior, is made up of 4 items concerning suicidal behavior and intent. Scale 1 is intended to assess actual mood, Scale 2 is intended for features related with the concept of endogenicity, Scale 3 is intended to assess neurovegetative signs, and Scale 4 assesses suicidality. There is considerable overlap among these scales, and individual items cover all of the major symptoms and signs of depression. To date, no factor analytic studies have been employed to validate the structure of these scales.

Early psychometric data on the SADS came from two samples: one from the NIMH collaborative program on the psychobiology of depression, and the other from a pilot study of 150 patients. While these samples were fairly large (104 and 150), they were insufficient for establishing norms, cut-offs, etcetera, and there were no data suggesting the consistency of structure of scales across subsamples, such as sex of subject. Cronbach alpha indices of internal consistency for the eight original subscales range from .47 to .97 (*N* = 150). With the exception of formal thought disorder (alpha = .47) and anxiety (alpha = .58), the remainder of the alphas were .79 or greater. Interrater reliabilities based on joint interviews with 150 patients ranged from interclass correlations of .82 to .99. Test-retest reliabilities based on two interviews given within a week of one another ranged from .49 to .93, based on an *N* of 60. Again, the formal thought disorder and anxiety scales were lowest at .49 and .67, respectively, and the remainder of the correlations were .78 or above. Concurrent validity for subscales has been established via correlations with the Katz Adjustment Scale ([KAS] relative and subject forms) and with the SCL-90. Correlations with the KAS-*R* (relative) ranged from .23 to .58, and those for the KAS-*S* (subject) ranged from .34 to .46. Correlations with SCL-90 scales ranged from .15 to .68. In general, these correlations are less than desirable for similar construct scales. The construct validity of the scales has received some degree of validation in studies comparing groups that receive different RDC diagnoses on nine criterion items. Several of these comparisons are given by Endicott and Spitzer (1978) who found that the prognostic indications of endogenous features were not supported.

While the SADS has been accepted and rapidly adopted by the research community, evidence for the subscales derived from the SADS is, to date, relatively slight and sometimes substandard. Pending further psychometric development, it might make more sense simply to use the index of meeting diagnostic criteria (current versions also allow DSM-III-compatible diagnoses) for inclusion in research studies, and, meeting criteria or not, for evaluation of outcome in psychotherapy studies. As an instrument to assess the presence or absence of syndromal depression, this instrument has quickly become the standard.

Diagnostic Interview Schedule (DIS)

The SADS may lose its position of prominence to the DIS (Robins, Helzer, Croughan, & Ratliff, 1981). The DIS was developed under contract with the National Institute of Mental Health, Division of Biometry and Epidemiology. It was intended for use in large-scale epidemiology studies and as such needed to be capable of administration by nonclinicians. The resulting scale is a highly structured interview that specifies all questions and probes. Attention is given to severity, frequency, distribution over time, and elimination of alternative explanations of symptoms in the construction of the DIS. A probe flow chart allows interviewers to make decisions about severity and alternative explanations. An interesting feature is that the DIS is set up to provide diagnostic informations in three diagnostic systems: the Feighner criteria, the RDC, and DSM-III. The interviewer records responses and a computer program determines which diagnostic criteria have been met according to the rules of the three separate systems. Symptom information is also obtained for five time frames: within the last 2 weeks, the last month, the last 6 months, the last year, or more than a year ago.

Robins et al. (1981) provide initial psychometric data on the DIS with a sample of 216 inpatients, outpatients, ex-patients and nonpatients. Using psychiatrists' diagnoses with the DIS as criteria, nonclinicians with 1 week training on the DIS achieved moderate to good agreement on diagnoses. Kappa coefficients were in the .60s for most disorders, with some better (e.g., anorexia and substance abuse disorders) and some poorer (e.g., schizophrenia, somatization, and panic disorders). The DIS has been employed in a large-scale epidemiological study, the National Institute of Mental Health Epidemiologic Catchment Area program (Eaton et al., 1984; Regier et al., 1984). Comparative data from the three sites (New Haven, Baltimore, and St. Louis) have also been reported (Robins et al., 1984; Myers et al., 1984). Thus, the scale is widely used, but little additional information on its psychometrics has accompanied these reports. The specificity of the DIS and the variety of information that can be derived from it may make it the preferred research instrument for diagnosis in the future. The complex scoring system requiring a computer program may limit its use in smaller research sites and in clinical settings. Although the DIS yields a total symptom count as a severity of psychopathology measure, this measure has not been evaluated and the scale in general has not yet been used as an outcome measure.

Other Clinician Rating Scales

Several other clinician rating scales should be mentioned. The Raskin Three Area Rating Scale (Raskin, Schulterbrant, Reatig, & McKeon, 1969; Raskin, Schulterbrant, Reatig, & Rice, 1967) was developed as a method for selecting research subjects. Three areas — "verbal report," "behavior," and "secondary symptoms of depression" — are each rated on a 5-point scale and summed. Normative and psychometric data are accumulating, and the scale may serve a variety of functions as a relatively global rating scale.

The Brief Psychiatric Rating Scale (Overall & Gorham, 1962) was originally developed to provide a rapid assessment technique of psychiatric symptoms for the purpose of evaluating change over time. Sixteen dimensions are rated on 7-point scales from "not present" to "extremely severe." While the intent is a broad coverage of psychiatric symptomatology, a number of the scales are relevant to depression: (1) somatic concern, (2) anxiety, (3) emotional withdrawal, (5) guilt feelings, (9) depressed mood, (13) motor retardation, and (16) blunted affect. While these dimensions include each of the standard areas, they do not assess the specific signs of depression. A total pathology score can also be obtained by summing the 16 ratings. Scoring weights are provided for evaluating improvement in 13 specific diagnostic types and include psychotic-depressive reaction and manic-depressive reactions depressive type. A second set of weights is given for three major patient populations: paranoid, schizophrenic, and depressive. Despite minimal initial psychometric development, the Brief Psychiatric Rating Scale has achieved some popularity for assessing change in psychiatric and psychological outcome research. For the purpose of assessing outcome in depression studies, it is doubtful whether simple ratings on so many scales would give an unbiased estimate of generalization of improvement. The weighting systems may prove helpful in making diagnostic distinctions.

The Feelings and Concerns Checklist (FCCL) is made up of 47 items selected and revised on the basis of pilot work (Grinker, Miller, Sabshin, Nunn, & Nunally, 1961). Each item is rated on a 4-point scale, from 0 (not present) to 3 (markedly present). The content of the items is entirely cognitive. Five factors derived from a factor analysis of 96 depressed patients are scored separately. The factors are labeled (1) dismal, hopeless, bad feelings; (2) projection to external events; (3) guilty feelings; (4) anxiety; and (5) clinging appeals for love. Reliability data are generally good, and the FCCL has been used in a number of psychotherapy outcome studies. Lewinsohn and colleagues have used the instrument in several studies, primarily as a subject selection criterion. Lewinsohn and Biglan (1975) and Lewinsohn, Weinstein, and Alper (1970) also report pre-post differences on the FCCL. Padfield (1976) reported that the FCCL discriminated between treatment conditions in a psychotherapy outcome study, suggesting that the FCCL is sensitive to clinical change. This instrument had an initial psychometric development and has been used to some degree in depression research (e.g., Simon, 1966) but has not enjoyed sufficient popularity to accrue a body of additional psychometric support. Its cognitive content could make it useful in combination with other scales.

Mentioned under self-report instruments were the clinician rating alternate forms of the Social Adjustment Scale (Weissman & Paykel, 1974) and the SCL-90 (i.e., the Hopkins Psychiatric Rating Scale; Derogatis, 1977). The Social Adjustment Scale consists of 42 items grouped within six role areas by five qualitative areas. Social interpersonal content is most heavily weighted, but other areas of depressive behavior are included as well. Psychometric data are minimal but promising. The Hopkins Psychiatric Rating Scale consists of nine anchored rating scales paralleling the nine subscales of the SCL-90. The parallel nature of data collected from two perspectives is important for each.

Direct Observational Methods

Coding Verbal Behavior
A number of studies have focused on specific aspects of depressed verbal

behavior as modification targets. Robinson and Lewinsohn (1973b) identified a slowed rate of speech as a depressive target behavior in a chronically depressed psychiatric patient. In therapy interviews, the number of words per 30-second interval was tabulated with a hand counter by an observer behind a one-way mirror. Rate of speech appeared to be a fairly stable response characteristic brought under reinforcement control. Ince (1972) used a verbal conditioning procedure to increase positive self-references over 17 therapy sessions; however, no reliability data are presented for the rating of positive self-statements. Aiken and Parker (1965) provided reinforcement contingencies for positive self-evaluation response choices to a written sentence-completion task, but no reliability or validity data are presented.

Lewinsohn (1968), Lewinsohn et al. (1970), and Libet et al. (1973a, 1973b) have evolved a method of coding the verbal interaction behavior of individuals in group and home settings. Pursuing the general hypothesis that depression represents a deficit in social skills, these researchers have attempted to validate a series of objective measures of skill in verbal interactions.

Lewinsohn et al. (1970) selected depressed undergraduate subjects on the same MMPI criteria, along with a set of criteria derived from the FCCL factors. Five female and four male subjects were seen for 18 sessions of group therapy. Interaction data on four social skill variables were collected by two observers at each session. These variables were: (a) total amount of behavior emitted by and directed toward each individual; (b) use of positive and negative reactions by each individual; (c) interpersonal efficiency ratio, defined as the number of verbal behaviors directed toward an individual relative to the number of verbal behaviors the individual emits; and (d) range of interactions with others. Interrater reliabilities were deemed satisfactory, although figures are only given for the number of actions ($r = .97$) and reactions ($r = .99$) given by an individual. Group treatment in this study consisted of weekly feedback to subjects of their coded interpersonal data from the prior week. These data served as a basis for discussion, goal formulation, and change efforts on the part of each subject. As such, the meaning of changes on these variables is difficult to interpret, and only representative graphs of selected variables for individual subjects are presented. Pre- and post-therapy scores on the MMPI and Grinker factors suggest improvement of depression, although no statistical tests are presented.

Libet and Lewinsohn (1973) selected "depressed," "nondepressed, psychiatric," and "normal" control subjects on the basis of MMPI and FCCL interview criteria. Using a similar system, interpersonal verbal behavior was coded for two groups over a number of sessions. Interrater reliabilities ranged from .63 to .99. Depressed subjects were found to have lower activity levels, although this effect was significant for only one group during its earlier sessions. Depressed subjects emitted fewer positive reactions to others but did not differ on negative reactions. No differences were found for the interpersonal efficiency measure, and interpersonal range was found to be narrower only for depressed males. An additional measure, action latency, indicated that depressed subjects were significantly slower in responding to another's reaction.

In an elaborate and statistically sophisticated study of social skill variables in group- and home-observation settings, Libet, Lewinsohn, and Javorek (1973) coded the interpersonal behavior of depressed, nondepressed psychiatric, and normal control subjects in 5 self-study groups and 18 visited homes. Again, subjects were identified on the basis of MMPI and FCCL interview criteria but included referrals and subjects solicited by newspaper ads for this study. Nineteen social skill and six criterion variables were defined in this study. Interrater reliabilities were generally good, although the authors noted that temporal stability was low for many of the variables. Situational differences between the two settings were also apparent. Depressed males in the groups were found to emit and initiate fewer questions (a functionally reinforcing event), were silent more often, and were slower in reaction response than the other two male groups. They were also more affected by aversive reactions and elicited fewer positive reactions. Results for females in the group were generally the same, but nonsignificant. Depressed males at home emitted fewer actions but initiated more. This reversal was attributed to less participation in ongoing conversations initiated by others. In addition, depressed males were more silent, slower to respond to reactions, and elicited a lower rate of positive reinforcement. Depressed females were less active, slower to respond to reactions, and elicited a lower rate of positive reinforcement than the other two female groups. Interestingly, the authors concluded on the basis of other analyses that social skills do not seem to be evidenced by higher ratios of positive to negative reactions elicited. This ratio tended to remain constant regardless of the total number of elicited reactions. This finding may relate to the nature of the studied situations.

Lewinsohn and colleagues have used their behavioral coding system as part of the assessment and evaluation in a series of clinical cases. As an assessment tool, the method has been used to identify problem areas that then become targets for behavioral intervention. Sample problem areas in the case studies include generally low activity level in the family (Lewinsohn et al., 1970), few initiations to the client (Lewinsohn & Atwood, 1969; Lewinsohn & Shaffer, 1971), low rates of mutual reinforcement (Lewinsohn & Shaw, 1969), and negative reactions from spouse (Lewinsohn & Shaffer, 1971). Lewinsohn and Shaffer (1971) point out that the use of home observations as a basis for assessment also provides advantages for subsequent therapy interventions by providing data that can be used as objective feedback to clients. Also, home observations focus attention on the interpersonal behavior of the client and his or her family. In two controlled studies (Johansson, Lewinsohn, & Flippo, 1969; Robinson & Lewinsohn, 1973a), the content categories in the coding system were used as target response classes in an interview setting. In applications of the Premack Principle, high-frequency response classes were made contingent on the prior occurrence of a low-frequency response class.

As described, these methods are somewhat cumbersome for most clinical uses, requiring multiple, well-trained observers in home or group settings. McLean, Ogston, and Grauer (1973) describe a simplified method based on Lewinsohn's coding system. Patients were required to make half-hour recordings of problem discussions with their spouses at home. These recordings were divided into 30-second intervals and coded for positive and negative initiations and reactions. Scores were calculated as proportions of interaction for both participants. Interrater agreement ranged from 73% to 97%, with an average agreement of 88%. Couples in the experimental group who received a behaviorally oriented training procedure decreased significantly in negative reactions and in negative actions and reactions on the posttest. A mixed control group did not change significantly on these measures.

Fuchs and Rehm (1977) videotaped 10-minute segments of therapist-absent interaction among groups of depressed subjects in a therapy study. The number of statements made in 10 minutes was counted as a simple assessment of verbal activity level. Interrater agreement ranged from 83% to 100%, with a mean of 87%. Experimental subjects increased in verbal activity level significantly more than placebo therapy controls from pre- to post-testing. Rehm, Fuchs, Roth, Kornblith, and Romano (1979) coded 9 verbal and nonverbal behaviors from group-therapy observations during first and last therapy sessions. Posttherapy scores, with pretherapy scores covaried, significantly differed between therapy conditions for negative self-references, negative references to others, and an overall depression rating. Rehm et al. (1981) found therapy effects for 2 of 11 verbal and nonverbal behaviors coded from pre- and post-therapy interviews (expressivity and latency). Of these same measures, only loudness and latency differentiated between depressed and normal subjects (Lamparski, Rehm, O'Hara, Kornblith, & Fitzgibbon, 1979).

Observations from structured interviews were also employed by Andreasen and Pfohl (1976), who found depression-associated differences on dimensions of the use of power, overstatement, and achievement words. Hinchliffe, Lancashire, and Roberts (1970, 1971a, 1971b) found differences on personal references, negators, direct references, expressions of feeling, nonpersonal references, speech rate, eye contact, and gaze duration.

Coyne (1976) set up telephone interviews between depressed and nondepressed persons. He found differences in behavior codes (such as time spent talking about self versus others) and also elicited social-interpersonal evaluations of each subject from the interview partner.

Jacobson (1981) described a coding scheme used in assessing small groups. He found that certain codes discriminate better between depressed and nondepressed subjects when they are viewed in terms of conditional probabilities rather than absolute frequencies (i.e., probability of a self-disclosure following a self-disclosure of another rather than frequency of self-disclosure per se).

In a German study Hautzinger, Linden, and Hoffman (1982) examined the verbal interactions between distressed couples in a clinical setting. In one group of 13 couples, 1 member of each couple was depressed; in another group of 13 couples, neither partner was depressed. Twenty-eight codes were extracted from 8 conversations of up to 45 minutes each on 8 different topics. Six-second intervals were rated for an average of 312 minutes per couple. Included were 2 codes of nonverbal affect expression, 7 codes of self-related verbalizations, 9 interaction verbalization codes, and 10 information categories. Couples with a depressed partner showed a more uneven, negative, and asymmetrical verbal relationship with frequent focus on somatic and psychological complaints by the depressed spouse. From an analysis of the pattern of these interactions, Hautzinger et al. suggest an insidious interaction pattern in depression where depressive complaints coercively control the interaction in the short run, but lead to the dissatisfaction of each member of the couple in the long run.

In summary, a number of different verbal behaviors have been coded in a variety of experimental conditions. Some codes appear to differentiate depressed subjects with some reliability, but failure to replicate differences in coding procedures and situational differences leaves many unanswered questions concerning the utility of coding verbal behavior as an assessment procedure. More systematic work and a standard set of codes will be required before such procedures can be adopted on a regular basis in research or clinical practice.

Coding Overt Motor Behavior

Several of the verbal behavior studies mentioned include nonverbal codes as well (e.g., eye contact and smiling). Using an interview observation similar to the procedures carried out in the previous review, Ranelli (1978) found differences between depressed and nondepressed subjects on head nods (fewer for depressed) and head aversions (more for depressed). Waxer (1974, 1976) found posture differences, and Ekman and Friesen (1974) found differences in gestures.

In a very sophisticated observational study in Germany, Fisch, Frey, and Hirsbrunner (1983) observed 13 depressed patients in interviews at admission and discharge. Time-series coding of 32 body movements in half-second intervals of 3-minute segments yielded summary scores for Mobility (percentage of time in motion), Complexity (simultaneous movement), and Dynamic Action (rapidity of start and stop of actions). Mobility increased from admission to discharge with large individual differences. Complexity increased and was correlated with doctors' ratings of depression. Dynamic Action was more rapid at discharge. Interestingly, the interviewer's Mobility and Complexity also increased at discharge but was unrelated to patient measures. The authors concluded that within-subject differences would be more valuable clinically than between-subject measures.

Assertion skill behaviors, some of them verbal, have been assessed in two therapy studies. Rehm et al. (1979) used an audiotaped situation test and found that — in comparison with a self-control therapy — assertion training with depressed subjects produced greater changes in speech duration, requests for new behavior, statements of opinion, loudness, fluency, and overall assertion. The self-control condition, however, improved more on depression measures. Wells, Hersen, Bellack, and Himmelhoch (1977) found changes in a behavioral assertion test that corresponded with depression improvement in four single-subject cases.

Observations of inpatients have employed direct observation measures of depressive behavior. Reisinger (1972), in a single-subject reversal design study, described the use of token reinforcement and response cost to increase smiling and decrease crying behavior, respectively. Careful behavioral definitions of the responses led to interrater reliabilities above 90% for observation periods of up to 2 hours. Token control was demonstrated and later faded.

There have been two attempts to develop scales with inpatients. Bunney and Hamburg (1963) developed a rating scale for use by nurses and psychiatrists in assessing ward behavior. Twenty-four dimensions are rated on 15-point scales within an 8-hour time frame. Subscales for depression, anger, anxiety, psychotic behaviors, somatic complaints, and physical activity can be derived. Unfortunately, reliabilities are relatively low, with intraclass rs ranging from .11 to .83 with a median of .36.

Williams, Barlow, and Agras (1972) describe the use of behavioral assessment procedures for 10 depressed psychiatric inpatients. At randomly determined points during each half-hour from 8 a.m. to 4 p.m., a trained observer noted the presence or absence of each of the following four response classes: (a) talking, (b) smiling, (c) motor activity, (10 subclasses further define this behavior), and (d) time out of room. Interrater reliability of 96% was reported. An analysis of the correlations among the four behavioral measures yielded a Kendall's coefficient of concordance of .70($p < .01$). On this basis, scores were summed and treated as a single index of depression severity. Comparisons were made between the behavioral index, Beck

Depression Inventory, and Hamilton Rating Scale at 3-day intervals during the course of the patients' hospitalizations. Mean correlations (calculated with appropriate Fisher's z-transformations) between the measures were as follows: Beck and Hamilton, $r = .82$; Hamilton and behavioral index, $r = .71$; Beck and behavioral index, $r = .67$. On the basis of follow-up information for 5 patients, the authors suggest that the course of overt behavioral improvement during hospitalization is more predictive of posthospitalization improvement than either the Beck or the Hamilton. Hersen, Eisler, Alford, and Agras (1973) used this behavior rating scale to assess improvement of 3 patients on a token economy ward. In three single-subject reversal designs, improvement on the behavior rating scale was shown to occur when patients were under token reinforcement conditions. No self-report measures were taken.

A technically sophisticated method of assessing overt motor activity level has been employed by a group of psychiatric researchers. Kupfer, Detre, Foster, Tucker, and Delgado (1972) described an apparatus which permits 24-hour telemetric recording of activity in an inpatient setting. A miniature transmitter containing a ferromagnetic ball in an inductance coil is encased in a cylinder 2.2 cm in diameter and 6.7 cm long. The transmitter is worn on a wrist band and has a range of 100 feet. Receivers transform the data into pulses, which are read out digitally as number of counts per minute. A reliability of 91.7% agreement is reported for five subjects wearing transmitters on each wrist for 1 hour. Kupfer et al. (1974) reported a .73 reliability for wrist and ankle transmitters. This research has shown correlations between activity level and various sleep parameters such as electroencephalograph (EEG) movement, minutes awake, time asleep, rapid-eye-movement (REM) time, and REM activity (Kupfer et al., 1972; Kupfer & Foster, 1973; Weiss, Kupfer, Foster, & Delgado, 1974). Kupfer et al. (1974) found differences between unipolar and bipolar depressives prior to drug treatment; unipolars had much higher levels of activity. No drug effects were found, but clinically improved unipolars ($N = 4$) decreased in activity level. This is the only study reporting relationships between the telemetered activity level and any conventional depression measure. No significant correlations were obtained with self-rating depression items on the KDS-1 (Kupfer & Detre, 1971), a general psychiatric self-report form. A correlation of .85 was found, however, with self-rated anxiety on the KDS-1 during drug treatment. This correlation is not surprising in light of the fact that a number of patients showed increased agitation during drug treatment. This was reflected by the anxiety rating. O'Hara and Rehm (1979) found no correlation with either anxiety or depression using simple pedometers. Further validational evidence will be needed in order to clarify relationships between retarded or agitated psychomotor activity and depression or anxiety. Correlations between telemetered psychomotor activity and other well-validated measures of depression would be helpful. If they are to be used as standard instruments, further work is needed on any of these methods for assessing overt motor behavior.

Activity Schedules

The use of activity schedules in depression research deserves comment, although it might be questioned whether these devices can be properly considered depression assessment instruments. In general, they involve a self-recording of overt events or activities; since depression involves decreased activity, these techniques do assess it. However, since there is usually an additional assumption that some specific activities or events are particularly important as determinants of depression, occasionally the putative cause is assessed rather than depression per se.

The best-developed instrument of this type is the MacPhillamy and Lewinsohn (1971, 1972a, 1972b, 1976) Pleasant Events Schedule (PES). The PES is based on Lewinsohn's theoretical model of depression, which accounts for depression as a lack or loss of response-contingent positive reinforcement. As such, the PES is intended to assess the amount of external positive reinforcement the individual receives. The PES consists of 320 events generated from lists of positive events elicited from 66 subjects (MacPhillamy & Lewinsohn, 1972a). A revised form III used another 70 subjects (Lewinsohn & Graf, 1973). The instrument is used in two ways: as a retrospective report of the events of the last 30 days and as the basis for daily logs of ongoing behavior. As a retrospective instrument, subjects are first asked to indicate how frequently each item occurred within the last 30 days on a 3-point scale: 0 = not happened, 1 = happened a few times (1–6 times), and 2 = happened often (7 or more times). Subjects then go through the list a second time indicating how pleasant and enjoyable each event was or potentially would be, again using a 3-point scale: 0 = not pleasant; 1 = somewhat pleasant; and 2 = very pleasant. Three scores are derived from these ratings: Activity Level, defined as the sum of the frequency ratings; Reinforcement Potential, defined as the sum of the pleasantness ratings; and Obtained Reinforcement, defined as the sum of the frequency and pleasantness ratings for each item. Test-retest reliabilities for 37 subjects over a 4–8 week span were .85, .66, and .72 for the three respective scores (MacPhillamy & Lewinsohn, 1972a, 1972b). Alpha coefficients of internal consistency were .96, .98, and .97 for the same scores. Norms for male and female college students are given by MacPhillamy and Lewinsohn (1972b, 1976).

Evidence for the validity of the instrument was also presented by MacPhillamy and Lewinsohn (1974, 1976), who found that all three scores statistically differentiated between depressed individuals and both psychiatric and normal controls, defined by MMPI and FCCL factor ratings.

The entire PES has also been used by Lewinsohn and his co-workers to generate shorter lists specific to individuals. Lewinsohn and Libet (1972) and Lewinsohn and Graf (1973) selected the 160 most pleasant items for individual subjects and had subjects use these lists as daily activity checks for 30 days. Significant intraindividual correlations were found between number of pleasant events and mood as measured by the DACL. In the Lewinsohn and Graf (1973) study, depressed subjects were found to engage in fewer pleasant events.

The use of individualized PES in therapy has been described by Lewinsohn (1976). Schedules of 160 items derived as above were kept for 30 days by 10 depressed patients. The 10 items most highly correlated with mood were then selected as targets for behavior-change efforts and reinforced with minutes of psychotherapy time. Target activities increased significantly more than did a set of control activities.

Ad hoc activity schedules or logs have been reported in case studies by Lewinsohn and Atwood (1969) and Rush, Khatami, and Beck (1975). The latter report employed activity schedules as a part of the therapy program. Patients' daily logs served as a basis for correcting cognitive distortions of their own behavior. In a controlled psychotherapy outcome study, Fuchs and Rehm (1977) employed an activity schedule procedure in a self-control therapy program. Using the PES as an item pool, a shortened list containing 20 classes of reinforcing behavior was constructed. Items on this list, the Positive Activities Schedule, were designed to emphasize the active role of the subject in producing potential reinforcement. Experimental subjects kept daily activity logs using the Positive Activities Schedule as a guide. These logs served as a basis for (a) attempts to modify distortions of self-observation, (b) selection of target behaviors to be increased, and (c) selection of behaviors to be used as contingent self-reinforcement. In addition, this study used the PES as a pre- and post-therapy outcome measure in comparisons among the experimental group, placebo therapy, and waiting-list controls. Increases in self-reported pleasant events over the last 30 days tended to be greater for the experimental group. This effect was replicated in Rehm et al. (1979, 1981).

More recently, the Unpleasant Events Schedule has been developed (Lewinsohn & Talkington, 1979) that also correlates with daily mood. This finding was replicated by Rehm (1978) with a less sophisticated daily log procedure and again by O'Hara and Rehm (1979) using similar lists.

In sum, event schedules are good examples of behavioral measures that have been subjected to careful psychometric development and analysis. The Pleasant Events Schedule has considerable promise as an instrument for use in treatment planning. Questions regarding reactivity of self-monitoring and possible depressive distortion in recall of events place a limit on these schedules as veridical measures of activity rate in depression.

Comments on Overt Behavioral Assessment

Much still needs to be done before overt behavioral assessment methods can be added to a depression assessment battery on a regular basis. Generally, coding systems and other methods need further replication, psychometric refinement, and standardization. Before these methods can be considered behavioral measures of actual depression, much more attention to breadth of content coverage will be necessary. The methods reviewed touch on most of the content areas; negative self-references, for example, are verbal-cognitive behavior; smiling or weeping is an affective behavior; activity level is an overt motor manifestation; and Coyne's (1976) ratings by conversational partner focus on social-interpersonal aspects of depression. No reviewed method, however, covers more than two, or perhaps three, such areas. Many areas important in depression have not been considered at all, such as somatic complaints or behavior associated with major depressive signs such as sleep, eating, and sexual behavior. It would be quite possible for important scales to include sleep and eating behavior. Self-recording logs could be used with outpatients. Little of the methodological advances from other areas of behavioral assessment research (e.g., obesity research measures of eating behavior) are seen in the assessment of overt behavior. Much further research is needed here.

Informant Measures

This category of instrument is included because of its potential special importance in depression assessment. Since depressed persons can be expected to distort their experiences, the veridicality of certain aspects of interview information may be doubtful. A relative or other significant informant can provide reliability checks on self-report. Such a person is likely to have a much larger sample of observation than that tapped by most of the overt behavior assessment samples. Significant others in the depressed person's life represent a direct source of evaluation of social interpersonal problems associated with depression.

Despite the need, very little work has been done in this area. McLean, Ogston, and Grauer (1973) used an audio-taped direct sample of an interaction with spouses, but did not collect spouse evaluations. Coyne (1976) collected some ratings from strangers in his phone-call procedure. Rush, Khatami, and Beck (1975) reported having a spouse monitor specific behaviors on the part of a patient as counterevidence to distorted self-report, but this was an individually tailored procedure. No fully developed scale has appeared for significant other reports; however, one other general scale includes considerable representation of depressive content.

Katz Adjustment Scale (KAS)

The KAS (Katz & Lyerly, 1963) consists of two sets of scales. Five scales are to be filled out by the subject or patient, and an additional five by a relative as an outside informant. Most work on the scales has focused on the Relative Scales (or R Scales). The purpose of the scales is to measure both psychiatric symptoms and other indices of social behavior which may be relevant to social adjustment. The scales were developed with the intent of assessing adjustment pre- and post-hospitalization. The rationale for two sets of scales is that social behavior involves both subject and social environment perceptions. The Relative Scales attempt to minimize the effects of various kinds of biasing by constructing items descriptive of behavior rather than by asking for attitudes or evaluations. The first of the Relative Scales, form R1, consists of 127 items intended to cover symptomatology relevant to depression, anxiety, suspiciousness, belligerence, and withdrawal. Each item is rated on a 4-point frequency scale from "almost never" to "almost always." In the original Katz and Lyerly article (1963), a several-week and a 2-week time frame were used. Hogarty (1975) reported that more recently a three-week time frame has been employed. Form R2, Level of Performance of Socially Expected Activities, consists of 16 items describing typical social behaviors that are rated on a 3-point scale from "not doing" to "doing regularly." Form R3, Level of Expectations for Performance of Social Activities, consists of the same 16 items rated on a different 3-point scale, ranging from "did not expect him to be doing" to "expected him to be doing regularly." The intention is to obtain a discrepancy reflective of the participant's degree of satisfaction or dissatisfaction with the subject's level of activity. Form R4, Level of Free Time Activities, consists of 23 items covering hobbies, social and community activities, and self-improvement activities. These items are rated on a 3-point scale consisting of (1) frequently, (2) sometimes, and (3) practically never. Form R5, Level of Satisfaction with Free-Time Activities, consists of the same 23 items as R4 but rated as to degree of satisfaction on a 3-point scale consisting of (1) satisfied with what he does here, (2) would like to see him do more of this, and (3) would like to see him do less.

The Subject Scales (or S Scales) begin with form S1, Symptom Discomfort, which consists of 55 items describing somatic, mood, and psychoneurotic symptoms. Responses are made on a 4-point frequency scale. Form S2, Level of Performance of Socially Expected Activities; form S9, Level of Expectations; form RS4, Level of Free Time Activities; and form S5, "Level of Satisfaction with Free-Time Activities" are self-rating formats which are otherwise identical to the R Scales. All items are constructed with a fairly simple vocabulary level and with fairly straightforward instructions (Katz & Lyerly, 1963; Michaux, Katz, Kurland, & Gansereit, 1969).

In terms of the standard content areas, roughly 29 of the 127 items of the R1 form are descriptive of typical depressive symptomatology. Of these, the heaviest weight is on behavioral (approximately 13 items) and cognitive (approximately 10 items) symptomatology. Approximately 4 items refer to affective symptoms and 1 item each refers to somatic and interpersonal symptoms of depression. These estimates are only approximate because many additional items could be peripherally related to depression. It is interesting to note the predominance of behavioral symptoms, which have much less weight in most other scales. It is surprising that interpersonal content is not tapped more heavily, though the other subscales do so. In terms of the standard depressive signs, one item refers to sleep problems and two to suicide. There are no items for eating or sex-related problems, but RS4 covers certain work-related performance problems.

Normative data on a variety of psychiatric populations are available on the KAS but not always from easily obtained publications (see Hogarty, 1975). No specific cut-off scores have been established, although profiles are available for different populations.

Hogarty (1975) reported some unpublished data by Crook and Hogarty on interrater reliability for the KAS. The median correlation between parents of 15 schizophrenics on the R1 symptom clusters was .71, with coefficients ranging from .33 for "nervousness" to .84 for "helplessness." Correlations on forms R2, R4, and R5 were .85, .47, and .74, respectively. Form R3, "parental expectations," showed low correlations, although this might be expected. Katz and Lyerly (1963) present Kuder-Richardson reliabilities for two samples of schizophrenic patients. Reliabilities for 12 subscales of form R1 for the first sample ($N = 73$) ranged from .61 to .87; in the second sample ($N = 242$) reliabilities ranged from .41 to .81.

Katz and Lyerly (1963) presented data for 15 well-adjusted and 15 poorly adjusted ex-psychiatric patients identified by a research program involving follow-up of ex-hospitalized patients. All correlations were significant except for those in form S5, indicating that the self-ratings discriminate less well than the relative ratings between well- and poorly adjusted patients. Hogarty (1975) reported on unpublished data by Katz and Lowery in which independent global ratings of adjustment produced multiple rs of .70 (with R forms) to .83 (with R and S forms) in a series of multiple regression analyses.

Marsella, Sanborn, Kameoka, Shizuru, and Brennan (1975) reported correlations between a subset of depression-related items from the Katz Adjustment Scales' pool and several standard depression scales. Correlations with the (Multiple Affect Adjective Checklist) (MAACL) ranged from .48 to .72, with the MMPI-*D* from .46 to .70, and with the SDS from .32 to .73. This set of items, however, is not a standard scale but suggests that there is some covariance with depression represented within the KAS. Hogarty, Goldberg, and Schooler (1974) found significant effects on a number of KAS variables in a study comparing drug and sociotherapy in aftercare with schizophrenic patients.

In summary, the KAS has yet to be thoroughly developed psychometrically. Most work has been done with the relative forms, particularly in terms of behavioral symptoms. There appears to be no other scale specifically designed for use by relatives or other informants that is relevant both to depressive symptomatology and social adjustment, or that has any better psychometric background.

The Assessment of Core Deficits of Depression

One of the major developments in recent depression assessment research has been the instruments constructed to assess the core deficit of depression as hypothesized by new behavioral models of the disorder. A number of scales have been developed to assess the core deficits hypothesized by each model. These instruments will be briefly listed for each model.

MacPhillamy and Lewinsohn's (1976) Pleasant Events Schedule (PES) has already been described as a primary assessment technique for assessing response-contingent reinforcement as a central construct in Lewinsohn's behavioral model of depression. Lewinsohn et al. (1976) have suggested cut-off scores for choosing between activity increase and desensitization treatment modules. An Unpleasant Events Schedule (Lewinsohn & Talkington, 1979) was developed to complement the PES as a measure of the impact on mood of daily aversive events.

A number of authorities have hypothesized that social skills deficits are a core deficit in depression. Within Lewinsohn's theory this is one possible reason for low rate of reinforcement, and an Interpersonal Events Schedule (Zeiss, Lewinsohn, & Munoz, 1979) was added to the battery in an attempt to provide a measure specific to this therapy module. In most instances, assessment instruments have been adopted from the social skills research area for assessment of the skills of depressed persons. For example, Rehm et al. (1979) used the Wolpe-Lazarus Assertiveness Inventory (Wolpe & Lazarus, 1967) and a taped situation test, and Wells, Hersen, Bellack, and Himmelhoch (1977) used the Wolpe-Lazarus and a behavioral role-play test. For a more complete review of social skills assessment, the reader is directed to chapter 11 of this volume.

Several measures of cognitive distortion have been presented, which attempt to assess deficits hypothesized by Beck (1972) as the core of the depression. Weissman (1978) developed a Dysfunctional Attitudes Scale that asks subjects how much they agree with depressive attitude statements. Hammen and Krantz (1976) developed a Cognitive Bias Questionnaire that asks subjects to indicate which alternative reaction would be typical of them in a variety of situations. Depression and distortion of response can be scored separately. Hollon and Kendall (1980) developed an Automatic Thoughts Questionnaire to tap depressive thinking patterns. Lewinsohn and colleagues added a Subjective Probability Questionnaire to their battery of tests to assess negative biases in accord with Beck's model (Lewinsohn, Larson, & Munoz, 1982). Beck and colleagues (Beck, Weissman, Lester, & Trexler, 1974) offered the Hopelessness Scale as a measure of negative cognitive bias associated especially with suicidal tendencies.

Similar in some ways to the Beck model is the Ellis (1962) rational emotive model of psychopathology that postulates irrational beliefs as the cause of neurotic behavior. An Irrational Beliefs Questionnaire has been published by Jones (1968). At least some of these specific beliefs have been related to depression. Lewinsohn, Larson, and Munoz (1982) have also developed a Personal Beliefs Inventory to assess this aspect of depression, and they found this scale to represent a third factor independent of negative thoughts and positive thoughts.

Two methods of assessing Seligman's helplessness construct have been developed. Seligman, Abramson, Semmel, and Von Baeyer (1979) have described an Attribution Styles Questionnaire that demonstrated predicted differences between depressed and nondepressed groups. A child's version of this measure first developed by Kaslow and Tanenbaum, and referred to as the KASTAN (Seligman et al., 1984) is also available.

My colleagues and I (Fuchs & Rehm, 1977; Rehm et al., 1979; Rehm et al., 1981) have used a Self-Control Questionnaire in conjunction with a self-control therapy program for depression. Questionnaire scores were found to improve with treatment. Rosenbaum (1980) developed a general self-control scale (initially called the Self-Control Schedule and later renamed the Learned Resourcefulness Schedule) that measures general self-control capacities and has proved to be a positive predictor of coping with stress. Heiby (1982) constructed the Self-Reinforcement Questionnaire to assess the tendency to self-reinforce — a component of the self-control model of depression. The Cognitive Events Schedule (Lewinsohn et al., 1982) attempts to assess frequency of self-reinforcing thoughts.

Finally, mention should be made of two scales of multiple deficits hypothesized to be related to depression. The Coping Styles Scales (Beckham & Adams, 1984) consist of 10 scales measuring (1) Blame, (2) Emotion Expression, (3) Emotion Containment, (4) Social Support, (5) Religious Support, (6) Philosophical/Cognitive Restructuring, (7) General Activity, (8) Avoidance/Denial, (9) Problem Solving, and (10) Passivity. Berndt, Petzel, and Berndt (1980) constructed the Multiscore Depression Inventory with 10 subscales to assess depression with particular reference to theoretically relevant constructs. The 10 subscales are (1) Sad Mood, (2)

Fatigue, (3) Learned Helplessness, (4) Guilt, (5) Pessimism, (6) Social Introversion, (7) Irritability, (8) Instrumental Helplessness, (9) Low Self-Esteem, and (10) Cognitive Difficulty.

Generally, these instruments are new and should be assumed to be experimental at this point. Much more standardization and validation data will be necessary before they are fully usable in clinical situations.

CASE DESCRIPTION

Some of the issues involved in depression assessment can be illustrated by a case example. The following case is drawn from a recent research project involving a self-control behavior therapy program for depression (Rehm, Kaslow, & Rabin, in press). The program is carried out in a structured group format in which self-control deficits associated with depression are targeted over the course of 10 weekly 90-minute sessions. A more detailed description of this program can be found in Rehm (1981, 1984). Subjects for the study were recruited from the community by announcements in the news media asking for female volunteers who felt depression was a serious problem. Volunteers who were not currently in treatment were screened on BDI (> 20) and MMPI (> 70) criteria. They were then given a modified SADS interview, thus the resulting population manifested nonpsychotic, nonbipolar major affective disorder. Exclusion criteria for other psychological disorders were employed.

The sample case, Ms. O. F., was a single, 33-year-old librarian. She described episodes of depression dating back to age 22 but complained of more frequent and longer episodes in the last 3 years since breaking up with a boyfriend. Ms. O. F. maintained a cordial but distant relationship with family members and work associates but had little social life. Social withdrawal was a primary complaint. She had previously sought help at a community mental health center and had consulted a psychiatrist on one occasion. He had prescribed an antianxiety agent which Ms. O. F. still had and which she took about once a week.

The SADS interview indicated complaints of initial and middle-of-the-night insomnia, fatigability, anhedonia, self-criticism, concentration problems, and suicidal thoughts. Pessimism, brooding, feelings of inadequacy, irritability, dependence on others, and somatic complaints were also indicated. Pretest data are shown in Table 10.1. All four of the severity scales (BDI and MMPI-*D* self-report scales and Hamilton and Raskin clinician ratings) were in the moderate depression range. The Self-Control Questionnaire score was about two-thirds of a standard deviation below the mean for volunteers entering the depression therapy program, indicating a low endorsement of positive self-control principles. The PES scores indicated a very low frequency of engagement in pleasant activities but an adequate

TABLE 10.1. Pre- and Post-Test Scores for Sample Case.

SCALE	PRETEST	POST-TEST
Beck Depression Inventory	23	5
MMPI-*D* (*T* score)	96	63
Hamilton Rating Scale	21	7
Raskin Three Area Scale	9	4
Self-Control Questionnaire	4.24	5.58
Pleasant Events Schedule:		
Frequency	.45	1.27
Enjoyability	1.45	1.84
F × E	1.35	2.47

TABLE 10.2. Sample Case Activity, Mood, and Depression Measures During Therapy Program.

WEEK	MAIN DAILY POSITIVE ACTIVITIES	MEAN DAILY MOOD	WEEKLY BDI-SF
1	—	—	15
2	7.9	5.6	7
3	14.4	7.4	5
4	14.2	7.8	5
5	13.9	6.4	4
6	16.0	7.1	3
7		(session mixed)	
8	14.3	8.4	2
9	13.9	8.0	2
10	15.2	8.5	1

ability to experience pleasure. This pattern fits the Lewinsohn et al. (1976) criteria for recommending a program to increase pleasant activities, a major component of the self-control therapy program.

During the course of the program, participants were told to record daily their positive activities and indicate an average mood rating for each day. Such monitoring was aided by a list of positive activities categories which were used as a checklist to prompt items included in the daily log. Mood was rated on a simple 11-point scale from 0 (worst mood ever) to 10 (best mood ever). In addition, subjects filled out a short-form version of the BDI at the beginning of each therapy session. Average number of daily positive activities, average mood rating, and weekly BDI short-form scores are shown in Table 10.2 for the course of the therapy program.

The first 3 weeks of the program stressed self-monitoring of positive activities, including attention to positive activities as they occurred and awareness of the relationship between number of positive activities and

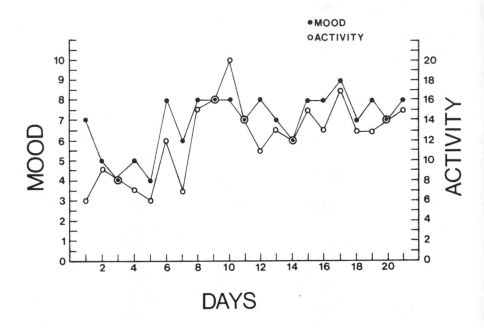

FIGURE 10.1. Daily number of events and mood ratings for first 3 weeks of the therapy program for the sample case.

mood. To illustrate this latter issue, participants constructed simple graphs of their weekly data. These data are shown for the first 3 weeks in Figure 10.1.

As can be seen, a correlation is evident between mood and activity in the first 3 weeks; an improvement on all weekly measures is evident after the first week. At this point the general rationale of modifying mood by increasing positive activities was presented, and 1 week's graph of the activity and mood data has been constructed by the participants.

The next three sessions focused on scheduling activities, setting behavioral goals, and breaking goals into specific subgoal activities. The aim was to modify self-evaluation behavior by teaching participants to set realistic self-evaluative standards and to make accurate attributions of responsibility for events. Ms. O. F. set goals of increasing outdoor physical activity and asserting herself more with colleagues at work (e.g., initiating conversations and insisting on her rights regarding work breaks). During this time period, Ms. O. F. evidenced improvement.

Weeks 7 and 8 involved teaching participants to use self-reinforcement contingently to reward their subgoal activities. Weeks 9 and 10 involved review and continuation of the program as a whole.

Posttest data demonstrate that positive self-control attitudes on the Self-Control Questionnaire improved by more than a standard deviation. PES scores all improved, most notably in the frequency score. Associated with these targeted changes is a general improvement on all four depression measures: All of these measures were in the normal range at posttest.

Since the therapy program in the described case is a complex package involving many procedures, it is not possible to isolate specific effects. (The case does illustrate the use of measures of targeted behavior along with measures of depression as a syndrome.) Changes in the targeted areas are a necessary validation of the therapy procedures.

FUTURE CONSIDERATIONS

From the perspective of behavioral measurement for clinical and research purposes, there are many problems with instruments currently available. Despite the heterogeneity of the phenomena of depression, virtually all the instruments reviewed produce a single severity score. None has developed subscales for specific sets of symptoms of subtype diagnoses. Subscales for the SADS are one development in this direction. Other scales can be broken into subscales based on the logic of their construction (e.g., the SDS). Coverage of content is quite variable. When compared against one another, the reviewed scales give very different weightings to different sets of symptoms. The depression scales generally neglect interpersonal symptoms, and in some instances they omit fairly basic diagnostic signs of depression. Content should be examined carefully in selecting instruments for different purposes.

The variation in content coverage also occurs across perspectives of evaluation. It is difficult to compare self-clinician, direct observation, and significant other reports when content as well as method varies. There are some instances of parallel forms across perspective, such as the SCL-90 and its self-report and parallel clinician rating forms; the SAS with self-report and clinician forms; and the KAS with self-report and significant other forms.

Format differences also create problems in comparing instruments. Some instruments offer statements and require a response, such as true-false or degree of agreement; others ask whether a symptom is present or absent or how frequently it occurs. Time frames vary from specific periods ("this last week"), to more general designations ("recently"), to other variations ("today" or "during the present episode"). These time frames may make a considerable difference in the response and the resulting severity index of the disorder.

Given the present status of development, instrument choice should be made with an eye to specific purpose. For the clinician, differential diagnosis is aided only partially by the available instruments. Severity can be well assessed against a variety of normative populations, but most instruments do not discriminate adequately between depression and other disorders.

The greater specificity of DSM-III diagnoses, together with the use of instruments such as the SADS, offer some decision rules for more reliable categorization. Little predictive validity has been established with the usual instruments. Evaluations of specific behaviors or constructs with the new instruments that attempt to measure depression core constructs may hold more promise for prediction of response to specific treatments. Instruments chosen for the evaluation of outcome should be considered in terms of content and perspective. Content should be surveyed to assure that syndromal depression is evaluated in a program focusing on specific targets. Perspectives should be surveyed in the context of the therapy situation (i.e., has change occurred from the perspective of the clinician, the patient, and the patient's significant others?).

For the researcher, population definition and description are especially important in depression since the disorder is heterogeneous and researchers may sample very differently. Populations should be defined by using instruments from more than one perspective. To assure comparability of disorder severity with other studies in a standardized fashion, subjects should meet criteria on at least one self-report and one clinician scale. The BDI, MMPI-*D*, and SDS are the most popular self-report instruments for this purpose. The SADS is probably the best instrument for research definition of a population. The Hamilton and Raskin scales are also popularly used for defining severity from the clinician's perspective.

Assessment for the purposes of differential treatment is an area much in need of attention by researchers. These is a need to look more generally at prediction in behavior therapy research, even in a post hoc manner. Outcome evaluation for research purposes presently necessitates a broad battery of assessment techniques to assess syndromal depression across content and perspective. Attention should be given to possible treatment by content or perspective interactions.

Future research will undoubtedly fill some of the voids in depression assessment. We are beginning to see new instruments assessing core constructs of depression which may provide treatment selection and prediction of response. We are also seeing instruments being developed for particular populations. For example, quite a few scales have been developed for assessing depression in children (Kaslow & Rehm, 1983; Rehm, Leventon, & Ivens, in press). A new assessment perspective may become more feasible as physiological procedures are developed. Promising research in at least two areas may soon produce useful methods: Schwartz, Fair, Salt, Mandel, and Klerman (1976) have demonstrated EMG differences in facial muscle patterns associated with both state and trait depression. Kupfer and Foster (1972) have demonstrated that EEG measurement of REM latency differs between depressives and normals and varies with clinical status. Most interestingly, Kupfer's research suggests that drug treatment response may be predicted from EEG response well before any clinical change is seen (Kupfer, Foster, Reich, Thompson, & Weiss, 1976). Biochemical assessments may also play more of a role in future.

What this area ultimately needs is a systematic battery covering important subsets of symptoms in parallel fashion across perspectives. Such a battery, in conjunction with instruments assessing core constructs, could provide the necessary comparability across many dimensions for clinical and research purposes.

SUMMARY

A number of problems can be identified relating to assessment of depression from a behavioral perspective. Depression is a heterogeneous construct assessed as a syndrome including many specific behaviors. A list of categories of depressive symptoms has been suggested for the purposes of the review. These include verbal-cognitive, overt motor, somatic, and interpersonal symptoms. Assessment instruments have been reviewed according to the perspectives of self-report, clinician rating, direct observation, and significant others. Instruments purporting to assess core deficits in depression were also reviewed briefly. Examples of the use of different assessment strategies in clinical studies were presented. Some of the deficiencies in existing instruments were pointed out and recommendations for the future were offered.

REFERENCES

Aiken, E. G., & Parker, W. H. (1965). Conditioning and generalization of positive self-evaluation in a partially structured diagnostic interview. *Psychological Reports, 17*, 459-464.

Aitken, R. C. B. (1969). Measures of feeling using analogue scales. *Proceedings of the Royal Society of Medicine, 62*, 989-993.

American Psychiatric Association. (1968). *Diagnostic and statistical manual of mental disorders: DSM-II.* Washington, DC: Author.

American Psychiatric Association. (1980). *Diagnostic and statistical manual of mental disorders: DSM-III.* Washington, DC: Author.

Andreasen, N. J. C., & Pfohl, B. (1976). Linguistic analysis of speech in affective disorders. *Archives of General Psychiatry, 33*, 1361-1367.

Bech, P., Gram, L. F., Dein, E., Jacobsen, O., Vitger, J., & Bolwig, T.G. (1975). Quantitative rating of depressive states. *Acta Psychiatrica Scandinavica, 51*, 161-170.

Beck, A. T. (1972). *Depression: Causes and treatment.* Philadelphia: University of Pennsylvania Press.

Beck, A. T., & Beamesderfer, A. (1974). Assessment of depression: The depression inventory. In P. Pichot (Ed.), *Psychological measurements in psychopharmacology. Modern problems in pharmacopsychiatry, Vol. 7.* Paris: Karger, Basel.

Beck, A. T., & Beck, R. W. (1972). Screening depressed patients in family practice: A rapid technique. *Postgraduate Medicine, 52,* 81–85.

Beck, A. T., Ward, C. H., Mendelsohn, M., Mock, J., & Erbaugh, J. (1961). An inventory for measuring depression. *Archives of General Psychiatry, 4,* 561–571.

Beck, A. T., Weissman, A., Lester, D., & Trexler, L. (1974). The measurement of pessimism: The hopelessness scale. *Journal of Consulting and Clinical Psychology, 42,* 861–865.

Beckham, E. E., & Adams, R. L. (1984). Coping behavior in depression: Report on a new scale. *Behaviour Research and Therapy, 22,* 71–75.

Berndt, D. J., Petzel, T. P., & Berndt, S. M. (1980). Development and initial evaluation of a Multiscore Depression Inventory. *Journal of Personality Assessment, 44,* 396–403.

Blumberry, W., Oliver, J. M., & McClure, J. N. (1978). Validation of the Beck Depression Inventory in a university population using psychiatric estimate as the criterion. *Journal of Consulting and Clinical Psychology, 46,* 150–155.

Blumenthal, M., & Dielman, T. (1975). Depressive symptomatology and role function in a general population. *Archives of General Psychiatry, 32,* 985–991.

Brown, G. W., & Harris, T. (1978). *Social origins of depression A study of psychiatric disorder in women.* New York: Macmillan Publishing Company.

Bunney, W. E., & Hamburg, D. A. (1963). Methods for reliable longitudinal observation of behavior. *Archives of General Psychiatry, 9,* 280–291.

Burrows, G. D., Foenander, G., Davies, B., & Scoggins, B. A. (1976). Rating scales as predictors of response to tricyclic antidepressants. *Australian and New Zealand Journal of Psychiatry, 10,* 53–56.

Caple, M. A., & Blechman, E. A. (1976). *Problem solving and self-approval training with a depressed single mother: Case study.* Paper presented at the meeting of the Association for Advancement of Behavior Therapy, New York, December 4, 1976.

Carroll, B. J., Fielding, J. M., & Blashki, T. G. (1973). Depression rating scales: A critical review. *Archives of General Psychiatry, 28,* 361–366.

Comrey, A. L. (1957). A factor analysis of items on the MMPI depression scale. *Educational and Psychological Measurement, 17,* 578–585.

Costello, C. G., & Comrey, A. L. (1967). Scales for measuring depression and anxiety. *Journal of Psychology, 66,* 303–313.

Coyne, J. C. (1976). Depression and the response of others. *Journal of Abnormal Psychology, 85,* 186–193.

Craig, T. J., & VanNatta, P. A. (1976a). Presence and persistence of depressive symptoms in patient and community populations. *American Journal of Psychiatry, 133,* 1426–1429.

Craig, T. J., & VanNatta, P. A. (1976b). Recognition of depressed affect in hospitalized psychiatric patients. *Diseases of the Nervous System, 37,* 561–566.

Dahlstrom, W. G., & Welsh, G. S. (1960). *An MMPI handbook: A guide to use in clinical practice and research.* Minneapolis: University of Minnesota Press.

Davies, B., Burrows, G., & Poynton, C. (1975). A comparative study of four depression rating scales. *Australian and New Zealand Journal of Psychiatry, 9,* 21–24.

Derogatis, L. R. (1977). *SCL-90 administration, scoring and procedures manual-I.* Johns Hopkins University Press.

Eaton, W. W., Holzer, C. E., Von Korff, M., Anthony, J. C., Helzer, J. E., George, L., Burnam, M. A., Boyd, J. H., Kessler, L. G., & Locke, B. Z. (1984). The design of the epidemiological catchment area surveys. *Archives of General Psychiatry, 41,* 942-948.

Ekman, P., & Friesen, W. V. (1974). Nonverbal behavior in psychopathology. In R. J. Friedman & M. M. Katz (Eds.), *The psychology of depression: Contemporary theory and research.* New York: Winston-Wiley.

Ellis, A. (1962). *Reason and emotion in psychotherapy.* New York: Stuart, 1962.

Endicott, J., & Spitzer, R. L. (1978). A diagnostic interview: The Schedule for Affective Disorders and Schizophrenia. *Archives of General Psychiatry, 35,* 837-844.

Endicott, N. A., & Jortner, S. (1966). Objective measures of depression. *Archives of General Psychiatry, 15,* 249-255.

Feighner, J. P., Robins, E., Guze, S., Woodruff, R. A., Winokur, G., & Munoz, R. (1972). Diagnostic criteria for use in psychiatric research. *Archives of General Psychiatry, 26,* 57-63.

Ferster, C. G. (1973). A functional analysis of depression. *American Psychologist, 28,* 857-870.

Fisch, H. U., Frey, S., & Hirsbrunner, H. P. (1983). Analyzing non-verbal behavior in depression. *Journal of Abnormal Psychology, 92,* 307-318.

Fuchs, C. Z., & Rehm, L. P. (1977). A self-control behavior therapy program for depression. *Journal of Consulting and Clinical Psychology, 45,* 206-215.

Green, B. L., Gleser, G. C., Stone, W. N., & Seifert, R. F. (1975). Relationships among diverse measures of psychotherapy outcome. *Journal of Consulting and Clinical Psychology, 43,* 689-699.

Grinker, R. R., Miller, J., Sabshin, M., Nunn, J., & Nunally, J. D. (1961). *The phenomena of depression.* New York: Harper & Row.

Grosscup, S. J., & Lewinsohn, P. M. (1980). Unpleasant and pleasant events and mood. *Journal of Clinical Psychology, 36,* 252-259.

Hamilton, M. (1960). A rating scale for depression. *Journal of Neurology, Neurosurgery and Psychiatry, 23,* 56-61.

Hamilton, M. (1967). Development of a rating scale for primary depressive illness. *British Journal of School and Clinical Psychology, 6,* 278-296.

Hammen, C. L., & Krantz, S. (1976). Effect of success and failure on depressive cognitions. *Journal of Abnormal Psychology, 85,* 577-586.

Harris, R. E., & Lingoes, J. C. (1955). *Subscales for the MMPI: An aid to profile file interpretation.* Unpublished manuscript, The Langley Porter Neuropsychiatric Institute.

Harrow, M., Colbert, J., Detre, T., & Bakeman, R. (1966). Symptomatology and subjective experiences in current depressive states. *Archives of General Psychiatry, 14,* 203-212.

Hathaway, S. R., & McKinley, J. C. (1942). A multiphasic personality schedule (Minnesota): III. The measurement of symptomatic depression. *Journal of Psychology, 14,* 73-84.

Hathaway, S. R., & McKinley, J. C. (1951). *MMPI manual* (Rev. ed., 1951.) New York: The Psychological Corporation.

Hautzinger, M., Linden, M., & Hoffman, N. (1982). Distressed couples with and without a depressed partner: An analysis of their verbal interaction. *Journal of Behavior Therapy and Experimental Psychiatry, 13,* 307-314.

Heiby, E. M. (1982). A self-reinforcement questionnaire. *Behaviour Research and Therapy, 20,* 397-401.

Hersen, M., Bellack, A. S., Himmelhoch, J. M., & Thase, M. E. (1984). Effects of social skill training, amitriplyline, and psychotherapy in unipolar depressed women. *Behavior Therapy, 15,* 21-40.

Hersen, M., Eisler, R. M., Alford, G. S., & Agras, W. S. (1973). Effects of token economy on neurotic depression: An experimental analysis. *Behavior Therapy, 4,* 392-397.

Hinchliffe, M., Lancashire, M., & Roberts, F. J. (1970). Eye contact and depression: A preliminary report. *British Journal of Psychiatry, 117,* 571-572.

Hinchliffe, M., Lancashire, M., & Roberts, F. J. (1971a). Depression: Defense mechanisms in speech. *British Journal of Psychiatry, 118,* 471-472.

Hinchliffe, M., Lancashire, M., & Roberts, F. J. (1971b). A study of eye-contact changes in depressed and recovered psychiatric patients. *British Journal of Psychiatry, 119,* 213-215.

Hogarty, G. E. (1975). Informant ratings of community adjustment. In I. E. Waskow & M. B. Parloff (Eds.), *Psychotherapy change measures.* Washington, DC: NIMH.

Hogarty, G. E., Goldberg, S. C., & Schooler, N. R. (1974). Drug and sociotherapy in the aftercare of schizophrenic patients, III. Adjustment of nonrelapsed patients. *Archives of General Psychiatry, 31,* 609-618.

Hollon, S. D., & Kendall, P. C. (1980). Cognitive self-statements in depression: Development of an automatic thoughts questionnaire. *Cognitive Therapy and Research, 4,* 383-397.

Humphrey, M. (1967). Functional impairment in psychiatric outpatients. *British Journal of Psychiatry, 113,* 1141-1151.

Ince, L. P. (1972). The self-concept variable in behavior therapy. *Psychotherapy: Theory, Research and Practice, 9,* 223-225.

Jacobson, N. S. (1981). The assessment of overt behavior in depression. In L. P. Rehm (Ed.), *Behavior therapy for depression: Present status and future directions* (pp. 279-299). New York: Academic Press.

Johansson, S., Lewinsohn, P. M., & Flippo, J. F. (1969). *An application of the Premack principle to the verbal behavior of depressed subjects.* Paper presented at the Meeting of the Association for Advancement of Behavior Therapy, Washington, DC.

Jones, R. G. (1968). *A factored measure of Ellis' irrational belief system.* Test Systems, Inc.: Wichita, KS.

Kaslow, N. J., & Rehm, L. P. (1983). Childhood depression. In R. J. Morris and T. R. Kratochwill (Eds.), *The practice of child therapy: A textbook of methods* (pp. 27-52). New York: Pergamon Press.

Katz, M. M., & Lyerly, S. B. (1963). Methods for measuring adjustment and social behavior in the community: Rationale, description, discriminative validity and scale development. *Psychological Reports, 13,* 503-535 (Monograph Supplement 4-V13).

Knesevich, J. W., Biggs, J. T., Clayton, P. J., & Ziegler, V. E. (1977). Validity of the Hamilton Rating Scale for Depression. *British Journal of Psychiatry, 131,* 49-52.

Kupfer, D. J., & Detre, T. P. (1971). Development and application of the KDS-1 in inpatient and outpatient settings. *Psychological Reports, 29,* 607-617.

Kupfer, D. J., Detre, T. P., Foster, F. G., Tucker, G. J., & Delgado, J. (1972). The application of Delgado's telemetric mobility recorder for human studies. *Behavioral Biology, 7,* 585-590.

Kupfer, D. J., & Foster, F. G. (1972). Interval between onset of sleep as an indicator of depression. *Lancet, 2,* 684–686.

Kupfer, D. J., & Foster, F. G. (1973). Sleep and activity in a psychotic depression. *Journal of Nervous and Mental Disease, 156,* 341–348.

Kupfer, D. J., Foster, F. G., Reich, L., Thompson, K. S., & Weiss, B. (1976). EEG sleep changes as predictors in depression. *American Journal of Psychiatry, 133,* 622–626.

Kupfer, D. J., Weiss, B. L., Foster, F. G., Detre, T. P., Delgado, J., & McPartland, R. (1974). Psychomotor activity in affective states. *Archives of General Psychiatry, 30,* 765–768.

Lamparski, D. M., Rehm, L. P., O'Hara, M. W., Kornblith, S. J., & Fitzgibbon, K. (1979, December). *Measuring overt behavioral differences in unipolar depressed, bipolar depressed and normal subjects: A multivariate analysis.* Paper presented at the meeting of Association for Advancement of Behavior Therapy, San Francisco, CA.

Lang, P. J. (1968). Fear reduction and fear behavior: Problems in treating a construct. In J. M. Shlien (Ed.), *Research in psychotherapy, III.* Washington, DC: APA.

Levitt, E. E., Lubin, B. (1975). *Depression: Concepts, controversies and some new facts.* New York: Springer.

Lewinsohn, P. M. (1968). *Manual of instruction for the behavior rating use for the observation of interpersonal behavior.* Unpublished manuscript, University of Oregon (revised, 1971).

Lewinsohn, P. M. (1974a). A behavioral approach to depression. In R. M. Friedman & M. M. Katz (Eds.), *The psychology of depression: Contemporary theory and research.* New York: Wiley.

Lewinsohn, P. M. (1974b). Clinical and theoretical aspects of depression. In K.S. Calhoun, H. E. Adams, & K.M. Mitchell (Eds.), *Innovative treatment methods of psychopathology.* New York: Wiley.

Lewinsohn, P. M. (1976). Activity schedules in treatment of depression. In J. D. Krumboltz & C. E. Thoresen (Eds.), *Counseling methods.* New York: Holt, Rinehart & Winston.

Lewinsohn, P. M., & Atwood, G. E. (1969). Depression: A clinical research approach. *Psychotherapy: Theory, Research and Practice, 6,* 166–171.

Lewinsohn, P. M. & Biglan, A. (1975). *Behavioral treatment of depression.* Paper presented at the Association for Advancement of Behavior Therapy, San Francisco.

Lewinsohn, P. M., Biglan, A., & Zeiss, A. M. (1976). Behavioral treatment of depression. In P. O. Davidson (Ed.), *The behavioral management of anxiety, depression and pain.* New York: Brunner/Mazel.

Lewinsohn, P. M., & Graf, M. (1973). Pleasant activities and depression. *Journal of Consulting and Clinical Psychology, 41,* 261–268.

Lewinsohn, P. M., Larson, D. W., Munoz, R. F. (1982). The measurement of expectancies and other cognitions in depressed individuals. *Cognitive Therapy and Research, 6,* 437–446.

Lewinsohn, P. M., & Libet, J. (1972). Pleasant events, activity schedules and depressions. *Journal of Abnormal Psychology, 79,* 291–295.

Lewinsohn, P. M., & Shaffer, M. (1971). The use of home observation as an integral part of the treatment of depression: Preliminary report and case studies. *Journal of Consulting and Clinical Psychology, 37,* 87–94.

Lewinsohn, P. M., & Shaw, D. A. (1969). Feedback about interpersonal behavior as an agent of behavior change: A case study in the treatment of depression. *Psychotherapy and Psychosomatics, 17*, 82–88.

Lewinsohn, P. M., & Talkington, J. (1979). Studies on the measurement of unpleasant events and relations with depression. *Applied Psychological Measurement, 3*, 83–101.

Lewinsohn, P. M., Weinstein, M. S., & Alper, T. (1970). A behavioral approach to the group treatment of depressed persons: Methodological contribution. *Journal of Clinical Psychology, 26*, 525–532.

Libet, J., & Lewinsohn, P. M. (1973). The concept of social skill with special reference to the behavior of depressed persons. *Journal of Consulting and Clinical Psychology, 40*, 304–312.

Libet, J., Lewinsohn, P. M., & Javorek, F. (1973). *The construct of social skill: An empirical study of several measures on temporal stability, internal structure, validity, and structural generalizability.* Unpublished manuscript, University of Oregon.

Lloyd, C. (1980). Life events and depressive disorder reviewed: II. Events as precipitating factors. *Archives of General Psychiatry, 37*, 541–548.

Lubin, B. (1965). Adjective checklists for measurements of depression. *Archives of General Psychiatry, 12*, 57–62.

Lubin, B. (1966). Fourteen brief Depression Adjective Checklists. *Archives of General Psychiatry, 15*, 205–208.

Lubin, B. (1967). *Manual for the depression adjective checklists.* San Diego: Educational and Industrial Testing Service.

Lubin, B., Dupre, V.A., & Lubin, A.W. (1967). Comparability and sensitivity of set 2 (Lists E, F, and G) of the Depression Adjective Check Lists. *Psychological Reports, 20*, 756–758.

Lubin, B., & Himmelstein, P. (1976). Reliability of the Depression Adjective Check Lists. *Perceptual and Motor Skills, 43*, 1037–1038.

Lubin, B., Horned, C. M., & Knapp, R. R. (1977). Scores on adjective check list, Eysenck Personality Inventory, and Depression Adjective Check List for a male prison population. *Perceptual Motor Skills, 45*, 567–570.

Lubin, B., Hornstra, R. K., & Love, A. (1974). Course of depressive mood in a psychiatric population upon application for service and a 3- and 12-month reinterview. *Psychological Reports, 34*, 424–426.

Lunghi, M. E. (1977). The stability of mood and social perception measures in a sample of depressed in-patients. *British Journal of Psychiatry, 130*, 598–604.

MacPhillamy, D. J., & Lewinsohn, P. M. (1971). *The pleasant events schedule.* Unpublished manuscript, University of Oregon.

MacPhillamy, D. J., & Lewinsohn, P. M. (1972a). *The measurement of reinforcing events.* Paper presented at the 80th Annual Convention of the APA, Honolulu.

MacPhillamy, D. J., & Lewinsohn, P. M. (1972b). *The structure of reported reinforcement.* Unpublished manuscript, University of Oregon.

MacPhillamy, D. J., & Lewinsohn, P. M. (1974). Depression as a function of levels of desired and obtained pleasure. *Journal of Abnormal Psychology, 83*, 651–657.

MacPhillamy, D. J., & Lewinsohn, P. M. (1976). *Manual for the pleasant events schedule.* Unpublished manuscript, University of Oregon.

Marone, J., & Lubin, B. (1968). Relationship between set 2 of the depression adjective checklists (DACL) and Zung Self-rating Depression Scale (SDS). *Psychological Reports, 22*, 333–334.

Marsella, A., Sanborn, K., Kameoka, V., Shizuru, L., & Brennan, J. (1975). Cross-validation of self-report measures of depression among normal populations of

Japanese, Chinese, and Caucasian ancestry. *Journal of Clinical Psychology, 31,* 281–287.

May, A. E., Urquhart, A., & Tarran, J. (1969). Self-evaluation of depression in various diagnostic and therapeutic groups. *Archives of General Psychiatry, 21,* 191–194.

McLean, P. D., & Hakstain, A. R. (1979). Clinical depression: Comparative efficacy of outpatient treatments. *Journal of Consulting and Clinical Psychology, 47,* 818–836.

McLean, P. D., Ogston, K., & Grauer, L. (1973). A behavioral approach to the treatment of depression. *Journal of Behaviour Therapy and Experimental Psychiatry, 4,* 323–330.

McNair, D. M. (1974). Self-evaluations of antidepressants. *Psychopharmacológia, 37,* 281–302.

McNair, D. M., Lorr, M., & Droppleman, L. F. (1971). *EITS Manual for the Profile of Mood States.* San Diego: Educational and Industrial Testing Service.

Mendels, J. (1968). Depression: The distinction between syndrome and symptom. *British Journal of Psychiatry, 114,* 1549–1554.

Mendels, J. (1970). *Concepts of depression.* New York: Wiley.

Mendels, J., & Cochrane, C. (1968). The nosology of depression: The endogenous-reactive concept. *American Journal of Psychiatry, 124,* (May supplement), 1–11.

Mendels, J., Weinstein, N., & Cochrane, C. (1972). The relationship between depression and anxiety. *Archives of General Psychiatry, 27,* 649–653.

Michaux, W. W., Katz, M. M., Kurland, A. A., & Gansereit, K. H. (1969). *The first year out: Mental patients after hospitalization.* Baltimore: Johns Hopkins Press.

Miller, W. R., & Seligman, M. E. P. (1973). Depression and the perception of reinforcement. *Journal of Abnormal Psychology, 82,* 62–73.

Myers, J. K., Weissman, M. M., Tischler, G. L., Holzer, C. E., Leaf, P. J., Orvaschel, H., Anthony, J. C., Boyd, J. H., Burke, J. D., Kramer, M., & Stoltzman, R. (1984). Six month prevalence of psychiatric disorders in three communities. *Archives of General Psychiatry, 41,* 959–970.

Neufeld, R. J., Rogers, T. B., & Costello, C. G. (1972). Comparisons of measures of depression by the experimental investigation of single cases. *Psychological Reports, 31,* 771–775.

O'Hara, M. W., & Rehm, L. P. (1979). Self-monitoring, activity levels, and mood in the development and maintenance of depression. *Journal of Abnormal Psychology, 88,* 450–453.

Overall, J. E., & Gorham, D. R. (1962). The brief psychiatric rating scale. *Psychological Reports, 10,* 799–812.

Padfield, M. (1976). The comparative effects of two counseling approaches on the intensity of depression among rural women of low socio-economic status. *Journal of Counseling Psychology, 23,* 209–214.

Perris, C. (1966). A study of bipolar (manic-depression) and unipolar recurrent depressive psychoses. *Acta Psychiatrica Scandinavica, 42,* (supplement 194), 7–189.

Radloff, L. (1975). Sex differences in depression: The effects of occupation and marital status. *Sex Roles, 1,* 249–265.

Radloff, L. S. (1977). The CES-D scale: A self-report depression scale for research in the general population. *Applied Psychological Measurement, 1,* 385–401.

Raft, D., Spencer, R. F., Toomey, T., & Brogan, D. (1977). Depression in medical outpatients: Use of the Zung scale. *Diseases of the Nervous System, 38,* 999–1004.

Ranelli, C. J. (1978). *Nonverbal behavior and clinical depression.* Unpublished doctoral dissertation, University of Pittsburgh.

Raskin, A., Schulterbrandt, J., Reatig, N., & McKeon, J. J. (1969). Replication of factors of psychopathology in interview, ward behavior and self-report ratings of hospitalized depressives. *Journal of Nervous and Mental Disease, 148,* 87–98.

Raskin, A., Schulterbrandt, J., Reatig, N., & Rice, C. E. (1967). Factors of psychopathology in interview, ward behavior, and self-report ratings of hospitalized depressives. *Journal of Consulting Psychology, 31,* 270–278.

Regier, D. A., Myers, J. K., Kramer, M., Robins, L. N., Blazer, D. G., Hough, R. L., Eaton, W. W., & Locke, B. Z. (1984). The NIMH epidemiologic catchment area program. *Archives of General Psychiatry, 41,* 934–941.

Rehm, L. P. (1977). A self-control model of depression. *Behavior Therapy, 8,* 787–804.

Rehm, L. P. (1978). Mood, pleasant events and unpleasant events: Two pilot studies. *Journal of Consulting and Clinical Psychology, 46,* 849–853.

Rehm, L. P. (1981). A self-control therapy program for treatment of depression. In J. F. Clarkin & H. Glazer (Eds.), *Depression: Behavioral and directive treatment strategies* (pp. 68–100). New York: Garland Press.

Rehm, L. P. (1984). Self-management therapy for depression. *Advances in Behavior Research and Therapy, 6,* 83–98.

Rehm, L. P. (in press). The measurement of behavioral aspects of depression. In A. J. Marsella, R. Hirschfeld, & M. Katz (Eds.), *The measurement of depression: Clinical, biological, psychological and psychosocial perspectives.* New York: Guilford Press.

Rehm, L. P., Fuchs, C. Z., Roth, D. M., Kornblith, S. J., & Romano, J. (1979). A comparison of self-control and social skill treatments of depression. *Behavior Therapy, 10,* 429–442.

Rehm, L. P., & Kaslow, N. J. (1984). Behavioral approaches to depression: Research results and clinical recommendations. In C. M. Franks (Ed.), *New developments in behavior therapy* (pp. 155–229). New York: Haworth Press.

Rehm, L. P., Kaslow, N. J., & Rabin, A. S. (in press). Cognitive and behavioral targets in a self-control therapy program for depression. *Journal of Consulting and Clinical Psychology.*

Rehm, L. P., & Kornblith, S. J. (1979). Behavior therapy for depression: A review of recent developments. In M. Hersen, R. M. Eisler, & P. M. Miller (Eds.), *Progress in behavior modification, Vol. 7.* New York: Academic Press.

Rehm, L. P., Kornblith, S. J., O'Hara, M. W., Lamparski, D. M., Romano, J. M., & Volkin, J. (1981). An evaluation of major components in a self-control therapy program for depression. *Behavior Modification, 5,* 459–490.

Rehm, L. P., Leventon, B. G., & Ivens, C. (in press). Depression. In C. L. Frame & J.L. Matson (Eds.), *Handbook of assessment in childhood psychopathology.* New York: Plenum.

Rehm, L. P., & O'Hara, M. W. (1985). Item characteristics of the Hamilton Rating Scale for Depression. *Journal of Psychiatric Research, 19,* 31–41.

Reisinger, J. J. (1972). The treatment of "anxiety-depression" via positive reinforcement and response cost. *Journal of Applied Behavior Analysis, 5,* 125–130.

Robins, L. N., Helzer, J. E., Croughan, J., & Ratliff, K. S. (1981). National Institute of Mental Health Diagnostic Interview Schedule. *Archives of General Psychiatry, 38,* 381–389.

Robins, L. N., Helzer, J. E., Weissman, M. M., Orvaschel, H., Gruenberg, E., Burke, J. D., & Regier, D. A. (1984). Lifetime prevalence of specific psychiatric disorders in three sites. *Archives of General Psychiatry, 41*, 949–958.

Robinson, J. C., & Lewinsohn, P. M. (1973a). An experimental analysis of a technique based on the Premack principle for changing the verbal behavior of depressed individuals. *Psychological Reports, 32*, 199–210.

Robinson, J. C., & Lewinsohn, P. M. (1973b). Behavior modification of speech characteristics in a chronically depressed man. *Behavior Therapy, 4*, 150–152.

Rosenbaum, M. (1980). A schedule for assessing self-control behaviors: Preliminary findings. *Behavior Therapy, 11*, 109–121.

Rush, A. J., Khatami, M., & Beck, A. T. (1975). Cognitive and behavior therapy in chronic depression. *Behavior Therapy, 6*, 398–404.

Schnurr, R., Hoaken, P. C. S., & Jarrett, F. J. (1976). Comparison of depression inventories in a clinical population. *Canadian Psychiatric Association Journal, 21*, 473–476.

Schwab, J. J., Bialow, M. R., & Holzer, C. E. (1967). A comparison of two rating scales for depression. *Journal of Clinical Psychology, 23*, 94–96.

Schwartz, G. E., Fair, P. L., Salt, P., Mandel, M. R., & Klerman, G. L. (1976). Facial muscle patterning to affective imagery in depressed and nondepressed subjects. *Science, 192*, 489–491.

Seligman, M. E. P. (1974). Depression and learned helplessness. In R. J. Friedman & M. M. Katz (Eds.), *The psychology of depression: Contemporary theory and research.* New York: Winston-Wiley.

Seligman, M. E. P. (1975). *Helplessness: On depression, development and death.* San Francisco: Freeman.

Seligman, M. E. P., Abramson, L. Y., Semmel, A., & Von Bayer, C. (1979). Depressive attributional style. *Journal of Abnormal Psychology, 88*, 242–247.

Seligman, M. E. P., Peterson, C., Kaslow, N. J., Tanenbaum, R. L., Alloy, L. B., & Abramson, L. Y. (1984). Attributional style and depressive symptoms among children. *Journal of Abnormal Psychology, 93*, 235–238.

Shipley, C. R., & Fazio, A. F. (1973). Pilot study of a treatment for psychological depression. *Journal of Abnormal Psychology, 82*, 372–376.

Simon, J. I. (1966). A study of feelings and concerns in depressed patients. *Archives of General Psychiatry, 15*, 506–515.

Snaith, R. P., Ahmed, S. N., Mehta, S., & Hamilton, M. (1971). Assessment of the severity of primary depressive illness. *Psychological Medicine, 1*, 143–149.

Spitzer, R. L., Endicott, J., & Robins, E. (1975). Research diagnostic criteria. *Psychopharmacologia Bulletin, 11*, 22–25.

Spitzer, R. L., Endicott, J., & Robins, E. (1978). Research diagnostic criteria: Rationale and reliability. *Archives of General Psychiatry, 36*, 773–782.

Waxer, P. (1974). Nonverbal cues for depression. *Journal of Abnormal Psychology, 83*, 319–322.

Waxer, P. (1976). Nonverbal cues for depth of depression: Set versus no set. *Journal of Consulting and Clinical Psychology, 44*, 493.

Weckowicz, T. E., Muir, W., & Cropley, A. J. (1967). A factor analysis of the Beck Inventory of Depression. *Journal of Consulting Psychology, 31*, 23–28.

Weiss, B. L., Kupfer, D. J., Foster, F., & Delgado, J. (1974). Psychomotor activity, sleep, and biogenic amine metabolites in depression. *Biological Psychiatry, 9*, 45–53.

Weissman, A. (1978, November). *Development and validation of the Dysfunctional Attitude Scale (DAS).* Paper presented at the meeting of the Association for Advancement of Behavior Therapy, Chicago.

Weissman, M. M., & Bothwell, S. (1976). Assessment of social adjustment by patient self-report. *Archives of General Psychiatry*, *33*, 1111–1115.

Weissman, M. M., & Paykel, E. S. (1974). *The depressed woman: A study of social relationships*. Chicago: University of Chicago Press.

Weissman, M. M., Pottenger, M., Kleber, H., Ruben, H. L., Williams, D., & Thompson, W. D. (1977). Symptom patterns in primary and secondary depression. *Archives of General Psychiatry*, *34*, 854–862.

Weissman, M. M., Prusoff, B. A., & Newberry, P. (1975). *Comparison of CES-D, Zung Self-Rating Depression Scale and Beck Depression Inventory*, Progress Report, Yale University New Haven, CA.

Weissman, M. M., Sholomskas, D., Pottenger, M., Prusoff, B. A., & Locke, B.Z. (1977). Assessing depressive symptoms in five psychiatric populations: A validation study. *American Journal of Epidemiology, 106,* 203–214.

Wells, K. C., Hersen, M., Bellack, A. S., & Himmelhoch, J. (1977, December). *Social skills training for unipolar depressive females*. Paper presented at the meeting of the Association for Advancement of Behavior Therapy, Atlanta.

Williams, J. G., Barlow, D. H., & Agras, W. S. (1972). Behavioral measurement of severe depression. *Archives of General Psychiatry*, *27*, 330–333.

Winokur, G. (1973). The types of affective disorders. *Journal of Nervous and Mental Disease*, *156*, 82–96.

Wolpe, J. (1979). The experimental model and treatment of neurotic depression. *Behavior Research and Therapy*, *17*, 555–566.

Wolpe, J., & Lazarus, A. A. (1967). *Behavior therapy techniques*. Oxford: Pergamon Press.

Woodruff, R. A., Jr., Goodwin, D. W., & Guze, S. B. (1974). *Psychiatric diagnosis*. New York: Oxford University Press.

Zealley, A. K., & Aitken, R. C. B. (1969). Measurement of mood. *Proceedings of the Royal Society of Medicine*, *62*, 993–997.

Zeiss, A. M., Lewinsohn, P. M., & Munoz, R. F. (1979). Non-specific improvement effects in depression using interpersonal, cognitive, and pleasant events focused treatments. *Journal of Consulting and Clinical Psychology*, *47*, 427–439.

Zung, W. W. K. (1965). A self-rating depression scale. *Archives of General Psychiatry*, *12*, 63–70.

Zung, W. W. K. (1967). Factors influencing the Self-rating Depression Scale. *Archives of General Psychiatry*, *16*, 534–547.

Zung, W. W. K. (1969). A cross-cultural survey of symptoms in depression. *American Journal of Psychiatry*, *126*, 116–121.

Zung, W. W. K. (1974). *The measurement of depression*. Milwaukee: Lakeside Laboratories.

Zung, W. W. K., Richards, C. B., & Short, M. J. (1965). Self-rating depression scale in an outpatient clinic. *Archives of General Psychiatry*, *13*, 508–515.

11
Assessment of Social Skills

Robert E. Becker
Richard G. Heimberg

A person's ability to behave effectively in the broad range of social situations encountered throughout life may be an important determinant of emotional well-being and mental health. In recognition of this fact, behavior therapists have developed a number of strategies for the development of social skills. Social skills training attempts to help an individual learn effective social behavior through a combination of behavioral instructions, modeling, behavioral rehearsals, corrective feedback, and positive reinforcement. Social skills training procedures have been successfully applied to the treatment of difficulties in assertive behavior, conversational behavior, and effective self-presentation in job selection interviews. A variety of patient populations, ranging from shy college students to severely impaired psychiatric inpatients, have benefitted from social skills training interventions.

Successful efforts at social skills training are dependent upon the adequacy of the behavioral assessment of social skills. While this may appear to be stating the obvious, assessment of social skills is a difficult and complex endeavor. In the first portion of this chapter, we review the major issues that must be addressed by the clinician or researcher who becomes involved in the assessment of social skills. Thereafter, we survey the major approaches to the assessment of social skills, with specific attention devoted to the clinical interview, self-report assessment, role play assessment strategies, and self-monitoring procedures. In this effort, we will draw most heavily from the literature on assertive and heterosocial behavior. In the final section, we examine the application of behavioral assessment of social skills to the treatment of a depressed individual.

THE CONCEPT OF SOCIAL SKILLS

Researchers in the area of social skills assessment and training have experienced considerable difficulty in defining the concept of social skills. In fact, a survey of several major books and articles on the topic (Arkowitz, 1981; Bellack, 1979, 1983; Bellack & Hersen, 1979; Curran, 1979; Curran & Monti, 1982; Curran & Wessberg, 1981; Eisler & Frederiksen, 1980; Kelly, 1982; Spence & Shepherd, 1983) reveals that their authors have generally refrained from offering specific definitions of social skills. Instead, they have chosen to discuss the major issues and conceptual questions that face the researcher or clinician who becomes involved in social skills training or assessment. We shall do the same.

The Skill-Deficit Hypothesis

Social skills assessment and training are based on the notion that inadequate social behavior is a result of an inadequate behavioral repertoire. It is often assumed that the individuals in question suffer from a "social skills deficit," that is, they perform to the best of their ability but simply do not possess the requisite behavioral competencies to stand a reasonable chance of obtaining positive social outcomes. Skill deficits are presumed to arise from insufficient interaction opportunities, punishment of social behavior at an earlier stage of development, or a variety of other untoward social experiences. Poor social performance and/or social anxiety are viewed as the reasonable side effects of a deficient behavioral repertoire, and appropriate training in relevant social skills may lead to improved social performance, more positive outcomes, and the amelioration of social anxiety. In the words of Goldsmith and McFall (1975), the social skills approach

> assumes that each individual always does the best he can, given his physical limitations and unique learning history, to respond as effectively as possible in every situation. Thus, when an individual's "best effort" is judged to be maladaptive, this indicates the presence of a situation-specific skill deficit in the individual's repertoire. . . . . Whatever the origins of this deficit (e.g., lack of experience, faulty learning, biological dysfunction) it often may be overcome or partially compensated for through appropriate training in more skillful response alternatives. Presumably, once these new skills have been acquired and reinforced, they will displace any competing, less reinforcing maladaptive behaviors. (p. 51)

While the presumed skills deficit certainly exists for a large number of persons, inadequate social behavior may be the final outcome of a multitude of factors in the individual's history and social environment. We may directly observe socially inadequate performance, but it does not automatically follow that these inadequacies arise from inadequate skills or an impoverished behavioral repertoire. In fact, poor social performance may result from anxiety, negative self-evaluation, inadequate knowledge of the rules of social discourse, negative outcome expectations, or a variety of other factors. These factors may inhibit the display of competent social behavior by a skilled individual, contribute to the development of skills deficits, or interact with skills deficits to influence the quality of social performance exhibited by the individual.

One way of distinguishing between poor performance due to inadequate skills and poor performance due to behavioral inhibition is to conduct behavioral assessment under varying stimulus conditions. Several studies have examined the effects of instructional demand on the quality of assertive behavior in role-played social situations. Demand has been manipulated by asking subjects to respond as they naturally would in the role plays (low demand) or to respond as assertively and effectively as they possibly could (high demand). In studies of the assertive behavior of college students, high demand instructions have resulted in more assertive performance (Kolotkin & Wielkiewicz, 1984; Nietzel & Bernstein, 1976; Rodriguez, Nietzel, & Berzins, 1980) and in greater self-reported assertiveness (Westefeld, Galassi, & Galassi, 1980). Since these subjects were able to produce more assertive behavior on demand, their nonassertive response style may be more easily attributable to behavioral inhibition than to deficient behavioral skills. However, Heimberg, Becker, Isaacs, and Cotch (1981) found nonassertive psychiatric patients to be unresponsive to similar high-demand instructions, a finding consistent with a skills-deficit formulation.

This general analysis has several implications. *First*, while this chapter will focus on the measurement of social *behavior*, complete assessment requires attention to the other variables noted above. Such broadly based assessment is of considerable importance since an individual whose social performance suffers as a combined result of anxiety, negative self-evaluation, and deficient social skills may require different and more extensive intervention than the individual whose social difficulties are a direct function of an inadequate repertoire of social skills. *Second*, since specific instructions may affect the "output" of role-play tests, such as those described later in this chapter, instructions may also influence the degree of correspondence between role-play and real-life performance. *Third*, since there is ample evidence that social skills training results in improved social behavior with a number of client populations (Kelly, 1982), it is likely that it produces its effects through multiple channels, affecting anxiety and self-evaluation as well as increasing behavioral proficiency. *Finally*, the literature's extreme focus on social *skills* may be somewhat misleading. As behavioral assessors, our goal is to pinpoint strengths and weaknesses in the person's social performance and to examine the effects of several independent variables upon it. While skills or competencies may be a very real part of that assessment, they are just that — only a part.

Consequences Versus Response Quality

How are we to evaluate the quality of social behavior? Is a behavior socially skilled if it is performed smoothly, with a minimum of anxiety, and well-integrated with the responses of others — or must a person achieve his or her specific goal in an interaction before it can be judged successful? This is a complex question that has not been adequately resolved. However, the behavioral assessor/clinician may have to answer it on a daily basis.

Libet and Lewinsohn (1973) defined social skill as "the complex ability to maximize the rate of positive reinforcement and to minimize the strength of punishment from others" (p. 311). This definition suggests a strong emphasis on the consequences of a behavior in determining its skillfulness or adequacy. However, in emphasizing the consequences of a response, we are neglecting its general appropriateness (Curran, 1979). As pointed out by Arkowitz (1981), strict adherence to a consequence-oriented definition would label as unskilled the person who assertively and persistently expresses an unpopular opinion, but it would label as skilled the juvenile delinquent whose false bravado and assaultive behavior are supported by his peer group. Surely, this is not the intent.

As behavior therapists, we must certainly pay attention to the consequences of social behavior. However, as Curran (1979) aptly points out, when we train our clients in social skills, we are teaching them not only to conquer specific social situations but also to exhibit behaviors which are generally appropriate and have a *high probability* of achieving positive interpersonal outcomes. In other words, we focus on *the quality of the response*, thinking that if the client can perform *well*, positive outcomes will most likely occur a reasonable percentage of the time. By focusing on the quality of the response, we may facilitate generalization and reduce client concerns about catastrophic consequences.

While the quality of a response must certainly be related to the consequences it brings, extreme emphasis on consequences places the evaluation of performance beyond the individual's ultimate control. For instance, we can very assertively and skillfully ask someone to modify troublesome behavior. We can do our very best. The person's behavior may or may not change. Should this modify our judgments of the skillfulness of the response or the clients' right to feel good about the quality of their efforts?

Obviously, both the quality of a response and its effectiveness at achieving various consequences must be considered. But are they actually considered by potential clients and counselors, and how are these two factors balanced against each other? To answer this question, Heimberg and Etkin (1983) developed a questionnaire that presents a series of interpersonal conflicts. Each situation consists of a transgression, a verbal response, and an interpersonal consequence. Transgressions are followed by either skilled or unskilled responses (attempts to get the transgressor to change his or her behavior), and these are followed by positive (compliance) or negative (defiance) consequences. Versions of the questionnaire were presented to samples of undergraduate students and mental health counselors who were asked to rate the "goodness" of each response. While counselors considered the quality of the response and its attendant consequences equally, students considered only the consequences of a response. Unskilled responses leading to positive consequences were rated as "good," while skilled responses leading to negative consequences were rated poorly. The judgments of assertive and unassertive students did not differ. While this finding requires further elaboration, it suggests that the extent of clients' reliance on consequence standards should be routinely evaluated and may be a useful target for cognitive restructuring interventions.

Situation Specificity

The behavioral approach to the assessment of social skills relies heavily on the concept of situational specificity. Social skills are not considered to be personality traits that may be manifested in all situations. Rather, we may observe that an individual may behave skillfully in some social situations but not in others. The behavioral components and overall quality of a response may vary as a function of the characteristics of the situation.

Several studies by Hersen and colleagues have demonstrated the impact of situational context on social skills, or, more specifically, on the execution of assertive responses. Eisler, Hersen, Miller, and Blanchard (1975) exposed male psychiatric patients to a variety of role-play situations that were systematically varied on several dimensions, including the gender of the interaction partner and the familiarity of the interaction partner with the subject. The responses of the subjects to the role-play situations differed dramatically as a function of the situational variables. For example, subjects complied more often in interaction with men and requested behavior changes more often from women. Differences also appeared on several nonverbal measures and on a measure of overall response quality. Similar results have been reported in studies with female psychiatric patients (Hersen, Bellack, & Turner, 1978) and college students (Chiauzzi, Heimberg, & Doty, 1982; Skillings, Hersen, Bellack, & Becker, 1978). Our own findings suggest that the influence of situational variables becomes more potent as task complexity increases (Chiauzzi et al., 1982).

The notion of situational specificity suggests that an individual's behavior differs from situation to situation. However, it does not imply the absence of individual differences in social skills. Most of the studies cited (e.g., Eisler et al., 1975) also report differences between groups of subjects defined as high or low on the dimension of general assertive skill. Also, in other areas of psychology, studies have shown that the variance attributable to either situational factors or individual differences may be quite small in comparison to the variance accounted for by the interaction of situations, response classes, and individual differences (Curran, 1979). Isolation of individual difference variables that interact with situational variables may increase our predictive ability and increase our understanding of social skills. A study by Trower (1980) provides an excellent example of the interaction between individual and situational variables. Psychiatric patients were first sorted into groups on the basis of social skills (skilled–unskilled, an individual difference variable). Each subject then participated in a social interaction with two experimental assistants. Each interaction consisted of several phases in which the experimental assistants were differentially responsive to the social interaction attempts of the subject. Analysis of behavioral data revealed that subjects in the socially skilled group adjusted their behavior dramatically in accordance with the behavior of the experimental assistants while unskilled subjects did not. In other words, the socially unskilled subjects were less responsive to situational demands than were the skilled subjects. Such responsiveness is an important part of social skills.

What are the implications of situational specificity for behavioral assessment of social skills? Most obviously, the assessor cannot assume that behavior in one situation is representative of the same class of behaviors in another situation. First, behavior noted in the initial interview should not be taken as representative of behavior in the natural environment. Second, the behavior of interest must be assessed in each potential setting. A person's ability to handle an interpersonal conflict with a friend does not predict an ability to do so with the boss, coworkers, parents, children, or a spouse.

Response Class Independence

Not only are social skills specific to the situation in which they occur, but they are generally unrelated to each other. Teaching one component of a behavioral response (e.g., eye contact or voice volume) should not be expected to produce changes in other component skills. In fact, these behaviors are minimally correlated, and a large number of studies reveal that component skills change only when they are specifically focused upon in treatment. Skills not receiving treatment do not change until they are specifically targeted (Heimberg & Becker, 1981).

Response class independence is also demonstrated in studies that have treated one particular behavior class (e.g., assertive refusal) and assessed generalization to new situations in the same class and to situations involving a different behavior class (e.g., requests for behavior change). While most studies have shown some degree of generalization to new situations of the same type, generalization across response classes has not been well documented. McFall and Lillesand (1971) found that refusal training did not enhance subjects' ability to make requests. Similarly, Kelly, Frederiksen, Fitts, and Phillips (1978) found only minimal changes in the positive assertive skills of an individual patient after he had been trained in negative assertive skills. However, St. Lawrence, Hughes, Goff, and Palmer (1983) did find evidence for generalization across different response classes. Of course, these studies underscore the need for complete assessment. Not only must we attend to clients' performance in all relevant situations but we must assess all subclasses of social behavior related to clients' presenting concerns.

Environmental Support of Social Behavior

The earlier quote from Goldsmith and McFall (1975) suggests that once social skills have been acquired, they will meet with a positive reception. It is assumed that new social behaviors will be positively reinforced and maintained by social consequences that naturally occur in the client's everyday environment. However, particularly in the area of assertive behavior, this cannot be taken for granted. Several studies have now been conducted that examine the reactions of the recipient to various types of assertive behavior. While a complete review of this growing literature is beyond the scope of this chapter, a brief summary can communicate its flavor (see Delamater & McNamara, 1986, for a review). Compared to passive behavior, assertion has been perceived as more skilled and competent but less likeable (Kelly, Kern, Kirkley, Patterson, & Keane, 1980) and as less polite, more hostile, and less satisfying to the recipient (Woolfolk & Dever, 1979). Females behaving assertively have been evaluated more negatively than males exhibiting the same behaviors (Kelly et al., 1980), especially if the evaluators maintained traditionally-oriented views of the role of women in society (Kern, Cavell, & Beck, 1985). These findings suggest that assertive behavior may not be supported in the client's natural environment. On the brighter side, however, these negative effects of assertive behavior may be softened by training the client to include a friendly and polite acknowledgment of the needs of the other person in his or her assertive responses (Woolfolk & Dever, 1979). Also, it appears that negative assertion (e.g., assertive refusals or requests for behavior change by the other person) may be more positively received if the asserter has previously acted in a positive fashion toward the other person (St. Lawrence, Hansen, Cutts, Tisdelle, & Irish, 1985).

The Dynamics of Social Behavior

The observational assessment of social skills is still at a primitive level of development. Most assessment strategies currently in use focus exclusively on the measurement of the frequency or duration of specific target behaviors. Relatively little attention has been paid to other factors that may influence social effectiveness. We will examine several efforts in the area of heterosexual-social anxiety.

Measures of the frequency or duration of specific target behaviors have shown inconsistent ability to discriminate between anxious and nonanxious subjects. However, these subject groups have been repeatedly and reliably separated by global impressionistic ratings (Arkowitz, Lichtenstein, McGovern, & Hines, 1975; see Conger & Farrell, 1981, for an exception). If this is the case, what are raters attending to? Fischetti, Curran, and Wessberg (1977) and Peterson, Fischetti, Curran, and Arland (1981) contend that the timing and placement of responses may be a more important aspect of social competence than the raw frequency with which a response is emitted. In their research, socially competent and incompetent males (Fischetti et al., 1977) and females (Peterson et al., 1981) tested their "reinforcing skill" by viewing a videotape of a person of the opposite sex discussing both general and personal topics. Whenever they believed that it would be an appropriate time to make a gestural or verbal response to the speaker, they were to press a switch. Reinforcing skill was defined as the extent to which subjects systematically placed their responses in time intervals frequently employed by a socially competent criterion group. Competent and incompetent subjects did not differ in the absolute frequency of gestural or verbal responses. However, incompetent subjects were less likely to hit criterion intervals (showed less reinforcing skill) than their more competent counterparts. The findings for males were somewhat stronger than the findings for females.

Gottman, Markman, and Notarious (1977) have emphasized the sequential and reciprocal nature of interaction between husbands and wives. These investigators conducted a detailed analysis of the conditional probabilities of one spouse's behavior given the prior occurrence of a specific behavior by the other spouse. A similar analysis of the behavior of heterosocially anxious males in interaction with a peer female was recently conducted by Faraone and Hurtig (1985). Male subjects conversed with female partners on any topic for a period of 15 minutes. Sequential analyses of audiotapes revealed several important differences between anxious and nonanxious males. Nonanxious (high skill) males were more verbally productive, producing the same number of words as the female partner and more words than anxious males. Nonanxious males talked more about themselves, taking longer conversational turns to talk about their own experiences. They assisted the female partner by asking more questions when she spoke about herself or when she appeared to be "stuck." They exerted more stimulus control over the partner's behavior than she did over theirs (i.e., the female partner's behavior was more predictable from the nonanxious male's behavior than vice-versa. The nonanxious males were more likely to make positive evaluations of the conversation topic and less likely to initiate negative topics. Their assertions were more likely to be followed by an animated response from the partner.

A full and complex picture of the social behavior of the male subjects was provided by this analysis. At present, these methods are not practical for routine behavioral assessment. However, development of efficient and cost-effective methods for sequential analysis is an important task for the future.

Levels of Measurement

When we decide to evaluate an individual's social skills, what should we measure? While the answer to this crucial question should depend upon the purposes of the assessment, two major approaches have appeared in the literature. The *molecular* approach focuses on the observation and measurement of the specific behavioral components of a socially skillful response (e.g., eye contact, facial expression, voice volume and tone, etc.). The *molar* approach focuses on the evaluation of responses at a more general level, emphasizing observer's ratings of the skillfulness of a total behavioral act. Each approach has advantages and disadvantages.

The molar approach has been thoroughly discussed by Curran (1979) and Curran and Wessberg (1981). Raters, who may or may not have received specific training in the dimensions to be judged, observe a sample of naturalistic or roleplayed behavior and provide their ratings on Likert-type scales. Often these raters are selected from the population of interest, and their ratings may represent a reasonable approximation to the evaluations that subjects may achieve in real life. This would be the case when a group of undergraduate women are asked to provide ratings of the performances of date-shy undergraduate men. As a result, molar ratings may provide important information about clients' baseline level of functioning or their overall response to treatment. Because it is difficult to determine the specific basis on which molar ratings are determined, however, they provide little direction for the conduct of skills-training procedures.

The molecular approach, most common in the study of assertive social skills, is well represented in the work of Hersen, Bellack, and colleagues (Eisler, Miller, & Hersen, 1973; Romano & Bellack, 1980). The total, integrated response of the individual is broken down into its several behavioral components, and each component is separately observed and scored. This approach to assessment often requires a great deal more effort than molar assessment but provides abundant information on specific responses. Thus, molecular assessment is described as a necessary prerequisite for the conduct of social skills training (Bellack, 1983).

Molecular ratings have been criticized because individual components are poorly correlated and may be poorly related to general ratings of social skills or performance (Curran, 1979). However, it is possible that past failures to relate molecular and molar scores may have suffered from problems of subject and task selection (Bellack, 1983). Also, while molecular ratings have a spotty history of discriminating between skilled and unskilled subject groups (Arkowitz et al., 1975), studies that have employed multiple regression approaches have been more successful (Conger & Farrell, 1981; Romano & Bellack, 1980). In Romano and Bellack's (1980) study, observer-rated component behaviors accounted for nearly 60% of the variance in the ratings of social skills provided by a panel of community judges. In another study (Rose & Tryon, 1979), subjects' judgments of an actor's assertiveness were dramatically affected by manipulating several components of the actor's response.

Molar ratings provide general evaluations but little else. Molecular ratings provide very specific information that is necessary for treatment, but their relationship to social impact has been questioned. Although one approach to resolving this conflict has been to develop qualitiative rating scales for specific behavioral components (Bellack, 1983; Wallander, Conger, & Conger, 1985), the safest approach at present is to include both global and specific measures in all assessments of social skill.

Cognitive Operations and Social Skill

As noted earlier, complete assessment of social skills requires attention to several additional variables. In our own work, we have focused on three cognitive factors that appear to influence social performance. These include self-statements, social perception skills, and outcome expectations. These factors may act to inhibit or distort a behavioral response whether or not the person possesses adequate social skills.

The possible role of covert self-statements has been explored with nonassertive and heterosocially anxious subjects (Cacioppo, Glass, & Merluzzi, 1979; Glass, Merluzzi, Biever, & Larsen, 1982; Chiauzzi & Heimberg, 1983; Heimberg, Chiauzzi, Becker & Madrazo-Peterson, 1983; Gottman, 1976). In general, performance difficulties have been associated with a preponderance of negative self-statements, that is, thoughts that focus on the individual's inadequacies, task difficulties, or untoward consequences.

Social perception — the ability to identify and accurately interpret the behavior, feelings, and motives of other persons — has been related to social skill by Morrison and Bellack (1981). They argue persuasively that skilled social performance is unlikely if one cannot accurately read the other person's mood, the demands of the situation, etcetera. In fact, measures of social perception are highly correlated with skillfulness of responses to role-played social situations among psychiatric patients (Fingaret, Monti, & Paxson, 1985) and college students (Fischetti et al., 1984). Social-perception training has been included as a component of multicomponent social skills training programs for depressed individuals (Becker & Heimberg, 1985; Hersen, Bellack, Himmelhoch, & Thase, 1984), but their specific contribution to treatment outcome has not been evaluated.

Several studies of assertive behavior have highlighted the role of outcome expectations (Eisler, Frederiksen, & Peterson, 1978; Fiedler & Beach, 1978; Kuperminc & Heimberg, 1983). Each of these studies suggests that unassertive individuals believe that little positive and much negative will result if they assert themselves. It also appears that unassertive persons devalue both the potentially positive consequences of assertion and the potentially negative consequences of passivity as compared to assertive individuals (Kuperminc & Heimberg, 1983).

ASSESSMENT OF SOCIAL SKILLS

In this section we shift from the general to the specific and review the major technical approaches to social skills assessment, including the clinical interview, role-play assessments, self-report questionnaires, and self-monitoring procedures.

The Clinical Interview

In most instances, behavioral assessment begins with an office consultation and a clinical interview. The interview develops a functional analysis of the client's presenting concerns. An interview conducted to assess social skills should attempt to accomplish the following goals: (a) determine the specific settings in which social behavior is problematic, (b) determine the specific behavioral competencies necessary for effective performance in each target situation, (c) determine whether or not the client possesses the necessary competencies, (d) examine the antecedents and consequences for skilled and unskilled performance in each setting, and (e) determine what additional assessment procedures will be necessary to complete the behavioral assessment.

Despite its central and essential role in behavioral assessment, the behavioral interview has not been subjected to the same empirical examination as have other behavioral assessment devices (see Chapter 4 on behavioral interviewing, this volume). As a result, its adequacy as a behavioral assessment device remains open to question. Also, as noted previously, the situationally specific nature of social behavior makes generalizations from the interview to behavior in the natural environment a risky business. Thus, the behavioral interview is best conceptualized as the starting point for assessment or, alternatively, as a device for generating hypotheses about the client's social behavior that may then be investigated or validated by other procedures. Overreliance on interview-generated data may lead the behavioral assessor to false conclusions.

In order to accomplish the five goals mentioned, we have utilized a semi-structured interview format that is derived from work on the behavioral assessment of assertiveness by Galasi and Galassi (1977). The guide for this interview is a simple matrix in which the columns represent various types of important social behaviors (negative assertion, positive assertion, conversational behavior) and the rows represent various persons with whom the client might interact (e.g., spouse, supervisor, friend). The client is questioned about the behavior required in each cell of the matrix (e.g., positive assertion with spouse) and asked to rate the difficulty he or she experiences performing the behavior in the target situation using a 1–100 Subjective Units of Discomfort Scale. After all cells in the matrix have received attention, the client is asked to reconsider his or her ratings and provide us with a rank ordered list of behavior-by-situation combinations. While reliability and validity data are not currently available for this procedure, it is our experience that client difficulties tend to cluster around specific behaviors, situations, or combinations. This procedure provides the behavioral assessor with the information necessary to construct personalized role-play assessments or to select situations and behaviors that the client may self-monitor.

Role-Play Assessment

It is often stated that the hallmark of behavioral assessment is the direct observation of the target behavior in the client's natural environment. It is important to observe the client's social behavior in order to best understand his or her behavioral deficits. However, in the context of social behavior, this is rarely practical. Social behaviors occur at unpredictable times and places; as a result, scheduling of behavioral observations may become a minor nightmare. Also, the very nature of social behavior is such that it may occur *only* when it is not being observed. Consider the practical and ethical dilemmas involved in observing heterosocial behavior or the impossibility of observing a client in assertiveness training request a raise from his boss.

In an attempt to circumvent these problems but maintain the ability to observe social behavior, researchers have developed a number of role-play assessment strategies. In role-play assessments, a situation is artificially created, and the client is asked to act as if it were actually happening. Behaviors observed in response to role-play stimuli are assumed to represent behavior as it might occur in the real situation. In this section, several of these strategies will be described and evaluated.

Role-play assessment procedures are many and varied. A complete review of available devices is beyond the scope of this chapter; however, they tend to fall into a number of categories that may be useful to describe. These are single-response role plays, multiple-response role plays, and naturalistic interactions. The first role-play tests to be developed were of the single-response variety (Eisler, Miller, & Hersen, 1973; Eisler et al., 1975; McFall & Marston, 1970). In the prototypical single-response role play, a stimulus situation is described to the client, a prompt line is delivered to the client by an experimental assistant (or by audiorecording), and the client is asked to make a response. After a brief response from the client, the situation is terminated, and a new one is introduced, etcetera, as illustrated in the following example from the Behavioral Assertiveness Test — Revised (Eisler et al., 1975):

> *Narrator:* You have been working for the same company for a year-and-a-half without a raise in pay. You feel that you have been doing very good work for the company and go in to see the boss about a raise.
> *Role Model Prompt:* "I'm not sure you really deserve a raise at this time."

One of the benefits of single-response role-play methodology is the relative ease with which a wide variety of stimulus situations may be assessed. Stimuli are easily standardized, and role-play personnel may perform their duties with a minimum of training. As a result of these and other factors, the literature is loaded with studies that utilize single-response role plays. Regardless of their good points, however, single-response role plays have been challenged on several grounds (Bellack, 1983). Single exchanges rarely occur in real-life interactions, and, as a result, subjects may feel extremely uncomfortable with this restricted format. Second, many individuals with interpersonal problems may not get into trouble unless the interpersonal partner is uncooperative. Many individuals may be able to assert themselves once, but if the first response is rebuffed, they break down. Obviously, this pattern cannot be detected with a single-response methodology. Third, as discussed in a later section of this chapter, studies have failed to support the validity of single-response role plays.

In a multiple-response role play, the subject's first response is followed by another prompt from the confederate. As the number of prompt-response couplets increase, the role play should increasingly come to resemble a real-life interaction. The following is an example of a multiple-response stimulus situation (Galassi and Galassi, 1977):

> You've gone to lunch at a restaurant. You've ordered a chef salad with thousand island dressing. However, when you get your salad, it has blue cheese dressing on it. You prefer thousand island. The waiter/waitress is approaching your area now.
> Waiter/Waitress: Is everything okay?
> Trainee:
> Waiter/Waitress: I distinctly remember you ordering blue cheese dressing.
> Trainee:
> Waiter/Waitress: I have it written right here on my slip — blue cheese.
> Trainee:
> Waiter/Waitress: All right, I'll be back in a few minutes. (p. 128)

In the multiple-response format, the behavior of the interpersonal partner becomes a more central focus. Bellack (1983), for instance, has questioned the common strategy of providing the role-play partner with a number of specific prompts that are to be delivered in a precise sequence. While this strategy insures consistency in confederate behavior, it also increases the likelihood that some subjects will receive confederate prompts that do not follow logically from their immediately previous response. Bellack (1983) suggests that confederates be trained to respond "within a narrow range, preventing excessive variability while insuring relevance" (p. 38). The wisdom of this statement is reflected in the results of three recent studies which demonstrated that the responsiveness of the confederate to the subject affected observer ratings of the subject's social skills (Mahaney & Kern, 1983; Moisan-Thomas, Conger, Zellinger, & Firth, 1985; Steinberg, Curran, Bell, Paxson, & Munroe, 1982).

Single- and multiple-response role plays have been most extensively utilized in the assessment of assertive behavior. As noted by Bellack (1979), these strategies may be best suited to assess the ability to make quick, pointed responses to a variety of different situations. In contrast, the assessment of heterosocial skill has relied most heavily on relatively unstructured "naturalistic" interactions. Typically, the subject is asked to interact with an opposite-sex confederate for a few minutes. A specific situation that the subject and confederate are to role play is sometimes described (e.g., they are together at a restaurant after seeing a movie together). Occasionally, the subject and confederate are simply instructed to get to know each other, and the confederate is trained to act in a positive, receptive manner but to leave the bulk of the conversational responsibility on the subject.

Regardless of the format adopted for role-play assessment, the behavioral assessor will be faced with a decision about the specific target behaviors to be assessed. As noted earlier, the wisest course may be to assess social performance at both the molar and molecular levels. However, we will focus our attention on molecular measurement. Since the early work of Eisler et al. (1973, 1975), molecular assessment has focused on the measurement of specific behavioral components. These measures have focused on the frequency (occurrence/ nonoccurrence) or duration of verbal and nonverbal events relevant to the specific class of behavior under investigation (e.g., positive or negative assertive skills). Typical measures have included response latency, response duration, voice volume, intonation, smiling, gazing, speech disruptions, requests for behavior change, compliance with unreasonable requests, expressions of praise or appreciation, gestures, etcetera. Multiple-response role plays sometimes include a measure of persistence (i.e., the number of responses a subject makes before yielding to an unreasonable request). Obviously, the number of potential measures is large. The task for the behavioral assessor is to determine which of these responses is relevant to the behavioral performance of the individual client.

These measures have historically been scored as if they fell on a linear dimension. That is, more (or less) of a specific behavior has been defined as skilled while less (or more) of a behavior has been defined as unskilled. However, history has taught us that this strategy is unwise, even naive. Some examples may serve to clarify this point. Among psychiatric inpatients, who tend to be withdrawn and unresponsive, an increase in response duration may be regarded as a positive treatment target. Among higher-functioning groups, such as unassertive college students, positive treatment outcome may be associated with a reduction in response duration. In the latter case, subjects may be trained to stop "beating around the bush" and get straight to the point, a far different goal than would be appropriate for many schizophrenic patients. In studies of depressed patients (Bellack, 1983; Hersen et al., 1984), the subject sample included both underresponsive and overresponsive subjects.

Measures like response latency, gaze, or voice volume may also be viewed from a curvilinear perspective. Too much or too little of the behavior may be maladaptive, whereas a moderate amount of the behavior may be optimal (Bellack, 1983; Trower, Bryant, & Argyle, 1978). Subjects who never look at the person they are interacting with are obviously deficient; subjects who never look away from the other person may also need to modify their behavior. Recent research suggests that skilled subjects look away from the listener while they are speaking but maintain gaze while listening to the other person (Duncan & Fiske, 1977). With this in mind, it is important to devise measures that will accurately pinpoint problematic behavior. One solution, suggested by Trower et al. (1978), is to utilize multidirectional rating scales. For instance, voice volume might be rated on a scale from 0 to 4. A score of 0 might represent normal volume. A score of 2 might represent volume that is too quiet (or too loud), and a 4 might represent volume that was extremely loud (or barely audible).

As noted earlier, role-play assessments are intended to replicate behavior that occurs in real life. That is, we should expect that role-play measures be externally valid and that they maintain a high correspondence to day-to-day behavior in similar situations. In the 1970s, such correspondence was simply assumed. A number of studies, particularly in the area of assertiveness, demonstrated that known groups of subjects could be discriminated against on the basis of their role-play performance and that subjects receiving assertiveness training improved on measures of role-play performance (McNamara & Blumer, 1982). However, several studies have now made us question the assumption of external validity. The initial series of studies was conducted by Bellack, Hersen, and colleagues and evaluated the external validity of the Behavioral Assertiveness Test — Revised (Bellack, Hersen, & Turner, 1978) or a similar device for the assessment of heterosocial skills (Bellack, Hersen, & Lamparski, 1979). The first study showed a dramatic lack of correspondence between role-play measures and criterion measures; the second showed only a moderate relationship.

These initial studies focused specifically on the evaluation of single-response role plays, and their results should not be generalized beyond. Variations in role-play methodology may affect the relationship between role play and criterion measures. In addition, these studies have been criticized because the role-play and criterion situations were not maximally similar (Curran, 1978; Higgins, Alonzo, & Pendleton, 1979). Bellack, Hersen, and Turner (1979) conducted a follow-up study in which they attempted to match single-response role-play situations and criterion situations and, again, failed to support the validity of role-play assessments.

Higgins and colleagues conducted a series of studies that focused on a limited number of situations but went to great lengths to assure the identity of role-played and criterion situations (Higgins et al., 1979; Higgins, Frisch, & Smith, 1983). In the first study (Higgins et al., 1979), subjects were confronted with an experimenter who attempted to withhold credit for experimental participation from subjects because a bogus second subject failed to appear. The experimenter engaged in a preprogrammed series of requests to reschedule the subject for a later session. In the second study (Higgins et al., 1983), subjects interacted with a confederate (posing as another subject), who made a series of escalating requests to borrow class notes. In both studies, some subjects were informed of the role-played nature of the interaction while others were led to believe it was real. In both studies, informed subjects behaved more assertively than uninformed subjects. However, a replication of Higgins et al. (1979) conducted by St. Lawrence, Kirksey, and Moore (1983) found no differences between subjects in informed and uninformed conditions.

Two studies by Kern (1982) and Kern, Miller, and Eggers (1983) suggest that role-play performances may more closely approximate naturalistic behavior under the right stimulus conditions. In the study by Kern (1982), waiting-room interactions between subjects and confederates were unobtrusively videotaped, and subject performance was compared to one of three types of role plays: (a) single-response, (b) extended interactions in which subjects and confederates acted as if they were at a pizza parlor after a date, and (c) "replication" role plays. In the replication role-play condition, subjects were told that the waiting-room interaction had been videotaped and that their goal was to behave as they had during that waiting-room period. As in the studies by Higgins and colleagues, all role plays resulted in higher levels of performance than the unobtrusive waiting-room measures. However, replication role plays achieved a close correspondence to the criterion. In the second, methodologically similar study (Kern et al., 1983), subjects again engaged in three types of role plays: (a) "typical" role plays, in which subjects were asked to respond as if they were in a waiting room, (b) replication role plays, and (c) specification role plays, in which subjects were asked to recreate three randomly chosen behavioral components of their waiting-room behavior. While typical role plays did not approximate behavior in the waiting room, replication role plays produced a much closer match, and specification role plays demonstrated the strongest relationship with the criterion. It appears, at least under these specific circumstances, that subjects can produce realistic samples of behavior during role-play assessments.

Several studies have demonstrated that subjects behave more skillfully while role playing than during more naturalistic interactions (Higgins et al., 1979, 1983; Kern, 1982). However, in the study by Kern et al. (1983), typical and replication role plays resulted in higher ratings of performance than did the criterion situation, whereas specification role plays did not. Kern et al. suggest that typical and replication role plays may sample response capabilities while specification role plays may tap naturalistic performance.

From another perspective, the importance of differences between performances in role-play and naturalistic interactions depends upon the rank ordering of subjects in both behavior samples. That is, the fact that individuals may behave more assertively during role play than criterion situations is less critical if they maintain their relative rank ordering in both assessments. Wessberg, Mariotto, Conger, Farrell, and Conger (1979), in a study of role-played heterosocial interactions, also reported that subjects behaved more skillfully during role plays than during unobtrusively observed waiting-room interactions. Subjects also rated the role plays as significantly less like real life and less like everyday heterosocial interactions than the waiting-room interactions. However, molar ratings of skill and anxiety in role plays were substantially correlated with similar measures from the waiting room ($rs = .62$, .68, respectively). Judges ranked subjects quite similarly on anxiety and skill across the two conditions.

There is some evidence that studies relying on molar measurement may demonstrate better external validity than studies focusing on molecular measures (McNamara & Blumer, 1982; Wessberg et al., 1979; Wessberg et al., 1981). However, this should not be regarded as surprising since it is the composite of molecular behaviors, rather than the behaviors individually, that comprise social skill. In a recent study by Blumer and McNamara (1982), canonical correlational procedures were used to relate molecular measures from role-play and criterion situations. This is a creative use of multivariate procedures to assess the total impact of molecular behaviors across the two situations. Canonical correlations for both verbal and nonverbal behaviors showed the two sessions to be highly related.

Bellack (1983) suggests that the data on the external validity of role-play assessments are sufficiently positive to justify their continued use, especially in the absence of viable alternatives. However, he contends that role-play stimuli should be made as relevant as possible for subjects. He suggests that subjects be allowed to preview and imaginally prepare for each interaction and that the scene content to be slightly altered to accommodate differences in subjects' experiences. Scene descriptions should be expanded to provide as much realistic information as possible. Such changes may increase the probability that subjects will make ecologically valid role-play responses. In addition, the relevance of role-play stimuli may be increased if the role-play situations are derived directly from the actual experiences of the individual subject.

This point was addressed in a study by Chiauzzi, Heimberg, Becker, and Gansler (1985). In this study, depressed patients were engaged in behavioral assessment, including two kinds of multiple-response role plays. The first was a set of standard role plays typical of those employed in social skills research. The second was a set of "personalized" role plays: that is, situations drawn from critical incidents in individual patients' lives and cast into the same format as the standard scenes. Patients reported greater discomfort while role playing personalized scenes. They also took longer to respond and spoke longer, at a lower volume, and with more speech disturbances. In other words, they performed less skillfully in response to personalized than standard scenes. Measures derived from personalized scenes also showed a stronger relationship to measures of depressed mood.

It is difficult to provide a succinct summary of the research on the external validity of role-play assessments. Studies have utilized a variety of research designs and role-play formats. However, the following conclusions appear warranted:

1. Single-response role plays have outlived their usefulness and should be retired.
2. Other role play strategies may enjoy a brighter future, but their specific configuration may determine their validity and clinical utility.
3. Role plays that maximize client involvement, that utilize personally relevant stimulus materials, and that instruct clients to replicate a specific behavioral event may have the greatest utility.

However, we must ask ourselves if we require too much of our assessment devices. Is it realistic to expect a close correspondence between role play and actual behavior when (a) behavior in both settings is situation specific, (b) when we have yet to agree on the most important parameters of the conduct of role plays, (c) when we have yet to agree on adequate measures of gathering behavior during role plays, and (d) when the criterion situations in external validity studies are unusual ones of potentially limited relevance to subjects? If we do not view role-play assessments with some caution, then we are naive. If we view them as invalid or as incapable of being valid, we have thrown out the proverbial baby with the bath water!

Maybe we should ask what role plays can tell us rather than try to determine their precise degree of correspondence with actual behavior. If a person exhibits a skilled social response in role play but fails to do so in real life, what have we learned? External validity is not a relevant question; if the person exhibits the skill, then it resides, by definition in his or her behavioral repertoire. The role play is not invalid, the person's behavior simply varied from role play to the other situation. We might then surmise that the person suffers from a variety of ills beyond the presumed skill deficit and assess for cognitive inhibition, poor social perception skills, low outcome expectations, prohibitive physiological arousal, etc. In this case, at least, the difference between role-played and actual behavior may aid the assessment process, not hinder it.

Self-Report Assessment

A large number of self-report devices have been developed for the assessment of general social functioning and for the major subclasses of social behavior such as assertiveness and heterosocial performance. Hersen and Bellack (1977) noted 18 such inventories, and several more have appeared in the intervening decade. Hence, a thorough review of the self-report assessment of social skills is a monumental task and one well beyond the scope of this chapter. This section highlights several of the issues important to the self-report assessment of social skills.

To begin, it is important to note that self-report assessment is just that. It is clients' or subjects' report of their *perceptions* of their behavior. Self-report scores therefore represent an important piece of a total assessment battery, but they should not be confused with veridical reports of behavior that may be expected to relate meaningfully to other indices of behavior. As we noted with role-play assessment, a mismatch between behavior and self-report should not automatically be taken as evidence for the invalidity of self-report. Rather, it may be viewed as useful information about the lack of concordance between a person's performance and his/her perception of that performance.

One crucial issue in any type of self-report assessment is (or should be) readability. Many self-report measures were originally developed on samples of college undergraduates but have come to be employed with clients in a broad range of settings. We simply cannot assume that clients in this more heterogeneous group can adequately read and understand these written materials. Andrasik, Heimberg, Edlund, and Blankenberg (1981) assessed the readability of 11 commonly used assertiveness inventories. Instructions for most scales required a high school reading level. Inventory items were generally more readable but spanned the range from 7th to 12th grade. A recent study by McCormick (1985) underscores the importance of readability for self-report assessment of assertiveness. Only 7% of a sample of offenders were able to successfully complete the Rathus (1973) Assertiveness Schedule while 97% could complete a simplified version of the scale.

Factor analytic studies of assertiveness scales (reviewed by Beck & Heimberg, 1983) reveal that most scales are multifactorial, with some studies reporting their scale to include as many as 12 independent factors (Hull & Hull, 1978). Yet investigators of assertiveness or assertion training persist in using total scale scores as an overall index of assertive behavior. Bellack (1979) and Beck and

Heimberg (1983) have raised serious concerns about this practice. Since scales consist of multiple factors that vary in number of items, total scores may obscure the meaning of responses for individual subjects. Also, since assertive behavior is situation specific, total scores may mask these situational variations. It may be more appropriate to report individual factor scores and ignore total scores. However, this strategy would require attention to the psychometric development of factor scores as well.

Bellack (1979) also notes similarity across scales in item *content* but wide variability among scales in item *format*. Inventories differ in how they ask questions. Some rely on yes-no or true-false formats while others use Likert-type rating scales. Some provide descriptions of scale points, others do not. Items may be directed at how subjects behave, how much difficulty they have, how frequently they emit various behaviors, how anxious they are, or how effectively they perform. To date, no studies exist which evaluate the impact of scale format on subjects' responses.

Traditional psychometric issues, such as social desirability response set, also deserve attention in the self-report assessment of assertiveness. Investigations of the relationship of social desirability and self-report of assertiveness have yielded conflicting results (Appelbaum, 1976; Rock, 1981). However, a study by Kiecolt and McGrath (1979) demonstrates how social desirability might affect the assessment of assertive behavior. After a course of assertion training, high scorers on a social desirability measure reported themselves to be more assertive on the Assertion Inventory (Gambrill & Richey, 1975) than low social desirability scorers. On a behavioral test, however, high scorers actually demonstrated less adequate behavior.

Beck and Heimberg (1983) review data on norms, reliability, and validity of eight commonly used assertiveness scales: the Wolpe-Lazarus Assertiveness Schedule (Wolpe & Lazarus, 1966); its revision by Hersen et al. (1979); the Assertion Inventory (Gambrill & Richey, 1975); the Adult Self-Expression Scale (Gay, Hollandsworth, & Galasi, 1975); the College Self-Expression Scale (Galassi, DeLo, Galassi, & Bastien, 1974); the Rathus (1973) Assertiveness Schedule; the Conflict Resolution Inventory (McFall & Lillesand, 1971); and the Assertion Questionnaire (Callner & Ross, 1976). A summary of their conclusions follows.

The inventories vary greatly in the amount of attention devoted to their psychometric development. The most extensive normative data base exists for the Rathus scale. Several samples of students have been reported, including z-scores and percentile ranks for both total and individual item scores (Quillen, Besing, & Dinning, 1977). Norms are also available for psychiatric patients (Rathus & Nevid, 1977) and criminal offenders (Heimberg & Harrison, 1980). No norms are available for several of the questionnaires, a situation that renders interpretation of results extremely hazardous.

Test-retest reliability coefficients have been reported for all scales except the original Wolpe-Lazarus. Only the revised Wolpe-Lazarus scales appear problematic in this regard. However, there is a need to examine temporal stability over more extended intervals than typically reported. Internal consistency analyses have been reported only for the Rathus and revised Wolpe-Lazarus scales.

Data on the validity of the assertiveness scales are much weaker than data on their reliability. Beck and Heimberg (1983) examined the scales' sensitivity to treatment effects, correlations among scales, and the relationship of scale scores to independent criteria. Five scales had received no attention. The Rathus Assertiveness Schedule, the Conflict Resolution Inventory, and the College Self-Expression Scale have been subjected to the most intensive analysis, and a base of validity information has been generated. The Conflict Resolution Inventory fares best in all areas, especially sensitivity to the differences among treatment and control groups. The other two scales, while showing similar promise, have not been as heavily utilized or scrutinized. Because of its specific focus on college students' ability to refuse unreasonable requests, however, the Conflict Resolution Inventory may have somewhat limited clinical utility.

An additional sobering note comes from a study by Wallander, Conger, Mariotto, Curran, and Farrell (1980), who examined the comparability of the four major self-report instruments for the assessment of heterosocial anxiety and performance: the Survey of Heterosexual Interactions (Twentyman & McFall, 1975), the Social Avoidance and Distress Scale (Watson & Friend, 1969), the Situation Questionnaire (Rehm & Marston, 1968), and the Social Activity Questionnaire (Arkowitz et al., 1975). After a variety of sophisticated statistical analyses, they concluded that subject samples derived by using each of the instruments were relatively independent from one other. That is, there was little advantage to knowing a subject's score on one instrument in predicting classification on another. Presumably, results from studies utilizing one selection instrument may not be safely generalized to samples selected with another. The difficulties this situation may pose to efforts for developing a meaningful fund of knowledge about heterosocial performance are vast.

Self-Monitoring of Social Behavior

Self-monitoring procedures have been extremely underutilized in the assessment of social skills. Self-monitoring has certain liabilities as an assessment strategy. For instance, it is known to produce reactive effects; that is, self-monitoring may actually produce changes in the target behavior (Kazdin, 1974; Nelson, 1977). While reactivity may have positive implications for the use of self-monitoring as a treatment intervention, its effect on the adequacy of clinical assessment information is unknown. Additionally, subjects may have difficulty with the accurate observation of their own behavior or may selectively attend to the behavior's negative aspects (Roth &

Rehm, 1980). They may fail to record behaviors as the behaviors occur, and records may be open to omissions and distortions of memory. Nevertheless, properly structured self-monitoring records may provide important information in several areas of interest to the behavioral assessor.

Self-monitoring may provide the only practical record of the frequency with which specific behavioral events occur in the natural environment. While a self-monitoring record is unlikely to provide meaningful information on the molecular components of social skills (e.g., eye contact or response latency), target events such as the number of conversations initiated with a member of the opposite sex, telephone calls, assertive behaviors, self-disclosures, etc., are more easily monitored. Similarly, subjective reactions to these events may be monitored by requesting subjects to provide ratings of anxiety or satisfaction with each targeted event.

Behavioral analysis of social performance deficits may be enhanced via the use of self-monitoring procedures. When the subject records the occurrence of a targeted event, several other characteristics of the event may be recorded, including: (a) the time of day, (b) the day of the week, (c) the location of the interaction, (d) the type of interaction, (e) the nature of the relationship with the interaction partner, (f) whether or not other persons were present, (g) whether or not other types of activity were involved, (h) the subject's anxiety or satisfaction with his/her performance during the interaction, (i) the subject's cognitions before and during the interaction, and so on. While difficulties in compliance may increase in direct relation to the complexity of the self-monitoring task, subjects are indeed capable of providing this information. By examining the frequency of targeted events, subjective reactions to them, and the covariation of subjective ratings with specific events, the timely establishment of treatment goals may be facialitated.

Dodge, Heimberg, Nyman, and O'Brien (in press) recently examined the self-monitored interactions of male and female subjects with self-reported high and low social anxiety. Subjects recorded all interactions with a peer of the opposite sex for a period of 2 weeks. Date; time; location; type of activity; type of relationship; with the person; topic of conversation; and ratings of anxiety, skillfulness, and satisfaction were recorded for each interaction. Subjects' gender had little effect on self-monitored interactions, but socially anxious subjects recorded fewer interactions, greater anxiety, and poorer self-evaluations than low anxious subjects. However, frequency of all types of interactions did not separate high and low socially anxious subjects, and the differences are revealing. Socially anxious subjects were less likely to engage in interactions that primarily revolved around conversation but did not differ from low anxious subjects in the frequency of structured activities such as attendance at movies, lectures, or sporting events. They also reported fewer interactions that occurred in classrooms or informal campus settings, interactions on weekdays, and interactions with friends or lovers. These differences in the interactions of socially anxious and nonanxious subjects suggest a number of starting points for the initiation of treatment for socially anxious students.

Self-monitoring procedures have also been utilized for the evaluation of treatment outcome. Most of these studies have focused on the treatment of heterosocial anxiety (e.g., Christensen, Arkowitz, & Anderson, 1975; Heimberg, Madsen, Montgomery, & McNabb, 1980; Twentyman & McFall, 1975) or social phobia (e.g., Marzillier, Lambert, & Kellett, 1976). We are aware of no studies that have utilized self-monitoring to evaluate the effectiveness of assertion-training procedures. Typically these studies reveal changes associated with treatment in the frequency and range of social interactions. For instance, male subjects receiving social skills training spent more time alone with more different women in more different situations than did subjects in a waiting-list condition (Twentyman & McFall, 1975). In our own study (Heimberg et al., 1980) that compared systematic desensitization, social skills training, and a structured homework-cognitive restructuring intervention to a self-monitoring-only condition for the treatment of socially anxious college males, several changes in self-monitored heterosocial behavior were noted. During the treatment period, significant increases in frequency and duration of heterosocial interactions and amount of time devoted to conversations occurred, and subjects' self-evaluations tended to improve. Curiously, frequency of interactions increased *most* for self-monitoring-only subjects while duration of interaction increased most for treated subjects. Speculatively, self-monitoring procedures led to a reactive increase in the frequency of interactions. However, in the absence of other (skill-teaching or anxiety-reducing) procedures, self-monitoring-only subjects could increase the frequency of interactions but not the quality (Heimberg et al., 1980).

A final area of concern is the validity of self-monitoring of social interactions. While little research has directly addressed this topic, Royce and Arkowitz (1978) report that scores derived from a self-monitoring log were significantly related to both scores on the Social Avoidance and Distress Scale and to peer ratings of social activity. Self-monitoring scores were also significantly related to observers' ratings of anxiety during a role-played social interaction (Twentyman & McFall, 1975). Further evaluation of self-monitoring measures is clearly required.

A CASE EXAMPLE OF THE ASSESSMENT OF SOCIAL SKILL

In this section we will describe the assessment of social skills of a patient who presented for the treatment of depression. Specifics of social skills training as applied to this case are outlined by Becker and Heimberg (1985), who provide this case description:

Joyce, a 43-year-old unmarried Caucasian female was self-referred to the Mood Disorders Clinic after an unremitting depression of several years' duration. At the initial intake she appeared composed, pleasant and alert, but quickly became tearful when questioned about her current job situation and her (virtually nonexistent) social life. She reported a variety of depressive symptoms, including prolonged sadness, low energy, poor concentration on household and occupational tasks, sleep-onset insomnia, and obsessive overconcern with her worth as a person. Joyce reported a moderately active but unsatisfying social life during college, but since that time, she has removed herself from the dating scene. She spends almost all of her nonwork hours in solitary pursuits, and although she endorses traditional desires for marriage and family, she has never had an intimate relationship. She characterizes herself as lonely and alone and spends considerable time berating herself for this state of affairs. In the absence of meaningful relationships, she has devoted herself almost entirely to her job, as an office manager for a local business executive. She works long hours at the job and is generally acknowledged as top-notch. She is also thought of as cold and unfeeling. Nevertheless, her relationships with her boss and co-workers represent the totality of her social network. The referral was precipitated by the client's recent declining mood pursuant to increasing conflict with her boss, who (according to Joyce) fails to provide her with adequate direction and then blows up at her when jobs are completed late or incorrectly. Further discussion revealed that Joyce reacts to these interactions by becoming angry and depressed and aimlessly struggling to do better. At the time of referral, she had begun to miss work for fear of being criticized by her boss. Additional discussion highlighted the client's need to develop a diversified social network. (p. 217)

Joyce received a diagnosis of dysthymic disorder. At pretreatment assessment her score on the Beck Depression Inventory (Beck, Ward, Mendelson, Mock, & Erbaugh, 1961) was 23. Her score on the 24-item Hamilton (1960) Rating Scale for Depression was 17.

Pretreatment assessment of social skills consisted of a behavioral interview, self-report questionnaires, and a detailed role-play assessment. The results of the behavioral interview were just reported in the case description. Use of the interview matrix described earlier revealed deficits in negative assertive behavior with her boss and in positive assertive and conversational behaviors with peers of both sexes.

Self-report assessment of social skills was restricted to assessment of her perceptions of her assertive abilities using the revised version of the Wolpe-Lazarus Assertiveness Schedule (Hersen et al., 1979). Her very low score on this scale suggested a self-perceived generalized deficit in assertive skill. Several other self-report measures (not described here) support this view.

Joyce also participated in a multiple-response role-play test that provided data on her behavioral performance in a variety of situations. Twelve scenes comprise a standard battery of role-play stimuli that are administered to all clients and assess responses to family, friends, and coworkers in positive and negative assertion situations. As suggested by Chiauzzi et al. (1985), additional scenes were derived from the behavioral interview and included situations that occurred in Joyce's own life and that were associated with an increase in her depressed mood. These included situations in which her boss failed to provide clear instructions, made extreme demands, or became unreasonably angry at her as well as situations that required her to initiate social interactions with the opposite sex.

In response to the set of personalized role plays with her boss, Joyce displayed extreme discomfort and several behaviors that made self-expression difficult. She bowed her head, avoided eye contact, stuttered, took a long time to respond, and, when she did respond, she simply offered a poor excuse. Examination of other negative assertion situations in the standard role-play battery revealed a similar but less extreme pattern. The client reported that this was a fairly typical response.

The first several sessions of treatment (see Becker & Heimberg, 1985) focused on interactions with the boss. In addition to the formal assessment of social skills just described, several additional role plays were conducted between client and therapist for the purposes of training the therapist in proper "boss behavior" and assessing Joyce's reactions to several situational variations. The first targeted situation involved a behavior of her boss that was extremely problematic. He would assign multiple tasks to Joyce but provide no information on relative importance, priority, or dates for completion. Her response to the boss's angry query, "Joyce, where's the memo I asked you to do? I need it now!" was examined. She took a long time to reply, stuttered, apologized profusely and avoided eye contact — a replication of her response in the assessment laboratory. She also reported feeling angry and depressed. Over the course of several rehearsals, her response was thoroughly analyzed and a constructive approach to the boss was formulated. It was suggested that she needed to (a) get his undivided attention, (b) point out the problem specifically, (c) suggest a solution to the problem, and (d) do it in a way that would not embarrass either party. The therapist modeled the response, and it was rehearsed several times. During each rehearsal, the therapist observed Joyce's response and evaluated it on response latency, eye contact, speech fluency, and the tendency to be overapologetic. Each time, the therapist's observations were relayed to Joyce and incorporated into the next rehearsal.

Self-monitoring procedures were also employed with Joyce: She was asked to keep a log of her interactions with her boss and her emotional reactions to them. Each week, this information was utilized to determine the course of the treatment session. Successes were rewarded and failures were carefully examined and utilized to design further rehearsals. Treatment continued to focus on the workplace until she reported that interactions with her boss were moving along and that they were no longer associated with a serious deterioration in mood.

Treatment also included an emphasis on social perception and self-reinforcement skills. After six sessions, her Beck Depression Inventory score had decreased to 11 and her Hamilton Rating Scale score had decreased to 6. Treatment then shifted to a focus on peer interactions.

SUMMARY

We have reviewed several important issues in the assessment of social skills, examined the major assessment methods, and described their application to a specific case. The reader may justifiably conclude that social skills assessment is a complex task and that it may be difficult to develop a valid and useful assessment of a client's social skills. Of course, this is true. As Bellack (1979) noted, we simply do not know as much about the assessment of social skills as we need to know. The current data on the validity of all assessment measures reviewed here are inadequate, and much remains to be done. However, we have made much progress since the publication of the second edition of this handbook, and that work continues.

REFERENCES

Andrasik, F., Heimberg, R. G., Edlund, S. R., & Blankenberg, R. (1981). Assessing the readability levels of self-report assertion inventories. *Journal of Consulting and Clinical Psychology, 49*, 142–144.

Appelbaum, A. S. (1976). Rathus Assertiveness Schedule: Sex differences and correlation with social desirability. *Behavior Therapy, 7*, 699.

Arkowitz, H. (1981). Assessment of social skills. In M. Hersen & A.S. Bellack (Eds.), *Behavioral assessment: A practical handbook* (2nd ed., pp. 296–327). New York: Pergamon.

Arkowitz, H., Lichtenstein, E., McGovern, K., & Hines, P. (1975). The behavioral assessment of social competence in males. *Behavior Therapy, 6*, 3–13.

Beck, A. T., Ward, C. H., Mendelson, M., Mock, J., & Erbaugh, J. (1961). An inventory for measuring depression. *Archives of General Psychiatry, 4*, 561–571.

Beck, J. G., & Heimberg, R. G. (1983). Self-report assessment of assertive behavior: A critical analysis. *Behavior Modification, 7*, 451–487.

Becker, R. E., & Heimberg, R. G. (1985). Social skills training approaches. In M. Hersen & A. S. Bellack (Eds.), *Handbook of clinical behavior therapy with adults* (pp. 201–226). New York: Plenum.

Bellack, A. S. (1979). A critical appraisal of strategies for assessing social skill. *Behavioral Assessment, 1*, 157–176.

Bellack, A. S. (1983). Recurrent problems in the behavioral assessment of social skill. *Behaviour Research and Therapy, 21*, 29–41.

Bellack, A. S., & Hersen, M. (Eds.). (1979). *Research and practice in social skills training*. New York: Plenum.

Bellack, A. S., Hersen, M., & Lamparski, D. (1979). Roleplay tests for assessing social skill: Are they valid? Are they useful? *Journal of Consulting and Clinical Psychology, 47*, 335–342.

Bellack, A. S., Hersen, M., & Turner, S. M. (1978). Roleplay tests for assessing social skill: Are they valid? *Behavior Therapy, 9*, 448–461.

Bellack, A. S., Hersen, M., & Turner, S. M. (1979). Relationship of roleplaying and knowledge of appropriate behavior to assertion in the natural environment. *Journal of Consulting and Clinical Psychology*, *47*, 670–678.

Blumer, C., & McNamara, J. R. (1982). The adequacy of a role play of a previous event as affected by high and low social anxiety and rehearsal. *Journal of Behavioral Assessment*, *4*, 27–37.

Cacioppo, J. T., Glass, C. R., & Merluzzi, T. V. (1979). Self-statements and self-evaluations: A cognitive-response analysis of social anxiety. *Cognitive Therapy and Research*, *3*, 249–262.

Callner, D. A., & Ross, S. M. (1976). The reliability of three measures of assertion in a drug addiction population. *Behavior Therapy*, *7*, 659–667.

Chiauzzi, E., & Heimberg, R. G. (1983). Effect of subjects' assertiveness level, sex, and legitimacy of request on assertion-relevant cognitions: An analysis by postperformance videotape reconstruction. *Cognitive Therapy and Research*, *7*, 555–564.

Chiauzzi, E. J., Heimberg, R. G., Becker, R. E., & Gansler, D. (1985). Personalized versus standard role plays in the assessment of depressed patients' social skill. *Journal of Psychopathology and Behavioral Assessment*, *7*, 121–133.

Chiauzzi, E. J., Heimberg, R. G., & Doty, D. (1982). Task analysis of assertive behavior revisited: The role of situational variables in female college students. *Behavioral Counseling Quarterly*, *2*, 42–50.

Christensen, A., Arkowitz, H., & Anderson, J. (1975). Practice dating as treatment for college dating inhibitions. *Behaviour Research and Therapy*, *13*, 321–331.

Conger, J. C., & Farrell, A. D. (1981). Behavioral components of heterosocial skills. *Behavior Therapy*, *12*, 41–55.

Curran, J. P. (1978). Comments on Bellack, Hersen, and Turner's paper on the validity of role-play test. *Behavior Therapy*, *9*, 462–468.

Curran, J. P. (1979). Pandora's box reopened: The assessment of social skills. *Journal of Behavioral Assessment*, *1*, 55–71.

Curran, J. P., & Monti, P. M. (Eds.). (1982). *Social skills training: A practical handbook for assessment and treatment*. New York: Guilford.

Curran, J. P., & Wessberg, H. (1981). The assessment of social inadequacy. In D. H. Barlow (Ed.), *Behavioral assessment of adult disorders* (pp. 405–438). New York: Guilford.

Delamater, R. J., & McNamara, J. R. (1986). The social impact of assertiveness: Research findings and clinical implications. *Behavior Modification*, *10*, 139–158.

Dodge, C. S., Heimberg, R. G., Nyman, D., & O'Brien, G. T. (in press). Daily heterosocial interactions of high and low socially anxious college students: A diary study. *Behavior Therapy*.

Duncan, S., & Fiske, D. (1977). *Face-to-face interaction: Research, methods, and theory*. New York: Erlbaum.

Eisler, R. M., & Frederiksen, L. W. (1980). *Perfecting social skills: A guide to interpersonal behavior development*. New York: Plenum.

Eisler, R. M., Frederiksen, L. W., & Peterson, G. L. (1978). The relationship of cognitive variables to the expression of assertiveness. *Behavior Therapy*, *9*, 419–427.

Eisler, R. M., Hersen, M., Miller, P. M., & Blanchard, E. B. (1975). Situational determinants of assertive behavior. *Journal of Consulting and Clinical Psychology*, *43*, 330–340.

Eisler, R. M., Miller, P. M., & Hersen, M. (1973). Components of assertive behavior. *Journal of Clinical Psychology*, *29*, 295–299.

Faraone, S. V., & Hurtig, R. R. (1985). An examination of social skill, verbal productivity, and Gottman's model of interaction using observational methods and sequential analyses. *Behavioral Assessment, 7*, 349–366.

Fiedler, D., & Beach, L. R. (1978). On the decision to be assertive. *Journal of Consulting and Clinical Psychology, 46*, 537–546.

Fingeret, A. L., Monti, P. M., & Paxson, M. A. (1985). Social perception, social performance, and self-perception: A study with psychiatric and nonpsychiatric groups. *Behavior Modification, 9*, 345–356.

Fischetti, M., Curran, J. P., & Wessberg, H. W. (1977). Sense of timing: A skill deficit in heterosexual-socially anxious males. *Behavior Modification, 1*, 179–194.

Fischetti, M., Peterson, J. L., Curran, J. P., Alkire, M., Perrewe, P., & Arland, S. (1984). Social cue discrimination versus motor skill: A missing distinction in social skills assessment. *Behavioral Assessment, 6*, 27–31.

Galassi, J. P., DeLo, J. S., Galassi, M. D., & Bastien, S. (1974). The College Self-Expression Scale: A measure of assertiveness. *Behavior Therapy, 5*, 165–171.

Galassi, M. D., & Galassi, J. P. (1977). *Assert yourself! How to be your own person.* New York: Human Sciences Press.

Gambrill, E. D., & Richey, C. A. (1975). An assertion inventory for use in assessment and research. *Behavior Therapy, 6*, 550–561.

Gay, M. L., Hollandsworth, J. G., & Galassi, J. P. (1975). An assertiveness inventory for adults. *Journal of Counseling Psychology, 22*, 340–344.

Glass, C. R., Merluzzi, T. V., Biever, J. L., & Larsen, K. H. (1982). Cognitive assessment of social anxiety: Development and validation of a self-statement questionnaire. *Cognitive Therapy and Research, 6*, 37–55.

Goldsmith, J. B., & McFall, R. M. (1975). Development and evaluation of an interpersonal skill-training program for psychiatric inpatients. *Journal of Abnormal Psychology, 84*, 51–58.

Gottman, J. G., Markman, H. J., & Notarius, C. I. (1977). The topography of marital conflict: A sequential analysis of verbal and nonverbal behavior. *Journal of Marriage and the Family, 39*, 461–478.

Hamilton, M. (1960). A rating scale for depression. *Journal of Neurology, Neurosurgery, and Psychiatry, 23*, 56–62.

Heimberg, R. G., & Becker, R. E. (1981). Cognitive and behavioral models of assertive behavior: Review, analysis and integration. *Clinical Psychology Review, 1*, 353–373.

Heimberg, R. G., Becker, R. E., Isaacs, K., & Cotch, P. (1981, November). *Instructional variations in the assessment of assertive behavior of psychiatric outpatients: A case of negative findings.* Paper presented at the Fifteenth Annual Convention of the Association for Advancement of Behavior Therapy, Toronto.

Heimberg, R. G., Chiauzzi, E., Becker, R. E., & Madrazo-Peterson, R. (1983). Cognitive mediation of assertive behavior: An analysis of the self-statement patterns of college students, psychiatric patients, and normal adults. *Cognitive Therapy and Research, 7*, 455–463.

Heimberg, R. G., & Etkin, D. (1983). Response quality and outcome effectiveness as factors in students' and counselors' judgments of assertiveness. *British Journal of Cognitive Psychotherapy, 2*, 59–68.

Heimberg, R. G., & Harrison, D. F. (1980). Use of the Rathus Assertiveness Schedule with offenders: A question of questions. *Behavior Therapy, 11*, 278–281.

Heimberg, R. G., Madsen, C. H., Montgomery, D., & McNabb, C. E. (1980). Behavioral treatments for heterosocial problems: Effects on daily self-monitored and role-played interactions. *Behavior Modification, 4*, 147–172.

Hersen, M., & Bellack, A. S. (1977). Assessment of social skills. In A.R. Ciminero, K. S. Calhoun, & H. E. Adams (Eds.), *Handbook of behavioral assessment.* New York: Wiley.

Hersen, M., Bellack, A. S., Himmelhock, J. M., & Thase, M. E. (1984). Effects of social skills training, amitriptyline, and psychotherapy in unipolar depressed women. *Behavior Therapy, 15*, 21–40.

Hersen, M., Bellack, A. S., & Turner, S. M. (1978). Assessment of assertiveness in female psychiatric patients: Motor and autonomic measures. *Journal of Behavior Therapy and Experimental Psychiatry, 9*, 11–16.

Hersen, M., Bellack, A. S., Turner, S. M., Williams, M. T., Harper, K., & Watts, J.G. (1979). Psychometric properties of the Wolpe-Lazarus Assertiveness Scale. *Behaviour Research and Therapy, 17*, 63–69.

Higgins, R. L., Alonso, R. R., & Pendleton, M. G. (1979). The validity of roleplay assessments of assertiveness. *Behavior Therapy, 10*, 655–662.

Higgins, R. L., Frisch, M. B., & Smith, D. (1983). A comparison of role-played and natural responses to identical circumstances. *Behavior Therapy, 14*, 158–169.

Hull, D. B., & Hull, J. H. (1978). Rathus Assertiveness Schedule: Normative and factor analytic data. *Behavior Therapy, 9*, 673.

Kazdin, A. E. (1974). Reactive self-monitoring: The effects of response desirability, goal setting, and feedback. *Journal of Consulting and Clinical Psychology, 42*, 704–716.

Kelly, J. A. (1982). *Social skills training: A practical guide for interventions.* New York: Springer-Verlag.

Kelly, J. A., Frederiksen, L. W., Fitts, H., & Phillips, P. (1978). Training and generalization of commendatory assertiveness: A controlled single-subject experiment. *Journal of Behavior Therapy and Experimental Psychiatry, 9*, 17–21.

Kelly, J. A., Kern, J. M., Kirkley, B. G., Patterson, J. N., & Keane, T. M. (1980). Reactions to assertive versus unassertive behavior: Differential effects for males and females and implications for assertiveness training. *Behavior Therapy, 11*, 670–682.

Kern, J. M. (1982). The comparative external and concurrent validity of three roleplays for assessing heterosocial performance. *Behavior Therapy, 13*, 666–680.

Kern, J. M., Cavell, T. A., & Beck, B. (1985). Predicting differential reactions to male's versus females' assertions, empathic assertions, and nonassertions. *Behavior Therapy, 16*, 63–75.

Kern, J. M., Miller, C., & Eggers, J. (1983). Enhancing the validity of roleplay tests: A comparison of three roleplay methodologies. *Behavior Therapy, 14*, 482–492.

Kiecolt, J., & McGrath, E. (1979). Social desirability responding in the measurement of assertive behavior. *Journal of Consulting and Clinical Psychology, 47*, 640–642.

Kolotkin, R. A., & Wielkiewicz, R. M. (1984). Effects of situational demand in the role-play assessment of assertive behavior. *Journal of Behavioral Assessment, 6*, 59–70.

Kuperminc, M., & Heimberg, R. G. (1983). Consequence probability and utility as factors in the decision to behave assertively. *Behavior Therapy, 14*, 637–646.

Libet, J. M., & Lewinsohn, P. M. (1973). Concept of social skill with special reference to the behavior of depressed persons. *Journal of Consulting and Clinical Psychology, 40*, 304–312.

Mahaney, M. M., & Kern, J. M. (1983). Variation in role-play tests of heterosocial performance. *Journal of Consulting and Clinical Psychology, 51*, 151–152.

Marzillier, J. S., Lambert, C., & Kellett, J. (1976). A controlled evaluation of systematic desensitization and social skills training for socially inadequate psychiatric patients. *Behaviour Research and Therapy, 14*, 225–238.

McCormick, I. A. (1985). A simple version of the Rathus Assertiveness Schedule. *Behavioral Assessment, 7*, 95–99.

McFall, R. M., & Lillesand, D. B. (1971). Behavior rehearsal with modeling and coaching in assertion training. *Journal of Abnormal Psychology, 77*, 313–323.

McFall, R. M., & Marston, A. R. (1970). An experimental investigation of behavior rehearsal in assertive training. *Journal of Abnormal Psychology, 76,* 295–303.

McNamara, J. R., & Blumer, C. A. (1982). Role playing to assess social competence: Ecological validity considerations. *Behavior Modification, 6,* 519–549.

Moisan-Thomas, P. C., Conger, J. C., Zellinger, M. M., & Firth, E. A. (1985). The impact of confederate responsivity on social skills assessment. *Journal of Psychopathology and Behavioral Assessment, 7,* 23–35.

Morrison, R. L., & Bellack, A. S. (1981). The role of social perception in social skill. *Behavior Therapy, 12,* 69–79.

Nelson, R. O. (1977). Methodological issues in assessment via self-monitoring. In J. D. Cone & R. P. Hawkins (Eds.), *Behavioral assessment: New directions in clinical psychology* (pp. 217–240). New York: Brunner/Mazel.

Nietzel, M. T., & Bernstein, D. A. (1976). The effects of instructionally mediated demand upon the behavioral assessment of assertiveness. *Journal of Consulting and Clinical Psychology, 44,* 500.

Peterson, J., Fischetti, M., Curran, J. P., & Arland, S. (1981). Sense of timing: A skill deficit in heterosocially anxious women. *Behavior Therapy, 12,* 194–201.

Quillen, J., Besing, S., & Dinning, D. (1977). Standardization of the Rathus Assertiveness Schedule. *Journal of Clinical Psychology, 33,* 418–422.

Rathus, S. A. (1973). A 30-item schedule for assessing assertive behavior. *Behavior Therapy, 4,* 398–406.

Rathus, S. A., & Nevid, J. S. (1977). Concurrent validity of the 30-item Assertiveness Schedule with a psychiatric population. *Behavior Therapy, 8,* 393–397.

Rehm, L. P., & Marston, A. R. (1968). Reduction of social anxiety through modification and self-reinforcement: An instigation therapy technique. *Journal of Consulting and Clinical Psychology, 32,* 565–574.

Rock, D. L. (1981). The confounding of two self-report assertion measures with the tendency to give socially desirable responses in self-description. *Journal of Consulting and Clinical Psychology, 49,* 743–744.

Rodriguez, R., Nietzel, M. T., & Berzins, J. I. (1980). Sex-role orientation and assertiveness among female college students. *Behavior Therapy, 11,* 353–367.

Romano, J. M., & Bellack, A. S. (1980). Social validation of a component model of assertive behavior. *Journal of Consulting and Clinical Psychology, 48,* 478–490.

Rose, Y. J., & Tryon, W. W. (1979). Judgments of assertive behavior as a function of speech loudness, latency, content, gestures, inflections, and sex. *Behavior Modification, 3,* 112–123.

Roth, D., & Rehm, L. P. (1980). Relationships among self-monitoring processes, memory, and depression. *Cognitive Therapy and Research, 4,* 149–157.

Royce, W. S., & Arkowitz, H. (1978). Multimodal evaluation of practice interactions as treatment for social isolation. *Journal of Consulting and Clinical Psychology, 46,* 239–245.

St. Lawrence, J. S., Hansen, D. J., Cutts, T. F., Tisdelle, D. A., & Irish, J. D. (1985). Situational context: Effects on perceptions of assertive and unassertive behavior. *Behavior Therapy, 16,* 51–62.

St. Lawrence, J. S., Hughes, E. F., Goff, A. F., & Palmer, M. B. (1983). Assessment of role-play generalization across qualitatively different situations. *Journal of Behavioral Assessment, 5,* 289–307.

St. Lawrence, J. S., Kirksey, W. A., & Moore, T. (1983). External validity of role play assessment of assertive behavior. *Journal of Behavioral Assessment, 5,* 25–34.

Schwartz, R. M., & Gottman, J. M. (1976). Toward a task analysis of assertive behavior. *Journal of Consulting and Clinical Psychology, 44,* 910–920.

Skillings, R. E., Hersen, M., Bellack, A. S., & Becker, M. P. (1978). Relationship of specific and global measures of assertiveness in college females. *Journal of Clinical Psychology, 34,* 346–353.

Spence, S., & Shephard, G. (1983). *Developments in social skills training.* London: Academic Press.

Steinberg, S. L., Curran, J. P., Bell, S., Paxson, M. A., & Munroe, S. M. (1982). The effects of confederate prompt delivery style in a standardized social simulation test. *Journal of Behavioral Assessment, 4,* 263–272.

Trower, P. (1980). Situational analysis of the components and processes of behavior of socially skilled and unskilled patients. *Journal of Consulting and Clinical Psychology, 48,* 327–339.

Trower, P., Bryant, B., & Argyle, M. (1978). *Social skills and mental health.* Pittsburgh: University of Pittsburgh Press.

Twentyman, C. T., & McFall, R. M. (1975). Behavioral training of social skills in shy males. *Journal of Consulting and Clinical Psychology, 43,* 384–395.

Wallander, J. L., Conger, A. J., & Conger, J. C. (1985). Development and evaluation of a behaviorally referenced rating system for heterosocial skills. *Behavioral Assessment, 7,* 137–153.

Wallander, J. L., Conger, A. J., Mariotto, M. J., Curran, J. P., & Farrell, A. D. (1980). Comparability of selection instruments in studies of heterosexual-social problem behaviors. *Behavior Therapy, 11,* 548–560.

Watson, D., & Friend, R. (1969). Measurement of social-evaluative anxiety. *Journal of Consulting and Clinical Psychology, 33,* 448–467.

Wessberg, H. W., Curran, J. P., Monti, P. M., Corriveau, D. P., Coyne, N. A., & Dziadosz, T. H. (1981). Evidence for the external validity of a social simulation measure of social skills. *Journal of Behavioral Assessment, 3,* 209–220.

Wessberg, H. W., Mariotto, M. J., Conger, A. J., Farrell, A. D., & Conger, J. C. (1979). Ecological validity of roleplays for assessing heterosocial anxiety and skill of male college students. *Journal of Consulting and Clinical Psychology, 47,* 525–535.

Westefeld, J. S., Galassi, J. P., & Galassi, M. D. (1980). Effects of role-playing instructions on assertive behavior: A methodological study. *Behavior Therapy, 11,* 271–277.

Wolpe, J., & Lazarus, A. A. (1966). *Behavior therapy techniques: A guide to the treatment of neuroses.* Oxford: Pergamon.

Woolfolk, R. L., & Dever, S. (1979). Perceptions of assertion: An empirical analysis. *Behavior Therapy, 10,* 404–411.

12
Assessment of Health-Related Disorders

Donald A. Williamson
C. J. Davis
Rita C. Prather

With the growth of behavioral medicine and health psychology has come a need for a diverse set of techniques and procedures for assessing behavior that is associated with health problems. For many health-related disorders, assessment must be directed at the physiological response that is dysfunctional (e.g., blood pressure with hypertension or peripheral circulation with Raynaud's disease). For other disorders, the individual's behavior is the primary determinant of the dysfunction and therefore health-related behavior must be the primary target for assessment (e.g., Type A Behavior Pattern and eating disorders).

This chapter reviews the assessment literature for most of the major health-related problems that have been studied by researchers in behavioral medicine and health psychology. As is typical in most areas of behavioral assessment, evaluations of these problems takes an idiographic approach whereby specific techniques have been developed for specific disorders. Also, in most cases, assessment is directly linked to treatment planning with the primary purposes of assessment being (a) diagnosis, (b) behavioral analysis, or (c) evaluation of treatment outcomes. Assessment of health-related disorders generally follows from a biobehavioral model (Williamson, Waters, & Hawkins, in press) whereby the assessment must be conducted at a variety of levels: biochemical, physiological, behavioral, and environmental. The chapter is organized by disorders. Each disorder is described and the assessment literature related to diagnosis and treatment planning are reviewed. At the conclusion, a case example is presented to illustrate how these behavioral assessment procedures may be applied to a health-related disorder.

SPECIFIC HEALTH-RELATED DISORDERS

Coronary Heart Disease

Description

Coronary heart disease (CHD) refers to any dysfunction of the heart muscle or to the arterial or venous system of the heart (Beeson, McDermott, & Wyngaarden, 1979). Annual deaths due to CHD have been estimated at 600,000 (Fishman, 1982). The primary clinical manifestations of CHD are angina, myocardial infarction (heart attacks), cardiac arrhythmias, and congestive heart failure (Blumenthal, 1982). Coronary heart disease has been linked to a number of biological and behavioral *risk factors* which predispose an individual to the development of CHD. The primary risk factors of interest to this chapter include hypertension, cholesterol, triglyceride level, Type A Behavior Pattern, and a number of lifestyle behaviors, e.g., overeating, sedentary habits, and smoking, which have all been shown to directly or indirectly cause biological changes which contribute to the development of CHD.

Assessment for Diagnosis

Coronary heart disease can only be diagnosed with a thorough medical examination. However, assessment of the presence of risk factors generally involves both medical and behavioral assessment (Blumenthal, 1982). For example, hypertension can be evaluated using one or more psychophysiological assessment methods that have been developed for measuring blood pressure (see chapter 7). The most common method for measuring blood pressure was developed by Korotkoff and employs a sphygmomanometer to establish the highest (systolic) and lowest (diastolic) pressure points. Systolic blood pressures above 140 mmHg and diastolic pressures above 90 mmHg are generally considered to be elevated in adult patients (Shapiro & Goldstein, 1982). For research purposes, the recording of blood pressure is often automated using chart or digital recording devices. Other risk factors that require medical assessment procedures are serum cholesterol and triglyceride levels. There are a variety of techniques for assaying these biochemicals, including electrophoresis and chromatography (Williamson et al., 1986). Cholesterol levels above 220 mg% and triglyceride levels above 150 mg% are considered to be clinically elevated (Blumenthal, 1982).

A variety of procedures have been developed for diagnosing Type A Behavior Pattern (TABP). TABP is generally considered to be a learned pattern of behavior (or behavioral style) that is characterized by time-urgency, hostility, competitiveness, aggressiveness, and restless motor mannerisms (Rosenman, 1978). The most well-developed and widely used procedure for assessing TABP is the structured interview (Rosenman et al.,

1964), which has recently been revised to allow for videotaping of the interview. The structured interview has been found to have satisfactory test-retest reliability and interrater reliability (Newlin, 1981). Also, its validity as a measure of TABP is widely accepted and is considered by many authorities to be the most valid method for assessing TABP (Blumenthal, 1982; Rosenman, 1978; Suinn, 1982).

There are several self-report inventories for assessing TABP. The most well-developed scales are the Jenkins Activity Survey (Jenkins, Rosenman, & Friedman, 1967) and the Framingham Type A Scale (Haynes, Feinleib, Levine, Scotch, & Kannel, 1980). Both scales were endorsed by the Review Panel on Coronary-Prone Behavior and Coronary Heart Disease (1981) as having satisfactory reliability and validity. Another rating scale, developed by Bortner (1969), has received less attention and is therefore less well developed psychometrically.

Lifestyle behaviors that must be evaluated when assessing CHD are eating habits, exercise habits, smoking habits, and drinking habits. For a more complete discussion of the evaluation of these behaviors, the reader should see chapter 15 (Assessment of Appetitive Disorders). Of particular interest to CHD is the patient's dietary habits. The consumption of excessive amounts of fats and sodium has been implicated in the development of CHD (Blumenthal, 1982). Therefore, analysis of these dietary factors would be especially important. Also, if obesity is diagnosed, it is important to determine whether the excessive weight is primarily due to excessive intake of food or inadequate exercise.

Assessment for Treatment Planning

Once CHD has been diagnosed and the presence of certain risk factors have been established, the next step is a comprehensive behavioral analysis which seeks to integrate these findings in order to account for the development of CHD and thereby establish the target behaviors for a rehabilitation program. Behavioral interviewing (see chapter 4) is the most common method for conducting this behavioral analysis. Also, self-monitoring of lifestyle behavior such as eating habits, exercise, smoking, and drinking can often elucidate the relationship between environmental, cognitive, and emotional events and behavioral reactions. Furthermore, role-play tests of assertiveness and other social behaviors may be used to obtain a sample of social behavior which might be related to the anxiety, anger, and competitiveness associated with TABP (Morrison, Bellack, & Manuck, 1985). In cases where stress and TABP are implicated, psychophysiological assessment using stressors such as competition can be used to evaluate the effects of environmental challenge upon cardiovascular reactions (E.L. Diamond et al., 1984).

Once the behavioral analysis is completed, specific health-related

TABLE 12.1. Measures Commonly Used to Evaluate Treatment Outcome for Coronary Heart Disease.

   I. Cardiovascular
       Systolic blood pressure
       Diastolic blood pressure
       Heart rate
  II. Biochemical
       Cholesterol (serum)
       Triglycerides (serum)
       Lipids (serum)
       Sodium (urinary)
 III. Type A Behavior Pattern
       Structured interview
       Jenkins Activity Survey
       Framingham Type A Scale
 IV. Lifestyle Behavior
       Eating habits
       Exercise
       Smoking
       Drinking
  V. Physical Characteristics
       Weight
       Skinfold measurements
       Physical fitness

---

behaviors should be targeted for modification. These behaviors and relevant physiological/medical variables (e.g., blood pressure, weight, cholesterol, etc.) should be monitored throughout treatment and follow-up to evaluate treatment outcome. Generally, the measures used for assessing CHD and the various risk factors have been used as outcome measures and have been found to be sensitive to treatment effects. Table 12.1 summarizes the measures which are commonly employed in research concerning the treatment of CHD.

Summary

Behavioral assessment methods for assessing behavioral and physiological risk factors associated with CHD are quite well developed. For most methods, adequate reliability and validity have been established. Most measures have been widely used for both research and clinical purposes and have been found to be both clinically useful and practical. Since CHD is one of our most serious health problems, it is likely that we will see, in the near future, the development of comprehensive, standardized assessment batteries for evaluating the risk factors associated with CHD. At present, there are signs that such batteries are in the developmental stages.

Headache

Description

Headache is a complaint that is often without any objective, measurable physiological markers. Due to the subjectivity of headache, a systematic assessment regarding the events surrounding the attack, as well as a thorough physical examination, is important in differentiating the nature of the headache, as well as in delineating appropriate treatment.

For the purposes of this chapter, the three most common types of headache will be discussed: migraine headache, muscle-contraction headache, and combined migraine and muscle-contraction headache. The reader is referred to Diamond & Dalessio (1982) for a thorough discussion of other types of headache. Table 12.2 summarizes the primary diagnostic criteria used for these three types of headache.

Approximately 8–12 million Americans report suffering from migraine headache (Diamond & Dalessio, 1982). Migraine may first be reported in childhood or middle age, with the most common age of onset being in the second decade (Diamond & Dalessio, 1982; Mathew, 1981). As shown in Table 12.2, there are two clearly differentiated types of migraine headache: common and classic. The primary diagnostic criterion differentiating these two types of migraine is the presence of clearly defined prodromal symptoms (usually a disturbance of vision prior to the onset of head pain) that occur in classic migraine. Also, unilateral pain is usually more evident with classic migraine, although it may occur with common migraine as well.

Muscle-contraction headache occurs more often than any other type of headache (Holroyd, Andrasik, & Westbrook, 1977). Although a tendency toward a positive family history has been noted for muscle-contraction headache sufferers (Friedman, 1979), many researchers have also hypothesized that stress and learning/modelling are factors in the acquisition of this type of headache (Diamond & Dalessio, 1982). The primary characteristic of muscle-contraction headache is a bilateral (not one-sided) dull, constant pain in the frontal or suboccipital areas. Combined headache, also referred to as mixed headache, has been described as "a combination vascular headache of the migraine type and muscle-contraction headache predominantly coexisting in an attack" (Ad Hoc Committee on Classification of Headache, 1962, p. 718). This mixed pattern can occur in various combinations, with the most common pattern being that of an almost-daily muscle-contraction type of headache, with periodic migraine headaches.

Assessment for Diagnosis

In diagnosing headaches, several forms of assessment may be utilized, including interview, physical examination, and questionnaire data. Information from these sources can then be analyzed, allowing the psychologist or physician to accurately diagnose the headache type based on the symptomatology described by the patient (see Table 12.2) and subsequently prescribe the most appropriate plan of treatment.

TABLE 12.2. Symptoms of Migraine, Muscle-Contraction, and Combined Headache.

DIAGNOSIS	PRESENTING SYMPTOMS FOR DIAGNOSIS	SYMPTOMS CONTRAINDICATED FOR DIAGNOSIS
Classic Migraine	1. Unilateral (one-sided) locus of pain 2. Throbbing/pulsating, severe pain 3. Possible nausea and vomiting 4. Prodromal symptoms, e.g., disturbances of vision prior to headache 5. Attacks are episode 6. Family history of migraines 7. For females, headache may increase during menses, and decrease or disappear during pregnancy and after menopause 8. Relief after sleep 9. Post-headache tenderness in affected areas which may last several days	1. Bilateral locus of pain 2. Constant, bandlike description of pain 3. Locus of pain near the jaw or ear, with bruxism or jaw popping
Common Migraine	1. Pain is more often bilateral than unilateral 2. Prodromal symptoms not well defined 3. Other symptoms similar to those of classic migraine	1. Constant, bandlike description of pain 2. Clearly defined prodromal symptoms 3. Locus of pain near the jaw or ear, with bruxism or jaw popping
Muscle Contraction Headache	1. Bilateral or diffuse pain beginning in the frontal or suboccipital area of the head 2. Constant, bandlike pressure around the head or stiffness and soreness in the neck 3. Wide range of pain intensity, varying from mild to severe 4. Pain is reduced by over-the-counter pain medications, e.g., aspirin 5. Pain intensity is reduced by relaxation of affected muscles	1. Pulsating or throbbing pain 2. Prodromal symptoms 3. Nausea and vomiting 4. Unilateral pain 5. Locus of pain near the jaw or ear, with bruxism or jaw popping
Combined Headache	1. Unilateral or bilateral pain 2. Bandlike pressure and, at other times, throbbing/pulsating pain 3. Other migraine *and* muscle-contraction headache symptoms present	1. Clearly defined migraine or muscle-contraction headache with no occurrence of the other style of headache 2. Locus of pain near the jaw

In Table 12.3, the important features of obtaining a thorough headache history are presented. Information may be obtained through interviews, questionnaires, and medical examinations. In the interview, a behavior-analytic approach should be used to assess the antecedents occurring prior to the headache and to obtain a description of the headache, of the behavior(s) occuring during the headache, and of the consequences of the headache (e.g., degree of disability and reactions of others). This approach is useful in determining to what extent, if any, the psychological factors (e.g., stress or reinforcement) are significant in either precipitating or maintaining the occurrence of the headache.

Most headache disorders are usually not associated with structural abnormalities of the brain (Saper, 1983). However, a complete physical examination insures that organic factors are ruled out and provides the patient with the assurance that a physical problem is not the causal factor of the headaches. Specific diagnostic tests include electroencephalograph (EEG), a complete neurological examination, computerized axial tomography (CT) scan (assisting in diagnosing neurological disease), angiography (used in patients with unilateral neurological disturbances accompanying headache), and lumbar puncture (used for assessing problems specifically diagnosed by cerebrospinal fluid or pressure). In addition to medical causes of headache, one must also rule out the presence of a major depressive disorder as the cause of headache (see chapter 10).

Headache questionnaires have proved to be useful in headache assessment in that they provide a method of documenting headache symptoms. They do not, however, replace the interview as the basic method for diagnosing headache in a structured, time-efficient way. In general, headache questionnaires reported in the literature have been similar in content, including demographic, medical, and medical history information. Several researchers have reported factor analysis of headache questionnaires (Arena, Blanchard, Andrasik, & Dudek, 1982; Granberry, Williamson, Pratt, Hutchinson, & Monguillot, 1981; Zeigler, Hassanein, & Hassanein, 1972). Similar factor structures were found in all three studies, including a vascular headache factor, a tension headache factor, and a duration factor. Only a follow-up investigation by Granberry (1985) has investigated the psychometic properties of the headache questionnaire, finding moderate to satisfactory test-retest reliability in most of the scales (factors).

Assessment for Treatment Planning

With a thorough assessment, an effective treatment plan can be constructed. However, it must be noted that assessment does not end with the initiation of treatment. Indeed, continued assessment is integral to successful treatment, allowing for modifications of the treatment process when needed.

One outcome measure that can be utilized for evaluation of treatment outcome is the self-monitoring procedure originally developed by Blanchard, Theobald, Williamson, Silver, and Brown (1978), which has been shown to be ecologically valid (Blanchard, Andrasik, Neff, Jurish, & O'Keefe, 1981). The reader is referred to Williamson, Ruggiero, & Davis (1985) for a more thorough description of this procedure and for the computations used for converting self-monitoring data into estimates of headache frequency, duration, and intensity.

The behavioral treatment of chronic headache can be broken down into three phases (Boudewyns, 1982). The first, aimed at modifying the stimuli that trigger pain, are called *stimulus control procedures*. Assessment in this phase must identify environmental situations that reliably precede headaches. These situations may include stress or certain behavioral habits such as drinking alcohol. The second aspect of treatment is targeted at changing *organismic* factors. Usually the patient is trained in relaxation using one of several techniques: progressive muscle relaxation (Jacobson, 1938), autogenic training (Sargent, Walters & Green, 1973), meditation procedures (Benson, 1975), or biofeedback (Williamson, 1981). Assessment of compliance with these procedures is important to insure integrity of treatment. Following relaxation training, the patient's maladaptive cognitions are often targeted for change. The reader is referred to chapter 6 for a complete discussion of these assessment procedures. The third aspect of treatment involves *contingency management*. The patient's own behavior (e.g., amount of pain medication consumed), as well as the behavior of significant others in the patient's life (e.g., reinforcing pain behavior) often require modification. Assessment of these factors can be accomplished via the behavior analytic interviews and self-monitoring. Using this type of analysis, a proper treatment plan can be developed and instituted so that all potential determinants of head pain are addressed.

Summary

As has been noted earlier, a thorough assessment of headache and all associated variables is integral in the successful treatment of head pain. Information from interviews, medical examinations, questionnaires, and self-monitoring procedures may provide a comprehensive analysis of the presenting problem, thereby allowing the psychologist or physician to help prescribe the most efficacious method of treatment. Most of the assessment techniques described in this section have been found to have adequate psychometric properties. Headache questionnaires and self-monitoring procedures have been found to have good reliability and validity. In combination with diagnostic interviews and medical/neurological evaluations to rule out other disorders, these procedures have proved to be useful for clinical and research purposes.

Chronic Pain

Description

Chronic pain is usually defined as pain which is not the result of a malignant disease process and has been present on a constant daily basis for at least 6 months. This pain is often the result of physical injury, trauma, or some other physical disorder. The pain is usually perceived to be quite severe and is often disabling.

Pain has been conceptualized as a subjective, private phenomenon (Gentry & Bernal, 1977), not lending itself to direct, observable measurement. It is different from many medical problems in that there is no objective diagnostic test to establish the quality or quantity of pain experienced by a patient. As Sternbach (1968) has stated, "it is necessary for the patient to do something . . . in order for us to determine that he is experiencing pain." Therefore, the most frequently used assessment techniques employed in the assessment of pain are those of patient's self-report of intensity, description, and location of the pain (Turk, Wack, & Kerns, 1985). Because of the biases inherent in self-report instruments and the lack of more objective measures, pain is a difficult construct to measure. However, since measurement of pain requires the "patient to do something," it is natural that behavioral assessment has played an important role in this area of medical evaluation.

Assessment for Diagnosis

Cinciripini, Williamson, and Epstein (1981) have noted that pain has three dimensions: a nociceptive-physiological dimension, a behavioral-motoric dimension, and a subjective-cognitive dimension. Most assessment procedures for chronic pain are directed at one of these three dimensions. The physiological dimension of pain includes information obtained from a medical assessment of the patient's pain. Information regarding the behavioral-motoric aspect of pain can be derived from non verbal observable behaviors such as gesturing (including limping, staggering, and abnormal posture), grimacing (facial gestures signifying discomfort), and touching the body part associated with pain (Cinciripini, 1985). The subjective-cognitive dimension is indicative of the patient's personal, private experience of pain, and is often assessed using rating scales and adjective checklists.

Pain intensity, location, and quality are three common indices of pain used in self-report methods (Keefe, Brown, Scott, & Ziesat, 1982). There are two commonly used rating measures of pain intensity: magnitude estimation (Swanson, Swenson, Maruta, & McPhee, 1976) and visual analog scales (Joyce, Zutshi, Hrubes, & Mason, 1975). Both ask the patient to rate the pain, either numerically or verbally. The VAS procedure has been found to be a more sensitive measure than the magnitude estimation scale (Joyce et al., 1975).

The McGill Pain Questionnaire (Melzack, 1975) is a measure of chronic pain that yields a measure of pain quality and intensity. It is an adjective checklist consisting of 102 adjectives. It has been used extensively for both clinical and research purposes (Leavitt, Garron, D'Angelo, & McNeil, 1979; Reading & Newton, 1978).

An alternative method for assessing the intensity of pain is through the use of stimulus-matching procedures whereby the patient demonstrates the relative degree of pain in various areas of the body using psychophysical scaling methods (Tursky, 1976; Gracely, McGrath, & Dubner, 1978). Also, the "pain map" (Keele, 1948) has been used to assess the location of chronic pain. The patient shades in the areas of pain on an outline of a human body. Scores obtained from pain maps have correlated highly with Minnesota Multiphasic Personality Inventory (Hathaway & McKinley, 1943) (MMPI) hypochondriasis and hysteria scales (Ransford, Cairns, & Mooney, 1976).

Traditional psychological tests are commonly used in the evaluation of patients with chronic pain because of the diversity of psychopathology seen in these patients. The MMPI is probably the most widely used of these tests. Patients with lower back pain have typically been found to have elevations on scales 1, 2, and 3, the "neurotic triad" (Gentry, Newman, Goldner, & von Baeyer, 1977; McCreary, Turner, & Dawson, 1977). An experimental scale of the MMPI, the Lower Back Pain scale, has also been used to differentiate between patients with known organic pathology and those with an absence of known pathology (Havnik, 1951). However, this scale has been found to have little clinical utility (Freeman, Caslyn, & Louks, 1976).

Other tests used with chronic-pain patients include the Symptom Checklist-90 — Revised (Derogatis, 1977; Derogatis, Rickles, & Rock, 1975), the Middlesex Hospital Questionnaire (Crown & Crisp, 1966), and the Health Index (Sternbach, Wolf, Murphy, & Akeson, 1973). All measure personality variables, and are symptom-oriented. They have proved useful for diagnostic assessment and for measurement of treatment outcome.

Self-monitoring of pain is one of the most commonly used methods of continuing assessment (Fordyce, 1976; Keefe & Brown, 1982). It is a useful procedure in that it is relatively inexpensive and provides a record of behavior when the patient is in naturalistic settings. Also, it serves to make the patient more aware of behaviors targeted for change. Fordyce and colleagues (Fordyce et al., 1973) have developed a system that monitors time spent reclining, walking, sitting, and standing. Other self-monitoring procedures have involved recording activity and exercise levels (Cairns, Thomas, Mooney, & Pace, 1976).

Direct observation, utilizing observation by hospital staff, family members, peers, and automatic recording devices are of utility in assessing the chronic pain patient. On the hospital ward, hospital staff are most commonly asked to rate medication consumption and pain behavior (Keefe et al., 1982). Observations by family members and peers are used to monitor certain aspects of the patient's pain behavior (Fordyce, 1976), thus providing a measure of this behavior in naturalistic settings. Automatic recording devices (Cairns, et al., 1976), which record activity level or time out of bed, do not have the psychometric problems inherent in observation procedures and have been shown to be both accurate and reliable. Therefore they provide a clear alternative to the use of observational procedures for recording behaviors related to activity on the ward or out of bed. Psychophysiological methods have also been used with chronic-pain patients. In particular, electromyography (EMG) has shown that muscular hypo- or hyper-activity may occur in the affected areas, indicating these muscle groups as targets for treatment using relaxation or biofeedback (Basmajian, 1978; Holmes & Wolff, 1952; Scott & Gregg, 1980).

Assessment of pain can be obtained through many avenues. The complete assessment should entail observations in naturalistic settings, in the hospital or clinic, and in the laboratory. Self-observation, observation by others, physiological assessment, and psychological tests are all methods which can be utilized in delineating the specific problem areas of individual pain patients. However, caution must be taken in placing too many demands on the patient. Overloading the patient with unnecessary evaluation procedures may produce compliance problems as well as sensitize the patient to the pain.

Assessment for Treatment Planning

Continued assessment of pain behaviors, levels of pain, and the psychological state of the patient may assist the professional in delivering the most effective treatment regime. Relaxation and biofeedback treatment, often utilized with chronic-pain patients (Gentry & Bernal, 1977), necessitates the continued monitoring of EMG levels. Pain behaviors (e.g., medication use, verbalizations of pain, or activity level) and the responses of others to those pain behaviors are also often targets for treatment. Continued assessment of these variables throughout treatment is useful for monitoring treatment efficacy in reducing the targeted pain behaviors.

Summary

The assessment and treatment of the chronic-pain patient is usually carried out by a multidisciplinary team, involving physicians, psychologists, social workers, physical therapists, and nurses. With an idiographic approach to assessment and treatment, those maladaptive behaviors exhibited by the pain patient can be effectively treated. Comprehensive assessment of the multitude of problem areas observed in chronic pain patients is essential for diagnosis, treatment planning, and treatment evaluation.

Many methods used in the assessment of chronic pain have been demonstrated to have adequate psychometric properties (e.g., McGill Pain

Questionnaire, automatic recording devices). However, there are several problems in the area of chronic-pain assessment. There is a lack of consensual agreement regarding which behaviors should be included in the construct of chronic pain. Also, there is little agreement regarding the procedures that are most appropriately used in the assessment of pain behaviors. In order to rectify these problems, more research is needed to establish the behavioral components of the construct of "pain behavior" and to establish the most reliable, valid, and convenient methods of assessing this construct (Turk et al., 1985).

Cancer

Description

Cancer is the second leading cause of death in the United States, causing approximately 300,000 deaths per year (Beeson, McDermott, & Wyngaarden, 1979). It is defined as "a general term frequently used to indicate any of various types of malignant neoplasms, most of which invade surrounding tissues, may metastasize to several sites, and are likely to recur after attempted removal and to cause death of the patient unless adequately treated" (*Steadman's Medical Dictionary*, 1976, p. 217). Approximately 80% of all cancers are related to environmental rather than genetic factors, it is thought (Beeson et al., 1979). There are various types of cancer affecting a wide variety of symptoms. Therefore, the professional associated with treatment of cancer patients must be aware of the unpredictability of both medical and psychological changes that may occur in the cancer patient.

Medically, cancer may lead to organ failure or obstruction, pain, diabetes, metabolic disorders, infections, endocrine disorders, cardiovascular disorders, respiratory disorders, and a variety of other problems (Beeson et al., 1979). Psychologically, anxiety, depression, and psychotic behaviors may result from both the diagnosis and direct effects of cancer (Lucas & Brown, 1982).

Because of the extensive range of medical problems associated with cancer, the assessment of these problems will not be covered in this chapter. The reader is referred to Beeson et al. (1979) for a thorough discussion of medical factors and complications associated with this disease. However, the assessment of psychological problems of patients and their families will be discussed.

Assessment for Diagnosis

Lucas and Brown (1982) have outlined six integral areas that may be assessed through the interview process with the cancer patient and family. They are:

1. the antecedent thoughts, feelings, and experiences which intensify the particular problems.

BA—N

2. the nature and severity of the problems as differentially perceived by the patient, the staff, and the family.
3. a history-taking of when the problems first appeared.
4. the duration of the problems and their pattern of occurrence.
5. past medical and behavioral interventions attempted to resolve problems, and the degree of success realized.
6. coping responses used by the patient and the effects of these responses both for the patient and significant others. (p. 360)

With the use of psychological tests — questionnaires, self-monitoring, and interviews with both the patient and the involved family members — a thorough assessment of the problems associated with the diagnosis, treatment, and disease process of cancer can be delineated clearly. With the clear definition of symptoms experienced by the patient, targets for treatment that are relevant to the patient's needs will become readily apparent.

With the diagnosis of cancer, and over the course of the disease, many psychologically related problems may appear. These problems include anxiety, depression, inactivity, sleep problems, sexual dysfunction, and nausea/vomiting resulting from chemotherapy. These, as well as other resulting problems, may also be assessed with the use of psychological tests.

Several psychological tests have been utilized in the literature describing assessment of cancer patients. They include the MMPI (Koenig, Levin, & Brennan, 1967), the Symptom Checklist-90 — Revised (Craig & Abeloff, 1974; Derogatis et al., 1983), the State-Trait Anxiety Inventory (Zook & Yasko, 1983), the Beck Depression Inventory (Zook & Yasko, 1983), and the McGill-Melzack Pain Questionnaire (Zook & Yasko, 1983). These assessment devices can be used to assess levels of depression, anxiety, and pain. A recently constructed questionnaire designed to assess the physical and psychosocial changes in cancer patients' lives associated with the diagnosis of cancer is the Health Survey (Frank-Stromburg & Wright, 1984), which may prove useful in delineating problems (e.g., self-image, sleep-problems, and weight problems) amenable to treatment. In the assessment of nausea and vomiting, rating scales measuring frequency, duration, and intensity of nausea and vomiting (Zook & Yasko, 1983) and the Morrow Assessment of Nausea and Emesis scale (Morrow, 1984) allow assessment of a patient's response and ability to tolerate chemotherapy. Assessment of nausea and emesis is necessary as they may contribute toward compliance problems, dehydration, fractures, and depression (Borison, Borison, & McCarthy, 1981; Morrow & Morrell, 1982).

Self-monitoring of problems associated with cancer and its treatment may also be used in the assessment process. A symptom checklist (McCorkle & Young, 1978) can be used to assess nausea, eating, sleep problems, affect, pain, bowel pattern, concentration, and appearance. Self-monitoring designed specifically to assess other problems of the patient (e.g., time in and out of bed, compliance with the medical regimen, activity level, and food consumed and kept) may also be utilized.

Assessment for Treatment Planning

Tentative evidence indicates that cancer patients with certain psychological characteristics (e.g., hopefulness, tendency to express feelings, high level of activity, self-confidence) are more successful in surviving cancer than those without these characteristics (Achterberg, Matthews, & Simonton, 1978; Derogatis, Abeloff, & Melisaratos, 1979; Grossarth-Maticel, 1980). Therefore, continued assessment of the patient's emotional state during treatment will not only guide the course of treatment to be taken, but may, with effective treatment, lead to an increased life expectancy for the patient (Lucas & Brown, 1982).

Those assessment techniques noted earlier (interview, self-monitoring, and questionnaires) provide measures of treatment efficacy and indices of other problem areas that may occur with the treatment of the disease.

Summary

Cancer is a disease that has historically been associated with a high degree of stress (Derogatis et al., 1983), perhaps due to the high rate of mortality associated with the disease. Even with successful treatment, the diagnosis and treatment of cancer is still associated with psychologically related problems. Due to the high rate of problems associated with this disease, a complete and thorough assessment is needed to adequately understand the nature of the problems presented by each individual, thereby allowing the planning and monitoring of the most effective treatment regimen for each patient. Much of the earlier research on the psychological reactions of cancer patients utilized more traditional psychological tests of psychopathology. Recently, there have been several assessment instruments developed specifically for cancer patients. These new instruments are in the early stages of development and therefore their psychometric properties have not yet been established.

Raynaud's Disease

Description

Raynaud's disease is a dysfunction of the cardiovascular system, involving episodes of vasoconstriction of the small blood vessels of the extremities, primarily in the fingers and/or toes. This vasoconstriction produces symptom changes that can be broken down into three phases: the affected area first blanches, then turns blue, and finally turns bright red as the spasm is relieved and normal blood flow resumes (Masur, 1977). During the spasms, the affected area feels cold to touch, produces pain, and can, if severe, lead to gangrene.

Allen and Brown (1932) developed the following criteria for the diagnosis of Raynaud's disease: (a) episodes of bilateral color changes precipitated by cold or emotion, (b) absence of severe gangrene, (c) absence of any systematic disease that might account for the attacks, and (d) duration of symptoms for at least 2 years.

The term *Raynaud's disease* refers to the primary form of the disorder, when the etiology of the disease is unknown (Freedman, Ianni, & Wenig, 1983). There is no accepted medical regimen that has proved effective for the treatment of this disorder (Freedman et al., 1983).

Assessment for Diagnosis

The assessment for Raynaud's disease falls into two categories: that of the patient's self-report and assessment of blood flow in the laboratory (Freedman, Lynn, & Ianni, 1982). The patient's self-report of symptoms can be assessed in an interview and through self-monitoring. In the interview, a complete description of presenting symptoms should be obtained, along with the antecedents and consequences of the attacks. Also, a complete medical and family history should be obtained to identify medical and emotional problems that may contribute to the maintenance of the disorder. Self-monitoring usually involves recording situations that precipitate vasoconstrictive attacks, symptom severity, emotional stress, skin color changes, duration of the attack, and methods used to abort the episode (Freedman et al., 1982).

In assessing the patient's emotional stress level, several psychological tests have been utilized, including the MMPI (Freedman et al., 1982) and the State-Trait Anxiety Inventory (STAI; Spielberger, 1983). It has been found that the STAI is more sensitive than the MMPI for measuring emotional antecedents of vasoconstrictive attacks.

The assessment of peripheral blood flow in the laboratory provides an objective measure of symptomatology without the inherent problems of self-report. Skin temperature, capillary microscopy, angiography, and plethysmography are all used to measure blood flow in the affected areas. Skin temperature is the most commonly used procedure, due to its simplicity and relative lack of expense. However, a problem with the skin temperature measure is that response time is rather slow. With capillary microscopy, observation of movement of the red blood cells in the affected area is permitted. This procedure is also of relatively low cost and allows for the assessment of momentary blood flow changes to specific stimuli (e.g., cold or stress). Angiography involves injection of radioactive contrast agents with subsequent X ray of arteries. However, this procedure is invasive and not without risk. Plethysmography allows the assessment of pulse waves and blood volume within tissue segments. The procedure only provides a relative measure of blood flow and is subject to error. However, it does allow assessment of the immediate vascular responses to cold stimuli or stressors.

Assessment for Treatment Planning

The unknown etiology of Raynaud's disease makes necessary a thorough assessment of all facets of probable contributing factors, such as life stressors, anxiety, and effects of cold stimuli. For proper treatment planning, one of the most important variables to be identified is the exact nature of the antecedents of vasoconstrictive attacks. By precisely identifying these situational variables, a treatment plan can be developed that targets the patient's response to these situations. For example, in some cases biofeedback and relaxation may be used for teaching the patient anxiety management skills. In other cases the personal problems of the patient (e.g., marital conflict), which are sources of stress, may be targeted for modification. Other patients may need to learn more effective means of avoiding cold stimuli (e.g., wearing gloves, wearing extra clothes, etc.).

Treatment efficacy can be monitored through repeated physiological and psychological assessments. Through continued self-monitoring, treatment gains or losses will also be readily apparent. Evaluation of treatment outcome should involve direct tests of changes in the patient's response to the antecedents of vasoconstrictive attacks, which were identified prior to the initiation of treatment. Also, it is important that the season of the year (e.g., cold vs. warm months) be considered when attempting to evaluate treatment outcome since it is well established that Raynaud's patients have much greater problems during the winter than during the summer.

Summary

The thorough assessment of Raynaud's disease involves an assessment of the patient's report of symptoms, psychological state of the patient, and physiological responses in the laboratory. This comprehensive assessment not only provides a measure of pretreatment symptomology, but also allows for proper treatment planning and provides a method of assessment of treatment efficacy. Although skin temperature seems to be both accurate and reliable, more research is needed to investigate the psychometric properties of self-monitoring procedures used. Also, there is no systematic interview method currently employed in assessing problems associated with Raynaud's disease. Therefore, more research is needed regarding these concerns in assessing patients with Raynaud's disease.

Diabetes Mellitus

Description

Diabetes mellitus is a major health disorder affecting approximately 5% of the American population (Pohl, Gonder-Frederick, & Cox, 1984). Thus, over 10 million Americans suffer from this disorder, and it is one of the most common chronic health problems (Surwit, Feinglos, & Scovern, 1983). This metabolic disorder is caused by either ineffective production or ineffective utilization of the hormone insulin, which is secreted by the pancreas. Two types of diabetes mellitus are currently recognized by the National Diabetes Data Group (1979). Insulin-dependent diabetes mellitus (IDDM) usually appears during childhood, and affected individuals are usually at or below normal weight. The pancreas produces little or no insulin and treatment requires daily injection of insulin (Surwit et al., 1983). Non-insulin-dependent diabetes mellitus (NIDDM) generally occurs after age 40. Approximately 60–90% of these patients are above normal body weight. The pancreas produces normal insulin, but either due to inefficient use of the insulin or increased demands on the insulin-secretory capacity (perhaps due to obesity) these patients cannot produce enough insulin. Additional insulin is occasionally required, but generally diet and oral hypoglycemia medications increase the body's use of its own insulin (Surwit et al., 1983). Non-insulin-dependent diabetes accounts for 80% of all diagnosed diabetes and occurs more frequently in women. The prevalence of IDDM does not differ by gender (Hartman & Reuter, 1984).

Assessment for Diagnosis

Following a medical diagnosis of diabetes, various psychological problems may follow, such as noncompliance to a self-care regimen, difficulty adjusting to a chronic disease, and poor stress management. Thorough history-gathering and behavioral interviews with the patient and significant others typically provides information necessary for targeting behavioral problems. Important variables to consider are nutrition and exercise (Pohl et al., 1984), presence and severity of stress (Surwit & Feinglos, 1984), and understanding and ability to carry out the self-care regimen (Fisher, Delamater, Bertelson, & Kirkley, 1982; Surwit et al., 1983; Turk & Speers, 1982). The self-care program is complex and demanding. It includes nutritional planning, weight management, monitoring of urine or blood glucose, special food care, extra precautions against commonly occurring illnesses such as flu and colds, and taking oral medications or insulin injections (Fisher et al., 1982).

Assessment for Treatment Planning

Intervention is normally directed toward behavioral manipulation of physiology for better control of glucose metabolism or at changing secondary behaviors related to diabetes (Surwit et al., 1983). Self-monitoring of lifestyle variables can target specific maladaptive behaviors that need changing such as diet, exercise, and preventative health care. Another useful assessment procedure is psychophysiological monitoring of autonomic nervous system changes under stress conditions. Commonly used physiological measures are galvanic skin resistance, skin temperature, electromyography, and heart rate. The autonomic nervous system plays a role in glucose metabolism (Vandenberg, Sussman, & Vaughan, 1967; Williams & Porte, 1974). It is therefore reasonable to enhance behavior regulation of stress reactions for better control of the body's ability to secrete insulin and metabolize glucose (Seeburg & DeBoer, 1980; Surwit & Feinglos, 1983; Young & Landsberg, 1979). Besides assessing the patient's understanding of the disease and the self-care regimen, additional areas to assess for intervention are the patient's ability to deal with problematic situations (problem-solving ability), reinforcement contingencies for carrying out the regimen, and assertiveness skills necessary for social interactions (e.g., refusing certain foods and drinks, leaving to administer insulin or complete glucose level checks, and telling their hosts that a specific type of meal is required).

Summary

Diabetes is one of very few health disorders that requires a great amount of responsibility because patient makes independent therapeutic decisions based on daily clinical observations. Insulin or oral hypoglycemic medication requirements are influenced by exercise, diet, and general physical and emotional health (Turk, Meichenbaum, & Genest, 1983). There is evidence to suggest that improvement of these behavioral factors results in better metabolic control and reduces long-term complications (Santiago, 1984). Effective diabetes care is complex and has presented new challenges for behavioral medicine's assessment and intervention measures. Assessment must be conducted to target the individual factors that affect diabetes mellitus.

Behavioral assessment procedures for diabetes involve both biological and behavioral variables. Medical procedures, such as determination of glucose levels, are very standardized and well developed. Behavioral procedures, on the other hand, have taken a more idiographic approach and are much less well developed.

Premenstrual Syndrome

Description

Although there is some variance in the definition of premenstrual syndrome (PMS) among researchers, it can be generally described as an emotional and behavioral disturbance occurring in some women during their premenstrual phase in the absence or any ongoing physical or psychological pathology (Steiner, Haskett, & Carroll, 1980). Early reports of the types of disturbances experienced have included many diverse symptoms and estimates of prevalence rates of PMS range from 20 to 90% (Altman, Knowles, & Bull, 1941; Green & Dalton, 1953; Pennington, 1957; Reid & Yen, 1981). A significant number of these women suffer symptoms sufficiently severe to interfere with interpersonal relationships and job performance (Reid & Yen, 1981).

Assessment for Diagnosis

A diagnostic interview must be carefully performed so that the interviewer does not lead the patient. Ruble (1977) found an increased report of physical symptoms in women misled to believe they were suffering premenstrual problems. Symptoms of PMS encompass three general areas of emotional, physical, and behavioral changes (Abplanalp, 1983) and may occur in any combination. Emotional states include depression or dysphoria, tension and anxiety, and irritability. Common physical complaints include headache, bloating and edema, and breast tenderness. Behavioral changes often include reduced social interaction, increased crying, and changes in work performance (Abplanalp, 1983; Sampson & Prescott, 1981). One questionnaire commonly used to assess PMS symptoms is the *Menstrual Distress Questionnaire* (MDQ) developed by Moos (1968, 1977) to assess affect, physiological, and behavioral changes in relation to the menstrual cycle. There are two forms of the MDQ, form C and form T. MDQ-C allows assessment of symptoms in three phases of the most recent menstrual cycle: four days before menstrual flow, during menstrual flow, and the remainder of the cycle. The MDQ-T enables description of symptoms for one or more specific days. Thus, form T is useful for repeated assessment over time (Moos, 1977). The MDQ-T has been shown to have satisfactory test-retest and split-half reliability (Markin, 1976). This questionnaire provides scores in eight specific areas as well as a global score. The eight subclasses are pain, concentration, behavior change, autonomic reactions, water retention, negative affect, arousal, and a control scale. Several studies have shown the questionnaire to differentiate symptom changes from the follicular to the premenstrual phase (Moos, 1968; Moos & Leiderman, 1978; Rouse, 1978; Sampson & Prescott, 1981). Steiner et al. (1980) also demonstrated a relationship between severity of the disorder and score on the MDQ.

Assessment for Treatment Planning

Since the menstrual cycle is different for each woman, self-monitoring basis of the symptom groups identified by the MDQ can help establish the temporal pattern of physical and emotional changes within the menstrual cycle. After obtaining a single cycle of monitoring, it is useful to compare it to consecutive cycles in the same individual (Sampson & Prescott, 1981). This baseline data is important not only to establish the presence and the pattern of PMS but also for evaluating symptom changes during treatment.

Summary

There is disagreement among researchers and clinicians concerning the criteria for a diagnosis of PMS. The current status of diagnosis requires one to recognize that PMS patients are a heterogeneous group and assessment of each patient must be on an individual basis. The current body of research has produced few definitive statements or assessment instruments and needs controlled research. Only the MDQ-C has been widely studied as an assessment device for PMS. Although it has been found to have satisfactory reliability, studies of its validity have only recently been reported. This topic badly needs more rigorous research related to the stability of PMS symptoms over several menstrual cycles and the development of procedures for differentiating subtypes of PMS.

Asthma

Description

Bronchial asthma is generally characterized by hyperresponsiveness of both large and small airways in the lungs and results in wheezing, coughing and shortness of breath. These attacks are episodic and may be so severe as to impede the patient's ability to walk or talk (Cluss & Fireman, 1985). The United States Department of Health, Education, and Welfare (NIAID Task Force, 1979) data suggests that 8.9 million Americans suffer from asthma. Studies have also indicated that from 2 to 30% of a family's income may be spent in the treatment of the asthmatic disorder (Vance & Taylor, 1971). As these figures show, it is a prevalent and very serious medical disorder.

Asthma attacks may be brought on by allergic or irritant stimuli (Williamson, McKenzie, Goreczny, & Faulstich, 1987) or by viral infections (Cluss & Fireman, 1985). These attacks are known as *extrinsic asthma*. *Intrinsic asthma* is so labeled because there are no identifiable allergens or viral infections. Many studies have shown that emotional factors and suggestions can precipitate or exacerbate an asthma attack (Levinson, 1979; Luparello, Lyons, Bleecker, & McFadden, 1968; Luparello, Leist, Lourie, & Sweet, 1970; Phillip, Wilde, & Day, 1972). Due to this psychological link, research in the area of behavioral medicine has included attempts to assess the emotional antecedents of asthmatic attacks and the emotional reactions of the patient and the family to asthmatic attacks.

Several studies have suggested that parental overprotection of an asthmatic child and reinforcement contingencies may play a role in the chronicity and severity of the disorder (Gardner, 1968; Lazar & Jedlikzka, 1979; Parker & Lipscombe, 1979). Therefore, assessment of the responses of the family members to asthmatic attacks is very important.

Assessment for Diagnosis

As with other health disorders, a medical evaluation is required to accurately diagnose asthma. The medical diagnosis of asthma is generally considered to be straightforward (Burrows, 1979). A careful history is an essential part of the diagnosis (Kaplan, Reis, & Atkins, 1985). A commonly used test for asthma is the use of a spirometer. This mechanical device measures the volume and flow of air in the lungs through the airways (Clausen & Zarins, 1982). These values can be compared to normal functioning values.

Several assessment measures have been developed to objectively assess differential responding to asthma symptoms. These include the Asthma Symptom Checklist (ASC), which describes five areas of subjective reports of asthmatic symptomatology: (a) panic-fear, (b) irritability, (c) fatigue, (d) airway obstruction, and (e) hyperventilation-hypnocapnia (Kinsman, Dahlem, Spector, & Staudenmayer, 1977). Test-retest reliability has been found to be satisfactory, with coefficients ranging from $r = .83$ to $r = .93$ (Kinsman, Luparello, O'Banion, & Spector, 1973; Kinsman et al., 1977). The Asthma Problem Behavior Checklist (APBC) was developed by Creer, Marion, and Creer (1983) to identify behavior problems that may contribute to the severity of asthma, to identify consequences of the disorder that affect the family system, and to define specific behaviors to be changed. The APBC has also been found to have high test-retest reliability with correlation coefficients above .90 (Creer et al., 1983). Also available is the Battery of Asthma Illness Behavior (BAIB), which is a combination of several measures. This instrument has been found to be reliable, independent of onset age and of objective medical aspects of severity of the disorder. Scores on the BAIB have been found to correlate with patient self-report of daily functioning and with noncompliance of the medication regimen (Dirks, Brown, & Robinson, 1982). These self-report instruments can be used for identifying target behaviors and for defining severity of the problem.

Assessment for Treatment Planning

These self-report instruments must be supplemented with a careful behavioral interview to identify antecedents and consequences which covary with asthmatic attacks. In some cases, specific environments or persons may precipitate attacks. In other cases, stress or emotional reactions may increase the probability of an attack. Regarding consequences, it is important to identify potential reinforcers (e.g., relief from responsibilities or escape from aversive environments which may maintain asthma attacks). Also, the emotional reactions of parents and family members may serve to heighten the anxiety of the asthmatic patient, thereby exacerbating the attack. Another variable that must be assessed is compliance with medical regimens (e.g., bronchial dilators, medications, etc.). Treatment outcome may be assessed via self-monitoring of asthmatic attacks, days missed from work or school, or frequency of emergency room visits. Also, self-report inventories such as the BAIB or the ASC may be used to evaluate treatment effectiveness.

Summary

Asthma can be a chronic medical problem complicated by psychological factors. Interviews, self-monitoring, pulmonary functioning tests, and self-report instruments which yield information about differential responding to asthma symptomatology as well as identify maladaptive behaviors should be the components of a complete battery for the assessment and treatment of the asthmatic condition. Several assessment instruments have been developed for evaluating asthmatic symptoms and behavioral problems associated with asthma. These instruments have all been investigated psychometrically and have been found to have satisfactory reliability and validity.

Sleep Disturbances

Description

Although there is considerable disagreement on how to categorize sleep disturbances, the basic definition can be summarized as any deviation from one's usual sleep pattern that results in impairment of that person's daily functioning. The prevalence rate of such disturbances is high, with figures ranging from 25.7% to 39.4% of the population (Bixler, Kales, Scharf, Kales, & Leo, 1976; Hammond, 1964; Price, Coates, Thoresen, & Grinstead, 1978).

There are four general categories of sleep disturbances recognized by the Association of Sleep Disorders Center, the Association for the Physiological Study of Sleep, and the American Psychiatric Association (APA). In the *Diagnostic and Statistical Manual of Mental Disorders* (DSM-III; APA, 1980), these include: (a) disorders of initiation and maintaining sleep (insomnia), (b) disorders of excessive somnolence (also known as hypersomnia), (c) disorders of the sleep-wake schedule, and (d) dysfunctions associated with sleep, sleep stages, or partial arousals (parasomnia).

In disorders of initiating and maintaining sleep (DIMS), the person generally complains of daytime fatigue, increased irritability, and other depressive symptoms. These problems occur due to reduced sleep time attributable to difficulty in falling asleep, staying asleep, and/or awakening early in the morning. Disorders of excessive somnolence (DOES) center around complaints of excessive sleepiness during the day that is not attributable to poor nocturnal sleep. Excessive nighttime sleep may also be reported. Disorders of the sleep-wake schedule include transient or persistent environmental changes, such as frequently changing workshift schedules. Parasomnias can be summarized as abnormal nocturnal behaviors (Coates &

Thoresen, 1981) and include behaviors that are performed during sleep. The three most common disruptive nocturnal behaviors are: sleepwalking, sleep terror, and sleep-related enuresis. Several other dysfunctions are included in this category such as nightmares, sleep-related bruxism, or impaired penile tumescence (APA, 1980). For a more complete discussion of these disorders, see Lawrence (1982).

Assessment for Diagnosis

A thorough medical exam should first be completed to rule out sleep disturbance as secondary to a physical disorder such as thyroid dysfunction or heart disease (Kales & Kales, 1974). Interviews with parent, spouse, and the patient should also be conducted to assess whether a neurological dysfunction such as sleep apnea, nocturnal myoclonous, restless legs syndrome, or narcolepsy is present (Frankel, Patten, & Gillen, 1974; Guilleninault, Eldridge, & Dement, 1973; Zarcone, 1975). Diaries and audio- and/or video-tapes of the sleep session can help confirm such diagnoses (Coates & Thoresen, 1981).

A very important step in diagnosis is to assess the patient's drug use history. Use of stimulants, alcohol, or hypnotic medications often lead to inferior sleep at night and excessive daytime fatigue. Hypnotics result in diminished rapid eye movement (REM) sleep and slow-wave sleep (Kales & Kales, 1974; Kales, Bixler, Tan, Scharf, & Kales, 1974; Kay, Blackburn, Buckingham, & Karacan, 1976). These disturbances can lead to daytime fatigue, frequent awakening, insufficient total sleep time, and inability to fall asleep.

Although all-night sleep recordings are important for sleep research and provide a wealth of clinical assessment data, they are expensive and time-consuming to perform. In some cases, however, all-night sleep recordings may be necessary to establish the presence of some sleep disorders, in particular, pseudoinsomnia. The pseudoinsomniac complains of insomnia even though the electroencephalograph (EEG) readings reflect normal sleep. Several studies have found that people complaining of insomnia often overestimate the latency of sleep onset as well as underestimate total sleep time and complain of daytime fatigue (Carskadon et al., 1976; Frankel, Coursey, Buchbinder, & Snyder, 1976; Pollak, McGregor, & Weitzman, 1975; Roth, Lutz, Kramer, & Tietz, 1977). An alternative to the all-night laboratory sleep recording is a procedure developed by Lichstein, Nickel, Hoelscher, & Kelley (1982) which requires the patient to respond to an auditory stimulus if he/she is awake. This procedure has been found to be a valid measure of sleep latency and duration and is much more convenient than laboratory assessments since it can be utilized in the patient's home.

In assessing sleep disturbances, a behavioral analysis is essential for establishing the impact of environmental, psychological, and physiological factors upon sleep. Behavioral assessment is also helpful in developing an appropriate treatment plan. Important areas to investigate are physical and mental bedtime activities, prebedtime activities, daytime activities and environment, the sleep environment, circadian rhythm, and diet (Coates & Thoresen, 1981). Also, ruling out a major depressive disorder is essential since it is well established that depression is associated with sleep onset insomnia and early awakening.

Assessment for Treatment Planning

A thorough behavioral interview with the patient and, if possible, significant others should yield relevant information concerning the patient's lifestyle and environment so that treatment can be focused on changing specific areas that contribute to sleep disturbance. Patient self-monitoring of these variables and perceived sleep time (often called sleep logs) can provide a baseline measure to assess the presence of these variables and can be used to assess treatment outcome. Lichstein et al., (1982) have shown that sleep data derived from sleep logs correspond very well to more objective measures of sleep time.

Areas of behavioral assessment should include physical and mental activity at bedtime. Physical tension may interfere with sleep and chronic tension during the day may result in fatigue. Common symptoms of physical tension are bruxism, tension headaches, and cramping. Mental activities that interfere with sleep may include worrying about transient or chronic problems (Coursey, Buchsbaum, & Frankel, 1975; Coates et al., 1980). Patients may also be thinking about their inability to sleep. Phobias about nightmares or loss of consciousness could also present problems in sleep quality. Daytime activities and environment should be assessed as chronic stress can lead to excessive physical tension or mental activity at bedtime. Certain prebedtime activity (such as exercise or arguments) may result in physical or mental activity and prolonged sleep onset. The sleep environment itself may also be interfering with sleep. Assessment of the noise level, light, and temperature of the room as well as the comfort of the bed may provide information on what needs to be changed. A commonly occurring problem with sleep disturbance is that the bedroom or bed becomes associated with thoughts or activities incompatible with sleep, such as reading or watching television. In such cases it is necessary to change the bedroom from a stimulus for activity to a stimulus for sleep (Bootzin & Nicassio, 1978). Changes in the sleep-wake schedule (i.e., workshift changes) may easily interfere with ability to sleep. Sleep disturbance may also result from abnormalities in the circadian cycle (Miles, Raynal, & Wilson, 1977). Normally, body temperature falls at bedtime and rises toward morning. The body temperature of the poor sleeper has been shown to fall at bedtime, rise again within a 5-hour period, then fall again. Sleep disturbances could reflect changes in this rhythmic cycle (Coates & Thoresen, 1981). Another important area of assessment is the food and drink taken before bedtime. High sugar and caffeine levels may interfere with sleep onset and sleep quality.

Summary

Sleep disturbance complaints are not often straightforward and usually require a comprehensive individualized assessment of relevant physiological, environmental, and psychological factors. An assessment that includes medical exams, careful history-gathering and behavioral interviews with the patient and significant others, audio or video taping, all-night sleep recordings (if possible), and self-monitoring of daily activities and diet should provide better understanding of the nature and cause of a sleep disturbance. Most of these procedures have been studied intensively and have been shown to be reliable and accurate as well as useful for differential diagnosis.

Eating Disorders: Anorexia Nervosa, Bulimia, and Obesity

Description

Both anorexia nervosa and bulimia are most often seen in white females between the ages of 13 and 20 (Halmi, Casper, & Eckert, 1979; Fairburn & Cooper, 1982). Obesity becomes more prevalent with age and is only slightly more common in females than in males (Brownell & Stunkard, 1980). Prevalence rates for anorexia are less than 1% of young women (American Psychological Association [APA], 1980), whereas bulimia is more common, with estimates of prevalence ranging from 1 to 13% (Mizes, 1985). Obesity has the highest prevalence rate with estimates of 24.2% of American men and 27.1% of American women evidencing clinical obesity (National Center for Health Statistics, 1980).

Anorexia nervosa diagnostic criteria include the loss of at least 25% of the body's weight, an intense fear of being fat, a distorted image of the body, and a refusal to maintain an appropriate body weight (APA, 1980). The main symptoms of bulimia include frequent binge eating, accompanied by fear of losing control over eating and feelings of depression and guilt following binge episodes. The binge eating usually consists of the consumption of large amounts of high-calorie foods. Some bulimics, however, consider only small amounts of "forbidden" foods, such as ice cream, to be binge episodes. A variety of other symptoms may accompany these primary symptoms: secretive eating, frequent weight fluctuation, self-induced vomiting, laxative abuse, and diuretic abuse in order to control weight are common secondary symptoms (APA, 1980). Similar to anorexics, bulimics appear to have distorted images of their bodies (Williamson, Kelley, Davis, Ruggiero, & Blouin, 1985).

Obesity is defined as an excessive amount of body fat (Rogers, Mahoney, Mahoney, Straw, & Kenigsberg, 1980). Due to the extra fat accumulation, the obese person is at a high risk for many health problems such as diabetes, hypertension, and cardiovascular illness.

Assessment for Diagnosis

Following the elimination of hormonal or endocrinological etiology for eating disorders by a complete medical evaluation, a variety of assessment procedures must be used to adequately differentially diagnose anorexia nervosa, bulimia, and obesity. Anorexics and purging bulimics share symptoms of body image distortion, fear of being obese, anxiety about eating, and the overuse of severe weight-control methods. Bulimics who do not purge (bulimic binge eaters) share symptoms with both the purging bulimics, such as frequent binge episodes, and with the nonbulimic obese, such as the use of frequent restrictive diets (Williamson, Kelley, Cavell, & Prather, in press).

Several self-report instruments are available to aid in assessment. The Eating Attitudes Test (EAT) was developed by Garner and Garfinkel (1979) to identify abnormal attitudes toward eating. This instrument has been shown to discriminate anorexics from normal subjects (Mann, Wakeling, Wood, Monck, Dobbs, & Szmukler, 1983). The Bulimia Test (BULIT) is a 32-item questionnaire useful in diagnosing bulimia (Smith & Thelen, 1984). Both of these instruments have been shown to have satisfactory reliability and validity. The BULIT has been shown to also be useful in differentially diagnosing the bulimic binge eater from the non bulimic obese (Prather, 1985).

Body image distortion is a problem that has been identified for anorexics and bulimics. Body image distortion involves perceiving oneself as being larger than is actually the case and wishing to be thinner than is normal. A variety of methods have been developed for assessing body image. These methods include the adjustable, body-distorting mirror (Traub & Orbach, 1964); the image-marking procedure (Askevold, 1975); the adjustable, body distorting television monitor (Allenbeck, Hallberg, & Espmark, 1976); and the visual size estimation method (Pearlson, Flournoy, Simonson, & Slavney, 1981). These procedures have generally been found to have satisfactory reliability and have been shown to demonstrate the predicted body image distortion in eating-disordered populations. However, all of these procedures are somewhat cumbersome to use and are difficult to implement in most clinical settings. Recently, Williamson et al. (1985) introduced a much simpler and more convenient method called the Body Image Assessment Procedure. This procedure uses nine silhouettes of female figures which vary in size from very thin to very obese. The silhouettes are placed in a random order and the patient is first asked to choose the figure that is closest to the patient's actual body size and is then asked (for a second random order) to choose the silhouette representing the patient's ideal body size. This procedure has been found to have satisfactory test-retest reliability (Davis, Williamson, & Ruggiero, 1984) and has demonstrated discriminant validity by differentiating bulimics from normals (Williamson et al., 1985) and bulimic binge purgers from bulimic binge eaters (Davis et al., 1984).

The concept of forbidden foods in eating disorders was recently discussed by Szmukler (1983), and the Food Survey (Ruggiero, Williamson, Jones, & Davis, 1984) was developed to help identify food types that lead to problem eating. The Food Survey has been found to be reliable and useful in differentiating bulimics who purge from obese subjects and bulimic binge eaters (Ruggiero et al., 1984).

The presence of anxiety following eating may be assessed using psychophysiological procedures during which changes in the client's heart rate, skin temperature, electromyograph, and peripheral vasomotor responses are monitored (Williamson, Davis, Ruggiero, Goreczny, & McKenzie, 1985; Williamson, Kelley, Davis, Ruggiero, & Veitia, 1985).

Self-monitoring of food intake and associated factors provides very useful information about the client's eating behavior (Schlundt, Johnson, & Jarrell, 1985). This procedure provides data on the frequency of eating, binging, purging, and fasting, as well as information on the type and amount of food eaten. Variables such as mood and activities engaged in prior to eating and secretiveness of the eating behavior can be identified. Concurrent validity of the self-monitoring was recently demonstrated by high correlations between self-monitoring data and scores on the EAT and BULIT (Prather, Upton, Williamson, Davis, Ruggiero, & Van Buren, 1985).

For a diagnosis of obesity, the percentage that one is overweight according to height and sex norms is one method that can be used. The most common criterion is 20% or more above statistically normal weight. However, researchers have used weight criteria as low as 10% overweight to define obesity (Coates, Jeffery, Slinkard, Killen, & Danaher, 1982). Skinfold thickness measure is an inexpensive method of accurately obtaining subcutaneous fat levels. This measure is more reliable and valid than the bodyweight measure for estimating body fat (Rogers et al., 1980). Four skinfold sites (biceps, triceps, subscapular, and suprailiac) are measured by skinfold calipers. An equation will then provide a body fat score. This score can be compared to age and sex norms (Durnin & Womersley, 1974).

Assessment for Treatment Planning

Many of the assessment methods used for diagnosis are also important for treatment planning. The severity of the eating-disorder symptoms will be reflected in the self-monitoring treatment data and will aid in targeting specific behaviors for treatment. The Food Survey and Body Image

Assessment Procedure can also provide information on necessary treatment components, such as nutritional education and body image desensitization (Prather, Mckenzie, Upton, & Williamson, 1985). Furthermore, the Food Survey can be used to target forbidden foods, which can be used in treatment via exposure with response prevention.

Recent research has indicated that eating-disordered clients display symptoms indicative of depression, anxiety, and other psychopathologies (Anderson, 1983; Calloway, Fonagy, & Wakeling, 1983; Williamson et al., 1985). The Minnesota Multiphasic Personality Inventory (MMPI), Symptom Checklist-90 — Revised (SCL-90), and Beck Depression Inventory (BDI) have been useful in identifying psychopathology for treatment. Williamson et al. (1985) found modest elevations (between 60 and 70 *T*-scores) on MMPI scales 1, 2, 3, 4, 7, and 8. These elevations suggest undue health concerns, depression, poor impulse control, anxiousness, negative self-evaluation, and poor self-esteem. The BDI revealed a mean score of 15.4 for bulimics (Williamson et al., 1985), whereas anorexics were found to average 28.6 (Garfinkel et al., 1983). Although the Williamson et al. (1985) research found obese subjects to score within normal limits on these measures, recent research from our clinic found that obese subjects evidence levels of psychopathology similar to bulimics (Prather & Williamson, in press). This difference has been attributed to the fact that the obese group of the Williamson et al. (1985) study was comprised of nonclinical subjects, and in our later research we employed clinical subjects who presented for treatment voluntarily (Prather, 1985). This hypothesis is currently being tested. These data suggest that psychopathology other than problems specific to eating disorders are relevant for treatment planning. Based upon these findings, it is recommended that comprehensive assessment of eating-disordered behavior as well as depression, anxiety, and personality disorders be conducted for these populations.

Summary

Recent research related to the assessment of anorexia nervosa, bulimia, and obesity suggest that there are many similarities and differences among these eating-disorder groups. Therefore, careful analysis of their eating-disordered behavior as well as more general psychopathology is recommended for proper treatment planning. Many of the present assessment procedures have been found to have good reliability and validity, and research is continuing to address the individual differences within these eating-disordered groups.

Failure to Thrive

Description

Failure to thrive (FTT) refers to a condition that is applied to infants who experience persistent growth retardation (Williamson, Kelley, Cavell, & Prather, in press). In classifying infants as FTT, criteria used are (a) weight persistently below the third percentile for age on standardized growth charts or (b) weight loss of two or more standard deviations below the mean of the normal growth curve for children (Bithoney & Rathbun, 1983). Often, FTT infants are socially withdrawn, hyperactive, irritable, developmentally delayed, and evidence eating problems (Bithoney & Rathburn, 1983; Williamson, Kelley, Cavell, & Prather, in press).

Assessment for Diagnosis

In assessing an FTT infant, several aspects of the infant's behavior, as well as the behavior of the primary caretaker, should be considered. Also, organic factors should be evaluated as causal factors in failure to grow. However, identification of organic factors is rare, as indicated by two studies that found that only 2% of all laboratory tests ordered on FTT infants proved to be positive (Berwick, Levy, & Kleinerman, 1982; Sills, 1978). Therefore, while ruling out organic factors, the assessment of nonorganic failures in the development and maintenance of FTT should be assessed concurrently (Bithoney & Rathbun, 1983).

In assessing the behavior of the FTT infant, feeding behavior is the most important variable to investigate. Often, the primary caretaker is questioned regarding the amount and frequency of food ingested by the infant. It should be noted that reliance on eating-behavior reports of others should be avoided because they are often of questionable validity. If at all possible, actual observation of the child's eating behavior should be conducted (Williamson, Kelley, Cavell, & Prather, in press).

Behavioral codes to score videotaped eating episodes have been developed (Klesges et al., 1983; Pollitt & Wirtz, 1981), as has been a system to assess the caloric and nutrient value of the food ingested (Traughber, Erwin, Risley, & Schnelle, 1983).

Mother–infant interactions must also be assessed with the FTT infant. Rosen, Loeb, and Tura (1980) have developed a system that measures the approach–avoidance behavior evidenced by infants interacting with examiners. This system does not directly assess the mother–infant interaction. It does, however, accurately differentiate between nonorganic and organic FTT infants.

A final area of assessment of the FTT infant is the psychological state and expectations of the primary caretaker. Depression, anxiety, isolation level, expectancies regarding management of the child, and financial problems should be assessed, identifying problematic areas that may be appropriate for intervention.

Assessment for Treatment Planning

Those procedures used to assess the FTT infant can be used as a measure of improvement during the treatment phase. For example, if caloric intake is found to be one targeted area for change, repeated assessments of caloric intake can provide important information regarding treatment efficacy. Also, the assessment of the parents' or primary caretaker's knowledge of appropriate nutrition and skill in parenting may provide important information for establishing target behaviors. Through interview and direct or taped observation of the parent–child interactions, specific problematic behaviors exhibited by either the infant or parent can be identified and, subsequently, treated.

Summary

The assessment of the FTT infant is quite complicated, requiring the assessment of (a) organic factors of the infant, (b) feeding behavior, (c) infant–primary caretaker interactions, and (d) the psychological state of the primary caretaker. For the most successful treatment, repeated assessments should be conducted throughout both the treatment and follow-up phases of therapy, insuring that treatment gains are initiated and maintained. However, assessment of FTT infants is relatively new, and more research is needed regarding the appropriate medical and psychological factors that should be assessed in these studies.

Food Refusal

Description

Food refusal is a problem of early childhood. There are several variations of food refusal, including a reluctance/refusal to eat foods outside of a select group of preferred foods or food textures; a refusal to eat enough food to produce weight gain; mealtime tantrums; and gagging, choking, or vomiting certain foods (Krieger, 1982; Linscheid, Oliver, Blyler, & Palmer, 1978; Williamson, Kelley, Cavell, & Prather, in press). The disorder may dissipate with maturation or may lead to malnutrition and retarded growth. In severe cases, it may result in a severe threat to the child's life.

Assessment for Diagnosis

While FTT infants never developed appropriate eating habits, children with food refusal problems usually have changed their eating habits. Interviews with parents can delineate any changes in dietary habits. In these interviews, a behavioral analysis of antecedents and consequences surrounding the refusal of certain foods should be conducted in order to establish the environmental conditions that are maintaining the refusal to eat. The Food Frequency Listing (Murray & Glassman, 1982) can help specify food flavor and texture preferences and can be utilized in conjunction with the interview to identify those foods which are eaten and those which are not.

Observation of the child while eating is helpful in developing or confirming hypotheses regarding factors that might be maintaining food refusal. For a less obtrusive procedure, videotaping can be utilized, allowing analysis of parent–child interactions during mealtimes.

Assessment for Treatment Planning

As with other disorders, assessment does not come with the onset of treatment. The assessment procedures noted above can be utilized not only to help delineate targeted behaviors for treatment, but also to assess treatment efficacy. The initial assessment should target the specific foods that are avoided, and treatment outcome may be evaluated by measuring changes in the eating of these foods. Other outcome measures that might be used are weight status and reduction of behaviors that are incompatible with eating.

Summary

Both the children exhibiting food refusal and the other family members (especially parents) are integral to both the assessment and treatment processes. Behavioral analysis of the child's eating (or noneating) habits, as well as the parenting/familial responses to the child's behavior, provide important information regarding appropriate targets for behavior change. In treating the food-refusing child, however, the parents may often be the primary focus of treatment and their behavior at mealtime may be a primary focus of assessment. Like assessment with FTT children, the development of assessment procedures for children with food refusal is in its early stages. Most of the assessment techniques for food refusal were developed in order to plan and evaluate treatment methods. Therefore, very little has been done to establish consistent or standardized procedures. Instead, the idiographic approach has predominated and will likely continue until the body of treatment literature concerning this problem is more extensive.

CASE EXAMPLE

Description and Presenting Problems

Susan was a 23-year-old white, married, female referred with a primary medical disorder of diabetes, which was exacerbated by a refusal to eat and complaints of nausea, stomach cramping, and vomiting after eating. Susan was diagnosed at age 2 as a severe case of juvenile-onset diabetes. She was very brittle and had been placed on an insulin pump 4 years prior to referral. The insulin pump enabled the medical team to stabilize her insulin requirements for about 1 year. At the time of referral she weighed 70 lbs., at a height of 4 ft, 11 in. She avoided eating almost all foods with a few exceptions: cooked carrots and boiled potatoes. When she attempted to eat other foods she consistently felt nauseous and developed stomach pain that appeared to be a result of cramping. If she ate even modest amounts of food, she vomited. At the time of referral she had been hospitalized and was being maintained on intravenous feeding with glucose. All medical tests and examinations had failed to explain the reasons for her failure to keep food down and her refusal to eat, despite the drastic health consequences of these habits.

Evaluation

A series of interviews were conducted and a battery of tests were administered while the patient was hospitalized in a general medical unit. The interviews were structured to obtain the patient's history, the history of her eating disorder, and a functional analysis of the factors which might be maintaining the disorder. From these interviews it was learned that she had been "pampered" all of her life due to her unstable diabetic condition. Prior to being placed on the insulin pump 4 years ago, she sought constant medical attention in order to be regulated properly. Her physicians believed that much of this behavior was motivated by the special medical attention that is naturally obtained by patients with severe medical conditions. Her insulin was well regulated for approximately 1 year when she developed the first evidence of an eating disorder. She began to feel nauseous and vomited several times after eating fatty meats. Soon afterward, she experienced the same symptoms, with stomach pain, in response to eating snack foods which tasted "greasy" (e.g., potato chips, corn chips, etc.). These behavioral reactions gradually generalized to a greater and greater variety of foods, which led to a severe restriction in her diet and overall caloric intake and resulted in a 25-lb weight loss over the year before her hospitalization. Prior to this time she had never been overweight and had no strong fear of losing control of her weight. During the interviews she was generally cooperative, though she often complained of lethargy, dizziness, and other symptoms that might "interfere" with her ability to remember events. Interviews with family members did, however, confirm the major historical events that she reported. At the time of referral, she ate very little — mostly cooked carrots and boiled potatoes. Efforts to eat other foods resulted in stomach pain and nausea and were avoided. She was able to manipulate her insulin level via the manual override on her insulin pump. In this manner she was able to keep her glucose level fairly stable, in the high normal range. Thus, she was generally able to avoid the hypoglycemia that would naturally result from constricted food intake and normal dosages of insulin. She preferred this high normal glucose level because she "had plenty of energy and never felt hungry."

A variety of behavioral assessment instruments and more traditional psychological tests were administered to complete this evaluation. In order to evaluate general psychopathogy, the MMPI, SCL-90R, and BDI were administered. Previous research (Williamson et al., 1985) had shown these instruments to differentiate bulimics from normals. These test results indicated that Susan was answering the MMPI questions in an honest and unbiased manner. The only abnormalities found were on Scale 3 (*Hy*) of the MMPI and the Somatic Complaints scale of the SCL-90R. There were no indications of depression or even a great deal of distress. In order to evaluate the nature of her eating disorder, three self-report instruments specific to eating disorders were administered. The BULIT, designed to assess bulimia, yielded a score of 35, which is not indicative of bulimia. Likewise, the score of the EAT, a test for anorexia, was 15, which is not indicative of anorexia. Examination of answers to specific questions on these two instruments showed that the patient positively endorsed questions related to starvation, weight loss, and vomiting, but did not endorse items pertaining to irrational beliefs about dieting, weight, foods, and body size. Administration of the Body Image Assessment Procedure (Williamson et al., 1985) yielded results which suggested that instead of striving for thinness, the patient wished to gain weight, which was congruent with statements made during the interviews. In order to assess the patient's eating behavior, the nursing staff was instructed to monitor the type and amount of food eaten as well as her reactions while eating. This observational procedure showed that she seldom ate. On the few occasions that she did eat, she reported nausea and stomach pain. Finally, a psychophysiological and behavioral observation procedure was conducted to evaluate autonomic and behavioral reactions to eating larger amounts of food than were normal for her. This assessment protocol involved recording heart rate and blood pressure, ratings of discomfort, ratings of nausea, and the occurrence of vomiting before and after eating a standard hospital lunch of approximately 550 calories. This evaluation indicated no autonomic signs of anxiety after eating: her heart rate was elevated about 6 beats per minute, and her blood pressure was unchanged, which is within normal limits. She required a great deal of coaxing to complete the meal. She complained of nausea and stomach pain, which was reflected in the ratings. After completion of the meal, she went to the bathroom where she vomited while under the observation of a staff member. It was reported that although she did not use a finger to elicit gagging, she did use postural and stomach contractions to induce vomiting. This purging required about 10 minutes of effort. Afterward she reported no discomfort or nausea.

Diagnosis and Case Formulation

The results of the assessment suggested that this was not a typical eating-disorder case. However, it did show that Susan's eating behavior was abnormal and that this behavior was likely under the control of psychological factors. For these reasons a diagnosis of atypical eating disorder exacerbating the diabetic condition was given. A diagnosis of bulimia or anorexia nervosa was not supported because the patient did not display many of the key diagnostic symptoms for these disorders (e.g., preoccupation with weight, food, and dieting; purging for weight loss; and body image distortion).

A more thorough behavioral conceptualization of the case suggested that eating most foods resulted in stomach cramping and nausea. Additional eating increased the severity of these symptoms, which were terminated by vomiting. It appeared that the vomiting was sometimes reflexive but was often an operant behavior serving the function of pain reduction. This behavior was apparently conditioned to greasy foods initially and gradually generalized to a much larger variety of foods. Eventually the patient came to avoid eating in order to avoid the discomfort. This starvation then produced the weight loss observed in the months before hospitalization.

There was another operant component to this case. It should be recalled that the patient's diabetic condition had served to gain much sympathy and attention. Furthermore, she had been relieved of many responsibilities because of this condition. At the time that the eating disorder began, Susan and her husband were house parents in a home for mentally retarded adults, a job which her husband enjoyed, but she despised. The deterioration of her health led to their voluntary termination of this job. It was also noted that the regulation of her insulin via the pump resulted in less medical attention, but allowed her to easily manipulate her insulin levels. In this manner she could avoid the immediate negative consequences of the eating disorder (i.e., hypoglycemia, by reducing her insulin doses).

Treatment Implications

The case formulation suggested both operant and respondent elements to the patient's eating disorder. However, before any behavioral program could be established, both Susan and her physician had to be convinced that part of her problem was psychological in nature. It was recommended that a conditioning explanation (an explanation presented in layman's terms) be presented and that she enter an inpatient, behaviorally oriented treatment program for eating disorders. From either an operant or a respondent conceptualization, treatment would have had to involve a gradual introduction of larger amounts and different types of food without her vomiting. It was recommended that the hierarchy of foods begin with those which had been problematic for the longest period of time. Also, she was to be trained in relaxation and self-instructional techniques to inhibit the nausea and reduce stomach cramping while simultaneously providing a set of coping behaviors which could be reinforced by the staff. These coping behaviors were incompatible with her illness behaviors and provided an alternative set of actions for the patient.

Assessment and Treatment Outcome

The efficacy of treatment was assessed both in the hospital and later as an outpatient, using a variety of measures. Weight gain was one objective measure of improvement. Also, monitoring of her eating habits, types and amounts of foods, number of meals, and frequency of vomiting were important variables for evaluating progress. While hospitalized, a checklist of "healthy" behaviors was completed by each nursing shift. As well, at selected individual treatment sessions, Susan completed a checklist for severity of stomach cramping and necessity of manipulating insulin levels. The rationale for conducting spot-checks of these problems was that we did not wish to draw her attention to these problems on a daily basis since she had a history of being preoccupied with her illness and using it for her own ends.

Summary

This atypical eating-disorder case illustrates how a comprehensive evaluation of behavioral and health factors can be conducted in order to properly treat a complex and potentially life-threatening medical condition. The assessment process drew from many areas of clinical practice, including eating disorders, the utilization of traditional personality tests, the recognition of illness behaviors (which is most widely studied in the area of chronic pain), and a general understanding of operant and respondent principles.

CONCLUSIONS

Behavioral assessment of health-related disorders has been developed only over the past 10 years. Given the briefness of this period, the assessment procedures are quite well developed. This area of behavioral assessment corresponds well to the history of behavioral assessment in general. Most assessment procedures were initially developed with the purpose of treatment planning and evaluation of treatment outcome as the primary focuses. As basic research concerning the influences of behavioral factors upon the disorder expanded, assessment procedures for differential diagnosis and behavioral analysis were initiated, and psychometric properties have begun to be investigated when warranted. At the time of this writing, most behavioral assessment techniques for health-related disorders still retain the idiographic focus that is consistent within the general area of behavioral assessment. However, for certain disorders (e.g., coronary heart disease, eating disorders, and headache) where there are many commonalities in the behavioral symptoms of patients, there is a growing body of literature describing standardized, psychometrically validated instruments for diagnosing the behavioral aspects of the disorder and for evaluating the efficacy of behavioral and medical treatments.

Another important characteristic of behavioral assessment in this area is its integration with traditional medical assessment. Many behavioral assessment techniques involve psychophysiological assessment of the biological responses of patients to psychological variables, such as stress. Other techniques take a straightforward approach to assessing the behavior which has been linked to pathophysiology through basic research. This integration of behavioral and biological factors in assessment and treatment is perhaps the strength of the general behavioral medicine movement, which stands in stark contrast to the approaches of earlier attempts to integrate psychology and medicine, for example, psychosomatic medicine.

It would appear that future development of this area should keep these two factors (i.e., behavioral and biological) as guiding principles. First, there must be a commitment to the idiographic approach with an appreciation for more standardized approaches where they are appropriate. Second, integration of behavioral and medical approaches must be recognized as the optimal method for advancing both areas. If these principles are applied, then we can only expect the next 10 years to be as fruitful as the preceding 10 years.

REFERENCES

Abplanalp, J. (1983). Premenstrual syndrome: A selective review. *Women & Health*, *8*, 107–123.

Achterberg, J., Matthews, S., & Simonton, D. C. (1978). Psychology of the exceptional patients who outlive predicted life expectancies. *Psychotherapy: Therapy, Research, and Practice*, *14*, 24.

Ad Hoc Committee on Classification of Headache. (1962). *Journal of the American Medical Association*, *179*, 717–718.

Allen, E., & Brown, G. (1932). Raynaud's disease: A critical review of minimal requisites for diagnosis. *American Journal of Medical Science*, *183*, 195–197.

Allenbeck, P., Hallberg, D., & Espmark, S. (1976). Body image — An apparatus for measuring disturbances in estimation of size and shape. *Journal of Psychosomatic Research*, *20*, 583–589.

Altman, M., Knowles, E., & Bull, H. (1941). A psychosomatic study of the sex cycle in women. *Psychosomatic Medicine*, *3*, 199–225.

American Psychiatric Association (1980). *Diagnostic and statistical manual of mental disorders* (3rd ed.). Washington, D.C.: Author.

Anderson, A. (1983). Anorexia nervosa and bulimia: A spectrum of eating disorders. *Journal of Adolescent Health Care*, *4*, 15–21.

Arena, J. G., Blanchard, E. B., Andrasik, F., & Dudek, B. C. (1982). The headache symptom questionnaire: Discriminant classificatory ability and headache syndromes suggested by a factor analysis. *Journal of Behavioral Assessment*, *4*, 55-69.

Askevold, F. (1975). Measuring body image. *Psychotherapy and Psychosomatics*, *26*, 71-77.

Basmajian, J. V. (1978). Muscle spasm in the lumbar region and the neck: Two double-blind controlled clinical and laboratory studies. *Archives of Physical Medicine and Rehabilitation*, *59*, 58-63.

Beeson, P. B., McDermott, W., & Wyngaarden, J. B. (1979). *Cecil textbook of medicine*. Philadelphia: W.B. Saunders.

Benson, H. (1975). *The relaxation response*. New York: Morrow.

Berwick, D. M., Levy, J.C ., & Kleinerman, R. (1982). Failure to thrive: Diagnostic yield of hospitalization. *Archives of Disease in Childhood*, *57*, 347-351.

Bithoney, W. G., & Rathbun, J. M. (1983). Failure to thrive. In Levine, Carey, Crocker, & Gross (Eds.), *Developmental behavior pediatrics* (pp. 557-572). Philadelphia: Saunders.

Bixler, E., Kales, J., Scharf, M., Kales, A., & Leo, L. (1976). Incidence of sleep disorders in medical practice: A physician survey. *Sleep Research*, *5*, 62.

Blanchard, E. B., Andrasik, F., Neff, D. F., Jurish, S. E., & O'Keefe, D. M. (1981). Social validation of the headache diary. *Behavior Therapy*, *12*, 711-715.

Blanchard, E. B., Theobald, D. E., Williamson, D.A., Silver, B. V., & Brown, D. A. (1978). Temperature biofeedback in the treatment of migraine headache — a controlled evaluation. *Archives of General Psychiatry*, *35*, 581-588.

Blumenthal, J. (1982). Assessment of patients with coronary heart disease. In F. Keefe & J. Blumenthal (Eds.), *Assessment strategies in behavioral medicine* (pp. 37-98). New York: Grune & Stratton.

Bootzin, R., & Nicassio, P. (1978). Behavioral treatment of insomnia. In M. Hersen, R. Eisler, & P. Miller (Eds.), *Progress in behavioral modification*. New York: Academic.

Borison, H. L., Borison, R., & McCarthy, L. E. (1981). Phylogenic and neurologic aspects of the vomiting process. *Journal of Clinical Pharmacology*, *21*, 235-295.

Bortner, R. (1969). A short rating scale as a potential measure of Pattern A behavior. *Journal of Chronic Diseases*, *22*, 87-91.

Boudewyns, P. A. (1982). Assessment of headache. In F. J. Keefe & J. A. Blumenthal (Eds.), *Assessment strategies in behavioral medicine*. New York: Grune & Stratton.

Brownell, K., & Stunkard, A. (1980). Behavioral treatment for obese children and adolescents. In A. Stunkard (Ed.), *Obesity* (pp. 415-437). Philadelphia: Saunders.

Burrows, B. (1979). Diseases associated with airway obstruction. In P. Beeson, W. McDermott, & J. Wynngarnder (Eds.), *Cecil textbook of medicine*. Philadelphia: Saunders.

Cairns, D., Thomas, L., Mooney, V., & Pace, J. B. (1976). A comprehensive treatment approach to chronic low back pain. *Pain*, *2*, 301-308.

Calloway, P., Fonagy, P., & Wakeling, A. (1983). Autonomic arousal in eating disorders: Further evidence for the clinical subdivision of anorexia nervosa. *British Journal of Psychiatry*, *142*, 38-48.

Carskadon, M., Dement, W., Mitler, M., Quilleminault, C., Zarcone, V., & Spiegel, R. (1976). Self-reports versus sleep laboratory findings in 122 drug-free subjects with complaints of chronic insomnia. *American Journal of Psychiatry*, *133*, 1382-1388.

Cinciripini, P. M. (1985). Behavioral treatment of chronic pain. In A.S. Bellack & M. Hersen (Eds.), *Dictionary of behavior therapy techniques* (pp. 39-43). New York: Pergamon.

Cinciripini, P. M., Williamson, D. A., & Epstein, L. H. (1981). Behavioral treatment of migraine headache. In J.M. Ferguson & C.B. Taylor (Eds.), *The comprehensive handbook medicine*. (Vol. II, pp. 207-227). New York: SP Medical.

Clausen, J., & Zarins, L. (1982). *Pulmonary function testing guidelines and controversies: Equipment, methods, and normal values*. New York: Academic.

Cluss, P., & Fireman, P. (1985). Recent trends in asthma research. *Annals of Behavioral Medicine, 7*, 11-16.

Coates, T., Jeffery, R., Slinkard, L., Keller, J., & Danaher, B. (1982). Frequency of contact and monetary reward in weight loss, lipid change, and blood pressure reduction with adolescents. *Behavior Therapy, 13*, 175-185.

Coates, T., Killen, J., Silverman, S., Marchini, E., Rosenthal, D., Sanchez, A., George, J., & Thoresen, C., (1980). *Problem-solving skills of persons complaining of insomnia and matched-control good sleepers*. Unpublished manuscript, The John Hopkins School of Medicine.

Coates, T., & Thoresen, C. (1981). Treating sleep disorders: Few answers, some suggestions and many questions. In S. Turner, K. Calhoun, & H. Adams (Eds.), *Handbook of clinical behavior therapy* (pp. 240-289). New York: Wiley.

Coursey, R., Buchsbaum, M., & Frankel, B. (1975). Personality measures and evoked responses in chronic insomniacs. *Journal of Abnormal Psychology, 84*, 239-249.

Craig, R., & Abeloff, M. (1974). Psychiatric symptomology among hospitalized cancer patients. *American Journal of Psychiatry, 131*, 1323-1325.

Creer, T., Marion, T., & Creer, P. (1983). Asthma Problem Behavior Checklist: Parental perceptions of the behavior of asthmatic children. *Journal of Asthma, 20*, 97-104.

Crown, S., & Crisp, A. H. (1966). A short diagnostic self-rating scale for psychoneurotic patients: The Middlesex Hospital Questionnaire. *British Journal of Psychiatry, 112*, 917-923.

Davis, C. J., Williamson, D. A., & Ruggiero, L. (1984). *Assessment of body image: Reliability and validity of a new measure or how do bulimics actually perceive themselves?* Paper presented at the annual meeting of the Association for Advancement of Behavior Therapy, Philadelphia.

Derogatis, L. (1977). *Manual for the Symptom Checklist-90, Revised*. Baltimore: John Hopkins University School of Medicine.

Derogatis, L., Abeloff, M., & Melisaratos, N. (1979). Psychological coping mechanisms and survival time in metastatic breast cancer. *Journal of the American Medical Association, 242*, 1504-1508.

Derogatis, L. R., Morrow, G. R., Fetting, J., Penman, D., Piasetsky, S., Schmale, A. M., Henrichs, M., & Carnrike, C. (1983). The prevalence of psychiatric disorders among cancer patients. *Journal of the American Medical Association, 249*, 751-757.

Derogatis, L. R., Rickles, K., & Rock, A. (1975). The SCL-90 and the MMPI: A step in the validation of a new self-report scale. *British Journal of Psychiatry, 128*, 280-289.

Diamond, E. L., Schneiderman, N., Schwartz, D., Smith, J. C., Varp, T., & Pasin, R. D. (1984). Harassment, hostility, and Type A as determinants of cardiovascular reactivity during competition. *Journal of Behavioral Medicine, 7*, 171-189.

Diamond, S., & Dalessio, D. J. (1982). *The practicing physician's approach to headache* (3rd Ed.). Baltimore: Williams & Wilkins.

Dirks, J., Brown, E., & Robinson, S. (1982). The Battery of Asthma Illness Behavior, II: Independence from airways hyperreactivity. *Journal of Asthma, 19*, 79-83.

Durnin, J., & Womersley, J. (1974). Body fat assessed from total body density and its estimation from skinfold thickness: Measurements on 481 men and women aged from 16 to 72 years. *British Journal of Nutrition, 32*, 77–97.

Fairburn, C., & Cooper, P. (1982). Self-induced vomiting and bulimia nervosa: An undetected problem. *British Medical Journal, 284*, 1153–1155.

Fisher, E., Delamater, A., Bertelson, A., & Kirkley, B. (1982). Psychological factors in diabetes and its treatment. *Journal of Consulting and Clinical Psychology, 50*, 993–1003.

Fishman, A. (1982). *Arteriosclerosis 1981* (Vol. 1: Report of the Working Group on Arteriosclerosis of the National Heart, Lung, and Blood Institute). Washington D.C.: U.S. Department of Health and Human Services.

Frank-Stromborg, M., & Wright, P. (1984). Ambulatory cancer patients perception of the physical and psychosocial changes in their lives since the diagnosis of cancer. *Cancer Nursing, 7*, 117–130.

Frankel, B., Coursey, R., Buchbinder, R., & Snyder, F. (1976). Recorded and reported sleep in chronic primary insomnia. *Archives of General Psychiatry, 33*, 615–623.

Frankel, B., Patten, B., & Gillin, J. (1974). Restless legs syndrome. *Journal of the American Medical Association, 230*, 1302–1303.

Freedman, R. C., Ianni, P., & Wenig, P. (1983). Behavioral treatment of Raynaud's disease. *Journal of Consulting and Clinical Psychology, 51*, 539–549.

Freedman, R., Lynn, S., & Ianni, P. (1982). Raynaud's disease. In F. Keefe & J. Blumenthal (Eds.), *Assessment strategies in behavioral medicine* (pp. 99–129). New York: Grune & Stratton.

Freeman, C., Caslyn, D., & Louks, J. (1976). The use of the MMPI personality inventory with low back pain patients. *Journal of Clinical Psychology, 32*, 294–298.

Friedman, A. P. (1979). Characteristics of tension headache: A profile of 1,420 cases. *Psychosomatics, 20*, 451–461.

Fordyce, W. E. (1976). *Behavioral methods for chronic pain and illness*. St. Louis: C.V. Mosby.

Fordyce, W. E., Fowler, R. S., Lehmann, J. R., Delateur, B. J., Sand, P. L., & Trieschmann, R. B. (1973). Operant conditioning in the treatment of chronic pain. *Archives of Physical Medicine and Rehabilitation, 54*, 399–408.

Gardner, J. (1968). A blending of behavior therapy techniques in an approach to an asthmatic child. *Psychotherapy: Theory, Research, and Practice, 5*, 46–49.

Garfinkel, P. E., Garner, M., Rose, J., Darby, P. L., Brandes, J., O'Hanlon, S., & Walsh, N. (1983). A comparison of characteristics in the families of patients with anorexia and normal controls. *Psychological Medicine, 13*, 821–828.

Garner, D., & Garfinkel, P. (1979). The Eating Attitudes Test: An index of the symptoms of anorexia nervosa. *Psychological Medicine, 9*, 273–279.

Gentry, W. D., & Bernal, G. A. (1977). Chronic pain. In R. B. Williams & W. D. Gentry (Eds.), *Behavioral approaches to medical treatment* (pp. 173–182). Cambridge, Mass.: Ballinger Publishing Co.

Gentry, W. D., Newman, M. C., Goldner, J. L., & von Baeyer, C. (1977). Relation between spinal block technique and MMPI for diagnosis and prognosis of chronic low back pain. *Spine, 2*, 210–213.

Gracely, R. H., McGrath, P., & Dubner, R. (1978). Ratio scales of sensory and affective verbal pain descriptors. *Pain, 5*, 5–18.

Granberry, S. W. (1985). *Development of a reliable and valid diagnostic assessment instrument for migraine and muscle-contraction headaches*. Unpublished doctoral dissertation, Louisiana State University, Baton Rouge.

Granberry, S. W., Williamson, D. A., Pratt, J., Hutchinson, F., & Monguillot, J. (1981). *An investigation of empirically derived categories of headache.* Paper presented at the annual meeting of the Association for the Advancement of Behavior Therapy, Toronto, Canada.

Green, R., & Dalton, K. (1953). The premenstrual syndrome. *British Medical Journal, 1,* 1007.

Grossarth-Matrice, K. R. (1980). Social psychology and course of the disease: First experience with cancer patients. *Psychotherapy and Psychosomatics, 33,* 129–138.

Guilleninault, C., Eldridge, F., & Dement, W. (1973). Insomnia with sleep apnea: A new syndrome. *Science, 181,* 856–858.

Halmi, K., Casper, R., & Eckert, E. (1979). Unique features associated with age onset of anorexia nervosa. *Psychiatry Research, 1,* 209.

Hammond, E. (1964). Some preliminary findings on physical complaints from a prospective study of 1,064,004 men and women. *American Journal of Public Health, 54,* 11–23.

Hartman, P. E., & Reuter, J. M. (1984). *The diabetic woman: Implications of gender for behavioral intervention.* Presented at the annual meeting of the Society of Behavioral Medicine, Philadelphia.

Hathaway, S., & McKinley, J. (1943). *Minnesota Multiphasic Personality Inventory.* Minneapolis: The University Press of the University of Minnesota.

Havnik, L. J. (1951). MMPI profiles in patients with low back pain. *Journal of Consulting Psychology, 15,* 350–353.

Haynes, S., Feinleib, M., Levine, S., Scotch, N., & Kannel, W. (1980). The relationship of psychosocial factors to coronary heart disease in the Framingham Study. III. Eight-year incidence of coronary heart disease. *American Journal of Epidemiology, 111,* 37–58.

Holmes, T. H., & Wolff, H. G. (1952). Life situations, emotions, and backache. *Psychosomatic Medicine, 14,* 18–33.

Holroyd, K. A., Andrasik, F., & Westbrook, T. (1977). Cognitive control of tension headache. *Cognitive Therapy and Research, 1,* 121–133.

Jacobson, E. (1938). *Progressive relaxation.* Chicago: University of Chicago Press.

Jenkins, C., Rosenman, R., & Friedman, M. (1967). Development of an objective psychological test for the determination of the coronary-prone behavior pattern in employed men. *Journal of Chronic Diseases, 20,* 371–379.

Joyce, C. B., Zutshi, D. W., Hrubes, V., & Mason, R. M. (1975). Comparisons of fixed interval and visual analog scales for rating chronic pain. *European Journal of Clinical Pharmacology, 8,* 415–420.

Kales, A., Bixler, E., Tan, T., Scharf, M., & Kales, J. (1974). Chronic hypnotic drug use: Ineffectiveness, drug withdrawal insomnia, and dependence. *Journal of the American Medical Association, 5,* 513–517.

Kales, A., & Kales, J. (1974). Recent findings in the diagnosis and treatment of disturbed sleep. *New England Journal of Medicine, 290,* 487–499.

Kaplan, R., Reis, M., & Atkins, C. (1985). Behavioral issues in the management of chronic obstructive pulmonary disease. *Annals of Behavioral Medicine, 7,* 5–10.

Kay, D., Blackburn, A., Buckingham, J., & Karacan, I. (1976). Human pharmacology of sleep. In R. Williams & I. Karacan (Eds.), *Pharmacology of sleep* (pp. 83–210). New York: Wiley.

Keefe, F. J., Brown, C. J., Scott, D. S., & Ziesat, H. (1982). Behavioral treatment of chronic pain syndromes. In P. Boudewyns & F. J. Keefe (Eds.), *Behavioral medicine in general medical practice* (pp. 321–350). Menlo Park, CA: Addison-Wesley.

Keele, K. D. (1948). The painchart. *Lancet*, *2*, 6–8.

Kinsman, R., Dahlem, N., Spector, S., & Staudenmeyer, H. (1977). Observations on subjective symptomatology, coping behavior, and medical decisions in asthma. *Psychosomatic Medicine*, *39*, 102–119.

Kinsman, R., Luparello, T., O'Banion, K., & Spector, S. (1973). Multidimensional analysis of the subjective symptomatology of asthma. *Psychosomatic Medicine*, *35*, 250–267.

Klesges, R. C., Coates, T. J., Brown, G., Sturgeon-Tillisch, J., Moldenhauer-Klesges, L. M., Holzer, B., Woolfrey, J., & Vollman, J. (1983). Parental influences on children's eating behavior and relative weight. *Journal of Applied Behavior Analysis*, *16*, 371–378.

Koenig, R., Levin, S., & Brennan, M. (1967). The emotional status of cancer patients as measured by a psychological test. *Journal of Chronic Diseases*, *20*, 923–930.

Krieger, I. (1982). *Pediatric disorders of feeding, nutrition, and metabolism*. New York: Wiley and Sons.

Lawrence, P. S. (1982). Behavioral assessment of sleep disorders. In F. J. Keefe & J. A. Blumenthal (Eds.), *Assessment strategies in behavioral medicine* (pp. 197–216). New York: Grune & Stratton.

Lazar, B., & Jedliczka, Z. (1979). Utilization of manipulative behavior in a retarded asthmatic child. *The American Journal of Clinical Hypnosis*, *21*, 287–292.

Leavitt, F., Garron, D.C., D'Angelo, C. M., & McNeill, T. W. (1979). Low back pain in patients with and without demonstrable organic disease. *Pain*, *6*, 191–200.

Levinson, R. (1979). Effects of thematically relevant and general stressors on specificity of responding in asthmatic and nonasthmatic subjects. *Psychosomatic Medicine*, *41*, 28–39.

Lichstein, K. L., Nickel, R., Hoelscher, T. J., & Kelley, J. E. (1982). Clinical validation of a sleep assessment device. *Behaviour Research and Therapy*, *20*, 292–297.

Linscheid, T. R., Oliver, J., Blyler, E., & Palmer, I. (1978). Brief hospitalization for the behavioral treatment of feeding problems in the developmentally disabled. *Journal of Pediatric Psychology*, *3*, 72–76.

Lucas, R., & Brown, C. (1982). Assessment of cancer patients. In F. Keefe & J. Blumenthal (Eds.), *Assessment strategies in behavioral medicine* (pp. 351–369). New York: Grune & Stratton.

Luparello, T., Leist, M., Lourie, & Sweet. (1970). The interaction of psychological stimuli and pharmacologic agents on airway reactivity in asthmatic subjects. *Psychosomatic Medicine*, *32*, 509–513.

Luparello, T., Lyons, H., Bleecker, E., & McFadden, E. (1968). Influences of suggestion on airway reactivity in asthmatic subjects. *Psychosomatic Medicine*, *30*, 819–825.

Mann, A., Wakeling, A., Wood, K., Monck, E., Dobbs, R., & Szmukler, G. (1983). Screening for abnormal eating attitudes and psychiatric morbidity in an unselected population of 15-year-old schoolgirls. *Psychological Medicine*, *13*, 573–580.

Markin, R. (1976). Assessment of the reliability of and the effect of neutral instructions on the symptoms ratings on the Moos Menstrual Questionnaire. *Psychosomatic Medicine*, *38*, 163–172.

Masur, F. T. (1977). Assorted physical disorders. In R. B. Williams & W. D. Gentry (Eds.), *Behavioral approaches to medical treatment* (pp. 209–248). Cambridge, MA: Balinger Publishing Co.

Mathew, R. J. (1981). *Treatment of migraine*. New York: SP Medical & Scientific.

McCorkle, R., & Young, K. (1978). Development of a symptom distress scale. *Cancer*

Nursing, 1, 373-378.

McCreary, C., Turner, D., & Dawson, E. (1977). Differences between functional versus organic low back pain patients. *Pain, 4,* 73-78.

Melzack, R. (1975). The McGill Pain Questionnaire: Major properties and scoring methods. *Pain, 1,* 277-299.

Miles, L., Raynal, D., & Wilson, M. (1977). Blind man living in normal society has circadian rhythms of 24.9 hours. *Science, 198,* 421-423.

Mizes, J. S. (1985). Bulimia: A review of its symptomatology and treatment. *Advances in Behavior Research and Therapy, 7,* 91-142.

Morrison, R. L., Bellack, A. S., & Manuck, S. B. (1985). Role of social competence in borderline essential hypertension. *Journal of Consulting and Clinical Psychology, 53,* 248-255.

Morrow, G. (1984). The assessment of nausea and vomiting. *Cancer* (Supplement), *105,* 2267-2280.

Morrow, G. R., & Morrell, B. S. (1982). Behavioral treatment for the anticipatory nausea and vomiting induced by cancer chemotherapy. *New England Journal of Medicine, 307,* 1476-1480.

Moos, R. (1968). The development of a menstrual distress questionnaire. *Psychosomatic Medicine, 30,* 853-867.

Moos, R. (1977). *Menstrual distress questionnaire manual.* Department of Psychiatry, Stanford University and Veterans Administration Hospital, Palo Alto, CA.

Moos, R., & Leiderman, D. (1978). Toward a menstrual cycle symptom typology. *Journal of Psychosomatic Research, 22,* 31-40.

Murray, C. A. R., & Glassman, M. S. (1982). Nutrient requirements during growth and recovery from failure to thrive. In P. J. Accordo (Ed.), *Failure to thrive in infancy and early childhood* (pp. 19-75). Baltimore: University Park Press.

NIAID Task Force (1979). *Asthma and the other allergic diseases* (NIH Pub. No. 79-387). Washington, D.C.: Department of Health, Education, and Welfare.

National Center for Health Statistics-Division of Health Examination Statistics (1980). *Health and nutrition examination survey for cycle 2 1976-1980, civilian, noninstitutionalized samples.* National Center for Health Statistics: Unpublished manuscript.

National Diabetes Data Group (1979). Classification and diagnosis of diabetes mellitus and other categories of glucose intolerance. *Diabetes, 28,* 1039-1057.

Newlin, D. (1981). Modifying the Type A behavior pattern. In C. Golden, S. Alcaparras, F. Strider, & B. Graber (Eds.), *Applied techniques in behavioral medicine* (pp. 169-190). New York: Grune & Stratton.

Parker, G., & Lipscombe, P. (1979). Parental overprotection and asthma. *Journal of Psychosomatic Research, 23,* 295-299.

Pearlson, G. D., Flournoy, L. H., Simonson, M., & Slavney, P. R. (1981). Body image in obese adults. *Psychological Medicine, 11,* 147-154.

Pennington, V. (1957). Meprobamate in premenstrual tension. *Journal of the American Medical Association, 164,* 638.

Philipp, R., Wilde, G., & Day, J. (1972). Suggestion and relaxation in asthmatics. *Journal of Psychosomatic Research, 16,* 193-204.

Phol, S., Gonder-Frederick, M., & Cox, D. (1984). Diabetes mellitus: An overview. *Behavioral Medicine Update, 6,* 3-7.

Pollak, C. McGregor, P., & Weitzman, E. (1975). The effects of flurazepam on daytime sleep after acute sleep-wake cycle reversal. *Sleep Research, 4,* 112.

Pollitt, E., & Wirtz, S. (1981). Mother-infant feeding interaction and weight gain in

the first month of life. *Journal of the American Dietetic Association*, *78*, 596–601.
Prather, R. C. (1985). *Differential diagnosis of eating disorders: Purgers, bingers, obese, and normals.* Unpublished master's thesis, Louisiana State University.
Prather, R., McKenzie, S., Upton, L., & Williamson, D. (1985). *A four component behavioral treatment for bulimics who purge.* Presented at the annual meeting of the Behavioral Medicine Special Interest Group, Houston.
Prather, R., Upton, L., Williamson, D. A., Davis, C. J., Ruggiero, L., & Van Buren, D. (1985). *Bulimia, depression, and general psychopathology.* Presented at the annual meeting of the Association for Advancement of Behavior Therapy, Houston.
Prather, R. & Williamson, D. A. (in press). Psychopathology associated with bulimia, binge-eating, and obesity. *International Journal of Eating Disorders.*
Price, V., Coates, T., Thoresen, C., & Grinstead, O. (1978). The prevalence and correlates of poor sleep among adolescents. *American Journal of Diseases of Children*, *132*, 583–586.
Ransford, A. O., Cairns, D., & Mooney, V. (1976). The pain drawing as an aid to the psychologic evaluation of patients with low back pain. *Spine*, *1*, 127–134.
Reading, A. E., & Newton, J. R. (1978). A card sort method of pain assessment. *Journal of Psychosomatic Research*, *22*, 503–512.
Reid, R., & Yen, S. (1981). Premenstrual syndrome. *American Journal of Obstetrics and Gynecology*, *139*, 85–104.
Review Panel on Coronary-Prone Behavior and Coronary Heart Disease (1981). Coronary-prone behavior and coronary heart disease: A critical review. *Circulation*, *63*, 1199–1215.
Rogers, T., Mahoney, M., Mahoney, K., Straw, M., & Kenigsberg, M. (1980). Clinical assessment of obesity: An empirical evaluation of diverse techniques. *Behavioral Assessment*, *2*, 161–181.
Rosen, D. W., Loeb, L. S., & Tura, M. B. (1980). Differentiation of organic from nonorganic failure to thrive syndrome in infancy. *Pediatrics*, *66*, 698–704.
Rosenman, R. (1978). The interview method of assessment of the coronary-prone behavior pattern. In T. Dembroski, S. Weiss, J. Shields, S. Haynes, & M. Feinleib (Eds.), *Coronary-prone behavior* (pp. 55–69). New York: Springer-Verlag.
Rosenman, R., Friedman, M., Straus, B., Wurm, M., Kositchek, R., Hahn, W., & Werthesson, N. (1964). A predictive study of coronary heart disease: The Western Collaborative Group Study. *Journal of the American Medical Association*, *189*, 103–110.
Roth, T., Lutz, T., Kramer, M., & Tietz, E. (1977). The relationship between objective and subjective evaluations of sleep in insomniacs. *Sleep Research*, *6*, 178.
Rouse, P. (1978). Premenstrual tension: A study using the Moos Menstrual Questionnaire. *Journal of Psychosomatic Research*, *22*, 215–222.
Ruble, D.N. (1977). Pre-menstrual symptoms: A reinterpretation. *Science*, *197*, 291–292.
Ruggiero, L., Williamson, D. A., Jones, G., & Davis, C. J. (1984). *Forbidden foods: The cognitive mediators of bulimia?* Presented at the annual meeting of the Association for the Advancement of Behavior Therapy, Philadelphia.
Sampson, G., & Prescott, P. (1981). The assessment of the symptoms of premenstrual syndrome and their response to therapy. *British Journal of Psychiatry*, *138*, 399–405.
Santiago, J. (1984). Effect of treatment on the long term complications of IDDM. *Behavioral Medicine Update*, *6*, 26–31.
Saper, J. R. (1983). *Headache disorders.* Boston: John Wright.

Sargent, J. D., Walters, E. D., & Green, E. E. (1973). Psychosomatic self-regulation of migraine headache. *Seminars in Psychiatry*, 5, 415–428.

Schlundt, D., Johnson, W., & Jarrell, P. (1985). A naturalistic functional analysis of eating behavior in bulimia and obesity. *Advances in Behaviour Research and Therapy*, 7, 149–162.

Scott, D. S., & Gregg, H. M. (1980). Myofascial pain of the temperomandibular joint: A review of the behavioral-relaxation therapies. *Pain*, 9, 231–241.

Seeburg, K., & DeBoer, K. (1980). Effects of EMG biofeedback on diabetes. *Biofeedback and Self-Regulation*, 5, 289–293.

Shapiro, D., & Goldstein, I. B. (1982). Biobehavioral perspectives on hypertension. *Journal of Consulting and Clinical Psychology*, 50, 841–858.

Sills, R. H. (1978). Failure to thrive. *American Journal of Diseases in Children*, 132, 967–969.

Smith, M., & Thelen, M. (1984). Development and validation of a test for bulimia. *Journal of Consulting and Clinical Psychology*, 52, 863–872.

Spielberger, C. (1983). *Manual for the State-Trait Anxiety Inventory*. Palo Alto, CA: Consulting Psychologists Press.

Steadman's Medical Dictionary (1976). Baltimore: Williams and Wilkins Co.

Steiner, M., Haskett, R., & Carroll, B. (1980). Premenstrual tension syndrome: The development of research diagnostic criteria and new rating scales. *Veta Psychiatrica Scandinavia*, 62, 177–190.

Sternbach, R. A. (1968). *Pain: A psychophysiological analysis*. New York: Academic.

Sternbach, R. A., Wolf, S. R., Murphy, R. W., & Akeson, W. H. (1973). Traits of pain patients: The low back "loser". *Psychosomatics*, 14, 226–229.

Suinn, R. (1982). Intervention with Type A behaviors. *Journal of Consulting and Clinical Psychology*, 50, 933–949.

Surwit, R., & Feinglos, M. (1983). The effects of relaxation on glucose tolerance in non-insulin-dependent diabetes. *Diabetes Care*, 6, 176–179.

Surwit, R., & Feinglos, M. (1984). Stress and diabetes. *Behavioral Medicine Update*, 6, 8–11.

Surwit, R., Feinglos, M., & Scovern, A. (1983). Diabetes and behavior: A paradigm for health psychology. *American Psychologist*, 38, 255–262.

Swanson, D. W., Swenson, M. W., Maruta, T., & McPhee, M. C. (1976). Program for managing chronic pain: I. Program description and characteristics of patients. *Mayo Clinic Proceedings*, 51, 401–408.

Szmukler, G. (1983). Weight and food preoccupation in a population of English schoolgirls. *Understanding anorexia and bulimia*. Report of the Fourth Ross Conference on Medical Research, pp. 21–27.

Traub, A. C. & Orbach, J. (1964). Psychophysical studies of body-image. *Archives of General Psychiatry*, 11, 53–66.

Traughber, B., Erwin, K. E., Risley, T., & Schnelle, J. F. (1983). Behavioral nutrition: An evaluation of a simple system for measuring food and nutrient consumption. *Behavioral Assessment*, 5, 263–281.

Turk, D., Meichenbaum, D., & Genest, M. (1983). *Pain and behavioral medicine: A cognitive behavioral perspective*. New York: Guilford Press.

Turk, D., & Speers, M. (1982). Diabetes mellitus: A cognitive-functional analysis of stress and adherence. In T. Burish & L. Bradley (Eds.), *Coping with chronic disease: Research and applications* (pp. 191–218). New York: Academic.

Turk, D. C., Wack, J. T., & Kerns, R. D. (1985). An empirical examination of the "pain–behavior" construct. *Journal of Behavioral Medicine*, 8, 119–130.

Tursky, B. (1976). The development of a pain perception profile: A psychophysical approach. In M. Weisenberg & B. Tursky (Eds.), *Pain: New perspectives in therapy and research* (pp. 171-194). New York: Plenum.

Vance, C., & Taylor, W. (1971). The financial cost of chronic childhood asthma. *Annals of Allergy, 29,* 455-460.

Vandenberg, R., Sussman, K., & Vaughan, G. (1967). Effects of combined physical-anticipatory stress on carbohydrate-lipid metabolism in patients with diabetes mellitus. *Psychosomatics, 8,* 16-19.

Williams, R., & Porte, D. (1974). The pancreas. In R. Williams (Ed.), *Textbook of endocrinology* (5th Ed., pp. 502-626). Philadelphia: W.B. Saunders.

Williamson, D. A. (1981). Behavioral treatment of migraine and muscle-contraction headaches: Outcome and theoretical explanations. In M. Hersen, R. Eisler, & P. Miller (Eds.), *Progress in behavior modification* (Vol. 11, pp. 163-201). New York: Academic.

Williamson, D. A., Davis, C. J., Ruggiero, L., Goreczny, A., & McKenzie, S. (1985). *Psychophysiological evaluation of the anxiety model of bulimia.* Presented at the annual meeting of the Association for Advancement of Behavior Therapy, Houston, TX.

Williamson, D. A., Kelley, M. L., Cavell, T. A., & Prather, R. C. (in press). Eating and eliminating disorders. In C. L. Frame & J. L. Matson (Eds.), *Handbook of assessment in childhood psychopathology: applied issues in differential diagnosis and treatment evaluation.* New York: Plenum.

Williamson, D. A., Kelley, M. L., Davis, C. J., Ruggiero, L., & Blouin, D. (1985). Psychopathology of eating disorders: A controlled comparison of bulimic, obese, and normal subjects. *Journal of Consulting and Clinical Psychology, 53,* 161-166.

Williamson, D. A., Kelley, M. L., Davis, C. J., Ruggiero, L., & Veitia, M. (1985). The psychophysiology of bulimia. *Advances in Behaviour Research and Therapy, 7,* 163-172.

Williamson, D. A., McKenzie, S., Goreczny, T., & Faulstich, M. (1987). Psychophysiological disorders. In M. Hersen & V. Van Hasselt (Eds.), *Behavior therapy with children and adolescents: A clinical approach* (pp. 271-300) New York: John Wiley and Sons.

Williamson, D. A., Ruggiero, L., & Davis, C. J. (1985). Headache. In M. Hersen & A. S. Bellack (Eds.), *Handbook of clinical behavior therapy with adults* (pp. 417-442). New York: Plenum.

Williamson, D. A., Waters, W. F., & Hawkins, M. F. (1986). Physiological variables. In R. M. Nelson & S. Hayes (Eds.), *Conceptual foundations of behavioral assessment* (pp. 297-327). New York: Guilford Press.

Young, J., & Landsberg, L. (1979). Catecholamines and the sympathoadrenal system: The regulation of metabolism. In S. Ingbar (Ed.), *Contemporary endocrinology* (Vol. 1, pp. 245-303). New York: Plenum.

Zarcone, V. (1975). Narcolepsy. *New England Journal of Medicine, 288,* 1156-1166.

Zeigler, D. K., Hassanein, R., & Hassanein, K. (1972). Headache syndromes suggested by factor analysis of symptom variables in a headache prone population. *Journal of Chronic Disease, 25,* 353-363.

Zook, D. J., & Yasko, J. M. (1983). Psychologic factors: Their effect on nausea and vomiting experienced by clients receiving chemotherapy. *Oncology Nursing Forum, 10,* 76-81.

13
Assessment of Marital Dysfunction

Gayla Margolin
Joseph Michelli
Neil Jacobson

This revision of our earlier chapter (Margolin & Jacobson, 1981) highlights the changes that have occurred during the past 5 years in the area of behavioral marital assessment. During the 1970s, we witnessed the introduction of an array of self-report and observational instruments. The reception was particularly enthusiastic for instruments that broke out of the mold of traditional assessment by focusing on dyadic as opposed to individualistic processes and that directly observed behavior rather than followed an indirect sign approach. The 1980s, in contrast, have been a time for critical reappraisal. Several new methodologies for collecting data have been introduced, and additional psychometric data on some of the older instruments have been made available. More important, significant issues have been raised and debated, such as the relevance and importance of observational data, the relative merits of using spouses as observers of themselves and each another, and the clinical significance of our treatment outcome data. Through dialogue on these and other issues, we continue to advance our measurement procedures to better meet the three basic purposes of marital assessment: to further our theoretical understanding of relationships, to identify what is wrong for a specific couple seeking therapy, and to measure relationship change as a function of therapy.

In this chapter, we first provide a brief history of behavioral marital assessment and review the constructs that have been posited as central to our understanding and treatment of marital distress. Further discussion of each

Preparation of this chapter was supported by NIMH Grant 1 R01 36595 and the Harry Frank Guggenheim Foundation.

construct includes descriptions of the assessment procedures designed to measure the construct. We then examine the important issues currently being debated in behavioral marital assessment. Our presentation of specific instruments focuses on how they have changed since 1981 and how they fit into the overall goals of behavioral marital assessment. Thus, this chapter is an extension of our previous one, which contained detailed descriptions of instruments and their characteristics. Additional descriptions of the instruments can be found in Jacobson, Elwood, and Dallas, 1981; Jacobsen and Margolin, 1978; Filsinger, 1983b; Filsinger and Lewis, 1981; Margolin, 1983a; Weiss and Margolin, 1986.

BRIEF HISTORY

The key constructs initially posited by behavioral marital therapists to account for marital disturbance were the rewards and punishments that spouses exchanged in their daily interactions, their communication effectiveness, and their subjective appraisals and feelings about the marriage (Patterson & Hops, 1972; Rappaport & Harrell, 1972; Stuart, 1976; Weiss, Hops, & Patterson, 1973). Connections between these constructs also were posited. The subjective appraisals were presumed to be a function of communication ineffectiveness and/or an overly punishing and unrewarding interaction. In return, it seemed likely that consistently negative appraisals might result in spouses' unwillingness to put much effort into rewarding or constructive interactions.

In fact, there has been considerable empirical evidence demonstrating the interrelationships among these constructs. Communication ineffectiveness has been shown to be a characteristic of couples who subjectively report marital dissatisfaction as opposed to satisfaction (Gottman, 1979; Gottman, Markman, & Notarius, 1977; Margolin & Wampold, 1981; Raush, Barry, Hertel, & Swain, 1974; Revenstorf, Vogel, Wegener, Hahlweg, & Schindler, 1980; Vincent, Friedman, Nugent, & Messerly, 1979; Vincent, Weiss, & Birchler, 1975). The level of punishing and/or rewarding behaviors in a couple's daily exchange has been related to global reports of marital dissatisfaction (Barnett & Nietzel, 1979; Birchler, Weiss, & Vincent, 1975; Margolin, 1981a) as well as to fluctuations in daily satisfaction ratings (Jacobson, Follette, & McDonald, 1982; Jacobson, Waldron, & Moore, 1980; Margolin, 1981a; Wills, Weiss, & Patterson, 1974). There is no evidence to date, however, regarding the association been communication effectiveness and the overall exchange of reinforcement and punishment between spouses.

Although these three constructs seem relatively straightforward, there were a number of factors to consider in deciding how to measure each one. The measurement of overall appraisals of satisfaction was least specific to the behavioral tradition, since this is a global construct that required spouses' self-reports. The goal in measuring behavioral exchange was to examine an array of rewarding and punishing behaviors that make up spouses' daily interactions. This required the identification and examination of specific problem areas (e.g., finances, sex, childrearing) as well as the evaluation of areas that are not sources of tension but that reveal the tenor of their lives together. Through early attempts to use outside observers to collect data on couples' behavioral exchanges, it became apparent that here, too, data collection needed to be done by the spouses themselves. Many of the behaviors of interest occurred in private or infrequently, thus they were unavailable to outside observers. Although the construct of communication effectiveness is of interest to all marital therapists, behaviorists have distinguished themselves in how they evaluate this dimension. Much of the behavioral work has taken a molecular approach that focuses on moment-to-moment interactional sequences. It is in this domain that the behavioral penchant for directly observable samples of behavior has been most clearly exhibited.

Interest in these three constructs has not diminished over time; however, the recent history of behavioral marital assessment has been marked by a broadening of its theoretical underpinnings and of the constructs to be assessed. The cognitive components of relationship distress — such as unrealistic beliefs and expectancies, causal attributions, and efficacy questions — have received increasing recognition. Second, the affective components of interaction, particularly the reciprocity of affect in the context of interactional sequences, has taken on increasing importance. Third, efforts to integrate family systems theory with behavioral marital therapy have resulted in attempts to define and measure trait-like constructs that characterize the marital system (e.g., dominance, cohesion, and flexibility).

The definition of what constitutes behavioral marital assessment clearly has shifted to be more all-encompassing. It was previously the characteristics of the instrument itself that resulted in its being included in the behavioral marital assessor's package (e.g., whether the instrument elicits information about behaviors that are operationally defined and directly observable). Now the criteria for inclusion reflect the purposes for which the instrument is used. Rather than there being behavioral techniques per se, behavioral marital assessment includes any instrument or procedure that contributes to an empirically based formulation of the etiology and treatment of marital dysfunctions.

HOW CONSTRUCTS TRANSLATE INTO SPECIFIC PROCEDURES

Overall Satisfaction

As Gottman and Levenson (1986) recently noted, there are a number of self-report questionnaires to measure marital satisfaction which have high levels of construct, discriminant, concurrent, and predictive validity, and which show high intermeasure correlations. The Marital Adjustment Scale (MAS; Locke & Wallace, 1959), once the most commonly used assessment of marital subjective well-being, has yielded some of its popularity to Spanier's Dyadic Adjustment Scale (DAS; Spanier, 1976; see Table 13.1 for sample items). The DAS, a 32-item measure, has been used both as a self-administered questionnaire and as an interview protocol. In his original validation study, Spanier indicated the existence of four subscales in the DAS: (1) Dyadic Cohesion, (2) Dyadic Satisfaction, (3) Dyadic Consensus. and (4) Affectional Expression. Recently, however, several groups of researchers have failed to replicate the existence of Spanier's original four subscale factors. Antill and Colton (1982) demonstrated a strong single factor and found some evidence for the Dyadic Consensus, Dyadic Satisfaction, and Dyadic Cohesion factors, but were unable to find factor cohesion for the Affectional Expression scale.

Sharpley and Cross (1982) similarly suggested that the DAS provides a predominant dyadic adjustment factor. They also noted that most of the original items on the DAS are unnecessary for reliably discriminating between maritally distressed and maritally satisfied couples and suggest that the DAS could more parsimoniously discriminate between these two groups with only six items. In a similar revalidation study on the MAS, Cross and Sharpley (1981) showed that most of the 15 items on the scale added little to discriminative validity of the measure. However, the following two items, taken together, could correctly classify 92% of the subjects as maritally satisfied or maritally distressed: "Rate your marriage, everything considered, from very unhappy to perfectly happy" and "If you had your life to live over, do you think you would marry the same person or a different one?"

Noting the limitations of existing measures of marital satisfaction, Snyder (1979) developed a self-report questionnaire that not only provided a global measure of satisfaction but additionally included information on important facets of marital interaction. The 280-item Marital Satisfaction Inventory (MSI) includes one validity scale, a global satisfaction scale, and nine other scales which address specific components of married life. These additional scales assess satisfaction with: (a) affective communication, (b) problem-solving communication, (c) time together, (d) discussions of finances, (e) sexual experiences, (f) childrearing practices, and (g) relationship with children; further, they measure marital attitudes and experiences that include (h) role-orientation, and (i) family history of distress (see Table 13.1 for sample items).

The original standardization studies reported in Snyder (1979) support the validity of the MSI's global distress scale by discriminating between couples seeking therapy and those not doing so. The global distress scale of the MSI correlated .75 with scores on the Locke-Wallace MAS. These studies also

TABLE 13.1. Sample Items and Corresponding Scale/Constructs of Marital Assessment Instruments

INSTRUMENT	SAMPLE ITEMS	CORRESPONDING SCALE CONSTRUCT
Dyadic Adustment Scale (Spanier, 1976)	Do you and your mate engage in outside interests together? (everyday — none of them)	dyadic cohesion
	Indicate the approximate extent of agreement or disagreement between you and your partner for each item (e.g., family finances, religious matters).	dyadic consensus
	Please circle the dot which best describes the degree of happiness (extremely unhappy — perfect)	dyadic satisfaction
	Do you kiss your mate (everyday — never)	affectional expression
Marital Satisfaction Inventory (Snyder, 1979)	At times I have very much wanted to leave my spouse.	global distress
	Sometimes my spouse just can't understand the way I feel.	affective communication
	There are some things my spouse and I just can't talk about.	problem-solving communication
	My spouse and I don't have much in common to talk about.	time together
	Our marriage has never been in difficulty because of financial concerns.	discussion of finances
	Our sex life is entirely satisfactory.	sexual experiences
	My spouse and I rarely disagree on when or how to punish the children.	childrearing practices
	Having children has increased the happiness of our marriage.	relationship with children
	The husband should be the head of the family.	role orientation
	I had a very happy home life.	family history of distress

Instrument	Category	Example
Spouse Observation Checklist (Weiss & Perry, 1979)	affection	Spouse hugged or kissed me.
	companionship	We listened to music on the radio or stereo.
	consideration	Spouse acted patient when I was cross.
	sexual fulfillment	Spouse rejected my sexual advances.
	communication process	Spouse consulted me on an important decision.
	couple activities	We invited a couple of our friends over to visit.
	child care	Spouse comforted baby, made him/her stop crying.
	household management	Spouse did household repairs or arranged to have them done.
	financial decision-making	Spouse bought something important without consulting me.
	employment/education	We discussed future employment opportunities.
	personal habits and appearance	Spouse left dirty dishes around the house.
	self and spouse independence	Spouse spoke positively about an experience from which I was excluded.
Couple Interaction Scoring System (Gottman, 1979)	agreement	Direct agreement, acceptance of responsibility, acceptance of modification, compliance, assent
	disagreement	Direct disagreement; yes — but disagreement with rationale; command, or order; noncompliance
	communication talk	Directing conversation back to topics, directing discussion toward resolution, statement about the discussion, request for clarification
	mindreading	Statements that attribute feelings, attitudes, opinions, or motives to spouse
	problem-solving	Specific or nonspecific plan, information exchange
	summarizing others	Summarizing previous statement of spouse
	summarizing self	Reviews own previous statement
	expressing feelings	Statement reveals immediate affective experience
	positive-negative affect	Smile–frown, tender voice–impatient voice, arms open–arms akimbo

Instrument	Item / Example	Category
Marital Interaction Coding System III (Weiss & Summers, 1983)	Problems stated within relationship or external to relationship	problem description
	Complain, criticize, negative mindread, put down	blame
	Proposal to increase or decrease the frequency of some behavior, compromise	proposal for change
	Agree, approval, accept responsibility	validation
	Disagree, deny responsibility, make no response	invalidation
	Paraphrase reflection, positive physical touch, smile/laugh	facilitation
	Normative but irrelevant speech or behaviors	irrelevant
	Physical positive, head nods, turning head away	nonverbal affect
	Attention, not tracking	listener attention
Relationship Belief Inventory (Epstein & Eidelson, 1981)	I cannot accept it if my partner disagrees with me	disagreements are destructive
	I do not expect my partner to sense all my moods	mindreading is expected
	A partner who hurts you badly once probably will hurt you again	relationships cannot be changed
Interaction Patterns Questionnaire (Sullaway & Christensen, 1983)	Sometime when A wants more attention from B, B seems to withdraw more. For example: (a) A might try to get more contact with B by being unusually affectionate or outgoing, or may ask favors of B; B reacts by initiating less contact. (b) When A asks for more attention, B sometimes feels crowded and doesn't respond. A doesn't understand this and feels hurt.	
Family Adaptability and Cohesion Scales — II (Olson, Russell, & Sprenkle, 1979)	We are supportive of each other during difficult times	cohesion
	We are flexible in how we handle differences	adaptability

provided normative values of the MSI. Scores on affective communication, problem-solving communication, and time together were shown to account for a considerable amount of the overall variance in the MSI global satisfaction scale. These correlations suggest that differences in overall marital satisfaction may be largely due to couples' communication competence and the quality of their shared time.

Clinically, the MSI seems to provide a finer gradation of marital distress than does the DAS or MAS, by indicating which components of marital life contribute to overall distress. Berg and Snyder (1981), for example, have demonstrated the ability of the MSI to discriminate between couples presenting marital distress as their primary treatment issue from couples who presented sexual concerns as their reason for seeking therapy. In addition, Snyder, Wills, and Keiser (1981) found significant correlations between MSI scales and clinicians ratings of relevant clinical criteria. While MSI profiles suggest specific foci for treatment, it is yet to be demonstrated whether different profiles lead to differential responsiveness on specific interventions.

Overall, while the problems of social desirability and other response biases inherent in global self-report measures still remain, the importance of measuring this construct of satisfaction cannot be denied. As stated most forcefully by Baucom (1983), "the criterion of marital satisfaction must remain central . . . we should not lose focus on the seemingly simple yet central issue of how each member of the couple feels about the spouse and the marriage when treatment is completed" (p. 93).

Behavior Exchange

Few studies have appeared in the literature since 1981 on behavioral exchange, perhaps due to the difficulty of measuring this construct. Theories surrounding the behavior exchange construct predict that distressed compared to nondistressed spouses will deliver fewer reinforcers, more punishers, and will exhibit a lower ratio of reinforcers to punishers. From an etiological perspective, it is suggested that global marital satisfaction is determined by the spouse's prior history of rewarding/punishing behavior exchanges. On a more immediate level, it is suggested that daily fluctuations in satisfaction are a function of daily fluctions in reward/punishment ratios (Jacobson & Moore, 1981a).

The primary instrument for measuring behavioral exchange in the natural setting has been the Spouse Observation Checklist (SOC; Weiss & Perry, 1979, 1983). This instrument was designed for spouses to continuously track their partners. The SOC is a 408-item instrument, consisting of 12 behavioral categories such as sex, household management, communication, and daily satisfaction rating (see Table 13.1).

Between 1973 and 1981, approximately 18 studies were published using the SOC. Several studies discriminated between maritally distressed and nondistressed couples by means of the SOC's "pleases to displeases ratio" (e.g., Birchler et al., 1975; Margolin, 1981a). Other studies investigated the frequency of positive and negative affectional and instrumental interchanges as a function of marital satisfaction (Barnett & Neitzel, 1979; Margolin, 1981a), while still others addressed the effects specific life events had on the couples' positive and negative behavioral exchanges. Vincent, Cook, and Messerley (1980), for example, used the SOC to predict the satisfaction of spouses with the birth of their first child; Weiss et al. (1973) and Margolin and Weiss (1978) used it to determine the effects of marital therapy.

Given these findings, which were routinely consistent with a behavioral exchange explanation of marital satisfaction, attention was then directed to testing a specific theoretical formulation of behavior exchange: that the presence or absence of aversive behaviors is the primary determinant of daily satisfaction in distressed couples whereas the presence of absence of positive behaviors is the primary controlling variable in nondistressed couples. Findings from three studies (Jacobson et al., 1980; Jacobson, Follette, & McDonald, 1982; Margolin, 1981a) consistently showed that unhappy couples are more reactive to negative behavior than are nondistressed couples. That is, negative behavior strongly affects distressed spouses' daily satisfaction. The Jacobson et al. (1982) findings further indicate, however, that distressed spouses are generally more reactive to recent events. In other words, they seem to function on the basis of immediate contingencies such that they are disenchanted by recent negative events but also enchanted by recent positive events.

As discussed below, there are considerable methodological challenges facing the SOC as a measure that relies on spouses as *observers* of their own interactions. Yet if we assume that a variety of classes of behavior, other than communication, are important to assess, then we must rely on instruments such as this. As Jacobson and Moore (1981a) conclude, classes of behavioral events that should concern us the most are communication, sex and affection, shared activities, and instrumental tasks. Although there are limitations to the conclusions that can be drawn differentiating distressed and nondistressed groups on the basis of the SOC, this instrument holds considerable promise in its ability to test hypotheses with specific couples. Using the SOC, the clinician can explore whether, by increasing specific classes of behavior, anticipated changes in daily satisfaction follow. Such data are essential as feedback on the effectiveness of clinical interventions.

Communication Effectiveness

With communication difficulties repeatedly linked to marital distress and dysfunction, marital therapies of all theoretical approaches have been dedicated to improving couples' communication effectiveness. The behavioral approach, however, has distinguished itself through the development of highly sophisticated coding systems designed to assess communication patterns. The Marital Interaction Coding System (MICS; Hops, Wills, Patterson, & Weiss, 1972; Weiss & Summers, 1983) and the Couples Interaction Scoring System (CISS; Gottman, 1979) continue to enjoy widespread use. In addition, several new coding systems have been developed, aimed at reducing the labor and cost involved in administration (see Table 13.1 for descriptions of MICS and CISS categories).

Gottman (1979) offers the most extensive review of the psychometric properties of the CISS as well as the data based on the CISS regarding the role of communication deficits in marital distress. Two recent reviews, however, examine clinical implications and new directions that are being taken with the CISS (Notarius & Markman, 1981; Notarius, Markman, & Gottman, 1983). The CISS, with its separate content and affect codes, has been used to examine two types of hypotheses regarding marital distress: the proportion of specific communication behaviors exhibited in maritally distressed and nondistressed couples and the sequential patterning of codes across time. CISS data have repeatedly pointed to affect, as opposed to content, codes as better discriminators of marital distress. They also point to differences in conflict resolution patterns; for example, distressed as compared to nondistressed couples are more likely to engage in cross-complaining and to use countercomplaints (Gottman et al., 1977). According to Notarius et al. (1983), the role of affect in the CISS is currently being reconsidered. Originally, CISS affect was based on an additive hypothesis such that each nonverbal channel (linguistic, facial, gestural, and proxemic) must be examined independently and then added together. Current modifications of the CISS are taking what Gottman (Gottman, 1982; Gottman & Levenson, 1986) calls a "cultural informants" view. In addition to examining physical features only, the observer also is trained to detect specific affects in specific cultures. Specific affects, such as anger and sadness, rather than just positive or negative affect are now examined.

The MICS coding system, recently in its third revision (MICS-III; Weiss & Summers, 1983), has also been used with videotaped problem-solving discussions and includes approximately 30 specific target codes. As summarized by Weiss and Summers, some version of the MICS has been used in 35 published studies, 10 unpublished papers and two studies on parent-child interaction. Most of these studies involve some or all of the following six collapsed categories: Problem Solving, Problem Description, Positive Verbal, Negative Verbal, Positive Nonverbal, Negative Nonverbal. Similar to the CISS, the MICS has been used to examine overall rates of behavior as well as the sequential patterning of behaviors in distressed and nondistressed couples. The MICS has been used as a treatment outcome measurement as well. Two limitations of MICS-II, which have provided the impetus for MICS-III, include (a) target codes that blend both content and affect and (b) the use of double codes, which increases the number of coded behaviors. Improvements found in MICS-III include (a) decision rules which hierarchically sort code functions (Behavior Unit Codes, Nonverbal Affect Carrying Codes, Modifier Codes, and State Codes); (b) definitions concerning functional supercode categories (Proposal for Change, Validation, Invalidation, Facilitation, Blame, Description, and Irrelevant), and (c) creation of the Dyadic Behavioral Unit (DBU). The DBU represents an innovation in dyadic coding as it organizes the data for both speaker and listener into a unified speaker/listener behavior, providing an unambiguous unit for all sequential lag analyses.

The Kategoriensystem fur Partnerschaftliche Interacktion (KPI; Hahlweg, Reisner, Kohli, Vollmer, Schindler, & Revenstorf, 1984) is a relatively new coding system designed to assess speaker and listener skills that are the basis of Halweg et al.'s communication and problem-solving treatment package. This system separately codes 12 content codes (e.g., Self-Disclosure, Positive Solution, Acceptance of Other) as well as a nonverbal rating based on a hierarchical scanning of face cues, voice tone, and body cues. A comparison between distressed and nondistressed couples showed significant group differences on 8 of the 12 content codes and on all 3 nonverbal categories. In addition, pre- to post-treatment changes from behavioral marital therapy, as contrasted with a waiting-list control group, showed significant changes for 5 of the content categories and 2 nonverbal categories, as well as changes approaching significance for another 4 content and 1 nonverbal category. Although data currently exist portraying the KPI as a reliable and valid system, its authors call for further investigation of the construct and predictive validity of the system as well as cross-validation studies of the results already presented.

Filsinger (1983a) reports on the Dyadic Interaction Scoring Code (DISC), a system designed to maximize computer technology. Based on codes from the MICS and the CISS as well as Olson and Ryder's (1978) Marital and Family Interaction Scoring System and Raush et al.'s (1974) Coding Scheme for Interpersonal Conflict, the DISC measures the duration of each speaking turn, the latency between speaking turns, and gaze duration. Scoring is done on a hand-held numerical keyboard, which offers the capability of interface with a computer into which data can be automatically inputted. Data regarding the utility of this system, however, are limited to a sample of 35 opiate-involved marital dyads whose overall marital satisfaction was not assessed (Filsinger, 1981).

Floyd and Markman (1984) developed the Communication Skills Test (CST), a measure such that, with a minimum of training, experienced observers can make reliable evaluations with only a single viewing of the interactional sequence. The CST defines its behavioral units as complete statements on the part of the spouse with the "floor." These statements can be either verbal or nonverbal, and are rated on a 5-point interval scale (very positive to very negative), with definitions provided for each of the ratings. Validation of this measurement is based on a sample of premarital couples participating in a study of relationship development. Posttest CST Scores were higher for couples who received the intervention than for a group of control subjects.

Though research on dyadic communication has extensively addressed issues related to the development of valid, economical coding systems, some research also has examined the validity of the communication task itself. Birchler, Clopton, and Adams (1984) investigated two commonly used conflict resolution tasks to determine the effects of task type. Both clinic and nonclinic couples participated in discussions of actual and hypothetical relationship problems. The hypothetical problems came from Olson and Ryder's (1970) research paradigm using the Inventory of Marital Conflicts. Their results, based on MICS coding, indicate that discussion of partners' own conflict leads to better discrimination between distressed and nondistressed couples. Recent attention to the influence of task on the assessment of communication effectiveness has led investigators to have couples engage in different tasks as part of the overall evaluation. Gottman, for example, has begun to use a three-part assessment technique in which the couple first shares the events of the day, then solves a salient relationship problem, and then has an enjoyable conversation (Notarius et al., 1983). Examining the transitions and carryover effects from one task to another offers important new dimensions in this type of assessment.

Finally it should be noted that, as a function of the proliferation of new coding schemes, several reviews have been written to compare and contrast the strengths and weaknesses of available systems (e.g. Hahlweg, Reisner et al., 1984; Markman, Notarius, Stephen, & Smith, 1981; Schaap, 1982, 1984). These reviews are quite useful in discerning the specific points of similarity and difference across systems and in summarizing the findings, both convergent and divergent, that derive from different systems. Comparisons across systems are limited, however, by the fact that there have not been empirical tests: two systems have not been applied to the same sample or to the same set of discussions. Moreover, all of these systems are derived from fairly similar theoretical perspectives and reflect considerable overlap in coding targets. Hopefully, these technologies eventually will be used to test a wider range of conceptualizations of marital dysfunction.

Cognition

The inclusion of cognitions within behavioral formulations of marital distress has been stimulated by clinical observations, theoretical concepts acknowledging the role of internal mediational processes, and research findings. Behavioral marital therapists have always argued that spouses are not simply passive receptors of stimuli from one another but actively evaluate and interpret such stimuli based on their personal cognitive sets (e.g., Jacobson, 1984b). Research findings lend support to this notion by showing that frequencies of behavior tell an incomplete story. It is not just that distressed spouses exhibit more negative behaviors than nondistressed spouses but, in addition, that they are more reactive to and do not show the same capacity for neutralizing such behaviors (e.g., Jacobson et al., 1980, 1982). Distressed spouses are also affected by a characteristic cognitive filter such that there are distortions between the intent of the message sent by one partner and the impact of that message on the other partner (Gottman et al., 1976). Finally, clinicians have repeatedly pointed to ways that dysfunctional cognitive processes subvert the process of change in marital therapy (Jacobson, 1984b).

In addition to data suggesting that distressed spouses have cognitive and perceptual biases, there has been a recent trend toward examining the specific irrational beliefs and attributions that characterize these couples. Following up Ellis's comment in the early 1960s (Ellis, 1962) regarding the role of irrational expectations in marital dissatisfaction, various researchers have systematically attempted to identify common marital beliefs that have a dysfunctional impact on married life. It has been posited that absolute expectations, such as "my partner must love everything about me" are what lead to disruptive emotions such as hurt and anger. The Relationship Beliefs Inventory (RBI; Eidelson & Epstein, 1982; Epstein & Eidelson, 1981) was developed to test five such dysfunctional beliefs about intimate relationships: disagreements are destructive to a marital relationship; spouses should know each other's feelings and thoughts without asking; relationships cannot be changed; sexual perfectionism is necessary in a marriage; and differences between the sexes cause marital conflict (see Table 13.1 for sample items). All five RBI scales were negatively correlated with marital adjustment, as measured by the MAS. Among a clinical sample, the RBI scales (except "the sexes are different") were negatively related to likelihood of improvement in therapy, desire to maintain versus end the relationship, and preference for conjoint versus individual treatment. Differences between clinic and nonclinic couples, however, were not as high as anticipated. These researchers concede that the RBI is in no way an exhaustive list of dysfunctional cognitions, but it does represent an initial step in the systematic assessment of cognitions and their relationship to marital therapy.

As Fincham (1985) points out, a number of theoretical papers on attributions in relationships have emerged recently despite the relatively meager data available on this topic. What has occurred over the past 5 years are attempts to translate attributional theory, which is concerned with how people make causal explanations, into the context of intimate relationships (e.g., Berley & Jacobson, 1984; Doherty, 1981; Fincham, 1985). Doherty was the first to identify five attributional dimensions that pertain to marital relationships: (a) source — which includes self, other, the relationship, and the external environment; (b) intent — which refers to purpose, ranging from positive to helpful to negative or destructive; (c) stability — which ranges from permanent to transitory and unstable; (d) voluntariness — which refers to the quality of deliberateness or purposefulness and ranges from voluntary to involuntary, and (e) specificity — which reflects whether the dimension in question is a narrow/specific or global characteristic of the source. Having reviewed the literature, Berley and Jacobson (1984) conclude that

> "There is some evidence that spouse/actors are more inclined toward situational, external, and variable attributions, whereas spouse/observers are inclined towards internal, dispositional, stable or traitlike attributions. However, these effects are qualified by the overall level of distress in the relationship, as well as by the valence of the behavior's impact. The results suggest a kind of expectancy, balance, or discounting effect in which distressed couples attribute expected negative behavior to partner's dispositions, while positive behavior is discounted and attributed to external or situational causes. Conversely, happy couples attribute positive behavior to stable, repeatable characteristics of the spouse while minimizing the impact of negative behavior by attributing it to situation factors." (p. 30)

The assessment of attributions has been conducted through a variety of instruments and tasks. Baucom, Bell and Duke (1982) developed two measures of marital attribution based on a revised version of Seligman's learned helpless model of depression (Abramson, Seligman, & Teasdale, 1978). The Dyadic Attributional Style Inventory (DASI), patterned after Seligman's Attributional Style Questionnaire, first describes a situation and then asks subjects to state a major cause of the situation and to make attributions based on internality/externality, stability/instability, and generality/specificity of the situation. The Partner Observation Attribution Checklist (POAC), patterned after the SOC, examines attributions for 102 behaviors that possibly occurred during the previous 24 hours. Spouses read through this list, indicating which behaviors occurred, specifying if the impact of the behavior was pleasing, neutral, or displeasing; listing the one most important cause for the occurrence of the behavior; and answering questions concerning attributions for the behavior. Data from both the DASI and POAC show a clear relationship between couples' attributions and marital satisfaction. However, counterintuitive findings regarding the internal/external scale led these investigators to reconceptualize this dimension for marital dyads. Rather than considering internal/external a single bipolar dimension, they recommend assessing each person plus outside circumstances.

Fincham and colleagues (Fincham & O'Leary, 1983; Fincham, Beach, & Nelson, 1984) have conducted a series of studies aimed at the further refinement of the role of attribution in marital satisfaction. Similar to Baucom, Fincham began by using hypothetical acts reflecting commonly occurring marital behaviors, had respondents name the major cause of each behavior, and then rated the act on four causal dimensions. Results from this study indicate that distressed spouses rate causes of negative behavior as more global, whereas nondistressed spouses consider causes of positive behaviors more global. In the next stage (Fincham et al., 1984), respondents were also asked to infer the extent to which the behavior reflected the spouse's positive or negative intention, was selfishly motivated, and was blameworthy or praiseworthy. The previous findings were replicated and, in addition, nondistressed spouses rated the causes of positive events as more stable than did distressed spouses. The validity of using hypothetical behaviors versus real behaviors was examined by Fincham (1985), when spouses were to write down the two most important difficulties they experienced in their marriage and then answer attributional questions pertaining to these difficulties. Here again, distressed spouses saw the causes of the difficulties as more global and were more likely to offer negative attributions for the difficulties. Since these results replicated those using hypothetical situations, this study diffuses some of the criticism of using hypothetical tasks as the task stimuli.

Jacobson and colleagues (Jacobson, McDonald, Follette, & Berley, 1985) take a different approach to the study of attributions by assessing spouses' attributions regarding the partners' behavior during a laboratory interaction. Unknown to one partner, the other partner was instructed to act positively or negatively during a conflict-resolution interaction. Following the discussion, the uninformed spouse was asked a series of attributional questions regarding the partner's behavior. While distressed spouses were particularly likely to attribute their partners' negative behavior to internal factors, nondistressed spouses were likely to attribute the partners' positive behavior to internal factors. In a follow-up study, Holtzworth-Munroe and Jacobson (1985) used direct and indirect probes in attempting to rule out the possibility that attributional activity occurs only when psychologists solicit it. Using spouses' response to a listing of SOC behaviors, the investigators were able to generate, for each subject, an individualized list of 20 partner-initiated behaviors. In the indirect probe, spouses were to imagine that the behaviors occur and to list their thoughts and feelings. In the direct probe, spouses went through the same list of behaviors and indicated what might be the cause of the partner's behavior. Lastly, subjects were asked to rate each behavior for perceived locus of causality, voluntariness, intentionality, trait vs. state, globality, stability, and attitude. The results from this study showed that while husbands in unsatisfying relationships reported more attributional thoughts than did happily married husbands, there were no differences between groups for wives. In general, behaviors with negative impact elicited more attributional activity than did positive behaviors. As anticipated, distressed couples discredited their partners' positive behaviors by attributing them to outside circumstances and by believing that the causes of such behaviors were unstable and specific. With respect to negative behaviors, distressed spouses attributed these behaviors to the partners' personality traits, saw them as having been done intentionally and voluntarily, and perceived them as stable and global.

In addition to attributions and unrealistic expectations, it has been suggested that different mechanisms of cognitive processing occur in distressed and nondistressed couples. As Revenstorf (1984) suggests, there are three mechanisms by which individuals can simplify incoming cognitive stimuli: deleting, distorting, and abstracting. The primary vehicle for assessing these notions is to obtain spouses' observations of their own communication process. Margolin (in press-b) describes a number of structures and formats for obtaining such data. Most frequently, spouses are asked to rate their reactions along a general positive-negative dimension either while interacting or during a videotape replay. One standardized procedure known as the "communication box" was introduced by Markman and colleagues (Markman & Floyd, 1980; Markman & Poltrock, 1982). Investigations using this procedure have shown that couples' impact ratings (a) are predictive of future relationship satisfaction for premarital couples (Markman, 1979, 1981), (b) show positive changes following intervention (Blew & Morgan, 1982), and (c) discriminate happily married couples from distressed couples (Floyd & Markman, 1983; Gottman et al., 1976). Weiss (1984) used a similar scale whereby spouses made 15-second ratings of perceived helpfulness from their partners. His results show that global measures of satisfaction, stability, and expectancy affect spouses' impact ratings. In addition, the impact ratings accounted for one-third of the variance in spouses' ratings of the outcome of the discusssion. These data, taken as a whole, indicate that cognitive distortions occur but do not identify the specific nature of the distortions that differentiate distressed and nondistressed couples.

The interest in cognitive phenomena and their relation to marital satisfaction is likely to intensify over the next few years. Thus far, the majority of the research has focused on the evaluation of long-standing cognitions, such as expectancies, beliefs, and attributions. As this field advances, it is likely to focus more on spontaneous cognitions and on cognitions that are connected to the ongoing processing of information. Finally, as several authors mention (e.g., Berley & Jacobson, 1984; Fincham,

1985; Holtzworth-Munroe & Jacobson, 1985), the findings have been restricted to correlational and cross-sectional data. It has not yet been determined whether cognitive variables cause important marital phenomena or are simply by-products of such phenomena.

Affect

One way of construing the history of the assessment of affect in behavior marital therapy is that, until recently, there have been very few efforts directed toward the systematic measurement of affect. Alternatively, one can argue that the study of affect, broadly conceived, influences most all aspects of marital assessment (Bradbury & Fincham, in press; Margolin & Weinstein, 1983). Questions about happiness and affection are found on most questionnaires regarding marital satisfaction. Furthermore, one self-report questionnaire designed explicitly to assess affect, the Positive Feelings Questionnaire (O'Leary, Fincham, & Turkewitz, 1983), has demonstrated to be sensitive to changes resulting from marital therapy (O'Leary & Arias, 1983).

Overall, however, the most direct assessments of affect are found in studies of spouses' immediate affective reactions as they engage in communication tasks. As previously described, the CISS (Gottman, 1979) was the first coding system designed to explicitly study affect as a separate communication channel. The importance of affect has been clearly supported in view of the CISS's ability to differentiate distressed from nondistressed couples (Gottman et al., 1977) as well as spouses' difficulty in faking this channel of communications (Vincent et al., 1979).

Early studies on the nonverbal communication of affect were aimed at testing the communication-deficit hypothesis and the related, but somewhat distinct, private-communication hypothesis. The first emphasizes communication deficits in distressed couples whereas the second emphasizes a personalized communication system in nondistressed couples. The research on this issue expanded upon a research paradigm first developed by Kahn (1970), in which the "sending spouse" was instructed to communicate an ambiguous message with either positive, neutral, or negative affect. Congruence in the way the message was sent and received depended upon the nonverbal communicative skills in both the sender and receiver. By comparing spouse-to-spouse accuracy and spouse-to-stranger accuracy, Gottman and Porterfield (1981) discovered receiver deficits for maritally dissatisfied husbands, and Noller (1980) discovered a sending/encoding deficit for dissatisfied husbands, particularly when sending positive affect. Further research by Noller (1981), in which couples decoded strangers, determined that the decoding deficits of distressed spouses found in earlier studies is not a trait but is specific to the relationship.

Gottman's (1979) structural model regarding the role of affect in the development of marital distress predicts that maritally distressed couples, compared to nondistressed couples, are likely to exhibit less positive affect, more negative affect, more negative affect reciprocity, and greater asymmetry in the predictability of affect from one spouse to the other. Although this model received support in a number of studies based on communication coding systems (e.g., Gottman, 1979; Margolin & Wampold, 1981; Revenstorf et al., 1980; Schaap, 1982), one component of it had not been investigated. Gottman had hypothesized that the observable components of affect which typify maritally distressed couples were paralleled by the couple's physiological response.

The productive collaboration of Gottman and Levenson has recently opened up new frontiers in the study of affect in marriage. In their first study (Levenson & Gottman, 1983), 30 couples engaged in two conversations at the end of their separate days, a low-conflict discussion in which they discussed the events of their days and a high-conflict discussion in which they attempted to resolve a disagreement. Four physiological measures (heart rate, pulse transit time to the finger, skin conductance, and general somatic activity) were monitored throughout the discussions. These data were the first demonstrations of "physiological linkage," that is, temporal predictability and reciprocity in spouses' physiological reactivity. These data indicate that 60% of the variance in marital satisfaction can be accounted for by physiological linkage variables. The relationship betwen physiological linkage and marital satisfaction held only for the high-conflict discussion, however. A three-year follow-up of 21 of these couples examined whether physiological measurements predicted change in marital satisfaction over this time period (Levenson & Gottman, 1985). The two findings which emerged were that negative affect reciprocity was a strong predictor of change in relationship satisfaction and that physiological arousal was highly predictive of declines in level of marital satisfaction. One interesting example is the .92 correlation between the husband's heart rate during the conflict discusssion and declines in marital satisfaction.

In addition to physiological measurements in this study, each spouse returned to the laboratory to view the videotape of these interactions and to provide a continuous self-rating of his or her own affect on a rating dial that represented a positive-through-negative scale. This procedure provided continuous ratings of affect without interrupting the flow of the conversation. Gottman and Levenson's (1985) report on the validity of this measurement indicated that it: (a) discriminated between high- and low-conflict discussion, (b) correlated with marital satisfaction and (c) showed statistical coherence between spouses' ratings of the same discussion. Couples' coding was additionally related to observers' coding of the couples' affect. These comparisons were based on Gottman's new specific affect-coding system (SPAFF), which classifies speech units as positive, neutral, or negative and then further classifies them into one of 11 specific affects (e.g., anger, disgust). The most powerful indicator of validity, however, was evidenced in the finding that physiological data obtained during the interaction session were significantly related to physiological data obtained during recall. In other words, subjects experienced the same sequence of emotions when viewing the videotapes as they had during the actual interaction.

Another innovative approach to the assessment of affect is found in Peterson's (1977) the Interaction Record procedure (IR), based on a critical incidents technique. As orginally described, this procedure asked spouses to independently describe the most important incident of the day, indicating where the incident took place, how the interaction started, what each person did and said during the incident, what each person was thinking and feeling, and how the interaction ended. Although Peterson (1979) initially described a complex coding system that included construals and expectations in addition to affect, he found that the affect coding carried most of the interpersonal meaning. Peterson and Rapinchuk (in press) report on patterns of affect from this procedure based on frequencies and sequential contingencies of four affects: affection, calm, anger, and distress. Comparing conflicts that end in a destructive versus a constructive outcome, they find that, in destructive conflicts, anger predominates by the second act, and continues to rise proportionally thereafter, while affection and calm all but disappear during this time. Constructive conflicts, in contrast, also begin with some distress and anger, but then calm emotions are proportionally more frequent and continue to rise until affection and calm have virtually replaced anger and distress. The sequential analyses provide further support for Gottman's (1979) affective reciprocity theory. Affection and calm were more commonly reciprocated in constructive than in destructive conflicts; anger and distress were more commonly reciprocated in destructive conflicts. Anger is also likely to follow calm approximately two-thirds of the time in destructive conflicts but virtually never follows it in constructive interactions.

Overall, the study of affect has progressed considerably over the past 5 years from looking at general or long-standing affects to immediate shifts in affect. The examination of sequential patterning of affect, through physiological measures and through spouses' self-reported affect, is beginning to address questions of what produces positive or negative emotions and what is the outcome of such emotions. Also, the study of affect has become more precise in that it no longer is limited to positive versus negative emotions but now examines specific categories of emotion, such as anger, disgust, fear, and so on. It still remains to be demonstrated, however, whether or not Bradbury and Fincham's (in press) prediction will hold true that affect will dominate the 1980s just as cognition dominated the 1970s.

Systems

Infusing a systemic perspective into the behavioral model means that the focus becomes interpersonal rather than intrapersonal. Systems, unlike individuals, do not have cognitions and feelings but do possess structure and functions. The implications of making the dyad or the relationship the unit of measurement and analysis are discussed by Margolin (1983). As Lederer and Jackson (1968) said in their seminal work on marital interaction, the system reflects more than the combined total of what individual participants contribute. Furthermore, based on the viewpoints that explanations of behavior are circular rather than linear and that individual actions derive meaning from larger sequences of exchange, it is difficult to segment behavior into meaningful units or to determine at what point a behavior begins or ends.

The investigation of interaction sequences has provided one solution to these dilemmas. In fact, an important point of convergence between social learning and systems perspectives is the emphasis on understanding reccuring patterns. Gottman's (1979; Gottman & Levenson, 1986) efforts to define cross-complaining, negative affect reciprocity, and physiological linkage are examples of systematic characteristics. Weiss's (1983) recent improvements with the MICS-III, particularly with the introduction of simultaneous speaker–listener behaviors, also reflect a more systemic perspective. Peterson's (1977) IR is founded on the systemic premise that any one behavior simultaneously (a) reveals something about the actor's state, (b) serves as a reaction to the other person's previous behavior, (c) is an action directed toward the other person, and (d) commands a response in return. Each of these efforts, however, has been directed toward identifying relationship structures through the microanalysis of interaction. The systems perspective, however, also calls for a more molar analysis of systemic characteristics.

In an attempt to assess more molar patterns. Christensen and colleagues (Christensen, Sullaway, & King, 1982; Sullaway & Christensen, 1983) developed a series of measures that define symmetrical and asymmetrical interaction patterns as well as dysfunctional communication cycles. Their goal was to see if couples recognize broad patterns in their relationships and whether any of these patterns were related to relationship satisfaction. The three measures used were the Interaction Patterns Questionnaire, which had the respondents indicate how frequently 12 complementary patterns occurred in their relationship (see Table 13.1); the Relationship Patterns Questionnaire, which had respondents indicate the extent to which six symmetrical patterns occurred in their marriage; and the Interaction Styles Questionnaire, which had respondents indicate which of Satir's four dysfunctional communication styles was most characteristic of themselves.

Agreement between spouses on each of these measures was described by Christensen et al. (1982) as "modest." However, a number of the patterns, particularly the asymmetrical ones, showed a strong correlation with relationship satisfaction. The following six patterns, for example, each accounted for 20–35% of the variance in relationship satisfaction: demanding/withdrawing; criticizing/hurt; engaging/avoiding; flirtatious/jealous; role-changer/role-stabilizer; and emotional/avoidant. Since this group of patterns is highly intercorrelated, Christensen et al. are continuing to work to obtain a small group of maximally orthogonal patterns that account for a maximal amount of the variance in relationship satisfaction.

The study of systems characteristics would be incomplete without mention of the Circumplex Model proposed by Olson and his associates (Olson et al., 1983; Olson & Portner, 1983; Olson, Russell, & Sprenkle, 1979). This model puts forth cohesion, adaptability, and communication as the three dimensions of family behavior that emerge from a conceptual clustering of over 50 concepts developed to describe marital and family dynamics. *Cohesion* is defined as the emotional bonding that family members have toward one another. *Adaptability* is the ability of a marital or family system to change its power structure, role relationships, and relationship rules. *Communication* is posited as a facilitating dimension, considered critical to movement on the other two dimensions. In order to classify couples and families along these dimensions, the Family Adaptibility and Cohesion Evaluation Scales (FACES II; Olson & Portner, 1983) was developed (with separate marital and family forms). These scales, which involve 30 true–false questions, provide separate measurements of cohesion (which spans disengaged, separated, connected and enmeshed) and adaptibility (which spans chaotic, flexible, structured, and rigid; see Table 13.1 for sample items). Organized into a four-by-four table, this model describes 16 types of marital systems, with chaotically-disengaged, chaotically-enmeshed, rigidly-disengaged and rigidly-enmeshed as the four extremes. It is generally hyopthesized that central rather than extreme levels of functioning on cohesion and adaptibility are more functional, although recent data show functional families as chaotically enmeshed (Olson et al., 1983). In addition to being able to compare the separate perceptions of both spouses, the instrument is designed so that it can be administered twice — once for how the spouses currently see their relationship (perceived) and once for how they would like it to be (ideal). Despite widespread use of this instrument in marital and family studies, it has not appeared in the behavioral marital literature. One possible direction would be to explore the association between cohesion or adaptability and process variables obtained through the examination of interaction samples.

In a behavioral-systems model of assessment, behavioral concepts can be applied at the relationship level of analysis or systems concepts can be operationalized and measured using behavioral technology. Thus far efforts have been directed to the former more than the latter. A concept such as reciprocity, for which there is considerable empirical support, is a behavioral concept that describes a characteristic of the relationship. Concepts coming out of systems theory, such as cohesion, homeostasis, boundary maintenance, scapegoating, and so on, have yet to be put to the empirical tests that characterize the behavioral approach. Hopefully, the methodologies that behaviorists have developed will eventually be used to examine concepts derived from theoretical approaches other than a behavioral model.

CURRENT ISSUES

The Role of Observational Data

Without question, the data from observational studies have contributed greatly to our understanding of the differences between satisfied and dissatisfied marriages. Nonetheless, the findings may be restricted since they are derived primarily from one type of observational strategy, that is, laboratory-based, time-limited discussions of problematic topics to which elaborate coding systems are applied by trained observers. By limiting observations to this particular context, we have no way of knowing whether the differences discovered are the only or are the most significant differences. Furthermore, it also can be asked whether the differences exhibited between distressed and nondistressed couples may, to some degree, be a function of the task itself. Even though distressed and nondistressed couples discuss an area of actual disagreement, and even though it may be the most severe disagreement in the marriage, can we conclude that the task is comparable for both sets of couples? Are the differences found actually a function of different conflict resolution processes in distressed versus nondistressed couples or a function of the intensity and complexity of that conflict as experienced prior to the interaction sample?

Jacobson (1985b, 1985c) has raised even more serious issues concerning the role of observational data with respect to treatment planning and treatment outcome. He argues that, despite our proclivity for the direct observation of behavior, *"we cannot assume that observational measures are superior to other types of measures simply because they are observational"* (Jacobson, 1985c, p. 324). He further indicates that the targets of primary interest may not be observable by an outsider. For example, communication effectiveness, which we typically measure through observation, may not reflect the problems that the couples bring to therapy. Even if communication difficulties are part of the presenting problem, our coding systems may not measure the presenting problem of a particular couple.

Furthermore, as an outcome measure, observational data may simply mirror the performance requirements of the treatment program rather than directly tap the issues brought in by the couple. In other words, observational measures may be better used to determine whether the communication skills taught in marital treatment actually were learned rather than used as a primary measure of whether or not the presenting problem and accompanying pain have lessened.

In reply to Jacobson's arguments, Weiss and Frohman (1985) and Gottman (1985) offer more optimistic appraisals of observational data but still seem to indicate that the full potential of these data is yet to be revealed. Weiss and Frohman (1985) focus on content validity issues, indicating that any observational system, just as any other assessment device, is dependent upon and constrained by its own structure and items. The goal for assessors of marital interaction is to "encode our best wisdom about these forms of human behavior by providing a language of constructs for 'seeing' reality" (pp. 312–313). These authors concede that we may not have encoded the most important behaviors and events in respect to affectional reactions and decisions, and they further recommend that cognitive, affective, and interactional events be included in future efforts.

Gottman (1985) agrees with Jacobson that the design of marital therapies is divorced from observational studies but, contrary to Jacobson, faults the treatments not the assessments. Taking a match-to-normal approach, he states that "the design of behavioral interventions needs to precisely reflect the *evidence* of how dissatisfied marital relationships differ from satisfied marital relationships, other than on the basis of dissatisfaction" (p. 319). He also points out that despite the validity of self-report instruments, their validity for the purposes of treatment outcome studies has yet to be demonstrated.

In a rejoinder to these two replies, Jacobson (1985c) questioned the wisdom of designing treatment strategies to conform to observational studies. He pointed out that the matching-to-sample strategy has serious shortcomings, including the tendency to overinterpret significant correlations as if they were of causal importance. In other words, simply because distressed couples exhibit certain interaction patterns does not, Jacobson contends, imply that these interaction patterns comprise the essential distinction between distressed and nondistressed couples. Moreover, the distinction is also made between primary and secondary outcome measures. The former constitute the basis for inferring treatment efficacy, while the latter are usually included for some other purpose. The relevance of this distinction, according to Jacobson, is that for some clinical problems, given the insensitivity of observational coding systems to a particular couple's presenting problem, the primary outcome measures will be self-reports of marital satisfaction. Finally, Jacobson advocates the continued use of moderate observational coding as opposed to the trend he sees toward observational methods addiction.

This debate, which is far more complicated than what has been summarized here, illuminates the difficulties that we face in attempting to translate our global constructs into measureable units. Although these authors differ as to where their skepticism is most forcefully directed, all three call for multidimensional assessments and for a more critical appraisal of our use of assessment instruments. Is it that overt behaviors no longer are the *sine qua non* of behavioral marital assessment, and they should take a parallel or secondary place with respect to cognitive and affective events, or should we redirect observations toward identifying variables that have better discriminative and predictive validity? These are not really either–or questions nor does the debate between the authors have yes–no answers. This series of articles, however, updates our consideration of observational procedures in light of the current status of marital research. It also defines the questions with which we must grapple in our continued use of observational procedures.

The Role of Spouses as Observers

In addition to questions about the usefulness of observational data as provided by trained observers, the degree to which spouses can provide useful observational data on their own relationship has been the subject of recent attention. Spouses' observations of themselves and one another have been labeled "quasi-observational" or "quasi-behavioral" (Weiss & Margolin, 1986), bridging the gap between one-time verbal report procedures and objective outsider observations. Rather than coming to the situation uninformed, a spouse brings the cumulative history of the relationship and all of its accompanying feelings to each new observation of the relationship. This, of course, makes objectivity with respect to these reports quite different from that of outside observers. Yet, these participant observational procedures are also quite distinct from one-time self-report tasks. The data are prospective rather than retrospective, involve repeated observations through monitoring rather than a singular response, refer to a limited time interval, and involve a carefully constructed format for recording observations (Margolin, in press-b).

The self- and spouse-monitoring procedures have been developed primarily to assess the nature and tone of spouses' behavioral exchange in the home as well as spouses' perceptions of their communication effectiveness. The SOC (Weiss & Perry, 1979), with its comprehensive listing of pleasing and displeasing relationship behavior, and the IR (Peterson, 1979), with its detailed recording of one critical relationship event for each day, are two of the most widely used and versatile methods for obtaining information about a couple's daily interactions. Procedures to elicit spouses' impressions of their own communication effectiveness have had spouses rate, along a positive-negative dimension, time intervals or content-based segments of interaction. Instructions in various studies have included ratings of the intent and expectations of the speakers, the perceived positive/negative impact on the listener, and general impressions of self and the partner (Notarius, Vanzetti, & Smith, 1981; Floyd & Markman, 1983; Markman & Poltrock, 1982; Gottman, 1979; Margolin, Hattem, John, & Yost, 1985; Weiss, 1984a; Weiss, Wasserman, Wieder, & Summers 1981).

In addition to the standardized formats for quasi-observations, these procedures can be tailored to meet the prerequisites of specific assessment situations. Procedures can be designed to monitor whatever individualized complaints or goals a client brings to therapy. The spouse who feels emotionally distant, for example, can be asked to appraise those feelings at regular intervals each day and to generate hypotheses about what factors contribute to each rating. Likewise, in understanding a spouse's dissatisfaction with communication, the spouse can generate his or her own referents for describing his or her reactions rather than being constrained by our targets and labels.

The advantage of this form of assessment is that information becomes available on interactional sequences that are inaccessible to outsiders and on private, internal states, such as thoughts and feelings. Another advantage is that with repeated observations there is a sequential dimension to these data. Thus, relationship characteristics can be looked at as fluctuating rather than stable and can be considered in conjunction with other conditions that also vary across time. To increase marital satisfaction, for example, one would identify conditions associated with upward as opposed to downward fluctuations, and then attempt to increase the likelihood of conditions concurrent with upward trends.

One controversy surrounding these data has to do with their reactivity, that is, whether the assessment processes per se lead to changes in the behavior being observed. With self- and spouse-monitoring, respondents receive immediate and direct feedback on their behavior. They also know exactly what is being observed. As Jacobson et al. (1981) point out, it is impossible to assess reactivity since there is no suitable baseline against which to compare these data. Changes might occur immediately with the initiation of assessment procedures. The only reactivity that can be measured is that which occurs between early and later periods of data collection. Collection of SOC data, for example, tends to show declines in behavioral frequencies over time (Robinson & Price, 1980; Wills et al., 1974), perhaps indicating an initial change in behavior that then receded, a change in behavior over time due to feedback through the SOC, or a fatigue effect. Certain reactive effects, such as behavior changes in a desired direction, are problematic for research purposes but are of course beneficial in the course of treatment. Patterson and Bank (1986) go so far as to suggest that the collection of molecular data by patients actually may be necessary for global judgments to become more sensitive to behavior changes and thus to reflect behavioral improvements.

The second controversy surrounding these measures has to do with problems of reliability. When two spouses are instructed to monitor the same behavior, agreement between them tends to be greater than chance but below the level usually considered acceptable for observation research. Level of agreement, furthermore, seems to be a function of relationship adjustment, with low agreement exhibited by persons in distressed relationships. Using a modified version of the SOC, for example, Christensen and Nies (1980) found that only 18% of the items had agreement levels greater than 70% and that most of the high-agreement items were pleasing events whereas the low-agreement items were displeasing events. Examining the same data for systematic sources of bias, Christensen, Sullaway, and King (1983) reported greater agreement in happy couples than in unhappy couples and higher consensus on items that were objective and molar rather than inferential and molecular. This study also revealed an egocentric bias in that spouses tended to overreport their own behavior and underreport their partner's behavior. Jacobson and Moore (1981b), also using the SOC, found a mean agreement rate of 47.8%, with the agreement for nondistressed couples (52%) significantly higher than the agreement for distressed couples (42%). Here, too, agreement was higher for behaviors that required little inference regarding the intent, or feeling state of the actor (e.g., companionship and sex).

When spouses' perceptions of communication effectiveness have been compared to codings by trained observers, there is also relatively low overall agreement. Gottman (1979) predicted low agreement, particularly in nondistressed couples, due their private-message systems. Using the "talk table," he found agreement scores between nonclinic couples and affect coders to be slightly lower than between clinic couples and the same coders. In a comparison between spouses' impact ratings and MICS coding, Weiss (1984a) found agreement between couples and coders about the occurrence of positive but not negative behaviors. Floyd and Markman (1983) also examined the relationship between spouses' ratings of one another and observers' ratings of the spouses. Although spouses' ratings of one another were not consistent with outsiders' ratings, spouses' ratings of the partner were consistent with outsiders' views of the spouse raters' own behaviors. Distressed wives, in particular, both produced the most negative ratings for their husbands and received the most negative ratings from outsiders. It thus appears that distressed wives perceived their husbands' behaviors as negative and then reciprocated with similar behaviors.

Comparisons between couples and outside coders also have been made having couples rate tapes other than their own. Weiss et al. (1981) found that couples' median correlation with outside coders on a positive tape of another couple was higher than on their own tape, but agreement on a negative tape was lower. Margolin et al. (1985) found consensus between couples and outside coders to be higher when coding other couples than when coding themselves. Agreement between the two spouses also was higher on the standardized tape than on self tapes. Thus, the personalized material of self-tapes, more than a consistent distortion in spouses' view of the relationship, is the source of the disagreements among observers. Furthermore, since agreement between the wife and husband was always higher than their agreement with trained coders, there is some evidence for Gottman's (Gottman, 1979; Gottman & Porterfield, 1981) hypothesis of a "private communication system" in couples.

As a whole, this body of research points to the conclusion that spouses' observations of themselves, both in the laboratory and at home, are affected by a variety of factors that develop through their history of repeated interactions and that are inaccessible to outside observers. As Margolin et al. (1985) suggest, the lack of agreement between insiders and outsiders does not mean that one or another observer source provides more accurate or more useful information but means that they measure different types of information. Similarly, the lack of agreement between the two spouses does not suggest that one set of data necessarily lacks accuracy. Important relationship phenomena are difficult to isolate, identify, and measure and are, in many instances, subject to interpretation. The same kiss may be counted as an affectionate act by one partner but ignored as a cursory gesture by the other.

The utility of these measures depends upon the purposes of the assessment. They are essential for assessments directed to understanding how the individual's perceptions guide his or her behavior. They are the key to understanding marital distress for those who believe that the cognitive appraisal of the behavior is more important for the relationship than the behavior itself (e.g., Revenstorf, 1984). Just as observations by trained coders are constrained by the researcher's underlying assumptions about marital interaction, these quasi-observations by spouses are affected by each spouse's perceptual biases. The difficulty in interpreting the observations comes from sorting out what really is a perceptual distortion and what reflects a spouse's ability to recognize the subtleties of behavior that are unavailable to an outsider.

Sex-Role Issues

Marital therapy in general and behavioral marital therapy in particular recently have come under attack for being insensitive to issues related to sex roles (Gurman & Klein, 1983; Jacobson, 1983; Margolin, Talovic, Fernandez, & Onorato, 1983). The less critical but still negative view of behavioral marital therapy is that sex role issues have simply been ignored. The more severe criticism portrays behavioral marital therapy as actively promoting relationship structures that are oppressive to women. In addition to the moral and ethical consequences, insensitivity to sex-role issues is counterproductive to the goal of relationship improvement. As recently demonstrated by Jacobson, Follette, and Pagel (in press), couples with traditional affiliation/independence patterns (i.e., a highly affiliative wife and a highly independent husband) were less likely to benefit from behavioral marital therapy.

Sex-role issues as they pertain to assessment take two predominant forms: Are sex-role preferences standardly assessed as part of our broad-based assessment strategies? Do our assessment instruments reflect sex-role biases? The answer to the first question, unfortunately, is no. Despite the flood of reviews and chapters on behavioral marital therapy during the past 5 years, and the myriad of suggestions as to what should be assessed, little attention has been paid to the assessment of sex roles. Somehow the behavioral marital assessment literature has been unaffected by the idea that spouses' gender identities and the cultural shifts regarding sex roles are an underlying source of conflict for most if not all couples (e.g., Goldner, 1985). We think this idea is quite compelling and believe that gender roles should be included as one of the important constructs in understanding marital dysfunction.

Our recommendation is that the assessment of all couples include inquiries pertinent to sex-role conflicts between the spouses and sex-role confusion within the individual. Just as one would not begin therapy without knowing whether sexual relations or finances are problematic for a given couple, sex roles deserve equal attention. The assessor must be aware, however, that spouses' concerns regarding sex roles may not be spontaneously forthcoming. Thus, this assessment means moving beyond presenting problems. Points of inquiry range from the ways gender is enacted in the day-to-day functioning of the marriage to spouses' fundamental feelings about themselves as individuals: Who controls what resources? What is the division of labor in the household? What are the discrepancies between expected and actual role assignments? What is the power structure of the relationship, how is it exhibited, and what are its consequences? How does the husband feel about himself as a man and, similarly, how does the wife feel about herself as a woman? Answers to these questions, and yet new questions, will come primarily from interviews as well as from directly observing the spouses in the session (e.g., Does one spouse capitulate to the other's point of view or check out his or her responses with the other?).

In answering these questions, it is not enough simply to label a couple as "egalitarian" or "traditional" or to identify one spouse as more powerful (e.g., Jacobson, 1983; Margolin et al., 1983). The assessment must go a step further and examine how the couple is affected by and copes with this situation. Do they inadvertently reinforce positions in one another that contradict their relationship ideals? How have their sex roles been affected by progressing into new life stages? Similarly, there is no one goal toward which to strive along the traditional versus egalitarian dimension. Some traditionally structured relationships promote positive outcomes such that each spouse maintains power in his or her domain and feels a sense of efficacy and control. Some egalitarian structures in which both are earning a salary and both are sharing in homemaking and childcare may result in two overly stressed and unhappy individuals.

The answer to the question regarding whether there is a sex-role bias in our assessment procedures most probably is yes. Laws' (1971) suggestion that assessment procedures be reexamined for sex bias still demands our attention today. As Margolin et al. (1983) point out, the Areas of Change Questionnaire includes items which read "help with the housework when asked" and "have meals ready on time," implying that such tasks are the responsibility of one person. If items were written without any sex-role presuppositions (e.g., "prepare meals" or "do housework"), there would be no assumption as to who was responsible for completing that particular task.

Objective coding systems also are subject to criticism for their emphasis on rational rather than emotional approaches to problem-solving. This model is, of course, stereotypically more masculine than feminine. Behaviors that are strongly valued in these systems are problem solutions and agreements. These is no recognition of the fact that problem resolutions sometimes are a function of premature, submissive, or coerced conciliations or reflect a compromise that neither spouse particularly desires. Moreover, expressions of dissension, such as criticisms, complaints, and sometimes even disagreements, are collapsed into negative summary scores. Yet for some spouses, particularly women in oppressive relationships, being able to fully express opinions and emotions may be a very constructive step.

In addition to these clinical issues, ideas about sex differences and their contribution to marital dysfunction are being shaped by findings from observational coding systems. The Floyd and Markman (1983) findings, for example, are being taken as evidence of wives as a "barometer" of a distressed marital system. This conclusion is made since wives are coded by outsiders more negatively than husbands and since wives also rate their husbands more negatively than husbands rate wives. An alternative explanation, however, is that wives are not simply acting more negatively but that they exhibit their dissatisfactions more directly, which the outside coders pick up, while men exhibit their dissatisfaction more covertly, which is recognizable to the wives but not to the outside coders.

The therapist as an instrument of assessment must also examine his or her behavior vis à vis sex-role issues. A number of authors have emphasized the importance of being aware of one's own biases regarding sex-role issues and clarifying these biases when they play a role in the assessment process (Berger, 1979; Gurman & Klein, 1980). As part of this, the assessor may need to monitor his or her own behavior for subtle signs that suggest that the husband and wife command different status. Are more inquiries made about the husband's work than the wife's work? Is equal attention paid to how the wife and the husband spend their independent days? Are questions about family finances automatically addressed to the husband while questions about the children are addressed to the wife? The process of assessment also determines at what level goals are defined. The behavioral literature has advocated accepting complaints at face value and then operationalizing those complaints into specific behavioral targets. Although this sometimes clears the path toward behavioral change, it may overlook an underlying unstated theme in a complaint, such as sex-role conflict. It is important that goals should not be accepted at face value simply because our techniques are geared more to that level and thus we feel more comfortable working at that level.

Emphasis on the Individual as well as the Couple

As indicated above, the recent history of behavioral marital therapy and assessment has shown a move toward systemic views (Weiss, 1980; Birchler & Spinks, 1980). We have embraced circular rather than linear explanations of relationship problems and thus plan interventions that involve change on the part of both individuals. We avoid labels that identify one spouse as the cause of the problem and focus on the present rather than on each spouse's individual histories prior to the relationship. Without diminishing all the benefits of intervening systemically, we wish to suggest that, in thinking systemically, we must be careful not to lose the individual altogether.

From an assessment perspective, there has been a tendency to use mean couple scores rather than individual scores. In comparisons between distressed and nondistressed couples, for example, it is common procedure to classify couples by an average or sum of the two spouses' scores on marital adjustment scales. With such procedures, a couple sum of 200 could result from two individual spouse scores of 100 or from one score of 80 and the other of 120. As Stevens, Arkowitz, Sladeczek, and Ridley (1985) recently demonstrated, the summation method is misleading whenever spouses are in disagreement and results in a loss of information. Other superior measurement recommendations made by these experimenters included difference scores and sum-to-difference ratios. Baucom and Mehlman (1984) similarly cast doubt on the utility of a summative method for handling data. Their objective was to examine data combination procedures to predict future marital status. What they label the "weak link" models, which focus on the least satisfied spouse, as well as using only wives' scores, proved to be better predictors than the summative model.

The recommendations by Jacobson, Follette, and Elwood (1984) echo a similar theme. They indicate that data should be reported for each spouse rather than for the couple as a unit and that data analyses should be augmented by an investigation of differential treatment effects as a function of spouses. While this presents certain problems regarding the nonindependence of subjects (O'Leary & Turkewitz, 1978), the problems are not insurmountable. Possible solutions include (a) treating individual spouses as repeated measures, with the unit of analysis remaining the dyad; (b) dividing the number of degrees of freedom in half; and (c) viewing each spouse as a separate univariate component in a multivariate analysis of variance (Baucom, 1983; Jacobson, Follette, & Elwood 1984; Kraemer & Jacklin, 1979).

From a clinical perspective, and regarding the gender issues already mentioned, one of the most important decisions in marital assessment is determining when a dyadically oriented treatment is inappropriate because it maintains a situation that is highly detrimental to one or both partners. This decision requires looking at spouses as individuals and thinking about the impact of therapy for each spouse separately. In all marital assessments, it is necessary to ascertain if one spouse is in an emotionally or physically abusive relationship or if one spouse is highly unlikely to change even though the other might make a considerable effort. Likewise, periodically in the course of marital therapy it is important to assess the outcome of therapy for each spouse separately. At any given point in time, it is not unusual to find that one spouse's satisfaction is increasing while the other's is not. If this situation persists, however, it may be necessary to alter the goals of therapy.

The interactional model of assessment proposed by Margolin (1983a) suggests that individual variables are mediating factors toward the criterion of relationship adjustment. In other words, intrapersonal variables, such as behavioral, affective, cognitive, physiological, and historical factors have a significant impact on relationship processes. Other factors are also to be considered, however, such as relevant determinants within the environment and the mutual learning history of the couple. We recommend the interactional model once the goal is determined to be relationship improvement. First, however, the assessor has to make the decision as to whether or not relationship improvement is a viable goal, which requires an assessment into the ways that the relationship affects the individual welfare to each spouse.

Assessing Treatment Outcome

Several investigators recently have been posing important and challenging questions about the effectiveness of treatment. Conclusions about improvement reflect our choice of measurement as well as our determination of the amount of change needed to designate a couple as "improved." The recommendation that uniformly appears regarding choice of measurement is a call for multidimensional measures. Dissension occurs, however, around the question as to what is the primary measurement, particularly if multiple measurements lead to divergent conclusions. Jacobson (1985a, 1985d) strongly advocates that change in the presenting problem be the primary criterion for successful therapy. He states that "if the family 'got what they came for' but the family interaction patterns were left unaltered, most people in the community (perhaps everyone except for family system theorists) would view the case as a success . . ." (Jacobson, 1985d, p. 164). In contrast to this call for individualized criteria, Baucom (1983) endorses marital satisfaction as a uniform criterion across all couples. He maintains that since most couples request marital therapy because they are unhappy or dissatisfied with the relationship, the ultimate criterion for treatment effectiveness is whether the two spouses leave therapy more satisfied with their relationship. Kniskern (1985), in direct response to Jacobson (1985a), maintains that the primary criterion for the evaluation of marital and family therapy be a change in interactional patterns. His criticism of presenting problems as the criterion is that attention will be directed away from the system and toward the identified patient. Thus, the controversy surrounds the question of whether variables identified by the therapist are the best criteria of effective functioning, as Kniskern suggests, or variables identified by the spouses are the best criteria, as Jacobson recommends.

Adding to these arguments, there may not be one answer to this question. Rather than conclude that there is one primary measure or that there is one source of that measure (i.e., either the therapist or the clients), the goals must be jointly negotiated between the therapist and both spouses. One concern not mentioned by Jacobson is that two spouses often do not agree on the presenting complaints. Thus, therapists often attempt to redefine spouses, presenting complaints to establish mutually acceptable goals. Redefinitions of the clients' problem by the therapist may also be used to focus attention on a unifying theme linking several complaints, such as sex-role concerns as opposed to individualized complaints, or on a core issue underlying the complaint of the problem (e.g., on increasing intimacy rather than the couple's goal of decreasing arguments). It can be argued endlessly whether or not the reframes are accurate representations of the problem or are done strictly for strategic purposes so that the problems can be better treated. More pertinent to the issue of measurement, however, is whether these more global or more core issues are accepted by the couple as reasonable goals. Decisions about the target of measurement should be a function of the joint decision of the couple and therapist about the level at which to address a problem.

To some extent, the decision regarding goals simply reflects a difference in language. Does the therapist convince the couple to adopt his or her viewpoint and language for discussing problems or does the therapist adapt his or her procedures to fit the clients' perspectives? It is those cases in which the therapist and clients cannot agree on a common language and common goals that are the important ones. If the couple is uninterested in altering fundamental relationship structures, then this is an inappropriate goal and an inappropriate assessment target. Yet, if the couple is willing to accept these fundamental changes as goals, it would be expected that these changes would be accompanied by changes as well in their more narrowly defined presenting complaints. This, however, should not be taken for granted but should be evaluated by assessing changes at both levels.

Coming to some agreement about goals and determining appropriate assessment targets should reflect both mediating and ultimate goals in marital therapy. According to Parloff (1976), "mediating goals are those which reflect the clinician's assumptions regarding the necessary steps and stages through which a patient must progress if the treatment is to be effective. These goals represent the postulated enabling or intermediate conditions which will permit the attainment of the ultimate goals" (p. 317). Thus, mediating goals generally are those steps specified by the therapist as a way to obtain the spouses' ultimate goals. Assessment criteria to assess these goals are what Jacobson (1985a) calls manipulation checks to document the success or failure of getting across the therapeutic message. For the therapist and couple to work together in therapy, they must agree on the ultimate goals. The therapist, however, generally identifies the mediating goals. It should be noted that what may be the ultimate goal for some couples (e.g., better communication) may be a mediating goal for others (e.g., better communication as a way to feel less distant). Often, a couple's decision of whether or not to stay together is a function of whether the mediating goals do indeed have the anticipated impact on the ultimate goals. A couple can develop very effective communication patterns but still be unhappy in their marriage. Examining the covariation between criteria representing the mediating goals and criteria representing ultimate goals can be an important part of the assessment and therapeutic process.

Issues regarding the amount of change required to identify a couple as improved bring up a different set of questions. Originally, the field was willing to accept as evidence of improvement any statistically significant difference between pretest and posttest measurements or between pretest and follow-up measurements. Efforts to make assessments more clinically relevant have resulted in the following questions: What do we use as a measure of clinical, rather than statistical, improvement? Is falling into the nondistressed range on a given measure the best criterion for efficacy? Alternatively, Is there a critical amount of change that would indicate that change is not due to chance?

Although we still await definitive answers, Jacobson and his colleagues have offered a number of recommendations regarding the way to present treatment outcome data in the marital field. In addition to reporting summary statistics, it is recommended that the percentages of couples and individual spouses who demonstrate clinically significant improvements also be provided (Jacobson, Follette, & Elwood, 1984). Jacobson, Follette, and Revenstorf (1984) elaborate upon this by recommending two criteria for determining clinically significant improvement: movement into a normative or nondistressed range and change of sufficient magnitude. There are three options proposed to determine whether clients move from the dysfunctional to the functional range: (a) Does the level of functioning at posttest fall outside the range of the dysfunctional population, where range is defined as extending to two standard deviations above (in the direction of functionality) the mean for that population? (b) Does the level of functioning at posttest fall within the range of the functional or normal population, where range is defined as beginning at two standard deviations below the mean for the normal population? (c) Does the level of functioning at posttest suggest that the subject is statistically more likely to be in the functional than in the dysfunctional population — that is, is the posttest score statistically more likely to be drawn from the functional than the dysfunctional distribution? The second criterion is whether there has been sufficient change during the course of therapy, thereby ruling out cases of little or no change despite a normal posttest level of functioning. A reliable change index (computed as the difference score (post-pre) divided by the standard error of measurement) larger than 1.96 is proposed as the criterion. Christensen and Mendoza (1986) have suggested substituting the standard error of the difference score in the denominator of this equation, a suggestion which Jacobson, Follette, and Revenstorf (1986) endorsed.

These proposals for measuring change are not the only ones but certainly are a step in the right direction and have been instrumental in initiating dialogue on these topics. Specific assumptions underlying these proposals, that is, that there are distinct distributions for the dysfunctional and functional populations, have been brought into question (e.g., Wampold & Jenson, 1986). Furthermore, as Jacobson, Follette, and Revenstorf (1984) observe, the methods proposed are only as good as the outcome measures available to the field: "Clinically significant change on a poor measure does not improve our ability to meaningfully interpret the findings from psychotherapy research" (p. 349). Finally, there is the dilemma posed by divergent findings among multidimensional measures where we cannot assume that there is a linear relationship among all criteria (e.g., when marital satisfaction deteriorates to the point of divorce, individual satisfaction may improve).

Decision-Making and Prediction

Decision-making and prediction are the primary reasons for conducting any assessment: to determine what types of couples are good candidates for marital therapy, to predict which couples will benefit from what types of intervention strategies and to identify what combination of factors will predict later marital distress. Preliminary data to help identify good candidates for behavioral marital therapy come from two large-scale treatment outcome studies. Data from the Munich marital therapy study (Halhweg, Schindler, Revenstorf, & Brengelmann, 1984) indicated that couples have an unfavorable prognosis when (a) both partners are thinking of separation or divorce or have been separated before, (b) the frequency of sexual intercourse is less than twice per month, (c) both partners score low on a scale of tenderness, or (d) the wife scores low on a scale of togetherness/ communication. These variables, reflecting emotional and affectional dimensions, proved more significant than demographic variables or variables describing the nature of the couple's conflict. It remains unknown, however, whether this finding applies to all marital therapies or only to the behavioral and communications training formats applied in this study.

Baucom and Aiken (1984) found that both masculinity and femininity are related to marital satisfaction and response to behavioral marital therapy. Wives' level of femininity prior to treatment was significantly correlated with increases in marital satisfaction for both husbands and wives at the end of treatment. Also, husbands' and wives' masculinity levels prior to treatment significantly predicted which couples would be living together 6 months after treatment was completed. Jacobson et al. (in press) found that patterns of affiliation/independence (i.e., a highly affiliative wife paired with a highly independent husband) predicted poor treatment outcome at posttreatment and at a 6-month follow-up. Depressive symptoms were associated with a positive treatment outcome immediately following treatment. Interestingly, in that study, age, femininity, and divorce potential were not predictive of treatment outcome after controlling for pretreatment marital distress.

Although these studies begin to shed light on the question of who benefits from behaviorally oriented treatment, their implications are somewhat limited. Although it is easy enough to assess these variables, we obviously would not use a score on femininity, affiliation-independence, etcetera, to recommend against treatment. Instead, the goal must be to use pretherapy assessment information to decide upon one type of treatment over another. In other words, we should be working toward models that predict the responses of particular types of client couples and specific clinical intervention strategies.

Jacobson, Follette, and Elwood (1984) argue that, rather than focus on demographic and severity variables, efforts should be made to categorize clients according to type of presenting problem or type of relationship. Specific dimensions that they recommend to build typologies of couple classification include types of communication deficits, differing needs for affiliation, different development histories leading up to the present distress, and different family histories for violence or substance abuse.

Margolin (in press-a) recommends using conflict strategy as a dimension along which to classify couples differentiating couples who escalate in conflict from those who withdraw from conflict. The assessment of such patterns would include affective factors (e.g., spouses' overall levels of anger arousal, their awareness of their own emotional arousal, their abilities to communicate anger as well as other emotions), cognitive factors (e.g., perceptual biases that lead to overly negative interpretations, beliefs about the role of conflict in relationships and the acceptableness of specific conflict behaviors), behavioral factors (e.g., the ability to be a careful listener, to assertively state one's own position, to be a creative problem solver), relationship factors (e.g., processes of influence and control in the relationship, repeating interactional sequences, and outcomes that arise from the couple's own attempts to solve the problem), and contextual and historical factors (e.g., the impact of environmental factors on conflict and spouse's individual histories of family conflict). Through such an assessment, an overall picture of conflict escalation or avoidance emerges, which then translates into specific treatment recommendations.

Just as there is considerable empirical work to be done before we have an actuarial matching of couple and treatment techniques, there is also considerable empirical work needed to predict marital distress and dissolution. This work is essential if our eventual goal is to help couples cope with the normal frustrations and disappointments in marriage and avoid severe marital dysfunction. Markman, Floyd, and Dickson-Markman (in press) call for a model of research that examines how couples behave during the identifiable transition periods in family life that are associated with increased stress. They recommend identifying variables that have predictive power but that also can be modified through preventative efforts.

Although preliminary progress has been made toward answering all three of the prediction questions posed above, knowledge base on these issues is still quite limited. While we have identified isolated characteristics that are associated with positive treatment outcomes and with the development of marital distress, there is little consistency across studies. Furthermore, the characteristics identified regarding treatment outcome and the development of marital distress do not lead to comprehensive theories upon which we can actually make decisions. It also should be noted that the characteristics studied are only a subset of what could be studied and represent variables that experimenters deemed important. As previously noted (Margolin &

Jacobson, 1981), couples are also engaged in evaluating and making relationship-related decisions. Perhaps we could expand our model by taking into account the variables that couples consider in coming to conclusions about their own relationships.

Overlap With Other Constructs

The assessment of marital dysfunction typically has been described as though it exists in isolation from other problems. We are faced with rapidly expanding evidence, however, that marital problems are associated with individual problems (e.g., Notarius & Pelligrini, 1984) and with problems in the family system (Emery, 1982; Margolin, 1981b). These associations with problems in the individual or larger family system are generally viewed as reciprocal and without a cause-effect explanation. With respect to the physical health of the individual partners, for example, there is evidence that poor health can lead to disturbed relationships, and conversely, that relationship problems may be detrimental to one's health (Margolin & Kingsolver, in press). Similarly, there is evidence that the marriages of depressed individuals are characterized by interpersonal friction, even after the depressive episode has ceased. Also, depressive episodes are more likely to occur in the wake of stressful life events, particularly those involving interpersonal tensions (Jacobson, 1984a). Furthermore, family theorists repeatedly have argued that there is a link between a dysfunctional marital system and the emotional as well as physical health of all family members, including the children (e.g., Minuchin, Rosman, & Baker, 1978).

We imagine that behavioral marital assessment procedures will play an important role over the next decade in gaining fuller understanding of these relationships. Although the bulk of the data supporting the relationship between marital problems and individual problems or systems problems comes from correlations on global self-report questionnaires, this trend is beginning to change. Researchers attempting to understand depression from an interpersonal context, for example, are examining the problem-solving interactions of the depressed spouse and his or her partner. Perceptions of these problem-solving attempts by both the depressed person and the spouse reveal less constructive problem-solving and more destructive behavior than perceptions of couples without a depressed spouse (Kahn, Coyne, & Margolin, 1985). Observations of similar interactions by outsiders reveal depressed women as displaying less problem-solving behavior than their husbands and both the husbands and wives revealing less self-disclosure than normal dyads (Biglan et al., 1985). Biglan and associates further found, through sequential analyses, that depressive behaviors function to reduce aversive behaviors from the spouse.

Margolin and Christensen (1985) used quasi-observational procedures to examine one spouse's perceptions of marital, parent–child, and sibling conflicts. Distressed families, but not nondistressed families, showed a tendency for conflict to move across intergenerational boundaries. That is, the sequential analysis of conflict patterns indicated that marital conflict increased the probability of parent–child and sibling conflict later in the day and that, vice versa, family and sibling conflict increased the probability of marital conflict.

The implications of these data for the behavioral marital assessor are twofold. First, as behavioral marital assessment procedures are used for expanding purposes, questions related to the reliability and validity of these measures are even more salient. Since all previous reviews on behavioral marital assessment have called for more data on the psychometric properties of these instruments, we will not belabor the point. We wish to emphasize the importance, however, of identifying what particular dimensions or scores of a given procedure are valid and recommended for widespread use. Second, it should be noted that the assessment task is expanded from what previously had been portrayed. It is the assessor's task to evaluate how individual functioning affects and is affected by the marital situation, and, if there are individual problems, to determine whether treatment should be directed toward marital or individual factors. It also becomes the marital assessor's task to evaluate whether the marital relationship is having untoward effects on others, particularly on the children, and to decide whether treatment of other family members or of the whole family system is warranted. Thus, before beginning any intervention, there is the fundamental question to answer about what unit to treat — the individual, the couple, or the family.

CASE EXAMPLE

Description of Couple

Bob and Bonnie S., ages 25 and 27, had been married for 5 years at the time they sought therapy. Both spouses had completed high school and currently were working for different branches of the same chain department store. They had previously been in therapy together but quit after five sessions, when they felt that their conflicts were intensifying. The content issues they presented during the intake session included the following:

1. *Jealousy*: Bonnie enjoyed the attention of men, particularly Bob's friends. When Bob worked into the evening, Bonnie sometimes invited other men over to their home. Until recently, Bob had steadfastly remained trusting of Bonnie, even in the face of hints from friends and relatives that he had better "keep an eye" on his wife.
2. *Anger*: Although Bonnie and Bob had a history of getting angry with one another, a recent argument was the first to involve physical violence.

TABLE 13.2. Bob and Bonnie's Preintervention Assessment Scores.

INSTRUMENT/ITEM	BONNIE	BOB
Verbal Coding (rate/minute)		
Positive behaviors	1.16	1.00
Negative behaviors	.16	000.80
SOC (rate/day)		
Pleases	20.33	20.33
Displeases	5.50	2.92
DAS	93.00	100.00

Neither was seriously injured but the incident was frightening enough that they decided to end their relationship if this situation recurred.

3. *In-law relationships*: Bob expressed annoyance at the extent to which Bonnie was involved with her parents. Her once-daily phone calls to her mother were a source of irritation, particularly when she called first thing in the morning. At the same time, Bob wished that they spent more time with his family.

4. *Household management*: Bonnie complained that Bob delayed in completing tasks he had agreed to do (fixing up their home and yard).

5. *Lack of appreciation*: Both partners felt that they contributed to the relationship in a positive way. However, they felt they received little acknowledgment of those efforts from one another.

Data Summary

Bob and Bonnie's 12-day preintervention assessment included the SOC, DAS, and an audiotaped sample of interaction, which was coded for nine verbal codes derived from the MICS and the CISS. Table 13.2 shows their scores.

Data Interpretation

The most notable features of the verbal coding data were the high rate of negative behaviors for Bob and the high rates of mindreading for both spouses. While communication skills such as Emotional Clarification, Accept Responsibility, and Agree were occurring at moderate rates, Problem Solution was particularly low, indicating this couple's inability to generate specific suggestions to their problems.

Examination of the self-report data indicate a moderate degree of marital distress. The SOC data translate into please/displease ratios of 3.7:1 for Bonnie and 7:1 for Bob. Bonnie's SOC data revealed low to average ratings of daily satisfaction while Bob's were generally above average. The DAS scores indicate average marital satisfaction for Bob and slightly below average satisfaction for Bonnie.

These data portray only part of the interaction patterns contributing to this couple's distress. Based on these data, Bob's behavior appeared to be more destructive to the marital relationship (e.g., emitting more displeases and negative communications). However, Bonnie's contributions to the relationship problem (i.e., her flirting and partying with other men) was a low-frequency event that carried extremely negative impact over a long period of time. Although that particular behavior did not occur during the baseline period and is thus not recorded anywhere in these scores, much of Bob's behavior reflects a cumulative reaction to Bonnie's past behavior.

Secondly, since this couple's difficulty with anger was not adequately assessed by these measures, they were instructed to monitor angry episodes by recording their somatic, affective, behavioral, and cognitive reactions to anger. This couple averaged three incidents of anger per week, ranging from minimal anger to intense anger. Although there were occasional threats of violence, expressions of anger during the assessment period were primarily limited to verbal behavior, such as blaming and criticism, with withdrawal from one another as the outcome. Spouses were asked to record these data for both themselves and the partner. Matching between spouses revealed little understanding or recognition of the partner's feelings or experiences during these incidents.

Treatment Planning

The composite picture of this couple based on pretherapy assessment plus ongoing feedback from the SOC and their anger records during therapy led to the following intervention strategies:

1. formulating an agreement that physical violence was totally unacceptable in this relationship
2. encouraging the couple to (a) express the variety of feelings (e.g., hurt, helplessness, frustration, anxiety) that typically were obscured by angry actions
3. training in listening to and reflecting the partner's feelings
4. having spouses practice showing appreciation during sessions and at home
5. formulating and writing a relationship contract outlining what they agreed as acceptable or unacceptable regarding outside heterosexual relationships
6. training in problem-solving that could be applied to issues regarding household management, inlaws, etcetera.

This brief summary is offered to illustrate how preassessment data are translated into treatment strategies. The reader is refered to Jacobson and

Margolin (1979) for more details on the clinically complex issues of getting beyond the spouses' hurt and hopelessness, raising positive expectancies, and preparing the couple for making behavior changes.

SUMMARY AND FUTURE DIRECTIONS

The reciprocal relationship between theory, assessment, and application, described so often in the behavioral literature, is exhibited in this review of recent trends in behavioral marital assessment. The three constructs that recently have received increased attention in assessment (cognition, affect, and systems) are important in our assessment endeavors precisely because of a recognized need for including them in theories of marital dysfunction and in treatment procedures. However, just as we let our theories and clinical observations guide the direction of the development and use of assessment procedures, data gathered through the assessment procedures lead to theoretical refinement and further clinical developments. Those who follow the treatment literature will find clear evidence of this in treatment procedures that integrate behavioral concepts with cognitive theory (Epstein, 1982; Jacobson, 1984b; Revenstorf, 1984), affective dimensions (Margolin, 1983b; Greenberg & Johnson, 1986), and systems theory (Birchler & Spinks, 1980; Wciss, 1980, 1984b).

The issues we continue to debate in behavioral marital assessment also reflect issues we still wrestle with in therapy: questions about the role of observational data reflect reconsideration of communication packages as standardized treatment components; questions about the usefulness of spouses as observers reflect varying opinions about the importance of spouses' perceptions and opinions as targets of treatment; sex role issues in assessment are receiving directly parallel considerations about how sex-role biases have influenced treatment and whether the balancing of sex roles is to be major target of treatment. Likewise, reaching a balance between systemic and individual variables in assessment mirrors the same striving for a sensitive, productive balance in therapy.

Part of our task as assessors is to translate concepts that are obvious to the astute clinician into a language and framework that can be studied empirically. The other part of our task is to test theoretical models as well as to help generate new models. Having completed this review, we believe that behavioral marital assessment has turned an important corner. At one time, much of our effort was spent devising instruments to demonstrate empirically what seemed fairly obvious to those working clinically with distressed couples. Thus, it came as no great surprise when we amassed empirical evidence that distressed couples exhibit more negative behaviors and fewer positive behaviors. At this point, however, we are able to examine dimensions that are not all that obvious, for example, physiological arousal, sequential patterning during important events in the home, naturally occurring attributions, and relationships among family subsystems. Advances such as these will not just confirm what we already believe to be true, but will actually advance our understanding of the intricacies and subtleties of marital interaction.

REFERENCES

Abramson, L. Y., Seligman, M. E .P., & Teasdale, J. D. (1978). Learned helplessness in humans: Critique and reformulation. *Journal of Abnormal Psychology, 87*, 49–74.

Antill, J. K., & Colton, S. (1982). Spanier's Dyadic Adjustment Scale: Some confirmatory analyses. *Australian Psychologist, 17*, 181–189.

Barnett, L. R., & Nietzel, M. T. (1979). Relationship of instrumental and affectional behaviors and self-esteem to marital satisfaction in distressed and nondistressed couples. *Journal of Consulting and Clinical Psychology, 47*, 946–957.

Baucom, D. H. (1983). Conceptual and psychometric issues in evaluating the effectiveness in behavioral marital therapy. In J. P. Vincent (Ed.), *Advances in family intervention, assessment and theory: An annual compilation of research (Vol. 3)*. Greenwich, CT: JAI Press.

Baucom, D. H., & Aiken, P. A. (1984). Sex role identity, marital satisfaction, and response to behavioral marital therapy. *Journal of Consulting and Clinical Psychology, 52*, 438–444.

Baucom, D. H., Bell, W. G., & Duke, A. G. (1982, November). *The measurement of couples' attributions for positive and negative dyadic interations.* Paper presented at the 16th Annual Convention of the Association for the Advancement of Behavior Therapy, Los Angeles.

Baucom, D. H., & Mehlman, S. K. (1984). Predicting marital states following behavioral marital therapy: A comparison of models of marital relationships. In K. Hahlweg & N. S. Jacobson (Eds.), *Marital interaction: Analysis and modification*. New York: Guilford.

Berg, P., & Snyder, D. K. (1981). Differential diagnosis of marital and sexual distress: A multidimensional approach. *Journal of Sex and Marital Therapy, 7*, 290–295.

Berger, M. (1979). Men's new family roles: Some implications for therapists. *Family Coordinator, 28*, 638–646.

Berley, R. A., & Jacobson, N. S. (1984). Causal attributions in intimate relationships: Toward a model of cognitive behavioral marital therapy. In P. Kendall (Ed.), *Advances in cognitive-behavioral research and therapy (Vol. 3)*. New York: Academic.

Biglan, A., Hops, H., Sherman, L., Friedman, L. S., Arthur, J., & Osteen, V. (1985). Problem solving interactions of depressed women and their husbands. *Behavior Therapy, 16*, 431–451.

Birchler, G. R., Clopton, P. L., & Adams, N. L. (1984). Effects of conflict resolution tasks on observed marital interaction. Unpublished manuscript. University of California Medical School, San Diego.

Birchler, G. R., & Spinks, S. H. (1980). Behavioral systems marital and family therapy: Integration and clinical application. *American Journal of Family Therapy, 8*, 6–28.

Birchler, G. R., Weiss, R. L., & Vincent, J. P. (1975). Multimethod analysis of social reinforcement exchange between maritally distressed and nondistressed spouse and stranger dyads. *Journal of Personality and Social Psychology, 31*, 349–360.

Blew, A., & Morgan, F. B. (1982, April). *Toward preventing relationship distress: A cognitive/behavioral communication enchancement program.* Paper presented at the meeting of the Western Psychological Association, Sacramento, CA.

Bradbury, T. N., & Fincham, F. D. (in press). Assessment of affect. In K. D. O'Leary (Ed.), *Assessment of marital discord.* Hillsdale, NJ: Erlbaum.

Christensen, L., & Mendoza, J. (1986). A method of assessing change in single subject designs: An alteration of the RC index. *Behavior Therapy, 17,* 305–308.

Christensen, A., & Neis, D. C. (1980). The Spouse Observation Checklist: Empirical analysis and critique. *American Jounal of Family Therapy, 8,* 69–79.

Christensen, A., Sullaway, M., & King, C. (1982, November). *Dysfunctional interaction patterns and marital happiness.* Paper presented at the annual conference of the American Association of Behavior Therapy, Los Angeles, CA.

Christensen, A., Sullaway, M., & King, C. (1983). Systematic error in behavioral reports of dyadic interaction: Egocentric bias and content effects. *Behavioral Assessment, 5,* 131–142.

Cross, D. G., & Sharpley, C. F. (1981). The Locke-Wallace Marital Adjustment Test reconsidered: Some psychometric findings as regards its reliability and factorial validity. *Educational and Psychological Measurement, 41,* 1303–1306.

Doherty, W. T. (1981). Cognitive processes in intimate conflict: I. Extending attribution theory. *American Journal of Family Therapy, 9,* 3–12.

Eidelson, R. J., & Epstein, N. (1982). Cognition and relationship maladjustment: Development of a measure of dysfunctional relationship belief. *Journal of Consulting and Clinical Psychology, 50,* 715–720.

Ellis, A. (1962). *Reason and emotion in psychotherapy.* New York: Lyle-Stuart.

Emery, R. E. (1982). Interparent conflict and the children of discord and divorce. *Psychological Bulletin, 92,* 310–330.

Epstein, N. (1982). Cognitive therapy with couples. *American Journal of Family Therapy, 10,* 5–16.

Epstein, N., & Eidelson, R. J. (1981). Unrealistic beliefs of clinical couples: Their relationship to expectations, goals, and satisfaction. *American Journal of Family Therapy, 9,* 13–22.

Filsinger, E. E. (1981). The Dyadic Interaction Scoring code. In E. E. Filsinger & R. A. Lewis (Eds.), *Assessing marriage: New behavioral approaches.* Beverly Hills: Sage.

Filsinger, E. E. (1983a). Choices among marital observation coding systems. *Family Process, 22,* 317–335.

Filsinger, E. E. (Ed.) (1983b). *Marriage and family assessment.* Beverly Hills: Sage.

Filsinger, E. E., & Lewis, R. A. (1981). *Assessing marriage: New behavioral approaches.* Beverly Hills: Sage.

Fincham, F. D. (1985). Attributions in close relationships. In J. Harvey & G. Weary (Eds.), *Attribution: Basic issues and applications.* New York: Academic.

Fincham, F. D., Beach, S., & Nelson, G. (1984). *Attribution processes in distressed and nondistressed couples. III. Causal and responsibility attributions for spouse behavior.* Manuscript submitted for publication.

Fincham, F., & O'Leary, K. D. (1983). Causal inferences for spouse behavior in maritally distressed and nondistressed couples. *Journal of Social and Clinical Psychology, 1,* 42–57.

Floyd, F. J., & Markman, H. J. (1983). Observational biases in spouse observation: Toward a cognitive/behavioral model of marriage. *Journal of Consulting and Clinical Psychology, 51,* 450–457.

Floyd, F. J., & Markman, H. J. (1984). An economical observational measure of couples' communication skill. *Journal of Consulting and Clinical Psychology, 52,* 97–103.

Goldner, V. (1985). Warning: Family therapy may be hazardous to your health. *The Family Therapy Networker, 9,* 18–23.

Gottman, J. M. (1979). *Marital interaction: Experimental investigations.* New York: Academic Press.

Gottman, J. M. (1982). Temporal form: Toward a new language for describing relationships. *Journal of Marriage and the Family, 44,* 943–962.

Gottman, J. M. (1985). Observational measures of behavior therapy outcome: A reply to Jacobson. *Behavioral Assessment, 7,* 317–322.

Gottman, J. M., & Levenson, R. W. (1985). A valid procedure for obtaining self-report of affect in marital interaction. *Journal of Consulting and Clinical Psychology, 53,* 151–160.

Gottman, J. M., & Levenson, R. W. (1986). Assessing the role of emotion in marriage. *Behavioral Assessment, 8,* 31–48.

Gottman, J., Markman, H., & Notarius, C. (1977). The topography of marital conflict: A sequential analysis of verbal and nonverbal behavior. *Journal of Marriage and the Family, 39,* 461–477.

Gottman, J., Notarius, C., Markman, H., Bank, S., Yoppi, B., & Rubin, M. E. (1976). Behavior exchange theory and marital decision making. *Journal of Personality and Social Psychology, 34,* 14–23.

Gottman, J. M., & Porterfield, A. L. (1981). Communicative competence in the nonverbal behavior of married couples. *Journal of Marriage and the Family, 43,* 817–824.

Greenberg, L. S., & Johnson, S. M. (1986). Affect in marital therapy. *Journal of Marital and Family Therapy, 12,* 1–10.

Gurman, A. S., & Klein, M. H. (1980). The treatment of women in marital and family conflict: Recommendations for outcome evaluation. In A. Brodsky & R.T. Mustin (Eds.), *Women & psychotherapy.* (pp. 159–190). New York: Guilford.

Gurman, A. S., & Klein, M. H. (1983). Marriage and the family: An unconscious bias in behavioral treatment? In E. A. Blechman (Ed.), *Behavior modification with women.* (pp. 170–189). New York: Guilford.

Hahlweg, K., Reisner, L., Kohli, G., Vollmer, M., Schindler, L., & Revenstorf, D. (1984). Development and validity of a new system to analyze interpersonal communication: Kategoriensystem fur Partnerschaftliche Interaktion. In K. Hahlweg & N. S. Jacobson (Eds.), *Marital interaction: Analysis and modification.* (pp. 182–198). New York: Guilford.

Hahlweg, K., Schindler, L., Revenstorf, D., & Brengelmann, J. C. (1984). The Munich marital therapy study. In K. Hahlweg & N. S. Jacobson (Eds.), *Marital interaction: Analysis and modification.* (pp. 3–26). New York: Guilford.

Holtzworth-Munroe, A., & Jacobson, N. S. (1985). Causal attributions of married couples: When do they search for causes? What do they conclude when they do? *Journal of Personality and Social Psychology, 48,* 1398–1412.

Hops, H., Wills, T. A., Patterson, G. R., & Weiss, R. L. (1972). *Marital interaction coding system.* Eugene, OR: University of Oregon and Oregon Research Institute.

Jacobson, N. S. (1983). Beyond empiricism: The politics of marital therapy. *American Journal of Family Therapy, 11,* 11–24.

Jacobson, N. S. (1984a). Marital therapy and the cognitive-behavioral treatment of depression. *The Behavior Therapist, 7,* 143–147.

Jacobson, N. S. (1984b). The modification of cognitive processes in behavioral marital therapy: Integrating cognitive and behavioral intervention strategies. In K.

Hahlweg & N. S. Jacobson (Eds.), *Marital interaction: Analysis and modification.* (pp. 285-308). New York: Guilford.

Jacobson, N. S. (1985a). Family therapy outcome research: Potential pitfalls and prospects. *Journal of Marital and Family Therapy, 11,* 149-158.

Jacobson, N. S. (1985b). The role of observational measures in behavior therapy outcome research. *Behavioral Assessment, 1,* 297-308.

Jacobson, N. S. (1985c). The uses versus abuses of observational measures. *Behavioral Assessment, 7,* 323-330.

Jacobson, N. S. (1985d). Toward a nonsectarian blueprint for the empirical study of family therapies. *Journal of Marital and Family Therapy, 11,* 163-166.

Jacobson, N. S., Elwood, R., & Dallas, M. (1981). The behavioral assessment of marital dysfunction. In D. H. Barlow (Ed.), *Behavioral assessment of adult disorders.* New York: Guilford Press.

Jacobson, N. S., Follette, W. C., & Elwood, R. W. (1984). Outcome research on behavioral marital therapy: A methodological and conceptual reappraisal. In K. Hahlweg & N. S. Jacobson (Eds.), *Marital interaction: Analysis and modification.* (pp. 113-132). New York: Guilford.

Jacobson, N. S., Follette, W. C., & McDonald, D. W. (1982). Reactivity to positive and negative behavior in distressed and nondistressed married couples. *Journal of Consulting and Clinical Psychology, 50,* 706-714.

Jacobson, N. S., Follette, W. C., & Pagel, M. (in press). Predicting who will benefit from behavioral marital therapy. *Journal of Consulting and Clinical Psychology.*

Jacobson, N. S., Follette, W. C., & Ravenstorf, D. (1984). Psychotherapy outcome research: Methods for reporting variability and evaluating clinical significance. *Behavior Therapy, 15,* 336-352.

Jacobson, N. S., Follette, W. C., & Ravenstorf, D. (1986). Toward a standard definition of clinically significant change. *Behavior Therapy,* in press.

Jacobson, N. S., & Margolin, G. (1979). *Marital therapy: Strategies based on social learning and behavior exchange principles.* New York: Brunner/Mazel.

Jacobson, N. S., McDonald, D. W., Follette, W. C., & Berley, R. A. (1985). Attributional process in distressed and nondistressed married couples. *Cognitive Therapy and Research, 9,* 35-50.

Jacobson, N. S., & Moore, D. (1981a). Behavior exchange theory of marriage: Reconnaisance and reconsideration. In J. P. Vincent (Ed.), *Advances in family intervention, assessment and theory: A research annual* (II). (pp. 183-214), Greenwich, CT: JAI Press.

Jacobson, N. S., & Moore, D. (1981b). Spouses as observers of the events in their relationship. *Journal of Consulting and Clinical Psychology, 49,* 269-277.

Jacobson, N. S., Waldron, H., & Moore, D. (1980). Toward a behavioral profile of marital distress. *Journal of Consulting and Clinical Psychology, 48,* 696-703.

Kahn, J., Coyne, J. C., & Margolin, G., (1985). Depression and marital disagreement: The social construction of despair. *Journal of Social and Personal Relationships, 2,* 447-461.

Kahn, M. (1970). Nonverbal communication and marital satisfaction. *Family Process, 9,* 449-456.

Kniskern, D. P. (1985). Climbing out of the pit: Further guidelines for family therapy research. *Journal of Marital and Family Therapy, 11,* 159-162.

Kraemer, H., & Jacklin, C. (1979). Statistical analysis of dyadic social behavior. *Psychological Bulletin, 86,* 2.7-224.

Laws, J. L. (1971). A feminist review of marital adjustment literature: The rape of the Locke. *Journal of Marriage and the Family, 33,* 483-516.

Lederer, W. J., & Jackson, D. D. (1968). *Mirages of marriage.* New York: Norton.

Levenson, R. W., & Gottman, J. M. (1983). Marital interaction: Physiological linkage and affective exchange. *Journal of Personality and Social Psychology, 45,* 587–597.

Levenson, R. W., & Gottman, J. M. (1985). Physiological and affective predictors of change in relationship satisfaction. *Journal of Personality and Social Psychology, 49,* 85–94.

Locke, H. J., & Wallace, K. M. (1959). Short-term marital adjustment and prediction tests: Their reliability and validity. *Journal of Marriage and Family Living, 21,* 251–255.

Margolin, G. (1981a). Behavior exchange in distressed and nondistressed marriages: A family cycle perspective. *Behavior Therapy, 12,* 329–343.

Margolin, G. (1981b). The reciprocal relationship between marital and child problems. In J. P. Vincent (Ed.), *Advances in family intervention assessment and theory: An annual compilation of research* (Vol. 2). Greenwich, CT: JAI Press.

Margolin, G. (1983a). An interactional model for the assessment of marital relationships. *Behavioral Assessment, 5,* 103–127.

Margolin, G. (1983b). Behavioral marital therapy: Is there a place for passion, play and other non-negotiable dimensions? *Behavior Therapist, 6,* 65–68.

Margolin, G. (in press-a). Marital conflict is not marital conflict is not marital conflict. In R. De V. Peters & R. McMahon (Eds.), *Marriage and families: Behavioral treatment and processes.* Champaign, Ill.: Research Press.

Margolin, G. (in press-b). Participant observation procedures in marital and family assessment. In T. Jacob (Ed.), *Family interaction and psychopathology.* New York: Plenum.

Margolin, G., & Christensen, A. (1985). *Everyday conflict in distressed and nondistressed families.* Manuscript submitted for review.

Margolin, G., Hattem, D., John, R. S., & Yost, K. (1985). Perceptual agreement between spouses and outside observers when coding themselves and a stranger dyad. *Behavioral Assessment, 7,* 235–247.

Margolin, G., & Jacobson, N. S. (1981). The assessment of marital dysfunction. In M. Hersen & A. S. Bellack (Eds.), *Behavioral assessment: A practical handbook* (pp. 389–426). New York: Pergamon.

Margolin, G., & Kingsolver, K. M. (in press). Disorders of family relationships. In E. Blechman & K. D. Brownell (Eds.), *Behavioral medicine in women.* New York: Pergamon.

Margolin, G., Talovic, S., Fernandez, V., & Onorato, R. (1983). Sex role considerations and behavioral marital therapy: Equal does not mean identical. *Journal of Marital and Family Therapy, 9,* 131–146.

Margolin, G., & Wampold, B. E. (1981). A sequential analysis of conflict and accord in distressed and nondistressed marital partners. *Journal of Consulting and Clinical Psychology, 49,* 554–567.

Margolin, G., & Weinstein, C. D. (1983). The role of affect in behavioral marital therapy. In M. L. Aronson & L. R. Wolberg (Eds.), *Group and family therapy 1982: An overview.* (pp. 334–355). New York: Brunner/Mazel.

Margolin, G., & Weiss, R. L. (1978). Comparative evaluation of therapeutic components associated with behavioral marital treatment. *Journal of Consulting and Clinical Psychology, 46,* 1476–1486.

Markman, H. J. (1979). Application of a behavioral model of marriage in predicting relationship satisfaction of couples planning marriage. *Journal of Consulting and*

Clinical Psychology, 47, 743–749.

Markman, H. J. (1981). Prediction of marital distress. A 5-year follow-up. *Journal of Consulting and Clinical Psychology, 49,* 760–762.

Markman, H. J., & Floyd, R. (1980). Possibilities for the prevention of marital discord: A behavioral perspective. *American Journal of Family Therapy, 8,* 29–48.

Markman, H. J., Floyd, F., & Dickson-Markman, F. (in press). Toward a model for the prediction and primary prevention of marital and family distress and dissolution. In S. Duck (Ed.), *Dissolving personal relationships.* London: Academic.

Markman, H. J., Notarius, C.I., Stephen, T., & Smith, R. J. (1981). Behavioral observation systems for couples: The current status. In E. E. Filsinger & R. A. Lewis (Eds.), *Assessing marriage: New behavioral approaches.* (pp. 234–262). Beverly Hills, CA: Sage.

Markman, H., & Poltrock, S. (1982). A computerized system for recording and analysis of self-observations of couples' interaction. *Behavior Research Methods and Instrumentation, 14,* 186–190.

Minuchin, S., Rosman, B., & Baker, L. (1978). *Psychosomatic families: Anorexia nervosa in context.* Cambridge: Harvard University Press.

Noller, P. (1980). Misunderstandings in marital communication: A study of couples' nonverbal communication. *Journal of Personality and Social Psychology, 39,* 1125–1134.

Noller, P. (1981). Gender and marital adjustment level differences in decoding messages from spouses and strangers. *Journal of Personality and Social Psychology, 41,* 272–278.

Notarius, C. I., & Markman, H.J. (1981). The Couples Interaction Scoring System. In E. E. Filsinger & R. A. Lewis (Eds.), *Assessing marriage.* (pp. 112–128). Beverly Hills: Sage.

Notarius, C. I., Markman, H. J., & Gottman, J. M. (1983). Couples Interaction Scoring System: Clinical implications. In E. E. Filsinger (Ed.), *Marriage and family assessment.* (pp. 117–136). Beverly Hills: Sage.

Notarius, C. I., & Pellegrini, D. S. (1984). Marital processes as stressors and stress mediators: Implications for marital repair. In S. W. Duck (Ed.), *Personal relationships 5: Repairing personal relationships.* (pp. 67–88). New York: Academic.

Notarius, C. I., Vanzetti, N. A., & Smith, R. J. (1981, November). *Assessing expectations and outcomes in marital interaction.* Paper presented at the meeting of the Association for the Advancement of Behavior Therapy, Toronto.

O'Leary, K. D., & Arias, I. (1983). The influence of marital therapy on sexual satisfaction. *Journal of Sex and Marital Therapy, 9,* 171–181.

O'Leary, K. D., Fincham, F., & Turkewitz, H. (1983). Assessment of positive feelings toward spouse. *Journal of Consulting and Clinical Psychology, 51,* 949–951.

O'Leary, K. D., & Turkewitz, H. (1978). Methodological errors in marital and child treatment research. *Journal of Consulting and Clinical Psychology, 46,* 747–758.

Olson, D. H., McCubbin, H. I., Barnes, H. L., Larsen, A. S., Muxen, M. J., & Wilson, M. A. (1983). *Families: What makes them work.* Beverly Hills, Sage.

Olson, D. H., & Portner, J. (1983). Family Adaptability and Cohesion Evaluation Scales. In E. E. Filsinger (Ed.), *Marriage and family assessment.* (pp. 299–316). Beverly Hills, CA: Sage.

Olson, D. H., Russell, C. S., & Sprenkle, D. H. (1979). Circumplex model of marital and family systems II: Empirical studies and clinical intervention. In J. Vincent (Ed.), *Advances in family intervention assessment and theory.* Greenwich, CT: JAI.

Olson, D. H., & Ryder, R. G. (1970). Inventory of Marital Conflicts (IMC): An experimental interaction procedure. *Journal of Marriage and the Family, 32,* 443-448.

Olson, D. H., & Ryder, R. G. (1978). *Marital and Family Interaction Coding System (MFICS): Abbreviated coding manual.* St. Paul: University of Minnesota.

Parloff, M. B. (1976). The narcissism of small differences — and some big ones. *International Journal of Group Psychotherapy, 26,* 311-319.

Patterson, G. R., & Bank, L. (1986). Bootstrapping your way in the nomological thicket. *Behavioral Assessment, 8,* 49-74.

Patterson, G. R., & Hops, H. (1972). Coercion, a game for two: Intervention techniques for marital conflict. In R. E. Ulrich & P. Mountjoy (Eds.), *The experimental analysis of social behavior.* New York: Appleton-Century-Crofts.

Peterson, D. R. (1977). A plan for studying interpersonal behavior. In D. Magnusson & N. Endler (Eds.), *Personality at the crossroads: Current issues in interactional psychology.* New York: Wiley.

Peterson, D. R. (1979). Assessing interpersonal relationships by means of interaction records. *Behavioral Assessment, 1,* 221-236.

Peterson, D. R., & Rapinchuk, J. G. (in press). Patterns of affect in destructive and constructive marital conflicts. *Journal of Personality and Social Psychology.*

Rappaport, A. F., & Harrell, J. (1972). A behavioral exchange model for marital counseling. *The Family Coordinator, 22,* 203-212.

Raush, H. L., Barry, W. A., Hertel, R. K., & Swain, M. A. (1974). *Communication, conflict and marriage.* San Francisco: Jossey-Bass.

Revenstorf, D. (1987). *Cognitive trend in behavioral marital therapy.* Unpublished manuscript. University of Tubingen, Psychological Institute.

Revenstorf, D., Vogel, B., Wegener, C., Hahlweg, K., & Schindler, L. (1980). Escalation phenomena in interaction sequences: An empirical comparison of distressed and nondistressed couples. *Behavioral Analysis and Modification, 4,* 97-115.

Robinson, E. A., & Price, M. G. (1980). Pleasurable behavior in marital interaction: An observational study. *Journal of Consulting and Clinical Psychology, 48,* 117-118.

Schaap, C. (1982). *Communication and adjustment in marriage.* Lisse, Germany: Swets & Zeitlinger.

Schaap, C. (1984). A comparison of the interaction of distressed and nondistressed married couples in a laboratory situation: Literature survey, methodological issues, and an empirical investigation. In K. Hahlweg & N. S. Jacobson (Eds.), *Marital interaction: Analysis and modification.* (pp. 133-158). New York: Guilford.

Sharpley, C. F., & Cross, D. G. (1982). A psychometric evaluation of the Spanier Dyadic Adjustment Scale. *Journal of Marriage and the Family, 44,* 739-741.

Snyder, D. K. (1979). Multidimensional assessment of marital satisfaction. *Journal of Marriage and the Family, 41,* 121-131.

Snyder, D. K., Wills, R. M., & Keiser, T. W. (1981). Empirical validation of the Marital Satisfaction Inventory: An actuarial approach. *Journal of Consulting and Clinical Psychology, 49,* 262-268.

Spanier, G. B. (1976). Measuring dyadic adjustment: New scales for assessing the quality of marriage and similar dyads. *Journal of Marriage and the Family, 38,* 15-28.

Stevens, J. J., Arkowitz, H. S., Sladeczek, I. E., & Ridley, C. A. (1985, August). *Measurement issues in the use of marital adjustment scales.* Paper presented at the 93rd Annual Convention of the American Psychological Association, Los Angeles.

93rd Annual Convention of the American Psychological Association, Los Angeles.

Stuart, R. B. (1976). An operant interpersonal program for couples. In D. H. L. Olson (Ed.), *Treating relationships.* (pp. 119–132). Lake Mills, IA: Graphic.

Sullaway, M., & Christensen, A. (1983). Assessment of dysfunctional interaction patterns in couples. *Journal of Marriage and the Family, 45,* 653–660.

Vincent, J. P., Cook, N. I., & Messerly, L. (1980). A social learning analysis of couples during the second postnatal month. *The American Journal of Family Therapy, 8,* 49–68.

Vincent, J. P., Friedman, L. C., Nugent, J., & Messerly, L. (1979). Demand characteristics in observations of marital interaction. *Journal of Consulting and Clinical Psychology, 47,* 557–566.

Vincent, J. P., Weiss, R. L., & Birchler, G. R. (1975). A behavioral analysis of problem solving in distressed and nondistressed married and stranger dyads. *Behavior Therapy, 6,* 475–487.

Wampold, B. E., & Jenson, W. R. (1986). Clinical significance revisited: Comment of Jacobson et al. *Behavior Therapy, 17,* 302–305.

Weiss, R. L. (1980). Strategic behavioral marital therapy: Toward a model for assessment and intervention. In J. P. Vincent (Ed.), *Advances in family intervention, assessment, and theory: An annual compilation of research* (Vol. 1, pp. 229–271). Greenwich, CT: JAI Press.

Weiss, R. L. (1984a). Cognitive and behavioral measures of marital interaction. In K. Hahlweg & N.S. Jacobson (Eds.), *Marital interaction: Analysis and modification.* (pp. 232–252). New York: Guilford.

Weiss, R. L. (1984b). Cognitive and strategic interventions in behavioral marital therapy. In K. Hahlweg & N. S. Jacobson (Eds.), *Marital interaction: Analysis and modification.* (pp. 337–355). New York: Guilford.

Weiss, R. L., & Frohman, P. E. (1985). Behavioral observation as outcome measures: Not through a glass darkly. *Behavioral Assessment, 7,* 309–316.

Weiss, R. L., Hops, H., & Patterson, G. R. (1973). A framework for conceptualizing marital conflict, a technology for altering it, some data for evaluating it. In L. A. Hamerlynck, L. C. Handy, & E. J. Mash (Eds.), *Behavior change: Methodology, concepts, and practice.* Champaign, IL: Research Press.

Weiss, R. L., & Margolin, G. (1986). Assessment of conflict and accord: A second look. In A. Ciminero (Ed.), *Handbook of behavioral assessment* (2nd Edition, pp. 561–600). New York: Wiley.

Weiss, R. L., & Perry, B.A. (1979). *Assessment and treatment of marital dysfunction.* Eugene, OR: University of Oregon & Oregon Martial Studies Program.

Weiss, R. L., & Perry, B. A. (1983). The Spouse Observation Checklist: Development and clinical applications. In E.E. Filsinger (Ed.), *Marriage and family assessment.* (pp. 65–84). Beverly Hills: Sage.

Weiss, R. L., & Summers, K. J. (1983). Marital Interaction Coding System III. In E.E. Filsinger (Ed.), *Marriage and family assessment.* (pp. 85–116). Beverly Hills: Sage.

Weiss, R. L., Wasserman, D. A., Wieder, G. R., & Summers, K. (1981, November). *Subjective and objective evaluation of marital conflict: Couples vs. the establishment.* Paper presented at the 15th Annual Convention of the Association for the Advancement of Behavior Therapy, Toronto.

Wills, T. A., Weiss, R. L., & Patterson, G. R. (1974). A behavioral analysis of the determinants of marital satisfaction. *Journal of Consulting and Clinical Psychology, 42,* 802–811.

14
Sexual Dysfunction and Deviation

Nathaniel McConaghy

Clinicians have traditionally assessed behavior by interview, as it enabled them to exercise their intuitive skills in eliciting and interpreting patients' self-reports, supplementing these with observation of nonverbal behaviors. The term *behavioral assessment* implies a preference for objective measurement of motor behavior, a preference noted, for example, by Neitzel and Bernstein (1981) in the demotion of subjective and visceral data in the assessment of anxiety in outcome studies of behavior therapy. In view of the major contribution of behaviorism to the development of behavior therapy in the United States and behaviorism's historical rejection of cognitive processes, it would seem inevitable that a trend to limit behavioral assessment to direct measurement of motor behavior would make an early appearance in the academic behavior therapy literature. It was sufficiently established by Hersen (1973) that clinicians could document the concern being expressed with the extant subjective appraisals and self-reports that were still being employed in evaluation of behavior modification techniques.

Subsequently, most behaviorists have returned to the more traditional concept of behavior. Indeed, if Nelson and Hayes (1981) are to be believed, they consider all forms of organismic activity — overt motor, cognitive-verbal and physiological — behavior. Certainly, for the majority, behavioral assessment encompasses all of these modalities, thus hormonal assessment, for example, will not appear out of place in this chapter. Nevertheless, the bias established in the earlier period — that of considering behavioral assessments by objective (rather than intuitive) methods both superior and virtually essential — persists in the academic behavior therapy literature and requires reevaluation.

Linehan (1977) stated that no outcome studies of behavior therapy had been found where the clinical interview was used as the sole data base for a behavioral assessment. Yet, as Nelson and Hayes (1981) pointed out, almost half of the practicing behavior therapists considered behavioral assessment strategies impractical in applied settings. Nelson and Hayes made this point while arguing that practicing clinicians should be encouraged to participate in clinical research. They did not conclude that this might require that the bias against the more intuitive assessments used by clinicians be reassessed. They recommended that behavioral assessments and single-case designs be developed, presumably by academics, for clinicians to use. Nelson and Hayes did not state whether they favored single-case designs because (a) the more complex and prolonged procedures necessary for objective behavioral assessment strategies are more practical when only a single subject is being investigated or (b) because U. S. academic behavior therapists favored this design. Single-case designs are of limited value in behavior therapy outcome research, particularly for assessing sexual dysfunctions and sexual deviations (McConaghy, 1977). Whatever their reason, clearly Nelson and Hayes considered that if clinicians were to carry out research acceptable to behavior therapy journals, they were to come to Mahomet. No attempt was made to determine if clinicians' intuitive skills, as were currently practiced could be researched by incorporating them in appropriate controlled group designs.

Bellack and Hersen (1985) also suggested that clinicians be encouraged to become involved in research and recommended that "clinical relevance must attain equal status with methodological purity in the planning and evaluation of research" (p. 16). There may be no necessary contradiction between the two ideals even if behavioral assessment as currently practiced by clinicians is used as the sole data base in outcome research. Given the readiness of physicians to use expensive and elaborate investigatory procedures in the treatment of physical illness, perhaps behavioral clinicians do not reject objectively scored behavioral assessments solely because of their greater impracticality. Clinicians may have learned from experience that such assessments lack the validity of those based on intuition. Certainly, the objective assessment of behavior by observation has greater face validity as compared to, "the generally suspect nature of self-report and peer-report data" (Linehan, 1977, p.31).

The faith of academic behavior therapists in this apparent validity was dramatically evidenced in the enthusiasm of their uncritical acceptance and immediate utilization of the initial laboratory assessment of the motor expression of emotional behavior — the Behavioral Avoidance Test (BAT), first used to measure snake phobia. Presumably because of this enthusiasm, the major and apparently obvious methodological flaws (McConaghy, 1970) and the unexplained alteration of the subjects' BAT scores in the two studies introducing the test (Lang & Lazovik, 1983; Lang, Lazovik, & Reynolds, 1965) were, and indeed continue to be, overlooked (Rachman, 1973; Kazdin, 1982). More important, the predictive validity of the BAT as an assessment of patients' behavior in natural settings was also unquestioned. Subsequently, its weaknesses — due to the operation of such factors as demand characteristics, social cues, and reactivity — have been repeatedly documented (Lick & Unger, 1977; Neitzel & Bernstein, 1981). Rosen, Glasgow, and Barrera (1976) reported superior prediction of natural behavior from patients' self-ratings, as compared to the BAT scores, following treatment. The readiness of behavioral academics to assume the predictive validity of behavioral observation, evidenced in the reception of the BAT, was also demonstrated in the BAT's use in role-play assessments. Subsequently, the validity of these assessments were also questioned. Bellack, Hersen, and Lamparski (1979), having reviewed the evidence, urged extreme caution in interpreting research based on role-play procedures. A similar readiness to accept validity of penile circumference changes as measures of sexual arousal will be documented when role-play procedures are discussed.

When validation of objectively scored behavioral assessments was attempted, the evidence supporting them was treated with far greater liberality than was demonstrated toward interview-based intuitive assessment. Intuitive assessment appears to have been rejected as inferior to other forms of behavioral assessment largely on its lack of face validity. It is apparent that some patients wish to please or gain the approval of their clinicians by reporting themselves as better than they are. Others may lie or conceal material about which they are ashamed. We do not know how much such distortions — which even experienced interviewers cannot detect or allow for — reduce the validity of assessments, considering that the majority of patients seek help voluntarily and are consciously motivated to provide the required information? The author is unaware of any research data answering this question, but clearly this would be desirable. Nevertheless, is it likely that the validity of clinicians' assessments would be reduced to the extent that they accounted for less than half of the variance of the behavior in which they were interested? Academics such as Linehan (1977) seem content with the validity of behavioral assessments established by relationships of this order:

> Concurrent validity of the behavioral ratings ranges from fair to good when compared to other behavioral ratings and observational data. For instance, Lentz, Paul, and Calhoun (1971) report correlations between .51 and .54 between the Minimal Social Behavior Scale and staff behavioral ratings. Mariott and Paul (1974) report substantial concurrent validity (no figure given) for the Inpatient Multidimensional Psychiatric Scale. (p.46).

Correlations of .51 to .54 mean of course that the scale is accounting for about 25% of the variance of the behavior validating it. Schiavi, Derogatis, Kuriansky, O'Connor, and Sharpe (1979) described 51 objectively scored, mainly self-rated assessments of sexual function and marital interaction, including data on reliability and validity, for about half the assessments.

Reliability was easily evaluated, presented mainly as correlations, generally in the range of .8 to .9. This was not the case for the validity data. Validity was usually described as adequate or as demonstrated by the test's ability to discriminate two groups. Only for one test was an actual figure given: a sexual anxiety scale which had a .62 validity coefficient with intensity of sexual dysfunction, accounting for about 36% of the variance.

Bellack et al. (1979) similarly criticized a role-play test of heterosocial skills considered to have moderate validity for female undergraduates:

> From a group classification perspective (e.g., high versus low skill), the significant correlations were quite substantial. However, in most cases less than 25% of the variance was accounted for in the analyses (p.341).

The academic distrust of interview-based assessments was further stimulated when the concept was advanced that three systems were independently involved in the expression of emotion: cognitive, motor, and physiological (Lang, 1968, 1971). This concept also was, at first, and uncritically accepted. As Nelson and Hayes (1981) pointed out, its implication was that thorough assessment required examination of all three systems. Again, the general acceptance of the concept was later revealed to be ill-founded. Cone (1979) pointed out that the apparent independence of responses in the three systems may be due to what he termed a system by method confound: for example, the use of self-report to assess cognitive responses, but direct observation to assess motor responses. Cone argued that if the same method were used in the different systems, the responses might be less independent. In any case, considerable independence is common between responses within the one system (Emmelkamp, 1982; Nelson & Hayes, 1981).

A recent strong statement that will hopefully modify the uncritical preference for noninterview-based behavioral assessment techniques was made by Nelson and Hayes (1981), who pointed out the lack of evidence for the acclaimed relationship between behavioral assessment and improved treatment and argued that assessment decisions must be tested with data, not just logic. They concluded that any assessment device claiming applied value should be regarded as unproven until its treatment validity has been experimentally demonstrated and that on this bases the applied value of virtually all behavioral assessment is still unproven.

In view of this lack of demonstrated treatment validity of behavioral assessment, clinicians under pressure to modify or supplement their customary intuitive assessment by interview face an ethical, not to mention a possible political, dilemma. Current requirements for informed patient consent would demand that clinicians inform the patient that they cannot accept the patient's reports of his or her responses to treatment as adequate, that they expect the patient to provide additional time and money for more objective investigations to determine the degree that the patient has actually improved with treatment, and that the value of these investigations is not established. A final irony is that behavioral assessment has been largely developed in the United States, the bastion of free enterprise founded on the belief that the individual is capable of arriving at accurate assessments of the value of goods and services on the basis of his or her own experience of such goods and services. Perhaps such experiences have led U. S. citizens to accept that they need outside help to make such assessments. Many of the author's patients, for example, would not take kindly to the idea that he was not prepared to leave it to them to decide if and when they had made an adequate response to treatment and that they would have to pay him not only for the treatment but also to determine by unproven methods if they had improved or not.

Noncompliance increases with the complexity, duration, and cost of therapy, at least with medical regimes (Appel, Saab, & Holroyd, 1985), so that even if patients are not informed concerning extra behavioral assessments, the use of such assessment is likely to reduce compliance and hence treatment efficacy. Patient drop-out is usually readily accommodated in research projects. Its accommodation is not so easy for clinicians who will certainly be affected adversely in immediate income and possibly in long-term reputation. Though they may never have thought the issue through consciously formulated their conclusions, clinicians, through their experience, would by trial and error have come to use the procedure most valid for assessing their patients' behavior while retaining the patients in therapy. Modifying or adding to this procedure could well reduce the clinicians' therapeutic efficacy.

This emphasis on increasing the therapeutic efficacy rather than the reliability of assessment highlights the difference in aims of clinicians and academics — a difference of fundamental importance. Research data are ultimately only accepted when they are adequately replicated. A primary aim of researchers must therefore be to ensure replicability of their findings. To do so they need to establish and maintain the reliability of their diagnostic and outcome criteria, abandoning, if necessary, procedures they intuitively believe to be more valid because their reliability is not and possibly cannot be established. Clinicians aim to provide the best treatment for their patients. The generally accepted belief, whether true or false, that clinicians vary significantly in skill, mainly due to differences in their intuitive judgments, means that clinicians will attempt to maximize their skill and obtain better results than their colleagues, usually by acting on intuition. The clinician whose intuitive diagnostic skill is superior to that of colleagues will make more valid diagnoses, which will lead to the choice of more appropriate treatment and better response. The more valid diagnoses will thus be inconsistent with those of colleagues. That is to say, the better the individual's assessment, the less reliable it is. The subtler aspects of clinicians' intuitions will usually not be able to be precisely formulated and therefore not replicable by others. Indeed, those techniques that are replicable no longer contribute to the clinician's individual clinical skill and hence reputation. Clinicians will therefore not willingly adopt procedures that interfere with their ability to exercise intuitive judgment. In essence, the researcher is likely to sacrifice validity to assessable reliability, whereas the clinician is likely to sacrifice assessable reliability to validity.

The significance attached by Nelson and Hayes (1981) to the treatment validity of behavioral assessments hopefully indicates the return of a readiness by academics to validate techniques in terms of their results, irrespective of whether the techniques are easily replicable or not. Bellack and Hersen (1985) point out that behaviorists seem to have made a 180-degree turn on the issue of the validity of patients' self-reports. This would appear to be true only for self-reports that are objectively assessed. Are behaviorists now ready to make a similar turn in regard to subjective assessment, at least to the extent of evaluating it in comparison to objective assessment?

A trend of this nature briefly emerged in the 1960s in the psychiatric literature. In 1966, Paredes, Baumgold, Pugh, and Ragland pointed out that in response to criticisms of their subjective bias and questionable reliability, clinicians' judgments were no longer being used in many psychopharmacological studies. At best, clinician participation was being restricted to rating behavior on scales. They found that in comparison to psychological tests, behavior ratings, and physiological measures, a psychiatrist's global assessment of patient improvement proved highly valid in determining which schizophrenic inpatients had been randomly assigned to chlorpromazine and which had been assigned to placebo in two successive double-blind cycles. This global assessment was not related to presence or absence of medication side effects. Factor analysis suggested it was closely related to patients' overt psychopathological behavior, subtle psychopathological changes, and disruptions of social functioning. Ratings by the psychiatrist on psychopathology rating scales did not prove as valid as his global assessment.

Paredes et al. (1966) concluded that, in their global assessments, clinicians are sensitive to a multitude of factors. When forced to rate patients along specific dimensions of behavior, clinicians narrow their perspective, reducing their ability to make valid intuitive judgments. Paredes et al. (1966) also considered that changes in patients' overall psychopathology do not fall along generally accepted dimensions, so that the whole is greater than the sum of its assumed parts. If these conclusions are correct, it would be impossible to match clinicians' intuitive judgment with analyses of patients' behavior on scales of assessed reliability, for the appropriate weighting of the scales, which would need to be different for each patient, would not be known. Lipman, Cole, Park, and Ricketts (1965) reported a similar study validating clinicians' global assessment as compared to various symptom-focused rating scales in detecting which patients were on a minor tranquilizer. They quoted two further studies that used antidepressants and tranquilizers, also validating clinicians' intuitive global assessment.

Little academic attention was given to the aforementioned research data, indicating the possible superiority of clinicians' intuitive assessments over less subjective and more replicable techniques. The appeal of the latter proved as irresistible to psychiatric as to behavioral researchers. The rejection of subjectivity by psychiatric academics was subsequently evidenced in their preference for the DSM-III diagnostic system based on operational definitions, despite what little evidence there existed suggesting the validity of such diagnoses (Kendell, Brockington, & Leff, 1979). Again, clinicians resisted this trend to objectivity. Psychiatric education, which remains under the clinician's influence, continues to emphasize the development of intuitive assessment skills. The alternative of basing clinical education on training in conducting structured interviews oriented to making operationally defined diagnoses would, of course, be much less time-consuming and more suited to reliable evaluation.

Clinicians' attachment to intuitive assessments may be completely justified. There would appear to be a real possibility that such assessments are of greater validity than are the more objective methods currently available. Furthermore, clinicians may have become intuitively aware of this superiority when acquiring their interviewing skills. It is, therefore, not entirely surprising that reliance on the intuitively interpreted clinical interview is not restricted to full-time behavioral clinicians. Several of the contributions to the recent *Handbook of Clinical Behavior Therapy with Adults* (Hersen & Bellack, 1985), who were presumably selected for being both clinicians and academics, emphasized the major role of the interview as compared to other methods of behavioral assessment:

> In my view, psychophysiological assessment and formalized pretreatment behavioral avoidance measures are not useful or economically viable procedures in ordinary clinical treatment of agoraphobia (Chambless, 1985, p.55)

> The major vehicle for assessing the obsessive-compulsive symptoms is the clinical interview (Grayson, Foa, & Stekette, 1985, p.139).

> The basic clinical interview is the mainstay of the appropriate assessment of depression (Hollon & Jacobson, 1985, p.172).

It would seem possibly inadvisable at present for behavioral clinicians to modify their current intuitively based assessment methods. The more objective techniques of behavioral assessment introduced by academics to improve the practice of behavior therapy clearly require further development and evaluation.

TECHNIQUES OF SEXUAL BEHAVIOR ASSESSMENT

The Clinical Interview

As the technique of the clinical interview is developed, largely intuitively, over years of experience, the masters of the art are likely to be full-time clinicians. Adequate accounts of their practice are unlikely to become available. It is possible to indicate how such clinicians can increase the validity of the patient's self-report by taking full advantage of the *flexibility* the interview allows them and to continually monitor and modify their responses to the patient's conscious and unconscious verbal and nonverbal behavior. Linehan (1977) has discussed this in some detail.

Observation of the Patient's Emotional State

By detecting that patients are becoming guilty, embarrassed, or reluctant to speak as certain topics, often aspects of their sexual behavior, are introduced, the clinician can respond with encouragement and support and thus elicit significant, indeed often crucial, information unlikely to be obtained with more structured techniques.

The Interpersonal Relationship

The interviewer is able to adopt a persona most likely to elicit a particular patient's trust, taking into account such factors as his or her sex; age; appearance; dress; socioeconomic background; intelligence; vocabulary; level of education; ethnic origin; and moral, ethical, and sexual attitudes and values. Clinicians adopt markedly different practices in this respect, presumably having learned what is most effective for them. Some modify their personality much more than others, changing their vocabulary, assertiveness and apparent ethical value structure and social status to become the person they feel the patient would relate to best.

Confidentiality

To obtain trust, the clinician establishes patients' confidence that he or she will not disclose, either deliberately or inadvertently, any information they give that could be damaging to them. The patient will otherwise withhold information and certainly will not commit it to paper, for example, in a questionnaire response. Such information is, of course, particularly common in relation to sexual disorders, which are often a sufficient enough source of concern to patients that they do not wish anyone other than the therapist to be aware of it. A technique used by many clinicians who make written records during the interview is to put down their pens when they become aware that a possibly sensitive area is being approached, so conveying to the patient that it will be remembered without being recorded.

Inadequate Communication Skills

Patients who are illiterate, schizophrenic, depressed, or suffering from brain damage may be unable or unmotivated to respond accurately or appropriately to questionnaires. The experienced clinician can usually obtain by interview the necessary information from such patients. This is particularly important with sexual offenders seeking treatment, a significant percentage of whom are intellectually impaired or psychotic (Berlin & Meinecke, 1981; McConaghy, Blaszcynski, & Kidson, 1986). Some patients without diagnosable psychopathology of this nature tend to convey information in an obscure or contradictory manner, possibly because of their mode of thought (McConaghy, 1985). The interviewers, by persistent focused questioning, can often determine what they wish to convey.

The *directivity* of the interview is another important aspect that clinicians can continuously modify in response to patients' behavior and so elicit information not easily obtained with more objective methods of assessment. The author's method in this regard is to commence with a partially nondirective technique, adopting a listening approach and asking a minimum of questions to encourage the patient to take charge of the interview. By not responding for brief periods after the patient appears to have finished talking, the interviewer is able to assess whether the patient shows some degree of anxiety in response to such periods of silence and, if so, how he or she expresses and deals with such anxiety. Patients may become obviously embarrassed and tongue-tied, may recommence talking in a fast and perturbed manner, may remain calm and silent, or may confidently start to direct the interview themselves, perhaps questioning or instructing the therapist about the treatment plan. In this way the interviewer obtains information to construct an initial hypothesis concerning the patient's personality. Is he or she somewhat dependent and inadequate, wanting the interviewer to direct the interview, or is the patient excessively assertive and authoritarian, needing to retain control throughout despite the cues the interviewer gives when it is considered appropriate to redirect the interview?

While adopting a nondirective technique concerning the overt control of the initial section of the interview, the author remains ready to be directive concerning its content so as not to waste interview time. He intervenes if patients commence to give information he considers irrelevant, judging this by intuition based on experience. Of course, the style and degree of both nondirectiveness and intervention must be used with control. The periods of silence should not be allowed to become so long that dependent patients begin to experience levels of anxiety that cause them to find the therapist unsupportive. Interventions should not threaten or antagonize assertive patients or allow obsessional or paranoid patients to conclude the interviewer is not concerned with the information the patient considers important.

In the initial section of the interview the author seeks to learn the reasons the patient has sought treatment. These include not only a complete concept of the patient's complaint, but the factors, including possible external pressures, that have prompted the patient to attend the particular session at the particular time. External pressures can vary from obvious legal ones to subtle social ones, at times requiring intuitive detection. For example, a woman may seek treatment for failure to reach orgasm with intercourse. Only after assessing her interaction with her partner does it become apparent she is doing so not because of her own dissatisfaction but to maintain his self-esteem. The patient's presentation of the reasons for treatment provides the initial information on which the interviewer bases his initial assessment of the patient's *motivation*, both conscious and unconscious. The author has briefly discussed the concept of unconscious motivation he employs elsewhere (McConaghy, 1985).

The author initiates the interview in standard form by asking patients what the problem is for which they are seeking treatment. He then responds only as much as is necessary to maintain the flow of information within reasonable limits of relevance. After having assessed the patient's response to being given control of the interview within these limits, he usually finds it necessary to become more directive to obtain the required information. For most patients this information is sought by following the structure of the standard interview — determining the past history of any problems similar to the presenting one, of other illnesses, of childhood and adolescent relationships with parents and siblings, of social and sexual relationships, and of educational and work experiences as well as current domestic, social, sexual, and occupational situations, including the nature and extent of interests and activities. Structured sexuality interviews (WHO Psychosocial Task Force Report, 1980) have been developed to ensure that all data considered relevant are collected while hopefully preserving adequate flexibility. It seems unlikely that these structured interviews are widely used outside research studies.

Usually within about 5 minutes from the commencement of the interview, the author has formulated hypotheses concerning the nature of the patient's problem and the aspects of his or her *personality* likely to be relevant in treatment. Information is collected during the rest of the interview in order to support or refute these hypotheses, and, equally important, all possible alternative hypotheses. The author finds it valuable to determine if patients with sexual dysfunctions or deviations show features indicative of one of two personality disorders — psychopathy and personality inadequacy (or asthenia).

Evidence of psychopathy is suggested early in the interview by the patient's level of confidence and failure to express ethical concerns (for example, in relation to the effect of his or her sexual activity on others). He or she is likely to give a history indicative of delinquency in early adolescence followed by an educational, occupational, social, and sexual record of behavior consistent with an ability to easily form relationships and to impress others with his or her capabilities but an inability to persist with activities or relationships once these become demanding or boring. Assessment of this behavior is of value, as these patients are likely to be consciously and unconsciously dishonest in their self-reports and to comply poorly with treatment. Nevertheless, the therapist may believe that treatment could be of definite help to them. For example, if the compulsive nature of their illegal sexual behavior could be reduced, they may cease to offend even if their motivation to cease is fairly slight. If treatment is planned, it is advisable to attempt to establish external constraints on these patients. If they are being assessed for a report to a court of law, it could be suggested that they be placed on probation for an extended period. In discussing the treatment plan with such patients, one stresses its advantages in making their lives more enjoyable by avoiding unpleasant social consequences or jail. No attempt is made to indicate that there are ethical aspects of their behavior they should consider. Any suggestion that the interviewer disapproves of some aspects of their behavior is likely to result in their not revealing further aspects which they think might provoke further disapproval.

Personality inadequacy, or asthenia (McConaghy, 1981, 1983), is associated with an inability to tolerate the usual levels of anxiety or depression associated with life's stressful situations or with a tendency to react to such situations with above-average levels of these emotions. Asthenia will be suggested in the interview by the patient's lack of confidence and increased anxiety and will be supported by a past history of inability to tolerate stress. This may be evidenced in avoidance of examinations at school, frequent terminations of employment when the job became demanding, and establishment of dependent social and sexual relationships. Illness behavior is a common means of avoidance and cause of seeking care. If these patients are to be maintained in therapy it will be necessary to cater to their needs for support while attempting, without excessive optimism, to replace the reinforcements for dependent and sick behavior with reinforcements for independent and healthy behavior.

Other personality traits are also noted in the interview, such as histrionicism and attention-seeking behavior. These can lead patients to distort their histories in an attempt to obtain sympathy from the interviewer with accounts of their having been sexually exploited, or to shock him or her with reports of socially unacceptable sexual behavior. The interviewer will be alerted by noting such traits, to seek evidence of their influence on the patients' past social and sexual behavior, and the patients' motivation for currently seeking treatment.

It is the author's belief that the simple behavior therapy techniques that have been developed for sexual dysfunctions and deviations are now sufficiently effective that when an appropriately chosen one fails, in the absence of organic causes for the problem, the failure is usually not due to inadequacies of the technique but to the patient not being sufficiently motivated to take advantage of his or her responses to it. This lack of motivation is commonly due to patients' personality problems, which are often associated with their being in pathological relationships with their partners. It is the development of techniques for assessment and modification of these personality and relationship problems that would appear to be the current major task of behavioral research. If this view is correct, sexual behavioral assessment should be focused at least as much on determining the complex factors influencing patients' motivation as on the nature of their usually clearly defined sexual problems.

Similar views appear to be developing among behavioral therapists treating other conditions. Hersen (1981) emphasized that all alcoholics are not from the same mold and drew attention to attributing importance in the response to treatment of alcoholics to such factors as dependency, avoidance of social responsibility, and lack of anxiety or guilt. Chambless (1985) found that agoraphobics who appeared to be basically healthy people responded excellently to treatment as compared with those whose phobic symptoms were intertwined with personal, interpersonal, and situational difficulties that made treatment less successful. Certainly, the term *personality* was avoided by these behavioral therapists. Indeed, Hersen (1981; Bellack & Hersen, 1985) suggested that the determinants of these complex behaviors were environmental variables that could be detected by protracted behavioral analysis and modified by package or multimodal approaches, using behavioral therapy methods currently in use. This has not been the author's experience in treating sexual disorders. In contrast to the majority of patients without organic problems who improve markedly in response to simple behavioral techniques, the minority who respond poorly show only minimal further gains when subjected to additional and often prolonged assessment and treatment, whether by the author or by other behavioral or nonbehavioral therapists. This experience has led the author to believe that there is a stability to the behaviors responsible for these patients' failure to respond, which will require that the concept of personality be incorporated in behavioral theory, under another name if necessary.

Traditionally, behaviorists have identified the concept of personality with psychodynamic or cognitive theories of development in which behavior was considered to be determined by relatively stable intrapsychic processes established in early childhood. This view was opposed to the behaviorist position that behavior was determined solely by current environmental variables. Another reason for the opposition of behaviorists to the concept of personality was their historical lack of interest in or rejection of constitutional individual differences. Nelson and Hayes (1981) considered that modern behaviorists have shifted to an interactionist view that behavior is a function of both current environmental and organismic variables. They included in the latter more remote environmental variables such as past learning and genetic and current physiological variables. Acceptance of such organismic variables, particularly genetic ones, which could be responsible for stable constitutional individual differences, suggests a preparedness by modern behaviorists to accept the possibility of a significant degree of behavioral stability not easily or perhaps not at all modifiable by manipulation of environmental contingencies. If behaviorists are not yet ready to use the term *personality traits* for such consistent behavioral patterns as dependency and lack of anxiety and guilt, there is growing awareness that these behavioral patterns are of sufficient prognostic significance to require behavioral assessment.

In view of the modification of the behaviorist position referred to by Nelson and Hayes (1981), does adequate consistency of approach remain among behavior therapists to identify a *behavioral clinical interview* in contrast to those carried out by therapists who are more eclectic or committed to alternative approaches? Nelson and Hayes (1981) considered that many of the variables which should be included in a behavioral assessment could be summarized under the headings Stimulus, Organism, Response, and Consequences. Demonstrating the persistence of tradition, Nelson and Hayes considered that there remained general agreement among behaviorists that behavior is generally situation specific. They gave most attention to Stimulus and Response variables and emphasized the need to identify the specific stimulus situations in which the patient's problematic responses were likely to occur. By problematic responses they appeared to mean the specific problem for which the patient sought treatment rather than those labeled personality problems by the author, which appear associated with a poor response of the specific problem to treatment.

In his assessment of sexual problems, the author has not found detailed identification of the specific stimulus situations in which the problems occur particularly necessary or useful. With sexual dysfunctions, the major behavioral treatment is systematic desensitization in reality or imagination to a hierarchy of situations of increasing physical intimacy culminating in reaching orgasm in intercourse (McConaghy, 1985). With sexual deviations, it is imaginal desensitization, used to reduce any compulsive urge the patient experiences to carry out the deviant behavior against his will (McConaghy,

1982; McConaghy, Armstrong, & Blaszczynski, 1985). The author appears to obtain results equivalent to those in the literature without detailed analysis of the specific stimulus situations in which the problem behaviors occurred. This view was supported in relation to compulsive behaviors by the demonstration that imaginal relaxation was equivalent to imaginal desensitization in the treatment of compulsive gambling (McConaghy, Armstrong, Blaszczynski, & Allcock, 1986). With imaginal relaxation, the patients imagined relaxing scenes, and there was no inclusion of situations in which the compulsive behavior occurred. It was suggested that the treatment acted by alteration of an Organism variable — the patients' level of arousal in relation to behavior completion mechanisms — rather than a Stimulus or Response variable (McConaghy, 1983). The author believes that his assessment varies from that of colleagues with nonbehavioral orientations in the greater emphasis he places on Consequences. Possibly because dynamically oriented therapists consider reinforcements for patients' specific problems and the more complex behaviors that appear to limit their treatment response as secondary rather than primary gains, these therapists commonly give little attention to such reinforcements. The author finds that he puts much more emphasis than do these therapists on obtaining a detailed account of the patients' activities throughout each day of the week. This often enables him to identify more completely both the reinforcements that are contributing to the maintainence of the patients' behaviors and those to be used to increase the frequency of alternative behaviors. These reinforcements are commonly the behaviors of the people with whom the patient interacts.

If it is correct that the simple behavioral treatments of specific sexual problems have been developed to virtually their maximal efficacy, it may be that behavioral assessment will be most clearly differentiated from that of other theoretical models and make its major contribution not to the assessesment of the specific problems themselves but of the more complex behavioral contexts in which they are embedded. Certainly, it is the assessment of these more complex problems that currently demands the intuitive skills of the experienced interviewer. If the aim of behavioral assessment is to replace intuitive with objective, easily replicable techniques, it is this area that requires their development. There are aspects of the specific sexual problems themselves that present difficulties to the interviewer, but more because there is insufficient objective knowledge concerning them than because of inadequacies of the method used in their assessment.

Sexual dysfunctions in the DSM-III classification include inhibitions of sexual desire, of sexual excitement, and of orgasm with vaginismus and dyspareunia in women and premature ejaculation in men. Frank, Anderson, and Rubinstein (1978) reported that in a happily married sample, sexual difficulties — such as inability to relax, inappropriate or insensitive arousal by the partner including too little foreplay, and attraction to persons other than the partner — were more common and more related to lack of sexual satisfaction than were dysfunctions. Such difficulties are less likely to be spontaneously reported in the clinical interview than are dysfunctions. This may not be important when difficulties are due to the common failure to communicate sexual needs and not part of a more complex emotional relationship with the partner. Failure to communicate sexual needs is dealt with routinely in the initial stages of the modified Wolpe/Masters and Johnson treatment of dysfunctions (McConaghy, 1985).

Dyspareunia experienced in mid or deep penetration is an indication for gynecological assessment. Pain experienced superficially and often associated with vaginismus is not, unless it persists following initiation of behavioral treatment. Impotence and premature ejaculation, the commonest sexual dysfunctions in men, often occur together. Premature ejaculation without impotence is rarely due to organic causes. Initial referral for neurological assessment is indicated only if the presentation is atypical. Typically, the patient reports that the condition does not occur with private masturbation but has been present to some extent since he initially attempted intercourse. He usually shows or reports evidence indicative of increased general anxiety. Unlike the situation a decade ago when most cases of impotence were considered to be due to psychogenic factors, it is now agreed most have a significant organic contribution (McConaghy, 1986). The expensive and unvalidated assessment of nocturnal penile tumescence (q.v.) to exclude organic factors continues to be widely recommended. The author usually finds the patient's self-report adequate. If the patient says that in private masturbation his erection remains of adequate rigidity for intercourse for several minutes, his impotence is psychogenic and due to anxiety related to intercourse. If his erection is not adequate in private masturbation, the interviewer should satisfy himself that the patient is not anxious in that situation due to guilt, a high general level of anxiety, or because he is masturbating to determine the quality of his erection. Usually this is not the case, and the author believes that inadequate erection with masturbation almost invariably means that organic factors are contributing. The patient and his partner should be asked about the quality of his erection during sleep and on awakening throughout the night and in the morning. If he does not have adequate persistent erections a few times a week, penile vascular studies are indicated. If he does, hormone studies should be carried out but are commonly normal in the absence of reduced sexual interest.

If the patient has inadequate erections with masturbation but normal nocturnal erections and hormone levels, and the rare "vascular steal" syndrome is excluded on his history, most clinicians currently appear to accept that the impotence is psychogenic. The author does not. Many, particularly older, patients with impotence of gradual onset have normal nocturnal erections and hormone levels but show no evidence of masturbatory anxiety to explain their poor erection upon masturbation. Nor do they show marked improvement in erection with treatment for psychogenic impotence. For adequate assessment of impotence more information is needed concerning the role of the neurological and vascular systems in erection and the effect of age upon this. Equivalent knowledge concerning sexual activity in women is even more lacking, preventing determination of the possible significance of biological factors in their reduced sexual arousal and failure to orgasm. In both sexes the patient's general health, physical fitness, diet, and use of drugs — both prescribed and recreational — appear important in the etiology of sexual dysfunctions and require assessment.

In determining *sexual orientation*, the author finds most adults can report the degree to which they are conscious of sexual attraction to strangers of either sex whom they see, say, walking in the street. This, in combination with the degree to which they use male versus female fantasy in sexual activities (including masturbation), generally enables an assessment of homosexual or heterosexual interest. Occasionally, a male adult reports that he is conscious of an interest in men's bodies, which he does not consider sexual. He explains it as due to feelings of inferiority concerning his own body, which cause him to compare his body with that of other men. In the author's experience, such patients show sexual arousal indicative of homosexuality with penile volume assessment (q.v.), and during treatment they usually become aware that their interest is sexual but repressed by guilt. Most adolescents are reluctant to admit the presence of homosexual or indeed of any socially disapproved sexual impulses, so this is one area of behavior where the validity of assessment by interview is suspect. The author believes this reluctance explains the marked discrepancy between (a) the consistent report by adults in surveys that about 50% were conscious when adolescents of a degree of homosexual feelings and (b) the findings of several sexuality studies by researchers that less than 5% of the adolescent experimental subjects and controls were aware of any homosexual feeling (McConaghy, 1984). The issue is discussed in more detail in the section in this chapter on *behavioral inventory assessment* of sex roles. Some professionals, particularly social learning theorists, consider the assessment of homosexuality should be based not on the subjects' sexual feelings but on their overt sexual behavior (Akers, 1973) or only on their self-identification as being homosexual (Hart & Richardson, 1981).

Interview assessment of *paraphilias* in adolescents present the same problem of reluctance to admit socially disapproved behaviors. When confronted with evidence of their paraphilic activity they often explain that they resist thinking about it in the hope that it will not recur, thus virtually denying its existence when not actively involved in the behavior. In the author's experience, the usual paraphilia for which adolescents seek treatment is fetishism involving female clothing, which is almost invariably combined with some degree of cross-dressing. Clothes may be stolen or taken from the patient's mother or sister, so the parents usually have evidence that the behavior is occurring. The continued involvement of at least one parent in the assessment of the patient's response to treatment is virtually essential and must be facilitated so that the patient accepts it without resentment.

In the author's experience, exhibitionists and voyeurs, unlike many pedophiles, usually seek treatment only after being legally charged with the paraphilic activity. They might therefore be expected to be less honest in self-reports. This does not appear to be so. Having been assured that the interviewer will not reveal any additional information they give, most appear to provide valid reports. Evidence of this validity was obtained in a recent study (McConaghy, Blaszczynski, & Taidson, 1986) in which sexual offenders' reports of the degree of reduction in their paraphilic urge following medroxyprogesterone treatment correlated significantly with reduction of their serum testosterone. The interviewer and patients were unaware of the testosterone levels.

When women patients report paraphilic urges, particularly of a dramatic nature such as sexually arousing impulses to harm children, or report having carried out such acts, the author has found these were commonly fabricated to gain attention. In this respect they were usually successful, as colleagues often reacted with considerable alarm to such reports, powerfully reinforcing them. In view of the rarity of paraphilias in women, it is wise to listen calmly to the patient's reports of such behaviors, subsequently attempting to corroborate them with the patient's significant others. Refusal by the patient to allow such corroboration for inadequate reasons is not unusual. On clinical interview, such patients commonly provide evidence of psychopathic or borderline personality disturbance. If this evidence is concealed by the more sophisticated patients prone to pathological lying, it may be obtained from records of the patients' previous treatment, the usual source of their sophistication.

Sexual role and identity require assessment in children with opposite-sex behaviors and in adolescent and adult transsexuals as well as retrospectively in the childhood of transsexuals, transvestites, and subjects with homosexual feelings. Effeminate behavior in boys is much more likely to disturb parents and lead them to seek help than the much commoner tomboyish behavior in girls. The parents' report of the child's behavior allows the interviewer to assess their attitudes concerning the opposite-sex behavior, as these will be a major factor in management of the problem. Effeminate behavior in men is rarely commented on by the men themselves or by their partners of either sex. The author's practice is only to discuss it if it seems appropriate. The patient is possibly unaware of or is denying it, and this may be a necessary defense for him.

Transsexuals often associate with each other, at times in formally organized clubs. These transsexuals learn the indications used by members of committees to recommend sex-conversion, and they may modify their history accordingly. One clinician may believe the ideal male candidate has been feminine but not effeminate since early childhood; another may believe that the patient can be a well-developed male (McConaghy, 1982). The interviewer should attempt to allow for possible distortion in the patient's account, where possible obtaining information from his parents and other appropriate sources.

Interview assessment clearly requires the clinician to be alert to the patient's conscious and unconscious distortions, and where relevant, as it usually is, to attempt to obtain information from other sources, often by interview also. This is commonly possible in patients with sexual dysfunctions whose partners are willing to be interviewed. Indeed, they are usually required to be involved in the treatment. When they refuse to attend assessment and treatment sessions the patient's reponse is generally compromised. If patients state that possible informants are not prepared to be interviewed, it is wise to ask permission to contact such possible informants directly by phone or letter. Often they agree to attend, and it becomes apparent that the patient did not desire this, consciously or unconsciously. Patients with paraphilias often do not wish their partners or other contacts to know of their behavior and frequently refuse to agree to their being interviewed.

The therapist must remain aware throughout the interview that its purpose is not only assessment but, and equally important, the establishment of the patient's motivation to accept and cooperate in the management that the therapist considers appropriate. Whether it is further interviews, investigations, a treatment program, or referral to another therapist, the skilled interviewer will plan the termination of the interview so as to maximize the likelihood that the patient will agree to the therapist's program. Patients must not be allowed to leave the interview feeling that they have been asked a lot of questions or have been allowed to talk freely but have received no answers. The therapist must make sure that patients are fully aware of what the management plan entails and why it, rather than alternatives, has been chosen. Any reservations that patients may have concerning the proposed plan should be dealt with fully so that by the end of the interview they commit themselves either to accepting the management offered or to making a decision within the next week as to whether they will or will not, which they will communicate to the therapist.

Behavioral Inventories

The advantages of behavioral inventories for researchers are that, in most, the data are collected in quantifiable form and thus are suited to statistical analysis, and most can be completed by the subject on his or her own and objectively scored. This avoids the criticism that the subject's report has been consciously or unconsciously distorted by the scorer. The disadvantage of such self-reports is that they do not allow clinicians to exercise their intuitive interviewing skills in the process of data collection. Some clinicians use self-report inventories to save time by asking patients to complete them prior to the interview. The clinician can use the information as a basis for further inquiry and thus clarify, expand, and intuitively interpret it. With this method, of course, the apparent advantage of objective scoring is lost, as it is for rating scales that the interviewer completes on the basis of the patient's self-reports. Conte (1983) has recently reviewed most of the established self-report assessments for sexual functioning.

The fact that self-reports are objectively scored does not exclude the possibility that the researcher or therapist using them has influenced them directly or indirectly. AuBuchon and Calhoun (1985) reported a study in which 18 women were asked to record their moods on a 16-item adjective checklist as twice-weekly test sessions for 8 weeks. Nine women, randomly selected, were informed that the study was to investigate a possible relationship between their behavior and their menstrual cycles. A negative relationship between mood and menstruation was found in their reports. It was not present in the reports of the 9 women not so informed. The authors attributed the difference to social expectancy and demand characteristics of the experiment. It is likely that some patients, suspecting or knowing their self-reports will be seen by their therapist, exaggerate their behavioral gains following treatment, particularly if the therapist tended in previous interviews with the patients to show a more positive reponse to reports of improvement. McConaghy, Armstrong, and Blaszczynski (1985) treated 20 subjects with desensitization or covert sensitization for sexual deviations. Treatment was given in 14 sessions over a 1-week period in the hospital. Patients were asked to complete ratings of their *expectancy* of improvement and of reduction in deviant urges at the end of the first, eighth, and fourteenth sessions, and at 1 month and 1 year following treatment. Reported reduction in urge correlated very highly with expectancy immediately following termination of treatment ($r = .93$ and $.96$), but less so after 1 month and 1 year. It was concluded that expectancy contributed significantly to patients' reported responses during treatment, but to a lesser degree to their responses following treatment because the patients became more aware of their actual reponse with the passage of time. From these results it would seem unwise to rely entirely on assessments of patients' self-report of response during treatment without follow-up data.

Patients' behavioral self-report in inventories can itself produce changes in behavior. LoPiccolo and Steger (1974) found that the magnitude of test-retest reliability correlations among subjects' scores on the Sexual Interaction Inventory were lower than hoped for. They referred to evidence that people's recording of their sexual activity leads to marked changes in the activity. They suggested that the completion by couples of the first Sexual Interaction Inventory would be likely to alter their behavior and hence their responses to the second inventory. If such an inventory is to be used to assess behavioral change due to treatment, it is necessary to deal with the problem that the inventory being used to monitor the change may itself be contributing to it. One solution is to administer the inventory on sufficient occasions prior to treatment for such *reactivity* to stabilize. However, the assessment of the patients' response to treatment at final follow-up is likely to still include an element of reactivity to the inventory. After that follow-up, when the patients cease to monitor their behavior by inventory, their behavior is likely to change in an unassessable manner.

A further problem with the use of self-report inventories to monitor treatment responses is lack of patient compliance. Barlow, Leitenberg and Agras (1969) reported a single-case study of two patients with sexual deviations. Both patients were asked to keep a small notebook in which to record each time they were sexually aroused. In subsequent single-case studies, patients were asked to record daily the incidence of sexual urges, fantasies, and behaviors (Barlow & Agras, 1973; Herman, Barlow, & Agras, 1974a). These researchers did not indicate whether reduced compliance was reponsible for the change from patients recording urges each time they occurred to recording them only daily. With single-case designs, only a few patients are studied and patient selection can be restricted to highly cooperative subjects. The therapists have more time to devote to the few patients and perhaps can maintain their compliance with daily record keeping for the relatively short duration that is usual with single-case studies.

The author, using randomized group designs for treatment evaluation, has found that many patients, particularly the mildly psychopathic or retarded, do not comply with requests to record their behavior daily. Yet such patients need to be accepted for treatment if a representative sample of patients is to be studied. Reading (1983) randomly allocated paid male volunteers to report details of their sexual behavior either by (a) interviews after 1 and 3 months ($N=21$); (b) interviews after 1, 2, and 3 months ($N=18$); or (c) diary card completed daily and returned every 3 days in addition to interviews at 1, 2, and 3 months ($N = 29$). Thirty-four percent discontinued with (c) as compared to 16% with (b) and 14% with (a). Another three dropped out prior to the first month with (c), considering that being required to complete diary cards was causing them potency difficulties.

Validation of daily written reports of coital frequency was attempted by requesting 58 black women to supply reports concerning whether they had menstruated and/or had coitus and/or orgasm in the past 24 hours. They were paid 50 cents daily to deliver the reports and first-morning urine specimens to a laboratory for a 90-day period (Udry & Morris, 1967). There were very few missing specimens and reports. Urine samples were examined for morphologically intact sperms. The positive sperm sighting was taken as evidence that coitus had occurred in the 48 hours prior to the urine being voided. Forty-two positive sightings were made on urine from 15 women. For 12 of the 15, all positive sightings were concordant with reported coitus. The authors concluded that the percentage of invalid reports did not appear excessive. The validity of the reports of the remaining 43 women could, of course, not be assessed in the absence of positive sperm sightings. An innovative method of validating patients' reports of their use of relaxation tapes was reported by Taylor, Agras, Schneider, and Allen (1983). Using a concealed electronic monitor in the tape recorders, it was found that 32% of patients falsely reported their use of the tapes on diary cards. Electronic monitors of sexual activity do not appear to have been used in this way to assess validity of self-reports.

The appeal to researchers of behavioral assessment by rating scale as opposed to global impression is understandable when subjects rate the behavior themselves, as scoring is objective and its reliability usually easily assessed. When the rating was carried out by the interviewer, it appears to have been preferred also, though why it should then be regarded as less subjective than global impression is difficult to understand. Paredes et al. (1966), in the study referred to earlier in this chapter, pointed out that in response to criticisms of subjective bias and questionable reliability of their global assessments, clinicians' participation in psychopharmacological studies was being restricted to rating behavior on scales. Researchers appeared to attribute greater face validity to such ratings compared to intuitive global assessments. Paredes et al. demonstrated that such ratings were in fact less valid. They attributed the reduction in validity to the narrowing of the clinician's perspective when forced to rate patients along specific dimensions. Similar considerations may apply to patients' global assessments. Women reported increased satisfaction in their sexual relationship by global assessment but decreased satisfaction when specific activities were measured by the Sexual Interaction Inventory (DeAmicis, Goldberg, LoPiccolo, Friedman, & Davies, 1984). Preference for behavioral assessment by rating scales rather than global intuitive evaluation has consistently distorted behavioral research findings.

In an excellently designed study, Birk, Huddleston, Miller, and Cohler (1971) randomly allocated eight homosexual males to avoidance conditioning and eight to a control procedure. Patients reported equal expectancy of improvement with the two procedures. All were concurrently receiving prolonged group psychotherapy. Response was assessed by clinical interview and rating scales. In interviews, five patients who received avoidance conditioning but no controls reported marked reduction or absence of homosexual urges, feelings, and behaviors. The difference in response remained statistically significant at 1 year. The authors termed these results "anecdotal." Kinsey ratings of the patients' sexual orientation altered in a heterosexual direction to a significant extent in the treated group as compared to controls in the first 2 months following treatment but not after 1 year. These were termed the "statistical" results and were given much more significance than the "anecdotal" results. The study was one of the relatively few behavioral therapy reports published in the *Archives of General Psychiatry*, which is widely read by American psychiatrists. It may well have contributed to the acceptance by these psychiatrists that such approaches to sexual offenses are "often disappointing ... brief changes in behavior are relatively easy to accomplish, but long-term maintenance of such change is achieved far less frequently" (Berlin & Meinecke, 1981, p. 603). In an editorial (1981b) on "The Ethics of Antiandrogen Therapy" for sexual offenders, the possibility of using behavioral approaches that raised no such ethical problems was not considered.

Review of the evidence (McConaghy, 1977, 1982) indicated that aversive therapy acts by reducing the compulsive aspects of homosexual subjects' urges or thoughts but does not alter their sexual orientation, as assessed by the degree to which they are attracted to members of one versus the other sex. Male patients commonly report, for example, that following treatment they are still attracted to men they see on the street but are no longer preoccupied with thoughts concerning them when they walk out of sight. The patients also report reduction in homosexual fantasy and in urges to become involved in homosexual acts against their will. Those already in heterosexual relations are likely to increase the frequency of heterosexual activities. These changes, particularly immediately following treatment, are likely when recorded on rating scales to indicate a shift toward heterosexuality. However, the patients show no specific change in penile volume responses (q.v.) to the pictures of nude men and women.

Premature closure on the concept that aversive therapy acted by altering patients' sexual orientation led other researchers besides Birk et al. (1971) to accept without question that rating scales of sexual orientation would provide valid assessments of homosexual subjects' response to aversive therapy. Feldman and MacCulloch (1971) used a Sexual Orientation Method (SOM) scale, stating it was not intended to supplant the clinical interview but to provide complementary data. They reported only SOM scores, not the interviewer's global impression of changes in patients' feelings. It would seem wise not to abandon global clinical assessment although it remains necessary to obtain as clear an idea as possible of patients' feelings and their change with treatment. Assessment by rating scale should not be relied upon until it is established that the scale is appropriate, in that it provides a *sufficiently sensitive* measure of the behavior being assessed. The confusion produced by the different assessments of response to aversive therapy is still not resolved. Recently, Emmelkamp (1982) stated that the usual outcome of aversive therapy was indifference to the conditioned stimulus.

Rating scales, when preferred to clinical global assessments, can distort or produce misleading research findings not only by being insensitive to the behavior being assessed, but by being *too sensitive*. LoPiccolo and Steger (1974), in introducing the Sexual Interaction Inventory, thought it would be of value in providing a more specific assessment of patients' change in sexual behavior with treatment than such commonly used global assessments as "much improved," "somewhat improved," and "no change." Recently, Jacobson, Follette, and Revenstorf (1984), discussing the gap between research and clinical practice, pointed out that most research evaluating psychotherapy outcome relies on statistical comparison of groups of patients' mean improvement on inventories. The studies provide no information concerning the response of individual subjects. Jacobson, Follette, and Revenstorf (1984) considered that descriptive statistics, such as the proportion of patients who improve, are at least as important as group means. If a rating scale is very sensitive to the change in behavior that follows treatment, differences in group means on that scale for patients receiving active treatment compared to those receiving placebo therapy could be highly significant statistically when the changes in the treated patients' clinical condition were trivial. Jacobson, Follette, and Revenstorf (1984) advanced as a correction to such misleading data application of statistical criteria to individual patient's scores. These criteria require knowledge of the norms, the mean, and the standard deviation of the scores of functionally well subjects on the rating scale used. Applying the criteria to studies of behavioral marital therapy, they found the mean improvement rate to be about 35%, considerably less than was generally believed (Jacobson, Follette, Revenstorf, Baucom, Hahlweg, & Margolin, 1984). In the absence of rating scales demonstrated to be valid for the behavioral changes being assessed and for which norms are available, it would seem reasonable to retain global assessments of individual patient's improvement in studies evaluating treatment. It is possible such clinician global assessment ratings of "much improved" and "no change," when used in comparison studies, are more reliable and valid than academic researchers are currently prepared to acknowledge. It was this type of assessment of improvement which correlated with reduced testosterone levels in paraphiliacs (McConaghy et al., 1986).

Preference for rating scales over interview assessments has also produced misleading research findings due to *reification* into categorical entities of the behaviors assessed on rating scales and inventories. The entry with the longest history in this respect is that of masculinity-femininity (M-F). Constantinople (1973) impressively reviewed the literature concerning M-F, pointing out the lack of a satisfactory theoretical definition or of a reliable empirical approach to its measurement:

> Anything that discriminated men from women, usually at a particular point in time in a particular culture, is taken as an indicator of M-F with no assessment of the centrality of that trait or behavior to an abstract definition of M-F....The relationship between a theoretical definition and the measures of M-F is further complicated by the confusion of such related terms as sex role adoption, sex role preference and sex role identity. (p.390)

Constantinople noted the relationship of the behaviors assessed by M-F scales to contemporary stereotypes and wondered whether the adjectives used to categorize subjects as "M" (hard-headed, humorless, self-centered) or "F" (dependent, sensitive, tolerant) were not really more appropriately seen as aspects of social sensitivity or even flexibility. She pointed out the low interscale reliability demonstrated when various tests of M-F were used to assess the same populations. Also discussed were such issues as whether M-F is a unitary trait to be measured with one total score or a set of subtraits better represented through profile scoring, and whether the assumption of inherent bipolarity in M-F could be supported.

In a more recent review of sex-role acquisition, Constantinople (1979) seemed content to ignore the penetrating criticisms she had made and treated sex role as an acceptable expression of M-F, namely, an unquestioned entity which was dichotomously distributed. Another development of the M-F concept that has also been uncritically accepted was the reification of M and F not as opposite poles but as two separate, orthogonal, and equally important aspects of human personality, so that individuals can be androgenous: that is, both M and F (Lenney, 1979). Lenney pointed out the confusion in studies of androgeny: subjects who obtained equal scores on both M and F scales were classified in earlier studies as androgenous whereas in later studies only subjects with high scores on both scales were so classified. The interscale reliability of the various androgeny scales was low. The major criticism remained that of Constantinople, namely, the lack of centrality of the concepts of M and F as related to some abstract definition. Clearly, at any time it is possible to develop a set of adjectives — loudspoken, tie-wearing, noncosmetic using — which will discriminate a sufficiently large number of men from women at a statistically significant level. Should this criterion of a statistically significant discrimination of men and women be considered adequate validation of an M-F scale, as has been the case? The alternative is that some theoretical reason be advanced justifying the rating scale items selected as being centrally related to some concept of M-F. All M-F behaviors have been recently defined as behaviors learned from social stereotypes (Heilbrun & Thompson, 1977). If this is accepted, a central group of such behaviors cannot be expected and need not be sought to establish a M-F scale. Any behavior can be socially stereotyped as M or F from this social learning point of view.

Increased rough-and-tumble play has been found to characterize boys as compared to girls not only in Western society but in societies as disparate as India, Japan, Mexico, Kenya, and the Philippines (Whiting, 1963). Reduction of such play in childhood has been reported in male homosexuals in retrospective studies of psychiatric patients (Bieber, 1962), prisoners (Holeman & Winokur, 1965), and members of homosexual organizations (Evans, 1969; Saghir & Robins, 1973) in the U.S.A., and nonpatient homosexuals in Guatmala and Brazil (Whitam, 1980). Prospective studies of effeminate boys revealed a similar relationship in that they were likely to become predominantly homosexual as adults (Bakwin, 1968; Money & Russo, 1979; Zuger, 1966, 1978, 1983). Several studies have reported increased rough-and-tumble play both in female higher primates and in girls exposed prenatally to increased male hormone (Ehrhardt & Money, 1967; Ehrhardt & Baker, 1974). In view of the consistency of these findings, their possible independence of a particular culture, and their relationship with a biological sexual determinant, it might be expected that workers interested in assessments of M-F or sex role would be prepared to examine whether rough-and-tumble play and related sex dimorphic activities could provide some centrality to these concepts. Heilbrun and Thompson (1977) and Pleck (1981) stated that few researchers have examined the relationship between sex-role deviation and homosexuality. They ignored the literature that consistently demonstrated this relationship and considered only that which sought and found no relationship between M-F or sex role scale scores and homosexuality. That is to say they identified sex-role deviation with the reified entity measured by rating scales but not with the effeminate behaviors of male children repeatedly assessed by interviewers from the subjects' or their parents' reports or from observation of the subjects' behaviors. This distortion or denial of research findings due to the reification of rating-scale assessment has been widely accepted.

> Masculinity and femininity are culturally defined attributes . . . and they have no demonstrable correlation with sexual orientation. (Katchadourian, Lunde, & Trotter, 1979, p.229).

There is, of course, question as to whether any sexual behavior past the most basically biological can be considered truly sex-dimorphic. (Editorial, 1981a, p.605).

What we do not know is the implications of these childhood differences (in sex-dimorphic behaviors) for adult masculinity and femininity. (Maccoby, 1980, p.239).

There is a lack of clear research on the relationship between early childhood behaviors and adult pathology or sex roles. (Resick, 1985, p.541).

Clearly, the history of behavioral assessment by inventory is a disaster area. However, the indications for the correct use of such inventories are being clarified, in particular the need to establish that (a) they appropriately measure the behavior under investigation and at an appropriate level of sensitivity and (b) the norms of healthy subjects' performance be available. Until these criteria are met for a particular rating scale, where experienced clinical judgment has been developed to assess the behavior, it would seem unwise to consider the scale superior to such judgment.

In addition to their advantages in enabling behavioral data to be collected outside the interview or observation period and to be quantified for statistical analysis, inventories provide a method of obtaining data anonymously from subjects who would not be prepared to provide it if they were identified. As previously discussed, adolescents are unlikely to report socially unacceptable sexual behaviors in the clinical interview. Most adults appear prepared to do so when they seek help as patients, but many would not in experimental investigations. In the past, data on the incidence of such sexual behaviors have been obtained from volunteers who may not be representative of the general population. Most surveys of this sort have investigated the incidence of homosexuality and found that 30–50% of the population have been aware of some homosexual feelings (McConaghy, 1984). In the final report of the American Psychological Association Task Force on Sexual Orientation (Paul, Weinrich, Gonsiorek, & Hotvedt, 1982), the findings of the surveys were generally accepted. Yet, sexuality researchers have continued to publish studies in which less than 5% of adolescent subjects reported having any homosexual feelings (Ehrhardt & Money, 1967; Ehrhardt & Baker, 1974; Green, 1985). Presumably, the researchers reject the representativeness of the survey data. Yet, if it is correct, the findings in these studies, which have been attributed considerable significance in supporting or rejecting theories of the etiology of homosexuality, must be invalid.

One possible method of obtaining representative data to resolve this conflict concerning the incidence of homosexual feelings was suggested by McConaghy, Armstrong, Birrell, and Buhrich (1979). Over 90% of second-year medical students at the University of New South Wales completed anonymous questionnaires on which they rated the degree of (a) their sexual interest in males versus females, (b) their involvement in various sex-dimorphic behaviors in childhood and adolescence, (c) their desire to be of the opposite sex, and (d) their sexual identity. The study was replicated over the 2 subsequent years. In each of the 3 years, over 50% of the males and females reported they were aware of some degree of homosexual feelings prior to 15 years of age, and over 40% were currently aware of such feelings. Of this 40%, over three-fourths were predominantly aware of heterosexual feelings. Significant correlations were in men found between the degree of current homosexual feelings and dislike of outdoor games, contact sports, and fighting during childhood and adolescence in all 3 years, supporting the validity of the reports. In view of the economy of this method as compared with that of other surveys that require the seeking out of homosexual subjects and the selection of appropriate controls, it was suggested that researchers could employ this method to investigate anonymously any groups available to them who would be representative of subsamples of the population. If similar results were obtained from all the subsamples, this would establish the validity of the original survey data on volunteers, and the findings of Ehrhardt and Money (1967) and Green (1985) would need to be rejected.

The data from the medical students rating their identity as men or women on a number of items in the questionnaire were used to investigate the concept of sexual or gender identity. This is another aspect of M-F which has been reified as an entity by researchers over the past 30 years, since the term was first used in relation to transsexualism. Once named, most researchers accepted that it existed as an entity without gradations (Ehrhardt & Baker, 1974):

> 35% of the (female) patients were undecided or thought that they might have chosen to be a boy . . . However . . ., none had a conflict with their female gender identity. (p.43).

The responses of the medical students to the items assessing their sense of sexual identity correlated with each other, with most at about .5 (McConaghy & Armstrong, 1983). The correlations were stronger in the subjects who reported some degree of homosexuality. These subjects also reported a greater degree of opposite-sex identity. It would appear that sexual identity is not a unitary entity, and it is less consistent in heterosexual subjects. The unitary concept of sexual identity is also weakened by the reports of transvestites who, when dressed as men, often experienced a male sexual identity, and when dressed as women, a female sexual identity (Buhrich & McConaghy, 1977).

Behavioral Observation

Social taboos have resulted in the observation of sexual behaviors that are not commonly used as assessment procedures by clinicians or researchers.

Masters and Johnson (1966) observed and described sexual responses of sexually functional male and female volunteers in the laboratory. Their research appeared to have a profound effect on U.S. psychology and psychiatry, liberating it from its psychoanalytically determined fixation on sexual theories to an interest in actual sexual behavior. However, Masters and Johnson's research observations do not appear to have significantly influenced the treatment of dysfunctional patients. Their theoretically most significant finding was that there was no difference in physical responses, heart rate, or blood pressure changes between the orgasms experienced by their women subjects with clitoral as compared to vaginal stimulation. This was considered to invalidate the analytic concept that there were two separate orgasms, clitoral and vaginal, associated with the phallic and genital stages of psychosexual development respectively. However, as Morokoff (1978) has documented, these data have not resolved the debate concerning the existence of two or even three different kinds of female orgasm.

Masters and Johnson did not observe the sexual behavior of subjects with sexual dysfunctions or deviations. The author believes that such observation could be of considerable value, but he has not progressed beyond seeking reports from female surrogate therapists concerning the potency of patients who appear obsessed about their erections not being satisfactory, even though, from the surrogate's account, they are adequate for intercourse. These patients are commonly rather eccentric in personality and do not have a regular partner prepared to give an independent report. Karacan (1978) recommended observation of the fullness of erections followed by assessment of their rigidity as part of assessment of penile nocturnal tumescence (q.v.). Other workers have emphasized this and also the observation of erections produced by masturbation (Wasserman, Pollak, Speilman, & Weitzman, 1980).

Maletzky (1980) reported the use of a temptation test for exhibitionists. A comely actress, unknown to the subjects, purposely placed herself in situations that previously had a high probability of eliciting their exposure behavior. The test was given at the end of treatment and 1 year later. All patients had been informed that experimental and unusual procedures would be employed.

The use of observation to assess effeminate behaviors in boys was, of course, part of the clinical interview (Bakwin & Bakwin, 1953; Bender & Paster, 1941). Subsequently, the observations of others were employed by researchers who requested that teachers (Kagan & Moss, 1962) and parents (Bates, Bentler, & Thompson, 1973) complete inventories recording their pupils' or sons' sex-dimorphic behaviors. Direct observation was used by Rekers and Lovaas (1974) in the treatment of an effeminate boy. The therapist observed the boy playing with boys' and girls' toys through a one-way mirror and instructed his mother through earphones to respond with appropriate reinforcement. Fagot (1977) reported the use of observers trained on videotapes, to a criterion of 90% agreement, to record the time spent by nursery school boys and girls in sex-dimorphic behaviors. The sex-dimorphic behaviors were selected on the basis that they were displayed significantly more frequently by members of one sex than another. The observers also recorded the responses of the teacher and peers to each child's behaviors. The validity of the technique was supported by the fact that peer reaction was significantly more negative to boys showing at least one standard deviation increase in incidence of feminine sex-dimorphic behaviors. A method for assessment of effeminate behaviors in adults by observation and recording has been described (Schatzberg, Westfall, Blumetti, & Birk, 1975), but does not appear to have been widely used, presumably because of its complexity.

Physiological Assessment

Genital Arousal

When the author first saw Brecht's play *Life of Galileo*, he had difficulty accepting the episode where Brecht represented the scholars of the period as refusing to look through Galileo's telescope to see evidence that the moons he had discovered revolved around the planet Jupiter. Instead, the scholars rejected the possibility and debated it, on the grounds that current philosophy required that all heavenly bodies revolved around the Earth. Surely, Brecht had departed too far from reality in his attempt to satirize academic man's willingness to shut his eyes to the evidence when it conflicts with his theories. This is not so. A similar reaction occurred to published graphs (McConaghy, 1974) of concurrent recordings of subjects' penile circumference and volume responses, till then assumed to be identical. The graphs made apparent that these responses were not identical; in fact, in some subjects they were almost mirror images, one indicating penile tumescence as the other indicated detumescence. It was suggested that the mirror image responses were due to the initial stage of tumescence in these subjects, which was associated with an increase in penile length too rapid for the associated increase in blood flow to maintain the penile diameter. While length and volume were increasing, circumference was decreasing, and the reverse was true in the final stage of detumescence. If this explanation was correct, and it seemed the only one possible, the penile volume (PV) but not the penile circumference (PC) measure was validly reporting the tumescence change in these subjects. In support of this conclusion, a graph was published subsequently (McConaghy, 1977), demonstrating a subject's PV increase commencing within a few seconds of his being shown a series of erotic slides, while PC showed a decrease for almost 2 minutes before it also began to increase. These findings indicated that penile circumference response in slight to moderate tumescence will be invalid in a percentage of subjects.

Rosen and Keefe (1978) considered that this graphic evidence, which questioned the validity of PCRs as measures of sexual arousal, should be interpreted with caution. No statistical comparisons had been reported and the number of subjects was small. PC assessments had until that time mainly been employed in single-case studies in which no statistical comparisons were made and the number of subjects were small. The irony of Rosen and Keefe's (1978) methodologically formalistic rejection of the visual evidence was probably lost on most of their readers. Certainly, PV and PC assessments continued to be viewed as identical (Abel, Blanchard & Barlow, 1981; Blader & Marshall, 1984), and the evidence validating penile volume response has entered academic consciousness as validating penile circumference response (Wincze & Lang, 1981):

> The assessment of male sexual arousal by direct measurement of changes in penile diameter or volume in response to erotic stimuli is now widely accepted as one of the most valid assessment techniques available. (p.313)

In fact, in contrast to PV assessment, the data available concerning PC, or penile diameter, assessment as a measure of sexual arousal has invalidated rather than validated it, both in many of the studies that attempted to differentiate sexually deviant groups and in 40–50% of subjects studied individually.

The use of PV assessment as a measure of male sexual arousal was introduced by Freund in Prague in the 1950s, though many academics seem unaware of this:

> it is only since the publication of *Human Sexual Response* (Masters and Johnson, 1966) [that] that current laboratory techniques have been applied . . . [to] . . . penile measurement. (Rosen & Keefe, 1978, p.374).

Freund (1963) was able to classify correctly all of 65 relatively exclusive heterosexual men and 48 of 58 relatively exclusive homosexual men from their PVRs to 13-second exposures of colored pictures of nude men, women, and children. When asked to fantasize, so as to produce sexual arousal, to pictures of members of the nonpreferred sex and to diminish arousal to those of the preferred sex, only 10 of 55 predominantly heterosexual and 6 of 24 predominantly homosexual men produced records which misclassified them.

McConaghy (1967) described a simpler apparatus for measuring PVRs and a relatively brief standardized procedure for presenting 20 10-second segments of moving pictures: 10 of nude women and 10 of nude men, presented in alternation at 1-minute intervals within a film of landscapes. The pictures of nudes were preceded by conditional stimuli, so providing measures of each subject's appetitive conditionability. The Mann-Whitney U test was applied to each subject's PVRs to the pictures of nudes. U scores of 77 or more indicated that the subject's 10 responses to pictures of women were significantly greater than his responses to pictures of men, demonstrating a statistically significant heterosexual response. U scores of 23 or less indicated a similar homosexual response. U scores between 23 and 77 were considered indicative of bisexuality. Studies reporting the reliability of this procedure and validating it in identifying men as predominantly heterosexual or homosexual and in discriminating bisexuals from predominant homosexuals, nuclear from fetishistic transsexuals, and nuclear from marginal transvestites have been reviewed elsewhere (McConaghy, 1982, 1987).

A potential source of error exists when the mean PVRs of a group of subjects to nudes of the nonpreferred sex are calculated. Negative PVRs occur in most self-defined heterosexual and some self-defined homosexual men to pictures of nudes of the nonpreferred sex. Freund, Langevin, Cibiri, and Zajec (1973) reported that such negative PVRs occurred to slides of members of the nonpreferred sex only when the slides were preceded by slides of members of the preferred sex. The author has found this not to be the case (McConaghy, 1977). Freund et al. (1973) reported that heterosexual men as a group showed minimal PVRs to pictures of nude men, and homosexual men as a group showed minimal PVRs to pictures of nude women. They concluded that it was rare for heterosexuals or homosexuals to show bisexuality. However, it seems likely that some individuals in both groups would have showed negative PVRs to pictures of the nonpreferred sex. If they did, other individuals must have shown positive PVRs to these pictures, indicating bisexuality, as when all PVRs were summed together the mean PVRs, on which Freund based his conclusions, were minimally positive.

A strain gauge measure of PC was introduced to assess penile tumescence during sleep (Fisher, Gross, & Zuck, 1965). Bancroft, Jones and Pullan (1966) assumed that with penile tumescence, PC increase would be proportional to increase in length, and stated that the strain gauge measured true volume changes and hence sexual arousal. No immediate attempt was made to validate these statements. In 1971 Bancroft reported that of 30 homosexual men whose PCRs to pictures of men and women were recorded, only 14 showed correlations between PCRs and subjective ratings of sexual arousal which reached significance ($r = .65 +$). The 14 whose PCRs were valid were mainly those subjects with mean penile diameter increases greater than .4mm. The lack of validity of PCRs in subjects whose PCRs were less than .4mm is consistent with the author's observation that PCRs associated with early tumescence are likely to be misleading. The mean responses of the total group of 30 to pictures of men were significantly greater than those to pictures of women, but the number of individuals whose responses were indicative of homosexuality was not given.

A similar low level of validity was demonstrated by Mavissakalian, Blanchard, Abel, and Barlow (1975). They found significant differences between the mean PCs of six homosexual and six heterosexual men to videos of same and opposite sex couples having sexual relations, but not to 2-minute black and white video pictures of nude women displaying provocative sexual behavior. By the time this report was published the use of PCRs to pictures of women was established as a measure of response in single-case studies of behavioral treatment in homosexuality (Barlow & Agras, 1973; Herman, Barlow, & Agras, 1974b; McGrady, 1973).

Laws and Rubin (1969) showed that some subjects were able to markedly reduce the extent of their PCRs in response to 10–12 minutes of erotic movies. PVRs are recorded for 10–13 seconds from stimulus onset. The longer duration of exposure to erotic stimuli needed to produce consistent PCRs is a probable factor in making PCRs more susceptable to voluntary control. With the longer period of exposure to the stimulus, subjects have the opportunity to fantasize and so, not necessarily deliberately, introduce stimuli into their fantasy at variance with that presented. This could explain the reports of homosexual subjects treated by regular exposure to pictures of women who developed 80% to complete erections to the pictures while experiencing no increase in their heterosexual feelings (Barlow & Agras, 1973; McGrady, 1973). The technique (Abel, Barlow, Blanchard, & Guild, 1977) of recording subjects' PCRs while they listen to a 2-minute audiotaped vivid description of sexual activity might reduce this uncontrolled aspect of the sexual fantasy and increase the validity of the procedure. However, Alford, Wedding, and Jones (1983) reported a subject who consciously used fantasy to alter his PCRs to such audiotapes very effectively.

Quinsey and Bergersen (1980) reported that normal subjects could influence their PCRs to pictures of nude adults and children so as to appear pedophilic. Quinsey, Steinman, Bergersen, and Holmes (1975) found that molesters of female children showed maximal PCRs to pictures of such children compared to males or females of other ages but failed to replicate the finding (Quinsey, Chaplin, & Carrigan, 1979). Murphy, Abel, and Becker (1980) reported that the PCRs of 16 exhibitionists to deviant images declined over four baseline sessions prior to treatment and concluded that such responses could be of no use to assess their response to treatment. Murphy, Krisak, Stalgaitis, and Anderson (1984) failed to replicate a report by Abel and colleagues differentiating rapists from nonrapists by their PCRs to 2-minute video scenes of consenting intercourse, rape, and aggression devoid of sexual connotations. They concluded the use of PCR assessment with certain populations is not highly valid.

Kockott, Feil, Ferstl, Aldenhoff, and Besinger (1980) carried out one of the few studies comparing PCRs to erotic film stimuli in sexually dysfunctional and control males. The Mean erection amplitude and latency of erection were significantly reduced for the group of patients with secondary psychogenic impotence and diabetes with impotence, but not for patients with primary psychogenic impotence or premature ejaculation. Correlations between PCRs and self-rated arousal were low in all groups.

Blader and Marshall (1984) recently confronted the considerable amount of evidence that penile response measures are inconsistent with subjective measures of sexual arousal. They accounted for the inconsistency by referring to the concept questioned earlier in this chapter, but which they label axiomatic, that the physiological, motor, and cognitive systems provide relatively independent valid measures of the same emotion. They considered it remained unclear which response (i.e., PCR or self-report) better predicted behavior. They did not say what behavior. They followed the lead of most academics in viewing PVRs and PCRs as identical and ignored the data at variance with this three-systems explanation of the low correlation between physiological measures and awareness of sexual arousal, namely, that PVRs have repeatedly been shown to correlate highly with individual subject's awareness of their degree of sexual arousal to one versus the other sex.

Hall, Binik, and DiTomasso (1985) also used the three-systems model to account for the inconsistency between PCRs and sexual arousal assessment found in their study. They recorded the PCRs of 20 university students to $4\frac{1}{2}$-minute audiotaped descriptions of heterosexual intercourse while the students continuously monitored the subjective level of arousal by moving a dial, a technique introduced by Wincze, Hoon, and Hoon (1977). Correlations between the two measures varied from .22 to .95. High correlations (> .70) occurred in subjects who showed greater penile arousal. These results would seem consistent with those of Bancroft (1971) with homosexual subjects as mentioned earlier. About half of the subjects showed significant correlations between PCRs and subjective arousal, showing greater PCRs. Hall et al. concluded that some subjects possess a synchrony between the two measures of arousal while others do not. They did not discuss why more subjects appeared to possess a synchrony when assessed by PVRs.

Although PCRs have been demonstrated frequently to lack validity and invariably to correlate significantly with subjective sexual arousal in only about half the individuals tested, studies reporting PCRs appear with increasing frequency. Invocation of the three-systems theory has obviated any need for further attempts at validation. The author's finding that the PCRs accompanying the commencement or termination of sexual arousal may be in the opposite direction to the actual tumescence or detumescence agrees with Bancroft's and Hall et al.'s findings of lack of validity of PCRs below a certain amplitude. If such responses are excluded from analysis, the validity of PCRs in discriminating groups might be improved. Also, it would seem wise to use highly arousing erotic stimuli to increase the validity of PCRs rather than the mildly arousing stimuli adequate for valid PVR assessment. In view of the frequent failures of replication of PCR studies, findings of such studies should be treated with more than the usual caution until they are replicated. When PCRs are used to investigate an individual subject, the 50% probability that they will correlate poorly with his subjective awareness of arousal should be kept in mind.

PCR assessment would appear to be of little clinical value. Kilmann, Sabalis, Gearing, Bukstel, and Scovern (1982) concluded that it was of questionable use in assessing outcome of treatment of paraphilias. As discussed previously, PVR assessments of subjects' sexual orientation did not change significantly following behavioral therapies for homosexuality (McConaghy, 1977, 1982). In view of the demonstrated validity of this assessment, it would be of theoretical value if those therapists who believe treatment does change male patients' sexual orientation (Masters & Johnson, 1979; Pattison & Pattison, 1980) demonstrated the change with this physiological measure.

Independent of their use in assessment of sexual arousal, PCRs are widely recommended to record nocturnal penile tumescence (NPT) in impotent subjects on the basis that those who show regular sustained erections with this procedure have impotence of psychogenic origin (Karacan, 1978). As discussed earlier, this did not seem to be true in a number of the author's patients. It was considered doubtful that this expensive assessment added significantly to an adequate clinical history. Fisher, Schiavi, Edwards, Davis, Reitman, and Fine (1979) concluded that some subjects with organic impotence obtained normal erections while asleep, but these were reduced in frequency and duration compared with those of subjects with psychogenic impotence. However, they also concluded that the latter subjects could show impaired nocturnal erections. It is not clear from their study how the subjects with organic and psychogenic impotence were differentiated. Marshall, Surridge, and Delva (1981) selected 20 patients, 10 with an established organic cause for impotence and no psychogenic factors and 10 with the reverse. By selecting cutting points that best discriminated the two groups, they could correctly classify 16 of the 20 on the basis of their maximum NPT and 19 on the frequency of their NPT, over 2 nights. They were aware that the study needed replication to be meaningful.

Procci and Martin (1984) reported NPTs from the second-night use of a portable monitor in 50 normal controls, 25 patients with nonrenal chronic illness and 48 with end-stage renal disease. Sexual function and NPT responses were unimpaired in the normal group. Five of the nonrenal chronically ill had impaired sexual function but normal NPT scores. Twenty-three of the renal patients had impaired sexual function, of whom 10 had abnormal NPT scores; 25 had normal sexual function, of whom 9 had abnormal NPT scores. In view of the virtual absence of a relationship between impaired sexual function and abnormal NPT scores in the renal patients, the authors' conclusion that the data were reasonably congruent seems remarkable.

If observation of a patient's erection and assessment of its rigidity is carried out when NPT indicates its presence, as Karacan (1978) advised, the technique may better discriminate psychogenic from organic impotence. Researchers interested in investigating NPT might prefer to commence with the less expensive method of having the subject place a ring of stamps around the penis before retiring (Barry, Blank, & Boileau, 1980).

Assessment of sexual arousal in women by measurement of genital physiological changes has been attempted using a variety of devices, including vaginal blood flow by thermistor, vaginal pulse amplitude and blood volume by photoplethysmograph, labial temperature by thermistor, clitoral blood flow by photoplethysmograph, and clitoral volume change by strain gauge. Hoon (1979) comprehensively reviewed the assessment of sexual arousal in women and concluded that color changes within the vagina measured by photoplethysmograph and labial temperature changes recorded by thermistor appeared to provide the most sensitive measures of arousal, in that they significantly distinguished the response of groups of women to erotic as compared to nonerotic stimuli. Correlations of these measures with subjective awareness of sexual arousal, presence of dysfunctions, and response to treatment have proved inconsistent, those with sexual arousal being lower than the equivalent correlations of PCRs with sexual arousal (Hatch, 1981; Wincze & Qualls, 1984). The inconsistent and lower correlations in women have been attributed to not instructing subjects to attend to bodily cues and to not using scaling methods (Korff & Geer, 1983). The useful three-systems explanation for such low correlations is, to the author's knowledge, yet to be employed.

Wincze and Qualls (1984) reported a significant difference in the mean maximum vaginal blood pressure amplitude of eight homosexual women measured by photoplethysmography to five 4-minute films. The greatest response was to the film with explicit lesbian sexual activity. The mean maximum responses to the films did not differ significantly. Individual correlations between maximal physiological and reported arousal to each film varied from $r = .26$ to $.89$; the average for the group was not significant. The equivalent correlations in eight homosexual men who viewed the same films while assessed by PCR were $r = .62$ to $.98$; the average was significant.

Recent studies of vaginal blood flow during orgasm used a heated oxygen electrode attached to the vaginal wall as a transducer rather than a photoplethysmograph, in response to the criticism that the latter is unsuitable for measuring vasoconstriction at high levels of sexual excitement.

Amberson and Hoon (1985) and Levin and Wagner (1985) both used the oxygen electrode to investigate orgasms produced in their subjects by self-masturbation in a laboratory. One-half of Amberson and Hoon's sample and two of Levin and Wagner's sample used a vibrator. In both studies subjects were asked to signal the onset and end of their orgasms. This provided the most intriguing result of the two studies. The duration of orgasm in the 17 American women, aged 23 to 46 years, studied by Amberson and Hoon ranged from 30 to 120 sec — mean = 48, SD = 30. The mean duration of orgasm of 26 Danish women of mean age 28, SD = 4, studied by Levin and Wagner, was 20 sec, SD = 12. Of the 17 U.S. subjects, 16 masturbated to orgasm in succession at least twice, 8 three times, 4 four times, and 1 seven times. It is not clear if they were specially selected. Levin and Wagner found no relation between vaginal blood flow (electrode power consumption) and intensity, duration, or latency of orgasm in their subjects.

Vaginal blood flow during REM sleep has been shown to be significantly increased, using both thermistors and plethysmographs. It was suggested this assessment may aid in determining if organic factors are contributing to sexual dysfunctions in women (Roger, Van de Castle, Evans, & Critelli, 1985).

At present it would seem that physiological measurement of genital arousal in women has no significant clinical value.

Other Physiological Responses

In 1971 Zuckerman fully reviewed the use of galvanic skin resistance (GSR), cardiovascular and respiratory function, pupillary size, skin temperature, evoked cortical potentials, and hormone levels, as well as penile erection measures and vaginal blood flow, to assess sexual excitement or response to erotic stimuli. He commented that the GSR had been the most favored psychophysiological toy of psychologists and there had been a flurry of interest in pupil size, but he stressed the lack of specificity of these responses as indices of sexual arousal. He pointed out the sensitivity of penile erection measures, demonstrated by the extensive studies of Freund using PVRs, but he unfortunately endorsed the assumption that PCRs provided identical measures of erection. Either in response to the review or the lack of specificity of the other physiological measures — or both — most attention since then has been paid to measures of genital arousal in assessment of sexual activity.

Two studies have reported successful differentiation of sexually anomalous subjects by GSR. Using the film developed by the author containing 10-second movie segments of nude women and men, Barr (1973) found that male transsexuals, unlike homosexual or heterosexual men, showed greater GSRs to the films of the nonpreferred rather than the preferred sex (in their case, women rather than men). Their PVR responses to the films of men as compared to women, assessed by U scores, were significantly greater than those of the homosexual subjects. The transsexuals stated that although they were not sexually interested in women, they were interested in their bodies. Kercher and Walker (1973) differentiated subjects convicted of rape from those convicted of nonsexual crimes by the significantly greater GSRs of the rapists to slides of subjects in romantic poses or involved in sexual activities.

In a previously mentioned study investigating the PCRs of sexually dysfunctional men to erotic and neutral films, Kockott et al. (1980) also recorded the subjects' GSRs and blood pressure. The erotic films produced marked increases in the mean systolic and diastolic blood pressure of all groups of subjects — those with primary and secondary impotence and premature ejaculation as well as controls — and in the number of spontaneous fluctuations in GSRs of all groups except those with primary impotence. The study indicated that the sexually dysfunctional were as emotionally reactive to the erotic films as the controls.

Hoenig and Kenna (1979) reviewed the literature reporting a relationship between temporal lobe electroencephalographic (EEG) abnormalities or epilepsy and sexual deviations, in particular fetishism, transvestism, and transsexualism. They carried out EEG examinations on 46 of 75 consecutive referrals for transsexualism. The EEGs were abnormal in 48% and borderline abnormal in a further 24%. However, no controls were used, and EEG assessment is notoriously subjective.

An anal probe has been used in men and women, along with a vaginal probe in the latter, to study the pattern of muscular contractions accompanying orgasm and their relation to its duration and intensity (Bohlen, Held, & Sanderson, 1980; Bohlen, Held, Sanderson, & Ahlgren, 1982). Strength of the pubococcygeal muscle in women was assessed by perineometer but contrary to previous findings did not correlate with frequency or intensity of orgasm (Chambless et al., 1982).

A number of techniques are used to determine the adequacy of the penile blood supply for erection, the most commonly employed being assessment of penile blood pressure. Metz and Bengtsson (1981) investigated the reliability and validity of penile strain gauge and ultrasonic pencil doppler for this assessment. Both are used to determine when blood flow returns to the penis as the pressure is reduced in an inflatable cuff around the penis. The indices of penile blood pressure used were the ratios of its measured values over brachial blood pressures determined concurrently. Mean indices from the two techniques in the group studied were .87 (SD +/- .11) and .83 (SD +/- .08), with a normal range of .7–1. The authors used the mean of the indices from both techniques for each individual patient. When the group was divided by age, the older men had significantly lower indices. In men with peripheral arteriosclerotic disease, the mean of 33 who were potent was .77

(SD +/- .13) and that of 32 who were impotent was .58 (SD +/- .15). Metz and Bengtsson recommended .60 as the dividing line below which the index indicated a penile blood pressure inadequate to maintain potency. The index misclassified 22% of their arteriosclerotic subjects in terms of their actual potency. The nature of the misclassification cannot be determined from the report, as the authors by error changed the number of the potent and impotent men. They concluded that an index below .60 in repeated determinations suggests that arterial insufficiency is a probable cause of impotence, but a higher index does not exclude it as a possibility. This conforms with the author's experience that penile blood pressure is not infrequently reported as adequate when organic vascular factors appear involved in patients' impotence. It would seem advisable for therapists who refer subjects for this investigation to discover the misclassification rate of the technique being employed. There is an unjustified tendency for psychotherapists to accept physical investigations as having a validity which psychological assessments lack.

Metz and Bengtsson (1981) recommended that other methods of determining the adequacy of the penile blood supply be employed when the penile blood pressure index indicates normal function. These methods involve arteriography and corpora cavernosography, procedures not without risk. If an organic cause is still suspected for impotence when medical, endocrine, and vascular causes have been ruled out, it has been recommended that the patient be referred for neurological investigation (Freund & Blanchard, 1981). In the author's experience, such referral has proved worthwhile only when obvious neurological symptoms were present. Impotence and other sexual dysfunctions have been shown to be related to peripheral and autonomic neuropathy in diabetic men and women (Hosking, et al., 1979; Jensen, 1981). Possibly, investigations such as the latency of the bulbocavernosus reflex and the latency and form of cerebral potentials evoked by glans penis and peroneal nerve stimulation will prove of value in demonstrating less apparent neurological causes of impotence (Ertekin, Akyurekli, Gurses, & Turgut, 1985).

The author has not been able to establish from clinicians or the literature the usefulness in the physically healthy of the available investigations in determining organic factors contributing to impotence. To balance this comment it should be pointed out that urologists have questioned the value of psychiatric or psychological assessment of patients seeking penile implant surgery for impotence (Blake, McCartney, Fried, & Fehrenbaker, 1983).

Hormone Assessment

Though it is accepted that hormones play a major role in maintaining sexual functions in men and women, the relationships between blood hormone levels and these functions have not been clarified. A reported rise in the frequency of intercourse and orgasm in women mid-menstrually and increased desire premenstrually have been attributed to high and low estrogen levels present at those times respectively (Morokoff, 1978). McCoy, Cutler, and Davidson (1985) found an association between hot flushes, declining frequency of intercourse, and declining estradiol levels in perimenopausal women. No studies appear to have related female sexual dysfunctions to hormone levels. Likewise, no relationship has been found between the frequency of men's sexual activity and testosterone levels. It has been suggested that the level in healthy men is well above the threshold necessary for sexual activity (McConaghy, 1984). This is consistent with the finding that the majority of men treated with medroxyprogesterone sufficient to reduce their testosterone by an averge of 70% maintained their potency and pretreatment frequency of heterosexual intercourse for the 6 months of treatment. They reported reduced sexual interest, the reduction in their paraphilic urges correlating significantly with reduction in their testosterone levels (McConaghy, Blaszczynski, & Kidson, 1986). Findings of significantly lower testosterone levels in men with impotence of organic as compared to psychogenic etiology have not been replicated (Schiavi & White, 1976). Both zero and positive correlations have been reported between reponse to behavioral therapy of impotent men and their pretreatment testosterone levels (Schwartz, Kolidny, & Masters, 1980; Takefman & Brender, 1984).

Reports of relationships between sexual orientation and hormone levels have been conflicting. Meyer-Bahlburg (1977, 1979) reviewed the relevant literature and concluded that no relationship had been consistently demonstrated in men, but about one-third of lesbian and transsexual women studies had elevated androgen levels. Doerner (1983) and Gladue, Green, and Hellman (1984) have both replicated Doerner's earlier finding of a positive estrogen feedback effect on luteinizing hormone (LH) in homosexual men but not in heterosexual or bisexual men. Doerner (1978) also reported a weak or moderate estrogen feedback effect on LH in transsexual women with homosexual behavior, as compared to the strong effect in heterosexual women. Gaffney and Berlin (1984) reported a marked LH response to LHRH (luteinizing-hormone releasing hormone) in seven mainly homosexual pedophiles, compared to five fetishists, exhibitionists, or voyeurs and five controls. The consistently reported relationship between tomboyism in girls and their prenatal exposure to increased levels of androgens (Ehrhardt & Money, 1967; Ehrhardt & Baker, 1974) does not seem to have been disputed, though its causal significance has. Loewit, Schwarz, and Voigt (1978) supported this significance, suggesting a link between urinary maternal testosterone levels in the 6th to 12th week of pregnancy and later tomboyism.

CASE STUDY: ASSESSMENT OF A PEDOPHILE

G. S. appeared for an interview, having failed to keep an initial appointment. A smartly dressed, good-looking youth with a confident manner, he appeared some years older than his age of 19. Early the previous year he had been charged with indecently assaulting some young boys in a park. He had been assessed by a psychologist, who in his report noted that the patient treated the interview as an imposition on his time. He told the psychologist of a previous conviction for a similar offense 2 years previously, and 8 to 10 other "experiences with young kids" for which he had not been apprehended. He confessed that his behavior was compulsive and that he had little control over it. The psychologist reported being alarmed by the patient's lack of concern for his deviant behavior. His major concern was with what would happen to him in court and what people would think of him. There were unspecified "cameo insights" which led the psychologist to believe that the patient had disturbing aspects to his personality, aspects which had their roots in his somewhat chaotic childhood and which required professional intervention.

A probation officer subsequently prepared a presentence report. The patient informed the officer of a disrupted childhood due to frequent residential changes, as his family shifted from one fast food business to another. His parents argued frequently with occasional physical altercations. The patient had nonexistent communication with his father, who provided no discipline. His mother was permissive and lenient, seeking the children's support. His education was disrupted by the residential changes and absenteeism due to involvement in the family business. His school performance was below his level of ability, and he left school at age 17 against his parents' advice. The offender showed a healthy attitude toward the need to work, having an unstated number of jobs as kitchen or counter hand in take-out food establishments. Five months previously he was made trainee manager, but also earned $300 a week selling artwork door to door. He had an outstanding debt of $6,000 on a car he was leasing. He also had outstanding fines and compensation payments to make for two offenses of false pretenses. A warrant had been issued for nonpayment of $450 compensation, but it was temporarily withdrawn when his father paid $240 of the amount. When seen by a psychiatrist 2 years prior for the first sexual offense, it had been considered due to "situational stress" and not indicative of "ongoing sexual perversion." He had no organized or constructive leisure activities, and though he claimed to have associates it seemed he was very much on the periphery of any group activities. He could offer no explanation for his behavior, which he acknowledged was very wrong but which he could not help. He claimed to have no homosexual persuasion and to have experienced normal heterosexual acts with a school friend 4 years previously. He impressed the probation officer as having little preparedness to be reflective and to confront the dilemma. It was concluded he had been adversely affected by his family and social environment and that he was isolated, insecure, and self-centered. In the home he was disruptive, manipulative, and temperamental. He did not have the psychological capacity to confront his conduct, but it seemed he might benefit from further psychological investigation and possibly treatment. His residing away from home under the supervision of the probation service was recommended. It was pointed out that he had not contacted the probation officer as instructed and had to be pursued at his place of employment.

The court accepted the recommendation of the probation officer, who subsequently referred the patient to a community psychiatric service. The psychiatrist there referred him to the author for possible aversive therapy for pedophilia, having told the subject his acceptance of this was voluntary. She provided the additional information that he had been convicted of a number of traffic offenses, and at age 13 he was required to appear in court due to his school absenteeism. She concluded that he displayed a significant number of antisocial traits and probably could be classified as suffering from personality disorder, a label she was reluctant to put on a 19-year-old boy.

The author is not reluctant to consider that psychopathic personality can be sufficiently established in 19 year olds that it will produce characteristic behavioral features for the next several years. Psychopathy is commonly associated with a history of disturbed parental relationships. The correlation could be causal, such relationships producing psychopathy. It could reflect the action of genetic factors, which produced both the parents' behaviors and the child's psychopathy. It could be due to an interaction between these environmental and genetic variables (McConaghy, 1979). In the author's experience, though most therapists believe psychopathy to be due to disturbed relationships, it is very difficult to find a therapist who will treat psychopathic patients in long-term intensive therapy. From previous reports, the author hypothesized that the patient was significantly psychopathic and that history-taking should reveal further evidence of minimal ethical values. If accepted for treatment, his compliance would be difficult to maintain and his self-reports would need to be treated with suspicion. Corroborative evidence should be sought, but the patient would be likely to make this difficult. All these predictions were verified.

Seeking details of the patient's daily activities in the initial interview, it was learned that he slept until 1 p.m. and then worked until 10 p.m. Asked if this limited his social activities, the patient responded that he socialized with customers, drinking beer or coffee with them, and added "you make them friendly." With nonjudgmental follow-up of this comment he somewhat boastfully said: "You must tell 50 or 60 lies in one house" and revealed that in selling paintings door to door he made up plausible stories to increase sales, such as that he was the painter, an impecunious student who used the money to work his way through art school. His employers encouraged this practice and employed a team of young people to sell mass-produced paintings for much more than their value. The patient made several hundred dollars a week, which was not declared for taxation. He subsequently produced a health card, revealing he was receiving government unemployment benefits. Apart from attempting to justify his behavior because of his debts, he showed no evidence of concern for the families he exploited, nor for the possible effects of his past sexual behavior toward children. He reported that he had on several occasions touched the genitals of boys 6 to 8 years of age, through their clothes, when they had been playing in the street and came up to the patient to pat his dog. The patient denied any pedophilic behavior since the offenses for which he was charged, but said he was aware of strong urges that he wished to control. He reported equal sexual interest in girls his own age and boys aged 6–8, both when he saw them in the street and in masturbatory fantasies. He said he had had intercourse with a few girls without difficulty and had seen one steadily for 8 months. He had no current relationship, and his main social life was with customers and his young work colleagues with whom he socialized after work from 10 p.m. to 12 a.m.

It is the author's practice to treat all patients who say they wish to control compulsive sexual urges provided they are not actively psychotic. The patient was therefore offered treatment. He replied that he knew about the sort of treatment he would be given and he certainly was not going to have it. He had been led to expect he would receive aversive therapy. He was offered medroxyprogesterone treatment, the details of which were explained. He was told if he accepted this he could discontinue treatment whenever he wished, but he would be expected to attend follow-up interviews at 1 and 2 years after treatment was initiated. As long as he accepted treatment, his probation officer would be informed if he failed to keep appointments regularly and could be expected to put pressure on him to attend. This proved necessary on a few occasions, as following his acceptance of treatment he regularly missed appointments, usually without prior cancellation, but subsequently providing plausible explanations, entertaining in their variety. He did risk exhausting his supply of ill or recently deceased relatives before termination of follow-up. As he had been convicted of several offenses, both sexual and nonsexual, in the previous two years, it was considered that further charges would provide a degree of negative or positive corroboration of his reports. He refused to allow any contacts to be interviewed, saying that none knew of his recent sexual offenses and they might learn of these if they were interviewed.

In the 2 years after treatment began he was not charged with any offenses. He reported marked reduction and good control of his pedophilic urges and the establishment of an 8-month heterosexual relationship, which terminated when the girl involved traveled overseas. Discussing the relationship he wondered if his sex drive was a bit high as he and his girlfriend were having intercourse daily. She had said, "You can't show affection without dragging sex into it." Whether this was evidence of the reality of the relationship or an example of his lying, one can only speculate. Lack of charges for criminal behavior is the only evidence to support the validity of this patient's report. There was no advantage to his lying to the author, as he had been assured that (a) the information he gave would remain confidential and therefore would not alter his legal management and (b) his decision in regard to treatment would always be accepted. As a research subject, he would seem unsuitable for single-case study. In a group design, his possible dishonesty would have less influence on the results of the total group, most of whom would be more likely honest. This was evidenced by the significant correlation of such subjects' reported responses to medroxyprogesterone treatment with the reduction it produced in their serum testosterone levels (McConaghy, Blaszczynski, & Kidson, 1986).

SUMMARY

The behaviorist rejection of intuitive assessment of patients' self-reports in favor of rating scale or objective assessment of their behavior is criticized, and evidence is advanced that intuitive assessment may be more valid. The intuitive assessments of the most able clinicians will differ from those of their colleagues, thus being less reliable and more valid. Unlike academics who are under pressure to sacrifice validity to demonstrable reliability, clinicians must aim to maximize validity in assessment at the expense of demonstrable reliability. Behavioral academics are beginning to stress the need to establish the treatment validity of assessment procedures, and many behavioral clinician-academics now rely on clinical interview as the major vehicle for assessment.

Ways in which the flexibility of the clinical interview allows the interviewer to increase the validity of subjects' reports are discussed. By modifying directiveness, the interviewer obtains information to establish hypotheses concerning the subject's motivation and personality. It is suggested that these are now the major determinants of patients' failure to respond to the available behavioral techniques for sexual disorders and dysfunctions, rather than inadequacies in the techniques themselves. If this is so, personality assessment must become a significant component of behavioral assessment, requiring re-evaluation of the historic opposition of behaviorism to the concept of personality. It is suggested that a behavioral interview for sexual problems may differ from a psychodynamic interview in the emphasis placed on the consequences — that is, the reinforcements — of the behaviors to be modified, rather than on the situations in which they occur or the detailed nature of the behaviors themselves. Establishment of the nature of the consequences requires knowledge of the patient's total lifestyle. Interview assessment of specific sexual disorders are discussed. Adolescents pose a particular problem. The use of the interview for assessment must not impair its role in maintaining the patient in treatment.

Reduction in the validity of behavioral inventories due to demand characteristics, expectancy, and reactivity are discussed, as are problems in patients' compliance with them. Research findings have been distorted due to ideological preference for rating scale rather than global intuitive assessment. Rating scales may be insensitive — as in assessment of the response to oversize therapy in homosexuality, or too sensitive — as in assessment of the response to behavioral marital therapy. Their use has led to reification of sets of responses into entities such as masculinity and femininity. The rating-scale assessment of these entities is then treated as having a unique validity greater than that of subjects' actual behaviors. This has resulted in academic rejection of the relationship between opposite sex dimorphic behavior in male children and their later homosexuality, found in numerous prospective and retrospective studies. Anonymous questionnaires may prove valuable in resolving disparities in the literature concerning the incidence of socially embarrassing sexual behaviors which many subjects, particularly adolescents, will not reveal in interviews. The major disparity of this sort is between the relatively high incidence of homosexual feelings reported in surveys as compared with the minimal incidence reported in etiological studies.

Observation of sexual behavior has rarely been employed in assessment of dysfunctions and deviations other than with sex-role behavior. Rejection of observation is presumably due to social taboos, which apply less to recording of physiological concomitants of sexual behaviors. That most commonly employed is the assessment of penile circumference responses (PCRs) to erotic stimuli. The evidence that PCRs can be mirror images of the accompanying penile volume responses (PVRs) has been virtually ignored, and the demonstrated validity of PVRs — particularly in assessing the sexual orientation of individual subjects — has been accepted as applying to PCRs. In only about half of the subjects investigated do PCRs correlate significantly with concurrent assessment of sexual arousal. Many subjects show negative PVRs to pictures of the nonpreferred sex, confounding research in which mean PVRs of groups of predominantly heterosexual and homosexual subjects are compared. PVR assessment of sexual orientation does not change significantly following behavioral therapy in homosexuality. PCRs do not appear to be of value in assessing response to treatment in paraphilias. PCR assessment of nocturnal penile tumescence is widely recommended to differentiate organic from psychogenic impotence, but this use has never been validated.

A variety of physiological measures has been used to assess sexual arousal in women, but these have proved less consistent than PCRs in men and have not yet been shown to possess clinical value. The use of other physiological responses in sexual assessment has been uncommon apart from penile blood pressure as an index of adequacy of blood supply in impotence. The misclassification rate of the method employed should be established. Reported correlations between hormonal measures and sexual behaviors have proved difficult to replicate in the past, but more recent findings of potential clinical significance may prove valid.

REFERENCES

Abel, G. G., Barlow, D. H., Blanchard, E. B., & Guild, D. (1977). The components of rapists' sexual arousal. *Archives of General Psychiatry, 34,* 895–903.

Abel, G. G., Blanchard, E. B., & Barlow, D. H. (1981). Measurement of sexual arousal in several paraphilias: The effects of stimulus modality, instructional set and stimulus content on the objective. *Behaviour Research and Therapy, 19,* 25–33.

Akers, R. L. (1973). *Deviant behavior: A social learning approach.* Belmont, CA: Wadsworth Publishing Co.

Alford, G. S., Wedding, D., & Jones, S. (1983). Faking "turn-ons" and "turn-offs." *Behavior Modification, 7,* 112–125.

Amberson, J. I., & Hoon, P. W. (1985). Hemodynamics of sequential orgasm. *Archives of Sexual Behavior, 14,* 351–360.

Appel, M. A., Saab, P. G., & Holroyd, K. A. (1985). Cardiovascular disorders. In M. Hersen & A. S. Bellack (Eds.), *Handbook of clinical behavior therapy with adults* (pp. 381–346). New York: Plenum Press.

AuBuchon, P. G., & Calhoun, K. S. (1985). Menstrual cycle symptomatology: The role of social expectancy and experimental demand characterics. *Psychosomatic Medicine, 47,* 35–45.

Bakwin, H. (1968). Deviant gender role behavior in children: Relation to homosexuality. *Pediatrics, 41,* 620–629.

Bakwin, H., & Bakwin, R. M. (1953). Homosexual behavior in children. *Journal of Pediatrics, 43,* 108–111.

Bancroft, J. (1971). The application of psychophysiological measures to the assessment and modification of sexual behavior. *Behaviour Research and Therapy, 9,* 119–130.

Bancroft, J., Jones, H. C., & Pullan, B. P. (1966). A simple transducer for measuring penile erections with comments on its use in the treatment of sexual disorders. *Behaviour Research and Therapy, 4,* 239–241.

Barlow, D. H., & Agras, W. S. (1973). Fading to increase heterosexual responsiveness in homosexuals. *Journal of Applied Behavior Analysis, 6,* 355–366.

Barlow, D. H., Leitenberg, H., & Agras, W. S. (1969). Experimental control of sexual deviation through manipulation of the noxious scene in covert sensitization. *Journal of Abnormal Psychology, 74,* 596–601.

Barr, R. F. (1973). Responses to erotic stimuli of transsexual and homosexual males. *British Journal of Psychiatry, 123,* 579–585.

Barry, J. M., Blank, B., & Boileau, M. (1980). Nocturnal penile tumescence monitoring with stamps. *Urology, 15,* 171–173.

Bates, J. E., Bentler, P. M., & Thompson, S. K. (1973). Measurement of deviant gender development in boys. *Child Development, 44,* 591–598.

Bellack, A. S., & Hersen, M. (1985) General considerations. In M. Hersen & A. S. Bellack (Eds.), *Handbook of clinical behavior therapy with adults* (pp. 3-19). New York: Plenum Press.

Bellack, A. S., Hersen, M., & Lamparaski, D. (1979). Role-play tests for assessing social skills: Are they valid? Are they useful? *Journal of Consulting and Clinical Psychology, 47,* 335-342.

Bender, L., & Paster, S. (1941). Homosexual trends in children. *American Journal of Orthopsychiatry, 11,* 730-743.

Berlin, F. S., & Meinecke, C. F. (1981). Treatment of sex offenders with antiandrogenic medication: Conceptualization, review of treatment modalities, and preliminary findings. *American Journal of Psychiatry, 138,* 601-607.

Bieber, I. (1962) *Homosexuality.* New York: Basic Books.

Birk, L., Huddleston,W., Miller, E., & Cohler, B. (1971). Avoidance conditioning for homosexuality. *Archives of General Psychiatry, 25,* 314-323.

Blader, J. C., & Marshall, W. L. (1984). The relationship between cognitive and erectile measures of sexual arousal in nonrapist males as a function of depicted aggression. *Behaviour Research and Therapy, 22,* 623-630.

Blake, D. J., McCartney, C., Fried, F. A., & Fehrenbaker, L. G. (1983). Psychiatric assessment of penile implant recipient. *Urology, 21,* 252-256.

Bohlen, J. G., Held, J. P., & Sanderson, M. O. (1980). The male orgasm: Pelvic contractions measured by anal probe. *Archives of Sexual Behavior, 9,* 503-521.

Bohlen, J. G., Held, J. P., Sanderson, M. O., & Ahlgren, A. (1982). The female orgasm: Pelvic contractions. *Archives of Sexual Behavior, 11,* 367-386.

Buhrich, N., & McConaghy, N. (1977). The clinical syndromes of femmiphilic transvestism. *Archives of Sexual Behavior, 6,* 397-412.

Chambless, D. L. (1985). Agoraphobia. In M. Hersen & A. S. Bellack (Eds.), *Handbook of clinical behavior therapy with adults* (pp.49-87). New York: Plenum Press.

Chambless, D. L., Stein, T., Sultan, F. E., Williams, A. J., Goldstein, A. J., Lineberger, M. H., Lifshitz, J. L., & Kelly, L. (1982). The pubococcygens and female orgasm: A correlational study with normal subjects. *Archives of Sexual Behavior, 11,* 479-490.

Cone, J. D. (1979). Confounded comparisons in triple response mode assessment research. *Behavioral Assessment, 1,* 85-95.

Constantinople, A. (1973). Masculinity-femininity: An exception to a famous dictum? *Psychological Bulletin, 80,* 389-407.

Constantinople, A. (1979). Sex-role acquisition: In search of the elephant. *Sex Roles, 5,* 121-133.

Conte, H. R. (1983). Development and use of self-report techniques for assessing sexual functioning: A review and critique. *Archives of Sexual Behavior, 12,* 555-576.

De Amicis, L. A. Goldberg, D. C., LoPiccolo, J., Friedman, J., & Davies, L. (1984). Three-year follow-up of couples evaluated for sexual dysfunction. *Journal of Sex and Marital Therapy, 10,* 215-228.

Doerner, G. (1978). Neuroendocrine aspects in the etiology of sexual deviations. In R. Forlei & W. Pasini (Eds.), *Medical Sexology.* (pp.190-198). Littleton, MA: PSG Publishing Co.

Doerner, G. (1983). Letter to the editor. *Archives of Sexual Behavior, 12,* 577-582.

Editorial. (1981a). Sex and physicians: Why is it so difficult to "tell it like it is?" *Journal of Nervous and Mental Disease, 169,* 605-607.

Editorial. (1981b). The ethics of antiandrogen therapy. *American Journal of*

Psychiatry, 138, 642–643.

Ehrhardt, A. A., & Baker, S. W. (1974). Fetal androgens, human central nervous system differentiation, and behavior sex differences. In R. C. Friedman & R. M. Richart (Eds.), *Sex differences in behavior.* New York: John Wiley & Sons.

Ehrhardt, A. A., & Money, J. (1967). Progestin-induced hermaphroditism: I.Q. and psychosexual identity in a study of ten girls. *Journal of Sexual Research, 3,* 83–100.

Emmelkamp. P. M. G. (1982). *Phobic and obsessive-compulsive disorders. Theory, research and practice.* New York: Plenum Press.

Ertekin, C., Akyurekli, O., Gurses, A. N., & Turgut, H. (1985). The value of somatosensory-evoked potentials and bulbocavernosus reflex in patients with impotence. *Acta Neurologica Scandinavica, 71,* 48–53.

Evans, R. B. (1969). Childhood parental relationships of homosexual men. *Journal of Consulting and Clinical Psychology, 33,* 129–135.

Fagot, B. I. (1977). Consequences of moderate cross-gender behavior in preschool children. *Child Development, 48,* 902–907.

Feldman, M. P., & MacCulloch, M. J. (1971). *Homosexual behavior: Therapy and assessment.* Oxford: Pergamon.

Fisher, C., Gross, J., & Zuck, J. (1965). Cycle of penile erection synchronous with dreaming (REM) sleep. *Archives of General Psychiatry, 12,* 29–45.

Fisher, C., Schiavi, R. C., Edwards, A., Davis, D. M., Reitman, M., & Fine, J. (1979). Evaluation of nocturnal penile tumescence in the differential diagnosis of sexual impotence. *Archives of General Psychiatry, 36,* 431–437.

Frank, E., Anderson, C., & Rubinstein, D. (1978). Frequency of sexual dysfunction in "normal" couples. *New England Journal of Medicine, 299,* 111–115.

Freund, K. (1963). A laboratory method of diagnosing predominance of homo- or hetero-erotic interest in the male. *Behaviour Research and Therapy, 1,* 85–93.

Freund, K., & Blanchard, R. (1981). Assessment of sexual dysfunction and deviation. In M. Hersen & A. S. Bellack (Eds.), *Behavioral assessment.* (pp.427–455). New York: Pergamon.

Freund, K., Langevin, R., Cibiri, S., & Zajac, Y. (1973). Heterosexual aversion in homosexual males. *British Journal of Psychiatry, 122,* 163–169.

Gaffney, G. R., & Berlin, F. S. (1984). Is there hypothalamic-pituitary-gonadal dysfunction in paedophilia? A pilot study. *British Journal of Psychiatry, 145,* 657–660.

Gladue, B. A., Green, R., & Hellman, R. E. (1984). Neuroendocrine response to estrogen and sexual orientation. *Science, 225,* 1496–1499.

Grayson, J. B., Foa, E. B., & Steketee, G. (1985). Obsessive-compulsive disorder. In M. Hersen & A. S. Bellack (Eds.), *Handbook of clinical behavior therapy with adults (pp.133–162).* New York: Plenum Press.

Green, R. (1985). Gender identity in childhood and later sexual orientation follow-up of 78 males. *American Journal of Psychiatry, 142,* 339–341.

Hall, K. S., Binik, Y., & Di Tomasso, E. (1985). Concordance between physiological and subjective measures of sexual arousal. *Behaviour Research and Therapy, 23,* 297–303.

Hart, J., & Richardson, D. (1981). *The theory and practice of homosexuality.* London: Routledge and Kegan Paul.

Hatch, J. P. (1981). Psychophysiological aspects of sexual dysfunction. *Archives of Sexual Behavior, 10,* 49–64.

Heilbrun, A. B., & Thompson, N. L. (1977). Sex-role identity and male and female homosexuality. *Sex Roles, 3,* 65–79.

Herman, S. H., Barlow, D. H., & Agras, W. S. (1974a). An experimental analysis of exposure to "explicit" heterosexual stimuli as an effective variable in changing arousal patterns of homosexuals. *Behaviour Research and Therapy, 12,* 335–345.

Herman, S. H., Barlow, D. H., & Agras, W. S. (1974b). An experimental analysis of classical conditioning as a method of increasing heterosexual arousal in homosexuals. *Behavior Therapy, 5,* 33–47.

Hersen, M. (1973). Self-assessment of fear. *Behavior Therapy, 4,* 241–257.

Hersen, M. (1981). Complex problems require complex situations. *Behavior Therapy, 12,* 15–29.

Hersen, M., & Bellack, A. S. (Eds.). (1985). *Handbook of clinical behavior therapy with adults.* New York: Plenum Press.

Hoenig, J., & Kenna, J. C. (1979). EEG abnormalities and transsexualism. *British Journal of Psychiatry, 134,* 293–300.

Holemon, R. E., & Winokur, G. (1965). Effeminate homosexuality: A disease of childhood. *American Journal of Orthomolecular Psychiatry, 35,* 48–56.

Hollon, S.D., & Jacobson, V. (1985). Cognitive approaches. In M. Hersen & A. S. Bellack (Eds.), *Handbook of clinical behavior therapy with adults* (pp.169–199). New York: Plenum Press.

Hoon, P. W. (1979). The assessment of sexual arousal in women. In M. Hersen, R. M. Eisler, & P. M. Miller (Eds.), *Progress in behavior modification:* (Vol. 7, pp.1–61). New York: Academic Press.

Hosking, D. J., Bennet, T., Hampton, J. R., Evans, D. F., Clark, A. J., & Robertson, G. (1979). Diabetic impotence: Studies of nocturnal erection during REM sleep. *British Medical Journal,* 1394–1396.

Jacobson, N. S., Follette, W. C., & Revenstorf, D. (1984). Psychotherapy outcome research: Methods for reporting variability and evaluating clinical significance. *Behavior Therapy, 15,* 336–352.

Jacobson, N. S., Follette, W. C., Revenstorf, D., Baucom, D. H., Hahlweg, K., & Margolin, G. (1984). Variability in outcome and clinical significance of behavioral marital therapy: A reanalysis of outcome data. *Journal of Consulting and Clinical Psychology, 52,* 497–504.

Jensen, S. B. (1981). Diabetic sexual dysfunction: A comparative study of 160 insulin treated diabetic men and women and an age-matched control group. *Archives of Sexual Behavior, 10,* 493–504.

Kagan, J., & Moss, H. A. (1962). *Birth to maturity.* New York: Wiley.

Karacan, I. (1978). Advances in the psychophysiological evaluation of male erectile impotence. In J. LoPiccolo & L. LoPiccolo (Eds.), *Handbook of sex therapy* (pp.137–145). New York: Plenum Press.

Katchadourian, H. A., Lunde, D. T., & Trotter, R. (1979). *Human sexuality.* New York: Holt, Rinehart, & Winston.

Kazdin, A. E. (1982). Methodological strategies in behavior-therapy research. In G. T. Wilson & C. M. Franks (Eds.), *Contemporary behavior therapy* (pp.403–442). New York: Guilford Press.

Kendell, R. E., Brockington, I. F., & Leff, J. P. (1979). Prognostic implications of six alternative definitions of schizophrenia. *Archives of General Psychiatry, 36,* 25–31.

Kercher, G. A., & Walker, C. E. (1973). Reactions of convicted rapists to sexually explicit stimuli. *Journal of Abnormal Psychology, 81,* 46–50.

Kilmann, P. R., Sabalis, R. F., Gearing, M. L., II, Bukstel, L. H., & Scovern, A. W. (1982). The treatment of sexual paraphilias: A review of the outcome research. *Journal of Sex Research, 18,* 193–252.

Kockott, G., Feil, W., Ferstl, R., Aldenhoff, J., & Besinger, U. (1980).

Psychophysiological aspects of male sexual inadequacy: Results of an experimental study. *Archives of Sexual Behavior, 9,* 477–493.

Korff, J., & Geer, J. (1983). The relationship between sexual arousal experience and genital response. *Psychophysiology, 20,* 121–127.

Lang, P. J. (1968). Fear reduction and fear behavior: Problems in treating a construct. In J. M. Shlein (Ed.), *Research in psychotherapy* (Vol. 3, pp.90–102). Washington, DC: American Psychological Association.

Lang, P. J. (1971). The application of psychophysiological methods to the study of psychotherapy and behavior modification. In A. E. Bergin & S. L. Garfield (Eds.), *Handbook of psychotherapy and behavior change* (pp.75–125). New York: Wiley.

Lang, P. J., & Lazovik, A. D. (1983). Experimental desensitization of a phobia. *Journal of Abnormal and Social Psychology, 66,* 519–525.

Lang, P. J., Lazovik, A. D., & Reynolds, D. J. (1965). Desensitization, suggestibility, and pseudotherapy. *Journal of Abnormal Psychology, 70,* 395–402.

Laws, D. R., & Rubin, H. H. (1969). Instructional control of an autonomic sexual response. *Journal of Applied Behavior Analysis, 2,* 93–99.

Lenney, E. (1979). Androgyny: Some audacious assertions toward its coming of age. *Sex Roles, 5,* 703–719.

Levin, R. J., & Wagner, G. (1985). Orgasm in women in the laboratory-quantitative studies on duration, intensity, latency, and vaginal blood flow. *Archives of Sexual Behavior, 14,* 439–449.

Lick, J. R., & Unger, T. E. (1977). The external validity of behavioral fear assessment. *Behavior Modification, 1,* 283–306.

Lineham, M. H. (1977). Issues in behavioral interviewing. In J. D. Cone & R. P. Hawkins (Eds.), *Behavioral assessment: New directions in clinical psychology* (pp.30–51). New York: Brunnel/Mazel.

Lipman, R. S., Cole, J. O., Park, L. C., & Rickels, K. (1965). Sensitivity of symptom and nonsymptom-focused criteria of outpatient drug efficacy. *American Journal of Psychiatry, 122,* 24–27.

Loewit, K., Schwarz, S., & Voigt, K. (1978). Fetal sex determination from early maternal testosterone excretion. In R. Forlei & W. Pasini (Eds.), *Medical sexology* (pp.202–209). Littleton, MA: PSG Publishing Co.

LoPiccolo, J., & Steger, J. C. (1974). The sexual interaction inventory: A new instrument for assessment of sexual dysfunction. *Archives of Sexual Behavior, 3,* 585–595.

Maccoby, E. E. (1980). *Social development.* New York: Harcourt, Brace, & Jovanovich.

Maletzky, B. M. (1980). Assisted covert sensitization. In D. J. Cox & R. J. Daitzman (Eds.), *Exhibitionism: Description, assessment, and treatment* (pp.289–293). New York: Garland STPM Press.

Marshall, P., Surridge, D., & Delva, N. (1981). The role of nocturnal penile tumescence in differentiating between organic and psychogenic impotent: The first stage of validation. *Archives of Sexual Behavior, 10,* 1–10.

Masters, W. H., & Johnson, V. E. (1966). *Human sexual response.* Boston: Little, Brown.

Masters, W. H., & Johnson, V. E. (1979). *Homosexuality in perspective.* Boston: Little, Brown.

Mavissakalian, M., Blanchard, E. B., Abel, G. G., & Barlow, D. H. (1975). Responses to complex erotic stimuli in homosexual and heterosexual males. *British Journal of Psychiatry, 126,* 252–257.

McConaghy, N. (1967). Penile volume change to moving pictures of male and female nudes in heterosexual and homosexual males. *Behaviour Research and Therapy, 5,* 43–48.

McConaghy, N. (1970). Results of systematic desensitization with phobias re-examined. *British Journal of Psychiatry, 117,* 89–92.

McConaghy, N. (1974). Measurements of change in penile dimensions. *Archives of Sexual Behavior, 3,* 381–388.

McConaghy, N. (1977). Behavioral treatment in homosexuality. In M. Hersen, R. M. Eisler, & P. M. Miller (Eds.), *Progress in behavior modification.* (Vol. 5, pp. 310–380). New York: Academic Press.

McConaghy, N. (1979). Maternal deprivation: Can its ghost be laid to rest? *Australian and New Zealand Journal of Psychiatry, 13,* 209–217.

McConaghy, N. (1981). Behavioral approaches to depression. *Australian and New Zealand Journal of Psychiatry, 15,* 217–222.

McConaghy, N. (1982). Sexual deviation. In A. S. Bellack, M. Hersen, & A. E. Kazdin (Eds.), *International handbook of behavior modification and therapy* (pp.683–716). New York: Plenum Press.

McConaghy, N. (1983). Agoraphobia, compulsive behaviors and behavior completion mechanisms. *Australian and New Zealand Journal of Psychiatry, 17,* 170–179.

McConaghy, N. (1984). Psychosexual disorders. In S. M. Turner & M. Hersen (Eds.), *Adult psychopathology and diagnosis* (pp. 370–405). New York: Wiley.

McConaghy, N. (1985). Psychosexual dysfunction. In M. Hersen & A. S. Bellack (Eds.), *Handbook of clinical behavior therapy with adults* (pp.659–692). New York: Plenum Press.

McConaghy, N. (1986). Learning approach. In J. H. Geer & W. T. O'Donohue (Eds.), *Approaches and paradigms in human sexuality.* New York: Plenum Press.

McConaghy, N. (1987). Penile volume response. In M. Hersen & A. S. Bellack (Eds.), *Dictionary of behavioral assessment techniques* (in press). New York: Pergamon Press.

McConaghy, N., & Armstrong, M. S. (1983). Sexual orientation and consistency of sexual identity. *Archives of Sexual Behavior, 12,* 317–327.

McConaghy, N., Armstrong, M. S., Birrell, P. C., & Buhrich N. (1979). The incidence of bisexual feelings and opposite sex behavior in medical students. *Journal of Nervous and Mental Disease, 167,* 685–688.

McConaghy, N., Armstrong, M. S., & Blaszczynski, A. (1985). Expectancy, covert sensitization and imaginal desensitization in compulsive sexuality. *Acta Psychiatrica Scandinavica, 72,* 176–187.

McConaghy, N., Armstrong, M. S., Blaszczynski, A., & Allcock, C. (1986). Behavioral completion, stimulus control, self-efficacy and expectancy in treatment of compulsive gambling. In press.

McConaghy, N., Blaszczynski, A., & Kidson, W. (1986). Treatment of sex offenders with imaginal desensitization and/or medroxyprogesterone. In press.

McCoy, N., Cutler, W., & Davidson, J. M. (1985). Relationship among sexual behavior, hot flushes, and hormone levels in perimenopausal women. *Archives of Sexual Behavior, 14,* 385–394.

McGrady, R. E. (1973). A forward-facing technique for increasing heterosexual responsiveness in male homosexuals. *Journal of Behavior Therapy and Experimental Psychiatry, 4,* 257–261.

Metz, P., & Bengtsson, J. (1981). Penile blood pressure. *Scandinavia Journal of Urology and Nephrology, 15,* 161–164.

Meyer-Behlburg, H. F. L. (1977). Sex hormones and male homosexuality in comparative perspective. *Archives of Sexual Behavior, 6,* 297–325.

Money, J., & Russo, A. J. (1979). Homosexual outcome of discordant gender identity/role in childhood: Longitudinal follow-up. *Journal of Pediatrics and Psychiatry, 4,* 27–41.

Morokoff, P. (1978). Determinants of female orgasm. In J. LoPiccolo & L. LoPiccolo (Eds.), *Handbook of sex therapy* (pp.147–165). New York: Plenum Press.

Murphy, W. D., Abel, G. G., & Becker, J. V. (1980). Future research issues. In D. J. Cox & R. J. Daitzman (Eds.), *Exhibitionism: description, assessment and treatment* (pp.339–392). New York: Garland Publishing.

Murphy, W. D., Krisak, J., Stalgaitis, S., & Anderson, K. (1984). The use of penile tumescence measures with incarcerated rapists: Further validity issues. *Archives of Sexual Behavior, 13,* 545–554.

Nelson, R. O., & Hayes, S. C. (1981). Nature of behavioral assessment: A practical handbook (2nd ed.). In M. Hersen & A. S. Bellack (Eds.), *Behavioral assessment* (pp.3–37). New York, Pergamon.

Nietzel, M. T., & Bernstein, A. D. A. Assessment of anxiety and fear. In M. Hersen & A. S. Bellack (Eds.), *Behavioral assessment: A practical handbook* (2nd ed., pp.215–245). New York: Pergamon.

Paredes, A., Baumgold, J., Pugh, L. A., & Ragland, R. (1966). Clinical judgment in the assessment of psychopharmacological effects. *Journal of Nervous and Mental Disease, 142,* 153–160.

Pattison, E. M., & Pattison, M. L. (1980). "Ex-gays": Religiously mediated change in homosexuals. *American Journal of Psychiatry, 137,* 1553–1568.

Paul, W., Weinrich, J. D., Gonsiorek, J. C., & Hotvedt, M. E. (1982). *Homosexuality.* Beverly Hills: Sage Publications.

Pleck, J. H. (1981). *The myth of masculinity.* Cambridge, MA: MIT Press.

Procci, W. R., & Martin, D. J. (1984). Preliminary observations of the utility of portable NPT. *Archives of Sexual Behavior, 13,* 569–580.

Quinsey, V. L., Chaplin, T. C., & Carrigan, W. F. (1979). Sexual preferences among incestuous and non-incestuous child molesters. *Behavior Therapy, 10,* 562–565.

Quinsey, V. L., Steinman, C. M., Bergersen, S. G., & Holmes, J. F. (1975). Penile circumference, skin conductance and ranking responses of child molesters and "normals" to sexual and non-sexual visual stimuli. *Behavior Therapy, 6,* 213–219.

Rachman, S. J. (1973). The effects of psychological treatment. In H. J. Eysenck (Ed.), *Handbook of abnormal psychology.* Belfast: Pitman Medical.

Reading, A. E. (1983). A comparison of the accuracy and reactivity of methods of monitoring male sexual behavior. *Journal of Behavioral Assessment, 5,* 11–23.

Rekers, G. A., & Lovaas, O. 1. (1974). Behavioral treatment of deviant sex-role behavior in a male child. *Journal of Applied Behavior Analysis, 7,* 173–190.

Resick, P. A. (1985). Sex role considerations for the behavior therapist. In M. Hersen & A. S. Bellack (Eds.), *Handbook of clinical behavior therapy with adults* (pp. 531–556). New York: Plenum Press.

Rogers, G. S., Van de Castle, R. L., Evans, W. S., & Critelli, J. W. (1985). Vaginal pulse amplitude response patterns during erotic conditions and sleep. *Archives of Sexual Behavior, 14,* 327–342.

Rosen, G. M., Glasgow, R. E., & Barrera, M. A. (1976). Unpublished manuscript, University of Oregon. Quoted in Lick and Unger (1977).

Rosen, R. C., & Keefe, R. J. (1978). The measurement of human penile tumescence. *Psychophysiology, 15,* 366–376.

Saghir, M. T., & Robins, E. (1973). *Male and female sexuality: A comprehensive investigation.* Baltimore: William & Wilkins.

Schatzberg, A. F., Westfall, M. P., Blumetti, A. B., & Birk, C. L. (1975). Effeminacy 1: A quantitative rating scale. *Archives of Sexual Behavior, 4,* 31–41.

Schiavi, R. C., Derogatis, L. R., Kuriansky, J., O'Connor, D., & Sharpe, I. (1979). The assessment of sexual function and marital interaction. *Journal of Sex and Marital Therapy, 5,* 169–224.

Schiavi, R. C., & White, D. (1976). Androgens and male sexual function: A review of human studies. *Journal of Sex and Marital Therapy, 2,* 214–228.

Schwartz, M. F., Kolodny, R. C., & Masters, W. H. (1980). Plasma testosterone levels of sexually functional and dysfunctional men. *Archives of Sexual Behavior, 9,* 355–366.

Takefman, J., & Brender, W. (1984). An analysis of the effectiveness of two components in the treatment of erectile dysfunction. *Archives of Sexual Behavior, 13,* 321–340.

Taylor, C. B., Agras, W. S., Schneider, J. A., & Allen, R. A. (1983). Adherence to instructions to practice relaxation exercises. *Journal of Consulting and Clinical Psychology, 51,* 952–953.

Udry, J. R., & Morris, N. M. (1967). A method for validation of reported sexual data. *Journal of Marriage and the Family, 29,* 442–446.

Wasserman, M. D., Pollak, C. P., Spielman, A. J., & Weitzman, E. D. (1980). Theoretical and technical problems in the measurement of nocturnal penile tumescence for the differential diagnosis of impotence. *Psychosomatic Medicine, 42,* 575–585.

Whitam, F. L. (1980). The prehomosexual male child in three societies: The United States, Guatemala, Brazil. *Archives of Sexual Behavior, 9,* 87–99.

Whiting, B. B. (1963). *Six cultures: Studies of child rearing.* New York: Wiley.

WHO Psychosexual Task Force Report. (1980). Acceptability of drugs for male fertility regulation. A prospectus and some preliminary data. *Contraception, 21,* 121–134.

Wincze, J. P., Hoon, P., & Hoon, E. (1977). Sexual arousal in women: A comparison of cognitive and physiological responses by continuous measurement. *Archives of Sexual Behavior, 6,* 121–132.

Wincze, J. P., & Lange, J. P. (1981). Assessment of sexual behavior. In D. H. Barlow (Ed.), *Behavioral assessment of adult disorders* (pp.301–328). New York: Guilford Press.

Wincze, J. P., & Qualls, C. B. (1984). A comparison of structural patterns of sexual arousal in male and female homosexuals. *Archives of Sexual Behavior, 13,* 361–370.

Zuckerman, M. (1971). Physiological measures of sexual arousal in the human. *Psychological Bulletin, 75,* 297–329.

Zuger, B. (1966). Effeminate behavior present in boys from early childhood. *Journal of Pediatrics, 69,* 1098–1107.

Zuger, B. (1978). Effeminate behavior present in boys from childhood: Ten additional years of follow-up. *Comprehensive Psychiatry, 19,* 363–369.

Zuger, B. (1983). Early effeminate behavior in boys. *Journal of Nervous and Mental Disease, 172,* 90–97.

15
Assessment of Appetitive Disorders

David W. Foy
Robert G. Rychtarik
Donald M. Prue

Substance abuse continues to be one of the most serious sociomedical problems among adolescents and adults in society today. Although millions of dollars are spent annually by consumers for alcoholic beverages, cigarettes, and prescription and "street" drugs, the costs to society in negative health and social consequences from these substances are even greater. Public awareness of potential health risks associated with drinking, smoking, and drug-taking has reached its highest level yet. A ready market exists for books and commercial programs for curbing these out-of-control appetites. Government agencies continue priority funding for a variety of substance-abuse research.

While these factors contribute to the growing need for improvements in substance abuse assessment and treatment methods, there remains much developmental work in assessment methodology. However, encouraging progress has been made in the 5 years since the second edition of this handbook was published. Accordingly, the purpose of this chapter is to present a current overview of behavioral assessment methods in appetitive disorders. Because our experiences and expertise are in alcohol and cigarettes, we will focus on empirical assessment related to these substances. Separate sections on smoking and alcohol use are designed to provide critical examinations of (a) self-reported rate measures, (b) objective rate and topography assessment methods, and (c) recent innovations in physiological and biochemical indexes of smoking and alcohol use and related health risks. The practical goal is to provide guidelines for the empirical clinician or substance-abuse researcher in designing assessment strategies and selecting appropriate dependent measures. Two case studies demonstrating multimodal assessment with alcoholism treatment are included, and critical issues are identified for future consideration.

The empirical clinician or researcher is faced with selecting the set of dependent measures that will (a) be acceptable to the client or subject, (b) accurately detect changes in substance use, (c) assess the degree of health risk, (d) be within budget and equipment limits of the clinic or laboratory, and (e) be comparable to measures used in previous and future studies with the substance. On each dimension there are several options available, each with its own advantages and limitations. No single measure currently exists for either alcohol consumption or cigarette smoking which adequately covers all dimensions. Accordingly, multimodal assessment techniques are recommended.

Self-report measures of rate of consumption remain of primary interest because existing literature for both substances is based upon their use. Assessing concurrent health risks is now seen as an important assessment issue as well. In this regard, physiological and biochemical measures of liver, lung, and cardiovascular functions as related to substance abuse are receiving increased attention. Unfortunately, equipment and supplies necessary for these measures are often costly and require technological sophistication beyond the reach of some clinical applications. Accordingly, health care providers are faced with the need to compromise between the advantages and disadvantages presented by the different methods for assessing each addictive behavior. These issues, the practical problems associated with them, and suggestions for solving some of the problems are presented for alcohol and smoking in the sections that follow.

SMOKING ASSESSMENT

There are a number of alternative strategies for the assessment of cigarette smoking. The recent development of sophisticated procedures for assessing smoking stems from limitations of rate measures as the sole measure of smoking exposure (Benfari, McIntyre, Benfari, Baldwin, & Ockene, 1977; Brockway, 1978; McFall, 1978; Densen, Davidow, Bass, & Jones, 1967; Frederiksen & Simon, 1979; Vogt, 1977). Newer methods of assessing smoking can be generally classified as more sophisticated microanalyses of smoking behavior per se or the assessment of biochemical variables. Specific measures in these two categories will be discussed and evaluated for their potential contribution to smoking assessment.

The initial section will review the advantages and disadvantages of rate measures. A number of suggestions will also be made to increase the validity of rate measurement. Then, two other categories of smoking behavior, substance and topography, will be reviewed. Again, the advantages and disadvantages of these two measures will be considered. Finally, three biochemical measures — nicotine, carbon monoxide, and thiocyanate — will be examined. Separate sections will cover the relationship of each of these measures to cigarette smoking and their advantages and disadvantages.

Self-report Measures

Rate

Rate measures have constituted the primary dependent variable in smoking research and treatment. Rate has been the focus of research because of the assumption that rate reflects smoking exposure and accompanying health risks. Rate measures have been obtained by retrospective self-report on questionnaires, by collecting physical products of smoking (e.g., cigarette butt counts), or by having smokers self-monitor the number of cigarettes smoked. (For a comprehensive review of smoking rate measurement, see Frederiksen, Martin, & Webster, 1979; Prue, Scott, & Denier, 1985.)

A voluminous literature (U.S. Public Health Service, 1979) on the dose response relationship between self-reports of cigarette consumption and numerous diseases substantiates historical reliance on this variable. Additional reasons for the frequent utilization of rate measures include their ease of collection, temporal proximity to smoking behavior, and low cost to the smoker and clinician. Also, possible treatment effects of self-monitoring on subsequent rates of consumption, primarily related to the reactivity of self-monitoring, constitutes a presumed advantage and possibly accounts for its widespread use in applied research (Frederiksen & Simon, 1979).

Despite the many advantages of rate measures, there are a number of serious disadvantages that tend to limit the value of these measures. The disadvantages have plagued rate measures regardless of how the measures have been obtained (e.g., questionnaire, self-monitoring). The first disadvantage concerns the questionable accuracy of smokers' self-reports (McFall, 1970). Although attempts (e.g., corroboration of significant others) have been made to make self-reports more reliable, such steps may be intrusive or subject to collusion (Pechacek, 1979). A second major limitation of rate, when collected via estimated self-reports or self-monitoring, has been smoker distortion of reported rate. Although always a problem in any self-monitoring procedure, distortion has played a particularly important role in smoking research when self-report measures of smoking have been used to evaluate smoking treatment. Although there are conflicting reports, some studies indicate that from 20 (Delarue, 1973) to 48% (Ohlin, Ludh, & Westling, 1976; Sillett, Wilson, Malcolm, & Ball, 1978) of smokers continue to smoke despite reporting abstinence following completion of smoking treatment programs. The primary implication of these data is that past research in smoking treatment may be misleading because of the unreliability of its data base.

Another limitation, and one that directly questions the validity of even accurate measurement of rate, is that rate has been considered a poor index of the health risks of smoking (Benfari et al., 1977; Densen, Davidow, Bass, & Jones, 1967; Vogt, 1977). Vesey (1981) concluded that rate data can be used to measure potential health risks on a group basis but the procedure fails to accurately identify those at risk. The importance of substance and topography variables in determining levels of smoking exposure often make simple rate measures misleading indices of smoking. The final disadvantage of self-report of smoking rate involves the response cost of self-monitoring to the smoker. Although there has been very little work on the effects of having smokers keep track of their rate of cigarette consumption, a study by Moss, Prue, Loma, and Martin (1982) indicates that when smokers are required to record cigarette consumption, clinic dropout rates range from 30 to 60%. When self-monitoring is not required of smokers, the dropout rate is less than 10%. A final disadvantage of rate measurement is the reactive effects of self-monitoring when rate is obtained during baseline assessments (King, Scott, & Prue, 1984).

Future rate measurement may be improved by addressing the identified problems. For instance, rate can be corroborated by more objective biochemical indices of smoking exposure, which are less intrusive than the corroboration of significant others and are not subject to collusion. In fact, research on treatment needs to provide supplemental biochemical measures because of the high rate of distortion in past reports. Another way to improve smokers' recording of rate is to make the recording procedure less reactive. Alternative methods of obtaining rate, such as daily phone checks or having smokers keep their empty cigarette packs, may be less reactive, have a lower response cost to smokers (Frederiksen, Epstein, & Kosevsky, 1975), and also lead to decreased drop-out rates. The accuracy of self-monitoring may also be improved by employing electronic or mechanical devices for self-monitoring (Azrin & Powell, 1968; Catchings, 1982; Frederiksen, personal communication) or by insuring timely recording of the behavior by requiring daily mailing of rate data to the clinic (Prue, Krapfl, & Martin, 1981). Both of these variations in monitoring procedures improve the accuracy of rate measurement. Last, when treatment programs are evaluated, treatment differences should be reported in terms of number of subjects who abstained from smoking following treatment (McFall, 1978). The validity of smokers' self-reports of abstinence can be easily verified by employing biochemical indices when it is difficult to verify particular rates of cigarette consumption. In spite of the limitations noted above, the past reliance on rate suggests that if comparisons of future research with past reports are to be made, then it will be necessary to continue to obtain rate measures.

Substance

Reports of the types or brands of tobacco consumed have been virtually ignored in smoking research despite their significant role in smoking-related health risks. Differences between types of cigarettes have not been considered as important as rate of cigarette consumption. Yet, epidemiological data (Gori, 1972, 1976) and machine testing (Ross, 1976a, 1976b) indicate that cigarettes differ widely in potential health effects because of differences in levels of tar and poison gases. In fact, differences in brand may account for more variance in health effects than differences in rates of cigarette consumption (Jaffe, Kanzler, Cohen, & Kaplan, 1978; Prue et al., 1985; Turner, Sillett, & Ball, 1974). Future research should consider this very significant but neglected variable. Also, substance should be easy to assess via direct observation at clinic sessions or by the collection of empty cigarette packs. Both these methods are likely to be reactive, yet the importance of substance variables indicates that they should be monitored in future research.

Smoking Topography Assessment

Another important dimension of smoking behavior is smoking topography (Frederiksen, Miller, & Peterson, 1977). Topography is a summary term that refers to variables related to how people smoke, including number of puffs, puff volume, puff length, interpuff interval, amount of cigarette consumed, etc. Topography variables have been monitored because much of the health risk associated with smoking is presumably related to how a person smokes. As Frederiksen et al. noted, if two smokers are consuming equal numbers of the same brand of cigarette, then any differences in exposure would be related to topography variables. Topography measurement also allows a much more detailed analysis of a smoker's idiosyncratic patterns of smoking (Comer & Creighton, 1982; Frederiksen, 1979; Henningfield & Griffiths, 1979). Finally, since changes in a smoker's topography represent an alternative treatment goal for risk reduction (Frederiksen, 1977; Royal College of Physicians, 1971), the use of pre- and post-treatment measures of topography would be helpful in evaluating treatments with noncessation goals.

There are a number of disadvantages with topography as a measure of exposure which have limited its usefulness to smoking researchers and clinicians. First, there is reason to believe that smokers cannot accurately report their smoking topography on at least some variables (Vogt, 1977; Wald, Idle, & Bailey, 1978) when this dimension is assessed via self-report.

This suggests that objective instruments need to be employed to assess topography. Unfortunately, topography measures obtained in the laboratory and in field research using electronic monitoring equipment are reliable (Henningfield & Griffiths, 1979) but the equipment is expensive to obtain and the procedures are very reactive. In fact, a recent report has provided data questioning the generalizability of laboratory measures of topography (Comer & Creighton, 1978). Finally, topography variables have not correlated well with measures of biochemical exposure in humans (Henningfield & Griffiths, 1979; Turner, Sillett, & Ball, 1974). This may be attributable to the complex interrelations among the topography variables (Dunn & Freiesleben, 1978) as well as to interdependencies between smoking topography, substances consumed, and rate of cigarette consumption when assessing smoking exposure. Additionally, the important topography variables — puff volume and duration of lung exposure to smoke — are typically not measured even in basic laboratory research studies (Prue et al., 1985).

In summary, the technology of present topography measurement is intrusive, costly, and of questionable generalizability to the natural environment. Thus, future research must document the value not only by examining the basic mechanisms of topography variables and correlations between topography and increased health risk but by demonstrating clinically significant changes in this variable following treatment.

Biochemical Measures

Nicotine and Cotinine

Nicotine is one of the primary determinants of cigarette consumption (Armitage, 1978; Jarvik, Popek, Schneider, Baer-Weiss, & Gritz, 1978; Russell, 1978; Schachter, 1977). Nicotine has been monitored in the blood (Zeidenberg et al., 1977) and urine (Paxton & Bernacca, 1979) of smokers as well as individuals who take snuff or chew tobacco. The accurate assessment of nicotine allows clinicians and researchers an objective evaluation of tobacco consumption. However, nicotine is rapidly metabolized by the body, giving it a short half-life of 30 minutes (Langone & Van Vunakis, 1975; Zeidenberg et al., 1977), which in turn makes nicotine levels extremely sensitive to the amount of time elapsed since a smoker's last cigarette (Armitage, 1978; Paxton & Bernacca, 1979). These factors make assessment of cigarette exposure based on nicotine monitoring impractical. The fact that even heavy smokers can abstain from smoking for a couple of hours could lead to distortion of their nicotine levels, Thus, while nicotine levels have a number of disadvantages that limit their usefulness, recent research has documented the value of cotinine assessment. Cotinine is the primary metabolite of nicotine and can be monitored in the blood, urine, or saliva of smokers (Hengen & Hengen, 1978; Lader, 1978; Langone & Van Vunakis, 1975; Zeidenberg et al., 1977). Studies have reported a dose-response relation between cotinine and number of cigarettes smoked (Rickert & Robinson, 1981) and the nicotine rating of brand smoked (Hill & Marquardt, 1980). Future research will surely define more closely the parameters of smoking that produce variations in cotinine levels. For now, cotinine is most useful in discriminating smokers from nonsmokers and, when repeated single-subject measures are obtained, as an index of changes in tobacco exposure.

Carbon Monoxide

A biochemical measure that has received the most attention in smoking research is carbon monoxide (CO). Carbon monoxide levels are important because of their documented relation to rate of cigarette consumption (Frederiksen & Martin, 1979; Vogt, 1977), topography variables (Robinson & Forbes, 1975), and substance smoked. Additionally, CO has been identified as critical in the etiology of numerous smoking-related diseases (e.g., chronic obstructive pulmonary disease, chronic heart disease). Carbon monoxide can be measured in the expired air or blood of smokers. The primary advantage of CO is ease of measurement when CO is assessed in expired air. Another advantage is that aside from the initial expense of purchasing equipment to measure CO in expired air, the assessment of carbon monoxide is inexpensive. Finally, the results of CO assessments are available within minutes after sampling and can be used to provide immediate feedback to smokers on their health risk.

The disadvantages of using carbon monoxide parallel those of nicotine assessment because carbon monoxide also has a short half-life in the body (2–4 hours). This short half-life leads to diurnal variability and sensitivity to amount of time since a smoker's last cigarette. This sensitivity can lead to subject distortion of carbon monoxide checks through short periods of abstinence prior to CO sampling. Variations in CO have also occurred because of ambient CO levels and smoker's activity levels (Wald & Howard, 1975). Both these factors can lead to the inadvertent distortion of assessments.

Despite drawbacks in CO assessment, the measure provides a reliable and direct measure of biochemical exposure to cigarette smoke. As a result of its many advantages, CO is perhaps the most widely employed objective measure of smoking behavior in both basic and applied research. (For a comprehensive review see Frederiksen & Martin, 1979.)

Hydrogen Cyanide

The third and final biochemical index of smoking exposure is the measurement of hydrogen cyanide gas consumed during smoking. Measures of hydrogen cyanide intake are obtained by assessing its metabolite, thiocyanate (SCN), in the blood, urine, saliva, or perspiration of smokers. Comparisons of the four fluids indicate that saliva and blood levels of SCN appear to be the most reliable and valid methods of sampling this metabolite.

Thiocyanate assessment is important because of its relationship to rate of cigarette consumption (Butts, Kueuhneman, & Widdowson, 1974; Tenovuo & Makinen, 1976; Vogt, 1977), topography (Barylko-Pikielna & Pangborn, 1968), and substance smoked (Prue, Martin, Hume, & Davis, 1981). Additionally, hydrogen cyanide gas has been implicated in the etiology of stomach cancer (Boyland & Walker, 1974; Lederer, 1976) and certain respiratory disabilities (Ross, 1976b; U.S. Public Health Service, 1979).

The primary advantage of SCN assessment, like CO assessment, is that it can be used as an objective measure of smoking exposure. Another advantage of SCN is its extended half-life in the body (10–14 days), which makes it less sensitive to transient rate fluctuations and subject distortion. Finally, the well-documented relation between smoking parameters and SCN levels makes it a useful screening device (Prue, Martin, & Hume, 1980; Vesey, 1981).

There are also a number of disadvantages of SCN assessment. *First*, research has noted a great deal of intrasubject variability in single-subject repeated measures of SCN. This variability has been particularly notable in multiple daily measures. Although the reasons for such variability have not been determined, a number of possible contributing factors have been suggested (Prue, Martin, Hume, & Davis 1981), including methodological inconsistency in assessment and analysis procedures. *Second*, variations in diet can have an impact on SCN levels because certain foods (e.g., broccoli, cabbage) contain naturally occurring thiocyanate (Densen et al., 1967). Dietetic influences can lead to inadvertent distortions in SCN levels. As in the case with CO, there is always the remote possibility that ambient levels of hydrogen cyanide gas lead to elevated levels. *Finally*, SCN assessment requires relatively sophisticated laboratory equipment. Despite these disadvantages, SCN offers some promise, especially as a supplementary measure of long-term abstinence when used in combination with CO (Vogt, 1977).

Comment

The assessment of smoking has recently become more sophisticated as researchers move away from a sole reliance on rate measures. Rate measures are being supplemented by the measurement of new dependent variables. Importantly, these new measures provide a more objective analysis of smoking. In the case of biochemical measures, the variables are also more reliable and direct measures of exposure and health risk. The treatment of smoking has been constrained by primitive, often unreliable, and perhaps invalid measurement procedures. Hopefully, newer approaches to assessment will result in new developments in smoking treatment.

ALCOHOL ASSESSMENT

It is becoming increasingly apparent that assessment of alcohol abuse requires attention to variables other than simply rate or amount of alcohol consumption. Evidence indicates that a change in drinking status is not necessarily correlated with improvements in other areas of life functioning (e.g., Emrick, 1974). Appropriate clinical assessment for the problem of alcohol abuse therefore requires behavioral assessment with respect to social skills, marital adjustment, vocational stability, and intrapersonal adjustment in addition to alcohol consumption. Assessment of many of these areas are presented elsewhere in this volume and therefore will not be covered here. This section will be limited to assessment of the actual drinking response or physiological indicants of it. In this respect, the following assessment modalities are presented: (a) self-report, (b) analog laboratory procedures, (c) topographical/observational drinking measures, and (d) biochemical drinking indices.

Self-Report Measures of Drinking

Self-reported drinking continues to be the most frequently used behavioral measure of alcohol consumption in alcoholism treatment and research. Yet, reliance on self-reported drinking poses special problems for both the clinician and the researcher. First, due to the stigma attached to drinking behavior, individuals may be reluctant to accurately report their drinking habits, and alcoholics, in particular, have a notorious reputation — whether justified or unjustified — for underreporting the extent of their alcohol consumption. Second, baseline measures of drinking behavior typically have to be obtained through retrospective reports of drinking behavior and thus may be additionally susceptible to the confounding effects of the passage of time and the distortion or lack of recall. Both ethical and practical reasons, nevertheless, account for this heavy reliance on retrospective drinking reports. Alcoholics, often present for treatment only when confronted with a crisis (e.g., severe medical problems, family crisis, legal difficulties, etc.) and it would be of questionable ethical practice to instruct the alcoholic to continue his/her typical drinking pattern for the next few weeks so as to obtain an accurate baseline of drinking behavior. Certainly, such a practice could be of potential risk to the individual (e.g., exacerbation of medical problems) and others (e.g., victims of drunk driving). Given these special problems in alcoholism treatment and research, it is no wonder that the reliability and validity of self-reported alcohol consumption remains an area of considerable concern and controversy.

Self-reported drinking behavior has usually been obtained through either a structured interview or questionnaire format. The two most frequently used and accepted methods are the time-line follow-back procedure (Sobell et al., 1980) and the quantity-frequency method (Armor & Polich, 1982). In the time-line follow-back procedure, the individual is presented with a calendar of the period to be covered (ranging from the past 30 days to the past 365 days) and is asked to indicate the amount of alcohol consumed on *each* day during the interval, with special event dates (e.g., holidays, birthdays, etc.) used to aid recall. Data from this method are usually presented in the form of the number of days within different drinking (e.g., abstinent, light, moderate, abusive), and involuntary nondrinking dispositions (e.g., alcohol- and non-alcohol-related incarcerations and hospitalizations). In the quantity-frequency method, the individual is asked to estimate the number of days over a specified period (e.g., last 30 days) during which either beer, wine, or liquor was consumed, and the amount of the different beverages *typically* consumed on a drinking day. Drinking indices for larger periods of time may be obtained by comparing the initial period to prior periods of time and similar questions asked for those periods during which drinking was reported to be more often or less often. Variations on the quantity-frequency method may also include questions as to the number of drinking days when alcohol consumption was above or below certain predetermined levels. Data from the quantity-frequency method are usually presented in the form of the number of days drinking or abstinent during the period, a typical quantity index representing the typical amount of absolute alcohol consumed on a drinking day over the period (i.e., total absolute alcohol during the period divided by the total number of days drinking), and the quantity-frequency index (QFI) which represents the typical amount of absolute alcohol per day (i.e., total amount of absolute alcohol consumed divided by the total number of days in the period covered, including both drinking and non-drinking days).

Although few comparisons exist, available data suggest a moderate to high degree of consistency between the two methods for assessing drinking behavior in the 30 days prior to treatment (Maisto, Sobell, Cooper, & Sobell, 1982; Sobell, Cellucci, Nirenberg, & Sobell, 1982). The time-line method may have the advantage of more precisely identifying an individual's drinking pattern; however, it takes over twice as long to administer than does the quantity-frequency method (Sobell et al., 1982). The time commitment required for the time-line method may, therefore, not be highly applicable in clinical settings with limited staff or in treatment outcome research where the success of long-term follow-up is highly dependent on the voluntary cooperation of individual subjects.

Reliability of Self-Reported Drinking

The instability of drinking patterns over time, particularly in alcoholics, poses an important source of error in measurements of self-reported drinking behavior. Increasing evidence suggests that alcoholics' drinking status may show considerable variability (Polich, Armor, & Braiker, 1980; Watson & Pucel, 1985). Drinking behavior at one point in time (e.g., the previous 30 days) may not be a reliable (i.e., representative) measure of drinking behavior over longer periods. Size of the time interval covered by the self-report method, therefore, appears to be an important variable. The few studies that have investigated this issue suggest, for example, that a pretreatment baseline using only the 30 days prior to treatment may not adequately represent typical drinking behavior (Cooper, Sobell, Maisto, & Sobell, 1980; McCrady, Duclos, Durbreuil, Stout, & Fisher-Nelson, 1984). Alcoholics in residential treatment centers (presumably representing more serious alcohol abusers) have been found to report significantly more days of abusive drinking in the 30 days prior to admission than during other periods in the pretreatment year (Cooper et al., 1980). Individuals attending outpatient alcohol treatment programs, on the other hand, appear to report more days of abstinence in the 30-day pretreatment period than is representative of the pretreatment year (McCrady et al., 1984). Similarly, small posttreatment intervals may not be representative of overall posttreatment functioning. Short periods of abstention (i.e., less than 3 months) have not been found to represent stable abstention over longer periods of time (Polich et al., 1980). It is, therefore, generally recommended that pretreatment and posttreatment intervals of no less than 6 months, and preferrably 12 months, be used in alcohol treatment outcome research. Moreover, proportion of days abstinent, moderate, and heavy should be adjusted to rule out bias as a result of periods of involuntary abstention due to hospitalization or incarceration (Cooper et al., 1980).

Test-retest reliabilities for self-reported drinking measures do appear quite reliable, at least when the same measurement period is used (e.g., the 6 months pretreatment) at both test and retest. This appears to be the case whether the population is one of outpatient alcoholics (Maisto, Sobell, Cooper, & Sobell, 1979; Sobell & Sobell, 1975; Sobell, Maisto, Sobell, & Cooper, 1979), alcoholics in residential or inpatient treatment programs (Maisto, Sobell, Cooper, & Sobell, 1979; Holland, Datta, Izadi, & Evenson, 1979; Davidson & Stein, 1982), female obstetrical patients (Blumhagen & Little, 1985; Streissguth, Martin, & Buffington, 1976; Little, Mandell, & Schultz, 1977), or the general population (Williams, Aitken, & Malin, 1985). Available data also suggest that, in general, when discrepancies do occur there is no particular response bias. The strength of the reliability of self-report drinking measures, however, may vary somewhat with the population under consideration and the type of questions asked. Maisto, Sobell,

Cooper, and Sobell (1979), for example, found a tendency for fewer test-retest discrepancies among alcoholic outpatients, as well as some differences in reliabilities between outpatients, inpatients, and individuals in residential treatment programs depending on the particular measure used (i.e., abstinent days, abusive drinking days, days of limited consumption, etc.). Blumhagen and Little (1985) report some evidence to suggest that even when large periods of time separate test and retest (e.g., 3–12 months), there are still high test-retest reliabilities in self-report drinking measures. As noted, however, this correspondence may not be the case with all measures. In the case of the Blumhagen and Little (1985) study, the amount of alcohol consumption reported during the second interview was significantly lower than at pretest, and reports of periods of binge drinking were not reliable.

Validity of Self-Reported Drinking

Contrary to popular opinion, and despite continuing controversy (see Maisto & O'Farrell, 1985; Watson, 1985; Watson, Tilleskjor, Hoodecheck-Schow, Pucel, & Jacobs, 1985), converging data on the validity of self-report drinking measures suggest that, as a group, alcoholics and others, for that matter, give fairly accurate reports of their drinking behavior. As with reliability, however, just how accurate these measures are may vary somewhat with the population under consideration, the time of measurement, the variables used, the types of questions asked, and the criteria upon which validity is evaluated (see Midanik, 1982). For example, although drinking history data have generally been reported to be quite accurate, alcoholics have been found to frequently overreport the number of drunk driving arrests or arrests for public drunkeness when compared to actual legal records — possibly due to confusion over the distinction between arrests and actual convictions (e.g., Sobell & Sobell, 1975; Sobell & Sobell, 1978; Sobell, Sobell, & Samuels, 1974). Interestingly, Sobell and Sobell (1975) found that those individuals with only one or two arrests were less likely to report them than those individuals with four or more arrests. Cooper et al. (1980), although finding a high degree of correspondence between self-reports and official records (i.e., hospitalizations, arrests, etc.), reported that when discrepancies occurred with inpatients, they were typically overreports; outpatients, on the other hand, tended to give underreports.

To overcome potential problems with sole reliance on self-reports, relatives and/or acquaintances having some knowledge of the client's drinking behavior have been used as collaterals to corroborate client-reported drinking. Accumulating evidence suggests that, in general, there is a high degree of agreement between patients and collaterals, with no particular tendency for patients to underreport or overreport when discrepancies occur (Hesselbrock, Babor, Hesselbrock, Meyer, & Workman, in press; Maisto, Sobell, & Sobell, 1979; McCrady, Paolino, & Longabaugh, 1978; Miller,

Crawford, & Taylor, 1979; O'Farrell, Cutter, Bayog, Dentch, & Fortgang, 1981; Polich, 1982). Unfortunately, the validity of collateral reports themselves has not been addressed. In fact, available evidence suggests that measurement error may not be greatly reduced through the use of collateral reports in alcoholism treatment outcome research. For example, Polich (1982) reports that in only 1 case out of 128 (i.e., 1% of the sample) did an alcoholic deny drinking while the collateral reported it. On the other hand, in 11 cases (9% of the sample) the subject reported drinking whereas the collateral denied it or was uncertain. Thus, on the question of whether the alcoholic did or did not drink there appears to be a high degree of agreement between the subjects and collaterals, and when disagreement occurs, it is more likely due to error in the collateral report rather than to underreporting by the alcoholic. Such a high level of agreement is not the case with all measures, however. Less noticeable measures (e.g., amounts of alcohol consumed, impairment) are what appear to be less easily validated by collaterals due to collaterals' uncertainty and underreporting. Similar results have been reported with college students. Stacy, Widaman, Hays, and DiMatteo (1985) found that an individual's level of alcohol intake as reported by one's peers was of questionable validity when compared to self-reported ratings of drinking behavior and self-reported alcohol intake. Finally, the extent of patient–collateral discrepancies and their direction may depend on the relation of the collateral to the patient. Freedberg and Johnston (1980) found that clients' reports were more negative than reports of spouses serving as collaterals and more positive than that of counselors used as collaterals.

Self-reported drinking has also been compared to more objective measures of alcohol consumption, such as breath or urine testing. As with collateral reports, reports of abstention generally appear to be in considerable agreement with these objective measures (Polich, 1982; Sobell, Sobell, & VanderSpek, 1979). Polich (1982) notes, for example, that of patients reporting their last drink as 30 days to 6 months ago, only 6 out of 100 cases had a positive blood alcohol level (BAL) on the last day of assessment. Alcoholics who have been drinking recently (i.e., within the last 24 hr), however, have been found to report inaccurate consumption measures, particularly over the past 24 hr (Orrego, Blendis, Blake, Kapur, & Israel, 1979; Polich, 1982; Sobell, Sobell, & VanderSpek, 1979). In the sample described by Polich (1982), among those who drank recently (i.e., within the last 24 hr), there was a large number (35%) who underreported the *amount* of alcohol consumed when compared to breath test measures. If the actual level of consumption over the past 24 hr (derived from objective BAL measures) is taken as representative of the typical amount consumed over the period, Polich (1982) found that 24% of the sample underreported typical quantities consumed over the past month, and suggests that this 24% rate of underreporting may be the best available conservative (i.e., cautious) estimate of underreporting in alcoholism treatment outcome research.

Although a 24% rate of underreporting amounts consumed may have significant impact when this measure is used alone, its impact may be considerably minimized when subjects are classified as problem drinkers, high consumers, low consumers or abstainers according to multiple measures, e.g., presence or absence of dependence symptoms, adverse health and social consequences, and typical amount of alcohol consumption (Polich, 1982; Stacey et al., 1985). Polich (1982), for example, has shown that when these multiple measures are used in combination for classification, only about 2% of the sample would be misclassified because of underreporting. Thus, although alcoholics' self-reports on most measures appear quite valid, the accuracy of outcome classifications can be maximized by incorporating multiple self-report measures.

Comparison of self-reported alcohol consumption in general population surveys with more objective drinking indices (e.g., beverage sales records) have indicated considerably higher rates of underreporting. The extent of underreporting when compared to sales records ranges from 50% to 20% (Armor, Polich, & Stambul, 1978; Room, 1971; Polich & Orvis, 1979). The discrepancy between alcohol consumption estimates in population surveys and alcohol beverage sales records may be at least partially accounted for by inadequate sampling procedures. For example, population surveys frequently will miss portions of the population who are typically high consumers (e.g., transients, etc.).

In summary, self-report methods in alcohol assessment have generally been found to be quite reliable and valid. Of course, exceptions do occur. As the above discussion suggests and as others have pointed out (Maisto & O'Farrell, 1985; Midanik, 1982), the question to really ask is for what populations, with what methods, under which conditions can accurate and reliable self-reports of drinking behavior be obtained. Although progress has been made in the last few years, the answer to this question is far from definitive. In the interim, problems with self-report methods may best be attenuated by relying on multiple drinking measures in outcome classifications and, where possible, by the inclusion of objective drinking indices discussed later.

Analog Assessment Procedures

The earliest behavioral methods of assessing alcohol consumption were operant in nature. The subject was required to make a response (e.g., lever pressing) according to a certain reinforcement schedule in order to obtain fixed amounts of alcoholic beverage. The approach is considered somewhat analogous to the natural setting, where a person must work to pay for drinks. Thus, the operant assessment method provides a means of assessing motivation to drink by quantifying how much and how frequently the subject will "work" for alcohol. Operant techniques such as these have been successfully employed to obtain a descriptive analysis of alcoholic drinking (Mello & Mendelson, 1971), to distinguish drinking behavior of alcoholics from social drinkers (Nathan & O'Brien, 1971), and to evaluate the influence of interpersonal stress on alcohol consumption (Miller, Hersen, Eisler, & Hilsman, 1974).

Despite the apparent internal validity of such operant approaches, their obtrusiveness and susceptibility to experimental demand make external validity questionable. In response to these validity problems, Marlatt, Demming, and Reid (1973) and Miller and Hersen (1972a) independently developed an alcohol assessment technique presented under the guise of a taste-rating task. In the taste-rating task, the subject is placed at a table and presented with a number of glasses containing either alcoholic or nonalcoholic beverages. Unaware that consumption is being monitored, the subject is asked to rate each beverage along a variety of dimensions (e.g., from strong to weak). The subject is then allowed to drink as much or as little as needed while sip rate and amount of alcohol consumption are monitored. This unobtrusive taste-test measure has successfully been employed in research on the influence of stress (Higgins & Marlatt, 1973), sexual arousal (Gabel, Noel, Keane, & Lisman, 1979), modeling (Caudill & Marlatt, 1975; Hendricks, Sobell, & Cooper, 1978), and expectancy (Marlatt et al., 1973) on alcohol consumption.

Though there are many advantages to analog drink assessment procedures (i.e., good reliability, experimental control, unobtrusiveness), other problems remain. Specifically, the extent to which drinking in such disguised situations under laboratory conditions is representative of drinking in the natural environment remains to be investigated. Moreover, while such methods have greatly contributed to our knowledge of the determinants of alcohol consumption in the laboratory, they appear to be of little practical utility for developing treatment planning in the clinical setting. One retrospective study suggests that alcoholics' consumption of alcohol during either operant tasks or taste-tests may be predictive of drinking disposition upon completion of treatment (Miller, Hersen, Eisler, & Elkin, 1974), and Miller and Hersen (1972b) reported measures on the taste-test to be sensitive to treatment changes during and following aversive conditioning treatment. However, until further research on these measures as predictors or indicators of treatment outcome is conducted, their clinical utility is undetermined and their use will likely remain confined to the laboratory setting.

Observational Drinking Measures

The notion that "in the behavioral approach the behaviors evaluated during the course of assessment are the very ones subjected to modification procedures in treatment" (Hersen, 1976, p. 10) becomes most apparent in the assessment of alcoholic drinking topography. In this procedure, the client is placed in either a simulated bar setting (Sobell & Sobell, 1973) or a casual living room environment (Miller, Becker, Foy, & Wooten, 1976) and provided with his/her favorite alcoholic beverage. Instructions are given to drink as usual. The client's drinking is then videotaped from an adjoining room. Upon completion of the session, the amount of alcohol consumed is determined and videotapes are subsequently rated to obtained measures of number of sips, length of intersip interval, and mix ratio.

Assessment of drink topography grew out of attempts by investigators to observe drinking behavior in settings more closely resembling those in the natural environment. Sobell, Schaefer, and Mills (1972) systematically observed the drinking behavior of 26 male alcoholics and 23 male normal drinkers in a simulated cocktail bar. Results indicated that alcoholics, when compared with normal drinkers, consumed significantly more, preferred straight drinks, drank faster, and consumed larger amounts per sip. These results have been replicated generally elsewhere (Schaefer, Sobell, & Mills, 1971; Williams & Brown, 1974). Such quantitative differences in drinking behaviors between alcoholics and normal drinkers suggested an operational definition of alcohol abuse. Furthermore, it implied that alcoholics might actually be capable of learning the drinking style (topography) of normal drinkers. In this regard, Miller et al. (1976) assessed and trained specific drinking skills (e.g., sip rate, etc.) in an alcoholic by employing a simulated drink setting. Unfortunately, recent research suggests that chronic alcoholics' acquisition of controlled drinking skills in the laboratory may not generalize to the posttreatment environment (Foy, Nunn, & Rychtarik, 1984; Rychtarik, Foy, Scott, Lokey, & Prue, in press). Research with less severe problem drinkers, however, has been more promising in this area (Miller & Hester, 1980).

Clearly, assessment of drinking topography in simulated settings offers advantages over other analog procedures. First, the assessment setting simulates more closely actual natural drinking environments. Second, results of the drinking assessment procedure provide direct information for treatment intervention with nonabstinent-oriented clients. However, it again remains unclear how representative the drinking measures obtained in simulated settings are of those in the natural environment. Some support for the validity of simulated drinking environments is found in evidence that natural drinking rates (i.e., number of drinks per hour) observed in the general population are quite similar to those obtained for nonalcoholics in the simulated setting (Reid, 1978). Moreover, modeling influences obtained in simulated settings (Garlington & Dericco, 1977) have recently received some external validation in a pilot investigation of modeling and naturalistic drinking behavior in the general population (Reid, 1978). On the other hand, a recent comparison of *ad lib* drinking topography among college males in a regular laboratory with drinking in the barroom revealed that barroom drinking was characterized by significantly greater alcohol intake and faster rates of consumption (Strickler, Dobbs, & Maxwell, 1979). As these findings indicate, drinking behavior appears to be somewhat more complex than initially construed. Research suggests that drinking in nonalcoholics may be influenced by such factors as sex (Hunter, Hannon, & Marchi, 1979; Rosenbluth, Nathan, & Lawson, 1978), socioeconomic status (Hunter et al., 1979), and the social context of drinking (Cutter & Storm, 1975; Rosenbluth et al., 1978; Sommer, 1965). With respect to this latter point, it is interesting to note that naturalistic studies have found that nonalcoholics consume more when drinking in a social versus solitary context. Solitary versus group social environment, however, does not appear to affect the drinking of alcoholics in the simulated lab (Foy & Simon, 1978). Unfortunately, investigations of drinking topography have typically employed nonalcoholic populations. Thus, additional information is required on the natural and laboratory drinking of both normal and alcoholic drinkers.

Two additional problems remain with drinking topography assessment procedures. First the methods employed to date typically have been too long (3–4 hr), require considerable staff time, and present notable patient risk (e.g.,consumption of large amounts of alcohol) to be of practical utility in the clinical setting. In response to this problem, Foy, Rychtarik, Nunn, and Webster (1979) have presented normative information on the drinking styles of alcoholics in a brief 30-minute drinking assessment paradigm. This shortened procedure appears sensitive to abusive drinking patterns in alcoholics and yet circumvents practical problems associated with lengthier methods. Finally, if the external validity of simulated drinking environments is firmly documented, the issue of whether the assessment information obtained is necessary or relevant for treatment requires attention. Recent data (Sanchez-Craig, Annis, Bornet, & MacDonald, 1984) suggest that drink training procedures may not be the critical treatment variable in determining moderate drinking dispositions in problem drinkers following treatment.

Behavioral assessment procedures reviewed thus far have relied primarily on observation of actual drinking in analog or simulated environments. Though evidence suggests that measures such as these may be used for purposes of evaluating treatment outcome, their use appears to be only appropriate for less severe problem drinkers who choose a goal of controlled/responsible drinking. Requiring individuals whose goal is total abstinence to engage in drinking for the purpose of obtaining outcome measures poses potential ethical and clinical problems. Observational drinking outcome measures, therefore, appear to be of practical utility with only a select portion of the alcohol-abusing population. Biochemical indices of drinking may be more widely applicable with respect to treatment goal and outcome.

Observational ratings or staff judgments of intoxication have also been reported in the alcohol assessment literature. However, judging on the basis of observations alone whether an individual is actually intoxicated or not, or whether he/she has been drinking recently (i.e., has a positive BAL) may actually be rather difficult. Drunken behavior may be easily observed in an individual who has yet to develop much tolerance to alcohol (e.g., the inexperienced high school or college student). On the other hand, individuals who, due to frequent heavy alcohol consumption, have acquired considerable tolerance for alcohol often fail to evince obvious drunken behavior even at high blood alcohol levels. Drinking in this latter group may therefore go undetected. Sobell, Sobell, and VanderSpek (1979) found that trained mental health interviewers using a 4-point level of intoxication rating failed to identify anywhere from 22.2% to 55% of patients with positive blood alcohol levels. More promising findings have recently been reported by Teplin and Lutz (1985) in the development of an 11-item checklist of behaviors associated with intoxication (e.g., smell of alcohol, impairment of fine motor control, red eyes, sleepiness, etc.) These authors found that when the presence of 3 or more items on the checklist was used as the criterion, 88% of a cross-validation sample of emergency-room patients with a BAL of .05 or more were correctly identified as having a positive blood alcohol level. Furthermore, 92 of individuals without a positive blood alcohol level were also correctly identified. While validation of the checklist is required using other populations, the instrument shows promise for use in clinical as well as research settings (e.g., naturalistic observations), where more objective measures of recent drinking (discussed later) are not available or are impractical.

Biochemical Measures

Blood Alcohol Level

In the breath analysis procedure, a small sample of alveolar air is collected and analyzed for alcohol content via various chemical or electrochemical methods (Cravey & Jain, 1974; Jain & Cravey, 1974). The procedure provides a direct indication of blood alcohol level (BAL) and is typically presented as a percentage of ethyl alcohol to blood volume (e.g., .10 percent BAL = 100 mg/100 ml). Recently, breath analysis instruments have become considerably more sophisticated. Instruments are now available ranging from inexpensive portable (though less accurate) models to larger machines that are accurate to plus or minus .01 percent. Overall, the breathalyzer provides a highly reliable, valid measure of recent drinking behavior.

Blood alcohol levels obtained via breath analysis have been employed as therapeutic outcome measures (Foy et al., 1984; Sobell & Sobell, 1973), as criteria for determining consequences for drinking (Miller, Hersen, Eisler, & Watts, 1974), and as a means of training alcoholics to discriminate varying blood alcohol levels (Lovibond & Caddy, 1970). Despite advantages of breath analysis, however, certain problems exist. Since alcohol is metabolized by the body at the rate of approximately one ounce per hour, breath analysis is sensitive to detecting consumption of large amounts of alcohol for only a period of 24 hr. Abusive drinking occurring 3–4 days prior to breath analysis would not be identified. A client may therefore pace drinking so that a breath test administered at a regularly scheduled appointment would not register a positive breath test. Outcome studies have employed unannounced probe breath tests or tests with little advance warning to overcome this reactive problem (Sobell & Sobell, 1973; Miller, Hersen, Eisler, & Watts, 1974). However, random breathalyzer probes may also discourage drinking, so results obtained in outcome research may actually be attributable to the assessment procedure itself as opposed to the treatment program being evaluated. Random probes also require considerable staff time and therefore may not be practical in the typical treatment program. Pacing of drinking episodes so as to avoid detection by regularly scheduled breath tests remains an empirical question. Evidence suggests, at least, that regularly scheduled breathalyzer tests during aftercare do not negatively influence aftercare attendance rates in chronic alcoholics (Nunn, Foy, & Rychtarik, 1980). Finally, use of the breathalyzer in research on drinking patterns in the natural environment may result in unrepresentative samples. Williams (1978), for example, reported that only 51% of barroom patrons would actually agree to a breath test.

An alternative source for detection of alcohol consumption is through the collection of perspiration, one avenue through which alcohol (ethanol) is excreted from the body. Phillips and McAloon (1980) report on the use of an adhesive, watertight sweat patch worn on the skin. This patch collects perspiration continuously for up to 10 days and may be easily tested for the presence of alcohol (Phillips, 1982) as a means of detecting drinking. Early work with the sweat patch suggested that alcohol collected in this manner was directly related to the amount of alcohol consumed and could correctly discriminate drinkers from nondrinkers (Phillips & McAloon, 1980). Recent research on the sweat patch, however, failed to replicate these findings (Philips, Little, Hillman, Labbe, & Campbell, 1984). It would appear that this test is still in a developmental stage and not yet ready for clinical or experimental application.

Biochemical and Hematological Markers

Since breath analysis is sensitive to abusive drinking only within 24 hr of occurrence, investigators have recently considered other biochemical indicants of abusive drinking. Within the past several years, attention has been given to the possible use of blood serum enzymes and other hematological measures to supplement self-reports and BAL indications of alcohol consumption. Moreover, such biochemical measures have been viewed as promising screening tests for use in identifying early stage problem drinkers who might otherwise go unnoticed until their alcohol abuse has become more severe. Although several such biochemical tests have been proposed as markers for alcohol abuse (Kricka & Clark, 1979), the test that has received the most attention is gamma-glutamyl transpeptidase (GGT), a liver enzyme normally found at low levels in the blood stream. This measure appears to be significantly elevated by heavy alcohol consumption and may require several weeks to return to normal, thus providing an index of drinking in the recent past. Research in this area, however, has not always found significant correlations between GGT and alcohol consumption (e.g., Garvin, Foy, & Alford, 1981; Poikolainen, Karkkainen, & Pikkarainen, 1985), and when significant correlations have been found, they have been relatively low (.16–.46) (Chick, Kreitman, & Plant, 1981; Papoz et al., 1981; Pomerleau & Adkins, 1980; Reyes & Miller, 1980; Sanchez-Craig & Annis, 1981; Sanchez-Craig et al., 1984; Warnet et al., 1984). Moreover, as a marker for the presence or absence of alcohol abuse, GGT, and other tests for that matter, lacks sensitivity. Specifically, the proportion of alcohol abusers correctly identified by these measures has often been disappointing (.34–.63) (Cushman, Jacobson, Barboriak, & Anderson, 1984; Chick et al., 1981; Eckardt, Ryback, Rawlings, & Graubard, 1981; Garvin et al., 1981; Gluud et al., 1981; Mayfield & Johnston, 1980; Sanchez-Craig & Annis, 1981). Furthermore, false positive rates ranging from 11 to 50% have been reported (Chick et al., 1981). The problem appears, at least partially, to be that such tests, and in particular GGT, are elevated in the absence of alcohol by various physical conditions (e.g., liver disease, pancreatitis) and other drug use (e.g., barbiturates, opiates, Dilantin, etc.). Therefore, single biochemical markers such as GGT seem to lack satisfactory power for widespread use in identifying alcohol abuse. They may, however, be helpful in individual cases where repeated testing provides a baseline level of activity over time, to which subsequent tests may be compared for the purposes of detecting alcohol abuse (see the case studies that follow).

Since individual tests may be influenced by many factors other than just alcohol consumption, a more promising approach appears to be the use of multivariate hematological indices to obtain a composite profile for identification of alcohol abuse (Beresford, Adduci, Low, Goggans, & Hall, 1982; Bliding, Bliding, Fex, & Tornvist, 1982; Chalmers, Rinsler, MacDermott, Spicer, & Levi, 1981; Cowan, Massey, & Greenfield, 1985; Ryback, Eckhardt, & Pautler, 1980). Ryback et al. (1980), for example, used a quadratic multiple discriminant analysis of 24 frequently used blood chemistry tests and were able to classify 100% of medical ward alcoholics as alcoholic, 94% of treatment program alcoholics as alcoholic, and 100% of medical controls as nonalcoholic. Importantly, the discriminant functions were also able to accurately identify all patients with nonalcoholic liver disease as nonalcoholic. Similar results have been reported with healthy young college students of differing levels of alcohol intake (Cowan et al., 1985). Such procedures may not be applicable for identification of alcohol abuse in all populations, however. The discriminant procedure used by Ryback et al. (1980) was not effective, for example, in individuals over 65 years of age. Consistent with research on individual biochemical markers, evidence suggests that the discriminating power of such procedures decreases with the use of fewer laboratory tests (Beresford et al., 1982; Bliding et al., 1982; Eckardt et al., 1981; Ryback & Eckardt, 1982). Blood/biochemical profiling for the identification of alcohol abuse is an area of considerable promise, yet it is still in a rather experimental stage. At this point, if such methods are employed, they should be considered only as preliminary screening devices to be used in conjunction with other drink assessment measures for the identification of individuals with alcohol problems. Unfortunately, blood testing as a means of detecting alcohol abuse requires access to sophisticated automated laboratory equipment and therefore may not be easily implemented in nonmedical treatment facilities. Lag time between blood sample collection and availability of results may prevent the most effective use of these tests by delaying immediate feedback.

Carbon Disulfide

Up to this point, the discussion has centered primarily on biochemical indicants of drinking behavior. Another approach that appears promising is the assessment of disulfiram (Antabuse) intake, which would presumably be related to abstinence. Antabuse is a drug used in conjunction with alcohol treatment programs that results in flushing, headache, nausea, etcetera, when followed by the consumption of alcohol. Antabuse consumption may, therefore, serve as a deterrent to drinking. Assessment of disulfiram compliance, however, appears to be a major problem, and an area of promising research and clinical utility. A recent report indicated that self-report and clinical judgments of disulfiram compliance were often inaccurate (Paulson, Krause, & Iber, 1977). To overcome this compliance problem, various strategies have employed supervised administration of disulfiram on an outpatient basis (Bigelow, Strickler, Liebson, & Griffiths, 1976). Such methods, however, require considerable staff time and high client response cost. Monitoring of the number of disulfiram prescriptions filled by the client has been employed also (Keane, Foy, Nunn, & Rychtarik, 1984). This method avoids problems associated with daily monitoring of disulfiram intake, yet provides only an indirect measure of compliance.

Another approach to assessing compliance has been to detect disulfiram or its metabolites in blood, urine, and/or breath samples. To date, blood sample tests have not been highly successful in providing a practical, reliable measure of compliance. Although urinalysis procedures have been demonstrated to be useful for detecting disulfiram compliance, a breath test for carbon disulfide (CS_2), a metabolite of disulfiram, may be more efficient. In this procedure, the subject is required to exhale into containers holding various prepared chemical solutions. If CS_2 is present a chemical reaction ensues, yielding an immediate yellow color in the liquid. For more accurate continuous measures, the solution can then be analyzed via spectrophotometry. The advantage of such an assessment procedure is its ability to provide immediate, valid results. Paulson et al. (1977) found this test to be valid within 20/30 hr of disulfiram ingestion. Rychtarik et al. (1983) found that a similar but abbreviated breath test was highly sensitive in discriminating disulfiram administration. It would appear that this technique deserves added attention with respect to reliability and validity considerations. At present, however, it remains in a relatively primitive, not widely applicable, stage and may suffer from potential problems similar to those of the breathalyzer. Clients may pace drinking and disulfiram consumption so as to obtain a positive CS_2 test at regularly scheduled appointments only.

Comment

It is unlikely that there will ever be a single, objective measure of alcohol use that is totally satisfactory. Assessment of alcohol consumption, nevertheless, has advanced considerably in the past few years. Moving from sole reliance on self-reported alcohol consumption, direct observational and, in particular, biochemical indices have received mounting attention. Yet, each method has limitations. Which method is most appropriate and practical may greatly depend on the questions to be asked and the resources available. Given the current state of the art in measurement of alcohol consumption, research and treatment should strive to incorporate multiple measures, and conclusions should be drawn on the basis of the convergence of these. Further specification of parameters influencing self-report, observational, and biochemical measures will hopefully lead to more effective and efficient integration of these methods.

Case Studies

Patient 1

The patient was a 60-year-old black male who resided with his wife of 31 years. He reported taking his first drink at the age of 21 but reported a history of abusive drinking dating back 10–15 years. In the 2 years prior to his seeking treatment, he reported a marked increase in his consumption of alcohol, typically consuming 38–50 oz of 80 proof whiskey per day, every day, with the exception of a three-week period of abstinence a year earlier when he attempted to quit but resumed due to "extreme boredom." The patient's increase in consumption appeared to coincide with a layoff from his job as a mechanic. At the time of screening for participation in alcoholism treatment he considered himself disabled due to work-related back problems and had a pending claim for disability compensation. The patient's drinking history was essentially corroborated through interviews with his wife. The patient denied extreme withdrawal symptoms (i.e., DTs, seizures) but did experience tremulousness and nausea when attempting to quit. The patient reported that his last drink was the day prior to screening; a breathalyzer test administered at the time of screening revealed a BAL of .00, and blood chemistry tests administered on the same day revealed an extreme elevation in GGT level (see Figure 15.1). The patient reported seeking treatment at the time due to encouragement from a friend who had recently completed treatment. Retrospective self-reported drinking in the year prior to treatment was obtained using the quantity-frequency method. Quantity-frequency index (QFI) scores for the 1st, 6th, and 12th months prior to treatment were each 22.36. The patient was subsequently accepted for treatment and placed on a 2-week waiting list for inpatient treatment. In the interim, he was placed on an outpatient detoxification regimen and scheduled for one interim outpatient appointment 1 week prior to admission. The patient reported complete abstention from the date of screening to his admission 16 days later. This report of abstention was confirmed through three independent sources: (a) his wife's report of abstention, (b) negative breathalyzer results at the time of the interim appointment and admission, and (c) a dramatic reduction in GGT level from screening appointment to the date of admission. The GGT level at admission was still significantly elevated, presumably indicative of the slow recovery time for this measure. As is evident in Figure 15.1, decreasing GGT levels closely corresponded with decreasing QFI scores. Even though the patient had been abstinent, these latter scores are based on the 30 days prior to the assessment point and therefore still include days during which the subject was drinking abusively.

The patient was admitted to a 28-day inpatient alcohol treatment unit which followed a broad spectrum behavioral model and advocated an abstinence goal (Miller & Mastria, 1977). In addition to group components in

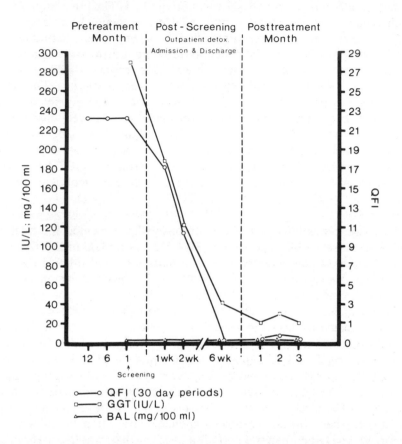

FIGURE 15.1. Case 1: Multimodal assessment across alcohol treatment phases using self-report and physiological measures.

problem-solving training, relapse prevention, and self-management training, individual treatment with this patient focused on involvement of the spouse in treatment and development of alternative activities (e.g., volunteer work, part-time employment, etc.) in order for the patient to cope with his idle time and boredom. There was no evidence of any alcohol consumption over the course of the patient's inpatient stay, and the spouse confirmed the patient's reports of abstinence on weekend passes. At the time of discharge, the patient's GGT level had been reduced further from that at the time of admission such that it was well within the normal range.

The patient subsequently entered the aftercare phase of treatment and self-reported drinking levels, breathalyzer tests, and GGT levels were obtained at the time of each aftercare appointment. Results of these assessments for the first 3 months of aftercare are shown in Figure 15.1. The breathalyzer test at each appointment was negative, and GGT levels remained stable within the normal range. The patient reported abstinence for the time period between his discharge and first appointment and this was confirmed by his spouse. At the time of his second appointment, however, he reported "testing" himself by taking a "swallow" of whiskey (estimated at 3 oz) on one day. This relapse was reportedly prompted by a visit to a local bar that he frequented prior to treatment. Estimates of the amount consumed were entirely based on the patient's self-report, as the wife suspected some light drinking but was unable to specify amounts. Some confirmation of the patient's self-reported low consumption level, however, can be obtained from the GGT level, which remained low and stable — indicative of the absence of alcohol abuse.

Patient 2

The patient was a 31-year-old white male who presented for treatment following his seventh conviction for DWI. He reported taking his first drink at the age of 12 and experimented with marijuana and other drugs as an adolescent. He reported that alcohol use became heavy during his military service in Vietnam and increased further upon his discharge from the service. In the 4 years prior to his presenting for screening for alcohol treatment, he had participated in three other alcohol treatment programs, and available records indicated a history of DSM-III Axis I diagnoses of schizophrenia (paranoid type, chronic) and posttraumatic stress disorder (PTSD) related to his combat experiences. At the time of screening, he had been unemployed for over a year and had a pending claim for disability related to his psychiatric diagnoses. The patient reported that his father, with whom he still had contact, also had a drinking problem, as did his wife, whom he had remarried 3 years earlier. Other than two periods during which he was hospitalized or in jail, the patient reported a steady, daily consumption pattern in the year prior to treatment which consisted of two six-packs of 12 oz beers daily and a 3–4 day period each month during when he consumed approximately two cases of beer per day. At the time of screening for alcohol treatment, the patient reported complete abstinence for the previous 30-day period due to his incarceration. His BAL at the time of the screening appointment was .00 and GGT was within the normal limits. He was subsequently accepted for treatment and scheduled for admission 1 week later. In the interim he was returned to jail. At the time of admission BAL and GGT both indicated abstinence in accordance with his own self-report.

The patient was admitted to the same broad-spectrum behavioral treatment program described in the first case study. In addition to standard treatment components discussed earlier, individualized goals focused on: (a) further differential diagnosis, assessment, and treatment of the patient's PTSD, (b) marital discord and the wife's own drinking problem, (c) the patient's lack of assertion with his father, who frequently stayed and drank at the patient's home, and (d) structuring the patient's idle time. The patient reportedly remained abstinent throughout the inpatient treatment program and during weekend passes at home, which was consistent with wife's report. At the time of discharge, BAL and GGT levels were consistent with this report as well (see Figure 15.2). One day after discharge, the patient relapsed into a 2-day binge during which he consumed a case of beer on each of 2 consecutive days. This binge appeared to be precipitated by an argument at a pool hall that he frequented. He reportedly stopped drinking after these 2 days and remained abstinent until his next appointment approximately 2 weeks later. His wife corroborated this report. At this appointment, his BAL was .00, but GGT was significantly elevated over the baseline GGT levels obtained during his screening, admission, and discharge — apparently reflecting the patient's binge 10 days earlier and the delay in recovery time for this measure. The patient was subsequently placed on disulfiram (Antabuse). Upon his return appointment about 6 weeks later, he reported abstinence since the last appointment and this appeared consistent with (a) the report of his wife, (b) his negative BAL, and (c) a GGT level well within the normal range (see Figure 15.2). This latter GGT level was somewhat lower than the baseline levels from screening, admission, and discharge. This discrepancy could be accounted for by the implementation of new, automated blood chemistry equipment, using slightly varied analysis procedures, in the medical center just prior to this appointment.

Case Study Summary

The two cases demonstrate the importance of incorporating multiple measures in the assessment of alcohol abuse. In both cases, the insensitivity of the breathalyzer to alcohol consumption beyond the past 24 hr is well documented. Had total reliance been placed on the BAL measure, our conclusions about treatment outcome in the few weeks following treatment would have been considerably different, particularly in the second case. For both patients, there was considerable correspondence between the 30-day QFI and GGT level. This strong relationship cannot be expected in every patient, particularly in those with complicating medical conditions. Nevertheless, as these two cases show, analysis of individualized GGT profiles may assist in the identification of relapses and the verification of self-reported drinking. Had the second patient failed to report his binge during the first aftercare visit, the significantly elevated GGT would have been a cue for treatment personnel to probe further and challenge the patient's self-report. Also important, GGT level was not significantly influenced by the relapse of the first subject. Given the relatively amount small of alcohol consumed on that one occasion, the GGT findings are consistent with other research that suggests that GGT may best be used in verifying abstention or

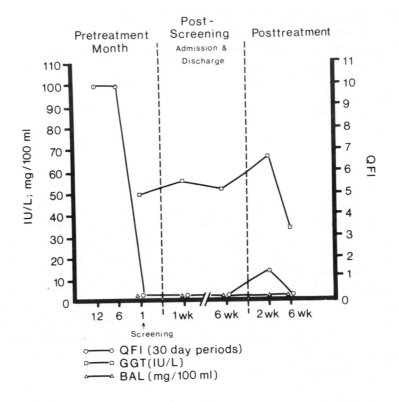

FIGURE 15.2. Case 2: Multimodal assessment across treatment phases.

abuse, and not moderate drinking episodes (Reyes & Miller, 1980).

SUMMARY

In both smoking and alcohol the need continues for including self-report measures of rate of consumption in clinical and research assessment procedures. For smoking applications, these measures may be improved by incorporating daily phone checks and having subjects keep their empty cigarette packages. Collateral sources can be used to verify self-reports for both smoking and drinking behavior when daily contact with the subject is possible, providing continuous opportunity for behavioral observation.

Laboratory-based direct observation of smoking and drinking behaviors appear to offer acceptable validity and reliability within that setting. However, the external validity with respect to natural environmental settings cannot be assumed. This limitation renders analog assessment methods most appropriate for basic studies conducted in laboratory settings. In alcohol applications, laboratory-based observations present an additional ethical consideration. Alcoholic clients for whom the treatment goal is abstinence may be reluctant to participate in any procedure requiring consumption of alcoholic beverages, even for evaluation purposes. Possible countertherapeutic effects and the client's right to refuse participation must be considered.

The latest development among behavioral scientists working with appetitive disorders is the addition of physiological or biochemical techniques in multimodal assessment approaches. In smoking, monitoring of nicotine, carbon monoxide, and thiocyanate levels is now possible. Methods to determine blood alcohol level, liver function, and alcohol consumption via GGT, and an objective test to determine Antabuse compliance are now available for alcohol assessment. While issues of reliability, validity, and complexity remain with these measures, they represent important advances beyond self-report and analog procedures in several respects. First, these measures relate actual substance use to physical impairment and health risk. Second, physiological indexes probably produce less reactivity and are less susceptible to subject distortion.

The need for individuals other than the subject to serve as collateral data providers is also reduced. Finally, further development of these more objective methods may provide a consistent set of dependent measures for use in future studies.

Smoking and alcohol assessment projects now need to be multimodal in design. Direct behavioral observations in the laboratory or clinic, reports of the target behavior in the natural environment by the subject and selected collaterals with daily contact, and newer physiological/biochemical measures need to be included to provide a balanced, comprehensive assessment approach.

REFERENCES

Armitage, A. K. (1978). The role of nicotine in the tobacco smoking habit. In R. E. Thornton (Ed.), *Smoking behavior: Physiological and psychological influences.* New York, Churchill Livingstone.

Armor, D. J., & Polich, J. M. (1982). Measurement of alcohol consumption. In E. M. Pattison & E. Kaufman (Eds.), *Encyclopedic handbook of alcoholism.* New York: Gardner Press.

Armor, D. J., Polich, J. M., & Stambul, H. B. (1978). *Alcoholism and treatment.* New York: Wiley.

Azrin, N. H., & Powell, J. (1968). Behavioral engineering: The reduction of smoking with a conditioning apparatus and procedure. *Journal of Applied Behavior Analysis, 1,* 193–200.

Barylko-Pikielna, N., & Pangborn, R. M. (1968). Effect of cigarette smoking on urinary and saliva thiocyanates. *Archives of Environmental Health, 17,* 739–745.

Benfari, R. C., McIntyre, K., Benfari, M. J. F., Baldwin, A., & Ockene, J. (1977).

The use of thiocyanate determination for indication of cigarette smoking status. *Evaluation Quarterly, 1,* 629–638.

Beresford, T., Adduci, R., Low, D., Goggans, F., & Hall, R. C. W. (1982). A computerized biochemical profile for detection of alcoholism. *Psychosomatics, 23,* 713–720.

Bigelow, G., Strickler, D., Liebson, I., & Griffiths, R. (1976). Maintaining disulfiram among outpatient alcoholics: A security-deposit contingency contracting procedure. *Behaviour Research and Therapy, 14,* 378–381.

Bliding, G., Bliding, A., Fex, G., & Tornqvist, C. (1982). The appropriateness of laboratory tests in tracing young heavy drinkers. *Drug and Alcohol Dependence, 10,* 153–158.

Blumhagen, J. M., & Little, R. E. (1985). Reliability of retrospective estimates of alcohol consumption during pregnancy by recovering women alcoholics. *Journal of Studies on Alcohol, 46,* 86–88.

Boyland, E., & Walker, S. A. (1974). Effect of thiocyanate on nitrosation of amines. *Nature, 248,* 601–602.

Brockway, B. S. (1978). Chemical validation of self-reported smoking rates. *Behavior Therapy, 9.* 685–686.

Butts, W. C., Kuehneman, J., & Widdowson, G. M. (1974). Automated method for determining serum thiocyanate to distinguish smokers from non-smokers. *Clinical Chemistry, 20,* 1344–1348.

Catchings, P. M. (1982). *Effects of using a portable smoking recorder on normal smoking topography.* Unpublished doctoral dissertation, University of Minnesota.

Caudill, B. D., & Marlatt, G. A. (1975). Modeling influences in social drinking: An experimental analogue. *Journal of Consulting and Clinical Psychology, 43,* 405–415.

Chalmers, D. M., Rinsler, M. G., MacDermott, S., Spicer, C. C., & Levi, A. J. (1981). Biochemical and haematological indicators of excessive alcohol consumption. *Gut, 22,* 992–996.

Chick, J., Kreitman, N., & Plant, M. (1981). Mean cell volume and gamma-glutamyl transpeptidase as markers of drinking in working men. *Lancet, 1,* 1249–1251.

Comer, A. K., & Creighton, D. E. (1978). The effect of experimental conditions on smoking behavior. In R. E. Thornton (Ed.), *Smoking behavior: Physiological and psychological influences.* New York: Churchill Livingston.

Cooper, A. M., Sobell, M. B., Maisto, S. A., & Sobell, L. C. (1980). Criterion intervals for pretreatment drinking measures in treatment evaluation. *Journal of Studies on Alcohol, 41,* 1186–1195.

Cowan, R., Massey, L. K., & Greenfield, T. K. (1985). Average, binge, and maximum intake in healthy young men: Discriminant function analysis. *Journal of Studies on Alcohol, 46,* 467–472.

Cravey, R. H., & Jain, N. C. (1974). Current status of blood alcohol methods. *Journal of Chromatographic Science, 12,* 209–213.

Cushman, R., Jacobson, G., Barboriak, J. J., & Anderson, A. J. (1984). Biochemical markers for alcoholism: Sensitivity problems. *Alcoholism: Clinical and Experimental Research, 8,* 253–257.

Cutter, R. E., & Storm, T. (1975). Observational study of alcohol consumption in natural settings; The Vancouver beer parlor. *Journal of Studies on Alcohol, 36* 1173–1183.

Davidson, R. S., & Stein. S. (1982). Reliability of self-report of alcoholics. *Behavior Modification, 6,* 107–119.

Delarue, N. C. (1973). The anti-smoking clinic: Is it a potential community service?

Canadian Medical Association Journal, 108, 1164-1165.

Densen P. M., Davidow, B., Bass, H. E., & Jones, E. W. (1967). A chemical test for smoking exposure. *Archives of Environmental Health, 14,* 865-874.

Dunn, P. J., & Freiesleben, E. R. (1978). The effects of nicotine enhanced cigarettes on human smoking parameters and alveolar carbon monoxide levels. In R. E. Thornton (Ed.), *Smoking behavior: Physiological and psychological influences.* New York: Churchill Livingston.

Eckardt, M. J., Ryback, R. S., Rawlings, R. R., & Graubard, B. I. (1981). Biochemical diagnosis of alcoholism: A test of the discriminating capabilities of gamma-glutamyl transpeptidase and mean corpuscular volume. *Journal of the American Medical Association, 246,* 2707-2710.

Emrick, C. D. (1974). A review of psychologically oriented treatment of alcoholism I: The use and interrelationships of outcome criteria and drinking behavior following treatment. *Quarterly Journal of Studies on Alcohol, 35,* 523-549.

Foy, D. W., Nunn, L. B., & Rychtarik, R. G. (1984). Broad spectrum behavioral treatment for chronic alcoholics: Effects of training controlled drinking skills. *Journal of Consulting and Clinical Psychology, 52,* 218-230.

Foy, D. W., Rychtarik, R. G., Nunn, L. B., & Webster, J. (1979, September). *Objective assessment of drinking behavior in alcoholic veterans.* Paper presented at the New Mexico Conference on Behavior Modification, Espanola, NM.

Foy, D. W., & Simon, S. J. (1978). Alcoholic drinking topography as a function of solitary versus social context. *Addictive Behaviors, 3,* 39-41.

Frederiksen, L.W. (1977). *But I don't want to quit smoking: Alternatives to abstinence.* Paper presented at the meeting of the Association for the Advancement of Behavior Therapy, Atlanta, December.

Frederiksen, L. W., Epstein, L. H., & Kosevsky, B. P. (1975). Reliability and controlling effects of three procedures for self-monitoring smoking. *The Psychological Record, 25,* 255-264.

Frederiksen, L. W., & Martin, J. E. (1979). Carbon monoxide and smoking behavior. *Addictive Behaviors, 4,* 21-30.

Frederiksen, L. W., Martin, J. E., & Webster, J. S. (1979). Assessment of smoking behavior. *Journal of Applied Behavior Analysis, 12,* 653-664.

Frederiksen, L. W., & Simon, S. J. (1979). Modification of smoking behavior. In R. S. Davidson (Ed.), *Modification of pathological behavior.* New York: Gardner Press.

Freedberg, E. J., & Johnston, W. E. (1980). Validity and reliability of alcoholics' self-reports of use of alcohol submitted before and after treatment. *Psychological Reports, 46,* 999-1005.

Gabel, P. C., Noel, N. E., Keane, T. M., & Lisman, S. A. (1979). *Effects of sexual versus fear arousal on alcohol consumption in college males.* Unpublished manuscript, State University of New York at Binghamton.

Garvin, R. B., Foy, D. W., & Alford, G. S. (1981). A critical examination of gamma-glutamyl transpeptidase as a biochemical marker for alcohol abuse. *Addictive Behaviors, 6,* 377-383.

Gluud, C., Andersen, I., Dietrichson, O., Gluud, B., Jacobsen, A., & Juhl, E. (1981). Gamma-glutamyltransferase, aspartate aminotransferase and alkaline phosphatase as markers of alcohol consumption in outpatient alcoholics. *European Journal of Clinical Investigation, 11,* 171-176.

Gori, G. B. (1972). Research in smoking and health at the National Cancer Institute, *Journal of the National Cancer Institute, 48,* 1759-1762.

Gori, G. B. (1976). Low risk cigarettes: A prescription. *Science, 19,* 1243-1245.

Hendricks R. D., Sobell, M. B., & Cooper, A. M. (1978). Social influences on human ethanol consumption in an analogue situation. *Addictive Behaviors. 3*, 253-259.

Hengen, N., & Hengen, M. (1978). Gas-liquid chromatographic determination of nicotine and cotinine in plasma. *Clinical Chemistry, 24*, 50-53.

Henningfield, J. E., & Griffiths, R. R. (1979). A preparation for the experimental analysis of human cigarette smoking behavior. *Behavior Research Methods and Instrumentation, 11*, 538-544.

Hersen, M. (1976). Historical perspectives in behavioral assessment. In M. Hersen & A. S. Bellack (Eds.), *Behavioral assessment: A practical handbook*. New York: Pergamon.

Hesselbrock, M., Babor, T. F., Hesselbrock, V., Meyer, R. E., & Workman, K. (in press). "Never believe an alcoholic?" On the validity of self-report measures of alcohol dependence and related constructs. *International Journal of the Addictions.*

Higgins, R. L., & Marlatt, G. A. (1973). The effects of anxiety arousal upon the consumption of alcohol by alcoholics and social drinkers. *Journal of Consulting and Clinical Psychology, 41*, 426-433.

Hill, P., & Marquardt, H. (1980). Plasma and urine changes after smoking different brands of cigarettes. *Clinical Pharmacology and Therapeutics, 27*, 652-658.

Holland, R., Datta. K., Izadi, B., & Evenson, R. (1979). Reliability of an alcohol self-report instrument. *Journal of Studies on Alcohol, 40*, 142-144.

Hunter, P. A., Hannon, R., & Marchi, D. (1979, December). *Observation of drinking behavior in a natural setting.* Paper presented at the meeting of the Association for Advancement of Behavior Therapy, San Francisco, CA.

Jaffe, J. H., Kanzler, M., Cohen, M., & Kaplan, T. (1978). Inducing low tar/nicotine cigarette smoking in women. *British Journal of Addiction, 73*, 271-278.

Jain, N. C., & Cravey, R. H. (1974). A review of breath alcohol methods. *Journal of Chromatographic Science, 12*, 214-218.

Jarvik, M. E., Popek, P., Schneider, N. G., Baer-Weiss, V., & Gritz, E. R. (1978). Can cigarette size and nicotine content influence smoking and puffing rates? *Psychopharmacology, 58*, 303-306.

Keane, T. M., Foy, D. W., Nunn, L. B., & Rychtarik, R. G. (1980). Improving antabuse compliance in alcoholic patients. *Journal of Clinical Psychology, 140*, 340-344.

King. A., Scott, R. R., & Prue, D. M. (1984). The reactive effects of assessing reported rates and alveolar carbon monoxide levels on smoking behavior. *Addictive Behaviors, 8*, 323-327.

Kricka, L. J., & Clark, P. M. S. (1979). *Biochemistry of alcohol and alcoholism.* New York: Halstead Press.

Lader, M. (1978). Nicotine and smoking behavior. *British Journal of Clinical Pharmacology, 5*, 289-292.

Langone, J. J., & Van Vunakis, V. (1975). Quantitation of cotinine in sera of smokers. *Research Communications in Chemical Pathology and Pharmacology, 10*, 21-28.

Lederer, J. (1976). Nitrosamines: A serious problem in alimentary hygiene. *Louvain Medical Journal, 95*, 135-143.

Little, R. E., Mandell, W., & Schultz, F. A. (1977). Consequences of retrospective measurement of alcohol consumption. *Journal of Studies on Alcohol, 38*, 1777-1781.

Lovibond, S. H., & Caddy, G. (1970). Discriminated aversive control in the moderation of alcoholics' drinking behavior. *Behavior Therapy, 1*, 437-444.

Maisto, S. A., & O'Farrell, T. J. (1985). Comment on the validity of Watson et al.'s "Do alcoholics give valid self-reports?" *Journal of Studies on Alcohol, 46,* 447–450.

Maisto, S. A., Sobell, L. C., Cooper, A. M., & Sobell, M. B. (1979). Test-retest reliability of retrospective self-reports in three populations of alcohol abusers. *Journal of Behavioral Assessment, 1,* 315–326.

Maisto, S. A., Sobell, L. C., Cooper, A. M., & Sobell, M. B. (1982). Comparison of two techniques to obtain retrospective reports of drinking behavior from alcohol abusers. *Addictive Behaviors, 7,* 33–38.

Maisto, S. A., Sobell, L. C., & Sobell, M. B. (1979). Comparison of alcoholic's self-reports of drinking behavior with reports of collateral informants. *Journal of Consulting and Clinical Psychology, 47,* 106–112.

Marlatt, G. A., Demming, B., & Reid, J. B. (1973). Loss of control drinking in alcoholics: An experimental analogue. *Journal of Abnormal Psychology, 81,* 214–233.

Mayfield, D. G., & Johnston, R. G. M. (1980). Screening techniques and prevalence estimation in alcoholism. In W. E. Fann, I. Karacan, A. D. Pokorny, & R. L. Williams (Eds.), *Phenomenology and treatment of alcoholism.* New York: Spectrum.

McCrady, B. S., Duclos, S., Dubreuil, E., Stout, R., & Fisher-Nelson, H. (1984). Stability of drinking prior to alcoholism treatment. *Addictive Behaviors, 9,* 329–333.

McCrady, B. S., Paolino, T. J., & Longabaugh, R. (1978). Correspondence between reports of problem drinkers and spouses on drinking behavior and impairment. *Journal of Studies on Alcohol, 39,* 1252–1257.

McFall, R. M. (1970). Effects of self-monitoring on normal smoking behavior. *Journal of Consulting and Clinical Psychology, 35,* 135–142.

McFall, R. M. (1978). Smoking cessation research. *Journal of Consulting and Clinical Psychology, 46,* 703–712.

Mello, N. K., & Mendelson, J. H. (1971). A quantitative analysis of drinking patterns in alcoholics. *Archives of General Psychiatry, 35,* 135–142.

Midanik, L. (1982). The validity of self-reported alcohol consumption and alcohol problems: A literature review. *British Journal of Addiction, 77,* 357–382.

Miller, P. M., Becker, J. V., Foy, D. W., & Wooten, L. S. (1976). Instructional control of the components of alcoholic drinking behavior. *Behavior Therapy, 7,* 472–480.

Miller, P. M., & Hersen, M. (1972a). *A quantitative measurement system for alcoholism and treatment.* Paper presented at the annual meeting of the Association for the Advancement of the Behavior Therapy, New York.

Miller, P. M., & Hersen, M. (1972b). Quantitative changes in alcohol consumption as a function of electrical aversive conditioning. *Journal of Clinical Psychology, 28,* 590–593.

Miller, P. M., Hersen, M., Eisler, R. M., & Elkin, T. E. (1974). A retrospective analysis of alcohol consumption on laboratory tasks as related to therapeutic outcome. *Behaviour Research and Therapy, 12,* 73–76.

Miller, P. M., Hersen, M., Eisler, R. M., & Hilsman, G. (1974). Effects of social stress on operant drinking of alcoholics and social drinkers. *Behaviour Research and Therapy, 12,* 67–72.

Miller, P. M., Hersen, M., Eisler, R. M., & Watts, J. G. (1974). Contingent reinforcement of lowered blood/alcohol levels in an outpatient chronic alcoholic. *Behaviour Research and Therapy, 12,* 261–263.

Miller, P. M., & Mastria, M. A. (1977). *Alternatives to alcohol abuse: A social learning model.* Champaign, IL: Research Press.

Miller, W. R., Crawford, V. L., & Taylor, C. A. (1979). Significant others as corroborative sources for problem drinkers. *Addictive Behaviors, 4*, 67–70.

Miller, W. R., & Hester, R. K. (1980). Treating the problem drinker: Modern approaches. In W. R. Miller (Ed.), *The addictive behaviors* (pp. 11-42). New York: Pergamon.

Moss, R. A., Prue, D. M., Lomax, D., & Martin, J. E. (1982). Implications of self-monitoring for smoking treatment: Effects on adherence and session attendance. *Addictive Behaviors, 7*, 381–385.

Nathan, P. E., & O'Brien, J. S. (1971). An experimental analysis of the behavior of alcoholics and non-alcoholics during prolonged experimental drinking. *Behavior Therapy, 2*, 455–476.

Nunn, L. B., Foy, D. W., & Rychtarik, R. G. (1980). *Measuring blood alcohol levels in alcoholics: Influences on alcoholics' aftercare attendance.* Unpublished manuscript, University of Mississippi Medical Center.

O'Farrell, T. J., Cutter, H. S. G., Bayog, R. D., Dentch, G., & Fortgang, J. (1981). Correspondence between one-year retrospective reports of pretreatment drinking by alcoholics and their wives. *Behavioral Assessment, 6*, 263–274.

Ohlin, P., Lundh, B., & Westling, H. (1976). Carbon monoxide blood levels and reported cessation of smoking. *Psychopharmacology, 49*, 263–265.

Orrego, H., Blendis, L. M., Blake, J. E., Kapur, B. M., & Israel, Y. (1979). Reliability of assessment of alcohol intake based on personal interviews in a liver clinic. *Lancet, 2*, 1354–1356.

Papoz, L., Warnet, J. M., Pequignot, G., Eschwege, E., Claude, J.-R., & Schwartz, D. (1981). Alcohol consumption in a healthy population: Relationship to gamma-glutamyl transferase activity and mean corpuscular volume. *Journal of the American Medical Association, 245*, 1748–1751.

Paulson, S. M., Krause, S., & Iber, F. L. (1977). Development and evaluation of a compliance test for patients taking disulfiram. *John Hopkins Medical Journal, 141*, 119–125.

Paxton, R., & Bernacca, G. (1979). Urinary nicotine concentration as a function of time since last cigarette: Implications for detecting faking in smoking clinics. *Behavior Therapy, 10*, 523–528.

Pechacek, T. F. (1979). Modification of smoking behavior. *Surgeon General's Report on Smoking and Health.* USDHEW: DHEW Publication No. 79-50066.

Phillips, E. L. R., Little, R. E., Hillman, R. S., Labbe, R. F., & Campbell, C. (1984). A field test of the sweat patch. *Alcoholism: Clinical and Experimental Research, 8*, 233–237.

Phillips, M. (1982). Sweat-patch test for alcohol consumption: Rapid assay with an electrochemical detector. *Alcoholism: Clinical and Experimental Research, 6*, 532–534.

Phillips, M., & McAloon, M. H. (1980). A sweat-patch test for alcohol consumption: Evaluation in continuous and episodic drinkers. *Alcoholism: Clinical and Experimental Research, 4*, 391–395.

Poikolainen, K., Karkkainen, P., & Pikkarainen, J. (1985). Correlations between biological markers and alcohol intake as measured by diary and questionnaire in men. *Journal of Studies on Alcohol, 46*, 383–387.

Polich, J. M. (1982). The validity of self-reports in alcoholism research. *Addictive Behaviors, 7*, 123–132.

Polich, J. M., Armor, D. J., & Braiker, H. B. (1980). *The course of alcoholism: Four years after treatment* (R-2433-NIAAA). Santa Monica: The Rand Corporation.

Polich, J. M., & Orvis, B. R. (1979). *Alcohol problems: Patterns and prevalence in the U.S. Air Force.* Santa Monica: The Rand Corporation.

Pomerleau, O., & Adkins, D. (1980). Evaluating behavioral and traditional treatment for problem drinkers. In L.C. Sobell, M.B. Sobell, & E. Ward (Eds.), *Evaluating alcohol and drug abuse treatment effectiveness* (pp. 93-108). New York: Pergamon.

Prue, D. M., Krapfl, J. E., & Martin, J. E. (1981). Biochemical exposure following changes to low tar and nicotine cigarettes. *Behavior Therapy, 12*, 400-416.

Prue, D. M., Martin, J. E., & Hume, A. (1980). A critical evaluation of thiocyanate as a biochemical index of smoking exposure. *Behavior Therapy, 11*, 368-379.

Prue, D. M., Martin, J. E., Hume, A. S., & Davis, N. S. (1981). Reliability of thiocyanate measurement of smoking exposure. *Addictive Behaviors, 6*, 99-105.

Prue, D. M., Scott, R. S., & Denier, C. A. (1985). Assessment of smoking behavior. In W. W. Tryon (Ed.), *Behavioral assessment in behavioral medicine.* New York: Springer Publishing Co.

Reid, J. B. (1978). Study of drinking in natural settings. In G. A. Marlatt & P. E. Nathan (Eds.,), *Behavioral approaches to alcoholism.* New Brunswick, NJ: Rutgers Center on Alcohol Studies.

Reyes, E., & Miller, W. R. (1980). Serum gamma-glutamyl transpeptidase as a diagnostic aid in problem drinkers. *Addictive Behaviors, 5*, 59-65.

Rickert, W. S., & Robinson, J. C. (1981). Estimating the hazards of less hazardous cigarettes. II. Study of cigarette yields of nicotine, carbon monoxide, and hydrogen cyanide in relation to levels of cotinine, carboxyhaemoglobin, and thiocyanate in smokers. *Journal of Toxicology and Environmental Health, 7*, 391-403.

Robinson, D., & Forbes, W. F. (1975). The role of carbon monoxide in cigarette smoking. *Environmental Health, 30*, 425-433.

Room, R. (1971). Survey vs. sales data for the U.S. *Drinking and Drug Practices Surveyor, 3*, 15-16.

Rosenbluth, J., Nathan, P. E., & Lawson, D. M. (1978). Environmental influences on drinking by college students in a college pub: Behavioral observation in the natural environment. *Addictive Behaviors, 3*, 117-121.

Ross, W. S. (1976a). Poison gases in your cigarettes: Carbon monoxide. *Readers Digest, 109*, 114-118.

Ross, W. S. (1976b). Poison gases in your cigarettes: Hydrogen cyanide and nitrogen oxides. *Readers Digest, 109*, 92-98.

Royal College of Physicians (1971). *Smoking or Health Now.* London: Pitman.

Russell, M. A. H. (1978). Self-regulation of nicotine by smokers. In K. Battig (Ed.), *Behavioral effects of nicotine.* Basel: S. Karger.

Ryback, R. S., & Eckhardt, M. J. (1982). Toward a biochemical definition of alcoholism. In I. Hanin & E. Usdin (Eds.), *Biological markers in psychiatry and neurology* (pp. 425-432). New York: Pergamon.

Ryback, R. S., Eckhardt, M. J., & Pautler, C. P. (1980). Biochemical and hematological correlates of alcoholism. *Research Communications in Chemical Pathology and Pharmacology, 27*, 53--550.

Rychtarik, R. G., Foy, D. W., Scott, T., Lokey, L., & Prue, D.M. (in press). Five-six year follow-up of broadspectrum behavioral treatment for alcoholism: Effects of training controlled drinking skills. *Journal of Consulting and Clinical Psychology.*

Rychtarik, R. G., Smith, P. O., Jones, S. L., Doerfler, L., Hale, R., & Prue, D. M. (1983). Assessing disulfiram compliance: Validational study of an abbreviated breath test procedure. *Addictive Behaviors, 8*, 361-368.

Sanchez-Craig, M., & Annis, H. M. (1981). Gamma-glutamyl transpeptidase and high-density lipoproteins cholesterol in male problem drinkers: Advantages of a composite index for predicting alcohol consumption. *Alcoholism: Clinical and Experimental Research, 5*, 540–544.

Sanchez-Craig, M., Annis, H. M., Bornet, A. R., & MacDonald, K. R. (1984). Random assignment to abstinence and controlled drinking evaluation of a cognitive-behavioral program for problem drinkers. *Journal of Consulting and Clinical Psychology, 52*, 390-403.

Schachter, S. (1977). Nicotine regulation in heavy and light smokers. *Journal of Experimental Psychology, General,106*, 5–12.

Schaefer, H. H., Sobell, M. B., & Mills, K. C. (1971). Baseline drinking behaviors in alcoholics and social drinkers, kinds of drinks and sip magnitude. *Behaviour Research and Therapy, 9*, 23–27.

Sillett, R. W., Wilson, M. B., Malcolm. R. E., & Ball, K. P. (1978). Deception among smokers. *British Medical Journal, 28*, 1185–1186.

Sobell, L. C., Cellucci, T., Nirenberg, T. D., & Sobell, M. B. (1982). Do quantity-frequency data underestimate drinking-related health risks? *American Journal of Public Health, 72*, 823–828.

Sobell, L. C., Maisto, S. A., Sobell, M. B., & Cooper, A. M. (1979). Reliability of alcohol abusers' self-reports of drinking behavior. *Behaviour Research and Therapy, 17*, 157–160.

Sobell, L. C., & Sobell, M. B. (1975). Outpatient alcoholics give valid self-reports. *Journal of Nervous and Mental Disease, 161*, 32–42.

Sobell, L. C., & Sobell, M. B. (1978). Validity of self-reports in three populations of alcoholics. *Journal of Consulting and Clinical Psychology, 46*, 901–907.

Sobell, M. B., Maisto, S. A., Sobell, L. C., Cooper, A. M., Cooper, T., & Sanders, B. (1980). Developing a prototype for evaluating alcohol treatment effectiveness. In L. C. Sobell, M. B. Sobell, & E. Ward, (Eds.), *Evaluating alcohol and drug abuse treatment effectiveness: Recent advances.* New York: Pergamon.

Sobell, M. B., Schaefer, H. H., & Mills, K. C. (1972). Differences in baseline drinking behavior between alcoholics and normal drinkers. *Behaviour Research and Therapy. 10,* 257–267.

Sobell, M. B., & Sobell, L. C. (1973). Individualized behavior therapy for alcoholics. *Behavior Therapy, 4*, 49–72.

Sobell, M. B., Sobell, I. C., & Samuels, F. H. (1974). Validity of self-reports of alcohol-related arrests by alcoholics. *Quarterly Journal of Studies on Alcohol, 35*, 276–280.

Sobell, M. B., Sobell, L. C., & VanderSpek, R. (1979). Relationships among clinical judgement, self-report, and breath-analysis measures of intoxication in alcoholics. *Journal of Consulting and Clinical Psychology, 47*, 204–206.

Sommer, R. (1965). The isolated drinker in the Edmonton beer parlor. *Quarterly Journal of Studies on Alcohol, 26*, 95–110.

Stacy, A. W., Widaman, K. F., Hays, R., & DiMatteo, M. R. (1985). Validity of self-reports of alcohol and other drug use: A multitrait-multimethod assessment. *Journal of Personality and Social Psychology, 49*, 219–232.

Streissguth, A. P., Martin, D. C., & Buffington, V. E. (1976). Test-retest reliability of three scales derived from a quantity-frequency-variability assessment of self-reported alcohol consumption. *Annals of the New York Academy of Sciences, 273*, 458–466.

Strickler, D. P., Dobbs, S. D., & Maxwell, W. A. (1979). The influence of setting on drinking behaviors: The laboratory versus the barroom. *Addictive Behaviors, 4*,

339–344.

Tenovuo, J., & Makinen, K. K. (1976). Concentration of thiocyanate and ionizable iodine in saliva of smokers and nonsmokers. *Journal of Dental Research, 55*, 661–663.

Teplin, L. A., & Lutz, G. W. (1985). Measuring alcohol intoxication: The development reliability and validity of an observational instrument. *Journal of Studies on Alcohol, 46*, 459–466.

Turner, J. A., Sillett, R. W., & Ball, K. P. (1974). Some effects of changing to low tar and low nicotine cigarettes. *Lancet*, (2), 737–739.

U.S. Public Health Service (1979). *Smoking and health: A report of the surgeon general: 1979.* Washington, DC: USDHEW, DHEW Publication No. 79–50066.

Vesey, C. J. (1981). Thiocyanate and cigarette consumption. In R. M. Greenhalgh (Ed.), *Smoking and arterial disease.* Bath, U.K.: Pitman Medical

Vogt, T. M. (1977). Smoking behavioral factors as predictors of risk. In M. Jarvik, J. Cullen, E. Gritz, T. Vogt, & L. West (Eds.), *Research on smoking behavior.* NIDA Research Monograph No. 17, DHEW Publication No. (ADM) 78–581.

Wald, N., & Howard S. (1975). Smoking, carbon monoxide and arterial disease. *Annals of Occupational Hygiene, 18*, 1–14.

Wald, N., Idle, M., & Bailey, A. (1978). Carboxyhaemoglobin levels and inhaling habits in cigarette smokers. *Thorax, 33*, 201–206.

Warnet, J. M., Papoz, L., Pequignot, G., Eschwege, E., Claude, J. R., & Schwartz, D. (1984). Alcohol consumption in healthy women: Relationship to gamma-glutamyl transferase activity, mean corpuscular volume and hormonal status. *Canadian Journal of Public Health, 75*, 285–288.

Watson, C. G. (1985). More reasons for a moratorium: A reply to Mastio and O'Farrell. *Journal of Studies on Alcohol, 46*, 450–453.

Watson, C. G., & Pucel, J. (1985). Consistency of posttreatment of alcoholics' drinking patterns. *Journal of Consulting and Clinical Psychology, 53*, 679–683.

Watson, C. G., Tilleskjor, C., Hoodecheck-Schow, E. A., Pucel, J., & Jacobs, L. (1985). Do alcoholics give valid self-reports? *Journal of Studies on Alcohol, 45*, 344–348.

Williams, A. F. (1978). Feasibility of determining blood alcohol concentrations in social drinking settings. *Journal of Studies on Alcohol, 39*, 201–206.

Williams, G. D., Aitken, S. S., & Malin, H. (1985). Reliability of self-reported alcohol consumption in a general population survey. *Journal of Studies on Alcohol, 46*, 223–227.

Williams, R. J., & Brown, R. A. (1974). Differences in baseline drinking behavior between New Zealand alcoholics and normal drinkers. *Behaviour Research and Therapy, 12*, 287–294.

Zeidenberg, P., Jaffe, J. H., Kanzler, M., Levitt, M. D., Langone, J. J., & Van Vunakis, H. (1977). Nicotine: Cotinine levels in blood during cessation of smoking. *Comprehensive Psychiatry, 18*, 93–101.

16
Assessment of Child Behavior Problems

Alan M. Gross
John T. Wixted

Child behavioral assessment emerged as an independent discipline only in the last decade, but in that time the field has progressed at a rapid pace. The range of assessment procedures available to the researcher and clinician, once restricted to naturalistic observation, has grown to include behavioral rating scales, self-report instruments, observation in clinic analog settings, and role-play tests of assertiveness. The rapid proliferation of child behavioral assessment strategies has been paralleled by an increased reliance on traditional psychometric analysis as a means of evaluating the utility of newly proposed assessment techniques (Cone, 1977, 1981; Hartmann, Roper, & Bradford, 1979; Linehan, 1980). This present chapter reviews the most commonly employed child assessment methods, considers their psychometric properties, and describes how these methods may be effectively administered on an individual basis.

The basic objectives of behavioral assessment, whether for children or adults, are to identify problems behaviors and their controlling variables, to measure changes in those behaviors as a result of treatment intervention, and to evaluate the durability of treatment gains after the intervention program has concluded. In addition to these shared goals, however, a number of important considerations are unique to child behavioral assessment. First, because children rarely refer themselves for treatment, an examination of the referral process itself is essential. Several experiments have found that the behavior of some clinic-referred children cannot be distinguished from that of nonreferred children on the basis of behavioral observations (Delfini, Bernal, & Rosen, 1976; Lobitz & Johnson, 1975a). In this regard, both marital discord and parental depression have been identified as contributing to perceptions of deviancy on the part of the child (Furey & Forehand, 1984; Oltmanns, Broderick, & O'Leary, 1977). Findings such as these indicate that the therapist should be sensitive to the possible existence of problems within the family that may supersede complaints about the child.

The rapid developmental changes occurring throughout childhood also present special difficulties for those concerned with the assessment of a child's behavior (cf. Edelbrock, 1984). The capabilities of younger children often differ greatly from those of children just a few years older. Therefore, it may be important to know whether the desired behaviors (e.g., appropriate social skills) are typically exhibited by children in the age group in question. In addition to varying capabilities, the behaviors that constitute a problem for children of one age may not be a problem for children of another. For example, bed-wetting three nights a week may be reason for concern if the child is 6 years old. The same in behavior in a 2-year-old, however, may be within normal limits. In dealing with questions of developmental strengths and limitations, the increased use of normative comparisons in child behavioral assessment has been of enormous benefit.

In addition to such practical considerations, a persistent and controversial conceptual problem involved in the assessment of childhood behavior is the issue of classification (Kazdin, 1983). Behavior analysts have generally eschewed traditional classification systems, such as DSM III, because of low interrater agreement, dubious empirical validity, the apparent implication of disease, and the undesirable social effects of labeling children (Ciminero & Drabman, 1977). Recently, however, a number of authors have advocated an alternative approach to classification that is empirically based (Achenbach & Edelbrock, 1978; Dreger, 1982; Quay, 1979). An empirical taxonomy is constructed by sampling a wide range of behavior (usually by means of behavioral rating scales) and subjecting the data to factor analyses to determine which deviant behaviors tend to appear together. The identification of consistent groups of behaviors, called "syndromes," usually entails no etiological assumptions and therefore may be consistent with a variety of therapeutic perspectives.

Achenbach and Edelbrock (1978) and Quay (1979) have noted considerable agreement between a very large number of studies using this methodology in identifying two broad-band syndromes termed *externalizing* and *internalizing*. Externalizing disorders are those characterized by behavioral excess, such as that exhibited by children referred to as conduct disordered, oppositional, or hyperactive. Internalizing disorders are characterized primarily by behavioral withdrawal, such as might be exhibited by children referred to as anxious/withdrawn or depressed. Although many instruments across many studies have distinguished externalizing and internalizing dimensions, agreement between studies on more specific syndromes is low. Nevertheless, those following the empirical approach to the classification of child behavioral problems hope that it will ultimately produce a much more reliable nosology than other available systems.

The most often cited advantages of an empirically based classification system are that it would: (a) encourage research aimed at identifying etiological factors involved in the disorder, (b) promote the development of effective interventions for specific child populations, and (c) eventually provide some information regarding the long-term prognosis for children with various behavioral disorders (Achenbach, 1978; Wells, 1981). Despite these potential benefits, Haynes and Wilson (1979) have cautioned against the hasty acceptance of an empirically derived diagnostic system. From a behavioral perspective, one difficulty with any diagnostic label is the implication that the identified behavioral syndrome will generalize across situations. Haynes and Wilson suggest that an empirical analysis of the cross-situational stability of each behavioral syndrome would be necessary in order for a diagnostic system to be consistent with behavioral principles. The likely outcome of such an analysis would be that certain syndromes would generalize across situations while others would be more situation specific (cf. Mischel, 1977).

Another important limitation of diagnostic labels is that they offer no information regarding possible situational variables that may be controlling the child's behavior. The diagnostic label "oppositional disorder," for example, provides some insight into what the problem behaviors are, but suggests nothing about what might be producing or maintaining those behaviors. Thus, while diagnostic categories may help in the communication about children who exhibit similar clusters of deviant behavior, the view that diagnosis should indicate the form of treatment in the absence of behavioral analysis is necessarily contrary to the behavioral approach to treating deviant behavior.

The following sections review the most widely employed child behavioral assessment procedures. The first section covers the primary indirect methods, which include the behavioral interview, behavioral rating scales, and self-report measures. The next section reviews direct methods of behavioral assessment, including observation in natural settings, observation of parent–child interactions in a clinic analog setting, and role-play tests for assessing children's social skills. The chapter concludes with a case study illustrating the integrated use of multiple assessment techniques.

INDIRECT METHODS

Behavioral Interview

A necessary element of every child assessment case is an interview with the primary referral source, usually the child's parent or teacher. The initial interview affords an economical means of identifying deviant child behavior, acquiring some understanding of the situational determinants of that behavior, and orienting the child's parent (teacher) to the types of assessment and treatment procedures that may be implemented at a later time (Wahler & Cormier, 1970). In addition, periodic interviews permit the therapist to roughly monitor the progress of treatment and to assess client perceptions of improvement after treatment has been completed (Gross, 1984).

In most cases, behavioral interviews are unstructured in that specific information is elicited at the therapist's discretion. Because the lack of structure permits rather extreme variability between therapists, a detailed psychometric analysis of this type of interview is almost impossible. However, because it is by far the most commonly employed assessment technique, the principles governing the unstructured interview will be described in some detail prior to a discussion of more standardized interview formats.

Unstructured Interviews

The unstructured interview is initiated by asking broad and open-ended questions about the nature of the presenting problem (e.g., "Please describe what your child does that concerns you"; "What problems have you been having with your child?"). Typically, parents will list a variety of concerns about their child using rather global and nonspecific terminology. An initial task of the therapist, therefore, is to help the parent describe the child's behavior as precisely as possible. Thus, for example, if a parent describes the child as suffering from a severe attitude problem, the therapist should inquire into exactly what the child does that leads the parent to that conclusion.

In order to gauge the severity of the presenting complaints, the parent or referral source should also be asked to provide estimates concerning the frequency (e.g., "How many fights has your son been involved with in the last month?"), duration (e.g., "How long do the temper tantrums usually last?"), and intensity (e.g., "How scared does he seem when you try to bring him to school?") of the identified problem behaviors (Witt & Elliott, 1983). The first behaviors targeted for treatment can be selected on the basis of this information. For example, behaviors that appear dangerous to the child or that appear to cause the child extreme distress can be targeted first. Otherwise, the parent or teacher may be asked to rank multiple problem behaviors in terms of priority.

An especially important objective of the initial interview is to identify the conditions under which the child's problem behaviors are most likely to occur. Such information may be difficult to obtain because most people are not accustomed to thinking of behavior as being situationally determined. Educating the parent in some of the basic principles of behavioral theory may facilitate this phase of the interview. Specific questions should be directed toward the setting in which the problem behaviors tend to occur (e.g., "How

Behavioral Assessment

does your child behave at home vs. at school?'') as well as toward typical antecedents and consequences (e.g., "What is likely to be going on just before she misbehaves?''; "What do you do in response to such behavior?'') of those behaviors.

In addition to identifying the environmental correlates of the child's deviant behavior, Nelson and Hayes (1979) recommend that the interviewer examine possible organismic controlling variables, a topic that is frequency overlooked by behavior analysts. For example, if a parent reports that a head injury to the child occurred at about the same time that the teacher began reporting attentional difficulties at school, medical rather than behavioral intervention might be indicated.

Following the survey of problem behaviors and possible controlling variables, the interviewer should encourage the parent or teacher to delineate acceptable behavioral alternatives. In some cases, the preferred behavior may not be in the child's behavioral repertoire, requiring that the behavior be shaped. In other cases, however, the child may exhibit appropriate behavior in a variety of situations, but this has simply gone unnoticed by the parents. Information on these matters can be obtained by asking the parent to list some of their child's behavioral assets (e.g., "Can you think of any situations in which he usually does what he is told?''; "When is he not a problem?''). In addition to providing some indication of the child's capabilities, an inquiry of this sort may help to ameliorate the parents' negative perceptions of the child.

For many cases, another important interview function is to identify potentially reinforcing stimuli for the child. The interviewer may inquire directly into preferred activities (e.g., "What does he like to do after school?''; "Does she like TV?'') or may request that the parent complete a reward survey schedule (e.g., Cautela, Cautela, & Esonis, 1983). In addition, both parents and teachers should be advised of the powerfully reinforcing effects of adult attention for most children.

A portion of the initial interview should also be reserved for surveying problem areas other than those already described by the parents (Haynes, 1978). In this regard, parents may simply be asked if there are any problems in the family that have not yet been dicussed. This information may help the therapist determine whether factors other than the child's behavior (e.g., marital difficulties) need to be further assessed. In some cases, problems with the child may turn out to be secondary to more pressing problems within the family.

The interview should be closed with the therapist providing a conceptualization of the child's problem behavior and a discussion of additional assessment techniques that may be necessary to augment information gathered in the interview. While most parents and teachers will agree to complete one or more behavioral checklists (discussed in the next section), they may object to the presence of unfamiliar observers in their home or classroom. In such cases, alternative assessment procedures, such as using participant observers to collect observational data or conducting observations in the clinic can be considered (see section on observational assessment in this chapter).

After meeting with the parents, a brief interview with the child alone is usually conducted (Gross, 1984). This interview can be initiated by asking why the child thinks the family has come to the clinic. Because children often feel uniquely blamed for family difficulties, the therapist should offer a nonthreatening rationale for therapy that does not single out one individual as the core of the problem. For example, the therapist might tell the child that the treatment will probably involve several family members and will help to make things more pleasant at home for everyone.

A meeting with the child also allows the therapist to roughly evaluate the child's social skills and deficits prior to treatment and to reassure the child that his or her concerns will not be ignored. Older children especially may be concerned about confidentiality, fearing that anything they say will be reported to their parents. One approach to this problem is to explain to the entire family in a joint session that, except in cases where the child's behavior appears to be dangerous, the child's right to privacy will be respected (Gross, 1984). Finally, children of all ages can be asked to complete a reward survey schedule in order to identify reinforcers to be used during treatment (e.g., Keat, 1979).

Structured Interviews

Although the unstructured interview possesses a high degree of face validity, its psychometric properties are essentially unknown (Gross, 1984). Structured interviews, which consist of a prearranged set of questions to be asked in sequential order, are much more susceptible to psychometric analysis. A number of structured interviews have been proposed in recent years, but only two, both designed for interviewing children, have received adequate psychometric evaluation.

The Diagnostic Interview for Children and Adolescents (DICA; Herjanic, Herjanic, Brown, & Wheatt, 1975) consists of 207 questions that cover four major areas: (a) factual information (e.g., age, address, etc.), (b) behavior, (c) psychiatric symptoms, and (d) mental status (e.g., orientation). For most of the questions, the child is required to simply answer yes or no. Herjanic et al. (1975) reported high interrater agreement (.89) and high agreement between the parent and child when they were interviewed separately (.80). Herjanic and Campbell (1977) also demonstrated that the DICA could discriminate normal children from those attending a psychiatric outpatient facility.

A second structured interview for children, The Child Assessment

Schedule (CAS), has been developed to provide information regarding content areas of dysfunction (e.g., school, friends, family, etc.) and DSM III diagnoses (Hodges, Kline, Fitch, McKnew, & Cytryn, 1981). Hodges, McKnew, Cytryn, Stern, and Kline (1982) summarized the results of several studies evaluating the psychometric properties of the CAS. Interrater agreement based on videotaped interviews has been found to be high (.90 and .91), and scores for children with differing levels of pathology (normal, psychiatric outpatient, and psychiatric inpatient) differed significantly. Further, in a test of concurrent validity, the total pathology score from the CAS was found to correlate highly with a similar score derived from a parent rating scale.

Both the DICA and the CAS may be employed clinically to help in the identification of specific problem behaviors and as screening instruments for referred children, though to date no normative data have been collected. Several structured interviews for parents of deviant children are also available, but none have been subjected to systematic psychometric evaluation. Two commonly used behavioral structured interviews, described by Holland (1970) and Patterson, Reid, Jones and Conger (1975), offer the advantage of analyzing both the behavioral and environmental aspects of a child's problem behaviors. Another popular structured interview, the Kiddie-SADS (Puig-Antich & Chambers, 1978), has been designed to assess severe depression and its concomitant symptoms in children. While some therapists may find these interviews useful, in the absence of psychometric data they appear to offer few advantages over an unstructured interview. Moreover, unstructured interviews allow the clinician more freedom to investigate potential controlling variables.

Behavioral Rating Scales

To supplement information derived from the behavioral interview, many therapists ask parents or teachers to complete a behavioral rating scale immediately prior to or following the first meeting. A typical rating scale lists a variety of specific behaviors or traits (e.g., fights) and the rater simply checks or rates those items that apply to the child. In most cases, a scale of this sort can be completed in less than 15 minutes.

Rating scales serve a number of functions in behavioral assessment, the most important of which are initial screening and treatment outcome evaluation. In many cases, the child's scores from a rating scale can be readily compared to those of a normative sample to help determine whether or not the identified problem behaviors are within normal limits. If the child's behavior does not deviate from that of other children, the parents may simply need to be informed of this fact. In other cases, an examination of family problems other than deviant behavior on the part of the child may be in order. On the other hand, if the child's scores are in the deviant range, further assessment and subsequent behavioral intervention would be warranted. At the end of treatment, a second rating scale may be completed to determine whether or not the child's behavior is now within normal limits.

Occasionally, the information derived from a rating scale is also used to select specific target behaviors for treatment. As noted earlier, behavioral rating scales are the primary means of empirically identifying behavioral syndromes. While the validity of specific syndromes is questionable, the information that they provide can be used clinically to identify possible clusters of deviant behavior that were not reported in the initial interview. For example, if the child receives a high score on the hyperactive dimension of a rating scale, the therapist may wish to further assess the behaviors that comprise that syndrome.

A very large number of rating scales are available for evaluating a child's behavior. The four considered here were chosen because they have been subjected to extensive psychometric evaluation and because normative data have been collected for each of them.

Behavior Problem Checklist

The Behavior Problem Checklist (BPC), developed by Peterson (1961), is a 55-item scale that can be completed by either parents or teachers in less than 15 minutes. The scale contains both specific, observable behavior problems (e.g., fighting), as well as global personality traits, such as feelings of inferiority and lack of self confidence. The more global items restrict the scale's utility in behavioral analysis, but its popularity warrants a brief discussion of its use in clinical assessment. A number of factor analytic studies have shown that the BPC yields four independent factors (conduct disorder, personality disorder, inadequacy/immaturity, and socialized/ delinquent personality), and manifests adequate concurrent validity, split-half reliabilities, and test-retest reliabilities (cf. Quay, 1977).

Although the BPC has been widely employed as a diagnostic screening instrument, its authors have recently revised the scale in order to broaden its diagnostic scope (e.g., to include psychotic behavior) and to increase the robustness of the identified factors by increasing the number of items comprising them (Quay & Petersen 1983). The *Revised Behavior Problem Checklist* (RBPC) consists of 89 items, each rated on a 3-point scale of severity. Several recent studies using the RBPC have all yielded similar factor structures: conduct problems, socialized aggression, attention problems, and anxiety withdrawal (Aman & Werry, 1984; Aman, Werry, Fitzpatrick, Lowe, & Waters, 1983; Quay, 1983). Two additional factors, psychotic behaviors and motor excess, appear less reliable.

Aman and Werry (1984) compared RBPC scores from 267 children from the community to 266 children referred to a psychiatric clinic and found that the clinic group received significantly higher scores on all six factors. Aman et al. (1983) and Quay (1983) have presented age-appropriate norms on each factor to enhance its ability to serve as a clinical screening instrument. Indeed, a parent-completed RBPC can quickly inform the clinician where the child stands in relation to normal and clinic-referred children.

Conners Teacher Rating Scale

Conners has developed a teacher rating scale (Conners, 1969) and a parent rating scale (Conners, 1970), both designed specifically for the assessment of hyperactivity in children. The current version of the teacher rating scale (TRS), which is used far more often than the parent rating scale (PRS), consists of 39 items rated on a 4-point scale (Conners, 1973). Most of the items refer to rather specific problem behaviors (e.g., "denies mistakes or blames others"), but others are more nebulous (e.g., "appears to lack leadership"). The TRS has been shown to discriminate normal children from those diagnosed as hyperactive (Werry, Sprague, & Cohen, 1975), and is senstive to changes in hyperactive behavior resulting from behavior modification (O'Leary & Pelham, 1978; O'Leary, Pelham, Rosenbaum, & Price, 1976) and stimulant medication (Conners & Werry, 1979). Trites, Dugas, Lynch, and Ferguson (1979) reported adequate test-retest and interrater reliability for this instrument.

Initial factor analyses on the TRS (Conners, 1969) yielded four orthogonal factors (conduct disorder, inattentive-passive, tension-anxiety, and hyperactivity), but a more recent analysis conducted on a very large sample of children (n = 9583) produced a somewhat revised factor structure: hyperactivity, conduct problem, emotional overindulgent, anxious-passive, asocial, and daydreams/attendance problems (Trites, Blouin, & Laprade, 1982). Trites et al. (1982) presented normative information on each factor according to age (4–12 years) and sex. Finally, Goyette, Conners, and Ulrich (1978) conducted an extensive normative study on somewhat shortened versions of the TRS and PRS (n = 383). The factor structure was similar to that reported by Conners (1969), and norms for each factor are presented according to age (3–17 years) and sex.

Child Behavior Problem Checklist

The Child Behavior Problem Checklist (CBCL) is one of the most thoroughly evaluated instruments of its type. Developed by Achenbach (1978; Achenbach & Edelbrock, 1979), the CBCL consists of 118 items describing specific behavior problems rated on a 3-point scale. In addition, several questions are included to evaluate the child's social strengths. For example, parents are asked to indicate whether or not the child engages in certain social activities and how well he or she interacts with peers. According to Achenbach (1978), the checklist requires only about 17 minutes to complete.

Thorough psychometric evaluations of the CBCL have been conducted for both boys and girls in one of three age ranges (4–5, 6–11, and 12–16 years). Achenbach and Edelbrock (1979) reported that 1 week test-retest reliabilities were high (.82–.89), though interparent agreement was somewhat lower (.54–.74). In a large-scale normative study, Achenbach and Edelbrock (1981) presented information on the discriminant validity of the CBCL. They collected CBCLs for 1,300 nonreferred children (50 boys and 50 girls for each age group between 4 and 16 years) and 450 children referred to mental health facilities for a variety of behavior problems. Significant differences between referred and nonreferred children were found on 108 of the 118 behavior problem items, with referred children scoring higher on all of them. Further, they presented cutoff scores for the total behavior problem and social competence ratings that may be used to classify children as deviant or normal. In their sample, the age-specific cutoff scores produced a misclassification rate of only 9% (2% for normal and 16% for referred children).

Achenbach and Edelbrock (1979) identified nine orthogonal factors for each age range studied. Although the specific factors differed between ages, somatic complaints, delinquent, and aggressive factors were common to all. Once the CBCL has been scored, individual T-scores based on the normative data provided by Achenbach and Edelbrock (1981) can be obtained for each factor to produce the Child Behavior Profile. Thus, instead of providing a single diagnostic label that may exclude potentially valuable behavioral information, a child's behavior on each dimension can be compared to that of normal children.

Eyberg Child Behavior Inventory

The Eyberg Child Behavior Iventory (ECBI) developed by Eyberg and Ross (1978) is a 36-item list of specific problem behaviors that was designed to assess the behavior of children labeled "conduct disordered." Some of the items include hits parents, yells or screams, and argues with parents about rules. The instrument requires that parents list the frequency (also termed "intensity") of each behavior on a 1–7 scale and indicate whether or not that behavior is a problem for them.

Eyberg and Ross (1978) initially tested the psychometric properties of the ECBI by comparing scores for children from a clinic-referred group, a community control group, and a group referred for intellectual or developmental assessment. On both the overall intensity and problem scores, the clinic-referred group significantly exceeded the other two groups (which were equivalent to each other). Further, following treatment at the clinic, the ECBI scores for 9 of the 10 conduct-disordered children decreased to levels commensurate with those of the children in the control group. Eyberg and Ross (1978) also report previously acquired reliability coefficients of .86 (test-retest) and .98 (internal consistency) for this instrument. Normative information for children aged 2–12 years (Robinson, Eyberg, & Ross, 1980) and for adolescents aged 13–16 years (Eyberg & Robinson, 1983) are available, along with proposed cutoff scores for identifying deviant child behavior.

Summary

As noted earlier, all of the scales considered can be employed clinically as screening devices for selecting children for treatment and, in some cases, for selecting specific target behaviors. Thus, for example, a child whose overall problem behavior score on the CBCL is very extreme compared to a normative sample may be seriously considered for treatment. On the other hand, if several raters indicate that the child's behavior is well within normal limits, a more thorough investigation of the sources of the parent or teacher's perceptions of deviancy would be indicated.

For general screening purposes, the TRS, RBPC, and CBCL are all useful instruments because they cover such a broad range of deviant behavior and because of the availability of extensive normative data. When an assessment of the child's social strengths is desired as well, however, the CBCL is clearly the best option. While all three scales provide information concerning problem behaviors, only the CBCL attempts to evaluate positive social behaviors. The ECBI, which was designed specifically to assess the behavior of conduct-disordered children, should be reserved for use with children referred for externalizing problem behaviors (e.g., conduct disorder, oppositional behavior, and hyperactivity).

In addition to serving a general screening function, the comparison of rating scale scores obtained prior to and immediately following treatment can provide one indication of the effectiveness of the treatment program. The TRS has been widely used in this regard in studies involving the treatment of hyperactivity. Indeed, both the TRS and the ECBI have been demonstrated to be sensitive to treatment intervention. In addition, although rarely used in this manner, rating scales offer a convenient method of long-term follow-up assessment.

Several difficulties with the use of rating scales in behavioral assessment should be noted. An obvious source of concern is the problem of rater bias. An individual rater may respond in such a way as to make the child appear very deviant in order to justify treatment. In other cases, the rater may try to make the child appear very well-behaved in order to avoid perceptions of deviancy. One solution to this problem is to have several individuals complete rating scales for the same child (e.g., both parents separately, teacher, etc.) and compare responses. If the ratings are substantially different, additional assessment methods may be employed to determine whether treatment is necessary.

Another important limitation of behavioral rating scales is that they offer no information concerning the variables that may be governing the child's deviant behavior. Because such information is vital to the design of an effective intervention program, rating scales should always be used in conjunction with other assessment techniques designed to identify these variables.

Self-Report Instruments

A relatively recent addition to the child behavioral assessment repertoire is the self-report measure. Like the behavioral rating scales already discussed, self-report instruments provide a convenient and inexpensive means of screening children in need of treatment, and they generally provide some information regarding the child's behavioral strengths and weaknesses. Self-report instruments usually require only a few minutes to complete and therefore may be used during the initial meeting with the child to supplement information derived from other assessment methods.

The field of behavioral assessment has been slow to incorporate self-report measures because they have long been considered to provide an unreliable estimate of actual behavior. However, in recent years, behavioral assessment methods have been increasingly judged on the basis of their demonstrated psychometric properties and not a priori on the basis of their procedural details. Thus, if a self-report measure of aggressiveness is found to correlate with teacher ratings and direct observations of aggressive behavior, then its inclusion as part of a behavioral assessment is warranted. However, because an individual rater may be biased, self-report measures should never be used in isolation.

Most of the self-report instruments described in the recent child behavioral assessment literature are intended to evaluate a child's mastery of social/ assertive skills. Additionally, two self-report instruments have been developed to aid in the assessment of the commonly reported childhood problems of fear and depression. In accordance with current trends in behavioral assessment, all of these instruments have recently been subjected to psychometric evaluation.

Social Skills

The assessment and treatment of social skills in children has received an increasing amount of attention in recent years. The interest in children's social skills stems from the notion that social skills deficits may result in both short- and long-term negative consequences (Ollendick, 1984). Three self-report measures of social skills in children have been developed and exposed to psychometric evaluation. The *Children's Assertiveness Inventory* (CAI) was designed to measure both positive and negative assertive behavior in children aged 6 to 12 years (Ollendick, 1984). The CAI consists of 14 items depicting a variety of social situations involving young children. The therapist reads a description of each situation and the child responds by simply stating yes or no.

Ollendick (1984) reports high 1-week and 3-month test-retest reliabilities (.76 and .61 respectively), but low internal consistency due to the heterogeneity of the 14 items. The CAI was also found to correlate positively with measures of self-concept, role-play assertion, and teacher ratings of positive social interactions but negatively with measures of anxiety. However, while the correlations between different measures were statistically significant, the actual values were rather low ($-.21$ to .54).

Another self-report scale, the *Children's Assertive Behavior Scale* (CABS), consists of 27 items dealing with complaints, empathy, requests, initiating conversations, and giving and receiving compliments (Michelson & Wood, 1980). For each situation depicted, the subject chooses one of five possible responses that range from very passive to very aggressive. Michelson and Wood (1982) summarized the results of several previously unpublished analyses of the psychometric properties of the CABS. Behavioral observations of assertiveness correlated significantly with the CABS total score ($r = .38$), and scores of fourth, fifth, and sixth graders correlated significantly with peer, parent, and teacher ratings of social competence, popularity, and overall social skills (r values were not reported). Michelson and Wood (1980) also found that the CABS could differentiate fourth grade children who had received social skills training from those who had not.

A third self-report measure of social skills, the *Children's Action Tendency Scale* (CATS), is designed to assess how a child would respond in situations involving provocation, frustration, loss, or conflict (Deluty, 1979). A description of each situation is followed by three response alternatives (aggressive, submissive, and assertive) presented in a paired comparisons format. The instrument yields three subscales (Aggressiveness, Assertiveness, and Submissiveness) that have been shown to correlate with peer and teacher reports of social behavior and to possess moderate split-half and test-retest reliabilities (Deluty, 1979). Deluty (1984) recently found moderate agreement between the CATS scale scores and measures of aggressiveness, assertiveness, and submissiveness obtained through direct observation of third- to fifth-grade boys in their school environments. For girls, however, only measures of submissiveness tended to coincide.

A major strength of the CATS is that it addresses a wide range of interpersonal conflict situations. However, it contains no provision for assessing positive assertive behavior. The CAI and the CABS, which address fewer interpersonal conflict situations, assess both positive and negative assertive behavior. Therefore, when evaluating social skills in children, the CATS would best be used in conjunction with another self-report instrument for a more complete clinical picture (Ollendick, 1984).

Fear

The behavioral assessment of children's fears has not received extensive evaluation. One instrument that may prove to be quite valuable in this regard is the Fear Survey Schedule for Children (FSSC; Scherer & Nakamura, 1968). The FSSC lists 80 specific items and events that children might fear (e.g., "being in a fight," "guns," etc.) that the child must rate on a numerical scale of severity. Originally, the instrument employed a 5-point rating scale, but Ollendick (1983) argued that a 3-point scale is more understandable to young children and is more consistent with other self-report instruments for children. Ollendick tested the psychometric properties of the revised FSSC and reported high internal consistency (.94) and 1-week test-retest reliabilities (.82). In addition, total fear scores correlated significantly with measures of trait anxiety, and scores for 25 school-phobic children were significantly greater than those for 25 matched control children.

Ollendick (1983) suggests that the FSSC be employed clinically as a normative instrument for selecting fearful children for treatment. Means and standard deviations of FSSC scores obtained from the clinical and normal samples in Ollendick's (1983) study may be used as a standard against which to compare the score of an individual child until more comprehensive normative information becomes available. The FSSC can also be used to identify specific fears in an individual child. All of the items are stated clearly enough to be targeted for treatment intervention without further translation.

Depression

Many clinicians and researchers have recently become concerned about the problem of depression in children. Although a clear definition of childhood depression remains elusive, many are convinced of its existence and some behavioral rating scales yield factors that have been labeled "depression." The most widely used self-report measure of depression in children is the *Children's Depression Inventory* (CDI; Kovacs, 1980/1981). The CDI contains 27 items, each of which consists of three sentences. These sentences describe a symptom of depression (e.g., sleep disturbance) in a manner ranging from normal to severely clinically significant. The child must select the sentence that best describes him or her over the past 2 weeks.

In an unpublished manuscript, Kovacs (1982) reported that the CDI can discriminate depressed from other emotionally disturbed children, and possesses high internal consistency and high 9-week test-retest reliabilities for both normal and depressed children. However, more recent comprehensive analyses of the CDI's psychometric properties have been less encouraging.

Saylor, Finch, Spirito, and Bennett (1984) found that while inpatients at a child psychiatric facility scored higher on the CDI than normal children, scores of children specifically diagnosed as depressed did not differ from those of other emotionally disturbed children. Saylor, Finch, Baskin, Furey, and Kelly (1984) used four methods (self-report, peer nomination, teacher nomination, and teacher rating) to measure two traits (depression and anger) in children. The self-report measure of depression was the CDI. In general, they found that correlations between measures using the same method (e.g., self-report of anger and self-report of depression) were about twice as high as correlations between measures of the same trait (e.g., self-report of depression and teacher ratings of depression). Kazdin, Esveldt-Dawson, Unis, and Rancurello (1983) reported similar findings. Finally, Kazdin, Esveldt-Dawson, Sherick, and Colbus (1985) compared behavioral measures of depression (social activity, solitary play, and affect-related expression) for inpatient children to both parent and child measures of depression. Although parent measures tended to agree with behavioral observations, scores from the CDI did not.

The difficulties with the CDI may derive from problems in deciding on acceptable criteria for defining childhood depression. At present, the instrument seems most useful as a device for identifying children with general emotional problems, but it does not seem to uniquely identify depressed children. However, in that regard, the CDI may be the only self-report instrument that serves a general screening function. Finch, Saylor, and Edwards (1985) provide normative data for the CDI based on scores obtained from 1,463 children in grades two through eight.

In general, the strengths and weaknesses of self-report instruments and behavioral rating scales are the same. Thus, while self-report measures may help in the screening of unassertive children, they are also subject to the problem of rater bias. More impatiently, self-report instruments offer little useful information to those concerned with a functional analysis of targeted behaviors. To this end, the direct methods of behavioral assessment are much better suited to identifying the variables that control the child's problem behaviors.

DIRECT METHODS

Cognitive behavior therapy notwithstanding, the goal of most behavioral intervention programs is to alter the probability of targeted overt responses. As such, the assessment strategy long considered to be of greatest utility in behavioral assessment is the direct observation and quantification of the child's behavior and surrounding events. Three approaches to observational assessment are common in child cases, the first involving observation in the child's natural setting (e.g., at home or in school), the second involving observation of parent–child interactions in a clinic analog setting, and the third involving observation of children's social skills by means of situational role plays. Because the practical considerations for these three methods differ in several important resepects, they will be treated separately.

Observation in Natural Settings

Due to the many behaviors exhibited by children and adults in their natural environments, the focus of an observational assessment must be restricted at the outset to those behaviors that bear on the current problem. The initial interview with the child's parents or teacher usually provides the most useful information concerning which child behaviors to include in the assessment. Unless perceptions of deviant behavior appear to be inaccurate, the only task is to translate descriptions of the child's behavior into specific and observable responses. The identification of the variables that may govern the child's deviant behavior, however, is often a more difficult task.

If the referral source is unable to pinpoint useful antecedent and consequent stimuli, the therapist may elect to target environmental events that are often associated with deviancy in children. For example, excessive commanding behavior on the part of a parent has been associated with oppositional behavior in children (e.g., Green, Forehand, & McMahon, 1979; Lobitz & Johnson, 1975b), and contingent teacher attention often serves to maintain a child's disruptive behavior in the classroom. Another option is for the therapist to conduct informal observations of the child during particularly difficult periods of the day. Several authors have even suggested that, as a preliminary step, an observer simply record in narrative fashion the behavior of the child in his or her natural setting, as well as the behavior of anyone who interacts with the child during the observational period (Barton & Ascione, 1984; Reid, 1978). The narrative may be subsequently translated in terms of antecedent stimuli, child responses, and consequent stimuli in order to generate hypotheses regarding factors governing the child's behavior.

Once the focus of the assessment is established, a method of collecting and recording the observational data must be selected. If the therapist wishes to record antecedent/response/consequent chains, the simplest approach is to assign codes or symbols to each individual and behavior targeted for observation (Haynes, 1978; Patterson et al., 1975). These codes can be easily used to succinctly record relatively complex behavioral interactions between parent and child. For example, mother, father, and child may be designated M, F, and C, respectively, and command, compliance, noncompliance, and praise as CO, CM, NC, and PR, respectively. To record a sequential interaction involving the mother issuing a command, followed by the child complying with the command, followed by praise from the mother, an observer would code M-CO, C-CM, M-PR.

As described above, the behavior coding system contains no indication of how closely in time successive behaviors occurred. In order to preserve the temporal relationships, the observation period is usually broken down into a series of smaller time units during which behaviors are recorded, a technique known as *interval recording*. For example, every 10 seconds the observer might switch to the next column on an observation sheet and continue coding the family's behavior. At the end of the session, the observational protocol will clearly indicate a series of different response chains separated by varying lengths of time.

When a record of sequential interactions is deemed unnecessary, simpler methods of recording the child's behavior may be employed. If only a few discreet behaviors are to observed (e.g., hitting and kicking), the simplest technique is to simply mark a tally sheet each time the targeted response occurs. This technique is termed *event* or *frequency* recording. If the onset and termination of a response is difficult to precisely specify (e.g., playing with blocks), *interval recording*, as described above, may be employed. In this case, the observer simply marks a tally sheet at the end of each interval (e.g., 10 sec) to indicate whether or not the behavior was occurring at any point during the previous 10 seconds. Finally, *duration recording* may be employed when the treatment intervention aims to alter the length of time that a child engages in a particular response (e.g., whining). This method simply entails recording the total amount of time of the child's behavior during an observation period.

When the range of behaviors to be assessed is relatively restricted, the development of an observational coding scheme tailored to an individual client, as mentioned previously, is an efficient option. When a more comprehensive assessment of family functioning is required, however, the use of an existing coding system may be a better choice (Forehand et al., 1978; Patterson, Ray, Shaw, & Cobb, 1969; Wahler, House, & Stambaugh, 1976). Patterson and his colleagues have developed and extensively employed an observation coding system known as the Family Interaction Coding System (FICS). The FICS, which was designed to measure behavioral interactions in families with conduct-disordered children, consists of 29 behavioral codes, including common problem behaviors (e.g., noncompliance, crying) and positive and negative parental responses (e.g., approval, ignoring). As typically used, an observer enters the home and targets each member of the family for at least 5 minutes of observation. During each 6-second interval, the observer codes the behavior of the targeted individual and the subsequent response of other family members. Jones, Reid, and Patterson (1975) summarized a number of experimental findings attesting to the psychometric strengths of the FICS.

Wahler et al. (1976) have also developed a comprehensive observational coding system for assessing family interactions in natural settings. This system covers a slightly wider range of child behaviors than the FICS (e.g., compliance, oppositional, autistic, play, work, and social behaviors), but has received much less empirical evaluation. Another coding system, developed by Forehand et al. (1978), can also be used to record family interactions. This system has been devised primarily for the assessment of noncompliance in children and has received substantial empirical validation in that regard (Forehand & McMahon, 1981). Therefore, if the presenting complaint is noncompliance and extensive family evaluation is required, the Forehand coding system may be the best choice.

In their experience in using the FICS, Patterson and his colleagues found that by following a few practical guidelines, observational assessment in the home can be greatly facilitated. These guidelines will probably improve any home-based assessment project even if only a few behaviors are targeted. Specifically, they recommend that (a) everyone in the family must be present, (b) the family be restricted to two adjacent rooms, (c) there be no outgoing telephone calls (incoming calls should be handled briefly), and (d) there be no talking to the observers while they are coding. Reid (1978) has presented much more detailed information on how to implement the FICS in practice. In addition, he provides age-appropriate norms for each behavioral category, although the normative sample is quite small.

All of the coding systems discussed require trained observers to conduct the assessment. If a simpler coding system is constructed for a specific case, a parent or teacher can be trained to use it, but more highly trained and experienced observers are a better option if resources permit. Even with trained observers, however, several threats to the integrity of observational data should be considered. One is the problem of *observer drift* in which observers gradually depart from the original definitions of target behaviors (e.g., Kent, O'Leary, Diament, & Dietz, 1974). This problem is usually solved by conducting periodic reliability checks and frequent observer training sessions (Kazdin, 1981).

Another issue that may complicate naturalistic observational assessment is the problem of *observer reactivity*, that is, when the behavior of the child or significant others is altered by the presence of an observer (Baum, Forehand, & Zegiob, 1979; Haynes & Horn, 1982; Johnson & Bolstad, 1973). Haynes and Horn (1982) provided the most recent review of studies that have detected reactive effects and offered several practical suggestions to deal with the problem, including using covert observational procedures, using video or tape recorders, minimizing subject–observer interaction, using participant observers, and allowing at least a short period of time for transient reactive effects to dissipate.

The use of participant observers, primarily for economical reasons, is quite common in child behavioral assessment. Parents, for example, are often trained in the use of a simple coding system constructed for an individual case. As long as the system is not very complicated, a minimally trained observer can collect data accurately without introducing the problem of observer reactivity. However, because participant observers are usually not subjected to rigorous reliability checks, other means of collecting observational data should be employed in order to supplement their reports if possible. One way to gather such information is to unobtrusively observe the child interacting with family members in a clinic analog setting.

Observation in Analog Settings

The direct observation of parent–child interactions in a clinic setting has been widely employed in recent years (Eyberg & Robinson, 1982; Hughes & Haynes, 1978; Forehand & McMahon, 1981). Typically, a parent and child are instructed to interact in a playroom equipped with toys and other age-appropriate objects while an observer records targeted behaviors from behind a one-way mirror. As with naturalistic observation, the therapist may devise an observational coding system for an individual case or may employ one of several systems that have been used for this purpose (Robinson & Eyberg, 1981; Forehand et al., 1978; Mash, Terdal, & Anderson, 1973). The Dyadic Parent–Child Interaction Coding System (DPICS), devised by Robinson and Eyberg (1981), is an easily implemented system that will be detailed here for illustrative purposes.

The DPICS consists of 22 parent and child behavior categories that were derived in part from Patterson's FICS. The system covers a range of negative child behaviors (e.g., whining, yelling, noncompliance) and parental antecedents and consequences (e.g., direct command, critical statements). In a test of its psychometric properties, Robinson and Eyberg (1981) used the DPICS to code the behavior of 20 families referred for conduct problems (disobedience, aggression, destructiveness, hyperactivity, or temper tantrums) and 22 normal families during clinic playroom interaction. In one session, the child was permitted to choose any activity, while in the other session the parent was instructed to direct the child's play. The purpose of structuring parent–child interaction is to ensure that the problem behaviors and parental responses occur at a high enough rate to be observed (Hughes & Haynes, 1978).

Interrater reliability averaged .91 for parental behaviors and .92 for child behaviors. The observations indicated that conduct-problem children exhibited more whining, yelling, and noncompliance than normal children and that their parents issued more critical statements and direct commands than the parents of normal children. These findings are in close agreement with those of other studies using a variety of other coding systems (e.g., Green et al., 1979; Lobitz & Johnson, 1975b). Eyberg and Robinson (1982) showed that a parent training program resulted in positive behavioral change in the clinic as assessed by the DPICS and at home as assessed by the ECBI behavioral rating scales.

More recent investigations of the DPICS have focused on whether or not observations conducted in the clinic agree with those conducted in the home. Zangwill and Kniskern (1982) derived four summary measures from the DPICS (parent rate of reinforcement, parent rate of punishment, child rate of compliance to commands, and child rate of deviant behavior) and compared scores obtained from the clinic and at home. Although absolute rates of responding differed in the two settings, they correlated highly for three of the four categories (except for child rate of deviant behavior). Kniskern, Robinson, and Mitchell (1983) conducted a similar experiment and concluded that the presence of siblings and the imposition of structure (i.e., both parent-determined and child-determined periods) were more important than the location of the assessment. Webster-Stratton (1985), however, reached a different conclusion. She found that only when both home and clinic observations were unstructured (i.e., parents instructed to behave normally) was there cross-situational agreement.

In light of the findings discussed above, the safest conclusions are that interobserver reliability, concurrent validity, and discriminant validity of the DPICS have been established. Despite its common practice, some question exists as to whether clinic observations should be structured or unstructured. Webster-Stratton (1985) suggests that perhaps both approaches should be followed until further research clarifies the important variables.

Role-Play Tests

Recent increased interest in social skills training for children has stimulated the search for efficient and psychometrically sound observational assessment techniques. One such technique is the behavioral analog role–play test in which a child is observed responding to various contrived social situations. The most widely used children's role-play test is the Behavioral Assertiveness Test for Children (BAT-C; Bornstein, Bellack, & Hersen, 1977, 1980), though two similar tests, the Behavioral Assertiveness Test for Boys (Reardon, Hersen, Bellack, & Foley 1979) and the Social Skills Test for Children (Williamson, Moody, Granberry, Lethermon, & Blouin, 1983), are also available. As originally presented, the BAT-C consisted of nine scenes, five involving a same sex role model and four involving an opposite sex role model. The scenes were designed to cover a range of situations that a child is likely to encounter in daily interaction with other children.

Due to practical and ethical difficulties involved in using children as role models, one female and one male adult generally serve as the models. The child is instructed to pretend that the described situations are real and to respond to the role models as if they were other children in the scene. The actual assessment proceeds as follows: a narrator reads a brief description of a scene (e.g., a description of children playing four square) over an intercom to the child and to two role models located in an adjoining room. After the scene is read, one of the role models issues a prompt (e.g., "It's my turn to serve") to which the child must respond. Following the child's response, the next scene is presented, followed by the next prompt, and so on. The role plays are recorded on videotape and various aspects of the child's behavior assumed relevant to assertiveness (e.g., eye contact, loudness of speech) are coded at a later time.

Initially, the validity of the BAT-C was assessed by demonstrating its sensitivity to social skills training in children (Bornstein et al., 1977, 1980). Bornstein et al. (1977), for example, showed that social skills training for four children resulted in increases in several components of assertive behavior, including eye contact, loudness of speech, and number of requests as measured by the BAT-C. In addition, after viewing the videotapes, independent observers rated each child as having increased overall assertiveness by the end of training.

Several recent investigations have more thoroughly evaluated the psychometric properties of this procedure. DiLorenzo and Michelson (1983) reported high interrater reliability, split-half reliability, and internal consistency using an expanded version of the BAT-C (46 scenes). However, Van Hasselt, Hersen, and Bellack (1981) found generally low 1-week test-retest reliabilities for a role-play assessment similar in structure to the BAT-C and showed that role-play behaviors did not correlate highly with the same behaviors occurring in more natural settings. Matson, Esveldt-Dawson, and Kazdin (1983) found that behaviors assessed by role play did not predict either teacher or child ratings of popularity. On the other hand, Hobbs, Walle, and Hammersly (1984) did find that several responses measured from the BAT-C correlated significantly with peer measures of likability, friendship, and admiration.

The mixture of findings on the BAT-C assessment procedure indicate that more work is needed in order to produce a truly sound role-play device. At present, role-play procedures do not seem to offer a valid indication of social skills in children. Indeed, no social skills assessment device has emerged as being particularly effective in this regard (Matson et al., 1983). By redefining the behaviors examined or the level at which they are measured, however, role-play procedures may eventually prove to be useful to the practicing clinician. It may prove necessary to measure sequences of behaviors thought to be relevant to social skills rather than to simply examine the probability of individual responses taken in isolation. In addition, role-play procedures may have to be devised that capture more of the essential elements of a typical child's social environment. In this regard, the use of one or more children as role models may be helpful. Until this technique is refined, the role-play assessment procedure will be of most interest to researchers interested in improving the assessment of children's social skills.

Many of the methods reviewed in this chapter can be employed for the assessment of a single case. Indeed, one definite trend in the field of behavioral assessment as a whole has been an increased reliance on multimethod assessment. The indirect assessment methods described earlier offer the advantages of economy and convenience at the expense of precise measurement and functional analysis. In addition, they are presently the only means of establishing whether or not the child's behavior deviates from that of other children from the same age group. The direct methods, on the other hand, are more expensive and difficult to implement, but they provide the information necessary for the design of an effective treatment program. The following case study illustrates the concurrent application of multiple assessment procedures.

CASE EXAMPLE

Michael is an 8-year-old boy in the third grade who was referred to a behavior management clinic by his mother (Mrs. W.) because of what she characterized as his increasing rebelliousness at home. Mrs. W. also reported that Michael's grades were falling recently and that his teacher had indicated that he could be more cooperative at school. Michael lived at home with both parents and a younger brother, age 6.

When Mrs. W. brought Michael to the clinic for an initial visit, she was asked to complete the CBCL while her son played in an adjoining playroom. During the ensuing interview, the therapist inquired into the nature of the problem and its historical development. Mrs. W. was unable to pinpoint exactly when the problems began, but she noted that his behavior at home had worsened since the start of school this year. In all other respects, Michael's developmental history was unremarkable. Because Mrs. W. used terms such as unfriendly and rebellious to describe her son, she was asked to clarify her meaning more precisely. For example:

Therapist: "What exactly does Michael do to cause you to describe him that way?"

Mrs. W.: "Well, I guess there are a lot of things. For one, he never has anything nice to say to me. I hardly know what he does at school everyday."

Therapist: "Is that what you mean by unfriendly?"

Mrs. W.: "Yes, and he is really rough on his brother. Michael always has to watch what he wants to watch on TV They fight constantly, sometimes physically, and Michael is much bigger than his brother."

Therapist: "What does he do that is rebellious?"

Mrs. W.: "He just doesn't do what he is told, ever."

Therapist: "Can you give me some examples?"

Mrs. W. "Well, he usually won't go to bed when I tell him to, or do his homework, and I have a lot of trouble getting him to clean up the messes he makes."

Further inquiry of this sort indicated that the most troubling issues were Michael's refusal to do homework (and the ensuing yelling match), nightly fights with his brother (mostly over which television shows to watch), and the lack of positive interpersonal interaction between Michael and the other family members. Therefore, increasing the rate of homework completion and decreasing the fighting over television were selected as initial goals. In addition, at least 5 minutes a day of positive discussion between Mrs. W. and her son were included in the behavioral objectives.

When asked about some of his positive characteristics, Mrs. W. replied that he had several friends with whom he got along very well. In addition, he could sometimes be a very charming young man at home, usually during vacations when schoolwork didn't interfere. The therapist suggested to Mrs. W. that Michael's negative behavior and her subsequent responses to him were probably reciprocally maintained. Her occasional acquiescence, for example, reinforced Michael's obdurate refusal to do his homework. In addition, her verbal scolding may have functioned as attentional reinforcement, further strengthening his refusal to cooperate. Moreover, Michael's occasional compliance with her angry demands probably reinforced her nominally punitive behavior.

The therapist informed Mrs. W. that a parent training program might be suitable for her but that additional behavioral assessment should be conducted before reaching a firm decision. To this end, Mrs. W. was scheduled for two clinic playroom observation sessions, and was provided with a simple observation form to record some of Michael's behavior at home. For now, she was instructed to record the behavioral sequence that surrounded her attempt to get Michael to do his homework each day. Mother and child were coded M and C, respectively, and simple codes were assigned to the following behaviors: requests to do homework, noncompliance, compliance, tantrum, and scold. Immediately following each episode, the coded sequence of behavior and the time of day were to be recorded.

After meeting with Mrs. W., the therapist spoke briefly with Michael. Michael understood that he was at the clinic because he and his mother tended to fight all of the time. The therapist explained that by working together, the whole family might be able to get along better, and Michael expressed a willingness to cooperate with the treatment program. When asked what sorts of things cause he and his mother to fight, he replied that she would never let him do his homework when he wanted to do it. Mrs. W. wanted Michael to do his homework after school, whereas he wanted to play then and do his homework before going to bed. In general, his descriptions of the interpersonal conflict with his mother coincided with the descriptions that she provided.

With Mrs. W's permission, the therapist arranged a visit with Michael's teacher at the school. The teacher reported that Michael was a restless boy who wasn't really a major problem, but that he did seem to be getting worse, both behaviorally and academically, as the year progressed. The biggest behavioral problem appeared to be a lack of cooperation when the teacher instructed him to stop bothering other children and start working. The teacher agreed to complete the Conners TRS and remained open to additional contacts with the therapist when they became necessary.

Michael's scores on the parent-completed CBCL indicated that many of the item's comprising the externalizing dimension were endorsed by Mrs. W. The highest scaled score was for aggressive dimension, which was almost two standard deviations above the mean for boys his age. The teacher-completed TRS indicated that Michael scored highly on both the hyperactive and conduct problem dimensions, each of which was about 1.5 standard deviations above the mean. This information corroborated the picture of Michael presented during the initial interview.

During the next two meetings, Mrs. W. was instructed to interact with Michael in the clinic playroom while the therapist recorded their behavior from behind a one-way mirror. For the first session, an unstructured format was employed. Mrs. W. was told to simply interact with Michael in a normal manner for 10 minutes. Structured observations were employed in the second meeting. For part of that session, Mrs. W. was instructed to permit Michael to play with whatever toy he desired, to refrain from commanding and questioning him, and to describe his actions out loud in narrative fashion (Eyberg & Robinson, 1982; Forehand & McMahon, 1981). When the therapist tapped on the window, however, she was to issue commands to Michael concerning what toys to play with, where to put them, and what the rules were. At the end of the session, she was to instruct Michael to clean up all of the toys.

The behavior of Mrs. W. and her son were recorded using the DPICS. The observational data revealed that Michael exhibited a level of noncompliance during the structured sessions commensurate with other children referred for conduct problems (Robinson & Eyberg, 1981), and that Mrs. W. issued a high level of commands and critical statements in both structured and unstructured sessions.

Based on the information derived from interviews, behavioral rating scales, and clinic observations, Mrs. W. was encouraged to participate in a parent training program offered at the clinic. The program basically consisted of training Mrs. W. in the use of contingent attention and other rewards for appropriate behavior, phrasing commands in a clear and unambiguous fashion, and employing brief time-out for inappropriate behavior (e.g., Peed, Roberts, & Forehand, 1977). Throughout the treatment program, clinic observations were conducted at weekly intervals and home observations were conducted by Mrs. W. on a daily basis in order to monitor treatment progress.

After several weeks of training, clinic observations indicated that Mrs. W. had greatly reduced the frequency of criticisms, had learned how to phrase commands appropriately, and how to impose time-out effectively. Her home observations indicated that refusals to do homework were consistently followed by time-out instead of strident verbal scolding and that the frequency of compliance had greatly increased. For the remainder of the training program, Mrs. W. was instructed to shift her attention to positive interpersonal interactions (e.g., talking about what went on in school that day) for observational recording. Once again, appropriate behavioral codes were selected for this purpose.

At the end of the training program. Mrs. W. reported that Michael's behavior was much improved and her own records indicated that the positive interactions she desired with her son had indeed begun to occur. At this point, she was again asked to complete the CBCL, the results of which also indicated that Michael's behavior had improved. His score on the aggressive scale was still high, but was within the normal range. A second TRS completed by his teacher also indicated some improvement in his behavior at school, although no program had been implemented to change his behavior in that setting. In addition, Michael's teacher indicated that his grades had improved slightly because he was completing his homework on a more consistent basis.

SUMMARY

The field of child behavioral assessment is a relatively new discipline that is experiencing rapid growth. The number and variety of assessment methods designed specifically for the assessment of child behavior have proliferated in the last decade. This present chapter has described the range of techniques available to those interested in the assessment of child behavior and has illustrated their coordinated application to an individual case.

The issue of the classification of childhood psychopathology, once rejected by behavior analysts, has re-emerged as the most pressing conceptual issue facing the field. The debate has been fueled by a new attempt to produce an empirically based classification system that addresses many of the traditional objections to disease-oriented diagnostic approaches. Thus far, this approach has succeeded in unambiguously identifying two syndromes: externalizing (characterized by behavioral excess) and internalizing (characterized by behavioral withdrawal). Whether a comprehensive system of classification can ultimately be produced by this method, however, remains to be seen.

The methods available for assessing children's behavior can be grouped into two categories, indirect and direct methods. The indirect methods include the behavioral interview, behavioral rating scales, and self-report instruments for children. The unstructured behavioral interview is probably the most commonly used assessment method, but its reliability and validity are difficult to evaluate. However, several structured interviews for children have recently been devised and found to possess acceptable psychometric properties. Because of the availability of normative data, rating scales and self-report instruments can serve a useful screening function in behavioral assessment and may also provide a convenient means of evaluating treatment outcome. However, because they offer no information about the variables that might be controlling a child's behavior, such instruments cannot substitute for a functional analysis.

The direct methods of assessment, which include naturalistic observation, observation in clinic analog settings, and role-play tests of assertive behavior, are better suited to reveal the situational variables that govern a child's behavior. A number of coding systems designed for the direct observation of children's behavior have been presented in this chapter along with specific principles to be followed in order to effectively implement them. Further, some typical problems encountered in observational assessment and some practical solutions to those problems have been considered.

REFERENCES

Achenbach, T. M. (1978). The Child Behavior Profile: I. Boys aged 6–11. *Journal of Consulting and Clinical Psychology, 4*, 478–488.

Achenbach, T. M., & Edelbrock, C. S. (1978). The classification of child psychopathology: A review and analysis of empirical efforts. *Psychological Bulletin, 85*, 1275–1301.

Achenbach, T. M., & Edelbrock, C. S. (1979). The Child Behavior Profile: II. Boys aged 12–16 and girls aged 6–11 and 12–16. *Journal of Consulting and Clinical Psychology, 47*, 223–233.

Achenbach, T. M., & Edelbrock, C. S. (1981). Behavioral problems and competencies reported by parents of normal and disturbed children aged four through sixteen. *Monographs of the Society for Research in Child Development, 46* (Serial No. 188).

Aman, M. G., & Werry, J. S. (1984). The Revised Behavior Problem Checklist in clinic attenders and non-attenders: Age and sex effects. *Journal of Clinical Child Psychology, 13*, 237–242.

Aman, M. G., Werry, J. S., Fitzpatrick, J., Lowe, M., & Waters, J. (1983). Factor structure and norms for the Revised Behavior Problem Checklist in New Zealand children. *Australian and New Zealand Journal of Psychiatry, 17*, 354–360.

Barton, E. J., & Ascione, F. R. (1984). Direct observation. In T. H. Ollendick & M. Hersen (Eds.), *Child behavioral assessment* (pp. 166–194). New York: Pergamon.

Baum, C. G., Forehand, R., & Zegiob, L. E. (1979). A review of observer reactivity in adult–child interactions. *Journal of Behavioral Assessment, 1*, 167–178.

Bornstein, M. R., Bellack, A. S., & Hersen, M. (1977). Social skills training for unassertive children: A multiple-baseline analysis. *Journal of Applied Behavior Analysis, 10*, 183–195.

Bornstein, M. R., Bellack, A. S., & Hersen, M. (1980). Social skills training for highly aggressive children: Treatment in an inpatient psychiatric setting. *Behavior Modification, 4*, 173–186.

Cautela, J. R., Cautela, J., & Esonis, S. (1983). *Forms for behavior analysis with children*. Champaign, IL: Research Press.

Ciminero, A. R., & Drabman, R. S. (1977). Current developments in the behavioral assessment of children. In B. B. Lahey & A. E. Kazdin (Eds.), *Advances in clinical child psychology* (Vol. 1, pp. 47–82). New York: Plenum.

Cone, J. D. (1977). The relevance of reliability and validity for behavioral assessment. *Behavior Therapy, 8*, 411–426.

Cone, J. D. (1981). Psychometric considerations. In M. Hersen & A. S. Bellack (Eds.), *Behavioral assessment: A practical handbook* (2nd ed., pp. 38–68). New York: Pergamon.

Conners, C. K. (1969). A teacher rating scale for use in drug studies with children. *American Journal of Psychiatry, 126*, 884–888.

Conners, C. K. (1970). Symptom patterns in hyperkinetic, neurotic, and normal children. *Child Development, 41*, 667–682.

Conners, C. K. (1973). Rating scales for use in drug studies of children. *Psychopharmacology Bulletin (Special Issue: Pharmacotherapy of Children)*, 24–84.

Conners, C. K., & Werry, J. S. (1979). Pharmacotherapy. In H. C. Quay & J. S. Werry (Eds.), *Psychopathological disorders of childhood* (2nd ed., pp. 336–386). New York: Wiley.

Delfini, C. F., Bernal, M. E., & Rosen, P. M. (1976). Comparison of deviant and normal boys in home settings. In E. J. Mash, L. A. Hamerlynck, & L. C. Handy (Eds.), *Behavior modification and families* (pp. 228–248). New York: Brunner/Mazel.

Deluty, R. H. (1979). Children's Action Tendency Scale: A self-report measure of aggressiveness, assertiveness, and submissiveness in children. *Journal of Consulting and Clinical Psychology, 47*, 1061–1071.

Deluty, R. H. (1984). Behavioral validation of the Children's Action Tendency Scale. *Journal of Behavioral Assessment, 6*, 115-130.

DiLorenzo, T. M., & Michelson, L. (1983). Psychometric properties of the Behavioral Assertiveness Test for Children (BAT-C). *Child and Family Behavior Therapy, 4*, 71–76.

Dreger, R. M. (1982) The classification of children and their emotional problems: An overview — II. *Clinical Psychology Review, 2*, 349–385.

Edelbrock, C. (1984). Developmental considerations. In T. H. Ollendick & M. Hersen (Eds.), *Child behavioral assessment* (pp. 20–37). New York: Pergamon.

Eyberg, S. M., & Robinson, E. A. (1982). Parent–child interaction training: Effects on family functioning. *Journal of Clinical Child Psychology, 11*, 130–137.

Eyberg, S. M., & Robinson, E. A. (1983). Conduct problem behavior: Standardization of a behavior rating scale with adolescents. *Journal of Clinical Child Psychology, 12*, 347–354.

Eyberg, S. M., & Ross, A. W. (1978). Assessment of child behavior problems: The validation of a new inventory. *Journal of Clinical Child Psychology, 7*, 113–116.

Finch, A. J., Saylor, C. F., & Edwards, G. L. (1985). Children's Depression Inventory: Sex and grade norms for normal children. *Journal of Consulting and Clinical Psychology*, *53*, 424-425.

Forehand, R., & McMahon, R. J. (1981). *Helping the noncompliant child: A clinician's guide to parent training.* New York: Guilford Press.

Forehand, R., Peed, S., Roberts, M., McMahon, R. J., Griest, D. L., & Humphreys, L. (1978). *Coding manual for scoring mother-child interaction* (3rd ed.). Unpublished manuscript, University of Georgia.

Furey, W., & Forehand, R. (1984). Maternal satisfaction with clinic-referred children: Assessment by use of single-subject methodology. *Journal of Behavioral Assessment*, *5*, 345-355.

Goyette, C. H., Conners, C. K., & Ulrich, R. F. (1978). Normative data on Revised Conners Parent and Teacher Rating Scales. *Journal of Abnormal Child Psychology*, *6*, 221-236.

Green, K. D., Forehand, R., & McMahon, R. J. (1979). Parental manipulation of compliance and noncompliance in normal and deviant children. *Behavior Modification*, *3*, 245-266.

Gross, A. M. (1984). Behavioral interviewing. In T. H. Ollendick & M. Hersen (Eds.), *Child behavioral assessment: Principles and procedures* (pp. 61-79). New York: Pergamon.

Hartmann, D. P., Roper, B. L., & Bradford, D. C. (1979). Some relationships between behavioral and traditional assessment. *Journal of Behavioral Assessment*, *1*, 3-19.

Haynes, S. N. (1978). *Principles of behavioral assessment.* New York: Gardner Press.

Haynes, S. N., & Horn, W. F. (1982). Reactivity in behavioral observation: A review. *Behavioral Assessment*, *4*, 369-385.

Haynes, S. N., & Wilson, C. C. (1979). *Behavioral assessment: Recent advances in methods, concepts, and applications.* San Francisco: Jossey-Bass.

Herjanic, B., & Campbell, W. (1977). Differentiating psychiatrically disturbed children on the basis of a structured interview. *Journal of Abnormal Child Psychology*, *5*, 127-134.

Herjanic, B., Herjanic, M., Brown, F., & Wheatt, T. (1975). Are children reliable reporters? *Journal of Abnormal Child Psychology*, *3*, 41-48.

Hobbs, S. A., Walle, D. L., & Hammersly, G. A. (1984). Assessing children's social skills: Validation of the Behavioral Assertiveness Test for Children (BAT-C). *Journal of Behavioral Assessment*, *6*, 29-35.

Hodges, K., Kline, J., Fitch, P., McKnew, D., & Cytryn, L. (1981). The Child Assessment Schedule: A diagnostic interview for research and clinical use. *Catalog of Selected Documents in Psychology*, *11*, 56.

Hodges, K., McKnew, D., Cytryn, L., Stern, L., & Kline, J. (1982). The Child Assessment Schedule (CAS) diagnostic interview: A report on reliability and validity. *Journal of the American Academy of Child Psychiatry*, *21*, 468-473.

Holland, C. J. (1970). An interview guide for behavioral counseling with parents. *Behavior Therapy*, *1*, 70-79.

Hughes, M. M., & Haynes, S. N. (1978). Structured laboratory observation in the behavioral assessment of parent-child interactions: A methodological critique. *Behavior Therapy*, *9*, 428-447.

Johnson, S. M., & Bolstad, O. D. (1973). Methodological issues in naturalistic observation: Some problems and solutions for field research. In L. A. Hamerlynck, L. C. Handy, & E. J. Mash (Eds.), *Behavior change: Methodology, concepts, and practice* (pp. 7-67). Champaign, IL: Research Press.

Jones, R. R., Reid, J. B., & Patterson, G. R. (1975). Naturalistic observation in clinical assessment. In P. McReynolds (Ed.), *Advances in psychological assessment* (Vol. 3, pp. 42–95). San Francisco: Jossey-Bass.

Kazdin, A. E. (1981). Behavioral observation. In M. Hersen & A. S. Bellack (Eds), *Behavioral assessment: A practical handbook* (2nd ed., pp. 101–124). New York: Pergamon.

Kazdin, A. E. (1983). Psychiatric diagnosis, dimensions of dysfunction, and child behavior therapy. *Behavior Therapy, 14*, 73–99.

Kazdin, A. E., Esveldt-Dawson, K., Sherick, R. B., & Colbus, D. (1985). Assessment of overt behavior and childhood depression among psychiatrically disturbed children. *Journal of Consulting and Clinical Psychology, 53*, 201–210.

Kazdin. A. E., Esveldt-Dawson, K., Unis, A. S., & Rancurello, M. (1983). Child and parent evaluations of depression and aggression in psychiatric inpatient children. *Journal of Abnormal Psychology, 11*, 401–413.

Keat, D. B. (1979). *Multimodal therapy with children.* New York: Pergamon.

Kent, R. N., O'Leary, K. D., Diament, C., & Dietz, A. (1974). Expectation biases in observational evaluation of therapeutic change. *Journal of Consulting and Clinical Psychology, 42*, 774–780.

Kniskern, J. R., Robinson, E. A., & Mitchell, S. K. (1983). Mother–child interaction in the home and laboratory settings. *Child Study Journal, 13*, 23-29.

Kovacs, M. (1980/1981). Rating scales to assess depression in school-aged children. *Acta Paedopsychiatry, 46*, 305–315.

Kovacs, M. (1982). *The Children's Depression Inventory*: *A self-rated depression scale for school-aged youngsters.* Unpublished manuscript, University of Pittsburgh.

Lineham, M. M. (1980). Content validity: Its relevance to behavioral assessment. *Behavioral Assessment, 2*, 147–159.

Lobitz, G. K., & Johnson, S. M. (1975a). Normal versus deviant children: A multi-method comparison. *Journal of Abnormal Child Psychology, 3*, 353–374.

Lobitz, G. K., & Johnson, S. M. (1975b). Parental manipulation of the behavior of normal and deviant children. *Child Development, 46*, 719–726.

Mash, E. J., Terdal, L., & Anderson, K. (1973). The response-class matrix: A procedure for recording parent–child interactions. *Journal of Consulting and Clinical Psychology, 40*, 163-164.

Matson, J. L., Esveldt-Dawson, K., & Kazdin, A. E. (1983). Validation of methods for assessing social skills in children. *Journal of Clinical Child Psychology, 12*, 174–180.

Michelson, L., & Wood, R. (1980). A group assertive training program for elementary school children. *Child Behavior Therapy, 2*, 1-9.

Michelson, L., & Wood, R. (1982). Development and psychometric properties of the Children's Assertive Behavior Scale. *Journal of Behavioral Assessment, 4*, 3–13.

Mischel, W. (1977). On the future of personality measurement. *American Psychologist, 32*, 246–264.

Nelson, R. O., & Hayes, S. C. (1979). Some current dimensions of behavioral assessment. *Behavioral Assessment, 1*, 1–16.

O'Leary, K. D., Pelham, W. E., Rosenbaum, A., & Price, G. H. (1976). Behavioral treatment of hyperkinetic children. *Clinical Pediatrics, 15*, 510–515.

O'Leary, S. G., & Pelham, W. E. (1978). Behavior therapy and withdrawal of stimulant medication with hyperactive children. *Pediatrics, 61*, 211–217.

Ollendick, T. H. (1983). Reliability and validity of the Revised Fear Survey Schedule for Children (FSSC-R). *Behaviour Research and Therapy, 21*, 685–692.

Ollendick, T. H. (1984). Development and validation of the Children's Assertiveness Inventory. *Child and Family Behavior Therapy*, 5, 1–15.

Oltmanns, T. F., Broderick, J. E., & O'Leary, K. D. (1977). Marital adjustment and the efficacy of behavior therapy with children. *Journal of Consulting and Clinical Psychology*, 45, 724–729.

Patterson, G. R., Ray, R. S., Shaw, D. A., & Cobb, J. A. (1969). *Manual for coding of interactions* (1969 rev.) New York: Microfiche.

Patterson, G. R., Reid, J. B., Jones, R. R., & Conger, R. E. (1975). *A social learning approach to family intervention: Vol. 1. Families with aggressive children*. Eugene, OR: Castalia Press.

Peed, S., Roberts, M., & Forehand, R. (1977). Evaluation of the effectiveness of a standardized parent training program in altering the interaction of mothers and their noncompliant children. *Behavior Modification*, 1, 323–350.

Peterson, D. R. (1961). Behavior problems of middle childhood. *Journal of Clinical Psychology*, 22, 337–340.

Puig-Antich, J., & Chambers, W. (1978). *Schedule for affective disorders and schizophrenia for school-aged children (6–16 years) — Kiddie-SADS*. New York: New York State Psychiatric Institute.

Quay, H. C. (1977). Measuring dimensions of deviant behavior: The Behavior Problem Checklist. *Journal of Abnormal Child Psychology*, 5, 277–288.

Quay, H. C. (1979). Classification. In H. C. Quay & J. S. Werry (Eds.), *Psychopathological disorders of childhood* (2nd ed., pp. 1–42). New York: Wiley.

Quay, H. C. (1983). A dimensional approach to children's behavior disorder: The Revised Behavior Problem Checklist. *School Psychology Review*, 12, 244–249.

Reardon, R. C., Hersen, M., Bellack, A. S., & Foley, J. M. (1979). Measuring social skills in grade school boys. *Journal of Behavioral Assessment*, 1, 87–105.

Reid, J. B. (Ed.). (1978). *A social learning approach to family intervention: Vol. 2: Observation in home settings*. Eugene, OR: Castalia Press.

Robinson, E. A., & Eyberg, S. M. (1981). The Dyadic Parent–Child Interaction Coding System: Standardization and validation. *Journal of Consulting and Clinical Psychology*, 49, 245–250.

Robinson, E. A., Eyberg, S., & Ross, A. W. (1980). The standardization of an inventory of child conduct problem behaviors. *Journal of Clinical Child Psychology*, 9, 22–28.

Saylor, C. F., Finch, A. J., Baskin, C. H., Furey, W., & Kelly, M. M. (1984). Construct validity for measures of childhood depression: Application of multitrait-multimethod methodology. *Journal of Consulting and Clinical Psychology*, 52, 977–985.

Saylor, C. F., Finch, A. J., Spirito, A., & Bennett, B. (1984). The Children's Depression Inventory: A systematic evaluation of psychometric properties. *Journal of Consulting and Clinical Psychology*, 52, 955–967.

Scherer, M. W., & Nakamura, C. Y. (1968). A fear survey schedule for children (FSS-C): A factor analytic comparison with manifest anxiety. *Behaviour Research and Therapy*, 6, 173–182.

Trites, R. L., Blouin, A. G. A., & Laprade, K. (1982). Factor analysis of the Conners Teacher Rating Scale based on a large normative sample. *Journal of Consulting and Clinical Psychology*, 50, 615-623.

Trites, R. L., Dugas, E., Lynch, G., & Ferguson, H. B. (1979). Prevalence of hyperactivity. *Journal of Pediatric Psychology*, 2, 179–188.

Van Hasselt, V. B., Hersen, M., & Bellack, A. S. (1981) The validity of role-play tests for assessing social skills in children. *Behavior Therapy*, 12, 202–216.

Wahler, R. G., & Cormier, W. H. (1970). The ecological interview: A first step in outpatient child behavior therapy. *Journal of Behavior Therapy and Experimental Psychiatry*, *1*, 279–289.

Wahler, R. G., House, A. E., & Stambaugh, E. E. (1976). *Ecological assessment of child problem behavior*. New York: Pergamon.

Webster-Stratton, C. (1985). Comparisons of behavior transactions between conduct-disordered children and their mothers in the clinic and at home. *Journal of Abnormal Child Psychology*, *13*, 169–184.

Wells, K. C. (1981). Assessment of children in outpatient settings. In M. Hersen & A. S. Bellack (Eds.), *Behavioral assessment: A practical handbook* (2nd ed., pp. 484–533). New York: Pergamon.

Werry, J. S., Sprague, R. L., & Cohen, M. N. (1975). Conners Teacher Rating Scale for use in drug studies with children: An empirical study. *Journal of Abnormal Child Psychology*, *3*, 217–229.

Williamson, D. A., Moody, S. C., Granberry, S. W., Lethermon, V. R., & Blouin, D. C. (1983). Criterion-related validity of a role-play social skills test for children. *Behavior Therapy*, *14*, 466–481.

Witt, J. C., & Elliott, S. N. (1983). Assessment in behavioral consultation: The initial interview. *School Psychology Review*, *12*, 42–49.

Zangwill, W. M., & Kniskern, J. R. (1982). Comparison of problem families in the clinic and at home. *Behavior Therapy*, *13*, 145–152.

PART 4

FUTURE DIRECTIONS

17
Future Directions of Behavioral Assessment

Alan S. Bellack
Michel Hersen

The second edition of this book reflected a gradual evolution of the field of behavioral assessment in the 5 years since the first edition was published. As indicated in the Preface to the second edition, the period from 1976 to 1981 was marked by increasing sensitivity to the importance of psychometrics, which resulted in a substantial refinement of techniques. In many ways, the second edition presented a more conservative and sophisticated perspective on assessment than did the first edition. Yet there was considerable overlap in the philosophy and tactics of assessment described in the two editions. In keeping with behavior therapy's operant tradition, the primary emphasis was on an idiographic approach to assessment (see Cone, chapter 2, this volume). Diagnosis and classification were substantially eschewed although the potential utility of DSM-III was acknowledged in the second edition (Nelson & Hayes, 1981). There was general support for the tripartite model in which behavior, cognition, and physiological activity were each assessed. But, behavioral observation was king. Any discrepancy between measurement categories was usually resolved in favor of the observational data. For the most part, clinical judgment, subjectivity, and overall ratings were seen as inferior to objective measures of specific (overt) behaviors.

This third edition reflects a more dramatic shift in the field. Behavior therapy in general has entered a period of critical self-evaluation. It has gradually become apparent that some of our most cherished beliefs and assumptions may not be valid and that other disciplines and models do have much to offer. This shift is especially marked in regard to assessment. Rather than continuing to simply revise and refine preexisting techniques, behavior therapists have begun to question the utility of even their most cherished tactics and the validity of the premises which underlie them. As indicated in

610

chapter 3, diagnostic classification is now viewed as a potentially valuable component of the behavioral assessment process. Clinical judgment, as employed in structured interviews and rating scales (Morrison, chapter 8, this volume), has lost much of its negative reputation and has become a standard assessment modality in most major clinical research programs (Bellack, 1986). In fact, DSM-III diagnoses and structured clinical interviews have become a *sine qua non* of NIMH-supported research, behavioral or otherwise (Maser, 1984). The clinical value (i.e., utility and external validity) of techniques that had been core approaches in some subject areas (e.g., marital therapy, chapter 13) have been questioned. Even the preeminence of behavioral observation is no longer accepted as given. Consider this recent statement by Jacobson (1985):

> Underlying this view regarding the superiority of observational measures is a presumption that functional analyses require or at least are greatly facilitated by such methods. The evaluation of observational methods becomes much more complicated when one considers the possibility that assessment process is independent of assessment modality. For example, there is now some consensus that self-report measures are acceptable to behavioral clinicians as long as they conform to the principles of a behavioral assessment process. This acceptance implies that the assessment process is independent of assessment modality . . . .
> A less often emphasized but equally plausible corollary is that observational methods may at times impede a functional analysis by focusing attention away from more relevant but less easily observed events. In fact, it could be argued that at times the behavior of interest, that inferential leaps remarkably consistent with those typically put forth in traditional assessments are often needed to retain observational measures, and that exclusive or primary focus on observational measures may at times negate many of the benefits which behavioral assessment was designed to foster. (p. 298)

This theme was echoed recently by several noted experts on behavioral assessment in a discussion about the selection of target behaviors for assessment and treatment. A repeated concern was that in striving for specificity and objectivity, we have frequently ignored our clients' most pressing concerns and focused instead on unimportant, albeit objectionable, targets (Evans, 1985; Kanfer, 1985). The following quote from Kazdin (1985) is illustrative of the questions raised about current practices:

> Although careful specification and operationalization of behavior in clinical work has been an obviously important methodological advance, it bears a familiar liability as well. What is ultimately assessed may depart considerably from the original complaint the client brings to treatment. The target behavior as assessed may only correspond imperfectly with the original

complaint or clinical problem that precipitated treatment. For example, children who are identified by parents, teachers, or others as extremely shy or withdrawn are often assessed for a variety of concrete behaviors. A behavioral role-play test is one measure commonly used where such behaviors as eye contact, voice volume, voice intonation, physical gestures, facial expression, and other concrete behaviors are assessed . . . . Questions can be raised about the extent to which the behaviors, as defined, relate to the problem that precipitated treatment. The specific behaviors and the conditions under which they are assessed may bear little or no relation to the social skills problems identified by the client or other . . . . There is no special reason to single out one area such as social skills and role-play performance . . . . Behavioral avoidance tests to assess anxiety, plethysmography to assess sexual arousal, or alcohol consumption in simulated bars to assess drinking, all depart from observations in the natural environment and may yield data about target behaviors that bear little relation to functioning in the domain (anxiety, arousal, drinking) that is problematic to the client. (pp. 34–35)

In sum, behavioral assessment is undergoing a dramatic reappraisal. The field has changed substantially in the last 5 years, and it promises to change even more in the next 5 years. Given that questions have been raised about fundamental premises and core procedures, it is especially difficult to predict what a fourth edition of this book might contain. There even is some question that behavioral assessment will continue to exist as an identifiable approach. There are a number of key issues that must be resolved if the field is to continue to survive and grow.

WHAT IS BEHAVIORAL ASSESSMENT?

Numerous specific controversies and problems have been identified throughout the preceding chapters, including the role of microbehavioral observation, clinical utility of techniques, the assessment of cognitive phenomena, and the criterion (external) validity of analog techniques. Each of these issues requires further study. However, they primarily impact on work in specific subareas of behavioral assessment. As such, they are secondary to a single, central issue confronting the entire field: the identity and definition of behavioral assessment. As pointed out by Cone (chapter 2, this volume), there is neither a single accepted definition of the field – or a consistent set of methods. In describing our approach, books and chapters on the topic typically present a set of guiding assumptions, followed by descriptions of a handful of prototype procedures (Barrios, chapter 1, this volume; Goldfried, 1982: Haynes, 1983; Nelson & Hayes, 1981).

Characteristically, behavioral assessment is said to emphasize objective measurement, reliability and validity behavior sampling, and a functional analysis of the individual case; it eschews inferential constructs, indirect (sign) measures, and traditional nomothetic/group classification approaches. However, in practice there are really two contrasting models of behavioral assessment: an idiographic-behavior approach and a nomothetic-trait approach (Cone, chapter 2, this volume). The former is characteristic of work with children and handicapped populations (e.g., the mentally retarded) in which intensive analysis of individual cases has predominated in both research and clinical work.

In contrast, the nomothetic-trait approach is the dominant model in research and clinical work with adult outpatients. Problems such as anxiety disorders, depression, addictive disorders, and interpersonal problems are all generally studied in group comparison designs where group means are more critical than are individual case analyses. Research and clinical work with these populations has always made extensive use of self-report inventories (e.g., the Beck Depression Inventory, Watson and Friend Social Anxiety and Distress Scale and Fear of Negative Evaluation Scale, the Fear Survey Schedule, etc.). Thus, while paying lip service to the fundamental behavior analytic principles, work in this area has *ipso facto* employed a trait-like model.

This conceptual discrepancy has been accentuated by recent trends. We have already referred to the increased use of standard diagnostic procedures, and to the associated adoption of structured interviews and subjective clinical ratings. Perhaps the most significant change has been the revival of interest in a long-standing behavioral anathema: cognition. In keeping with the development of cognitive behavior therapy, behavioral assessors have devoted increasing effort to development of methods for assessment of cognitions and cognitive functioning (Bowers & Meichenbaum, 1985; Kendall & Hollon, 1981; Rehm, chapter 10, this volume). What once was viewed as hopelessly inferential and unobjectionable has now become a core feature of research and clinical work on depression, anxiety, social skills, and addictions (to name just a few areas).

It is not our intention here to compare the two assessment models outlined by Cone (chapter 2, this volume) or to evaluate the increased use of nomothetic/subjective procedures. However, we do feel that the identity of behavioral assessment is in jeopardy. If we employ a standardized psychiatric interview to reach a DSM-III diagnosis, generate clinical ratings of symptom severity, administer self-report inventories, and assess cognitive style, is the assessment still "behavioral"? Is it behavioral simply because it is administered by a behavior therapist, or is there some necessary methodology that must be employed?   It has frequently been argued that the specific *methods* employed in assessment are less important than the *general processes* involved in the synthesis and utilization of information (Evans, 1985; Kanfer, 1985). Thus, an assessment would be considered behavioral as long as it adhered to behavioral tenets. While this argument certainly has merits, it does not really resolve the issue. Many core behavioral tenets, such as objectivity, reliability, and validity, are fundamental to any sound assessment approach. Defining behavioral assessment on that basis is tantamount to arguing that any assessment approach is behavioral if we choose to call it so, even if it was developed and is primarily employed by professionals who do not identify themselves as behavior therapists. For example, neuropsychologists use reliable and objective measures to sample behavior, do an intensive analysis of the individual subject, and do not infer the existence of hypothetical mediating variables to explain the client's behavior. Is the Halstead-Reitan battery therefore a behavioral assessment procedure and all neuropsychologists behavioral assessors?

Defining behavioral assessment on the basis of general processes fails to emphasize the unique and significant contributions of behavioral technology and, by so doing, risks the loss of any real identity for the behavioral approach. Behavioral therapists as individual scientists and clinicians can do much to improve diagnostic systems and advance the assessment of cognitive phenomena. But, we question whether behavioral assessment as a discipline can add much to these important areas. Moreover, we see no reason why it must. We have tended to view behavioral assessment as an all-encompassing approach. This is no longer a viable perspective. We must recognize that it is valid and useful for some purposes, but it is clearly not appropriate for others. Similarly, it also is no longer reasonable to contrast behavioral and nonbehavioral assessment in an either/or, good/bad manner. Rather, the reliability, validity, and utility of any procedure should be paramount, regardless of its behavioral or nonbehavioral development. We see no value in reifying behavioral strategies just because they are behavioral if they are not psychometrically sound and clinically useful. Conversely, sound nonbehavioral strategies can no longer be rejected out of hand.

The label "behavioral assessment" is not useful if behavioral and nonbehavioral assessors alike use the same procedures. We believe the term can be useful if it is limited to, for example, Cone's idiographic-behavior model, if for no other reason than it is most clearly identified with behavior therapy. However, we also believe that assessment techniques that fit this definition can no longer be considered to be primary for all assessment tasks. They may be best suited for a secondary stage of assessment when there is a need to do a functional analysis and develop objective measures of specific behaviors. The nomothetic–trait approach might be more suited to screening and to the initial phases of assessment, where it is often more important to categorize clients and develop an overall picture of their dysfunction and life situation. This is characteristically what happens in clinical practice. The clinician takes the first few sessions to develop a diagnostic formulation by interviewing the client and administering a battery of self-report inventories. Only when the general picture is clear does the clinician begin to search for environmental contingencies, develop specific treatment targets, and initiate behavioral observation (e.g., self-monitoring, role play).

Our position is based at least as much on our clinical experience as on existing data. Recognizing the limitations of clinical judgment, we hope that this issue is subjected to extensive debate and research before publication of the fourth edition of this series.

REFERENCES

Bellack, A.S. (1986). Schizophrenia: Behavior therapy's forgotten child. *Behavior Therapy, 17,* 199–214.

Bowers, K., & Meichenbaum, D. (Eds.). (1985). *The unconscious reconsidered.* New York: Wiley.

Evans, I. M. (1985). Building systems models as a strategy for target behavior selection in clinical assessment. *Behavioral Assessment, 7,* 21–32.

Goldfried, M. R. (1982). Behavioral assessment: An overview. In A.S. Bellack, M. Hersen, & A. E. Kazdin (Eds.), *International handbook of behavior modification and therapy.* New York: Pergamon.

Haynes, S. N. (1983). Behavioral assessment. In M. Hersen, A. E. Kazdin, & A. S. Bellack (Eds.), *The clinical psychology handbook.* New York: Pergamon.

Jacobson, N. S. (1985). The role of observational measures in behavior therapy outcome research. *Behavioral Assessment, 7,* 297–308.

Kanfer, F. H. (1985). Target selection for clinical change programs. *Behavioral Assessment, 7,* 7–20.

Kazdin, A. E. (1985). Selection of target behaviors: The relationship of the treatment focus to clinical dysfunction. *Behavioral Assessment, 7,* 33–48.

Kendall, P. C., & Hollon, S. D. (Eds.) (1981). *Assessment strategies for cognitive behavioral intervention.* New York: Academic.

Maser, J. D. (1984). Behavioral testing of anxiety: Issues, diagnoses, and practice. *Journal of Behavioral Assessment, 6,* 397–409.

Nelson, R. O., & Hayes, S. C. (1981). Nature of behavioral assessment. In M. Hersen & A. S. Bellack (Eds.), *Behavioral assessment: A practical handbook* (2nd ed.). New York: Pergamon.

Author Index

617

Subject Index

About the Editors and Contributors

THE EDITORS

Alan S. Bellack received his Ph.D. at Pennsylvania State University in 1970 and is professor of psychiatry at the Medical College of Pennsylvania and adjunct professor of psychology at Temple University. He was formerly professor of psychology and psychiatry and director of clinical psychology training at the University of Pittsburgh. He is a past president of the Association for Advancement of Behavior Therapy, and a fellow of Division 12 of APA. He is coauthor and coeditor of 18 books including *The Clinical Psychology Handbook, International Handbook of Behavior Modification and Therapy, Handbook of Clinical Behavior Therapy for Adults,* and *Schizophrenia: Treatment Management, and Rehabilitation.* He has published over 90 journal articles and has received numerous NIMH research grants on social skills, behavioral assessment, and schizophrenia. With M. Hersen, he is editor and founder of the journals *Behavior Modification* and *Clinical Psychology Review.* He has served on the editorial boards of numerous journals and has been a consultant to a number of publishing companies and mental health facilities, including the National Institute of Mental Health.

Michel Hersen, Ph.D., is professor of psychiatry and psychology at the University of Pittsburgh School of Medicine. He is past president of the Association for Advancement of Behavior Therapy. He has coauthored and coedited 50 books including *The Clinical Psychology Handbook, Behavior Therapy for Children and Adolescents: A Clinical Approach, Behavior Therapy for the Developmentally and Physically Disabled, Handbook of Developmental and Physical Disabilities, Handbook of Family Violence, Psychological Evaluation of the Developmentally and Physically Disabled,* and *Research Methods in Clinical Psychology.* He has also published more than 155 scientific journal articles and is coeditor of several psychological journals, including *Clinical Psychology Review, Journal of Anxiety Disorders, Journal of the Multihandicapped Person, Journal of Family Violence,* and *Behavior Modification.* His research interests include assessment and treatment of a variety of child populations, including multihandicapped children and their families, and family violence. Dr. Hersen is the recipient of several research grants from the National Institute of Mental Health, the Department of Education, the National Institute of Disabilities and Rehabilitation Research, and the March of Dimes Birth Defects Foundation.

THE CONTRIBUTORS

Billy A. Barrios received his Ph.D. in clinical psychology from the University of Utah in 1980. Since 1981 he has been on the faculty of the Psychology department at the University of Mississippi. He has served as an associate editor of *Behavioral Assessment* and as a consulting editor for *Behavior Therapy* and the *Journal of Consulting and Clinical Psychology.*

Robert E. Becker received his Ph.D. in clinical psychology from the State University of New York at Albany in 1966. His research interests have included the diagnosis and treatment of mood disorders, particularly depression. A second interest area focuses on anxiety disorders, particularly social phobia. He has served as director of the Mood Disorders Clinic, Albany Medical College. Currently he is director of the Chronic Depression Treatment Program and director of the Psychology Internship Program at the Medical College of Pennsylvania. He is the senior author of *Social Skills Training Treatment of Depression* (1987).

Debora J. Bell-Dolan received her B.A. from the University of Kansas in 1983 and is currently working toward a doctorate in psychology at West Virginia University. Her major areas of interest include assessment of children's peer relations and direct observation methodology.

Douglas A. Bernstein received his Ph.D. from Northwestern University in 1968 and is currently professor and associate head of the Department of Psychology at the University of Illinois at Urbana-Champaign. His research interests center on behavioral medicine, particularly the areas of reduction of general tension, elimination of anxiety relating to dental procedures, and prevention of serious diseases through the modification of smoking behavior. He is coauthor of *Progressive Relaxation Training* (1973), *Introduction to Clinical Psychology* (1980/1987) and *Psychology* (1988).

Donald A. Burge received his B.A. from Florida State University. He is currently employed at PRYDE of West Virginia, an agency that provides specialized foster care for disturbed youths. His interests include children's social skills and family-based foster care.

John D. Cone received his A.B. from Stanford University in 1964 and his Ph.D. in clinical psychology from the University of Washington in 1968. He has been chief psychologist, Madigan General Hospital, Tacoma, Washington, and a lecturer in psychology at the University of Puget Sound. Since 1970 Dr. Cone has been on the faculty of the child clinical psychology program at West Virginia University, and has twice been a visiting professor at the University of Hawaii. He is coeditor (with R. P. Hawkins) of *Behavioral Assessment: New Directions in Clinical Psychology* and cofounder (with Rosemery O. Nelson) and current editor of *Behavioral Assessment*.

C. J. Davis is a doctoral candidate in clinical psychology at Louisiana State University. Her major areas of interest are eating disorders and behavioral medicine.

Sharon L. Foster, Ph.D., is a faculty member in the Department of Psychology at West Virginia University. In addition to her position as associate editor for *Behavioral Assessment*, she serves on the editorial board of the *Journal of Consulting and Clinical Psychology, Behavior Therapy,* and *Behavior Modification*. She has published a number of articles and chapters on the assessment of children's social skills, parent–adolescent conflict, and direct observation.

David W. Foy received his Ph.D. from the University of Southern Mississippi in 1975 and is currently professor and director of clinical training, School of Psychology, Fuller Theological Seminary. His research interests include assessment and etiological factors in substance abuse and posttraumatic stress disorder and social skills training.

Sandra E. Gramling received her Ph.D. from the University of Mississippi in 1986 and is currently an assistant professor at Virginia Commonwealth University in Richmond, Virginia. She is affiliated with the behavioral medicine and behavior therapy specialty tracks in the Ph.D. clinical psychology training program at VCU. Her research interests include assessment and treatment of psychophysiological dysfunction, psychopharmacology, and coronary heart disease risk–factor reduction.

Alan M. Gross, Ph.D., Washington State University, is associate professor of psychology at the University of Mississippi. His research interests include self-management, child behavior therapy, and behavioral pediatrics. He is the recipient of several grants from NIH and is currently the Editor of *The Behavior Therapist*.

Richard G. Heimberg received his Ph.D. from Florida State University in 1977 and is associate professor of psychology at the State University of New York at Albany and research associate at the University's Center for Stress and Anxiety Disorders, where he directs the treatment program for individuals with social fears and phobias. He has published over 40 articles on the topics of depression, social anxiety, social skills training, and cognitive-behavior therapy.

Steven D. Hollon received his Ph.D. from the Florida State University, and was a predoctoral research associate at the University of Pennsylvania. He was on the faculty at the University of Minnesota from 1977 through 1985 before moving to Vanderbilt University where he is currently an associate professor of Psychology. His research interests focus on the affective disorders, both their psychopathology and treatment, with a special emphasis on the role of cognitive processes. He is the former editor of the journal *Cognitive Therapy and Research* (1981–1985), coeditor (with Philip C. Kendall) of *Cognitive-Behavioral Interventions: Theory, Research, and Practice* and *Assessment Strategies for Cognitive-Behavioral Interventions*, and coauthor (with Masters, Burish, and Rimm) of *Behavior Therapy: Techniques and Empirical Findings* (3rd ed.).

Neil S. Jacobson is full professor and director of clinical training in the clinical psychology program at the University of Washington, having received his degree in 1977 from the University of North Carolina. His primary research interests are marital and family therapy, cognitive and behavior therapies, and psychosocial aspects of depression. In addition to extensive publications in these areas, Jacobson has published *Marital Therapy: Strategies Based on Social Learning and Behavior Exchange Principles* (with G. Margolin), *Clinical Handbook of Marital Therapy* (with A. S. Gurman), *Marital Interaction: Analysis and Modification* (with K. Hahlweg), and *Psychotherapists in Clinical Practice.*

Gayla Margolin received her Ph.D. in 1976 from the University of Oregon and is currently associate professor in the Department of Psychology, University of Southern California. Her research interests center on marital and family interaction, with an emphasis on family violence. She is currently on a career development award sponsored by the Guggenheim Foundation and is coauthor with N. S. Jacobson of *Marital Therapy: Strategies Based on Social Learning and Behavioral Exchange Principles.*

Nathaniel McConaghy obtained his M.D. thesis from the University of Melbourne in 1966 and is currently associate professor of psychiatry at the University of New South Wales, Sydney, Australia. His research interests center on behavioral assessment and therapy of sexual and impulse disorders and cognitive styles in normals and schizophrenics.

Joseph Michelli is a doctoral student in clinical psychology at the University of Southern California and is doing his internship with the Family Interaction Unit at Atascadero State Hospital. His primary research interests include child eyewitness testimony and cognitive and behavioral marital assessment.

Kenneth P. Morganstern received his Ph.D. in psychology from the Pennsylvania State University in 1974. He was on the clinical psychology faculty at the University of Oregon in Eugene and is presently a member of the medical psychology department of the Oregon Health Sciences University. He is currently in private practice in Portland, and his major interests include behavioral interviewing and assessment, marital and sexual dysfunction, and the treatment of anxiety.

Randall L. Morrison received his Ph.D. from the University of Pittsburgh in 1982 and is currently assistant professor and associate director of the Behavior Therapy Clinic of the Department of Psychiatry of the Medical College of Pennsylvania at EPPI. His primary research interests are the assessment and rehabilitation of interpersonal deficits in schizophrenic patients. He is coeditor (with A. S. Bellack) of *Medical Factors and Psychological Disorders: A Handbook for Psychologists.*

Michael T. Nietzel received his Ph.D. from the University of Illinois (Urbana-Champaign) in 1973. From 1977 to 1985 he served as director of the Clinical Training Program in the Department of Psychology at the University of Kentucky, where he currently is professor of psychology. His research interests concentrate on social learning interventions for community problems, the assessment and treatment of anxiety-based disorders, the assessment of clinical significance, and forensic psychology. He is the author of *Crime and Its Modification* (1979), *Introduction to Clinical Psychology* (2nd edition, 1987, with D. A. Bernstein), and *Psychological Consultation in the Courtroom* (1986, with R. C. Dillehay).

Carlton W. Parks, Jr., received his Ph.D. from the University of Minnesota in 1985 and was a postdoctoral research associate at Vanderbilt University for two years before becoming an assistant professor of Psychology at Texas A & M University. His research interests include the structure and function of imagery, social influences on life-span cognitive development, and the role of cognitive processes in the expression of psychopathology. Dr. Parks combines backgrounds in developmental and clinical psychology and brings a developmental perspective to his studies of the psychopathological process.

Rita C. Prather is a doctoral candidate in clinical psychology at Louisiana State University. Primary research interests are in behavioral medicine and eating disorders.

Donald M. Prue received his Ph.D. at West Virginia University in 1978. He is currently senior scientist for the Division of Health Promotion Research at the American Health Foundation in New York, where he directs research on the cessation and prevention of smoking among nurses.

Lynn P. Rehm received his Ph.D. from the University of Wisconsin-Madison in 1970. He has been a member of the faculties of the Department of Psychiatry at the UCLA Neuropsychiatric Institute and the Departments of Psychology and Psychiatry at the University of Pittsburgh. Since 1979 he has been professor of psychology at the University of Houston.

Robert L. Russell received his Ph.D. at Clark University in 1984. With graduate degrees in both linguistics and philosophical psychology, he is mainly interested in language and cognitive processes as these affect adjustment and the course of psychotherapy. He is currently assistant professor of psychology at the New School for Social Research and has recently edited a book entitled *Language in Psychotherapy: Strategies of Discovery*.

Robert G. Rychtarik received his M.A. and Ph.D. degrees in clinical psychology from the University of Montana. He is currently senior research scientist at the New York State Research Institute on Alcoholism, Buffalo, New York, and research associate professor of psychology at the State University of New York at Buffalo. His interests include alcoholism treatment outcome research, assessment and broad-spectrum behavioral treatment of alcoholism, and study of factors contributing to alcohol abuse and relapse.

Ellie T. Sturgis received her Ph.D. from the University of Georgia in 1979 and is currently an assistant professor of psychiatry and behavioral sciences at the Medical University of South Carolina and program director of the Alcohol Dependence Treatment Program, Charleston Veterans Administration Medical Center. Her research interests include assessment and treatment of substance abuse problems, assessment and treatment of psychophysiological dysfunction, and the management of compulsive behavior patterns.

Donald A. Williamson received his Ph.D. in clinical psychology from Memphis State University in 1978 and is professor of psychology at Louisiana State University. He is also director of the Psychological Services Center at LSU. His primary research interests are eating disorders and behavioral medicine.

John T. Wixted is an instructor of psychiatry at the Medical College of Pennsylvania at EPPI. His research interests include social skills training with chronic psychiatric patients and basic operant processes. His most recent publications appear in the *Journal of the Experimental Analysis of Behavior* and *International Journal of Mental Health*.

Pergamon General Psychology Series

* Out of print in original format. Available in custom reprint edition.